EXPLORING THE COSMOS

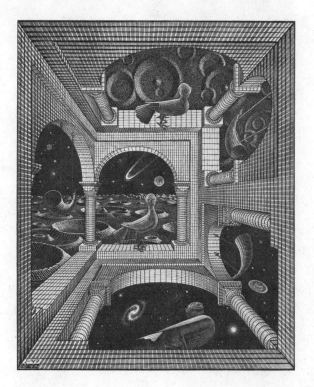

ANOTHER WORLD by M. C. Escher is a wood engraving printed from three blocks, 31.5 × 26 cm, revealing the interior of a cube-shaped building. As described by the artist, openings in the five visible walls give views of three different landscapes. Through the topmost pair one looks down, almost vertically, on the ground; the middle two at eye level show the horizon; through the bottom pair one looks straight up to the stars. Each plane of the building, which unites the nadir, horizon, and zenith, has a threefold function. For example, the rear plane in the center serves as a wall in relation to the horizon, a floor in connection with the view through the top opening, and a ceiling with respect to the view up toward the starry sky. (This description reprinted by permission of Reprinter *from the* Graphic Works of M. C. Escher, *Hawthorne-Ballantine edition.)*

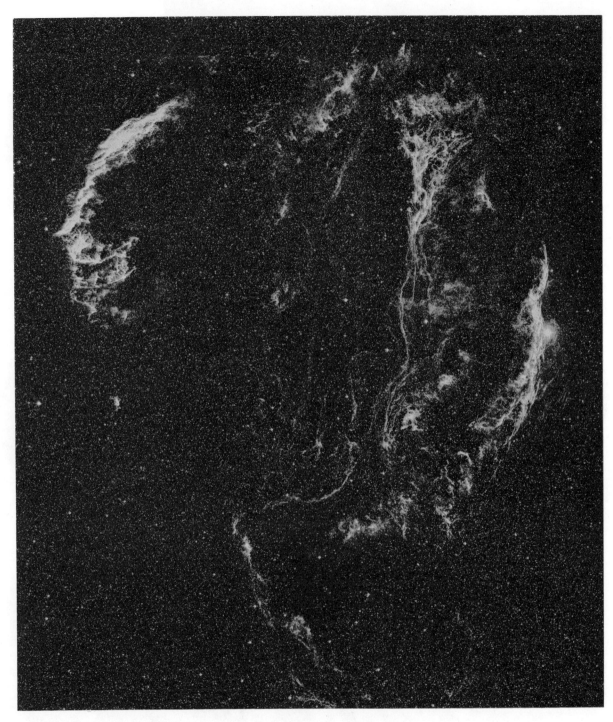

Loop nebula in Cygnus—the expanding gaseous relic from the violent explosion of a star.

EXPLORING THE COSMOS

LOUIS BERMAN

University of San Francisco

Little, Brown and Company Boston

Color plates 7, 9, 10, 11, 12, 13, 14,
15, 16, 17, 18, 19, 21, and 22:
Copyright by the California Institute of Technology
and the Carnegie Institution of Washington.
Photographs courtesy of the Hale Observatories.

Cover art: *Another World* by M. C. Escher
From the collection of C. V. S. Roosevelt

Production: Kenneth R. Burke and Associates
Design: James Stockton
Copyediting: Judith Fillmore
Illustrations: Basil Wood
Photo Research: Wendy Cunkle

PREFACE

Of all the natural sciences astronomy possesses the most universal popular appeal. This widespread interest in astronomy is evident in the large numbers of enthusiastic amateur telescope-makers enjoying their hobby; in the many active local and regional amateur astronomical societies that flourish; in the illustrated lectures, popular books, and periodicals that are available; and, not the least, in the various planetariums that serve the public interest in the field.

Yet in spite of its fascination and understandability in the past, the astronomical world is becoming more difficult for the layman to comprehend. The study of astronomy has changed from the descriptive telescopic work of yesteryear to the complicated instrumentation of today. Astronomical research, in large measure, now utilizes the technology of electronics, computers, and the sophisticated hardware of the laboratory. The enormous expansion of scientific knowledge has fashioned a discipline with its own distinctive jargon, its own brand of expertise, and a specialized style of reasoning that is alien to the humanistic world of thought. This is the predicament that faces the liberal-arts student who enrolls in an elementary course in astronomy. A primary goal of an introductory course in astronomy should be, therefore, to narrow the communications gap that separates the nonscientist from the scientist.

The object of this book is to acquaint the general reader with the role that astronomy has played in enriching man's cultural and scientific heritage; to provide him with the proper background for an understanding and appreciation of the recent fasci-

nating discoveries and burgeoning activities that have created a new era in astronomy; and, most importantly, to lay before him an enlarged perspective of his relationship with the universe. Astronomy affords the inquisitive student a superb opportunity, as no other science does, to search for the meaning of his own existence and to see where he fits into the scheme of things.

Although the style of presentation in *Exploring the Cosmos* is largely descriptive and as nontechnical as possible, the broad physical principles underlying the behavior of the cosmic forces and their interactions with matter and energy are not abandoned. There is a sparing amount of simple mathematics which the unprepared student may ignore without risk. In a few places where the explanations are somewhat technical or the mathematics beyond the scope of the reader, the student may skip the discussion and accept the statements of related fact or observation without loss in continuity. These sections appear in color.

The text departs somewhat from the traditional presentation of subject matter both in content and in emphasis. More attention is paid to contemporary research which, though rapidly changing, conveys to students a sense of the excitement and fervor that one finds on the frontiers of astronomy. Excluded entirely are the topics dealing with coordinate systems, certain phenomena related to the earth's rotation and revolution, geometrical optics, time, the seasons and the calendar, and eclipses. Omitted partially are the detailed descriptions of the constellations, the more involved portions of celestial mechanics, the more technical aspects of atomic structure and radiation, and the enumerative details of stellar types and properties.

The innovative treatment incorporated in the various chapters includes the following features. The first chapter stresses the usefulness of astronomy in particular and the role and relevance of science in general in the modern world. Astronomy lends itself well to this discussion because of its historical contributions to scientific thought. The dominant theme of Chapter 2 is the historical development of cosmology. In Chapter 5 the earth is viewed in a broader context, with brief incursions on the lithosphere (continental drift), the hydrosphere, the biosphere, the origin of life, and the ecology of the planet. Descriptions of the physical properties of the moon in Chapter 6 have been subdivided into the ground-based and extraterrestrial observations, including a summary of the Apollo findings; the discussion of the moon's origin is expanded. Chapter 7 on the planets contains the latest information from the Mars Mariner 9 orbiter. In Chapters 10 and 11 detailed descriptions of stellar species and stellar characteristics have been kept to a minimum in order to make room for a more generalized picture of the Galaxy as a whole. Treatment of the distinctions between the stellar populations, however, is not sacrificed. The newly discovered interstellar compounds are discussed in Chapter 11. Stellar evolution is given a somewhat more complete and up-to-date account in Chapter 12. In Chapter 13, which covers the galaxies and clusters of galaxies, galaxian evolution is also discussed. The high-energy sources, to which explanatory references have been made in the earlier chapters, are brought together in the single unifying Chapter 14 entitled "Cosmic Violence." Also included is a brief treatment on black holes. The highly controversial interpretations of the large red shifts observed in quasi-stellar objects provide students with a classic illustration of the clash of scientific opinions regarding a puzzling discovery. In Chapter 15 the simpler aspects of relativity theory are presented. This topic, which has been given little or no consideration in other comparable astronomy textbooks, is introduced because of its importance to cosmology. In most students' minds there is a mystique about relativity that challenges the imagination. Verbal descriptions and illustrations are favored where possible over mathematical presentations. Chapter 16 on cosmology is a natural follow-up. Here the student realizes that there is no firm handle to grasp on one of the great unsolved riddles: In what kind of universe do we exist? And therein lies a lesson for students to ponder: There is no interpretive finality about many of the well-entrenched statements in the astronomy textbooks. Chapter 17 on space astronomy is a new addition. As enlightened citizens, students should know how wisely the taxpayer's money is being spent on space research and what its benefits are to society-at-large. Chapter 18 on exobiology and Chapter 19 on interstellar communication are introduced because of the great popular interest and curiosity in these newly developing fields. Finally, Chapter 20 briefly considers man's scientific achievements and his role and position in the universe.

The liberal-arts student who is taking a science course for the first time will encounter the scientific methodology that often proves to be an obstacle to his comprehension of the natural laws and the description of physical phenomena. I have tried to ease the student's path through the brambles of astronomical knowledge in the present arrangement. Pity the poor reader who must wade through a morass of technicalities, strange words, and factual trivia without being able to see the forest for the trees. Better that the student carry with him a lifelong speculative interest in the majestic wonders of the astronomical universe and its grandeur than a head filled with the statistics of natural objects by name and form.

Lack of mathematical knowledge need not detract from the profitable reading of this book. Helpful rules in the use of powers of ten and in simplified algebraic procedures appear as memory refreshers in Appendices 1 and 2. Metric and English units are used interchangeably. These and other pertinent data appear in the other appendices. A list of student projects provides students with opportunities for research and self-expression where that is feasible. A glossary is also included.

To those who contributed to the leavening process through which the manuscript passed before evolving into its final form, I extend my sincere gratitude: to Charles Krieger who read the first draft and who kindly volunteered useful suggestions; to Cramer W. Schultz whose critique of the manuscript was helpful; to Harold Weaver and John Phillips who perused several chapters and with whom I had fruitful discussions; to J. McKim Malville and John Russell whose careful reading of the manuscript and whose critical comments led to worthwhile improvements. Last but not least I acknowledge my indebtedness to Kenneth Burke who was instrumental in the general design and format of the book and who shepherded it through the various labyrinths of production toward its eventual publication; and to Wendy Cunkle for her unstinting efforts in amassing the photographic illustrations that appear in the text.

Louis Berman

San Francisco
September, 1973

A biochemical laboratory, instrumented to detect the presence of micro-organisms rests on the surface of Mars while its detached orbiter component circles the planet. Results of the automated experiments will be telemetered from the lander to the earth via the orbiter. The first Viking spacecraft is scheduled for launch in mid-August 1975. A second Viking is expected to follow a month later. (Courtesy of NASA.)

CONTENTS

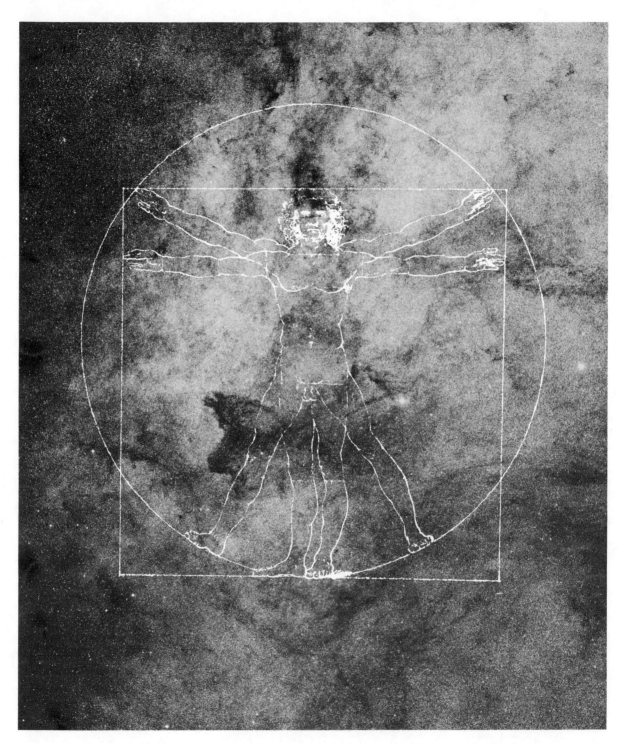

From the stars has descended man.

INTRODUCTION
TO THE COSMOS

Go, wondrous creature! mount where
    Science guides;
Go, measure earth, weigh air, and state the
    tides;
Instruct the planets in what orbs to run;
Correct old Time, and regulate the sun.
Go, teach Eternal Wisdom how to rule—
Then drop into thyself and be a fool!

    Alexander Pope (1688–1744),
    Essay on Man, Epistle 2

As man continues to probe the inner recesses of the atom and the outer reaches of the universe, he is still seeking to establish his place and role in the cosmos. While he investigates the origins of his past he wonders about his future fate on the third planet from the star he calls his sun, another star among the billions of other suns that exist within our Galaxy. It is the story of science—the unending thirst for knowledge stimulated by man's natural curiosity of the unknown with its roots buried in antiquity.

The practitioners of science share a common adherence to exacting standards and modes of operation in their investigations of natural phenomena. Experimental and observational data are continually refined, theories improved, and predictions rendered more precise in the attempt to unlock the secrets of nature. What has been the impact of scientific knowledge upon the world's culture, the interplay between science, technology, and the quality of life? Is there a dichotomy between the scientific and the humanistic communities? The moral and ethical aspects of science and technology are being questioned by some groups in our society, and concerned scientists themselves are wondering where science is headed and what its future may portend.

As one of the pure sciences astronomy has been largely divorced in the past, though less so now, from the practical mainstream of life because of the nature of its enterprise—the study of the cosmic environment. Despite its basic thrust as a pure science, many useful applications have materialized as the result of astronomical research in the pursuit of knowledge for its own sake. Above all else, as the oldest of the sciences, astronomy has given man a penetrating glimpse of the cosmos, a deeper understanding of the physical laws of nature, and a keener appreciation of the nature of his existence on earth.

1.1 THE COSMIC DESIGN

Deciphering the Heavens

Man has lived in the civilized state for a tiny fraction of his existence on earth. Four centuries ago he cast aside his self-centered view of the universe. The earth, man discovered, is not at the center of the solar system, much less at the center of the universe. Circling the sun are eight other planets: four like the earth of stony-metallic composition and four very large planets composed mainly of lightweight hydrogen and helium. In addition, thousands of small, solid bodies from asteroidal size to meteoroids orbit the sun; their total contribution amounts to but a small fraction of the earth's mass. Ranging widely about the sun are countless numbers of comets believed to be icy blobs of frozen gases and dust. A near vacuum of gas and tiny particles fills the empty spaces be-

Figure 1.1   Photograph of Mars taken by the Mariner 7 spacecraft at a distance of approximately 269,600 miles from the surface on August 4, 1969. The south polar cap at the bottom of this picture is very conspicuous. Prominent also is bright, ring-shaped Nix Olympica and the complex bright streaks of the Tharsis-Candor region. (Courtesy of NASA.)

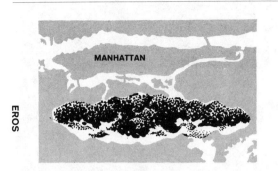

EROS

MANHATTAN

Figure 1.2 Drawing of the oblong asteroid Eros, approximately 15 miles long and 5 miles thick. (From the Life Nature Library book, The Universe, *published by Time-Life Books.)*

tween the planets. This is the overall picture of the solar system that man has gradually pieced together since he began to explore the heavens with a telescope more than three and a half centuries ago.

The sun, a hot globe of glowing gases large enough to contain one and one-third million earths, is but one star out of the approximately 200 billion suns that populate our Galaxy. Our earthbound view of the Galaxy is an edgewise presentation that forms the luminous girdle of stars familiar to us as the Milky Way. Its true shape is a spiral-structured disk so enormous in extent that it would take a light ray 100,000 years to traverse its diameter. Strewn along the spiral arms of our Galaxy are bright clumps of gas that we recognize as the gaseous nebulae; meandering lanes of dark dust, gas, and obscuring clouds known as the dark nebulae; knots of stars called star clusters, and countless individual stars frequently intermixed with the dust and gas. An eighteenth-century telescopic survey of the structure of the Milky Way indicated that our sun was located at its approximate center. Since the early part of this century man realized that the sun does not play a

centralized role in the Galaxy any more than the earth did in the geocentric system of the ancients. Our sun is actually located about two-thirds of the radius of the Galaxy from its center. Around this position all the stars revolve, like the planets around the sun. Our own star completes its nearly circular orbit around the galactic nucleus in 220 million years.

The Panoramic View of the Universe

At the beginning of this century astronomers wondered whether the many faint, nebulous patches of light appearing on their photographic plates were parts of one all-embracing galaxy or were other galaxies. By the mid-twenties the issue was settled in favor of the latter interpretation. The estimated number of galaxies capable of being photographed with the largest telescopes is in the billions. Although the structural forms of the galaxies are restricted to a few broad classes, their dimensions and luminosities vary widely. Our Galaxy ranks among the larger galaxies; others may be smaller by as much as one-

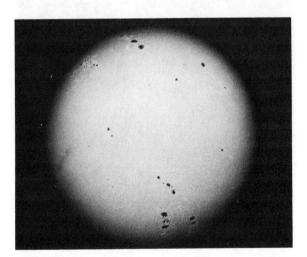

Figure 1.3 The sun photographed on September 15, 1957 under excellent conditions, showing a large number of sunspots. (Courtesy of Hale Observatories.)

Figure 1.4   Mosaic of the Milky Way from Cassiopeia to Sagittarius. (Courtesy of Hale Observatories.)

Figure 1.5   Spiral galaxy, M 81, in Ursa Major; photographed with the 120-inch reflector of the Lick Observatory. (Courtesy of Lick Observatory.)

Figure 1.6   Spiral galaxy, NGC 4565, in Coma Berenices, seen edge on; photographed with the 200-inch Hale reflector. (Courtesy of Hale Observatories.)

fiftieth of our size. In the spiral and irregularly shaped galaxies, gaseous clouds and dust are interspersed with the stars. In the more regular elliptical galaxies, the interstellar material is nearly or completely absent. Within the individual galaxies are myriads of stars of assorted sizes, colors, luminosities, masses, and ages arranged singly or in groups. Their numbers within each galaxy range from millions to billions.

In many regions of space, clustering of the galaxies over enormous dimensions is a widely observed pattern. In the hierarchal arrangement of class size, the clusters of galaxies rank as the largest organized collections of matter known. The most distant objects are believed to be the highly energetic, enigmatic quasars. The light by which we see some of them today presumably began its journey long before the solar system was formed some five billion years ago.

One of the greatest discoveries of the twentieth century is the knowledge that the universe is expanding, causing the galaxies to separate from each other. The most widely accepted cosmological interpretation of this phenomenon is that at about eighteen billion years ago, the universe began its expansion from the fireball explosion of a superhot, superdense core of highly energetic primeval matter out of which the galaxies were formed. How long the expansion of the universe is bound to continue, how much it may be slowing down due to its self-gravitation, and whether the expansion will eventually cease and contraction set in are presently unanswered questions.

From their studies astronomers have concluded that the universe possesses properties in like degree in all directions. Everywhere in space the chemical composition of matter is remarkably alike, mostly hydrogen and some helium; the same physical laws operate throughout; the gross structure of matter is similar; and the large-scale appearance of the universe

Figure 1.7   Cluster of galaxies in Hercules, photographed with the 200-inch Hale reflector. (Courtesy of Hale Observatories.)

1 INTRODUCTION TO THE COSMOS

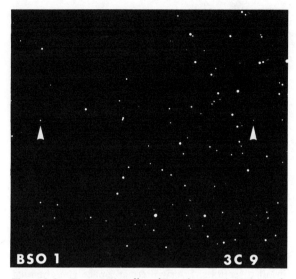

Figure 1.8 *Two quasi-stellar objects (quasars), BSO 1 and 3C 9, photographed with the 200-inch Hale reflector. Their identification is obtained from spectral analysis. (Courtesy of Hale Observatories.)*

Table 1.1   Compressed Time Scale of Certain Events

Epoch/Event	Compressed Time Scale
Age of earth	100 years
Life began on earth	65 years ago
First humanoid	25 days ago
Earliest civilizations	2 hours ago
Age of astronomical science	70 minutes old
Age of telescopic astronomy	4+ minutes old
Age of radio astronomy	10 seconds old
Man set foot on moon	2 seconds ago

is not very different from planet Earth than it is from planet X millions of light-years distant. When we probe more deeply into the structure of celestial matter we begin to observe variations as we are confronted with new cosmic riddles—the quasars, the exploding galaxies, the energetic x-ray and radio sources, the rapidly blinking radio objects called pulsars, and the presence of organic molecules within the interstellar clouds of our Galaxy.

Contracted Time Scale of Events during Earth's History

Some idea of the brevity of man's existence on this planet and his record of astronomical-space accomplishments may be gained by shrinking the age of the earth (4.6 billion years) to one century (see Table 1.1).

No longer does man look through a glass darkly. He has come to understand more clearly the intimate relationship between himself and his environment.

He is probing the structure of matter, living and non-living, on earth and in space with powerful tools. Soon he will be conducting a greater share of his celestial observations outside the atmosphere in space-orbiting laboratories and eventually on the moon. He has listened briefly for signs of coded intelligence possibly transmitted from other worlds. Our sun is destined to flourish for the next five billion years much as it has in the past before it begins its slow descent into oblivion. With almost limitless time ahead of him, will *Homo sapiens* evolve toward a level of superintelligence that may have been achieved already in interstellar societies? Or will the story of mankind come to an untimely and inglorious end? These are the questions which only the future can answer.

1.2   THE ROLE AND RELEVANCE OF SCIENCE IN MODERN SOCIETY

Origins of Science

Natural curiosity and the desire to understand, if not control, his environment are the stimuli that have driven man in the past to acquire systematic knowledge and to organize it into the many divisions that we call science. From this enterprise the general laws governing the natural phenomena have been derived for man's material welfare and for his intellectual enrichment. The word "science" is of relatively recent origin. Its precursor was natural philosophy which arose in ancient Grecian times from man's innate desire to explore his environment and to formulate concepts and principles relating to the behavior of the natural phenomena. Some of the physical ideas of the Greek philosophers, who preferred a-priori reasoning to experimentation, were mistakenly accepted at face value without experimental evidence.

This type of preoccupation, which preempted the testing of physical theories by logic instead of by trial and error, began to change with the passage of time. It was completely overthrown in the sixteenth and seventeenth centuries by the great experimental and observational pioneers: Copernicus, Brahe, Kepler, Galileo, Newton, and the others. Scientific societies were organized and laboratories were established while publications gave widespread distribution to ideas and discoveries. It was not until the nineteenth century that professional scientists and technologists were trained in any large numbers in the universities and technical institutes throughout Europe and later in this country and in other lands. It is from these beginnings that science has become such a dominant force in modern civilization in the twentieth century.

Workings of Science

As it stands today, science is neither a sacred cow that is above public criticism nor is it an elitist institution. The nearest thing to a scientific aristocracy in this country is a private organization, established in 1863 by a national charter, called the National Academy of Sciences. Its approximately one thousand individuals constitute the most prestigious members of the scientific community.

Science does not necessarily operate as a smooth-running machine. In its various branches it may advance fitfully, unpredictably, occasionally by quantum leaps, and it has been known even to regress. Scientific progress is replete with examples of brilliant and nonsensical speculation, inspirational hunches, hypotheses, theories, controversy, perceptivity, unorthodoxy, serendipity, creativity, plain plodding, and hard work. Yet out of this bewildering complexity of common effort, science has developed a universal technique from which there can be derived by observational, experimental, and theoretical means a common body of knowledge that transcends human imperfections. The acquired information does not remain a stagnant body of accumulated knowledge, but is continually refined, reassessed, and tested with increasingly sophisticated tools in the quest for the ultimate truth. In their interpretation of the natural phenomena scientists frequently strive to develop self-consistent structures of nature in the form of "models." The biologist constructs a model of the living cell; the physicist, a model of the atomic nucleus; the geophysicist, a model of the earth's interior; the cosmologist, a model of the universe, and so on. Universal acceptance of these models may come through the influence of a few strong individuals, by the bandwagon approval of the majority of scientists, or by the herd instinct which may later prove to be embarrassingly wrong.

In all these endeavors, the dedicated scientist takes pains, not always successfully, to heed one guiding principle: "Occam's Razor" (the principle of parsimony). William of Occam, a medieval logician, admonished that explanations should not be multiplied endlessly. Newton expressed it thusly: "Nature is pleased with simplicity and affects not the pomp of superfluous causes." Yet there is a price to pay for simplicity, as Einstein and his fellow worker, L. Infeld, pointed out: "The simpler and more fundamental our assumptions become, the more intricate our mathematical tool of reasoning." (They were referring to the subtleties in the physical world.) Nature may be artful and reveal her secrets only reluctantly, it is said, but never maliciously. Our perception of her conduct is limited by the inadequacy of our comprehension and the narrowness of our past experience.

Social Consequences of Science

The proceeds of science and its technological returns, which have brought luxury and comfort with questionable spiritual enrichment to only a portion of the world's inhabitants, are a matter of growing anxiety among many concerned scientists. Should scientists assume a moral obligation to ensure that the products of technology be wisely administered even to the point of exerting political pressure? This question has been openly debated from the podiums of many professional gatherings. The utilization of the power given to man by the fruits of science and technology carries with it the grave risk of its misuse without adequate safeguards. Certain elements in our society have concluded that technological progress can no longer be managed rationally. This feeling of insecurity has fostered a number of countercultures with anti-intellectual and anti-scientific tendencies. One by-product of this development has been the increasing ratio of astrologers to astronomers which was estimated in 1970 to be in the ratio of three astrologers to one astronomer.

Scientist-trained British novelist C. P. Snow speaks of two great cultures existing a world apart from each other with little in common intellectually, spiritually, and psychologically, and with no bond of communication between them: the scientific elements and the humanistic elements in our society.[1] This is perhaps too sweeping an indictment, for there are indeed scientists who share a deep appreciation and understanding of the humanistic values just as there are nonscience intellectuals who can comprehend the physical elegance of the natural world.

The taxpayers' contribution to science and technology amounts to many billions of dollars annually, for the federal government still carries the major financial burden in the support of all research and development. The development portion, which is largely military oriented, absorbs well over one-half of the total expenditures. Applied science accounts for about one-fourth of the total effort. The remainder, about one-seventh, goes for pure scientific research slightly more than half of which is conducted in the educational institutions.[1] Should there result a decline in expenditures in basic research that is allowed to continue indefinitely, it will adversely affect our role as a world leader in science. If we have learned one lesson about pure scientific research, it is that it cannot be made amenable to rigorous cost accounting in advance. The discovery of the fundamental laws of nature provides the key to power that is the nation's richest resource.

It has been estimated that scientific knowledge, including its trivialities, is presently doubling every fifteen years; the annual rate of increase in frontier science is about 2 per cent. The escalation of scientific and technological progress cannot continue indefinitely without recognition of the proper utilization of the natural resources and the attendant social and economic consequences of their misuse.

1.3 THE USEFULNESS OF ASTRONOMY AS A SCIENCE

The Study of Astronomy

The word "astronomy" derives from the combination of two Greek words signifying the law of the stars: *aster* (star) and *nomos* (law). Astronomers constitute a small minority within the scientific

---

[1] C. P. Snow, *The Two Cultures and the Scientific Revolution* (1959) and *The Two Cultures and a Second Look* (1969), Cambridge University Press.

[1] The proportionate amounts quoted vary somewhat from year to year.

community. In this country about one out of two hundred scientists is an astronomer. In physics the ratio is one out of ten; in chemistry, one out of three. The reason is obvious: Astronomy is basically a pure and culturally inspired science devoted primarily to acquiring knowledge about our cosmic environment. Yet impressive material benefits have come out of the discoveries made by astronomers as will be recounted shortly. Unlike the experimental sciences, astronomical science is still observational in scope whether conducted from earth-based observatories or from orbiting observatories. It is largely destined to remain that way despite the acquisition of lunar samples and the prospects of acquiring planetary specimens in the future. In the next century, the manned earth-orbiting laboratories, the establishment of a lunar scientific base, and the instrumented and possibly manned planetary missions will contribute immeasurably to astronomical knowledge. Nevertheless, astronomers will still be obliged to depend on the weak radiation from inaccessible celestial sources with the aid of powerful light-gathering instruments and sensitive detectors.

The Technological Harvest of Astronomy

Toward the close of the sixteenth century, before the invention of the telescope, one of the most impressive and far-reaching technological contributions of astronomy was forged. The high-quality observing instruments in Tycho Brahe's great observatory made possible the determination of sufficiently accurate planetary positions that enabled Kepler, Brahe's successor, to develop his planetary laws of motion. From these, half a century later, Newton derived his law of gravitation in the course of which he invented the powerful mathematics of the calculus. Newton's research was instrumental in laying the dynamical and mathematical foundations for the subsequent progress in the physical sciences and in engineering upon which much of our modern technology rests. Galileo's astronomical telescope, developed in the first decade of the seventeenth century, was the forerunner of the microscope. Thus the science of optics, which has branched into many practical applications, was aided in its development by astronomers who were eager to improve the quality and performance of their optical aids.

Other Practical Contributions

Timekeeping is an essential astronomical function. Time on clocks is constantly checked against the rotation of the earth at various governmental observatories by photographing the meridian crossings of selected stars near the zenith with a specially constructed telescope known as the photographic zenith tube. The national time services transmit accurate time signals throughout the world on assigned shortwave-radio frequencies for the benefit of science laboratories, astronomers, navigators, the railroads, the radio stations, and the utility power plants. In astronomical hands the constantly improved pendulum clock introduced in 1656 by C. Huyghens, the Dutch physicist, served as the most accurate timekeeping mechanism until the advent of the quartz crystal clock in 1928 with its thousand-fold increase in accuracy. In 1948 the first atomic ammonia clock went into operation; the present-day atomic cesium and rubidium atomic clocks have an accuracy of one part in 100 billion. (The high degree of precision attained in the quartz crystal clock depends on the very stable vibrating frequency of a piezoelectric crystal. The atomic clock is regulated by the naturally occurring vibrating frequencies of certain atoms or molecules.)

One important practical use of astronomy lies in the field of navigation. Application of the principles of nautical astronomy, combined with time-recorded sightings on the heavenly bodies with suitable measuring equipment (sextants, octants, etc.), leads to the precise determination of one's

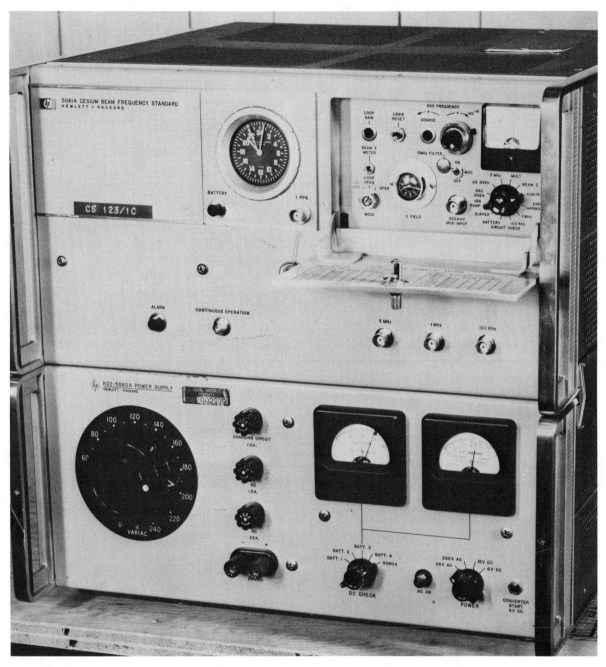

Figure 1.9 Cesium atomic clock, which can keep accurate time within one second for at least one thousand years. (Courtesy of U.S. Naval Observatory.)

position, whether on earth or in outer space. Certain kinds of astronomical observations that are commonplace in geodesy include large-scale surveying operations, determinations of latitude and longitude, and triangulation networks extending over long meridian arcs of the earth's surface. Accurate knowledge of the earth's exact shape has been derived from the observed gravitational deviations in the earth-orbiting satellite trajectories.

In 1800 Sir William Herschel's detection of the infrared solar radiation by positioning thermometers beyond the visible red end of the sun's spectrum foreshadowed the invention of more sensitive heat detectors. An electrical type of thermometer, called a bolometer, was constructed in 1881 by American astronomer S. P. Langley to investigate the extension of the solar spectrum into the deep infrared region. The present sophisticated wide-ranging bolometers and other types of heat sensors have extensive applications in the physical and space sciences, in the military, in medicine, and in industry. One of the most useful by-products of astronomical research has been the spectroscope, conceived in its present form by Joseph Fraunhofer, German optician, in 1814 to observe the sun's spectrum. When the principles of spectrum analysis were laid down a half-century later, rapid progress in the use of the instrument became possible. Since the replacement of the viewing eyepiece by the photographic plate toward the end of the nineteenth century, the device has become one of the most versatile tools employed in scientific and industrial research. The early photoelectric cell was exploited in the 1920's by astronomers seeking to improve their measurements on the brightnesses of the stars. Its successor some twenty years later, the photomultiplier tube, is now universally employed in a variety of ways in science and technology for many applications requiring instrumentation of great light sensitivity. The Schmidt astronomical camera and its modifications

have been used in aerial mapping, military photo-reconnaissance, and in the tracking of space vehicles.

Early in the century the pioneering work by astronomers revealed the close relationship between changes in the solar activity and electrical disturbances in the earth's upper atmosphere and in the earth's magnetic field. One very useful spin-off from these correlation studies over the years is found in the radio propagation forecasts and geophysical alerts accompanying the time signals. They are transmitted on 2.5, 5, 10, 15, 20, and 25 megahertz (megacycles) by the National Bureau of Standards through its stations WWV from Fort Collins, Colorado, and WWVH from Kaui, Hawaii. These radio forewarnings of disturbed propagation conditions are invaluable to the governmental, commercial, military, and amateur broadcast services. The joint cooperation of the solar optical and radio astronomers is leading to an improved understanding of the solar-terrestrial relationships and their possible effects on weather patterns that may some day provide long-range meteorological forecasts beneficial to agriculture and industry.

In the late 1930's when computer technology began its spectacular rise in science and industry, the American astronomer W. J. Eckert applied the newly developed IBM punched-card methods in scientific calculations. One of the earliest uses in science of modern high-speed electronic computers was by astronomers who constructed new planetary tables and recalculated the theory of the lunar motions in the early 1950's, ending up with thousands of pages of figures. The computational experience proved extremely valuable later in the decade in solving the complex equations dealing with the problems of stellar structure and evolution. The first inkling that large amounts of thermonuclear energy could result from the partial annihilation of matter in accordance with Einstein's famous equation,[1] $E = mc^2$, came from the study of stellar

[1] Energy equals mass multiplied by the square of the velocity of light.

interiors half a century ago. Astronomers were also the first to verify certain predictions of Einstein's theory of relativity many years ago.

A branch of astronomy that was quite useless in the technological sense suddenly blossomed into one of great practical expediency in the late 1950's. In the pre-Sputnik period only a handful of astronomers in this country were quietly working in the highly theoretical field of celestial mechanics. Following the orbiting of the first space vehicles in 1957–58, however, the urgent need arose to train more experts capable of applying the principles of gravitational astronomy to the solution of space-vehicle trajectories. This activity has now expanded into the large discipline of astrodynamics.

An interesting astronomical approach to the study of atmospheric pollutants has been developed by an interdisciplinary team of astronomers, atmospheric physicists, chemists, geophysicists, and engineers at the University of Washington. By comparing old and recent plates of the solar spectrum, which is modified by the presence of gases in the earth's atmosphere, it is possible to evaluate the growth of atmospheric contaminants over an interval of time. An analysis carried out by astronomer Paul Hodge indicated that the transparency of the air over the Mount Wilson observatory in southern California deteriorated 22 per cent in the ultraviolet and 10 per cent in the yellow colors during the half-century interval between 1911 and 1960–62.

Other Astronomical Activities

Astronomers cooperate with historians to fix the dates of historical events that occurred near the time of a recorded eclipse of the sun or moon; with archeologists to research the astronomical background of ancient structures (Stonehenge, pyramids, etc.); and with archivists and archeologists to track down in historical records or in cave inscriptions the ancient references to old supernovae (violently exploding stars that suddenly become very bright). Astronomers occasionally are called on to perform individual and community services: informing the public about special or unusual celestial happenings, delivering popular lectures on astronomy to many different kinds of audiences, hosting "open house" visits to observatories by the public, testifying as experts in court trials involving astronomical events, preparing almanacs of astronomical phenomena for certain publications, and combatting by indirection the spreading influence of astrology through science education.

1.4 THE MODERN REVOLUTION IN ASTRONOMY

The Old Astronomy

There was a time, not so many decades ago, when astronomy enjoyed a unique reputation. One distinction rested on the claim that astronomy was the oldest science in existence; another, that its principal observing equipment, the telescope, was the costliest single instrument of research; a third, that, unlike biology and chemistry, astronomers worked with clean, uncluttered instruments; and most significantly, that astronomical research was a rather "useless" but pleasant scientific pursuit.

The New Astronomy

As a result of the transformation that has overtaken it since the end of World War II, astronomy bears little resemblance to its past role. Its title to antiquity still remains unchallenged. The most expensive scientific tool of research on earth today is not the $5.5 million, 200-inch Hale reflector of recent years, nor the present giant radio-telescope array being constructed in New Mexico at a cost of $76 million. The most costly scientific tool is the particle accelerator used by physicists in the study of the atomic nucleus. (The approximate cost of the Stanford linear accelerator is $300 million; that of the proton

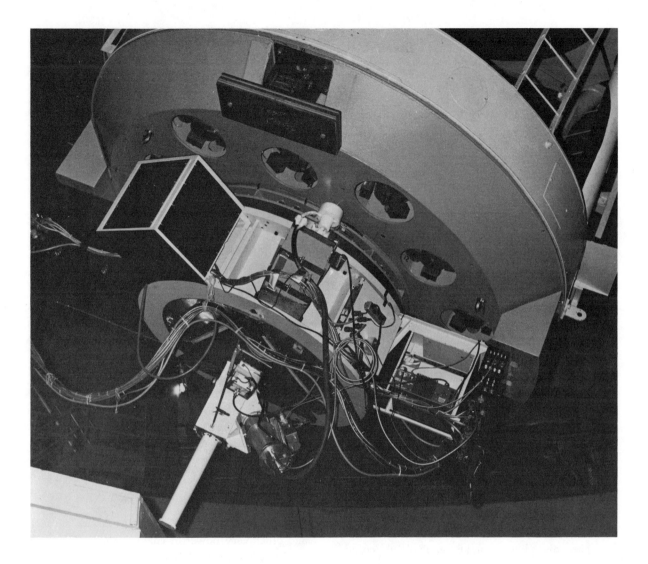

Figure 1.10   Cluttered end of a modern telescope. The long white apparatus at the lower end of the 120-inch Lick reflector is a grating spectrograph. The cylinder projecting out of its right side houses an image scanner. On the right side of the mounting cylinder at the base of the telescope mirror is a container carrying replaceable electronics for special instruments. To its right is a junction box for cabling observational data to a display unit or to the memory bank of a computer in the nearby readout room. (The astronomer may now sit in the warm, well-lighted readout room without suffering the discomfort of exposure to the cold air on a mountaintop.) The black box on the left side of the mounting cylinder contains electronics and controls. Below it and extending to the left is the television housing guider and field viewer. This does not exhaust the listing of attached parts! (Courtesy of G. H. Herbig.)

1 INTRODUCTION TO THE COSMOS

accelerator at the National Accelerator Laboratory near Batavia, Illinois, $250 million.) The telescopic use of sensitive detection devices and electronic accessories, together with their computerized system aids, have become an astronomer's way of life. A modern observatory is more like a physical laboratory than a place where an astronomer looks through a telescope. The descriptive adjective "useless" was employed in the past more for its shock value than for any literal significance associated with the term. Its use merely emphasized the impractical nature of astronomical science which has been concerned chiefly with the cultivation of celestial knowledge for its own sake.

The vigorous cross-fertilization of astronomy with the other sciences has revolutionized astronomical science. It began with the rapid expansion of radio astronomy which brought radio engineers, electronic specialists, and physicists into the profession after World War II. The 200-inch Hale reflecting telescope on Mount Palomar in California, completed in 1948, pushed the space frontier out to double its former value. Since then, powerful new telescopes, equipped with improved light-gathering devices, have been adding to our celestial storehouse of knowledge. In 1958 our first instrumented space vehicles opened up a new vista in the ultraviolet and x-ray celestial radiations hitherto inaccessible from the ground because of atmospheric absorption. Space astronomy is now allied with a number of emerging disciplines, notably exobiology, cosmic chemistry, and astrogeology. Some of the fascinating problems under study in these fields involve life on other worlds; the presence of amino acids in meteorites and organic molecules in the interstellar clouds of our Galaxy; and the extraterrestrial exploration of the solar system. Astronomy has been further enriched by the recent surge of theoretical physicists, specialists in high-energy physics, and relativists into the fields of cosmology and astrophysics per-

Figure 1.11   The Astronomer, painting by D. Owen Stephens. "In Nature's infinite book of secrecy/A little I can read." (Shakespeare, Antony and Cleopatra, *Act I, Scene 2.) (Courtesy of D. Owen Stephens, Hayden Planetarium.)*

taining to the quasars, exploding galaxies, pulsars, and other very powerful energy sources. Who can predict what practical fallouts will eventually materialize when the mechanisms underlying these explosive cosmic events are completely understood?

REVIEW QUESTIONS

1. Describe the role that astronomy has played in enlightening man's knowledge of himself and the universe, and in contributing to his intellectual enrichment.

2. Distinguish among the following designations: (a) pure science; (b) basic science; (c) applied science; (d) empirical science; (e) practical science; (f) experimental science; (g) natural science; (h) physical science; (i) life science; (j) pseudo-science.

3. List several practical achievements that have indirectly materialized as the result of astronomical research.

4. In what way, if any, is your notion of astronomy different from what you thought and what you have learned by reading this chapter?

5. List the principal classes of astronomical bodies existing in the universe, from the smallest to the largest.

6. Among the photographs in this chapter, which one interests you the most and why?

7. From your personal experience as a nonscience student, would you agree with C. P. Snow's contention that there is a polarization between the humanistic and scientific elements in your school?

8. Why are there so few astronomers in comparison with other researchers in the scientific profession?

9. In what way are astronomers justified in claiming that astronomy is the oldest science? Could not physics, chemistry, or biology claim priority?

10. Astronomy has also been classed as a cultural science—one with attached esthetic values. Can you give any reasons why this is so?

SELECTED READINGS

Campbell, N., *What Is Science?*, Dover, 1952.

Dubos, R., *Reason Awake*, Columbia University Press, 1970.

Friedlander, M. W., *The Conduct of Science*, Prentice-Hall, 1972.

Hoyle, F., *Of Men and Galaxies*, University of Washington Press, 1964.

Huxley, J., *What Dare I Think*, Harper, 1931.

Melsen, A. G., *Science and Responsibility*, Duquesne University Press, 1970.

Shapley, H., *The View from a Distant Star*, Basic Books, 1963.

Weaver, W., *Science and Imagination*, Basic Books, 1967.

Ptolemaic model of the universe from "The Cosmographical Glasse, conteinyng the pleasant Principles of Cosmographie, Geographie, Hydrographie, or Navigation," by William Cunningham, London, 1559.

DESCRIPTIONS
OF THE COSMOS

Hereafter, when they come to model heaven
And calculate the stars, how will they
    wield
The mighty frame, how build, unbuild,
    contrive
To save appearances, how gird the sphere
With centric and eccentric scribbled o'er,
Cycle and epicycle, orb in orb.

    John Milton (1608–1674),
    Paradise Lost, Book 8

To the ancient worship of the "celestial deities" we owe the deification of the planets, the depiction of the constellations, the signs of the zodiac, the origin of the days of the week, and the pseudoscience of astrology. The ancient civilizations constructed models of the universe centered on man and the earth. Beginning with the early Greek philosophers in the seventh century B.C., astronomy broke loose from the shackles of mythology and astrology and emerged as a pure science in its own right. The evolving concept of the earth-centered universe attained its final fruition in the celebrated model of the geocentric system described in its most elegant form by the last of the great Greek astronomers, Claudius Ptolemy, about A.D. 140. Despite its falsity, it remained steadfastly anchored as the supreme dictum of astronomical thought, bolstered by the great weight of Aristotelian and theological authority, for another one and a half millennia until it was seriously challenged by Copernicus in the sixteenth century. His heliocentric system was firmly established by the work of his successors, Brahe, Kepler, Galileo, and Newton in the century after Copernicus. The crowning achievement of this revolution in astronomy was Newton's discovery of the law of gravitation.

The eighteenth-century imaginative concept of other Milky Way systems as island universes and William Herschel's observational conclusion that our Milky Way was a stellar system in the shape of a grindstone led to further cosmological advances in the nineteenth century. The basic question asked at the beginning of this century was: Do we live in an all-inclusive, one-galaxy universe that embraces all the nebulae or in a multigalaxy universe of which the Milky Way is one representative? The question was firmly resolved in favor of the latter concept in the mid-1920's by Edwin Hubble of the Mt. Wilson Observatory. He proved that the Andromeda spiral nebula and other large spiral nebulae were indeed other Milky Way systems. We exist in an expanding universe filled with billions of galaxies.

2.1 ORIGINS OF ASTRONOMY

Astronomy in Ancient Times

Astronomy arose as a practical necessity when primitive man employed the recurring cycles of the sun, moon, and stars as daily, monthly, and yearly timekeeping mechanisms in regulating his activities. The resourceful use of astronomy by the ancients is seen in the preparation of celestial timetables for the sowing and reaping of crops; in the selection of certain bright stars as navigational guides for travel over the deserts and waters; in the north-south orientation of religious temples and observatories; in the invention of the gnomon (a shadow-casting pillar), the sundial, the water clock, and star-sighting devices for the tracking of time and the recording of seasonal astronomical events. Astronomical know-how was highly prized in all well-developed civilizations of the past.

In the clear skies of the Euphrates, Tigris, and Nile valleys, where the earliest large-scale civilizations flourished over five millennia ago, watchers of the heavens sought to account for the mysterious movements of the celestial bodies by endowing them with miraculous powers. In the constellation groupings of the stars, the ancients envisioned the outlined figures of mythological supermen, animals, and monsters who once reigned over heaven and earth. Religious shrines and observation temples were dedicated to the worship of the principal heavenly bodies: the sun, the moon, and the five known planets. These totaled the mystic number seven, out of which arose the naming of the days of the week.

Figure 2.1   Sunrise over the "heelstone" on the day of the summer solstice at Stonehenge, an ancient observatory constructed in three main stages of activity between 2000 B.C. and 1500 B.C., approximately. Its ruins lie on Salisbury Plain, Wiltshire, England. (Courtesy of Department of the Environment, England.)

The Seven Days of the Week

The origin of the days of the week is credited to the Babylonians. They arranged the seven celestial bodies according to their observed motions among the stars. Saturn took the longest time to complete its course in the heavens, and then in succession came Jupiter, Mars, the sun, Venus, Mercury, and the moon. Each body in turn controlled one hour of the 24-hour day as shown in Table 2.1. The "planet" that ruled over the first hour became the reigning deity of the day named after it. Thus Saturday was named after Saturn, Sunday after the sun, Monday after the moon, and so on.

The naming of the days follows the Latinized version in the Romance languages (French, Italian, Spanish) as shown in Table 2.2. In English and German, deviations exist in the naming of Tuesday, Wednesday, Thursday, and Friday.

Signs of the Zodiac

Observations by the priest-astronomers over the centuries revealed that the motions of the sun, moon, and planets were confined almost exclusively to a narrow zone in the heavens, sixteen degrees wide, centered on the sun's yearly path (the ecliptic). The band was divided into twelve equal constellational divisions or signs through which the sun passed monthly in succession during the course of the year. Several thousand years ago, the vernal equinox, which is located in the sign of Aries, lay in the constellation of Aries. Today the constellation of Pisces occupies the sign of Aries, the constellation of

Table 2.1   The Planetary Arrangement for the Hours of the Day

Saturn	Jupiter	Mars	Sun	Venus	Mercury	Moon
[1	2	3	4	5	6	7
8	9	10	11	12	13	14
15	16	17	18	19	20	21
22	23	24]	[1	2	3	4
5	6	7	8	9	10	11
12	13	14	15	16	17	18
19	20	21	22	23	24]	[1 etc.

Table 2.2   Origins of the Names for Days

Body	English	German	French	Italian	Spanish
Sun	Sunday	Sonntag	Dimanche[a]	Domenica[a]	Domingo[a]
Moon	Monday	Montag	Lundi	Lunedi	Lunes
Mars	Tuesday[b]	Dienstag[c]	Mardi	Martedi	Martes
Mercury	Wednesday[d]	Mittwoch[e]	Mercredi	Mercoledi	Miercoles
Jupiter	Thursday [f]	Donnerstag[g]	Jeudi	Giovedi	Jueves
Venus	Friday[h]	Freitag[h]	Vendredi	Venerdi	Viernes
Saturn	Saturday	Samstag	Samedi	Sabato	Sabado

[a]Means "day of the Lord."
[b]Named after *Tiw,* Norse-Germanic god of battle.
[c]Named after *ding* (assembly).
[d]Named after *Woden,* Norse god of wisdom.
[e]Means "middle of week."
[f]Named after *Thor,* Norse god of thunder.
[g]*Donner* is thunder in German.
[h]Named after *Frigga,* goddess of love and fertility.

Aquarius occupies the sign of Pisces, etc. The signs of the zodiac are thus out of step with the constellations of the same name due to the phenomenon of the precession of the equinoxes. It causes the equinoxes, including the signs, to slide westward along the ecliptic about fifty seconds of arc per year. The description of this phenomenon appears in Section 6.5.

2.2   ANCIENT COSMOLOGY

Early Accounts of Genesis

A familiar central theme that dominated a number of archaic cosmologies was the conviction that the universe was created out of a great void of darkness, necessitating the superhuman labors of the gods to fashion it into an existing world order before it could be occupied by mortal man. Another illusion shared by many peoples was one that could symbolically be called "egocentric," the natural inclination to place one's self and country at the center of the universe. Later, "egocentric" was transformed to "geocentric" when the earth as a whole was considered the hub of the universe.

We are all familiar with the Biblical version of Genesis: "In the beginning, God created the heavens, and the earth. And the earth was without form and void; and darkness was upon the face of the deep." And after six days of labor, everything was in place in the world as we know it. The Greek legend of Genesis begins with Chaos from whom issued Erebus,

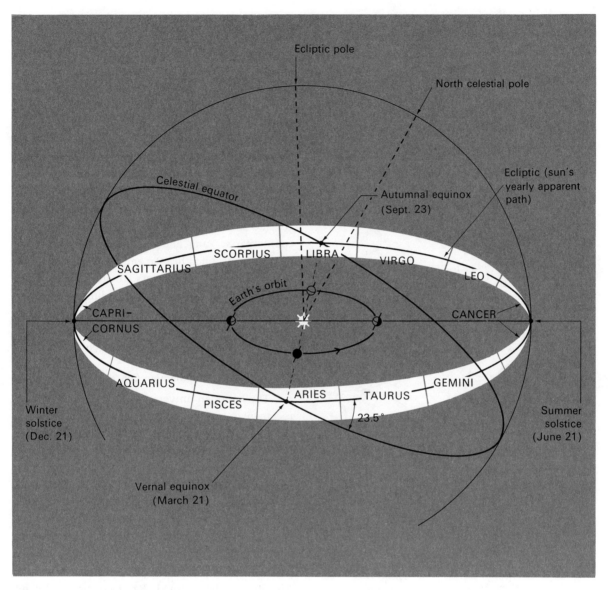

Figure 2.2 Signs of the zodiac. Each day as the earth moves eastward about one degree in its orbit, the sun, as we view it, appears to move about one degree eastward along a path called the ecliptic. *At the end of one year the sun therefore, because of the earth's orbital motion, appears to move completely around the sky 360 degrees. The ecliptic is inclined to the extension of the earth's equator in the sky, the celestial equator, by 23.5 degrees. This is the amount that the earth's axis is tipped from the vertical to the plane of the earth's orbit. The point of intersection between the ecliptic and the celestial equator, which the sun reaches about March 21, is called the* vernal equinox. *The opposite point of intersection in the sky, reached by the sun about September 23, is called the* autumnal equinox.

2 DESCRIPTIONS OF THE COSMOS

THE SPRING SIGNS

ARIES—The Ram TAURUS—The Bull THE PLEIADES Seven Sisters GEMINI—The Twins

THE SUMMER SIGNS

CANCER—The Crab LEO—The Lion VIRGO—The Virgin

THE AUTUMN SIGNS

LIBRA—The Scales SCORPIUS—The Scorpion SAGITTARIUS—The Archer

THE WINTER SIGNS

CAPRICORNUS—The Sea Goat AQUARIUS—The Water Carrier PISCES—The Fishes

Figure 2.3   Outline figures of the zodiacal constellations.

the darkness under Earth, and black Night who conceived Aether and Day. From Earth came the firstborn, Heaven, destined to harbor Earth's other children who, from their Olympian heights, fought among themselves for the mastery of the world. The Indian account of creation reverts to a familiar theme: In the beginning, all was without form and substance; darkness and space enveloped the undifferentiated waters. Father Sky and Mother Earth conceived the gods who molded the geography of the earth. The ancient Chinese had no clearly defined description of the origin of the universe. Nature was considered to be divided into male and female counterparts, Yang and Yin. They were the vital force that sustained heaven and earth, supplied light to the sun, moon, and stars, rotated the sky, and held the earth motionless. According to Egyptian legend, the earth-god, Sibu, and the sky goddess, Nuit, were originally joined together as mates until the god of sunshine forcibly separated them.

Egyptian and Mesopotamian Concepts of the Universe

The Egyptian universe was conceived as a large rectangular box whose known terrestrial portions, the Mediterranean area and its fringes, lay at the bottom with Egypt naturally occupying the center. Above stretched the vault of the sky from which hung the celestial lamps of the stars that were invisible in the daylight. Supporting the dome of the heavens at the four cardinal points of the compass were lofty peaks connected by a procession of mountains. Around the base of the mountains circulated a great celestial river whose principal branch was the Nile River. The sun-god, Ra, accompanied by his attendants, was carried daily westward in the solar boat along the celestial river at a uniform speed. At the close of the day he disappeared behind an eternally shrouded, dark region, reappearing in the east on the following day.

Across the Red Sea from the land of the pharaohs

Figure 2.4 *The ancient Hindu universe. The Hindu universe was enclosed by a giant cobra. The tortoise, symbol of force and creative power, floated on a sea of milk. Upon its back stood four elephants supporting the earth at the east, west, north, and south points of the horizon. It was crowned by the triangle from whose top gleamed the symbol of creation. (Courtesy of The Bettman Archive.)*

Figure 2.5 *The early Egyptian universe. The sun-god Ra is shown in the upper left traveling along the celestial river in his boat. The star lamps, suspended from the ceiling of the sky, were lit and extinguished by the gods. (Courtesy of American Museum of Natural History.)*

dwelt two other civilized peoples in ancient Mesopotamia, the Babylonians and the Chaldeans. Their concept of the universe resembled that of the Egyptians: an enclosed chamber with their part of the world at the center. The earth floated on the surrounding eternal waters beyond which rose a great circular wall that served as the supporting structure for the metal dome of the sky. The dawn-god, Shamosh, sallied forth from the eastern gate of the wall in his chariot at the appointed time, accompanied by two divine attendants, to begin his daily drive across the heavens before disappearing at twilight into a tunnel at the western terminus.

The Practice of Astrology

Although the Egyptians and the Babylonians indulged in astrology, the Chaldeans raised it to a fine but misleading art. The notion that the stars and the planets exercise some kind of secret control over human affairs by virtue of their particular configurations is a preposterous delusion. Shakespeare discredits astrology in the following words (sonnet 14):

> Not from the stars do I my judgement pluck;
> And yet methinks I have astronomy,
> But not to tell of good or evil luck,
> Of plagues, of dearth, or season's quality.

The Chaldean priest-astrologers performed their nightly rites from the temple observatories convinced that they must constantly watch the movements of the heavenly bodies in order to interpret the will of the gods for the benevolent guidance of mankind. According to historians, the Tower of Babel[1] served as a Chaldean religio-astronomical observatory. It was a pyramidal edifice constructed of seven different colored-stone layers, one for each principal celestial body. The lowest story, in black stone, represented Saturn; then in ascending order rose Jupiter in orange, Mars in red, the sun in gold, Venus in yellow, Mercury in blue, and the moon in silver. The top of the tower served as an observing platform from which the priest-astrologers studied the movements of the heavenly bodies.

2.3   GREEK COSMOLOGY; THE GEOCENTRIC SYSTEM

The Earth Takes Shape

Much of early Greek astronomy, including astrology, was inherited from the contemporaneous Egyptians and Babylonians. From the seventh century B.C. onward, under the tutelage of wise philosophers, astrological influences were purged from astronomy which emerged as a true science in its own right. Astronomical attitudes were then directed into more rigorous channels that paved the way for a more rational approach to celestial phenomena.

The early philosophers pictured the earth as a flat disk floating in water or riding in air like a kite. Succeeding philosophers, realizing that the earth was spherical because it cast a circular shadow on the moon during a lunar eclipse, conceived of the earth as an immovable globe surrounded by the outermost fixed sphere of the heavens. Next in sequence was

the rotating star sphere which accounted for the daily rising and setting of the celestial bodies. There remained the problem of interpreting the varying motions of the sun, moon, and the five "wanderers" or planets among the stars. It was noted that the planets would sometimes temporarily reverse their normal eastward motion among the stars and execute a closed or open loop (↶ or ꞩ) before resuming their eastward journey.

Development of the Geocentric System

Greek philosophical doctrine dictated that the observed celestial movements be accountable on the basis of various combinations of uniform circular motions centered on the earth. Nature, it was reasoned, displayed her celestial wares in the form of the "perfect" geometrical figure of the sphere, combined with flawless circular movement. One acceptable solution proposed in the fourth century B.C. utilized twenty-seven uniformly rotating concentric shells centered on the earth: one for the stars, three each for the sun and moon, and four each for the five planets. The outside spherical shell of the stars accounted for the daily westward rotation of the sky. Each prime body required a set of separate shells whose poles could rotate independently of the pole of the sky. The exterior shell in each set produced the daily westward motion along with the stars. The remaining inner shells rotated at different rates, some in opposite directions, to produce the observed nonuniform easterly motions of the sun and moon, and the looped motions of the planets. Subsequently, Aristotle (384–321 B.C.) employed a total of fifty-five concentric shells in order to account more accurately for the complex motions of the sun, moon, and the planets. Two major deficiencies of the Aristotelian scheme were its inability to explain the changes in the observed brightness of the planets and to interpret satisfactorily the variable motions of the sun, moon, and the planets.

---

[1] The Chaldean translation is "Gateway to the Highest God"; in Hebrew, "Babel" signifies "confusion."

Final Form of the Geocentric System

A new chapter in astronomy began with the transfer of Hellenistic culture from its previous center in Athens to Alexandria in Egypt about 300 B.C. The Alexandrian astronomers undertook the task of improving the geometric model of the geocentric system in order to reduce the discrepancies between observation and theory. The final version appeared in the *Great Syntaxis of Astronomy*, renamed *The Almagest* in the Arabian translation. It was a thirteen-volume astronomical encyclopedia compiled by the last of the Alexandrian astronomers, Ptolemy (A.D., c. 90–168).

In the Ptolemaic system, each planet was imagined to move uniformly around a small circle called an *epicycle*. Its center in turn revolved uniformly around the earth on the circumference of a large circle called the *deferent*. The rotary motion of the planet on the circumference of the epicycle, com-

bined with the revolution of the center of the epicycle around the earth, produced a loop with retrograde movement. The moon and sun possessed no epicycles. They completed their respective journeys around the earth in 27.3 days and $365\frac{1}{4}$ days. Each of the three outer planets (Mars, Jupiter, and Saturn) moved around in its epicycle once a year, maintaining a parallelism between the line joining the planet to its epicycle center and the moving earth-sun line. The center of the epicycle completed its journey along the deferent in the planet's orbital period around the earth. Each of the two inner planets (Mercury and Venus) moved around its epicycle once in its orbital period while the center of the epicycle, located on the earth-sun line, described a complete revolution around the earth in one year. This resulted in Venus and Mercury swinging from one side of the sun to the other in accordance with their observed motions as morning and evening "stars." An added refine-

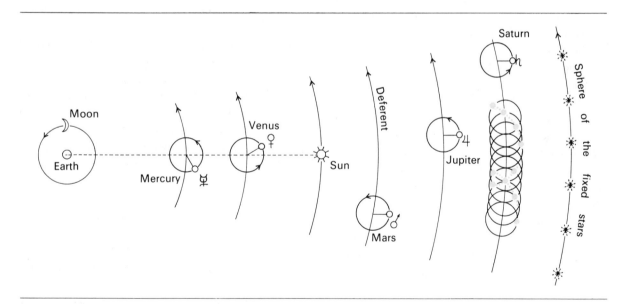

Figure 2.6   Schematic of the Ptolemaic system. The looped motion of Saturn is shown as its epicycle rotates while the center of the epicycle moves along the deferent.

2 DESCRIPTIONS OF THE COSMOS

ment (not shown in the diagram) was to place the earth slightly off-center of the deferent system in order to account better for the planetary variations and for the nonuniform motions of the sun and the moon. As conceived by Ptolemy and his predecessors, the geocentric system was in reality a mathematical representation rather than an actual physical model of the planetary configurations.

2.4 MEDIEVAL COSMOLOGY

Decline of Astronomy

The golden era of Greek astronomy ended with the major destruction of the famed Alexandrian library in A.D. 390 by Bishop Theophilus, who conspired with the Roman conquerors to eradicate its works under the delusion that the heathen Greek library was a menace to the growth of Christianity. The early Christian fathers, imbued with their religious zeal and unversed in the ways of science, had little use for the pagan (Greek) philosophical methods of inquiry. The heavens, they insisted, were not a great sphere but a vault whose stars were moved by the angels.

The Romans disdained astronomy but readily adopted astrology. The most eloquent orator, Cicero, was a firm believer in the geocentric system. He proclaimed the universe to be composed of nine globes that move. He described the function of each star, planetary, sun, and moon globe in turn and concluded that the earth remained motionless at the center of the universe. On the other hand, the Roman philosopher Seneca questioned whether the earth stood still or rotated. He suggested, as had a few others before him, that the risings and settings of the celestial bodies occurred because men themselves rise and set with the rotating earth.

Revival of Astronomy

When the Arabians became masters of the previously Roman-dominated Byzantine empire dur-

ing the disintegration of the Roman conquests in the seventh century, they resurrected the science of astronomy under the benign patronage of the caliphs. Our knowledge of Ptolemaic cosmology derives indirectly from the Arabian translation of Ptolemy's original work which was lost; the Arabian translation was called *The Almagest* (The Greatest). Although the Arabians were diligent observers and skillful calculators, they did not expound any new astronomical concepts, preferring to elaborate on the Ptolemaic representation of the universe.

By the mid-thirteenth century, knowledge of astronomy had spread throughout medieval Europe as an increasing number of the works of the Greek masters were translated into the Latin language in the newly founded universities where many scholars were gathered. Unlike the preceding centuries of the Dark Ages, secular knowledge was becoming fashionable and reconciled with Christian beliefs. In Spain, under the aegis of Alfonso X (1221–1284), who displayed a keen interest in astronomy, astronomers compiled a comprehensive encyclopedia of astronomical knowledge. The king found the system of Ptolemy hopelessly unmanageable as epicycles were added to epicycles in vain attempts to harmonize the planets' observed positions with the predicted positions given by the theory. "Had I been present at the creation of the universe," Alfonso declared before a gathering of bishops, "I could have given good advice on constructing it in a less complicated manner."

2.5 THE COPERNICAN REVOLUTION

Dissatisfaction with the Ptolemaic System

The invention of the printing press in 1430 accelerated the proliferation of cultural thought—astronomy was no exception. Astronomers working in the newly established European universities were finding increasing inconsistencies in the Ptolemaic

Figure 2.7 Medieval cosmology. Old woodcut shows a curious traveler poking his head through the dome of the sky to discover the celestial machinery that actuates the heavenly bodies.

system and were beginning to raise serious doubts about its validity. Its final coup de grace was administered by the Polish astronomer Nicholas Copernicus. After nearly four decades of study on the problem, he published his monumental work entitled *The Revolutions of the Heavenly Orbs*. It appeared in the year 1543 as he lay on his deathbed. In the preface to his book, which he dedicated to Pope Paul III, he stated that people would cry out that his theory be rejected and that he be subjected to contempt because of the novelty and apparent absurdity of his viewpoint.

The impact of the revolutionary Copernican theory upon the Church was considerably softened by the theologian in charge of the book's printing, Andreas Osiander. He disarmed criticism by anonymously inserting in the text an apologetic note to the reader that read in part: "It is consequently permissible to imagine causes [of the planetary motions] arbitrarily under the sole condition that they should represent geometrically the state of the heavens, and it is not necessary that such hypotheses should be true or even probable."

The Copernican System

Copernicus pointed out that the observed movements of the sun, moon, and the planets with their looping motions could be more accurately represented by placing the sun at the center of the solar system instead of the earth. The orbital motions of these bodies around the sun were being viewed from the moving platform of the earth revolving around the sun. Copernicus was unable to divest himself completely of the Aristotelian insistence of circularity of motion. He was forced to inject into his system, in order to account for the minor deviations from uniformity of motion, a number of epicycles and other mathematical artificialities.

The European religious leaders rejected the heliocentric model as being contrary to the scriptural revelations. Man at the center of the universe was now being relegated to a position of secondary importance in the new scheme. Heretics who defied the authority of the Church by publicly advocating views contrary to its established doctrines would be punished. This fate befell the eminent philosopher Giordano Bruno, who lectured on the Copernican theory and proclaimed that the universe was infinite and contained stars like the sun with orbiting planets that might be inhabited. In 1592 he was charged with heresy and apostasy by the Inquisition. When he refused to recant his views in order to save his soul, he was imprisoned, tortured, and later burned at the stake in the year 1600.

2.6 THE COPERNICAN SUCCESSORS: BRAHE, KEPLER, AND GALILEO

Brahe's Contributions

As sometimes happens throughout the history of science, the right man for the next logical advance appears at the opportune time. Such an individual was the Danish nobleman turned astronomer, Tycho

---

2 DESCRIPTIONS OF THE COSMOS

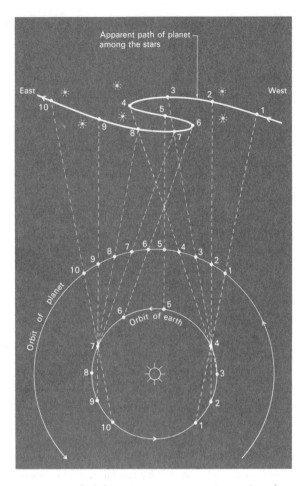

Figure 2.8   The heliocentric arrangement, showing looped planetary motion.

Figure 2.9   Tycho Brahe at work in his observatory on the island of Hven. An observer at the extreme right reads on the great mural quadrant the altitude of the star whose light is projected through an opening in the panel on the left. One assistant checks the clock while another records the measurement. (Courtesy of The Bettmann Archive.)

Brahe. With financial assistance from King Frederick II of Denmark, he constructed in 1582 a superbly equipped observatory on the Island of Hven, about twenty miles northeast of Copenhagen. It was furnished with the most accurate pretelescopic observing instruments ever designed. They enabled Brahe to determine the positions of the heavenly bodies with a precision of two minutes of arc ($\frac{1}{30}$ degree), far surpassing any previous measurements.

Brahe's carefully laid plan was to observe the sun, moon, planets, and stars regularly instead of haphazardly as had been the custom in the past. An uninterrupted record of their movements over many years would then be available for study and analysis. In spite of his careful measurements he had certain reservations about adopting the heliocentric theory in its entirety. He accepted the revolutions of the five planets around the sun as correct but he could not bring himself to believe that the heavy and sluggish earth moved; otherwise its motion could be felt, he argued, and besides, a moving earth was contrary to scriptural belief. He was reinforced in his views by his inability to detect the orbital motion of the earth by means of the parallactic shifts in the brighter stars. Consequently, his cosmological system was a compromise: the planets orbited the sun while the sun and moon in turn orbited a fixed earth.

Johannes Kepler and the Laws of Planetary Motion

Brahe's original scheme to observe the moving celestial bodies methodically eventually bore fruit. His ingenious German assistant, Johannes Kepler, who succeeded Brahe, employed his predecessor's long series of observations to make a number of historic discoveries pertaining to the planetary motions. After twenty-five years of incredible labor, during which he tried and rejected many ideas, none of which satisfied the observational data within acceptable limits, Kepler made known in two separate publications (1609 and 1619) the true nature of the planets' movements. His uncompromising objective that a theoretical model must satisfy the observational facts completely or fail mark him as a scientist in the truest modern sense. "By the study of Mars," Kepler wrote, "we must either arrive at the secrets of astronomy or forever remain in ignorance of them."

The frustrations associated with Ptolemy's ensnaring epicyclic mechanisms were forever banished when Kepler made the great discovery that the orbits of the planets were ellipses and not circles, and that their varying motions were related to their distance from the sun. These results are embodied in the first two of his laws. The third law expresses a relationship between the orbital period of the planet and its distance from the sun.

Kepler's laws of planetary motion are:

Law 1 (Law of Trajectory): Each planet moves in an elliptic orbit around the sun, which occupies one of its two foci.*

Law 2 (Law of Areal Velocity): The imaginary line connecting the planet to the sun sweeps over equal areas of the ellipse in equal intervals of time.

Law 3 (Harmonic Law): The square of the period of orbital revolution of a planet is proportional to the cube of its mean distance from the sun.

In mathematical form Kepler's third law may be written: $P^2 = ka^3$ where k is the constant of proportionality, P is the period of revolution, and a is the mean distance. If we express the period of the planet in years and its mean distance in units of the earth's mean distance from the sun (92,956,000 miles = 1 astronomical unit), the constant $k = 1$ and the formula becomes $P^2 = a^3$.

Example: Calculate the period of Jupiter which orbits the sun at a mean distance of 5.2 astronomical units.

$$P^2 = (5.2)^3 = 140.6$$
$$P = \sqrt{140.6} = 11.86 \text{ years}$$

Significance of Kepler's Laws

Kepler's laws are universal. They apply to any two bodies gravitationally bound to each other whether in the solar system or elsewhere in space. The notion that the planets moved in circular orbits because nature decreed "perfection" in the movements of the heavenly bodies was finally buried forever. This does not preclude the possibility that bodies may move in circular orbits when the focus of the attracting body lies at the center of the circle, which is the limiting form of the ellipse. Kepler did not know why the planets moved in accordance with

*An elipse may be drawn by looping a string taut around two separated tacks (the foci) and a moving pencil.

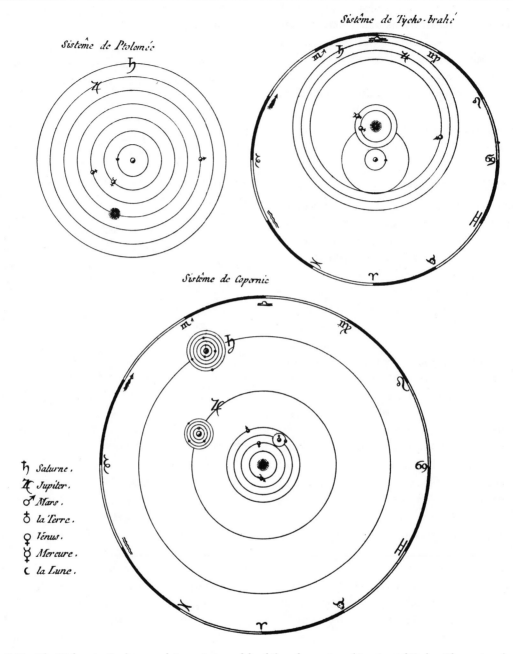

Figure 2.10   The Ptolemaic, Brahean, and Copernican models of the solar system. (Courtesy of Yerkes Observatory.)

his empirically established laws. He had a vague idea that bodies have a natural magnetic affinity for each other and guessed that the sun possessed an attractive force. It remained for Newton to account for the planetary behavior a half-century later.

One major fallout of Kepler's achievement lay in substituting a dynamic planetary model in place of a purely geometrical model. It helped to set the stage for the introduction of the modern concepts of physical science relating to the mathematical analysis of forces in motion and their mutual reactions. One of the chief exponents of this new movement was the Italian physicist-astronomer, Galileo Galilei, whose basic experiments with bodies in motion and the forces governing them laid the foundations of modern mechanics.

Galileo and His Telescope

In another direction, Galileo revolutionized the study of astronomy through the skillful use of an "optic tube" of his own construction in 1609. As the first telescopic explorer of the heavens, he made many exciting observations: the four large satellites of Jupiter; the craters and the mountains on the moon; the sunspots; the phases of Venus; the resolution of the Milky Way into stars. Kepler demonstrated the theoretical validity of the heliocentric system, and Galileo provided some observational support of it. The movements of Jupiter's satellites around the planet were analogous, on a miniature scale, to the motions of the planets around the sun. The discovery that Venus exhibited the complete cycle of phases offered the most convincing

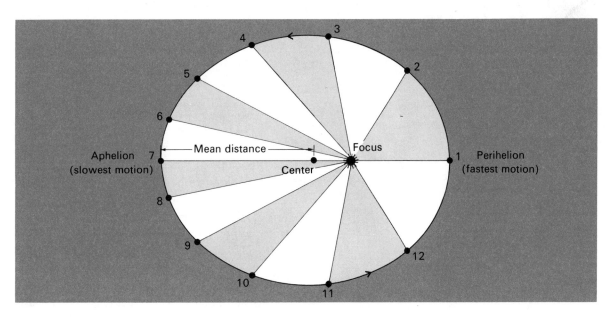

Figure 2.11 Kepler's law of trajectory and law of areas. Since all sectors, shaded and unshaded, are equal in area, the planet passes through the successive numbered positions in equal intervals of time. The mean distance is equal to one-half the length of the major axis whose end points are 1 and 7.

2 DESCRIPTIONS OF THE COSMOS

evidence. According to the Ptolemaic arrangement, the phases of Venus were confined between the new and crescent phases.

In his widely read work published in 1632, *The Dialogues of Galileo Galilei on the Two Principal Systems of the World: the Ptolemaic and the Copernican*, Galileo had presented the heliocentric system as an unproven alternative to the geocentric system as Pope Urban VIII had earlier admonished him to expound it. Subsequently, the Church felt he had cast the Ptolemaic system in an unfavorable light and accused him of expressing opinions which were contrary to Holy Scripture. The Holy Office of Rome had issued the following decree in February 1616:

> The following propositions are to be censured: (1) that the Sun is at the center of the world and the universe. . . . Unanimously, this proposition has been declared stupid and absurd as a philosophy, and formally heretic because it contradicts in express manner sentences in the Holy Scripture. . . . (2) that the Earth is not at the center of the world and motionless, but changes its place entirely according to its diurnal movement. Unanimously, this proposition is declared false as a philosophy. . . .

Galileo's book was officially banned and in 1632 the great scientist was publicly humiliated by a papal tribunal, forced to recant his heretical views, and placed under house detention in his declining years until his death in 1642. The official condemnation of Galileo was lifted in 1965 by the Ecumenical Council called by Pope John XXIII. The ban on his *Dialogues* was removed from the *Index of Prohibited Books* in 1835.

2.7 ISAAC NEWTON AND THE LAW OF GRAVITATION

The final and most imposing groundwork in laying the foundations of physical astronomy was provided by Isaac Newton through his development

Figure 2.12   Galileo's telescopes, now displayed in a museum in Florence, Italy. The smaller telescope is the first of his "optic tubes." (Courtesy of Yerkes Observatory.)

of the physical laws relating to matter, force, and motion and to his celebrated discovery of the law of gravitation. With the aid of a powerful mathematical tool, the calculus, which he invented,[1] the entire field of celestial mechanics became ripe for analysis by his successors. Guided by Kepler's laws, he deduced the basic universal law that governs all motion in space originating from gravitational forces. The results of his remarkable investigations are incorporated in his famous publication, *The Principia*, published in 1687 with the generous assistance of his good friend, Edmund Halley, the illustrious English astronomer.

[1] The German philosopher and scientist G. W. Leibnitz also invented the calculus (1675) without knowledge of Newton's earlier unpublished results.

Newton's Laws of Motion

The laws of motion are basic to the development of the law of gravitation. We begin with a statement expressing each of Newton's laws of motion. These laws rest upon the labors of previous experimenters, Galileo in particular.

First Law: A body remains at rest or moves along a straight line with constant velocity so long as no external force acts upon it.

Second Law: A body acted upon by a force will accelerate in the direction of the applied force. The greater the force or the smaller the mass, the greater will be the acceleration.

Third Law: A body subjected to a force reacts with an equal counterforce on the applied force, that is, action and reaction are equal and oppositely directed.

Mass should not be confused with *weight*. Mass is a measure of the total matter content of a body whose value remains unaltered, regardless of its position in space—whether on the earth, the moon, or in some other galaxy. The weight of an object is a measure of the gravitational force that the attracting body exerts on the object. For example, a man weighing 180 pounds on the earth's surface would weigh 30 pounds on the moon's surface because the moon's gravitational pull is one-sixth that of the earth's gravitational pull. His mass content is the same, whether on the moon or on the earth.

Newton's Derivation of the Law of Gravitation

In order to follow Newton's reasoning in establishing the law of gravitation, we shall adopt a simplified, descriptive approach to the problem without complicating it mathematically. From Kepler's first law of planetary motion, Newton inferred with the aid of his second law of motion that if a planet moves in a curved path, in this case an ellipse, there must be a force acting on it. From the mathematical analysis of Kepler's second law of areal velocity, Newton showed that the force acting on the planet is a central force, namely the sun. He deduced that the only kind of force that would satisfy Kepler's requirement that the sun must be at the focus of the ellipse and be consistent with Kepler's harmonic law is an inverse-square law. This implies that the force varies inversely as the square of the distance between the planet and the sun. Several of Newton's contemporaries suspected an inverse-square relationship but could not prove it. Finally, making use of his third law of motion, Newton put his results together into one comprehensive statement, the law of gravitation. He demonstrated its universality by proving that it applied to the falling apple and the earth, to the motion of the moon around the earth (in reality, another body falling earthward about $\frac{1}{10}$ in/sec^2), and to the revolution of the planets around the sun. Indeed, he imagined gravitation to be operative beyond the limits of the solar system, the proof of which was later verified.

The Law of Gravitation

Expressed in words, the law of gravitation states:

Objects in the universe attract each other with a force that varies directly as the product of their masses and inversely as the square of their respective distances from each other.

If m_1 represents the mass of one body, m_2, the mass of a second body, d, the distance between their centers, F, the mutual force of gravity between them, and G, the constant of gravitation, the law in mathematical form becomes:

$$F = \frac{Gm_1 m_2}{d^2}$$

In dealing with spherical bodies, Newton proved that such bodies act as if their gravitational mass is concentrated at their centers, thus enormously simplifying their mathematical treatment. Examples

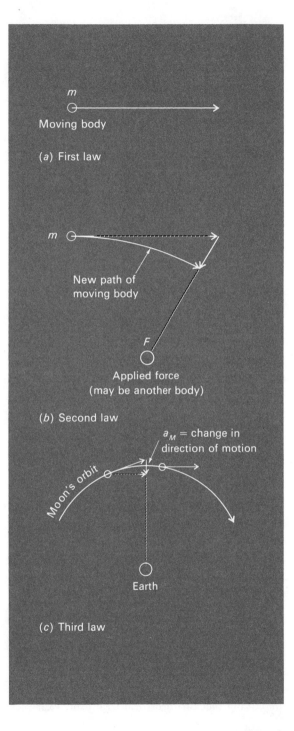

m
Moving body

(*a*) First law

m

New path of
moving body

F

Applied force
(may be another body)

(*b*) Second law

a_M = change in
direction of motion

Moon's orbit

Earth

(*c*) Third law

Figure 2.13   Illustrations of Newton's laws of motion. (a) First law: rectilinear uniform motion when no force is applied; hence acceleration is zero. (b) Second law: acceleration effect; moving body undergoes change in direction or speed or both. Acceleration = force/mass or a = F/m or F = m · a. (c) Third law: earth exerts a gravitational force on the moon which is exactly counterbalanced by the moon's force on the earth and oppositely directed, although the respective accelerations are different. From the second law, force on moon by earth, F_M, equals mass of moon, m_M, times acceleration of moon, a_M, or $F_M = m_M \cdot a_M$. Force on earth by moon, F_E, equals mass of earth, m_E, times acceleration of earth, a_E, or $F_E = m_E \cdot a_E$. From the third law, force on moon equals force on earth or $F_M = F_E$. Hence, $m_M \cdot a_M = m_E \cdot a_E$. Since the mass of the moon is 1/81 of the earth's mass, its acceleration is 81 times greater than the earth's acceleration. From knowledge of the moon's orbit, one calculates that the actual value of the moon's acceleration, a_M, is 0.1 in/sec^2. This agrees with the value derived from the law of gravitation as Newton first demonstrated, thus confirming the validity of the law.

Figure 2.14   Comparison of gravitational forces.

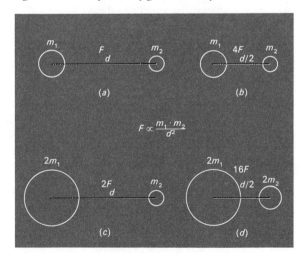

m_1 F m_2
        d

m_1 $4F$ m_2
        $d/2$

(*a*)

(*b*)

$$F \propto \frac{m_1 \cdot m_2}{d^2}$$

$2m_1$ $2F$ m_2
               d

$2m_1$ $16F$ $2m_2$
              $d/2$

(*c*)

(*d*)

showing how the force of gravity varies under different circumstances are shown in Figure 2.14.

The constant of gravitation, G, is one of the fundamental constants of nature.[1] One method of evaluating it makes use of a torsion balance, a device consisting of a lightweight rod suspended at the center by a fine quartz fiber and carrying a small sphere at each end. A large mass brought close to one of the spheres causes the fiber to twist as a result of the gravitational attraction between the two bodies. From the known masses of the two bodies (m_1 and m_2), their separation (d), and the measured gravitational force (F) given by the amount of twist, the constant G in Newton's law is calculated. Its numerical value in the metric system is 0.0000000667 (6.67 $\times 10^{-8}$) cm^3/g · sec^2.

Newton also derived the accurate expression of

[1] Sections such as this that appear in color are optional and may be skipped if too technical for the student.

Figure 2.15   Permissible orbits under the law of gravitation.

Kepler's third law by evaluating the constant k in terms of basic physical units. The comparison appears as:

$$P^2 = ka^3 \qquad \text{(Kepler's version)}$$

$$P^2 = \frac{4\pi^2 a^3}{G(m_\odot + m_p)} \qquad \text{(Newton's version)}$$

where $k = 4\pi^2/[G(m_\odot + m_p)]$, $m_\odot$ is the mass of the sun, m_p is the mass of the planet, P is the orbital period, and a is its mean distance from the sun. Note that k is not quite a true constant since the mass of each planet, though a small fraction of the solar mass, is different for each planet.

Permissible Orbits under the Law of Gravitation

Newton went on to prove that the orbit of a body revolving around another is one of a family of curves called *conic sections*. They are so called because they are formed when a plane is passed through a right circular cone at different angles. The ellipse of a planetary orbit is one example of a conic section. The ellipse is obtained when the cutting plane inter-

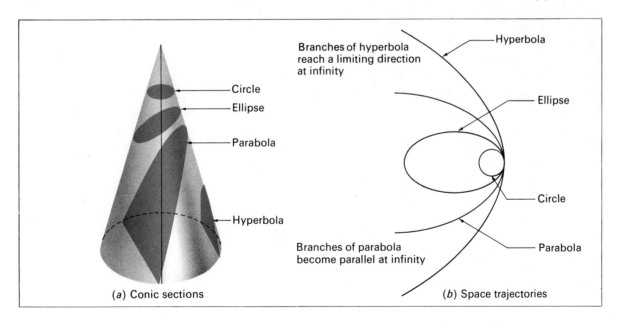

Circle
Ellipse
Parabola
Hyperbola

Branches of hyperbola reach a limiting direction at infinity

Hyperbola
Ellipse
Circle
Parabola

Branches of parabola become parallel at infinity

(a) Conic sections   (b) Space trajectories

2 DESCRIPTIONS OF THE COSMOS

sects both sides of the slant edge of the cone. The circle is derived when the plane cuts the cone at right angles to the vertical axis. The remaining two conic sections are open-ended. The parabola is formed when the plane is passed through the cone exactly parallel to its slant element, and the hyperbola is obtained when the cone is intersected at a smaller angle with the vertical axis. In either the parabolic or hyperbolic trajectory, the body will orbit the attractive central force only once, never to return as it recedes toward infinity. The solar family obviously consists of those members that move around the sun in the closed paths of an ellipse or a circle. An object approaching the sun from outside the solar system would, if undisturbed, theoretically travel around the sun in the open-ended trajectory of a hyperbola or parabola.

2.8 COSMOLOGICAL ADVANCES IN THE POST-NEWTONIAN ERA

Expansion of Astronomical Knowledge

By the end of the seventeenth century the true nature of the solar system and its obedience to the law of gravitation had been settled to a fair degree of understanding. Astronomers had accumulated a century of observational data with improved telescopes on the bodies composing the solar system, the individual stars, the nebulae, and the Milky Way. The universe was no longer the simple earth-centered, one-world universe. In 1718 Edmund Halley obtained proof that the stars were not fixed but in motion. On comparing the positions of the bright stars Sirius, Arcturus, and Procyon with those given in the catalogs of Hipparchus and Ptolemy some 1,700 years earlier, he discovered that these stars had shifted their positions slightly in the sky. It was realized that the stars were at unfathomable distances from the earth. Not until 1837–39 did astronomers succeed in measuring the parallaxes of three stars and deriving

their distances: Alpha Centauri (3 light-years); 61 Cygni (10 light-years); Vega (13 light-years).[1] Today we know the distances of many thousands of stars from a variety of methods.

Cosmological Speculations

In 1576 the English astronomer Thomas Digges had wondered, as had Bruno, whether the universe "have his boundes or bee in deed infinite and without boundes" in his book, *Perfit Description of the Celestial Orbes.* Several decades later Galileo was to advance the notion of an infinite and unbounded universe in his *Dialogues.* He had already noted in his telescope that the Milky Way consisted of myriads of stars.

What was the true nature of the Milky Way? The Swedish philosopher Emanuel Swedenborg hinted in 1734 that the stars formed a vast single system of which the solar system was but one constitutent. Thomas Wright of England theorized in his work, *An Original Theory of the Universe,* in 1750 that the Milky Way was a disk-shaped, star-studded structure in which the individual stars, including the sun, revolved around its center similar to the planets' revolution around the sun. The physical similarity of the stars to the sun, however, was not demonstrated until the early part of the nineteenth century by Joseph Fraunhofer in his spectral examination of the brighter stars. Immanuel Kant, the famous German philosopher, expanded Wright's concept by suggesting in 1755 that the small, oval, nebulous objects observed in telescopes were other Milky Way systems or "island universes," a phrase that was to capture the popular fancy a century and a half later.

The Grindstone Concept of the Milky Way

Turning all prior speculations aside, one might ask: What observational evidence was there regard-

[1] The modern values of the distances are, respectively: 4.3, 11, and 26 light-years.

Figure 2.16 *A cluster of distant galaxies in Corona Borealis, photographed with the 200-inch Hale reflector. The small, fuzzy, lens-shaped objects are the galaxies. (Courtesy of Hale Observatories.)*

2 DESCRIPTIONS OF THE COSMOS

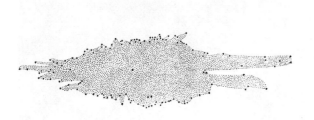

Figure 2.17 Herschel's grindstone model of the Milky Way. The sun is the star at the approximate center. The cleavage at the right end is caused by the obscuring Great Rift that divides the Milky Way into two branches between Cygnus and Centaurus.

ing the structure of the Milky Way? In 1785 William Herschel of England provided the first quantitative proof that the Milky Way was a disk-shaped, stellar structure in the form of a grindstone. He did this by conducting a "Gallup poll" method of sampling star counts within strategic selected areas of the sky. Because his telescopic vision was limited, he placed the sun at the center of the stellar system whose diameter he estimated as 20,000 light years, one-fifth the actual diameter. Herschel ventured the opinion that many of the misty, lens-shaped nebulae observed in his telescope were the island universes that Kant had envisioned earlier.

A Cosmic Hierarchy?

A contemporary of Kant, the Alsatian philosopher-scientist Johann H. Lambert, gave full rein to his imagination by suggesting that our own universe was only one system in a hierarchy of other universes filled with stellar bodies. This type of argument reached its zenith in the early part of the twentieth century when Swedish astronomer C. V. L. Charlier proposed his hierarchal system of successive orders

of complexity. Might not the simplest clumped form of matter begin with a star cluster, followed in order by a single galaxy, a cluster of galaxies, and so on? Some observational evidence at present suggests that clusters of clusters of galaxies (superclusters) exist, but that seems to be the limit.

2.9 DEVELOPMENT OF MODERN COSMOLOGY

Nineteenth-Century Views

In 1826 German astronomer H. W. M. Olbers uncovered a puzzling situation. He had proved mathematically that the combined light of an infinite number of stars uniformly distributed in an infinite static universe would lead to a sky that was not dark at night. We now know that Olbers' paradox, as it was called, has a ready explanation. The expansion of the universe reddens the starlight traveling over vast distances, thereby weakening the energy of the starlight and accounting for the dark of the sky.[1]

As additional nebulosities came to light during the nineteenth century, the general consensus was growing that they belonged to one system, our Galaxy. Large numbers of nebulous objects were found to be resolvable in the form of gaseous clouds, filamentary or ring-shaped structures, and star clusters. The spectroscopic examination revealed numbers of nebulae to be truly gaseous. In addition, the symmetrical distribution of the nebulae with respect to the Milky Way and the mixed appearance of stars and gas in the same nebula were advanced as arguments against the existence of external galaxies.

Early Twentieth-Century Views

At the start of this century the introduction of photography began to provide more accurate and detailed views of the nebulae than all the previous

[1]The energy of light grows weaker with increasing wavelength, that is, toward the red (described in Section 4.2).

visual observations had been able to muster. Thousands of nebulae, including many spirals, were recorded on the plates of the 36-inch Crossley reflector of the Lick Observatory. Published distances for the Great Nebula in Andromeda (the nearest large spiral) ranged from 1,600 to 30,000 light-years, an underestimate by a factor of fifty or more. Figures for the diameter of our Galaxy ranged from 6,000 to 15,000 light-years, an underestimate by seven to fifteen times. The nature of the Milky Way and the nebulae, and their status with respect to each other and to the Milky Way, remained uncertain at this stage.

In 1922 Dutch astronomer J. C. Kapteyn, employing statistical methods based on photographic star counts and mean stellar distances and brightnesses, derived a sun-centered model of the Galaxy, 50,000 light-years in diameter and 6,000 light-years thick. Five years earlier, American astronomer Harlow Shapley had concluded from his analysis of some sixty globular star clusters, photographed with the 60-inch Mt. Wilson reflector, that they formed a spheroidal system centered on our flattened stellar system; that the overall dimensions of the Galaxy were 300,000 light-years across and 30,000 light-years thick; and that the sun was located 65,000 light-years from the center of the system. The eccentric position of the sun was a startling result not readily accepted at the time. The diameter of the Galaxy, however, was overestimated by a factor of 300 per cent.

In a historic debate before the National Academy of Sciences on April 26, 1920, between Shapley of the Mt. Wilson Observatory and H. D. Curtis of the Lick Observatory, both of whom had substantial photographic data at their disposal, Shapley advocated the one-galaxy concept while Curtis favored the multigalaxy concept. Shapley argued that the spiral nebulae recorded on the photographic plates were some 10,000 light-years distant and only a few

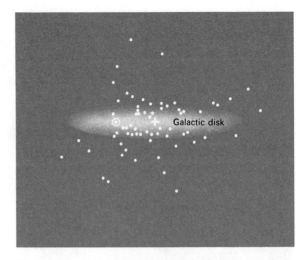

Figure 2.18   Shapley's globular cluster distribution (1917). The globular clusters are represented as white dots, the sun is shown as a circle with a concentric dot, and the cross marks the center of the Milky Way.

hundred light-years in diameter. Curtis maintained that these objects were galaxies similar to our Galaxy.

Modern Twentieth-Century View

In 1923 the true nature of the spiral nebulae was revealed by Edwin Hubble, the Mt. Wilson astronomer, from a careful photographic analysis of the Great Nebula in Andromeda and another great spiral in Triangulum. He had succeeded in resolving their outer portions into multitudes of stars on plates taken with the 100-inch reflector which had recently been placed in operation. Among their stars were numbers of supergiant stars called *cepheids* whose periodic variations of light were similar to those observed in our Galaxy. Employing these cepheids as "standard candles" whose luminosities had previously been calibrated within our own Galaxy, Hubble derived a distance, two years later, of 900,000 light-years for the two spirals, an underestimate of about 100 per cent. No longer was there any doubt that the spiral nebulae were indeed island universes as Kant

Figure 2.19   The nearby spiral galaxy, M 33, in Triangulum. Its distance is slightly more than two million light-years, photographed with the 200-inch Hale telescope. (Courtesy of Hale Observatories.)

had so long ago imagined. Today we are aware of the existence of billions upon billions of galaxies spread out over the vast reaches of space, often in giant clumps. The galaxies, their characteristics, and their evolution are explored further in Chapter 13.

REVIEW QUESTIONS

1. Describe briefly how man's view of the universe has changed from antiquity to modern times.

2. How did the ancients differentiate between a planet and a star?

3. In what way did the early Greek philosophers improve upon the astronomical concepts of their Egyptian and Babylonian predecessors?

4. How did the signs of the zodiac originate?

5. What restrictions were imposed on the earth-centered model of the universe according to Greek philosophical doctrine?

6. How did the Greek astronomers account for the looped motions of the planets? The nonuniform motions of the sun and moon?

7. Describe the Ptolemaic system and explain its mechanics.

8. Why is the heliocentric system a better representation of the planetary system than the geocentric system?

9. What observational evidence was there that the Copernican system was the correct interpretation of the planetary motions?

10. What was Tycho Brahe's major contribution to astronomy?

11. State in your own words, with the help of a diagram if necessary, Kepler's three laws of planetary motion.

12. List Galileo's contributions to astronomy.

13. Describe how Newton arrived at his law of gravitation.

14. If the effect of gravity is not noticeable between persons, why is it so obvious in the planetary movements or in the motion of the moon around the earth?

15. Discuss the evolving ideas in astronomical thinking concerning the nature of the universe from the beginning of the twentieth century to the present time.

SELECTED READINGS

Abetti, G., *The History of Astronomy*, Abelard-Schuman, 1952.

Berry, A., *A Short History of Astronomy*, Dover, 1961.

De Vaucouleurs, G., *Discovery of the Universe*, Macmillan, 1957.

Koestler, A., *Sleepwalkers*, Grosset and Dunlap, 1963.

Kopal, Z., *Widening Horizons*, Taplinger, 1970.

Ley, W., *Watcher of the Skies: An Informal History of Astronomy from Babylon to the Space Age*, Viking, 1969.

Lindsay, J., *Origins of Astrology*, Barnes and Noble, 1971.

Lockyer, J. N., *Dawn of Astronomy*, M.I.T. Press, 1964.

Thiel, R., *And There Was Light*, Knopf, 1957.

Astronomer at the prime focus position in the observing cage of the 200-inch Hale reflector. The guiding eyepiece is just to the left of his right hand in which he has the plateholder. (Courtesy of Hale Observatories.)

TELESCOPES AND OBSERVATORIES

The giant Hale 200-inch telescope on Mount Palomar could easily record the images of a million galaxies in the bowl of the Big Dipper.

Harlow Shapley (1885–1972),
Beyond the Observatory, Scribner, 1967

Modern astronomers rarely study the heavenly bodies by looking through a telescope. Instead, they use the telescope to photograph the celestial bodies, frequently through color filters, or to register the objects' radiation with specialized instruments whose sensitivity and range of wavelengths enormously exceed human vision. The automatic recording and display of the observational data with minicomputers is changing the direction of astronomical research.

Celestial radiation is studied with different kinds of telescopes appropriate to the spectral region under investigation. Optical astronomers working in the visible wavelengths employ refracting telescopes, reflecting telescopes, and Schmidt cameras. For investigation of the ultraviolet and infrared extensions beyond visible radiation, conventional or specially designed reflecting telescopes are the most efficient collectors of light. Radio astronomers, working in the wavelength region that lies between the much longer millimeter and meter radiations, use radio telescopes of various configurations: large parabolic dishes, rows of smaller dishes, and various antenna arrays. The larger antenna installations are spread over many acres. Increasing the diameters of optical and radio telescopes not only intensifies the amount of received energy but sharpens the resolution of detail. Astronomers working in the ultraviolet, x-ray, and gamma-ray spectral regions employ laboratory detection devices that are sensitive to radiation of the shortest wavelengths. Since this radiation is obstructed by the earth's atmosphere, the ultraviolet, x-ray, and gamma-ray telescopes must be mounted in balloons, rockets, and space vehicles.

The astronomer's work with the telescope is normally routine and uneventful. His main labors are confined to analyzing and interpreting the recorded observational data afterward. It is during this period, unless he obtains real-time processed data, that something exciting may be discovered. The domain of astronomical research varies so extensively that astronomers can specialize in only some of its fields.

Optical observatory sites are chosen with great care. Usually located on mountaintops possessing optimum sky conditions, they must also be sufficiently removed from population centers to avert light pollution. Radio observatory sites, also carefully selected, must be located in isolated areas that are free from terrestrial radio interference and that have favorable climatic conditions.

3.1 HOW ASTRONOMERS DO THEIR WORK

Working Conditions

A popular misconception of the astronomer has been that he spends all his working hours with his eyes glued to the eyepiece of a telescope. Actually, most work performed with conventional telescopes involves the recording of light in the spectral region covering the ultraviolet, visible, and infrared wavelengths by means of photographic exposures or measurements with attached specialized equipment. The sophisticated observing instruments and the use of automatic recording, storage, and display of the observational data with small computers have improved the efficiency of the optical telescope.

The cosmic radiation collected in the long wavelengths with radio telescopes and in the very short wavelengths with ultra violet, x-ray, and gamma-ray telescopes in space vehicles is also automatically recorded and displayed on printout sheets or in other ways. An astronomer may spend weeks and possibly months analyzing and interpreting the results of a few hours of operation with the telescope.

Not all astronomers work with telescopes. Some try to develop by mathematical methods a theoretical explanation of the observed phenomena based on the physical laws. Other astronomers are equally proficient in both the theoretical and observational fields. A successful theory must satisfactorily account not only for the observational phenomena presently known but also for any relevant discoveries in the future.

Fields of Astronomical Research

The whole extent of astronomy is too vast a domain for any individual to comprehend thoroughly its entirety. Consequently, astronomers specialize in a selected number of fields or their subdivisions. This was not so marked in the early years of this century when there were fewer fields of investigation. Since astronomy and physics are closely intertwined, it is not surprising that many physicists also engage in astronomical research. The principal areas of astronomical research include the following categories:

1. *Astrometry* deals with the determinations of the precise positions, the distances, and the real and apparent motions of the celestial bodies.

2. *Astrophysics*, with a very large number of participants engaged in various specialties of the subject, broadly involves the measurement of the energy distribution and polarization of the electromagnetic radiation emitted by astronomical sources, and the investigations of their physical characteristics, structures, and compositions. It touches nearly all fields of astronomy.

3. *Cosmology* pertains to the origin and evolution of the universe and the galaxies, and the birth of the primordial elements. It applies the principles of relativity theory to the solution of a world model of the universe consistent with the observational data.

4. *Dynamical astronomy* concerns the analysis of the motions of the stars and gas within our Galaxy, the stability of star clusters, the mechan-

ics of the spiral-arm structure, the interactions between neighboring galaxies, and other related activities under the influence of various forces. An important related field, *celestial mechanics*, treats of the gravitational forces and motions primarily between the material bodies of the solar system.

5. *Extragalactic astronomy*, a large active field with many ramifications, deals with the types, space distributions, motions, distances, physical characteristics, and compositions of the galaxies, quasars, and extragalactic radio sources.

6. *Galactic astronomy*, covering a broad general area with many branches, concerns the physical characteristics and behavior of the different classes of stars and star clusters in our Galaxy; the chemistry, structure, and evolution of the stars and the stellar populations; the nature, distribution, and composition of the gaseous clouds and the interstellar medium; and the structural form and rotation of the Galaxy.

7. *High-energy astrophysics* deals with the nature and physical developments of the supernovae, pulsars, quasars, and x-ray sources, and their powerful radiations; and the origin, composition, and energy distribution of the cosmic rays.

8. *Infrared astronomy* involves the study of astronomical sources in the wavelength regions between about one micron (one-thousandth of a millimeter) and several hundred microns. The development of sensitive new types of heat-sensing detectors has spurred interest in this field. Areas of research include the infrared radiation from the planets, cool stars, planetary nebulae, stellar envelopes, interstellar dust, the galactic center, the galaxies, and the quasars.

9. *Neutrino astronomy*, one of the newer fields, concerns the theoretical analysis of the production of neutrinos and their practical detection

on earth. Neutrinos are elusive, penetrating particles that shower the earth profusely from the sun but weakly from the distant stars. They are difficult to detect because they move so freely through matter. If detected in sufficient numbers, they would provide us with important astrophysical information on the thermonuclear processes inside the stars.

10. *Radio astronomy* relates to the study of radiation with radio telescopes in the millimeter to meter wavelengths from sources throughout space. It is one of the largest and most active branches of astronomy. Important areas of investigation include the study of radio emissions from the sun, Jupiter, stars, supernovae, pulsars, interstellar clouds, galaxies, and quasars; and exploration of the hydrogen distribution in our Galaxy and in other galaxies. A related field, *radar astronomy*, uses the technique of bouncing earth-transmitted radio waves from objects in the solar system. The reflected waves from the surfaces of Mercury and Venus, for example, are analyzed to yield their accurate distances, rotation periods, and the nature of their terrain.

11. *Solar-system astronomy* is another large general field with many subdivisions. One principal area of research is *planetary astronomy*, which deals with the surface features and atmospheric conditions of the planets and their satellites, and their interior structures; the nature, distribution, and physical conditions of the comets, asteroids, meteoroidal bodies, and the interplanetary medium; the chemistry and biology of the planets; and the origin of the solar system. An important activity, *solar physics*, deals with the descriptive and physical study of the sun and its effect upon the terrestrial environment.

12. *Space astronomy* began with the exploration of the moon, the sun, the planets, and the interplanetary spaces by extraterrestrial spacecraft. It has since expanded to include galactic and extragalactic phenomena not visible from the earth's surface. An important, growing division of space astronomy involves ultraviolet, x-ray, and gamma-ray investigations of cosmic sources by means of specialized detection devices in balloons, rockets, and space vehicles.

3.2 OPTICAL TELESCOPES

Image Formation and Brightness

Before proceeding to a description of modern telescopes and their uses, it will be helpful to examine briefly the optics of lenses and mirrors. A simple convex lens or a concave mirror produces an image of a distant object at the focal position as shown in Figure 3.2. Note that the light rays are bent or refracted in passing through a lens and reflected from a mirror. Note also that the image is inverted (Figure 3.2c and d). In the reflector a plane mirror or a right-angle prism can be mounted in the converging beam in front of the prime focus to bring the reflected image to one side of the framework of the telescope for the viewing convenience of the observer (Figure 3.2f). The viewing eyepiece magnifies the image as a reading glass magnifies small print (Figure 3.2e and f).

The brightness of a point source is proportional to the amount of light intercepted by the telescope objective (lens or mirror). Hence it is proportional to the area or to the square of the aperture (diameter) of the objective. The brightness is not related to its focal length. Doubling the telescopic aperture reduces the exposure time by one-fourth since four times as much light falls on the objective.

In photographing an extended object such as the moon or a planet, both the aperture and the focal length are involved. In this instance the exposure

Figure 3.1   Aerial view of the Lick Observatory on Mount Hamilton, California, near San Jose. The large white dome in the foreground houses a 36-inch refractor; the one directly behind it houses a 120-inch reflector. (Courtesy of Lick Observatory.)

3 TELESCOPES AND OBSERVATORIES

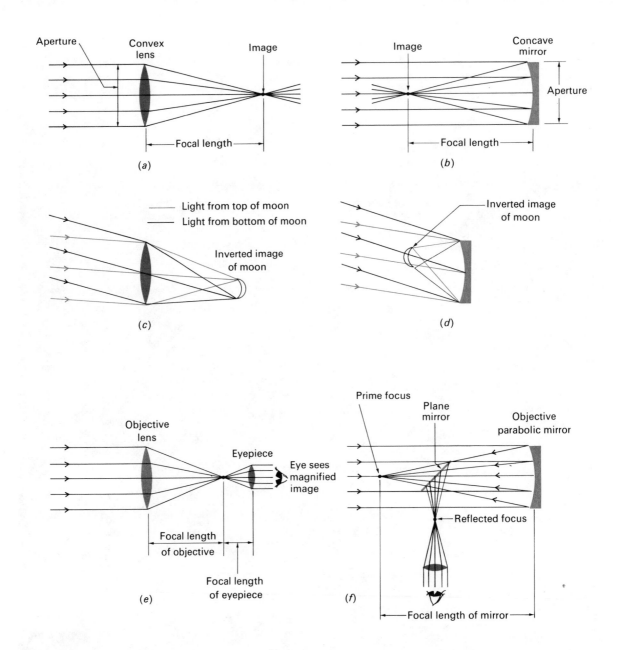

Figure 3.2   Image formation in lenses and mirrors. (a) Image of star formed by simple convex lens; (b) image of star formed by concave mirror; (c) image of extended object formed by convex lens; (d) image of extended object formed by concave mirror; (e) simple refracting telescope; (f) reflecting telescope. The magnifying power of a telescope = focal length of objective/focal length of eyepiece. Eyepieces of different focal lengths provide various powers of magnification.

time is proportional to the focal ratio squared. The focal ratio is the ratio of the focal length, f, to the aperture, a, ($= f/a$). In the camera trade, the focal ratio is called the f number. The smaller the f number, the shorter is the exposure time required. (The iris diaphragm in your camera is used to adjust the aperture of the camera lens to provide the proper focal-ratio setting for the correct exposure time). An $f{:}2$ lens, in which the aperture is one-half the focal length, requires an exposure time one-fourth as long as an $f{:}4$ lens, and one-ninth as long as an $f{:}6$ lens, in order to obtain the equivalent surface brightness of an extended object.

The image size of an extended object is proportional to the focal length of the objective, regardless of its aperture. A two-inch lens with a focal length of four inches produces an image of the moon with a diameter equal to one-thirtieth inch. A four-inch lens with a focal length of eight inches doubles the image size of the moon. Both lenses require the same exposure time to obtain the equivalent surface intensity of the moon's image since the f number is the same, $f{:}2$.

Resolving Power

The ability of a telescope to discriminate clearly between two adjacent objects or to delineate fine detail is called the *resolving power*. No amount of magnification by the eyepiece will increase the resolution of the image. The wave nature of light causes a point source of light in the focal plane of the telescope to appear as a bright spot called a *diffraction disk*, surrounded by progressively fainter circular fringes. The larger the aperture of the telescope, the smaller is the size of the spurious disk, thereby improving the resolution of closely adjoining features, or of a close pair of stars. In the latter instance, when the smaller diffraction disks of the two stars no longer overlap each other, it is possible to see two separate stellar images.

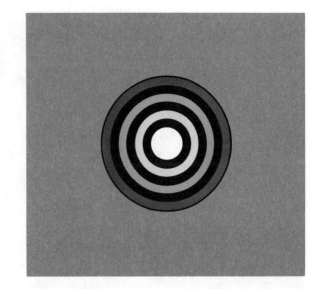

Figure 3.3 Diffraction pattern of a point source of light (enlarged). The alternating bright and dark fringes are produced by the reinforcement and cancellation of the light waves with each other. The diffraction disk is the central white image where most of the light is concentrated.

The resolving power is defined as the least angular distance between two stellar images that can just be separated in a telescope. The formula for this angle is:

$$d'' = 2.1 \times 10^5 \frac{\lambda}{a}$$

where d (seconds of arc) is the critical angular separation, λ is the observed wavelength, and a is the aperture of the telescope in the same unit of measurement. For visible light, the equation becomes:

$$d'' = \frac{4.5}{a} \quad (a \text{ in inches})$$

According to the second equation, it would take a 4.5-inch lens to resolve the components of a close double star whose angular separation is one second of arc. To resolve two adjacent sources one second apart in the sky with a radio telescope that operates on a wavelength of ten centimeters, the aperture

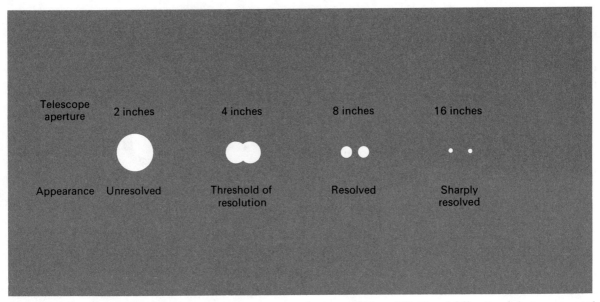

Figure 3.4   Image resolution of double star components separated one second of arc (1″). Size of diffraction disks is exaggerated for purposes of illustration.

would have to be thirteen miles. This is so because the radio waves are 180,000 times longer than the light waves and the resolution deteriorates with increasing wavelength.

The Achromatic Refractor

The simple seventeenth-century refracting telescopes possessed a number of optical deficiencies. Two major defects were: *spherical aberration*, the inherent inability of the objective to form a sharp image; and *chromatic aberration*, its failure to bring all the colors to a common focus (Figure 3.5a and c). In 1735 the English optician John Dolland overcame these handicaps by placing a concave lens of denser flint glass of the proper curvature behind the original convex lens of crown glass[1] (Figure 3.5c). Compared to the crown lens, the denser concave flint lens exerts a greater effect on the violet than on the red

and offsets the difference in deviation of the two colors introduced by the crown lens. Thus the two extreme colors (violet and red) are brought very nearly to the same focal position somewhat beyond the focal settings of the crown glass alone. In practice, two adjoining colors, usually yellow and green, are brought to an identical focus with the remaining colors falling very close to their focal setting. A color-corrected compound lens, known as an achromatic lens, besides virtually eliminating chromatic aberration, also minimizes spherical aberration. Achromatic lenses are employed in other optical systems

[1] The manufacture of seventeenth-century glass in England was licensed by the Crown—hence the name. The ingredients consisted of sand fused with a mixture of soda, potash, and lime. Later, another kind of glass was made in which flint nodules containing lead were substituted for the sand. Although different ingredients have since been added to both kinds of glass, the names persist.

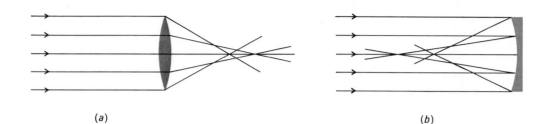

(a)   (b)

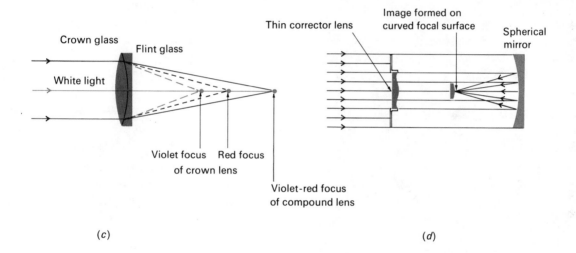

Crown glass
          Flint glass

White light

Violet focus   Red focus
of crown lens

Violet-red focus
of compound lens

(c)

Thin corrector lens

Image formed on
curved focal surface

Spherical
mirror

(d)

Figure 3.5   Spherical and chromatic aberrations and achromatic systems. (a) Spherical aberration in a lens: light rays passing through the outer portions of the lens are bent more sharply than those passing through the center section. (b) Spherical aberration in a spherical mirror: light rays hitting the outer portions of the mirror are reflected back at a sharper angle than those reflected from the center portion. (c) Achromatic objective: the single crown glass fails to bring the violet and red colors together to a common focus because of chromatic aberration. (d) Schmidt telescope: light rays entering the corrector lens from different directions than that shown in the diagram fall on different parts of the spherical mirror so that the entire surface of the mirror is utilized in producing bright images over a wide field of view.

3 TELESCOPES AND OBSERVATORIES

ranging from cameras to microscopes. The viewing eyepiece of the telescope is also a compound lens; this further improves the quality of the observed image. Eyepieces of different focal lengths provide various powers of magnification (Figure 3.2e and f). A photographic plate inserted in the focal plane of the objective in place of the eyepiece transforms the telescope into a giant camera.

The Reflecting Telescope

The previously mentioned aberrations are avoided in a reflecting mirror by making its surface parabolic, although other minor deficiencies remain. The reflecting telescope was conceived in principle by James Gregory of England and N. Cassegrain of France in the 1660's. In 1668 Isaac Newton constructed the first reflector, a miniature two-inch "toy."

Figure 3.6   Automatic camera attached to the base (eye end) of the 36-inch Lick Observatory refractor. (Courtesy of Lick Observatory.)

Figure 3.7   Newton's "toy" reflector; the mirror is nearly two inches in diameter. (Courtesy of The Science Museum, London.)

Large modern telescopes are of the reflecting type for a number of reasons. The glass for a reflector need not be of the high optical purity and homogeneity as that required for a large lens. Consequently, the melting of a large amount of molten material and its casting are less cumbersome and expensive. There is only one surface to grind in a mirror compared to four in an achromatic objective. To minimize the temperature changes that affect the focal setting of the telescope throughout the night, fused quartz, or a zero-expansion glass called *Cervit*, is currently used in the casting of large mirrors. The surface of the mirror is coated with a thin layer of metallic aluminum of high reflectivity.

The focal arrangement of the reflector depends on the type of observation to be performed. The prime focus is used in the photography, photometry, and spectroscopy of the faintest objects in order to lessen the exposure time with a small focal ratio. The Newtonian focus is useful for direct visual study. In both arrangements the observer works at a considerable height above the observatory floor. In the Cassegrain version, the secondary convex mirror reduces the rate of convergence of the rays; this effectively increases the focal length of the telescope several hundred per cent. The interposition of the small secondary mirror and its supports, or the observer's cage, does not result in any significant loss of light nor does it affect the quality of the images. In the older type reflector without the central hole, an additional flat secondary mirror is placed a small distance above the primary mirror to deflect the converging rays toward the side of the telescope. Equipment that is too heavy or bulky to be attached to the back side of the primary mirror can be placed in a room below the observatory floor to receive the long converging beam via the Coudé arrangement. An auxiliary flat mirror diverts the beam down the interior hollow portion of the polar axis around which the telescope rotates. This permits the focal position to remain fixed in position no matter which way the telescope points.

The greatest advantages that the reflector possesses over the refractor are its complete lack of chromatic aberration, which makes it ideal for all-purpose photography and spectroscopy, and its adaptability to various focal settings. Refractors do, however, possess certain conveniences. Because of their flatter field of good definition and stable optics, they are well suited for visual examination of the sun, moon, and planets. Their normally large focal ratio (f:10 or greater), combined with their wide field of good images, makes them particularly suitable for photographic measurements of small angles and star positions in astrometry.

The Schmidt Camera or Telescope

A wide-angle telescopic system that provides excellent definition over the entire field of view was invented in 1930 by the German optician Bernhard Schmidt at the Hamburg observatory. The great advantage of the Schmidt camera lies in its extensive sky coverage through its superb light-gathering capability with short exposure times owing to its small focal ratio. The scale of the plate is reduced because of its relatively short focal length. A thin corrector plate with negligible chromatic aberration, placed at the center of curvature of a spherical mirror, is shaped to compensate for the spherical aberration introduced by the mirror (Figure 3.5d). By making the mirror aperture appreciably larger than the diameter of the correcting lens, bright images are secured over a large field of view. Larger corrector plates than those presently in use (up to about fifty inches) introduce annoying aberrations into the optics of the system. Since the light rays come to a focus approximately midway between the mirror and the corrector plate on a spherically shaped surface, the photographic plate must be slightly curved to be in focus, a slight working disadvantage. Several variations of the original design are extant, including

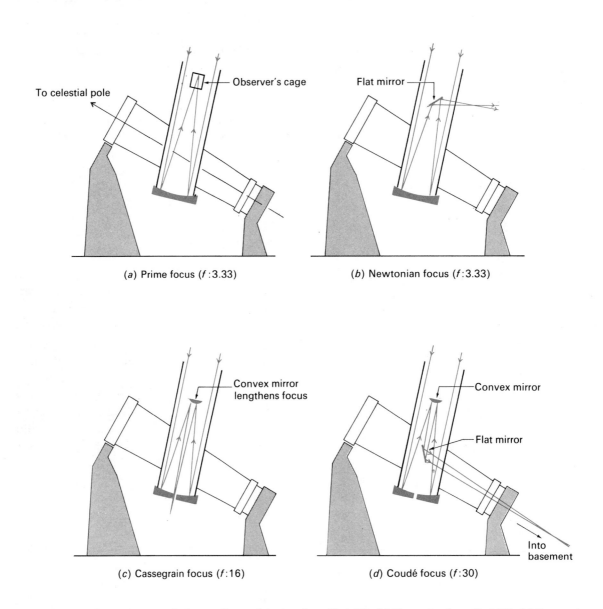

Figure 3.8 Focal arrangements of a large reflector: (a) prime focus (f: 3.33); (b) Newtonian focus (f: 3.33); (c) Cassegrain focus (f: 16); (d) Coude focus (f: 30). The focal ratios are those of the 200-inch Hale reflector.

Figure 3.9   The 200-inch Hale reflector is in a vertical position. The horseshoe collar on the left, resting on a film oil pad, slowly rotates the great telescope about its polar axis to keep pace with the apparent rotation of the sky. (Courtesy of Hale Observatories.)

some that straighten out the focal surface through further optical refinement. A Cassegrain version of the Schmidt design is used for optical viewing as well as for photography.

Telescope Mounts

Astronomical optical telescopes are mounted equatorially to follow the apparent rotation of the sky and to permit them to be conveniently pointed toward any direction of the sky. There are two degrees of freedom in the equatorial mounting system regardless of the mounting style. One permits the telescope to be rotated around the polar axis (in line with the earth's axis of rotation) in an east-west direction parallel to the equator of the sky; the other permits the telescope to be swung in a north-south direction about a perpendicular declination axis pivoted to the rotating framework of the polar axis. The smaller telescopes possess a pair of setting circles for positioning the object by hand; the largest telescopes are set electronically from an operating console and guided into exact position with hand electronic controls by the observer from his operating position. Once properly positioned, an electronic clock drive slowly turns the telescope around its polar axis at the same rate that the sky turns westward, thus keeping the celestial object centered in the field of view. (Appendix 13 contains information on acquiring your own telescope.)

3.3 RADIO TELESCOPES; X-RAY AND GAMMA RAY TELESCOPES

Radio studies of the heavens came to astronomers by an indirect route. In 1931 a Bell Telephone engineer, Karl G. Jansky, was attempting to locate the source of interference that was disrupting the

Figure 3.10   The 48-inch Schmidt telescope, Mount Palomar, California. The observor looks through the guiding telescope, keeping the object centered, while the picture is being taken. (Courtesy of Hale Observatories.)

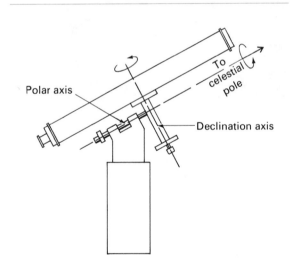

Figure 3.11   Schematic of equatorially mounted refracting telescope.

transatlantic radiophone circuits. He discovered that the radio noise was extraterrestrial in origin and that one significant source came from the direction of the Milky Way. An Illinois radio engineer, Grote Reber, pursued the phenomenon further by building the world's first parabolic radio reflector, thirty-one feet in diameter, in 1936. With this device he succeeded in constructing the first radio map of the sky. He found that the strongest signals were coming from the region of the rich star clouds in Sagittarius in the direction of the center of the Galaxy. At that time astronomers were not generally aware of the full significance of Reber's work since they were chiefly preoccupied with the use of optical equipment.

In 1942, while tracking down the source of intermittent interference experienced by British radar operators during World War II, British scientists discovered that the source of interference was attributable to radio emission from the sun. After the war the young field of radio astronomy quickly accelerated as physicists, radio engineers, and astronomers joined forces to build larger and more efficient radio telescopes. These instruments could detect radio signals from faint sources both inside and outside our Galaxy. Radio astronomy, which has grown tremendously since that time, has led to a number of startling discoveries: the quasars, radio galaxies, pulsars, and the interstellar molecules.

Radio-Telescope Design

Radio telescopes assume a variety of forms. One of the most common types, the dish-shaped antenna, is very similar to the reflecting optical telescope. The reflecting material consists of fine open-wire mesh or solid metal with a paraboloidal contour to fit the bottom and sides of the dish. The radio waves are reflected from the bowl of the dish and collected at the focal region where a collector antenna in the shape of a horn absorbs the concentrated energy. From there it is fed by cable to a building which

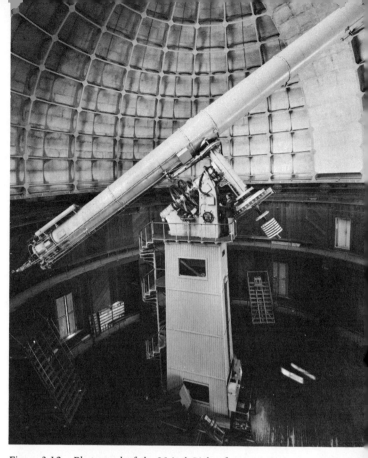

Figure 3.12   Photograph of the 36-inch Lick refractor showing both the polar and declination axes. Compare this photograph with Figure 3.11. (Courtesy of Lick Observatory.)

houses the receiving equipment where the signal is processed and passed on to a printer that records the output data in one form or another. The received signal is so weak that every precaution is taken to extract the desired signal from the accompanying noise pattern (like trying to single out one person's voice in a yelling crowd at a football game). The unwanted noise arises from atmospheric and man-made static, internal receiver noise, and thermal radiation from surrounding objects. A radio map of the central portions of the Galaxy processed through a computer appears in Figure 3.13.

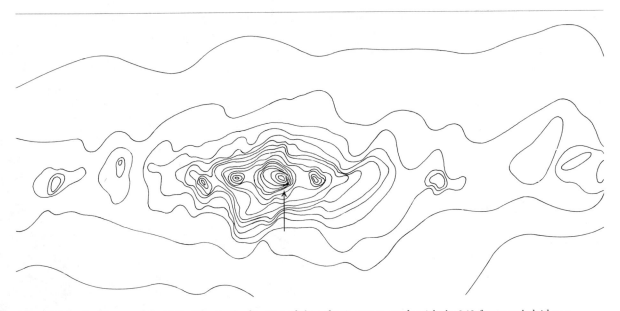

Figure 3.13   Radio map of the Milky Way in the direction of the galactic center, made with the 140-foot paraboloid on a wavelength of six centimeters at the National Radio Astronomy Observatory in Green Bank, W. Va. The contour lines are lines of equal radio strength. The more closely spaced the lines, the more intense is the radiation. Arrow points to center of Galaxy.

Certain antenna assemblies have been constructed in the form of a single line of smaller dishes, or two such arrays crossing at right angles to each other, or helical-wound antenna, or dipole configurations. The larger the capture area of the dish, or the more components that constitute a larger array, the higher is its sensitivity and the more pronounced is its pinpointing accuracy or resolution because of the reduction in the size of the diffraction disk which narrows the receiving beam of the telescope (Figure 3.14). The largest single radio telescopes have a resolution of about one-thirtieth degree, comparable to that of the eye.

Because of its large dimensions, the radio telescope is remotely controlled. The radio astronomer can direct its various functions from an operating console within the building where the receiving and recording equipment is located. The moderate-sized radio telescopes, up to 150 feet in diameter, are mounted equatorially to follow the rotation of the sky in the same manner as the optical telescopes. The larger ones employ an alt-azimuth mounting whose vertical and horizontal movements are synchronized by a computer with the rotation of the sky. There are too many engineering problems to overcome within reasonable economic considerations in attempting to construct an equatorially mounted dish greater than about 150 feet in diameter. In the biggest and most unwieldy structures, the installation remains in a fixed position on the ground while the rotation of the sky permits a considerable portion of the heavens to pass in review within the beam pattern of the antenna. The beam lobe can be shifted to certain other limited directions of the sky by remote mechanical motion of the collector antenna. The world's largest fixed installation at Arecibo, Puerto Rico

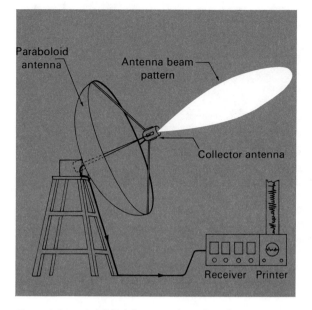

Figure 3.14 Simplified diagram of a radio-telescope system. The antenna-beam configuration represents the response pattern of the radio telescope to sky radiation. It corresponds to the central image of the diffraction pattern of a telescope discussed in Section 3.2. The larger the size of the dish, the narrower the beam pattern and the greater is the resolving power of the telescope.

(Figure 3.18), consists of a metal reflecting dish contoured out of a natural bowl in the ground, 1,000 feet in diameter. In this arrangement the sky can be surveyed within twenty degrees of the zenith, covering about 40 per cent of the sky.

Radio-Telescope Interferometers

It was noted earlier that larger telescopes can resolve minute details better than smaller telescopes. Observing at small wavelengths also improves the resolution, as the resolving formula in Section 3.2 indicates. For example, a radio telescope receptive to waves 100,000 times longer than light waves would require an aperture of 325 miles to equal the resolving power of the Hale 200-inch telescope. One method of obtaining a high degree of resolution is based on the phenomenon of interference. In the radio arrangement, two separate radio antennas are connected by cabling or a radio link with a common time standard (an atomic clock). The ability to discriminate between two closely spaced sources increases directly with the separation between the two antennas. The signals from each antenna are mixed in an electronic device, called a *correlator*, for proper analysis.

Referring to Figure 3.19, note that the wave crests of the signals arrive at slightly different times at antennas A and B because of the slightly different path lengths between each antenna and the emitting source. In certain directions at a given instant, the crest of a wave arrives at antenna A in phase with the crest of the same wave, or a succeeding wave, at antenna B and the signal is reinforced. This corresponds to the maximum position of the lobes, equivalent to the bright fringes in the diffraction pattern. In a slightly different direction, the crest of a wave arrives at antenna A while the trough of the same wave, or a succeeding wave, arrives at antenna B and the signal is canceled. This corresponds to the null position between the loops, equivalent to the dark spacings (or fringes) between the bright fringes. The path lengths to each antenna from a radiating source in the sky constantly change with the rotation of the sky, resulting in a set of changing interference fringes recorded as variations in signal strength with time on a moving strip of paper. From the analysis of the changing fringe pattern it is possible to determine whether the radio source is resolvable or not.

By separating two antennas over distances measured in thousands of miles, even on separate continents, the resolution of minute radio sources exceeding by many times that of the largest optical telescopes is possible. In practice, a magnetic-tape recording of the received signal is made at each station equipped with its own atomic clock. The two timed tapes are

Figure 3.15 *The 16-element crossed arrays of the Stanford Radio Astronomy Institute provide a high degree of resolution at an operating wavelength of 9.1 centimeters. Each leg is 375 feet long. (Courtesy of Stanford Radio Astronomy Institute.)*

Figure 3.16 *The 300-foot paraboloid radio telescope at the National Radio Astronomy Observatory in Greenbank, W. Va. This telescope has an alt-azimuth mounting and is movable only in a north-south elevation. (Courtesy of National Radio Astronomy Observatory.)*

Figure 3.17   *The 600 × 400-foot radio-reflecting trough of the University of Illinois, Vermillion River Observatory. (Courtesy of G. W. Swenson, Jr.)*

Figure 3.18   *The 1,000-foot fixed dish at the National Astronomy and Ionospheric Center at Arecibo, Puerto Rico. (Courtesy of The National Astronomy and Ionosphere Center.)*

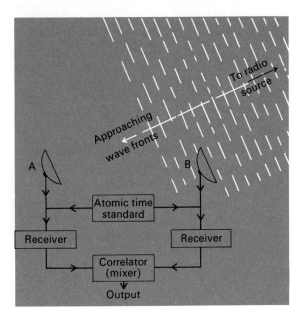

Figure 3.19 Simplified schematic of radio-telescope interferometer.

passed through a general-purpose computer that carries out millions of involved electronic functions for processing and synthesizing the received information. The final result may appear in the form of a display map such as a contour map representing the variations in radio intensity within the source as in Figure 3.13, or some other tabulation of the data. The technique described here is called *very long baseline interferometry* (VLBI). Another method of obtaining high resolution, which will not be described here, is *aperture synthesis*. Although it is a slower process, it permits the economic use of smaller antennas that can be shifted about at various separations. In effect, the aperture of a very large radio telescope is simulated by combining—that is, synthesizing—the contributions from a series of movable smaller antennas.

X-Ray and Gamma-Ray Telescopes

Except for the grating type, the telescopic equipment used in space vehicles to record extraterrestrial

Figure 3.20 The high-resolution radio interferometer at the Stanford Radio Astronomy Institute. The five 60-foot paraboloids are equatorially mounted and spaced along a 675-foot, east-west base line. The operating wavelength is 2.8 centimeters with a resolution of 20 seconds of arc. (Courtesy of Stanford University.)

EXPLORING THE COSMOS

radiation in the shortest wavelengths bears no resemblance in shape or construction to that employed in conventional telescopes. The instrumentation consists of sophisticated laboratory detectors with a collimating arrangement that permits the electronic measurement of the intensity of the x-ray or gamma-ray radiation in a given direction. In this capacity they do perform like ordinary telescopes in their ability to pinpoint the locations of small sources or extended objects on the sky. The devices used to detect the shortest waves are described in Section 4.6.

3.4 OBSERVATORIES

Selection of Modern Observatory Sites

Modern observatory locations are chosen with great care after exhaustive observing tests of a likely site have been conducted over a long period of time. The ideal specifications of an optical observatory include these requirements: (1) a mountaintop, preferably with a high degree of atmospheric transparency and dry air; (2) as dark a sky as possible; (3) freedom from future sky deterioration by any

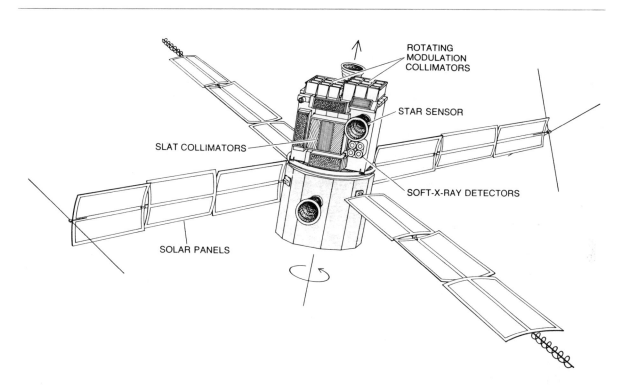

Figure 3.21   Small Astronomical Satellite (SAS-C) carries x-ray telescopes to search for soft x-rays in the galactic plane and to locate x-ray sources in our Galaxy and in other galaxies. (From "The X-Ray Sky" by Schnopper and Delvaille. Copyright July 1972 by Scientific American, Inc.)

source; (4) steady (nonturbulent) atmospheric conditions; (5) maximum number of clear days and nights; (6) minimum amount of wind; (7) accessible site to minimize the cost of construction and the building of a road to the top.

The choice of a radio-observatory site is equally stringent, with climatic conditions a prime factor. The principal considerations are: (1) dry air, which has less effect on the scattering of radio waves than moist air; (2) as little snow as possible to minimize the weight load on the reflecting dish; (3) freedom from strong winds for good mechanical stabilization of the antenna; (4) a radio-quiet area away from a population center to avoid interference from broadcast and television stations and from static caused by electrical machines.

Sky Pollution

A century ago most astronomical observatories were located in the vicinity of sparse population centers or in the countryside not too far removed from such areas. During the last few decades optical astronomers have labored under an increasing environmental hazard brought about by urban and suburban sprawl, resulting in the deterioration of sky conditions. Metropolitan smog and the general night illumination of the city lights affect the quality of their photographs. The spectral lines of mercury street lights and neon signs are recorded along with the fainter spectral lines of the photographed celestial body. Also, direct photographs are fogged in the longer exposures.[1]

Present and Projected Large Telescopes

Some of the older major observatories in this country, such as the Lick Observatory in northern California, the Hale Observatories on Mt. Wilson and Mt. Palomar in southern California, the Yerkes

[1] Lament of the astronomer: "Star bright, street light, which will I see tonight?"

Observatory in Wisconsin, and the McDonald Observatory in Texas, were founded by grants from wealthy individuals. The chief financial angel available today is the U. S. government. In the 1960's government funding through the National Science Foundation aided in the establishment of the Kitt Peak National Observatory in Arizona and its inter-American branch in Chile. The National Radio Astronomy Observatory in Green Bank, West Virginia, and the National Astronomy and Ionosphere Center in Puerto Rico are also financially supported by the National Science Foundation. Other mutual efforts involving private and governmental agencies in this country and in Europe have cooperated in establishing large observatories in the southern hemisphere whose sky has not been as extensively explored as that in the northern hemisphere.

The largest optical telescope in the world is the 236-inch (6-meter) alt-azimuth mounted reflector nearing completion at a site in the Caucasus mountains (USSR), 6,900 feet high. Next in size is the 200-inch Hale reflector on Mt. Palomar at an altitude of 5,500 feet in southern California. The world's highest observatory (13,800 feet), the Mauna Kea Observatory, was completed in 1970 on the island of Hawaii. It houses an 88-inch reflector. The air is so thin that oxygen breathing units are available, if desired. By the mid-1970's several reflectors with apertures between 140 and 160 inches will be in operation throughout the world. There are two reflectors in the range of 100 to 120 inches in this country, one in the Soviet Union, and one in England, and about thirty reflectors in the 60- to 90-inch range in different parts of the world. The two largest refractors still are the 40-inch at the Yerkes Observatory and the 36-inch at the Lick Observatory, constructed many decades ago. There are fourteen other refractors with apertures between 24 and 28 inches scattered around the world. The two largest Schmidt telescopes are the 53-inch convertible arrangement in Germany at the

Figure 3.22 *Night view of the valley below Mount Wilson, showing the lights of Los Angeles, Hollywood, and over forty other cities and towns. The glare of the night sky has rendered the 60-inch and the 100-inch telescopes virtually useless for research on the frontier problems of astronomy involving the faintest objects. (Courtesy of Hale Observatories.)*

Figure 3.23 *Moonlight view of the 200-inch Hale telescope dome with the shutter open. (Courtesy of Hale Observatories.)*

Tautenburg Observatory[1] and the 48-inch on Mt. Palomar. Besides the main telescope at a major observatory, there is usually an assortment of smaller telescopes within various domes plus a cluster of shops, laboratories, and other buildings on the grounds.

Among the largest steerable radio telescopes are the 326-foot dish in Bonn, West Germany, the 300-foot (semi-steerable) dish at the National Radio Observatory in Green Bank, West Virginia, the 250-foot dish at Jodrell Bank in England, and the 210-foot dish in Australia. There are about two dozen paraboloids between 85 and 150 feet in diameter around the world. The world's largest dish (not steerable), dug out of a naturally shaped bowl and lined with metal

[1] By removing the 53-inch corrector lens, the 80-inch reflector becomes a standard reflector.

Figure 3.24   Aerial view of the Mount Wilson Observatory site. The two tower structures on the left are the solar observatories. The smaller dome houses a 60-inch reflector, the larger dome, a 100-inch reflector. (Courtesy of Hale Observatories.)

panels, measures 1,000 feet across; it is located at the National Astronomy and Ionosphere Center in Arecibo, Puerto Rico. The largest antenna installations in terms of physical size consist of the multi-element arrays spread out over a large acreage or in-line arrays extending over several miles. A very large array (VLA) consisting of 27 dishes each 82 feet in diameter should be ready for use in New Mexico within a few years, according to present plans of the National Radio Astronomy Observatory. The interferometer will resemble a Y configuration with nine movable dishes mounted on each branch of the Y. The entire structure encompasses a circular area extending over 25 miles in diameter. Appendix 7 lists the largest telescopes in use or projected for the future.

REVIEW QUESTIONS

1. Can you name any fields of research listed in Section 3.1 in which activities have been mentioned in the public press or in magazines during the last several months?

2. If you were given the choice of a ten-inch refractor or a ten-inch reflector, which telescope would you prefer and why?

3. Why are achromatic lenses used in optical equipment, including astronomical telescopes?

4. Explain how the f number of a camera that you may possess can be altered by means of an iris diaphragm.

5. Why does the Coudé arrangement of the reflector result in a larger picture of the moon than in the other focal arrangements?

6. Why are large reflectors preferred over large refractors in the construction of modern telescopes?

7. Under what conditions is it preferable to employ a Schmidt telescope instead of a refractor or a reflector?

8. Why are optical telescopes mounted equatorially? Why cannot all radio telescopes be mounted equatorially?

9. Explain how it is possible to sharpen the beam pattern of a radio telescope. What is the advantage of a narrow pencil lobe in the beam pattern?

10. How can the resolution of tiny radio sources be improved with radio telescopes?

11. Name all the advantages that accrue from the use of large-aperture telescopes, radio or optical.

12. What is the best site for an optical telescope? For a radio telescope?

13. In what way does an x-ray telescope differ from a conventional telescope?

14. What are some of the configurations used in radio-antenna systems?

15. Why cannot the ordinary Schmidt telescope be employed visually?

SELECTED READINGS

Collins, A. F., *The Greatest Eye in the World—Astronomical Telescopes and Their Stories*, Appleton-Century, 1942.

Kopal, Z., *Telescopes in Space*, Hart, 1970.

Land, B., *The Telescope Makers*, Crowell, 1968.

Page, T., and L. W. Page, eds., *Telescopes*, Macmillan, 1966.

Piper, R., *Big Dish: The Fascinating Story of Radio Telescopes*, Harcourt Brace Jovanovich, 1963.

Smith, F. G., *Radio Astronomy*, Penguin, 1960.

Woodbury, D. O., *The Giant Glass of Palomar*, Dodd, Mead, 1970.

Control room for the 300-foot radio telescope at the National Radio Astronomy Observatory in Green Bank, W. Va. Instructional commands may be relayed to a computer programmed to provide for completely automatic operation of the telescope. (Courtesy of the National Radio Astronomy Observatory.)

CELESTIAL RADIATION
AND THE ATOM

I believe most simply in the nobility of this great effort to understand nature, and what we can of ourselves, that is science.

J. Robert Oppenheimer (1904–1967),
The Need for New Knowledge, 1959.

The visible light of the heavenly bodies constitutes only a tiny fraction of the entire range of radiation arriving at the earth's surface from outer space. The complete scope of radiation, called the electromagnetic spectrum, *extends from the shortest waves (gamma rays) continuously to the longest waves (radio) over an interval of wavelengths from one-trillionth of a centimeter to several million centimeters. The earth's atmosphere obstructs the passage of most of these waves except in the visible region, in certain portions of the infrared, and in the radio region. Information about the universe in the past has come mainly through the optical and radio "windows." At present it is being considerably augmented in the hitherto inaccessible spectral regions by telemetered data received from balloons, rockets, and space vehicles.*

The analysis and interpretation of the received observational data rest upon a knowledge of the properties of light, the laws of spectrum analysis, the structure of the atom, and the interaction between matter and energy. The study of radiation requires the use of detectors that are sensitive to different spectral regions. Telescopes collect and feed the concentrated celestial radiation into various detection devices and accessories such as photometers, spectrographs, electronic cameras, radio receivers, and infrared, ultraviolet, x-ray sensors. The instrumentally recorded or stored observational data are later studied and analyzed by the astronomer for proper interpretation.

4.1 ELECTROMAGNETIC RADIATION

The ordinary light that we see around us is an insignificant fraction, but an extremely important one, of the electromagnetic radiation present in the universe. The human eye is sensitive only to the visible light rays composed of the rainbow colors from red to violet. Radiation outside the range of visible light must be investigated with many different kinds of specialized detection devices. Today, x-ray and radio astronomers can measure the celestial radiation at wavelengths respectively 10,000 times shorter and 100 million times longer than the visible wavelengths.

The Electromagnetic Spectrum

Infrared radiation heats our bodies, ultraviolet light burns our skin, x-rays and gamma rays damage our tissues and cells, but television and radio broadcast waves fall harmlessly upon us. These and all the other wavelengths of radiated energy constitute the *electromagnetic spectrum* as shown in Figure 4-1.

Most of the harmful ultraviolet radiation is effectively screened out by an absorbing layer of ozone ten to twenty miles above the earth's surface. The still more dangerous x-rays and gamma rays are effectively filtered out by molecular oxygen and nitrogen at greater altitudes and by their dissociated atoms at the highest levels between 60 and 120 miles. In the partially obscured infrared region, molecular oxygen, carbon dioxide, and water vapor are the principal absorbers at heights up to ten miles. At the long-wavelength end of the electromagnetic spectrum, the radio waves longer than about 25 meters are reflected back into space by an ionospheric (electrified) atmospheric layer. Our knowledge of outer space in the past was confined mainly to the two transparent windows, one in the narrow visible spectral portion and the other in the very wide radio spectral region. Since midcentury the radiations hitherto inaccessible from the ground have been intensively explored by means of instrumented sounding balloons, sounding rockets, and space vehicles. The major portion of astronomical research will continue to be confined to earth-based observations because it still remains very profitable; besides, that is where much of the expensive capital equipment is invested.

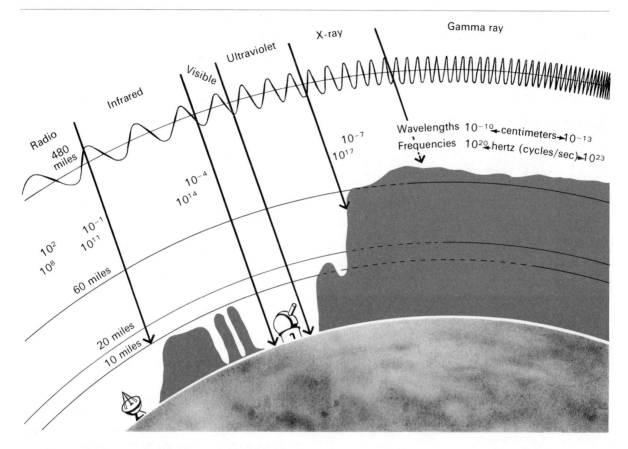

Figure 4.1   The electromagnetic spectrum (adapted from a NASA diagram). The blue areas represent the atmospheric regions where celestial radiation is obstructed at different elevations.

4.2   PROPERTIES OF RADIATION

Wave Theory of Light

Light may be visualized as being propagated spatially at a speed of 186,300 miles per second from a radiating source in the form of spreading concentric waves. The action resembles the outward movement of water ripples in a pond when a stone is dropped into the pond. The wavelength, λ, is the distance between the successive wave crests or troughs. The frequency, f, represents the number of wave crests passing by a fixed point each second. It is clear that the shorter the wavelength, the greater is the number of waves going by, or the higher is the frequency of the passing waves. This important relationship may be expressed as follows:

$$\lambda \cdot f = c \quad \text{or} \quad \lambda = \frac{c}{f} \quad \text{or} \quad f = \frac{c}{\lambda}$$

λ = wavelength, f = frequency, c = velocity of light (3×10^{10} cm/sec; 186,300 mi/sec).

Example: What is the wavelength radiated (a) by

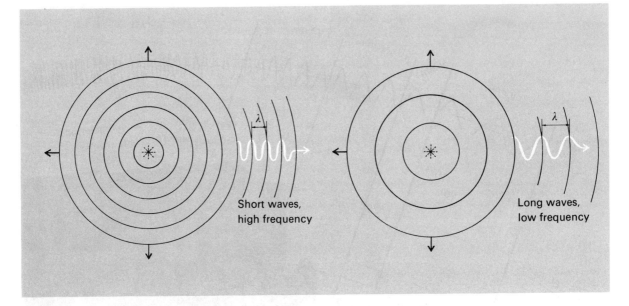

Figure 4.2 Waves of different lengths or frequencies.

a broadcast station whose dial setting is 930 kilocycles (kilohertz)? (b) By a television station on VHF channel 11 at 200 megacycles (megahertz)? (One hertz equals one cycle per second.)

(a) Broadcast station

$$\lambda = \frac{c}{f} = \frac{186,300}{930 \times 1000} = 0.2 \text{ mile}$$

(b) Television station

$$\lambda = \frac{3 \times 10^{10}}{200 \times 10^{6}} = 150 \text{ cm} = 1.5 \text{ meters}$$

It may be difficult to imagine that in the very room you occupy, radio waves from a local broadcast station, one-fifth mile long at the rate of 930,000 waves per second, are rushing by you at the speed of 186,300 miles per second.

Photon Concept of Light

At the beginning of the century, M. Planck and A. Einstein demonstrated that there is another aspect of light—a particlelike characteristic called a *photon*, possessing a *quantum*, or unit bundle, of energy. In 1923 the American physicist A. H. Compton showed that a photon colliding with an electron acted like a particle in imparting energy to the electron and bouncing off with reduced energy. A continuous radiating source may also be pictured as emitting photons of differing discrete energies spreading out as energized packets in all directions. The dual manifestations of light, photon or wave, are complementary to each other and mutually exclusive. Light appears in one or the other of its guises, depending upon the experiment, but *never* both ways at the same time.

Photons retain their original parcels of energy in traveling through space. Their arrival rate or flux at any point in space decreases with the square of the distance from the radiating source. A photon-actuated device, such as a photoelectric photometer, can be attached to a telescope to measure the bright-

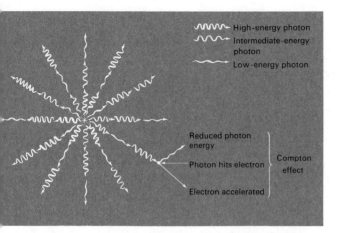

High-energy photon
Intermediate-energy photon
Low-energy photon

Reduced photon energy
Photon hits electron
Electron accelerated
Compton effect

Figure 4.3   Photon concept of light. The wavelets depicting the photons of different energies are only diagrammatic and should not be construed as literal representations—photons cannot be chopped off. Photons thin out with distance but retain their original energy.

ness of a star. The energy of each photon, *E*, is proportional to its frequency, *f*. It is also inversely proportional to its wavelength, λ. Thus:

$$E = h \cdot f = \frac{h \cdot c}{\lambda}$$

where *c* is the velocity of light and *h* is called the Planck constant (its numerical value is 6.625 × 10^{-27} erg · sec). The Planck constant is one of the fundamental constants of nature along with the constant of gravitation, *G*, and the velocity of light, *c*. From the above relation it follows that the shorter the wavelength, the more energetic is the radiation. That is why very high-frequency x-rays and gamma rays can destroy molecular structures within living tissue and ordinary light cannot.

Polarization of Light

The polarized nature of light is best understood in terms of its wave action. Most natural radiating sources emit waves that vibrate in all planes; their light is said to be unpolarized. A polaroid filter placed in the path of a light beam acts like the slats in a Venetian blind in permitting the wave vibrations to pass through in one direction only. When unpolarized radiation is viewed through a polaroid filter that is rotated in its own plane, there is no change in the intensity of the resulting plane-polarized light. Reflected or scattered light is likely to be partially polarized and the intensity of the transmitted light will vary as the polaroid filter is rotated. A position can be found where the transmitted light is a minimum, as shown in Figure 4.4. The percentage of polarization is obtained by comparing the minimum and maximum intensities. In polaroid sunglasses, the polarizing material is oriented to reduce the glare of the partially polarized sunlight by blocking the passage of the horizontal vibrations.

A celestial body that emits polarized radiation can be analyzed in a polarizing instrument to obtain some information concerning the nature of the emitting source. Polarization studies also provide clues to the properties of the planetary surfaces or atmospheres and to the interstellar medium by the manner in which the light is scattered by their particles.

4.3   SPECTRUM ANALYSIS

Production of a Spectrum

The analytical study of visible radiation became possible with the invention of the *spectroscope* by British chemist-astronomer W. H. Wollaston in 1802 and its subsequent improvement by German optician J. Fraunhofer in 1814. (The working arrangement of the instrument is described later in Section 4.6.) We are concerned here with the action of its principal component, the prism in the form of a triangular block of glass. When white light is passed through a prism, it is dispersed into a spectrum of rainbow

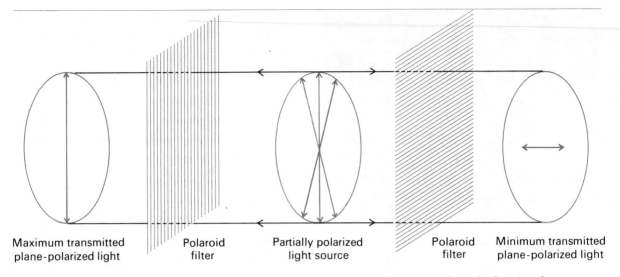

Maximum transmitted
plane-polarized light

Polaroid
filter

Partially polarized
light source

Polaroid
filter

Minimum transmitted
plane-polarized light

Figure 4.4   Polarized radiation. The light from the radiating source is propagated at right angles to the direction of its vibration. The polaroid filter on the right is rotated 90 degrees with respect to the polaroid filter on the left.

colors. The dispersion is not uniform; the violet end is spread out more than the red.

Another widely used device that produces a spectrum is a *diffraction grating.** One common type of grating employed in astronomical spectroscopy consists of an aluminized glass plate containing thousands of fine, closely spaced, parallel grooves to the inch. It is called a *reflection grating.* A beam of white light falling on the grooved surface of the plate reflects back spectral colors which can be photographed. In another type of grating known as a *transmission grating*, the grooves are ruled on a transparent glass plate. In this instance, light passing through the grating is dispersed into the spectral colors. The normally ruled grating spreads the light into a line pattern of repeating spectra

---

*Unlike a glass prism, which is transparent only to visible light, the grating is useful over the broad spectral range from the x-ray to the infrared wavelengths. An explanation of the production of a spectrum by means of a diffraction grating, which involves the phenomenon of light interference, can be found in any elementary physics textbook.

called spectral orders. By ruling the grooves in a special way it is possible to concentrate the light into a single spectral order. Such a grating is called a *blazed grating*, a necessity in the spectroscopy of the ordinarily weak celestial radiation.

Laws of Spectrum Analysis

The classification and interpretation of celestial and laboratory spectra (Plate 1) are based on certain guiding principles independently enunciated by the German chemist G. Kirchhoff and the American astronomer W. Draper over a century ago. These principles are:

1. *Continuous spectrum*: A radiating solid, liquid, or highly pressurized gas exhibits a continuous spectrum ranging through the various wavelengths. The lighted filament of an electric light bulb shows this kind of spectrum.

2. *Emission or bright-line spectrum*: A rarefied

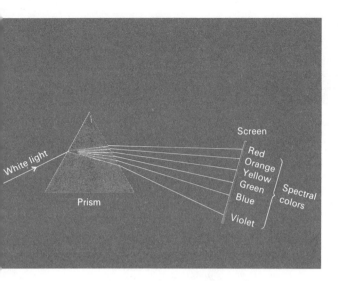

Figure 4.5   Formation of a spectrum by a glass prism.

radiating gas exhibits a discrete set of isolated bright-colored lines whose pattern is characteristic of the chemical composition of the gas. A glowing neon street sign displays a bright-line spectrum. (Molecules, which consist of two or more bound atoms, produce a complicated pattern of closely spaced lines forming a banded structure.)

3. *Absorption or dark-line spectrum*: Light from a radiating source producing a continuous spectrum will undergo selective absorption in certain wavelengths characteristic of any cooler gas that happens to lie in front of the radiating source. The continuous spectrum is crossed by dark lines which indicates that the light of these wavelengths is highly attenuated. The sun and stars exhibit this kind of spectrum.

Identification of the Elements

A celestial source will contain a mixture of different atoms each with its own set of spectral lines.

It is possible, with the aid of previous laboratory spectral analysis of each separate element, to identify the atoms present in the celestial body from the measured wavelengths of their spectral lines. The photographic plate on which the spectrum is recorded with the telescope and its attached spectrograph is called a *spectrogram*. A bright-line spark spectrum of a vaporized source (iron or titanium or neon) is photographed for comparison above and below the spectrum of the celestial body being photographed. The spark spectrum is recorded at the telescope in a matter of seconds during the course of the object's exposure, which may be in minutes or hours. The impressed reference system of comparison lines, whose wavelengths are known, enables the astronomer to determine with a special measuring engine the wavelengths of the object's spectral lines on the spectrogram.*

The Doppler Effect

The motion of an observer relative to a radiating source produces a displacement of the spectral lines from the normal position as shown in Figure 4.7. This is the Doppler phenomenon. If an observer at point O is moving toward a fixed radiating source S, he will encounter more wave crests passing him each second at a higher frequency than will the stationary observer at Q. If another observer at P is moving away from the same source, he will record fewer wave crests passing by him each second at a lower frequency. The wavelengths are shifted to the violet on approach and to the red on recession. The amount of displacement is proportional to the velocity of the observer. In reality, it is immaterial whether the source is in motion or the observer or both. The Doppler displacement can be measured only in a

*Henry Norris Russell, a distinguished American astronomer once remarked: "Analyzing a spectrum is exactly like doing a crossword puzzle, but when you get through with it, you call the answer *research.*"

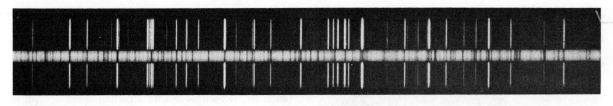

Figure 4.6   A portion of the spectrum of Alpha Persei obtained with a three-prism spectrograph attached to the 36-inch refractor of the Lick Observatory. Note the coincidence of the comparison spectral lines of titanium with those in the star's spectrum. (Courtesy of Lick Observatory.)

source that emits a bright- or dark-line spectrum. The actual amount of shift is generally so slight for most celestial bodies that it must be viewed through a magnifying eyepiece to see it in the spectrograms. A special measuring apparatus, which may be the same type employed in the determination of the wavelengths, enables the line shift to be easily measured with respect to the undisplaced comparison lines of the local source.

The formula expressing the Doppler shift is:

$$v = -\frac{\Delta\lambda}{\lambda}\,c \quad \text{(approach)}$$

$$v = +\frac{\Delta\lambda}{\lambda}\,c \quad \text{(recession)}$$

where $\Delta\lambda$ (delta lambda) is the measured shift in wavelengths; λ, the undisplaced wavelength; c, the velocity of light (186,300 mi/sec); v, the relative velocity of observer to light source (radial velocity). Expressed in words, the formula states that the shift in wavelength is the same fraction of the undisplaced wavelength that the radial velocity is of the velocity of light. Optical and x-ray astronomers find it convenient to state the wavelengths in *angstrom* units rather than in centimeters (1 angstrom $= 10^{-8}$ cm). Infrared astronomers prefer to use *microns* (1 micron $= 10^{4}$ angstroms $= 10^{-6}$ meter). Radio astronomers express the radio wavelengths in millimeters, centimeters, or meters.

Example: the measured red shift of a spectral line

at 5000 angstroms in a certain star was found to be 0.5 angstrom. What is the radial velocity of the star relative to the earth? From the preceding formula

$$v = +\,c\,\frac{\lambda\,\Delta}{\lambda} = +\frac{186{,}300 \times 0.5}{5000}$$

$$= +\,18.63 \text{ mi/sec, recession}$$

(A correction depending on the date of the observation is customarily applied to obtain the radial velocity relative to the sun; this eliminates the variable effect of the earth's annual motion around the sun.)

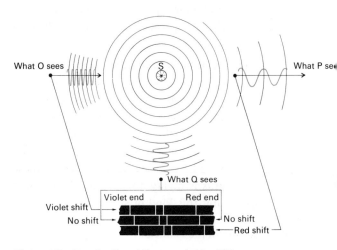

Figure 4.7   Doppler line shifts recorded by different observers.

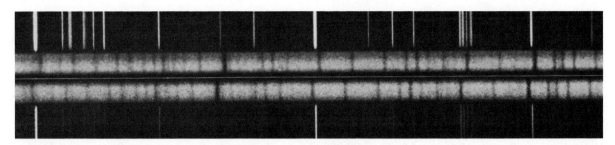

Figure 4.8   The spectrum of the spectroscopic binary α^1 Geminorium photographed at two different times, showing the change in Doppler shift arising from its orbital motion. (Courtesy of Lick Observatory.)

4.4   ATOMIC STRUCTURE

Early Research on Atomic Structure

It will be helpful at this point to review briefly the developments that led to the modern concept of an atomic model before discussing the mechanism responsible for the production of atomic radiation. The pioneering research on the structure of the atom was conducted by E. Rutherford in England during the early years of this century. The bombardment of atoms with fast-moving alpha particles (helium nuclei) ejected from radioactive elements indicated that the atom behaved like a fairly empty structure. It was found to consist of a central positively charged nucleus and a number of outlying negatively charged electrons circulating around the nucleus. The refined concept that gradually emerged accounted satisfactorily for the periodicities of atomic properties (the periodic table of the elements) and for many of the various physical and chemical processes associated with atomic behavior in general.

The Structure of the Atom

Each atom is distinguished by the number of protons and neutrons it carries within its nucleus and the corresponding complement of surrounding electrons equal in number to the protons. The proton possesses a unit positive electrical charge, the electron an equal but negative electrical charge, and the neutron a zero charge. The mass of the atom is concentrated in the nucleus because the mass of the proton or neutron is 1,836 times greater than the mass of the electron. The proton weighs 1.00728 mass units and the neutron, 1.00866 mass units. One atomic mass unit by convention is equal to one-twelfth the mass ($= 1.6604 \times 10^{-24}$ gram) of the most common species of carbon whose nucleus contains six protons and six neutrons (see Table 4.1).

The "trademark" of each element lies in the number of protons contained within the nucleus. Beginning with the simplest element, hydrogen has the atomic number of 1; that of helium is 2; that of lithium is 3; and so on down to the last natural element, uranium, whose atomic number is 92.

Isotopes

Although the nucleus of a given element contains a fixed number of protons, it may have different numbers of neutrons. The different atomic species of a particular element are called *isotopes* (Table 4.1). There are some 300 naturally occurring isotopes, of which about 25 are radioactive. Over 1,000 different radioactive isotopes (radioisotopes) have been artificially created by man. Since all but twenty of the elements consist of an unequal mixture of two or more isotopes, their measured atomic weights depend on the relative proportion of their isotopes (note column 5 in Table 4.1). For example, the atomic

---

4 CELESTIAL RADIATION AND THE ATOM

Table 4.1   Some Representative Isotopes

Element	Atom No.	Atomic Nucleus Symbol[a]	Atomic Weight	Per cent Abundance of Isotopes[b]	Total No. Natural Isotopes	Inside Nucleus		Outside Nucleus
						No. Protons	No. Neutrons	No. Electrons
Hydrogen	1	$_1$H^1	1.0078	99.985	2	1	0	1
Deuterium	1	$_1$H^2	2.0140	0.015		1	1	1
Helium	2	$_2$He^4	4.0026	99.99987	2	2	2	2
Carbon	6	$_6$C^{12}	12.0000	98.89	2	6	6	6
Carbon	6	$_6$C^{13}	13.0034	1.11		6	7	6
Oxygen	8	$_8$O^{16}	15.9949	99.759	3	8	8	8
Aluminum	13	$_{13}$Al^{27}	26.9815	100.00	1	13	14	13
Iron	26	$_{26}$Fe^{56}	55.9349	91.66	4	26	30	26
Uranium[c] 235	92	$_{92}$U^{235}	235.0439	0.72	3	92	143	92
Uranium[c] 238	92	$_{92}$U^{238}	238.0508	99.27		92	146	92

[a]Subscript refers to number of protons or element number; superscript refers to atomic weight, rounded to a whole number.
[b]Relative contribution of isotope to total content of that element.
[c]Radioactive isotopes.

weight of iron is 55.847, which results from an unequal mixture of four isotopes. A complete listing of the elements appears in Appendix 6.

4.5   ATOMIC RADIATION

The Bohr Model of the Atom

One problem plaguing the early twentieth-century physicists concerned the mechanism that caused the atom to emit a discrete pattern of spectral lines. It was argued that an orbiting electron would be forced to spiral inward toward the positively attracting nucleus, emitting radiation continuously in the process, until it fell into the nucleus. By 1913, when the internal structure of the atoms had become sufficiently known, Niels Bohr, the Danish theoretical physicist, found a way out of the difficulty based on the structure of the simplest atom, hydrogen: a single electron orbiting around a proton. He developed certain empirical rules under which the electron is permitted to occupy a selected number of prescribed concentric stationary orbits. According to his reasoning, the electron normally circulates in the lowest energy orbit closest to the nucleus. When the atom absorbs energy, the atom is *excited* as the electron is raised to one of the higher permissible orbits. The atom may acquire energy in a variety of ways: by collisions with another particle, from electrical or thermal sources, or by interaction with a light photon. An atom whose electron is momentarily lodged in an orbit of large radius has "swallowed" a larger chunk of energy than one whose electron has been placed in an orbit of smaller radius. Because the atom tends to remain in the lowest energy state (that is, in the orbit closest to the nucleus), it will almost immediately disgorge the captured energy. Like a ball bouncing down a staircase, the electron cascades down into one or more lower energy orbits on its way toward the bottom resting orbit. With each downward quantum jump a light photon is emitted

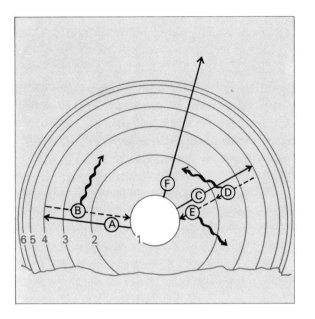

Figure 4.9 Atomic absorption and emission. Examples of modes of energy production: (1) atom normally remains in lowest energy orbit 1 (level or state). (2) Atom absorbs energy quantum Ⓐ and is excited to upper level 4 (1 → 4). This is equivalent to the electron jumping from orbit 1 to orbit 4. Within 10^{-8} second, atom radiates photon Ⓑ of same energy and is deexcited to level 1 (4 → 1). This is equivalent to the electron dropping from orbit 4 to orbit 1. The photon is usually radiated in a different direction from the original direction of absorption. (3) Atom absorbs energy quantum Ⓒ and is excited to upper level 3 (1 → 3). It falls back at once to level 1 in two jumps as it radiates photon Ⓓ (3 → 2) and photon Ⓔ (2 → 1) in rapid succession. The two emitted energies are equal to the original absorbed energy. (4) Atom absorbs a sufficient amount of energy Ⓕ to lift the electron beyond the last orbit. The electron detaches from the atom as the atom becomes ionized and assumes a positive charge since it has lost one negative charge (the electron).

representing the energy difference between the two levels associated with the transition. The greater the jump, the greater is the amount of energy released and the shorter the resulting wavelength. A photon may be emitted in any direction, regardless of the original direction of the absorbed energy. Exceedingly small atomic transitions in the outermost energy levels of the atom produce radiation in the radio spectral region. Small transitions give rise to radiation in the infrared region; moderate transitions in the middle and outer energy levels produce radiation in the visible and ultraviolet regions. Large transitional changes in the lowest energy levels give rise to the x-ray emissions. Gamma rays generally originate from energy changes inside the nucleus.

We may picture atoms in the gas to be constantly absorbing and emitting energy in their own haphazard way in a rapid hop, skip, and jump action. A rough analogy in the emission process is to imagine how a sack of marbles dumped down a staircase would randomly tumble down the steps. The released energies of the various photons involved in the many different transitions taking place within the billions upon billions of atoms contribute toward the total radiation of the emitting source. Although we know today that electron orbits do not exist as such in the atom, they constitute a useful crutch in visualizing the radiation processes within the atom. It is more accurate to say that the atom possesses discrete energy states or levels corresponding to the electron orbits.

The Hydrogen Spectrum

An energy-level diagram for hydrogen appears in Figure 4.10. The level numbers correspond to the electron orbit numbers. The uppermost levels, representing the highest energy states of the atom, crowd together toward a head called the *series limit*. The hydrogen line spectrum in the visible region, known as the Balmer series, figures prominently in the spec-

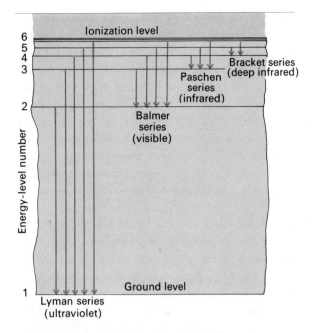

Figure 4.10 Energy levels and series in hydrogen atom. Each series occupies a different portion of the electromagnetic spectrum, and each series comes to a head known as the series limit. Downward transitions shown here give rise to emission lines; upward transitions give rise to absorption lines.

tra of most stars. It arises from transitions originating or terminating on the second level of the atom, depending on whether absorption or emission processes are taking place. In the same way, transitions involving the ground level give rise to the Lyman series in the ultraviolet; those involving the third level give rise to the Paschen series in the infrared; and so on for the remaining series whose lines appear in the deep infrared or microwave spectral region.

When the hydrogen atom absorbs energy in excess of that required to raise it to the highest energy level, the electron is ejected from the atom with a net amount of kinetic energy, and the atom is said to be *ionized*. It now possesses a positive electrical charge. In this condition the ionized atom is incapable of absorbing or reradiating energy in the form of discrete lines until it captures a stray electron. This is not generally true of other atoms with a greater complement of electrons even though they have undergone multiple ionizations so long as they retain some of their electrons.

Atomic Radiation in General

Each atom possesses a unique set of differently spaced energy levels. Consequently, the resulting pattern of spectral lines originating in the electronic transitions between the various levels differs for each element, as does the amount of energy needed to liberate an electron—that is, to ionize the atom. For example, to remove the first electron from helium requires five times as much energy as to remove the first electron from sodium. Furthermore, each additional ionization requires a greater amount of energy to free those electrons in the tighter orbits since they are more closely bound to the atomic nucleus.

In the stellar atmospheres, atoms are excited to upper levels from two sources: (1) thermal or heat energy involving photons of the right wavelengths; (2) kinetic energy involving collisions with other atoms. Excited atoms may reemit the energy spontaneously or they may be induced to reradiate the energy in the presence of a field of radiation; or, prior to emission, they may less frequently encounter another atom and deexcite by transferring the energy without radiation to their colliding neighbor.

Wave Model of the Atom

The Bohr model of the atom, despite later improvements, including the introduction of elliptical orbits and other refinements, was less successful in accounting for the spectral behavior of the more complex atoms. In 1924 the French physicist L. de

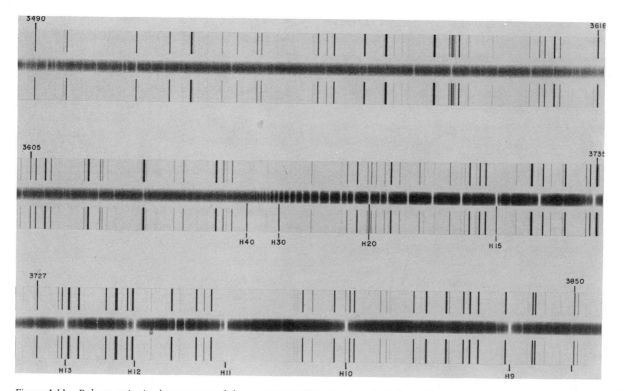

Figure 4.11   Balmer series in the spectrum of the star HD 193182, showing the hydrogen lines converging toward the series limit to the left of H 40 at 3646 Å. Beyond that extends the Balmer continuum (continuous spectrum of diminishing intensity) produced by the removal of the electron from the atoms. (Courtesy of Hale Observatories.)

Broglie clarified the concept of the dual nature of light (photons and waves) by pointing out that elementary particles have waves associated with them and that light waves in turn possess a particle nature. This notion was shortly verified in laboratory experiments with electrons. It is now an accepted fact of nature that matter and radiant energy possess mutual wave properties and particle properties. Seizing upon de Broglie's concept, E. Schrödinger, an Austrian physicist, and W. Heisenberg, a German physicist, independently constructed mathematical theories of atomic radiation about the same time (1925). The two theories, Schrödinger's wave mechanics and Heisenberg's matrix mechanics, were consolidated by P. A. M. Dirac, the English physicist, into the mathematical formulation of the present-day quantum mechanics. It represents the most rational and logical approach to the processes involving the behavior of atomic phenomena so far developed. The newer concepts are beyond the scope of this book. In reality, there are no electron orbits. Inside the atom the electron is spread out in the form of a vibrating cloud in three dimensions around the nucleus. It acts as a point charge only when it is detected outside the atom. Within the hydrogen atom, for example, there exist spherical regions surrounding the proton within which the electron is spread out into a set of integral electron waves. The innermost zone (corresponding to the first orbit) accommodates exactly one wavelength of the electron wave. The second zone (corresponding to the second orbit) contains two whole electron waves which fill a larger space; the third zone, three whole electron waves which occupy an even larger volume, and so on. The atom can accommodate only one set of integral wavelengths at any one instant; this corresponds to a specific energy level within the atom. It is this distribution of integral wavelengths that accounts for the discrete spacing of the energy levels within the atom as shown in Figures 4.9 and 4.10.

4.6 TELESCOPIC INSTRUMENTATION

Recording of Celestial Radiation

Without the use of auxiliary equipment attached to the telescope, astronomers would know little about the physical nature of the heavenly bodies. It was not until man expanded his vision with instrumental aids that he brought a new order of insight into his observations of celestial phenomena.

Many of the telescopic accessories employed are light-sensitive devices capable of detecting electromagnetic radiations both in the visible and nonvisible regions with an accuracy surpassing visual efforts thousands of times. The function of the telescope in this kind of usage is to collect and feed the concentrated light into the appropriate apparatus equipped with an output recording device or suitable electronic contrivance for storing the data. The earliest storage method, the photographic plate, has many advantages over human vision: It is cumulative in its action, that is, longer exposures enhance the fainter details; the accurate brightnesses of many stars can be measured on a single plate; it covers a wide range of spectral sensitivity from the x-rays to the infrared; it provides a lasting and accurate record of the night's observations. Unfortunately, the photon efficiency of the photographic plate is very low. Only 1 to 2 per cent of the incident light photons activate the photographic emulsion. Astronomers therefore have sought other means, mostly electronic in nature, to improve the performance of their telescopes. One such electro-optical device is the photoelectric photometer.

The Photoelectronic Photometer

This instrument has a higher light-action efficiency and provides more precise determinations of brightnesses than the photographic plate. Its principal disadvantage is that the measurements of starlight must be confined to one object at a time, a time-consuming process. Its action is similar in principle to that of an exposure meter in camera photography. Light is converted into photoelectrons whose current flow is measured with a meter. The essential components consist of a photomultiplier tube about the size of a small radio tube, a power supply system, an output current amplifier, and a recording device.

Starlight entering the telescope is focused on a light-sensitive metalized surface (C), called a photocathode. A dislodged electron is attracted toward anode plate 1 which is slightly more positively charged than the negative cathode. Upon impact of the attracted electron, two or more electrons are splashed out from anode 1 and are directed toward the more positive anode 2. More electrons are splashed out from anode 2 and head for anode 3, etc. A multiplying cascade of at least one million electrons is collected by the positive collector plate (P). The electron current, which is directly proportional to the stellar brightness, is thus internally amplified within the tube about one million times. It is further amplified externally before its intensity is recorded by a pen moving on a strip of paper or by some other display mechanism. A more recent development is the multichannel photomultiplier array

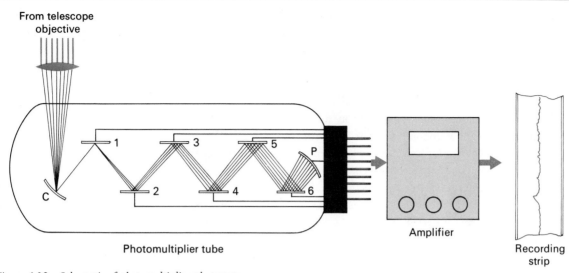

Figure 4.12   Schematic of photomultiplier photometer.

containing a string of photocells sensitive to different spectral regions. When used in combination with appropriate color filters, it permits an accurate sampling of the spectral-energy distribution of the celestial body.

The Electronic Camera

The most efficient present-day method of recording weak celestial light is by means of electronic intensification through the use of an image tube or a vidicon tube. Exposures are speeded up by a factor of fifty to a hundred times over conventional systems. Electronic amplification of starlight within the evacuated image tube is obtained in the following manner: Starlight from the telescope is focused on a photocathode surface which ejects electrons. The electrons are accelerated by means of high voltages and magnetically focused on a phosphor screen which converts the image, thus intensified, back into light. By placing a photoemitting surface behind the phos-

Figure 4.13   Schematic of electronic camera (cascade-image-tube system): 1, photocathode; 2, accelerating electrodes; 3, focusing magnet; 4, photo-emitting surface (phosphor screen photocathode combination); 5, phosphor screen; 6, camera lens; 7, photographic plate.

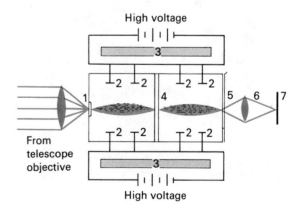

4 CELESTIAL RADIATION AND THE ATOM

phor screen, the electron flow can be further intensified and focused on a second phosphor screen where an electronic image of the exposed star field is produced. A camera lens and photographic plate record the images.

Several types of the newer, commercially produced television cameras employing vidicon tubes have been adopted by astronomers in the study of very faint objects. In the vidicon tube, the light from stellar images is converted into electrical charges that are impressed on a target plate. An electron beam scans the charged plate, producing a series of electrical pulses that are converted back into a light pattern of the star field or of the star's spectrum.

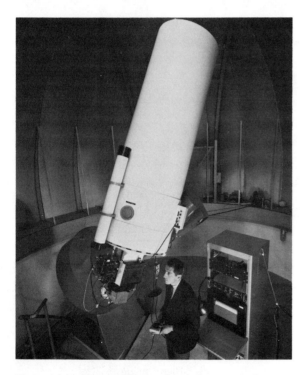

Figure 4.14   Electronic camera attached to a 24-inch reflecting telescope at the Lick Observatory. (Courtesy of Lick Observatory.)

Not only is the efficiency of the vidicon system many times higher than that of the photographic plate, but also it is receptive to a wider range of wavelengths. If desired, the picture elements can be stored on videotape for later computer processing.

The Spectrograph

Unlike other light-analyzing devices which register the integrated light, the spectrograph disperses the wavelengths of radiation into a spectrum. In the prism spectrograph, the incoming light from the telescope objective is focused at the entrance slit. The diverging light enters a collimator lens placed at a distance equal to its focal length from the slit so that a beam of parallel rays passes through the prism. The camera lens forms a spectral image in the focal plane where the photographic plate is positioned. The entire apparatus is enclosed in a light-tight metal box rigidly mounted in position at the eye end of the telescope. Temperature is regulated during the exposure to prevent spurious displacements of the spectral lines. Only a small percentage of the original starlight arrives at the plate; some is lost by absorption in the optical system, but most is lost at the entrance slit which must be narrowed to a few thousandths of an inch to form a spectral pattern with clearly resolved lines. In place of prism spectrographs, grating spectrographs are now widely employed in astronomy. They are more convenient to use and more efficient, particularly in the spectroscopy of faint objects (note spectrographs in Plate 2 and Figure 1.10).

An objective (slitless) prism spectrograph is a useful arrangement for quick preliminary spectral analysis of an entire star field. (In the slit spectrograph described earlier, only one star's spectrum can be photographed at a time.) When used in conjunction with a refractor or a Schmidt camera, the objective prism spectrograph becomes an excellent survey

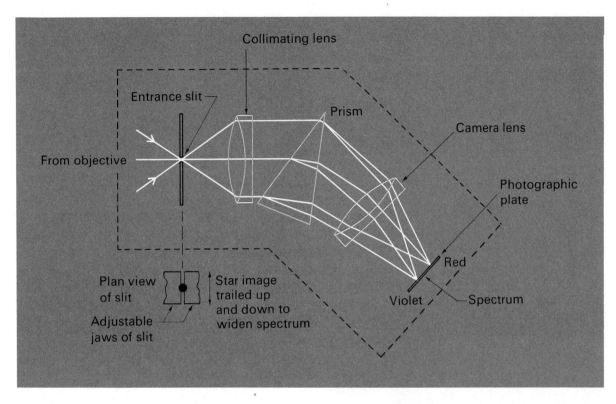

Figure 4.15   *Single-prism spectrograph.*

Figure 4.16   *Exposed view of the Bruce three-prism spectrograph of the Yerkes Observatory. The collimator tube is at the bottom with the three prisms on the left and the camera tube at the top. (Courtesy of Yerkes Observatory.)*

4 CELESTIAL RADIATION AND THE ATOM

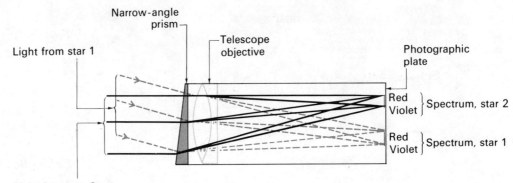

Figure 4.17 *Objective-prism spectrograph.*

tool in probing the skies. It suffers from the disadvantage that the dispersion is on a small scale and it is not practical to place a comparison spectrum above or below the spectrum of an individual star.

Infrared Detectors

Two kinds of heat-sensing detectors commonly used in the past to investigate the infrared radiation of the sun and the stars were the *thermocouple* and the *bolometer*. The former device consists of two strips of dissimilar metals joined together at one end. When the junction is heated by an infrared source, a small flow of electric current is generated which can be read by a meter attached to the free ends of the strips. The bolometer originally consisted of a blackened metal foil which absorbed heat radiation. The resulting increase in its electrical resistance could be measured in an electrical circuit. The modern heat-sensing instruments far surpass in sensitivity and spectral range the older thermocouple and bolometric devices. A germanium crystal forms the resistive element of one current type of bolometer. When

shielded against extraneous heat by cooling with liquid helium, the detection assembly is capable of measuring a temperature change of 1/10,000,000° Celsius. A second type of heat-sensing detector employs a photoconductive crystal which releases electrons when it absorbs infrared photons. A current-measuring instrument measures the flow of the electrons; the measured current is proportional to the intensity of the emitting source.

Detection of Radio Waves

Unlike light waves, the much longer radio waves from celestial sources are barely affected by propagation through the gas and dust of space. The earth's atmosphere provides a broad radio window for the passage of these waves in the spectral region between 5 and 25,000 millimeters (25 meters). Below 5 millimeters the air strongly scatters the waves and above 25 meters the ionosphere reflects them back into space.

Except for the difference in frequencies, a radio telescope coupled to a receiver functions essentially

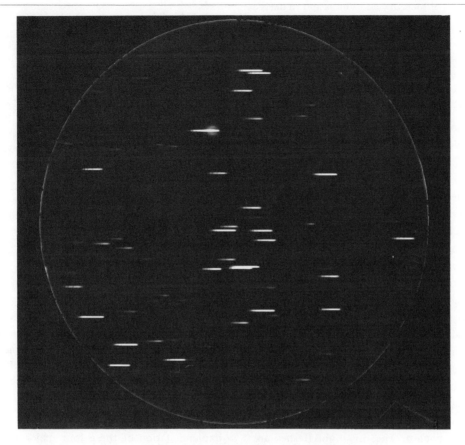

Figure 4.18   Objective-prism spectrogram of a star field. (Courtesy of University of Michigan.)

in the same manner as an antenna connected to a home receiver. The radio-telescope receiver, however, is vastly more sophisticated and elaborate than the home receiver. This is because the cosmic signals are very weak and are accompanied by undesirable noise; also, receiver stability is more difficult to attain at the higher frequencies. Once tuned in, the desired signals are electronically processed through the receiver components in such a way as to minimize the accompanying noise and filter out the unwanted frequencies. After amplification the signal variations

from the receiver's output are impressed on a moving chart by a recording pen, or punched on tape, or registered by printed numbers. The signal changes also can be fed into a computer for analysis.

In the allied field of radar astronomy, powerful pulses of radio energy are transmitted from large antennas toward distant bodies. The signals reflected back to earth are distorted in various ways, depending on the type of object. Radar echoes have been received from meteors, the aurorae, the moon, and the nearer planets. The technique has been used to map the surfaces of Mercury and Venus and to derive their accurate rotation periods. Radar studies have also resulted in an improved determination of the astronomical unit, the mean distance between the earth and the sun.

Detection of Very Short Wavelengths

Observations of extraterrestrial radiation in the shortest wavelengths are conducted with laboratory equipment modified for use in atmospheric sounding balloons, rockets, and orbiting spacecraft. The direct solar ultraviolet and x-ray radiation has been photographed with passband filters that admit the narrow passage of selected spectral regions. In addition, the continuous ultraviolet and x-ray spectral distribution of the sun has been electronically recorded with grating spectrographs. X-ray and gamma-ray detection devices employ photomultipliers, proportional counters, and scintillation counters. A proportional counter contains a gas-filled tube with a voltage across it. When a gamma or x-ray photon enters the tube, it ionizes the gas and renders it electrically conducting. The momentary pulse of electric current is amplified and recorded. A scintillation counter has a substance that momentarily glows when struck by a high-frequency photon. The tiny light flashes are amplified by a photomultiplier tube and electronically counted to provide a measure of the intensity of the light source. In all instances, precautions must be exercised to ensure that the background or other unwanted radiations are removed or reduced to a tolerable minimum.

Astronomy and Astrophysics for the 1970's

The growing concern for new research facilities required to exploit the frontier problems of astronomy was expressed in a report prepared by the Astronomy Survey Committee of the National Academy of Sciences in 1972. The panel recommended that federal funding be made available for the

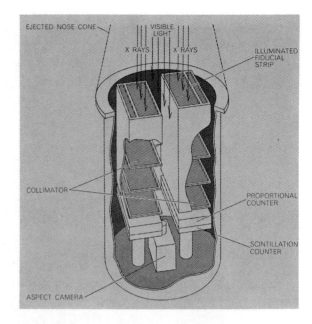

Figure 4.19   X-ray detector. The two banks of wire-screen collimators help to pinpoint the direction of the x-ray source. The aspect camera records the star fields in the vicinity of the x-ray source in order to establish its location on the sky. (From ''X-Ray Stars'' by R. Giacconi. Copyright December 1967 by Scientific American, Inc.)

implementation of these four major programs: the building of a very large radio-telescope array in New Mexico for which money has been authorized; the development of improved types of electronic cameras combined with computer-handling facilities; the construction of a good-sized infrared telescope in each hemisphere; and several high-energy space observatories to investigate the x-ray, gamma-ray, and cosmic-ray sources. These high-priority programs, together with a number of recommended lesser projects, would increase the average governmental expenditure in basic astronomical research to about $355 million per year during the next decade. This is about $85 million higher than the previous annual funding.

REVIEW QUESTIONS

1. Describe the electromagnetic spectrum. What information can be derived by analyzing the electromagnetic radiation from celestial sources?

2. Which portions of the electromagnetic spectrum are completely or partially blocked by the earth's atmosphere? What are the physical reasons for these obstructions?

3. Give a brief resumé of the kinds of tools and accessories used by astronomers to observe the different regions of the electromagnetic spectrum.

4. Can you explain in terms of atomic excitation what happens when you strike the phosphorus tip of a match to light it?

5. Discuss the properties of light as a wave phenomenon; as a photon phenomenon. Give instances of where each manifestation can be observed.

6. A student claimed that since the line frequencies of a rapidly approaching luminous body increase because of the Doppler shift toward the violet, the energy of the body increases because the energy of radiation is proportional to the frequency. Is this argument valid?

7. If you could examine the city neon signs at night with a simple transmission grating, what kind of spectra would you observe? What determines the color of the neon signs?

8. What is the purpose of recording the comparison spectrum of some known element on either side of the stellar spectrogram?

9. Describe the Doppler effect. How do astronomers determine the line-of-sight velocity by means of this phenomenon?

10. Can you explain why the atomic weight of argon (atomic number 18) is greater than the atomic weight of potassium (atomic number 19)? (Refer to Table of Chemical Elements in Appendix 6.)

11. Give a simplified account of how an atom absorbs radiation and reemits it.

12. What makes the photomultiplier tube used in photoelectric photometry so sensitive to light?

13. Define the following: (a) excitation; (b) ionization; (c) photon; (d) isotope; (e) neutron.

14. Describe in terms of the Bohr model how the spectral lines of the Balmer series of hydrogen are produced.

15. In how many different ways can an atom absorb energy?

SELECTED READINGS

Asimov, I., *Inside the Atom*, Abelard-Schuman, 1966.

Cohen, B. L., *The Heart of the Atom: The Structure of the Atomic Nucleus*, Doubleday, 1967.

Hale, G. E., *Signals from the Stars*, Scribner, 1931.

Hewish, A., ed., *Seeing beyond the Visible*, American Elsevier, 1970.

Hoffman, B., *Strange Story of the Quantum*, Dover, 1959.

Miczaika, G. R., and W. M. Sinton, *Tools of the Astronomer*, Harvard University Press, 1961.

Pendray, G. E., *Men, Mirrors, and Stars*, Harper, 1946.

Stokley, J., *New World of the Atom*, Washburn, Ives, 1971.

The earth from 22,300 miles in space on November 10, 1967. Portions of four continents are visible while the Antarctica continent is blanketed under cloud cover. South America appears between 6 and 9 o'clock; North America, between 10 and 12 o'clock; Europe, at about 1 o'clock; and Africa, at 2 o'clock. (Courtesy of NASA.)

OUR BLUE-WHITE PLANET: EARTH

Here is the world, sound as a nut, not the smallest piece of chaos left, never a stitch nor an end, not a mark of haste, or botching, or second thought; but the theory of the world is a thing of shreds and patches.

Ralph Waldo Emerson (1803–1882)

Our planet was created about 4.6 billion years ago, it is believed, within a contracting solar nebula that gave birth to our planetary system. Its age has been derived from radioactive dating of terrestrial rocks. Analyses of seismic recordings of earthquakes, whose vibrations penetrate deeply into the earth before reemerging at distant points, have disclosed the composition of the earth's interior. It has a nickel-iron core, solid at the center and liquid farther out, which is surrounded by a rocky mantle and a thin granite crust. Worldwide studies of the ocean-bottom configurations have verified an old concept of continental drift through sea-floor spreading. There is strong evidence this drift began with the breakup of a single huge land mass into separate continents about 200 million years ago, a process that is still going on.

Great forces and vast circulatory movements also appear in the earth's hydrosphere (water portion) and atmosphere. Two atmospheric regions that have received special attention in recent years are the ionospheric (electrified) layers in the upper atmosphere and the magnetosphere (magnetic-field envelope) surrounding the earth. The origin of the earth's magnetism is apparently linked with rotational differences within the interior of the earth, but it is not known why the earth's magnetism has reversed itself many times in its past. The earth's day has imperceptibly lengthened over geologic time as a result of the frictional effects of the sun- and moon-generated tides sweeping over the rotating earth. Superimposed on the earth's slowdown are minute irregularities, not yet completely understood, in the earth's rotation.

The biosphere (zone of life) interacts with the atmosphere, hydrosphere, and soil of the earth. How did life originate within the biosphere? One line of reasoning, based in part on laboratory experiments, suggests that a primeval atmospheric mix of methane, ammonia, hydrogen, and water vapor, sparked by ultraviolet solar radiation or other energy sources, led to the formation of the amino acids. These products then formed the basis for the subsequent complex organic molecular compounds that constituted the first primitive organisms. In the warm, watery broth of the ancient seas, they found a favorable haven for their continued evolutionary development. In time, the primitive organisms discovered the photosynthetic process of sustaining themselves through the closed carbon-oxygen cycle about three billion years ago. The evolutionary track of development then entered on a new revolutionary course that has taken life through the increasingly complex biological orders on to man. Evolution of the species, according to Darwinian theory, proceeds by the process of natural selection and cumulative mutation. The blueprint plans and instructions for cell growth and reproduction lie in the genetic code supplied by the DNA molecule.

Man is beginning to render his habitat more unlivable through the misuse of the earth's natural resources, the pollution of his environment, and overpopulation. The social consequences of this ecological crisis, if not checked, may affect the quality of life on this planet.

5.1   THE EARTH'S DEVELOPMENT AS A PLANET

Introduction

The study of the earth as a whole has taken on a new meaning since our recognition that many diverse influences shape the history of our planet. In this chapter we shall consider briefly the biological and ecological aspects as well as the physical aspects of our world. The earth is a common laboratory in which scientists from many disciplines can pool their talents to solve problems of mutual interest. For example, astronomers are allied with geophysicists in their studies of continental drift and the earth's slight wobbling on its axis of rotation. The movement of continents is presently being checked by astronomers with laser beams reflected back to earth from the corner reflectors left on the moon by the astronauts. Astronomers stationed on different continents can measure the minute change in their locations by timing the round-trip path of a laser beam telescopically transmitted from each observatory. Geophysicists are attempting to determine whether there is any connection between the earth's wobble, seismic disturbancies, and minute irregularities in the earth's rotation. An interdisciplinary group of scientists, including an astronomer, has been studying the effects of atmospheric pollution (mentioned in Section 1.3). These are only a few samples of the coordinated efforts by scientists seeking to unravel the complexities of our planet.

The discoveries of amino acids in meteorites and of organic molecules in interstellar clouds have stirred a lively interest in the field of exobiology. Before we can grapple with the possibilities of life on other worlds, we must have a clearer understanding of its origin and development on earth. How are planetary systems formed and what factors endow a planet with living organisms? What effect does man, nature's youngest major and most complex species, have upon the ecology of his planet? Astronomers predict a long future for the earth, but how will man modify his environment and his existence on the best of all possible worlds in the solar system?

Early History of the Earth

The earth and the other planets were created about 4.6 billion years ago, according to radioactive dating of meteorites and terrestrial rocks. The planets are believed to have evolved within the rapidly contracting disk portion of a rotationally flattened solar nebula whose central portion became the sun. One common version is that a cool, uniuniformly composed earth was formed from a coalescence of different-sized bodies that had solidified within the turbulent disk. As the temperature of the earth's interior rose because of gravitational compression during many millions of years, a critical temperature was reached which melted the core material and liquefied the outer portions. In this molten condition, the heaviest elements, iron in particular, sank toward the center after separation from the lighter magnesium-rich silicates which rose to form the mantle layer surrounding the central core. (Silicates are chemical combinations of silicon and oxygen in various proportions.) The more volatile material flowed to the top where the granitic slag cooled on a bed of molten basalt and hardened into the continental land masses. How this picture of the structural and chemical composition of the earth's interior was derived from seismic studies will be considered in Section 5.2.

Age of the Earth

One of the better known facts about the earth's early history is its age. In 1654 Archbishop Usher of Ireland claimed from his study of the Scriptures that the earth was born on October 26 at 9 A.M. in the year 4004 B.C. During the latter part of the nineteenth century, scientific estimates of the earth's age soared from twenty million to fifty million years. Even the latter figure proved to be far too low on the basis of geological evidence which had accumulated by the end of that century. From 1900 to the present time the figure for the calculated age of the earth kept increasing at the rate of 800 million years each successive decade up to the present value of 4.6 billion years where it has now stabilized.

Accurate age-dating of the earth was freed from theological considerations and more rational but inadequate methods at the beginning of the twentieth century with the discovery of natural radioactivity. Radioactive elements such as uranium and thorium spontaneously break down into the lighter radioactive elements at regular rates. They end up as stable isotopes of lesser atomic weights. In principle, the age of a rock sample is found by determining the percentage of the final stable isotope relative to the remaining parent material from which the isotopes descended, combined with the known rate of disintegration. According to Table 5.1, half of the original uranium 238 decays in 4.51 billion years into lead 206. If examination of the oldest rocks revealed a 50-50 proportion of uranium 238 to lead 206, the age of the rock sample would be about 4.5 billion years if no lead 206 were present at the beginning. Analysis of the oldest meteorite specimens shows that some primitive lead 206 was originally present when the planetary system was formed. After proper allowance for the primordial lead abundances in the earth's rocks, geophysicists have derived a value of 4.6 billion years since the earth was formed.

5.2 THE GEOSPHERE

Earth's Size

The earth's dimensions follow from the geodetic measurement of the number of miles between parallels of latitude one degree apart. Suppose for the sake

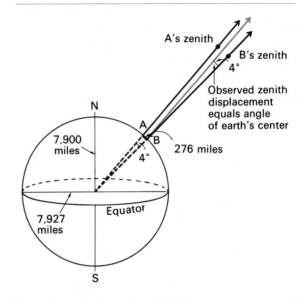

Figure 5.1   Measuring the earth's size.

of illustration that a star appears in the zenith (overhead) at station A. It will not be observed at the zenith at station B due north or south of station A. The amount of angular displacement of the star relative to the zenith depends on the distance in miles between the two stations. If, for example, the observed zenith displacement at station B is four degrees and the distance between A and B is 276

Table 5.1   Representative Radioactive Elements

Radioactive Atom	Atomic No.	Half-life in Billions of Years[a]	Final Stable Decay Isotope Products	Atomic No.
Uranium 238	92	4.51	Lead 206, helium	82
Uranium 235	92	0.71	Lead 207, helium	82
Thorium 232	90	13.9	Lead 208, helium	82
Rubidium 87	37	47	Strontium 87	38
Potassium 40	19	1.31	Argon 40	18

[a]Time required for 50 per cent of the original amount to decay into final products.

EXPLORING THE COSMOS

miles, the number of miles to one-degree change of latitude is 276/4 = 69 mi/deg.

Measurements made in different parts of the world reveal that the number of miles in one degree of latitude increases slightly from the equator (68.7 miles) toward the poles (69.4 miles). This indicates that the earth has the shape of an oblate spheroid with a diameter longer in the equatorial direction than in the polar direction. The earth's average circumference is equal to 69 miles times the number of degrees around the earth, or 69 × 360 = 24,840 miles. The earth's equatorial diameter is 7,927 miles; its polar diameter is 7,900 miles. The slight spherical deformity of the earth (one part in 300) is a consequence of the earth's axial rotation.

Earth's Mass and Density

There are several experimental ways of finding the earth's mass. The methods are based on Newton's law of gravitation. Once the mass is known, the mean density of the earth follows from the ratio of the mass to its volume. The mass of the earth is found to be 6.6×10^{21} tons. The mean density of the earth by calculation is 5.5 times the density of water.

One method of evaluating the mass of the earth is as follows: A body of mass m at the surface of the earth, subjected to the earth's gravitational force F, undergoes an acceleration $g = F/m$ (Newton's second law of motion, Section 2.7). From Newton's law of gravitation, the gravitational force between the body and the earth is $F = GmM/R^2$ where G is the gravitational constant, m is the mass of the body, M is the mass of the earth, and R is the distance from the body to the center of the attractive force, that is, the radius of the earth. Hence

$$g = \frac{F}{m} = \frac{GmM}{mR^2} \quad \text{or} \quad M = \frac{gR^2}{G}$$

The observed acceleration, g, of a body falling at the earth's surface is 980 cm/sec^2 (= 32 ft/sec^2). From the known values of the gravitational constant (6.67×10^{-8} cm^3/g · sec^2) and the earth's radius (6.38×10^8 cm), we find on substitution

Mass of earth

$$M = \frac{980 \times (6.38 \times 10^8)^2}{6.67 \times 10^{-8}}$$

$$= 5.98 \times 10^{27} \text{ grams or } 6.6 \times 10^{21} \text{ tons}$$

The average density of a spherical body of mass M and radius R is obtained by dividing its mass by its volume. For the earth we find

Average density of earth

$$\frac{\text{mass}}{4/3\pi R^3} = \frac{5.98 \times 10^{27} \text{ g}}{1.08 \times 10^{27} \text{ cm}^3} = 5.5 \text{ g/cm}^3$$

The Earth's Interior

Nature has provided geophysicists with a probing tool: the seismic waves which spread out in all directions from the site of an earthquake disturbance. From the manner of their propagation through the earth, their periods and amplitudes of vibration, and their arrival time at each station, scientists can deduce the earth's internal structure. Two kinds of penetrating seismic waves are recognized: pressure (P) waves and shear (S) waves. The speed with which the P and S waves travel through the earth (3 to 8 miles per second) depends upon the density, compressibility, and rigidity of the material. The P waves alternately compress and rarefy the substances through which they pass along the direction of their travel in a manner similar to the passage of sound waves through the air. The S waves, which move somewhat slower than the P waves, cause the material through which they pass to vibrate perpendicular to their line of travel, like water waves. Unlike the P waves, they are incapable of being transmitted through liquids which absorb their vibrations. As the waves penetrate the different layers, their speed increases with depth and they bend or are reflected on reaching an

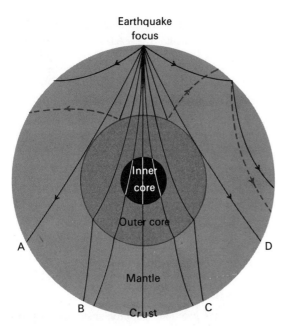

Earthquake
focus

Inner
core

Outer core

A

D

Mantle

B

C

Crust

Figure 5.2   Refraction (bending) and reflection of seismic waves inside the earth. Zones AB and CD are the shadow zones for P waves (in black color) where no P waves are found. Those that travel through the inner core are sharply bent back as they emerge from the outer core. Large zone covering ABCD is the shadow zone for S waves (blue color) where no S waves enter because they are absorbed by the outer fluid core.

interface (boundary between two zones). The observed shadow-zone phenomena for both kinds of waves, together with other data relating to the speeds and curvature of the wave fronts, have led to the discovery of the earth's layered construction. This structuring was brought about during the formative period of the earth by a melting process that separated the ingredients into the stratified zones according to their relative weight and volatility.

The prevailing model of the earth's central portions is that of a hot, highly compressed *inner core*, presumably solid, about 1,500 miles in diameter; it is believed to be composed mainly of nickel-iron.

The central core is surrounded by a molten shell of liquid nickel-iron chiefly, about 1,400 miles thick, with lighter liquid material on top. The outer envelope, the *mantle*, is nearly 1,800 miles deep; it consists mostly of solid rock in the form of olivine, an iron-magnesium silicate. A thin coat of granitic composition called the *crust* forms the outermost skin of the earth. A summary of the pertinent geophysical data appears in Table 5.2.

5.3   THE LITHOSPHERE

The Earth's Crust

The crust has a maximum depth of twenty miles under the continents and a minimum depth of a mile or two below the ocean floor. The main composition of the continental blocks is a relatively light granitic rock rich in the silicates of aluminum, iron, and magnesium. On top of the igneous strata constituting those portions of the continents not subject to volcanic activity or mountain-building lies a thin veneer of river-borne material such as sedimentary rocks and soil deposited during the past ages. In the coastal region, on the continental margin, the sedimentary material consists of mud and clay washed down from the land by the rivers and waves.

Sandwiched between the upper mantle and the continental land masses and ocean beds is a layer of igneous basaltic rock, several miles thick. It consists mainly of iron and magnesium silicates derived from the lava flow issuing from the earth's mantle. The boundary between the basaltic layer and the crust is called the *Mohorovicic discontinuity*, named after the Yugoslavian seismologist who discovered its existence in 1909 from the abrupt alteration in speed of the seismic waves at this point.

Sea-Floor Spreading—Continental Drift

Evidence has now accumulated that the lithosphere is segmented into a number of major plates some fifty to eighty miles thick and many minor

Table 5.2 The Layers of the Earth

Layer	Depth below Surface (mi)	Density relative to Water (g/cm³)	Pressure (tons/sq in)	Approx. Temp. (°C)	Main Composition
Crust	0–20	2.5–3.3	0–75	20–600	{ Continents: granite; or water
Mantle	20–1800	3.3–5.8	75–10,000	600–2500	{ Basaltic rocks: magnesium and iron silicates
Outer core	1800–3200	5.8–9.6	10,000–22,500	2500	{ Molten nickel iron
Inner core	3200–3960	9.6–17	22,500–25,000	3600	{ Solid nickel-iron

plates floating on the earth's mantle. They are slowly separating from each other across the ocean beds, carrying the continents with them, at an average rate of an inch or two per year. This phenomenon goes by the name of *continental drift*. The new science that it has generated is called *plate tectonics*. Further confirmation of plate movements is obtained from the shape, geological structure, and paleontology of the continents. Additional evidence is found from the orientation of the magnetic fields frozen in the ancient igneous rocks which match up between separated continents across the oceans.

Exploration of the ocean bottoms by means of sounding techniques has led to the discovery of a mid-ocean ridge system, thousands of miles long. Deep central rifts up to ten miles in width run north-south through the Atlantic and Indian ocean basins. The Pacific Ocean is marked by a number of deep trenches bordering its edges and a disoriented network of ridges, troughs, and fractures. The rifts and trenches coincide with some of the major seismic belts of the earth.

As molten magma is forced upward into the mid-ocean fracture, it pushes out laterally to form volcanic cones which are displaced to one side or the other by the separating plates to form the ridges. Deep core samples from depths of five miles below sea level confirm the judgment that the youngest volcanic rocks to have been laid down are found in the vicinity of the mid-ocean ridge. Here the fresh material from the mantle has welled up through the mid-rift and has spread laterally to settle and harden later in the oceanic basins adjoining the continental margins. One commonly favored mechanism for transporting the plates on which the continents ride is by means of the horizontal flow of convection currents which form convection cells circulating within the upper, softer portion of the mantle. When the leading edge of the continental plate encounters an oceanic plate, it will be pushed downward and disappear into the mantle to form a deep trench. Material rising from the mantle region will form a coastal mountain belt similar to the Andes. Mountain chains like the Alps, according to tectonics theory, are believed to have been created from the succession of encounters between the European and African plates when the Atlantic Ocean first began to widen.

The theory of continental drift did not gain many adherents when it was first seriously proposed by the German geologist A. L. Wegener in 1912. But

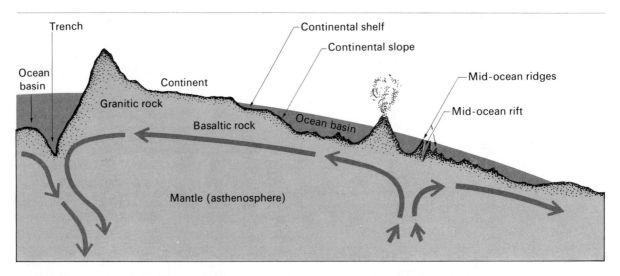

Figure 5.3   Schematic profile view of a portion of the lithosphere.

now after extensive exploration of the sea bottom, his idea has been confirmed and the picture that has emerged is the following one. The last great mass movement of the continents began about 200 million years ago. At that time there existed but one consolidated land mass called *Pangaea*. Some 20 million years later, sea-floor spreading had separated the supercontinent into two segments: northern *Laurasia* and southern *Gondwana*. About 45 million years later, the North Atlantic and Indian oceans had widened considerably and South America had begun to separate from Africa while India was drifting northward. During the next 70 million years (from 135 to 65 million years ago), the South Atlantic ocean had widened into a major ocean; the Mediterranean Sea had begun to open up and the separation of North America from Eurasia had just begun. In the last 65 million years, almost half of the oceans were created. Greenland had split from North America which had completed its cleavage from Eurasia as the Atlantic ocean widened. Northward-drifting India collided with and joined Asia; a

developing rift detached Australia from Antarctica. According to a computerized solution projected for the next 50 million years, the Atlantic and Indian oceans will enlarge while the Pacific ocean will contract. Australia will continue to drift northward toward a possible collision with Eurasia. The northward movement of Africa will seal the Bay of Biscay and doom the Mediterranean. Lower California and a sliver west of the San Andreas fault will be torn from the California mainland and begin to drift in a northwesterly direction. In 10 million years, Los Angeles will have moved far enough to become abreast of San Francisco. It will eventually slide into the Aleutian trench in about 60 million years.

5.4   THE HYDROSPHERE

Introduction

The hydrospheric composition of the earth includes all forms of water: the liquid phase in the oceans, rivers, lakes, streams, underground waters, and the falling rain; the solid phase in the glacial deposits, icebergs, snowpacks, and frozen water; the gaseous phase, principally in the atmosphere where it condenses in the form of clouds, and in the dew and frost on the ground. The hydrosphere occupies about 74 per cent of the earth's surface, with all but 2 per cent contained in the oceans.

The lithosphere, hydrosphere, and atmosphere interact constantly with each other. The circulation of the waters produces weathering on the land masses and transports the soil over land and into the seas. Plants transpire, bodies of water evaporate, and the saturated water vapor precipitates out from the clouds as rain. Rain that falls on land infiltrates the soil or runs off in streams and rivers. It acts as an erosive agent before returning its liquid contents to their original sources, thus closing the hydrologic cycle. The excellent heat-storing capabilities of the oceanic waters produces a moderating influence on the world's temperature; their circulation and interaction with the atmosphere profoundly influence the world's climate.

Lunisolar Tides in the Hydrosphere

The gravitational pull of the moon on the hydrosphere produces two tidal bulges on opposite sides of the earth in line with the moon. To understand why the two high tides are formed, let us refer to an idealized representation of the earth entirely surrounded by water. The moon attracts that part of the water closest to it more strongly than the earth. The water on the opposite side of the earth, which is farthest from the moon, is attracted less strongly than the earth. Thus there is a larger acceleration of the oceans at point A than at point C relative to the earth at point B. This causes the waters to move toward the moon at point A and to recede from the moon at point C relative to the earth as a whole. Consequently, the waters pile up in the form of an ellipsoid whose long axis is directed toward the moon. Midway between the high tides are the low tides from which

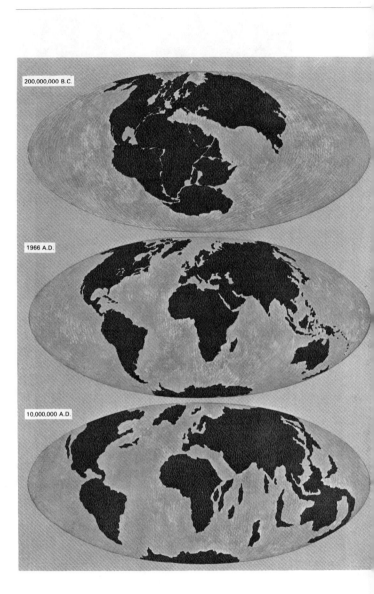

Figure 5.4   The drifting continents. From the Life Science Library book, The Planets, *published by Time-Life Books. Drawing by Paul Calle.*

5 OUR BLUE-WHITE PLANET EARTH

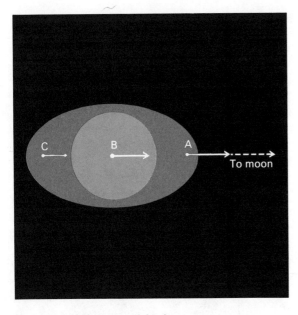

Figure 5.5 The earth's tidal bulge.

the waters have ebbed toward the flood tides. The 24-hour rotation of the earth underneath the tidal bulges results in the alternating high and low tides twice each day. After one complete rotation of the earth, the moon has moved about thirteen degrees farther eastward in its orbit. The earth must turn eastward on its axis for another fifty minutes to bring the *same* high tide back to the same place on the earth's surface. The average interval between successive high or low tides is, therefore, $1/2 \times 24^{hr}$ 50^{min} or $12^{hr} 25^{min}$. Since the earth rotates faster than the moon revolves, it drags the tidal bulges somewhat ahead of the line joining the centers of the moon and the earth.

The sun's contribution to the tides amounts to nearly one-half that of the moon. When the sun and moon are in line, as at new or full moon, their combined gravitational pull on the waters of the earth is at a maximum, producing so-called *spring tides*. These highest tides occur twice each month at approx-

imate intervals of two weeks. When the sun and moon are positioned at right angles to each other, as at first and last quarter of the moon, their gravitational pulls partly offset each other. This results in the lowest high tides, called *neap tides*, which occur about one week before or after the spring tides.

5.5 ROTATIONAL AND MAGNETIC PHENOMENA

Earth's Rotation

The constant friction generated by the lunisolar tides sweeping over the rotating earth has gradually slowed down the earth's rotation. It is calculated that during the past several billion years the period of rotation changed from its original value of several hours to its present value of twenty-four hours. This process of dissipating the earth's rotational energy is destined to continue indefinitely. The present average rate by which the day is lengthening amounts to 0.0016 seconds per century. In fifty-four centuries the *accumulated* effect adds up to a difference of twenty-four hours between a clock regulated to the length of the day fifty-four centuries ago and one regulated to the length of the present day. In other words, our clock would have lost twenty-four hours on the earlier clock in 5,440 years. This concept can be clarified by calculating the total amount a clock would lose at the end of a ten-day interval if it loses one additional second per day. It is *not* ten seconds but fifty-five seconds.

The slowdown in the length of the day is not uniform. Irregularities have been uncovered, particularly in recent years since the introduction of atomic clocks against which the earth's rotation is compared. First, there is an approximate ten-year fluctuation of a few milliseconds ascribed to a transfer of rotational energy between the earth's liquid core and the mantle (one millisecond = 0.001 second). Second, there is a slowing down of the earth in the spring of our northern hemisphere and a speeding up in the fall by about thirty milliseconds, apparently resulting from seasonal variations in the atmospheric winds and ocean tides. Third, sudden, unexplained changes up to ten milliseconds occur at unpredictable intervals. As the earth turns, it wobbles slightly on its rotational axis over a roughly circular path at the poles some fifty feet in diameter during a fourteen-month period. This phenomenon, known as the *Chandler wobble*, is believed to be sustained by the occurrence of major earthquakes; otherwise, according to calculations, the motion would die down in the short time of twenty years.

Earth's Magnetism

Another puzzling problem relates to the origin of the earth's magnetic field. It is believed that the earth acquired its magnetism as a result of the differential rotation existing between the electrically conducting molten core and the mantle. This produces a dynamo action that generates the earth's magnetic field. Over geologic time the magnetic field has changed directions many times. During the last ten million years, the reversals have come on an average of once every 220,000 years. This is revealed from studies of the frozen magnetism embedded in the ancient rocks of different ages. Iron particles buried in molten lava beds tend to align themselves in the direction of the existing magnetic poles. After solidifying, the rocks retain the fossilized magnetism indefinitely. The cause of the geomagnetic reversals is presently unknown. One suggestion is that they may have been initiated by meteorite or asteroidal impact; another, that they may be related in some vague way with changes in the earth's rotational motion.

The Magnetosphere

The magnetosphere may be visualized as the magnetic field surrounding the earth in which it exercises electromagnetic control over charged particles entering its domain. Our knowledge of the magnetosphere has come by way of instrumented satellites monitoring the strength, direction, and composition of the field at various distances from the earth. The magnetosphere has been found to consist of several concentric zones populated by charged particles (protons and electrons). Most of these particles are ejected from the sun in the form of the solar wind; as they enter the earth's atmosphere, they become trapped by the earth's magnetic field.

The principal zones, known as the Van Allen radiation belts, encircle the earth in two doughnut-shaped regions centered about 2,500 and 10,000 miles from the earth's surface. They are named after their discoverer, the American physicist J. A. Van Allen, who first disclosed their existence in 1958 from Explorer satellite data. The collision between the solar wind and the earth's magnetosphere creates a shock-wave disturbance that distorts and compresses the field on the sunlit side and stretches it into a long tail on the nighttime side of the earth.

5.6 THE ATMOSPHERE

Role of the Atmosphere

The atmosphere plays a vital role in the preservation of life on earth. Sunlight passing through the air warms the ground which reradiates the solar energy in the form of heat waves. Their passage outward into space is restricted by atmospheric absorption due to the presence of ozone, carbon dioxide, and water vapor, producing the well-known *greenhouse effect*. This provides a biologically favorable temperature range for life. The upper atmosphere screens us from harmful ultraviolet and x-ray solar radiation. It also volatilizes the meteoroids in their flight through the air and lessens the severity of the incoming highly energetic particles (mostly protons) that we call cosmic rays. The diffusion and selective scattering of the harsh solar radiation by the lower atmosphere creates

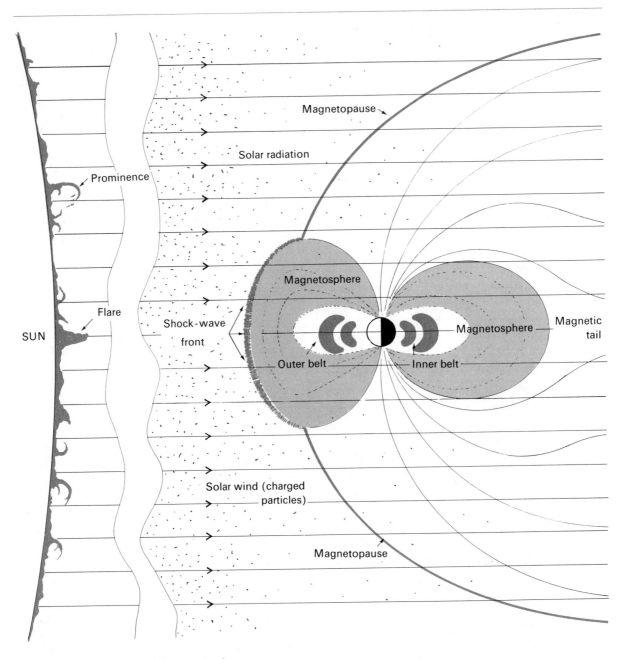

Figure 5.6   Cross-section of the magnetosphere.

the soft blue appearance of the sky. The sky appears blue because the atmospheric gases reflect the blue colors of sunlight in all directions much more energetically than the other colors.

Atmospheric Properties

The atmosphere possesses several distinct layers characterized by their unique thermal, physical, chemical, and electrical properties. The bottom layer, known as the *troposphere*, extends to an average altitude of seven miles above the earth's surface; our weather occurs in this region. Above the troposphere lies a narrow layer known as the *stratosphere* where the temperature remains constant at $-67°F$. Within the next zone, the *mesosphere*, the temperature rises toward a maximum of about $50°F$; thereafter, it rapidly declines toward a minimum value of $-90°F$ at its upper limit of sixty miles. Above this height, the temperature climbs steadily to very high values throughout the *thermosphere* and into the *exosphere* toward the atmospheric fringe several hundred miles above sea level. These high temperatures are the gas-kinetic temperatures resulting from the rapid motions of the gas atoms which have freely absorbed the solar energy at these lofty altitudes.

Up to sixty miles there is no diffuse separation of the gases. Here the chemical composition remains nearly constant: nitrogen, 78 per cent; oxygen, 21 per cent; argon, nearly 1 per cent; carbon dioxide, 0.03 per cent; water vapor, variable up to several per cent in the troposphere. Minute traces of other gases exist in the upper air, including sodium, methane, ammonia, and nitrous oxide. At extreme heights a rarefied layer of helium extends from 600 to 1,500 miles above the earth's surface. This, in turn, is topped by a highly attenuated hydrogen layer that gradually merges into interplanetary space. Approximately one-half of the atmosphere is contained in the first 3.5 miles; all but 1 per cent of the air lies below the twenty-mile limit.

The atmosphere is suffused with a faint, permanent light called the *airglow*, which spreads its soft luminescence throughout the sky. Its spectrum has been recorded during the twilight and dark hours of the sky. On long-exposure photographs it fogs the astronomers' plates and reduces the contrast between the faintest celestial images and the sky background. The gaseous constituents responsible for the production of the airglow involve the molecules of hydrogen, nitrogen, the hydroxyl OH, and the atoms of oxygen, sodium, and calcium. These gases absorb the ultraviolet sunlight and reradiate the energy in a small number of wavelengths confined to the green, red, and infrared spectral regions.

The well-known aurorae are most frequently observed in the auroral zones that lie between $65°$ and $70°$ north and south magnetic latitudes. They originate from encounters between the upper atmospheric atoms of oxygen and nitrogen with the Van Allen particles that are precipitated out of the magnetosphere into the auroral latitudes. The collisions stimulate these gases to radiate in the familiar pale green and occasional bright red spectral colors. The auroral phenomenon is most intense during the peak period of the eleven-year sunspot cycle when the sun is most active. At the time of a major solar outburst the "northern lights" can sometimes be seen as far south as the middle latitudes.

The Ionosphere

The atmosphere is stratified into several electrified layers known by the general name of the *ionosphere*. These are the D, E, F_1, and F_2 ionospheric levels as shown in Figure 5.7. The electrical activity of these regions is maintained by the solar ultraviolet and x-ray radiation that removes electrons from the neutral atoms and molecules. This process ionizes the air and renders it electrically conducting. Radio waves from ground stations entering the ionosphere cause the free electrons to vibrate and to reradiate

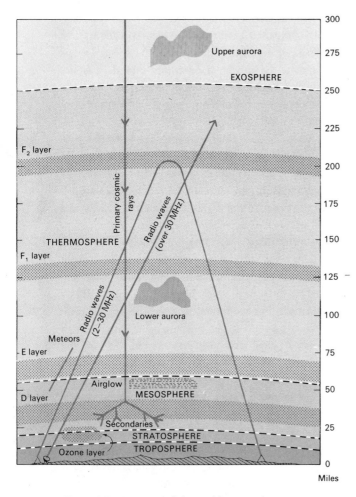

Figure 5.7   Structure of the earth's atmosphere.

energy at the same frequency as the incident waves. As these waves penetrate more deeply into the denser portions of the ionosphere, the oscillating electrons propagate their energy more in the backward direction toward the earth's surface than in the same direction as the incident radio waves. Finally, the higher ionospheric density retards the wave energy so that it can no longer propagate in the forward direction. As a result, radio waves at frequencies less than about 30 megahertz transmitted from the earth's surface are turned back by the various ionospheric layers. (The D layer turns back the frequencies below 500 kHz; the E layer, those between 500 kHz and approximately 2MHz; and the F_1 and F_2 layers, the frequencies approximately between 2 MHz and 30 MHz.) Reflection of the radio waves makes possible long-distance communication between widely separated stations on the earth's surface. Frequencies higher than 30 megahertz pass through the ionosphere into space with little or no bending. Since these line-of-sight frequencies are unaffected by ionospheric disturbances caused by enhanced solar activity, they have been widely employed in the synchronous communications satellites[1] for point-to-point instantaneous transmissions between continents.

Atmospheric Scintillation and Refraction

The presence of unsteady air in the lower atmospheric levels causes the image of a star observed in the telescope to waver. The various layers of differing air density drifting across the line of sight continuously displace and blur the observed stellar image. With reduced atmospheric turbulence there is less twinkling of the stars and the "seeing" is improved. On the other hand, a planet shines with a steady light because each point of its tiny disk twinkles differently and is therefore out of step with its neighbor, so the observer sees only the constant average effect of all the twinkling points of the disk.

As starlight enters the atmosphere it undergoes an increasing amount of bending or refraction toward the vertical. The object is apparently observed slightly closer to the zenith than its true direction in space. The amount of refraction is naturally a

[1] A synchronous satellite orbits the earth in the same period that the earth rotates, therefore hovering over the same region of the earth continuously. Such communication satellites are now stationed over the Indian Ocean and over the mid-Atlantic and mid-Pacific equatorial areas.

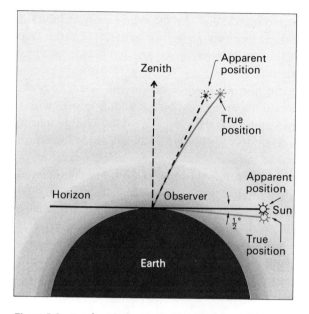

Figure 5.8 *Bending (refraction) of starlight or sunlight.*

maximum for a body observed near the horizon where the path length through the air to the observer is longest. The angle of refraction at the horizon is one-half degree. The rising or setting sun and moon are, in reality, below the observer's horizon, but because of refraction they are raised above the horizon by an amount equivalent to their apparent diameter, which happens to be one-half degree.

5.7 THE BIOSPHERE

Early Primitive Conditions

The biosphere is the life zone extending from three miles below sea level to four miles above sea level. It is critically dependent for its existence on the supply of oxygen and carbon dioxide in the earth's atmosphere and the water content of the earth. The primordial atmosphere of the earth is thought to have consisted principally of a mixture of hydrogen, ammonia, methane, and water vapor out of which the amino acids and simpler organic com-

pounds were synthesized by irradiation of solar ultraviolet light and other energy sources. This stage of chemical metamorphosis has been reproduced in various laboratory experiments.

Subsequent cooling of the molten rocks about 3.4 billion years ago released large amounts of water vapor, carbon dioxide, and nitrogen into the air by outgassing from the earth's interior, thus replacing most of the original atmosphere. Further cooling condensed the water vapor to create the warm, shallow seas that were destined to provide a safe haven for the evolutionary development of the first organic compounds.

Development of Life

The first primitive organisms sustained themselves in the warm oceanic broth by utilizing the ambient organic compounds through a simple fermentation process that released the alcohols, acids, and carbon dioxide. As additional carbon dioxide accumulated biologically and from volcanic venting, the more successful living organisms, by the repeated processes of trial and error, developed the more efficient mode of photosynthesis. This process, which utilizes solar energy, the existing carbon dioxide, and water to synthesize the sugars and starches necessary for growth, yields free oxygen by respiration. Evidence of these photosynthesizing organisms has been found in certain microscopic, one-cell, algae-type fossils deposited in the sedimentary South African rocks about 3.3 billion years ago. Some additional oxygen may have been released also through the dissociation of water vapor into oxygen and hydrogen by ultraviolet solar radiation.

Eventually, a protective atmospheric layer of ozone was formed, thus cutting off the more harmful solar ultraviolet light and permitting life to develop more freely closer to the surface of the oceans. Without the proper temperatures, an available supply of nutrients, and the self-regulating recycling mechanisms evolved by the organisms, life in the biosphere would have been unable to develop and sustain itself. The complete sequence of events leading from the inorganic compounds present in the primordial soup of the primitive oceans to the hereditary, self-duplicating molecular structures containing the genetic code remains obscure. The probable course of development from the primitive raw materials to the first living forms is presented in Table 5.3.

Biological History

The further accumulation of biologically produced oxygen in the earth's atmosphere set the stage for the development of the more complex forms of life, with the first invertebrates appearing some 600 million years ago. Table 5.4 has been constructed from paleontological and geological evidence to show the biological course of evolution from the first living organisms to the advent of man.

The Carbon-Oxygen Cycle

The sun is the prime source of energy in the cycle of life. Animals consume food energy and plants produce and store it. Within the biosphere the utilized materials of plant organisms are recycled back for further reuse through the processes of respiration by animals and dead organic matter and transpiration by water sources. The photosynthetic operation active in this cycling system involves water, carbon dioxide, and solar energy to form the organic compounds for the growth of plants and vegetation. Molecular oxygen is released as a by-product.

If the photosynthetic process were to cease, animal life in the biosphere would be in peril within two millennia, the recycling period of atmospheric oxygen. It is not likely that the oxygen in the oceans and in the atmosphere can be seriously depleted by anything man could do in polluting his environment. The recycling period for carbon dioxide is a short three hundred years. During geologic time, animals and plants have reached an equilibrium stage in which they work together in harmony. Thus appreciable change in the environmental status quo would upset the delicate equilibrium now existing between the two species. This possibility is discussed in Section 5.9.

5.8 THE LIVING CELL AND THE GENETIC CODE

Darwinian Concept of Evolution

Evolution in plants and animals proceeds through the interaction of the environment with the hereditary material present in the genes. It is constantly being modified by the process of natural selection and the chance mutations that enable the species to survive. Mutations occur at random; the unfavorable ones are weeded out by the inability of the host

Table 5.3   Early Evolutionary Sequence of Life

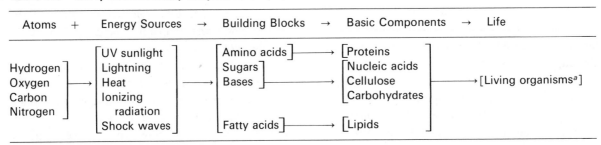

Atoms	+	Energy Sources	→	Building Blocks	→	Basic Components	→	Life
Hydrogen Oxygen Carbon Nitrogen		UV sunlight Lightning Heat Ionizing radiation Shock waves		Amino acids Sugars Bases Fatty acids		Proteins Nucleic acids Cellulose Carbohydrates Lipids		[Living organisms[a]]

[a]Chemical content of living matter is approximately 77 per cent water, 15 per cent protein, 5 per cent fat, and 2 per cent carbohydrate.

Table 5.4   The Geological-Biological Timetable

Time Scale (millions of years ago)	Geological Events or Era	Species
4,500–4,000	The earth forms; primeval atmosphere present	
4,000–3,000	Oldest crustal rocks; oceans develop	First lime deposits
3,000–1,500	Oxidized atmosphere replaces reducing atmosphere	Algal microorganisms; change to oxygenic life
1,500–700	Precambrian	Fossilized algae
700–600	Cambrian	Invertebrates
600–220	Paleozoic	First reptiles; first amphibians; first fishes; ferns
220–80	Mesozoic; fragmentation of huge single land mass (Pangaea) into the separate continents	Flowering plants; giant reptiles; first mammals; first birds
80–3	Cenozoic	Mammalian evolution; Man-ape (4 million years ago)
3-present	Pleistocene Recent	*Homo erectus* *Homo sapiens*

organism to adapt to its environment. It is this natural, relentless experimentation through cumulative mutation and natural selection, first clearly enunciated by Charles Darwin in 1859, that has produced the great diversity of life on our planet. It is estimated that a total of about four billion different species have inhabited the earth at one time or another.

Cell Structure

All living organisms contain diverse cells equipped to perform specialized functions within the organism. The individual cell is made up of a jellylike substance called the *cytoplasm* enveloping the *nucleus* which contains long, thin, ropelike strands called *chromosomes*. In the ordinary cell the chromosomes occur in pairs, and their number is fixed in every species. In man their total number

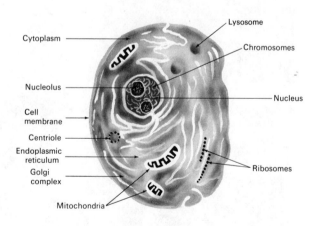

Figure 5.9   Configuration of a cell. (Redrawn by permission from Time, *April 19, 1971.)*

within each cell is forty-six. The human body contains about 180 billion cells; every minute millions of them disintegrate and must be replaced. The hereditary information contained within the chromosomes is passed on by the nuclear DNA (deoxyribonucleic acid), a double-twisted helix of many genes that specifically determines the characteristics of the living organism.

Amino Acids and Proteins

The building blocks of life are the amino acids, twenty varieties in all. They are composed principally of complex combinations of hydrogen, carbon, oxygen, and nitrogen. During cell production they arrange themselves into various long molecular sequences called *proteins*. The arrangement of the amino acids in the protein molecule determines its specific characteristic. Proteins serve as structural material and as *enzymes*, the chemical catalysts that govern the metabolism of the cell. They are needed in the production of bone, blood, hair, or whatever the genetic code in the DNA molecule specifies.

The Nucleotides

The proteins in turn link up in the proper order to form the long chains consisting of the nucleotides. A nucleotide is a combination of a base (A, T, C, or G), a sugar (S), and a phosphate (P) as shown in Figure 5.10. Each nucleotide base, with its alternating associated side units, (P and S) in one strand, is hooked through a system of hydrogen bonds with its complementary number in the opposite strand in a definite way: only A with T or T with A and only C with G or G with C. A single human cell, for ex-

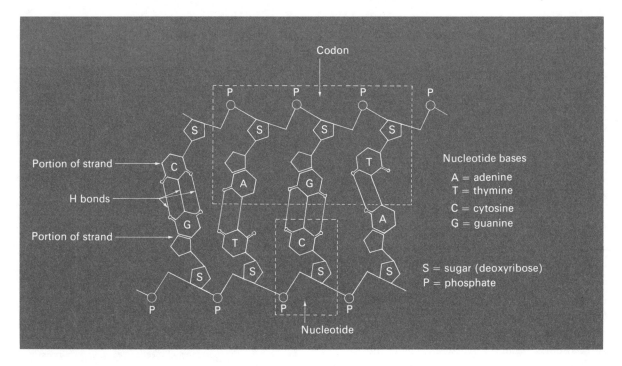

Figure 5.10   Portion of DNA structure.

EXPLORING THE COSMOS

ample, contains a minimum number of six billion nucleotide-base pairs. If straightened out and laid end to end, the total amount of DNA in the cell would be about six feet in length.

A triplet of nucleotides, called a *codon*, specifies one of the twenty amino acids in the chain. The codons are arranged in various sequences along the DNA strands to form the thousands of different protein molecules synthesized within the cell. If the nucleotides correspond to the letters of the alphabet, the amino acids to three-letter-word groups, and the proteins to whole sentences, then the DNA molecule might be considered to express the idea conveyed in an entire paragraph.

The Double-Twisted Strands of DNA

The structure of the DNA molecule was first worked out jointly by J. D. Watson of Harvard and F. H. C. Crick of Cambridge University in 1953. A representation of its configuration in the form of the double-twisted strands appears in Figure 5.11. Each strand of the twisted molecule consists of the four nucleotide bases (A, T, C, G) repeated over and over in a long sequence of codons (triplets). If a section of one strand contains the bases C, A, G, T, T, and C

in that order, the opposite section of strand consists of the sequence G, T, C, A, A, and G in the order shown.

The function of the DNA molecule is twofold: it passes the hereditary information on to daughter cells by self-replication and it directs the synthesis of protein manufacture within the cell with the aid of the single-stranded messenger and transfer RNA (ribonucleic acid) molecules. The long sequence of the bases constituting the rungs of the twisted ladder of strands determines whether a man or a mouse is created. Certain combinations of nucleotides, not yet tried by nature, may be attempted by man in the future when he learns to manipulate the genetic code artificially.

5.9 THE ECOLOGICAL CRISIS

The Population Explosion

For most of the two million years or so of his existence on this planet, man struggled just to survive by utilizing his skills as a herbivore, scavenger, and hunter. In the last 10,000 years since man learned to domesticate animals, grow crops, and live in clustered domiciles, his numbers have increased drama-

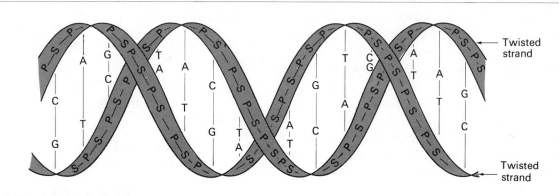

Figure 5.11   The DNA double helix.

tically. It is estimated that the world's population rose from about ten million in ancient times to about 500 million by the eighteenth century. Since that time the world's population has reached a current total of three and a fraction billion inhabitants. By the year 2200, at the present rate of growth, the world's population will total 500 billion people crowded together in the urban density now existing in the large cities. The increasing population expansion, if allowed to continue in the face of enormous pressures for food, water, and breathing space, obviously will have a devastating impact on man's future existence. The grim prospects of overpopulation with the increased demands on the world's resources were emphasized as early as 1799 by Thomas Malthus in his famous work, *An Essay on Population*. It is more likely that social restraints and inhibitions will contrive with other compelling forces to limit the population growth within tolerable limits.

Environmental Pollution

During the past one hundred years, the environmental changes wrought by man in the burning of fossil fuels, in the clearing of large forest areas, and in the exploitation of the land and water regions have been enormously accelerated. Exact knowledge pertaining to the processes by which the biosphere is being contaminated and damaged by man-made pollution is far from complete. What are the environmental effects of pesticides, waste disposal and oil pollution in the waterways, gaseous emissions and particulate effluents from industry, agriculture, homes, automobiles, and aircraft? In short, what is the extent of ecological injury to our planet and how will it affect the quality of life? The answers are now being sought by experts in the fields of biology, chemistry, engineering, metallurgy, geology, physics, ecology, the social sciences, and the legal profession.

Nature automatically operates within a closed ecological system. Energy is utilized by vegetation which is consumed by animal life which in turn diverts its products back into the air and soil to be recycled. On the other hand, man operates within an open-ended system that terminates in a dump or sewer without benefit of recycling. Unless he can achieve a proper population balance and a state of ecological equilibrium with nature, man may encounter serious difficulties in the future. The earth is indeed a great spaceship endowed with a finite life-support system that can optimally accommodate only a limited number of occupants, who must learn, therefore, to utilize its resources wisely.

REVIEW QUESTIONS

1. Explain how we derive the age of the earth from its oldest radioactive rocks.

2. How have geologists been able to arrive at a comprehensive picture of the earth's interior?

3. Describe the phenomenon of sea-floor spreading within the lithosphere. How is continental drift accounted for?

4. Why is the west coast of North and South America earthquake-prone?

5. Describe the closed-cycle system that operates in the hydrosphere.

6. How are tides produced within the hydrosphere by the gravitational attraction of the sun and moon on the earth?

7. How do we know that the earth has reversed its magnetic polarity many times in the past?

8. Describe the magnetosphere, including its composition, structure, extent, and interaction with the solar wind.

9. Name the principal atmospheric divisions and discuss their chemical and physical properties.

10. What role does the ionosphere play in the propagation of radio waves between transmitted and received signals from ground stations?

11. Describe the phenomenon of atmospheric refraction and that of atmospheric scintillation or twinkling.

12. What is the approximate chemical composition of the earth's principal atmospheric gases at sea level? At great heights?

13. Describe the early evolutionary steps that are believed to have led to the synthesis of the first living organisms from the primeval atmospheric mix of gases containing hydrogen, methane, ammonia, and water vapor.

14. What biological improvement resulted when the secondary oxidized atmosphere replaced the primordial reducing atmosphere during the early period of the earth's history?

15. Describe the roles of carbon dioxide, oxygen, and solar energy in sustaining most forms of life on earth by means of the carbon-oxygen cycle.

16. What is the Darwinian concept of evolution?

17. What is the relationship between the amino acids, proteins, and nucleotides in the formation of cell growth?

18. What determines within the genes whether a man or a monkey is to be created?

19. Name the factors underlying the population and ecological problems that the world faces today.

20. What is the difference between a closed cycle and an open-ended cycle of operation?

SELECTED READINGS

Beiser, A., *The Earth*, Life Nature Library (Time, Inc.), 1962.

Carson, L. R., *The Sea around Us*, Oxford University Press, 1953.

Dobson, G. M. B., *Exploring the Atmosphere*, Oxford University Press, 1968.

Eisley, L., *The Invisible Pyramid*, Scribner, 1970.

Gamow, G., *Planet Called Earth*, Viking, 1970.

Haber, H., *Our Blue Planet*, Scribner, 1969.

Meadows, D. L., ed., *The Limits to Growth*, Universe Books, 1972.

Nicks, O. W., ed., *This Island Earth*, NASA (U.S. Government Printing Office), 1970.

Scientific American, Inc., *The Planet Earth*, Simon and Schuster, 1957.

Astronaut Irwin of Apollo 15 at Hadley Base beside American flag with Lunar Roving Vehicle and Lunar Excursion Module viewed against the background of the Apennine mountains. (Courtesy of NASA.)

THE MOON:
A MARRED WORLD

The moon is nothing
But a circum-ambulatory aphrodisiac
Divinely subsidized to provoke the world
Into a rising birth rate.

Christopher Fry (1907–   ),
The Lady's Not for Burning

The earth-moon system could be regarded as a double planet because of the relatively large size of our satellite compared to the earth. These two dissimilar worlds exist in close proximity: a lively, variegated earth and a lifeless, barren moon. The difference in their development results chiefly from the earth's being eighty-one times more massive. The moon was formed about the same time as the earth, some 4.6 billion years ago, according to radioactive dating of terrestrial and lunar rocks. Because its mass is insufficient to retain an atmosphere, the moon's surface has changed little during the passage of time—in contrast to the earth whose topographical features have undergone constant change as a consequence of weathering and geologic processes.

Astronomers know a great deal about our satellite's general behavior, its distance, its complex orbital motions, its rotation, and the mutual gravitational interactions between the moon and the earth. Yet most persons have only the vaguest notions about the moon's phases, and its real and apparent motions. Despite the fact that the moon has been thoroughly observed in great detail with earth-based telescopes, new surprises continue to spring from extraterrestrial exploration of the moon. Rock samples brought back by Apollo astronauts reveal a number of chemical physical, and mineralogical differences from terrestrial rocks. The youngest rocks so far returned are slightly over three billion years old. Extraterrestrial evidence indicates that the moon passed through a period of great geological and thermal activity during the first 1.5 billion years of its existence. Since that time it has remained more or less physically quiescent.

In the last few years we have acquired more solid knowledge concerning the moon's past history and the formation of lunar craters and maria than in all of the preceding centuries. The hind side of the moon is now better known than the earth's ocean bottom! One major mystery is the different appearance of the terrain caused by the scarcity of maria on the far side of the moon. Although we comprehend more clearly the general physical nature of the moon, we still have no firm understanding of the origin of the earth-moon system.

6.1 LUNAR STUDIES

Observing Epochs

The study of the moon may be divided into two major observing periods, ground-based and extraterrestrial:

1. Earth-based observations
   (a) Pretelescopic, from antiquity to 1609
   (b) Telescopic, from 1609 to present (visual, photographic, photometric, spectrographic, radio/radar)
2. Extraterrestrial observations
   (a) Photographic observations and data collection from 1964 to present (flybys, landers, and orbiters)
   (b) Manned landings from 1969 to present (lunar samples, experiments, placement of automated instruments)

Following Galileo's first telescopic examination and drawings of the lunar surface in 1609, a number of astronomers vigorously pursued the study of the moon in succeeding centuries. They identified hundreds of additional features that were incorporated in the newer and more detailed lunar maps of the period. In time, the novelty of the subject wore off—after all, nothing much seemed to change on the moon. Except for a handful of astronomers, this lagging interest in the moon continued up to the present mid-century. Since the launchings of the

American and Soviet lunar vehicles in the late 1950's, preoccupation with the moon has naturally skyrocketed. The new field of lunar science has branched into a multidisciplined activity that has brought together many different scientific groups engaged in the common study of the moon. Prior knowledge of our extraterrestrial environment had come from the study of the celestial electromagnetic radiations, from the study of the cosmic rays (the highly energetic particles that crash through the earth's atmosphere from outer space), and from the analysis of meteorites. Now for the first time we can hold in our hands and examine the extraterrestrial samples returned by our astronauts from another body in space.

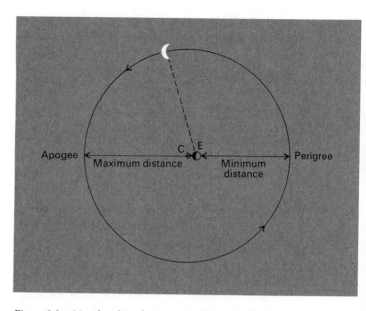

Figure 6.1   Moon's orbit relative to the earth. C shows the center of the orbit and E shows the position of the earth.

6.2   ORBITAL MOTION AND ROTATION

The Lunar Orbit

The moon revolves around the earth in an ellipse of small eccentricity with the earth at one focus (Figure 6.1). During its orbital period of 27.32 days, the moon approaches within 222,000 miles of the earth at *perigee* and recedes to a maximum distance of 253,000 miles at *apogee* nearly two weeks later. The moon's path is inclined to the plane of the ecliptic (i.e., the earth's orbit) by about five degrees. The two points of intersection where the moon crosses the plane of the ecliptic are called the *nodes* (Figure 6.2). The node through which the moon passes on its way north is the *ascending node*; nearly a fortnight later it crosses the *descending node* on its way south.

Figure 6.2   Nodes of the moon's orbit.

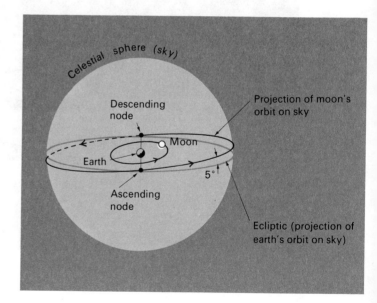

Measuring the Moon's Distance

The mean distance between the moon's center and the earth's center is 238,860 miles (384,400 km). The earliest reliable method of finding the distance of the moon involved measurement of the apparent displacement (parallax) of the moon among the stars observed from two widely separated points on the earth's surface. Let us suppose that the observations are being conducted simultaneously from the two observatories in opposite hemispheres as shown in Figure 6.3. The apparent displacement of the moon observed from the two stations at A and B—that is, the parallax angle, AMB—combined with knowledge of the earth's radius leads to a geometric solution of the moon's distance, CM. A more accurate determination was made in 1946 by bouncing a radar signal from the moon. By electronically timing the interval between the transmission of a sharp radar pulse from the earth and the return of its echo from the moon about 2.5 seconds later, the lunar distance was obtained with an accuracy of about one mile. More recently the moon's distance has been measured within an accuracy of six inches by reflecting a laser beam from a square array of corner reflectors placed on the moon by the Apollo astronauts. Several

observatories are cooperating in the lunar ranging experiment. The operation is providing precise evaluations of the many complex lunar motions, as well as data on the earth's Chandler wobble and the rate of continental drift.

The Sidereal and Synodic Months

The orbital period of the moon (27.32 days) is called the *sidereal month*. The period of the lunar phases during the calendar month (29.53 days) is known as the *synodic month*. The reason why they differ is made clear in Figure 6.4. Although the moon has completed its revolution around the earth at the end of the sidereal month, it has failed to reach the line joining the earth and the sun; its phase is not yet full. Consequently, a little more than two days of travel time around the sun is required by the earth-moon system to bring the moon in line with the earth and the sun. When the moon is again full, the synodic month is complete.

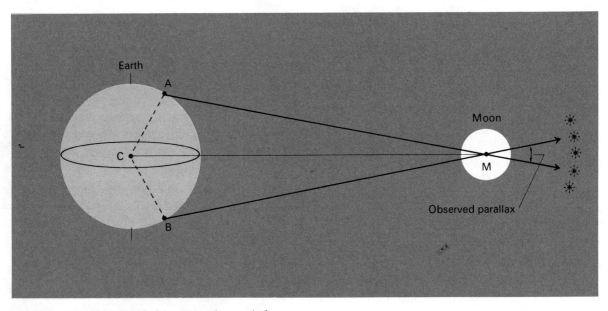

Figure 6.3   Parallax method of measuring the moon's distance.

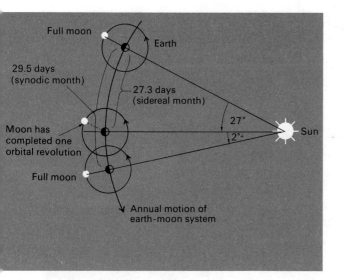

Figure 6.4   Sidereal vs. synodic months.

The Rotation of the Moon

Because the moon turns on its axis in the same time that it completes its orbit around the earth, the same hemisphere is always facing the earth. A simple way of illustrating this is to walk around a stool while continually watching the stool. Next walk around the stool *without turning*. In the first instance you have rotated once while you have revolved once, just as the moon does. In the second instance you have not rotated about your axis. If the moon behaved in this fashion, we could see all sides of the moon during the month. Actually, our lunar view from the earth encompasses about 59 per cent of the moon's surface. The bonus of an extra 9 per cent arises chiefly from two causes: (1) the slight tilt of seven degrees in the moon's axis enables us to look over the poles as the north and south poles are alternately tipped from us at intervals of two weeks; (2) the nonsynchronization between the uniformly

rotating moon and its variable revolution permits us to "peek" around the east and west edges alternately during the course of the month.

The equality between the period of the moon's rotation and the period of its orbital revolution (27.32 days) is not accidental. The tidal actions between the earth and the moon over the eons of time have resulted in a spin-orbit lock that has caused the moon to present the same hemisphere to the earth. It is calculated that originally both bodies were much closer, perhaps about 5 to 10 per cent of the present distance, and rotating more rapidly than at present. The earth-day was then about five hours long and the month less than a week in length. Owing to the greater tidal force of the earth, the moon's rotation has slowed down more rapidly than the earth's. The earth's rotational energy is gradually being transferred by the lunar tides generated on earth to the orbiting moon. This causes the moon to recede slowly from the earth about one inch per year. Calculations indicate that the earth will eventually slow down into a locked configuration with the moon. The earth and moon will then face each other with equal periods of rotation and revolution of about forty-seven days at a distance of 350,000 miles. The time for this event to happen, about fifty billion years, exceeds the probable lifespan of the earth-moon system by a large factor.

6.3   LUNAR PHASES AND APPARENT MOTIONS

The Moon's Changing Phases and Positions in the Sky

The two most obvious lunar phenomena are the night-to-night alterations in the position of the moon in the sky and the progressive changes in its phase. These are a consequence of the moon's eastward revolution around the earth during the course of the month. Let us examine the lunar aspects during the month.

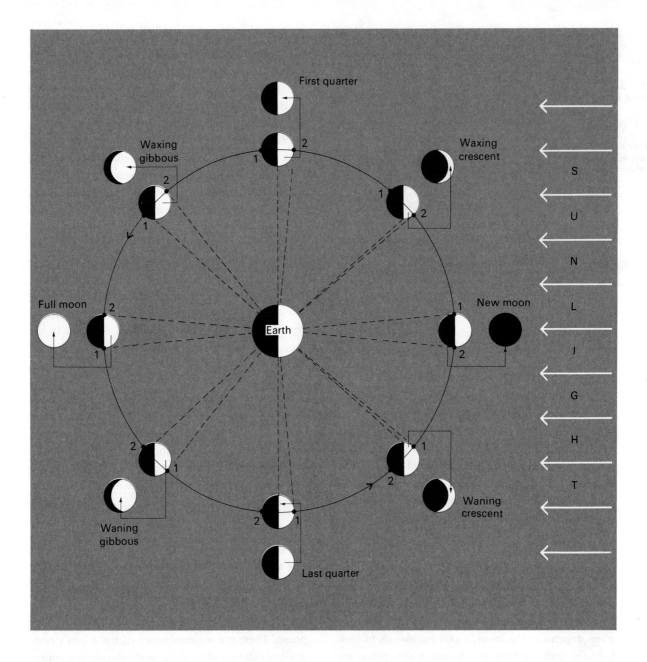

Figure 6.5   Lunar phases during synodic period (29.5 days). The portion between the dashed lines facing earth represents the visible part of the moon during the month, excepting the new moon. The effect of the moon's rotation is shown by the numbers 1 and 2.

The parallel rays of the distant sun always illuminate one-half of the moon's sphere as well as one hemisphere of the earth. At the time of new moon, when the moon is between the earth and the sun, its dark side is presented toward the earth and it is therefore invisible from the earth. Although it rises and sets with the sun, it is not usually in a direct line with the sun to produce a solar eclipse because its orbit is inclined to the ecliptic plane. (At least twice a year at intervals of nearly half a year this does happen and a complete or partial solar eclipse occurs somewhere on the earth's surface.) A couple of days later the thin crescent of the moon appears low in the western sky after sundown because of the rapid eastward orbital motion of the moon. During the next few days the waxing crescent appears higher in the sky after sunset and therefore sets later on consecutive nights. One week after the new moon the moon is at first quarter on the ob-

server's meridian at sundown; it will set about six hours after the sun. In the following week the gibbous moon waxes toward full as it continues its easterly orbital movement around the earth. Two weeks after new moon the moon is full and on the opposite side of the earth in relation to the sun; it rises approximately at 6 P.M. and sets approximately at 6 A.M. One week later the last-quarter moon rises at about midnight and sets at about noon. The fifty-minute average delay in moonrise on successive nights exists during the entire period of lunation and arises because the moon moves thirteen degrees farther east in a twenty-four-hour period. Consequently, the earth must rotate an additional thirteen degrees, which takes fifty minutes to bring the moon to the eastern horizon again.[1] Finally, the

[1] Around the time of the full moon in September, owing to the small angle that the moon's path makes with the eastern horizon, the "harvest moon" rises with very little delay on successive nights.

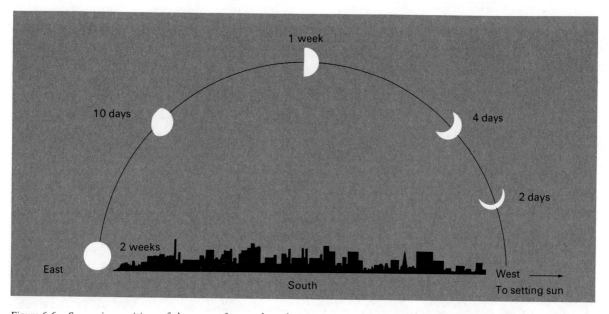

Figure 6.6   *Successive positions of the moon after sundown between new and full moons. The moon moves about 13 degrees eastward around the earth each day. The age of the moon is counted from the date of the new moon.*

6 THE MOON: A MARRED WORLD

waning crescent moon rises shortly before sunup as the moon is about to overtake the sun one month from the start of the new moon.

The Moon's Changing Altitude and Orientation

During the winter months in the northern hemisphere, the sun describes a low diurnal path in the sky. Since the full moon is in the opposite direction from the sun, the moon "rides high" in the nighttime winter sky. In the middle latitudes it never reaches the zenith. During the summer months the reverse is true; the sun appears highest in the sky while the moon "rides low." The orientation of the moon's setting crescent in the spring and autumn months is quite different. The horns of the crescent must always point *away* from the sun. In the spring, the setting crescent lies on its back with the horns pointing upward. In the fall the setting crescent lies on its side with the horns pointing toward the left as viewed near the western horizon. This difference in orientation of the moon's horns depends on the angle that the ecliptic (and very nearly the moon's orbit) makes with the western horizon throughout the year. In the spring the angle is highest at evening twilight; in the fall it is lowest at evening twilight. The lack of knowledge concerning proper lunar behavior has led to astronomical errors in prose and poetry.[2]

6.4 PHYSICAL PROPERTIES OF THE MOON

The following list summarizes physical data about the moon:

1. Mean diameter: 2,160 miles

2. Mass: 1/81.3 of the earth's mass

3. Average density: 3.3 g/cm^3 or 3.3 times that of water

[2] An example of a triple-compounded error appears in Dorothy Canfield's novel, *Seasoned Timber*, whose locale is in Vermont. According to her description, the great disk of the full moon rises after midnight; about an hour later, it is overhead. Can you find the three mistakes?

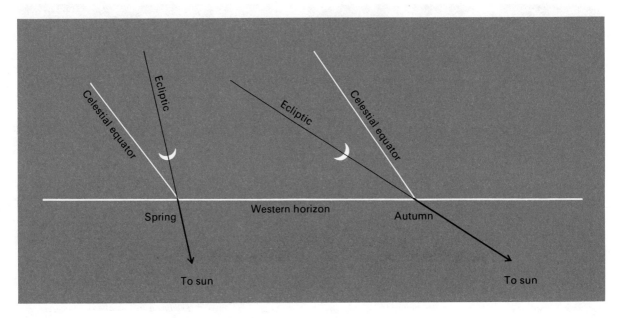

Figure 6.7   Orientation of the setting crescent in the spring and autumn.

4. Surface gravity: 1/6 that of the earth's surface gravity

5. Escape velocity: 1.5 miles per second

6. Atmosphere: virtually absent ($\sim 10^{-13}$ of earth's sea-level pressure)

7. Surface reflectivity (albedo): 7 per cent

8. Water: nonexistent in returned lunar rocks; may be present in interior

9. Maximum day temperature: $+265°F$ ($+130°C$)

10. Minimum night temperature: $-275°F$ ($-170°C$)

11. Magnetic field: generally weak; stronger in certain localized regions up to a fraction of 1 per cent of the earth's field strength

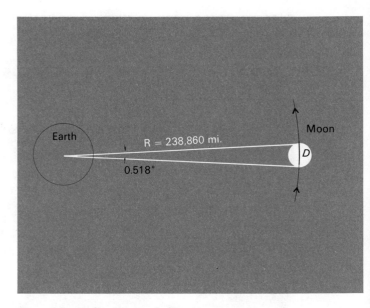

Figure 6.8   Finding the moon's diameter.

Diameter of the Moon

The moon does not quite span the width of the United States. Its diameter is found by simple trigonometry from its known distance and the angle that it subtends in the sky. We can avoid the use of trigonometry, however, by legitimately assuming in Figure 6.8 that the earth is at the center of a circle whose radius is the moon's average distance, 238,860 miles. The arc of this circle intercepted by the moon is so small in comparison with the circumference of the circle that it may be considered a straight line. Hence by simple proportion:

$$D : 0.518° = 2\pi R : 360°$$

where $2\pi R$ is the circumference of the moon's orbit and 0.518 degrees is the moon's apparent angular diameter. On substituting the numerical values and solving for D, we obtain:

$$D = \frac{2 \times 3.1416 \times 238,860 \times 0.518}{360} = 2,160 \text{ miles}$$

Mass of the Moon

The mass of our satellite is 1/81 of the mass of the earth. It is found by analyzing the motion of the earth relative to the common center of mass of the earth-moon system. This point, which lies on the line joining their centers, is called the *barycenter*. It is the point that most closely orbits the sun annually in accordance with Kepler's laws. The barycenter corresponds to the center of balance of an imaginary rod supporting the earth at one end and the less massive moon at the other end.

The center of the earth describes a small monthly orbit around the barycenter in comparison with the moon's much larger orbit around the barycenter. (Imagine how the earth and moon revolve as the bar in Figure 6.9*a* is swung around its fulcrum.) Because of this motion, telescopic observations from the surface of the earth reveal a monthly displacement of the nearer objects, such as the planets or asteroids. From the observed magnitude of this monthly shift,

6 THE MOON: A MARRED WORLD

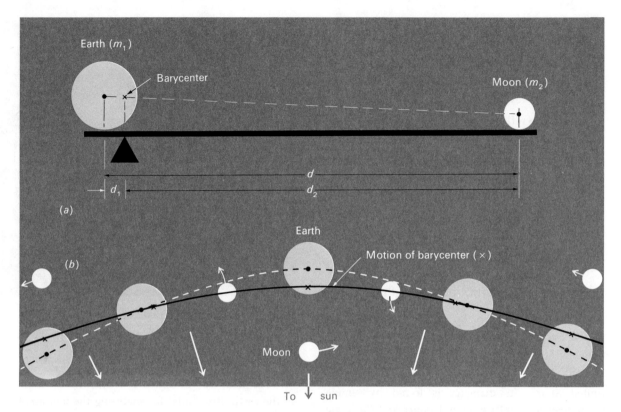

Figure 6.9   Center of mass of the earth-moon system. (a) *Finding the moon's mass from the location of the barycenter:*
d = 238,860 miles; d_1 = 2,900 miles; d_2 = 235,960 miles; m_2/m_1 = d_1/d_2 = 2,900/235,960 = 1/81.3. (b) *Motion of the
earth-moon system.*

it is found that the barycenter lies 2,900 miles from the center of the earth. The ratio of the moon's mass to that of the earth is in the inverse ratio of their respective distances from the barycenter. Hence the moon's mass is equal to 2900/235,960 or 1/81.3 of the earth's mass. This value has been confirmed by measuring the lunar gravitational accelerations imparted to space vehicles as they approach the lunar neighborhood.

The moon's mean density is easily found by dividing its mass by its volume. The result is 3.3 g/cm^3. This may be compared with the earth's mean density of 5.5 g/cm^3.

The smaller lunar mass and radius result in a lower acceleration of gravity on the lunar surface compared to that of the earth. The surface acceleration of a body is proportional to the mass divided by the square of the radius ($\propto m/r^2$), a result that is easily verified from Newton's law of gravitation. The lunar value is 5.3 ft/sec^2 compared to the earth's 32.2 ft/sec^2, or about one-sixth of the earth's gravity.

The escape velocity of an object from an attracting body is proportional to the square root of the attracting body's mass divided by the square root of its radius ($\propto \sqrt{m/r}$). For the moon the value is 1.5 mi/sec compared to the earth's value of 7 mi/sec.

Other Lunar Properties

The virtual absence of an atmosphere and the lack of surface water have been confirmed by direct observations and from analysis of the rock samples returned by the Apollo astronauts. Water may be trapped, however, in the underground lunar material. The day-to-night surface temperatures were previously determined with the aid of heat-sensing detectors attached to earth-based telescopes. Now they have been more accurately recorded by placing temperature-recording equipment on the lunar surface and telemetering the data back to earth. The lunar temperature ranges from a maximum of +265°F (about 50°F above the boiling point of water) during the nearly two-week daytime period to −275°F (almost 300°F below the freezing point of water) during the nearly two-week period of darkness. Photometric measurements of moonlight made from the earth reveal that, on the average, only 7 per cent of the sunlight is reflected from the moon's surface. The reflectivity is lowest from the maria (∼5 per cent) and highest from the upland crater regions (∼10–15 per cent). The observed lunar reflectivity is similar to that of terrestrial granitic rock. Sensitive magnetometers installed in orbiting spacecraft first revealed that the magnetic field of the moon as a whole is extremely weak.

6.5 LUNISOLAR GRAVITATIONAL INFLUENCES

Precession of the Equinoxes

Both the sun and the moon tend to pull the equatorial bulge of the earth into the earth and lunar orbital planes respectively. The rotating earth acts like a spinning gyroscope in resisting any force that would compel its axis to change direction. The net effect of the sun's and moon's action causes the earth's axis to gyrate slowly westward around the pole of the ecliptic in a period of about 26,000 years, a phenomenon called the *precession of the equinoxes*. As a consequence of the precession, the celestial equator (which is the projection of the earth's equator upon the sky) shifts its position along the ecliptic in a westerly direction at an annual rate of about fifty seconds of arc. This causes the equinoxes, the points of intersection of the celestial equator and the ecliptic (refer back to Figure 2.1), to precess completely around the ecliptic in the period of 26,000 years. The phenomenon of precession was discovered by the Greek astronomer Hipparchus in the second century B.C. Upon comparing the positions of the principal stars in the zodiac with those of astronomers 150 years earlier, he found that the vernal equinox had shifted westward two degrees along the ecliptic. The physical explanation of the phenomenon was given by Newton.[1] The axis of the earth retains its tilt of 23.5 degrees throughout the cycle. It is presently directed toward a point on the sky less than one degree from the star we call Polaris. In ancient Egypt the axis pointed in the general direction of the

[1]Its explanation, which involves physical principles beyond the scope of this book, can be found in any advanced astronomy textbook or first-year physics textbook.

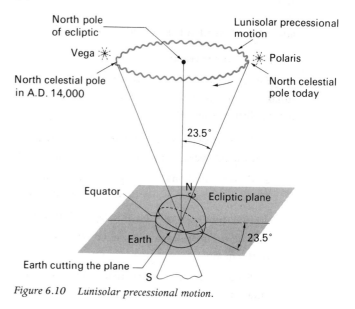

Figure 6.10   Lunisolar precessional motion.

star Alpha Draconis (Thuban), which was then only a few degrees from the pole around which the heavens rotated. About A.D. 14,000 the very bright star Vega will be the "north star" around which the sky will turn.

Nutation

Primarily because of the sun's gravitational disturbance of the orbiting moon, the lunar-orbit plane shifts its position with respect to the plane of the ecliptic. It maintains its inclination angle of five degrees to the ecliptic plane while the direction of inclination changes through 360 degrees in 18.6 years. This motion causes the moon's nodes to slide westward or regress along the ecliptic nearly twenty degrees per year (refer back to Figure 6.2). The regression of the moon's nodes introduces a small periodic variation in the moon's gravitational effect on the earth's equatorial bulge. It results in a slight ripple called *nutation* that is superimposed on the earth's average gyrational motion. Each complete ripple lasts 18.6 years (Figure 6.10).

6.6 LUNAR SURFACE FEATURES

Category of Lunar Features

Earth-based and extraterrestrial observations of lunar features disclose a wealth of details. Principal surface features include:

1. Maria (seas): sixteen on side facing earth, including one ocean; three on far side of the moon

2. Craters: millions, ranging from 150 miles in diameter to inches on both sides of the moon

3. Mountains: twenty on side facing the earth

4. Isolated mountain peaks: ten on the front side of the moon

5. Rilles (crevices): more than 1,000 on both sides of the moon

6. Ray systems: several radiating from prominent craters, mostly on the front side of the moon

As the preceding list shows, there are more than a dozen large, dark-colored circular areas called *maria* or *seas*. Several mountain ranges, isolated mountain peaks, countless craters, ringed plains, cliffs, rilles, and crater-associated ray systems are easily visible even in moderate-sized telescopes. The best resolution obtainable with telescopes from the earth is about one-half mile. The roughest portions of the lunar terrain are found in the south polar area where the surface is pitted and broken up with innumerable craters. Until recently the number of designated lunar formations on the front side totaled about 6,000, as sanctioned by a commission of the International Astronomical Union. In 1970 that body authorized the naming of some 500 additional craters on the far side of the moon according to the past custom of naming the craters after prominent, deceased physical scientists or certain other distinguished individuals.

Lunar Maria

In the pretelescopic days it was thought that the dark, round basins were bodies of water; they were accordingly given the imaginative names of seas. To the naked eye the pattern of the seas at the time of the full moon forms the face of the "man in the moon." Large-scale, earth-based photographs of the seas reveal relatively smooth circular floors, darker than the surrounding highlands and wrinkled toward the edges with serpentine ridges. They are indented here and there with shallow-appearing craters suggestive of an inundating overflow of lava that engulfed the older features.

Lunar Craters

The tremendous numbers of circular craters that pit the moon bear witness to the cataclysmic events

Figure 6.11   Full moon photographed at the Lick Observatory. Note that the moon as it is photographed by a telescope is inverted. (Courtesy of Lick Observatory.)

Oceanus Procellarum—Ocean of Storms
Mare Humorum—Sea of Moisture
Mare Nubium—Sea of Clouds
Mare Imbrium—Sea of Showers
Mare Frigorus—Sea of Cold

Mare Serenitatis—Sea of Serenity
Mare Vaporum—Sea of Vapors
Mare Crisium—Sea of Crises
Mare Nectaris—Sea of Nectar
Mare Foecunditatis—Sea of Fertility

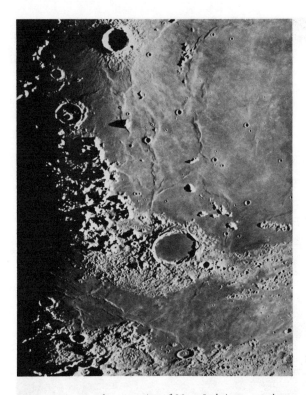

Figure 6.12   Northeast section of Mare Imbrium near the sunrise line, photographed with 120-inch Lick reflector. The large, smooth-bottomed crater immediately below the center is Plato. Near the left edge, center, is the Alpine Valley, appearing as a long, dark streak across the Alp mountains. (Courtesy of Lick Observatory.)

Figure 6.13   Giant crater Clavius and surrounding region, photographed with the 200-inch Hale reflector. The crater is approximately 150 miles in diameter. (Courtesy of Hale Observatories.)

that have altered the moon's crust during its past history. Over 30,000 are visible from ground-based telescopes. The estimated total number, down to bushel-basket size, may well exceed one million. The great walled plains or super craters with low profiles like Clavius or Grimaldi possess a general structure resembling the maria except on a smaller scale. Their diameters are about 150 miles.

Next in size on the front side are some three dozen craters ranging in diameter from 50 to 120 miles. One-third of them are conspicuously marked by light-colored streaks radiating outward in all directions without interruption up to distances of several hundred miles. The well-known ray craters—Tycho, Copernicus, Kepler, and Aristarchus—represent this latter group. Many of the secondary small craters appearing beyond the rim apparently were formed by a rain of debris ejected from the primary crater following the impact with a large colliding body. The larger craters have terraces on their inner

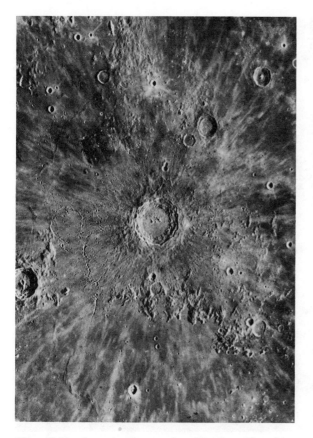

Figure 6.14　Copernicus crater, about 50 miles wide and its associated ray system. The prominent crater near the left edge below center is Eratosthenes. (Courtesy of Lick Observatory.)

Figure 6.15　Crater Tycho. Note its terraced walls on the left side. (Courtesy of NASA, Lunar Orbiter 5.)

walls and frequently possess a fairly smooth floor out of which rise a few low peaks. The crater rim often has a wavy appearance possibly created by the material that was pushed out of the crater at the time of impact. Most of the moderate-sized craters, like the larger ones, have high-rise walls. Some have floors out of which rise mountain peaks; in others the floors are bare. In places where these craters are the most numerous, as in the southern highlands on the front side of the moon, they frequently overlap.

Lunar Mountains

The majority of the mountain chains are found at or near the periphery of the circular maria. The mountains bordering the maria rise more precipitously on the side facing the seas than on the other side. They are frequently surmounted by lofty peaks occasionally rising to heights of 25,000 feet above the surrounding plains. The height of a lunar mountain can be determined by trigonometry from the length of its shadow, combined with knowledge of the sun's

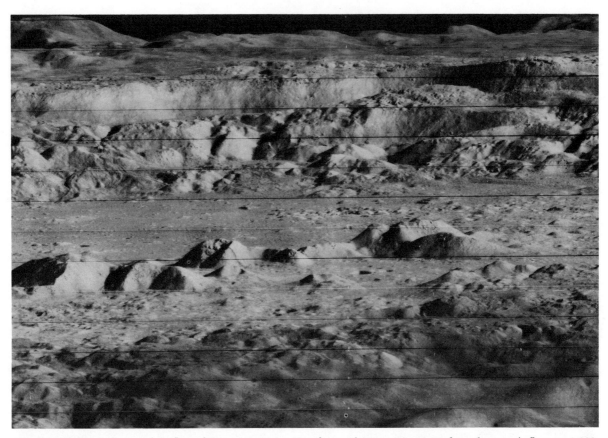

Figure 6.16   Close-up view of the floor of Copernicus over a 17-mile stretch. Mountains rising from the crater's floor are 1,000 feet high with slopes up to 30 degrees. Cliffs on the crater's rim are 1,000 feet high and undergoing continual downslope movement of material. (Courtesy of NASA, Lunar Orbiter 2.)

calculated angle of elevation above the lunar horizon.

Other Lunar Features

An interesting feature long noted in earth-based telescopes is the narrow valley cutting across the Alps mountains beyond the eastern edge of Mare Imbrium. The Alpine valley photographed by a lunar-orbiter spacecraft reveals a deep trough two to six miles wide and about eighty miles long. (Compare Figure 6.12 with Figure 6.17.) Narrow channels called *rilles* appear to resemble chasms or gorges; they have been photographed cutting across the lunar terrain, frequently without interruption, for many miles. Other shorter rilles frequently pursue tortuous paths. Some of them may be lava channels or collapsed tubes partly filled with rubble from lava flows. The rille running lengthwise down the middle of the Alpine valley is very conspicuous. The walls of the 1200-foot-deep canyon known as Hadley rille near the base of the Apennine mountains and their lower slopes were observed by astronaut D. R. Scott of Apollo 15 to be stratified into a number of parallel tilted layers.

Figure 6.17   *The Alpine Valley is about 80 miles long and up to 6 miles wide. Note the rille running centrally along its floor. Compare this view with the earth-based view in Figure 6.12. (Courtesy of NASA, Lunar Orbiter 4.)*

One interpretation of this layering is that the large object which impacted to create Mare Imbrium heaved up tilted blocks of earlier lava-flow substrata that had impregnated the lunar crust.

What appear as wrinkles on the surface of the maria turn out to be, upon closer examination, sinuous ridges. They were evidently piled up from the plastic material flow activated by long-extinct compressional waves that spread out from the sites of the giant impacts that created the maria. Evidence of past volcanic activity is clearly present in the numbers of small domes and cinder cones and their associated lava flows in the maria flatlands.

6.7   RESULTS FROM EXTRATERRESTRIAL OBSERVATIONS

Thousands of remarkably clear photographs of all parts of the moon were secured during the period 1964–1968 by three U. S. Ranger hard landers, five Surveyor soft landers, and five lunar orbiters. The USSR employed Lunas and Zonds for similar purposes.

6 THE MOON: A MARRED WORLD

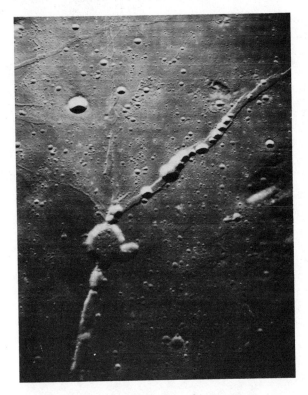

Figure 6.18   Hyginus Rille consists of two segments radiating from the Hyginus crater, seven miles in diameter. The evenly spaced craterlets along the rille suggest a volcanic origin rather than an impact origin. (Courtesy of NASA, Lunar Orbiter 4.)

Lunar Mascons

During passes over the major maria the speed of the lunar orbiters would unexpectedly increase, apparently as the result of a stronger gravitational force. Such a gravitational irregularity is attributed to a concentration of mass beneath the surface. The excess mass has been given the name of *mascon*, an abbreviation for mass concentration. The present evidence supports the view that the mascon is a large, disk-shaped formation lying less than twenty miles below the surface rather than the fractured remnant of an impacted iron meteorite embedded below the surface.

Lunar Terrain on the Far Side

The topography on the far side of the moon differs strikingly from the near side. There are craters everywhere but few with steep slopes or basins filled with lava. There are no tall mountains and no large lava-flooded maria like Mare Imbrium on the front side. Only three smaller maria have been discovered, but there are some large shallow depressions pitted with numerous craters and lighter in tone than the maria on the front side.

The relative ages of different portions of the lunar topography can be evaluated on the basis of overlapping of one feature by another or of the relative worn-down smoothness from constant meteoric bombardment. The Mare Orientale "bullseye" basin with its concentric craters appears to be one of the youngest formations. It is in an excellent state of preservation with very little encrustation, erosion, and disarrangement (Figure 6.21).

Apollo Findings

The lunar samples returned by the Apollo astronauts consisted of: (1) fine soil called *fines* embedded with glassy, crystalline, and tiny iron-meteoritic fragments; (2) basaltic rocks containing either fine or coarse mineral grains; (3) *breccias*, which are compacted mixtures of soil and rock fragments. Physical, chemical, mineralogical, geological, and biological experiments conducted by several hundred scientists on the lunar specimens permit some tentative conclusions to be formed.

The chemistry of the Apollo 11 Sea of Tranquility site and the Apollo 12 Ocean of Storms site was found to be fairly similar. The minerals in the samples consisted mostly of plagioclase and pyroxene, two crystalline minerals common in volcanic rocks. (Plagioclase is a calcium-sodium-aluminum silicate; py-

Figure 6.19   Domes in Oceanus Procellarum. They are best seen on the left of the picture. Varying from 2 to 10 miles in diameter and from 1,000 to 1,500 feet in height, they resemble the volcanic domes of northern California and Oregon. The large crater in the upper right is Marius. (Courtesy of NASA, Lunar Orbiter 2.)

Figure 6.20   Far side of the moon. The area at left center is Mare Moscoviense (Sea of Moscow). (Courtesy of NASA, Lunar Orbiter 5.)

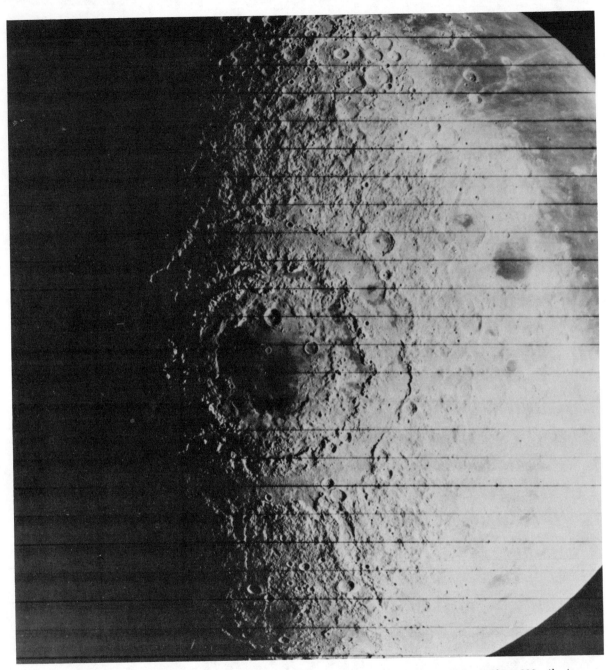

Figure 6.21   Mare Orientale basin photographed on the back side of the moon. The sea's outer scarp is about 600 miles in diameter. The dark portion in the upper right is Oceanus Procellarum. (Courtesy of NASA, Lunar Orbiter 4.)

roxene is a calcium-magnesium-iron silicate.) About two dozen elements and a dozen oxides plus small amounts of the noble gases (helium, neon, etc.) were detected. The rock samples from the Apollo 14 Fra Mauro site, near a highland area (the lighter, rougher part of the moon's surface), showed many differences in their metallic compositions from the mare locations of Apollo 11 and 12. They also contained more plagioclase. This was also found to be true of the Apollo 15 highlands site near the base of the Apennine mountains. The region contained a high abundance of aluminum and sparse amounts of magnesium and iron as did the Apollo 16 highlands site near the crater Descartes. This is the opposite of the distribution in the mare basins. No traces of water and no organic compounds indicative of life processes were discovered in any of the rock samples. The landing site chosen for the final Apollo flight of December 7, 1972 (Apollo 17) was the Littrow-Taurus region, beyond the eastern edge of the Sea of Serenity. It was the longest and most experimentally ambitious of all the Apollo missions.[1]

Radioactive dating points to an origin, similar to that of the earth, of about 4.6 billion years ago, most likely from the accretion of the planetesimal debris within the contracting solar nebula. The moon appears to have undergone large-scale melting followed by partial chemical separation shortly after its creation. It is believed that this was due to the heating effects arising from gravitational compression, radioactivity, and meteorite impacts. From more refined radioactive analysis, it appears that a second partial melting occurred about 3.1 to 4.0 billion years ago. The subsequent flooding of the primitive basins with lava created the maria as we know them today.

The variety of rocks and their ages strongly suggest that a number of cataclysmic events took place during the first 1 to 1.5 billion years of the

moon's existence. The rock specimens carry the marks of explosive events attributable to shattering, melting, and subsequent solidification. The great Mare Imbrium basin apparently was formed about 3.9 billion years ago by the impact of a large object about the size of Rhode Island. It may have been left over from the earlier space-cluttering debris that existed within the solar nebula out of which the planetary system was formed. Following the upheaval that splashed out a thick layer of rocks and rubble, molten basalt from below welled upward to flood the ravaged area. The Apennine mountains, which border the basin, may have been created by material pushed upward by the tremendous internal pressure created by the shock of the impact. Nearby Hadley rille could have resulted from fracturing or lava flows. Radioactive dating indicates that the last lava flow in this region occurred about 3.3 billion years ago. During the moon's violent period catastrophic events of different orders of magnitude recurred throughout the moon in the same regions. Evidence of this buildup in stages is revealed in the successive lava flows that have inundated the mare basins at different times and in the encroachment of new craters on older craters. In the last three billion years it is believed that thermal and geological activity on the moon has been relatively quiescent. Although most volcanism appears to have ceased about 1.5 billion years ago, some volcanic activity and seismic disturbances continue.

The seismographs left on the lunar surface by the astronauts have recorded seismic signals whose patterns differ from those on earth. Moonquakes, rare meteorite impacts, and artificially produced vibrations (grenade explosions and crash landings of discarded spacecraft parts) are transmitted through the lunar material at a very slow rate. They build up gradually and take up to an hour to subside. The origin of some seismic disturbances has been traced to geologic movements within the rilles. This suggests

[1] At the time of writing no details were available.

Figure 6.22 Apollo lunar rock sample, classified as a glass-coated breccia. (Courtesy of NASA.)

Structure of the Moon

It is conjectured that the original source of heat that led to the moon's chemical separation of its surface layers came from the energy supplied by planetesimal accretion during the early formative period of the moon. The crustal material solidified into the lower-density rocky structure that now rests on top of the higher-density rocks below. The topmost layer consists mainly of a substance called anorthosite, a granular rock rich in the silicates of aluminum and calcium. It forms the crust of the moon and is found in its cratered portions. Seismic data indicate that it is about forty miles thick, twice the thickness of the earth's crust. The basaltic material of the maria was formed later by partial melting of the iron-rich regions below the crustal layer.

With the further accumulation of heat by gravitational compression and radioactivity, some melting must have occurred at progressively lower depths. It is not known if the innermost lunar material reached melting temperatures. Seismic velocities reveal the existence of a uniformly structured mantle nearly 600 miles deep underlying the lunar crust. The present evidence indicates that the core of the moon is partly molten, perhaps not over 1500°C.

6.8 THE ORIGIN OF THE MOON

Despite the wealth of new information the moon's origin remains a mystery. Various proposals either of a catastrophic or noncatastrophic nature have been advanced to account for the earth-moon system without any of them gaining universal acceptance.

Fission Theory

The earliest theory of the moon's origin imagines that eons ago a rapidly spinning earth flattened

that they may be faults in the moon's crust. The tidal stress applied to the moon by the earth's gravity apparently triggers a series of moonquakes when the moon is near the perigee and apogee points in its orbit.

The general magnetic field of the moon is only about 1/10,000 that of the earth. This very low figure suggests that the moon does not presently possess a molten nickel-iron core which is believed to be a prerequisite in the formation of a magnetic field comparable to that of the earth. It does not rule out the possibility that the moon may have possessed a stronger magnetic field early in its history. Random magnetic fields up to about 0.6 per cent of the earth's field intensity have been detected with portable magnetometers at different sites by the Apollo astronauts. The reason for such magnetic anomalies is not well understood.

Figure 6.23   Astronaut Young of Apollo 16 replaces tools at the rear of the Lunar Roving Vehicle. Smoky Mountain with the large Ravine crater on its slope is in the left background. (Courtesy of NASA.)

sufficiently to become dumbbell-shaped because of rotational instability, perhaps as a consequence of unequal internal movement within the earth's molten core. The smaller end of the dumbbell broke away to become the moon. Both earth and moon resumed their ellipsoidal forms and have been separating ever since. This theory accounts for a lunar density comparable to that of the earth's crust and upper mantle. It cannot explain why only a small fraction of the original rotational energy of the rapidly spinning earth and moon was transferred to the earth-moon system. Sufficient differences exist in the chemical composition of the moon and the earth to reject the notion that the two bodies descended from a single body.

Separate-Formation Theory

This version supposes that the earth and moon were formed simultaneously out of the same primordial blob of gas and dust. The blob subsequently split into two unequal halves forming a binary system. The fact that the oldest lunar rocks and the earth are of comparable ages (around 4.6 billion years old) is a strong point in this theory's favor, but the theory does not account for the differences in composition and density unless some unknown process of differentiation of the material existed prior to the time of the rupture. In the catastrophic version of separate formation, the moon passed through the limit of tidal instability, known as the *Roche limit*, about 10,000 miles from the earth. This close approach to the earth created enormous tidal bulges that caused the moon's surface layers to melt through friction and to partially disrupt into fragments that were hurled into the lunar orbit. These fragments were intercepted by the moon, mostly near the apogee of its orbit where the earth's gravity was weakest, to produce the lunar cratering upon impact with the moon's surface. In the noncatastrophic version, the earth and moon approached

each other outside the Roche limit, resulting in the creation of nondisruptive tides. Consequently, the lunar structure was not radically altered and the heating of the moon and earth was negligible. The lunar craters were formed afterward by asteroid or meteorite impact.

Capture Theory

According to this concept, the moon and the earth evolved as separate bodies out of the solar nebula, independently pursuing their individual elliptical orbits around the sun. About four billion years ago, the moon approached the earth on a near-collision course. It was captured by the earth and forced to move around it in a far-flung elliptical orbit ranging from 10,000 miles at perigee to hundreds of thousands of miles at apogee. Tidal disruptive forces near the Roche limit tore fragments from the lunar surface and led to subsequent cratering by their infall near the apogee of the moon's orbit. For several thousand years thereafter, the moon's highly elongated orbit decayed into a gradually shrinking, more nearly circular orbit outside the Roche limit. Since that time it has slowly spiraled outward to its present distance of 239,000 miles and will continue to do so into the distant future.

REVIEW QUESTIONS

1. Define the following terms : (a) perigee ; (b) apogee ; (c) barycenter; (d) nodes of the moon's orbit; (e) eccentricity of the moon's orbit.

2. What is the principle involved behind the parallax method of deriving the moon's distance ? Behind the laser-ranging method ?

3. Explain the phases of the moon with the aid of a diagram.

4. About what time does the moon set at first quarter ? About when does the full moon rise ? Can

the last-quarter moon be seen in the early evening hours? Explain your answer.

5. Why is the calendar month about two days longer than the true period of the moon's revolution around the earth?

6. Why can we see only about half of the moon's surface from the earth?

7. Why do we divide the moon into a near side and a far side?

8. What is the cause of lunisolar precession?

9. Does the earth rise and set as seen from the moon? Explain your answer.

10. Name and briefly describe the kinds of lunar features observed with earth-based telescopes.

11. How does the back side of the moon differ from the front side?

12. What is the chemical composition of lunar soil?

13. Explain why a baseball pitcher could not throw a curve on the moon.

14. What is strange about the seismic disturbances recorded by the seismometers left on the moon by the astronauts?

15. Would a human body buried on the moon's surface decompose? Explain your answer.

SELECTED READINGS

Alter, D., *Lunar Atlas*, Dover, 1968.

Branley, F. M., *Exploration of the Moon*, Natural History Press, 1964.

Cherrington, E. H., Jr., *Exploring the Moon through Binoculars*, McGraw-Hill, 1969.

Cooper, H. S. F., *Moon Rocks*, Dial, 1970.

Gamow, G., and H. G. Stubbs, *Moon*, Abelard-Schuman, 1971.

Kopal, Z., *New Photographic Atlas of the Moon*, Taplinger, 1971.

Levinson, A. A., and S. R. Taylor, *Moon Rocks and Minerals*, Pergamon, 1971.

Match, T. A., *Geology of the Moon*, Princeton University Press, 1970.

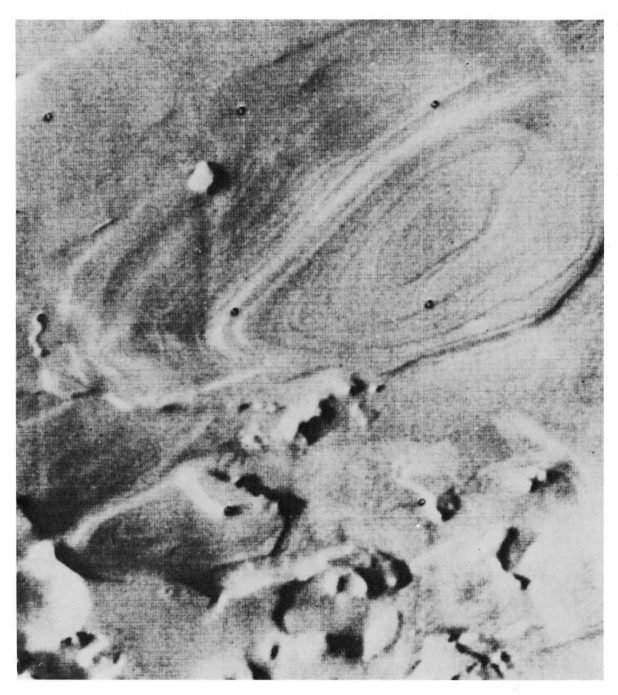

Layered oval tableland near Martian south pole, photographed by Mariner 9, February 28, 1972. Large amounts of water ice may be concealed below this formation. Near the bottom of the frame is an older and unlayered deposit, deeply etched with jagged pits and grooves. (Courtesy of NASA.)

THE SOLAR SYSTEM: PLANETS AND SATELLITES

The heavens themselves, the planets,
  and this center
Observe degree, priority, and place,
Insisture, course, proportion, season, form,
Office, and custom, in all line of order.

  Shakespeare (1564–1616),
  Troilus and Cressida, Act I, Scene 3

There are two distinct kinds of planets. First are the inner, smaller, denser planets, some with and others without atmospheres: Mercury, Venus, Earth, Mars, and the most distant planet, Pluto, which may have been a former satellite of Neptune. Second are the outer, larger planets with low densities and very thick atmospheres containing large amounts of hydrogen and helium: Jupiter, Saturn, Uranus, Neptune.

William Herschel's discovery of Uranus in 1781 was the first planet discovered in recorded history. Neptune was found in 1846 through its gravitational disturbances upon Uranus, from mathematical computations by J. C. Adams in England and U. J. J. Leverrier in France, working independently. The discovery of Pluto in 1930 was inspired by the research of the American astronomer Percival Lowell, who believed that an unseen planet was gravitationally disturbing both Uranus and Neptune.

The orbital motions, physical properties, and distinguishing features of each planet and the various satellites have been intensively studied telescopically from ground-based observatories for many decades. Astronomers employ a variety of techniques in observing the planets, including visual, photographic, photometric, spectral, and radio/radar. In recent years, significant new findings concerning Venus and Mars have been revealed from telemetered data received via instrumented American Mariner flyby and orbiter vehicles and from Soviet flyby and entry probes. Pioneer 10 should provide significant Jovian data when it reaches the giant planet's neighborhood late in 1973. Future planetary exploration by spacecraft will yield important new facts about the solar system—such as the biological environment of Mars, the possibility of living organisms in Jupiter's atmosphere, and the hidden surface features of Venus.

7.1 MEMBERS OF THE SOLAR SYSTEM

The Sun

The sun contains 99.86 per cent of the total mass of the solar system and that is why the planets, the asteroids, the comets, and the minor particulate matter are gravitationally forced to orbit around it. The satellites, on the other hand, are gravitationally bound to their planetary primaries because of their relative closeness. Even so, the sun exerts a sufficiently strong attractive force to appreciably disturb the motions of the satellites, particularly the outermost satellites.

Like any other normal star, the sun is kept going by the thermonuclear reactions within its hot central core. Its giant sphere of gas, glowing at a surface temperature of 5,800°K (11,000°F) stretches across a diameter 109 times greater than the earth's, encompassing a mass one-third million times greater than the earth's mass. Out of the prodigious solar energy that floods the solar system (380 sextillion kilowatts), its family of planets can intercept only a minute fraction. It is an intriguing thought that its light may be observed as a faint star by a distant viewer living on another planet light-years away.

The Planets

The nine planets monopolize the major share of the mass outside the sun. There exists a chemophysical segregation of the planetary bodies into two well-defined categories. One consists of an inner group composed chiefly of metallic and rocky material with an occasional overlay of atmospheric gases: the terrestrial planets, Mercury, Venus, Earth, Mars, plus the outermost planet Pluto. They possess earth-like dimensions and masses, and relatively high densities. An outer second group, known as the Jovian planets, consists of the more elemental substances, mostly hydrogen and helium, with extensive atmospheres: Jupiter, Saturn, Uranus, and Neptune.

They rotate more rapidly, possess lower densities (near that of water), are more massive and considerably larger in size.

All the planets have certain orbital characteristics in common. They revolve around the sun in the same easterly direction in roughly circular, regularly spaced orbits lying nearly in the same plane. The innermost and outermost planets, Mercury and Pluto respectively, exhibit the greatest departure from this regularity; they move in the most eccentric orbits, which are also the most highly inclined to the earth's orbital plane. The planets orbit the sun at mean distances of from two-fifths the earth's distance from the sun to forty times the earth's distance, with orbital periods of revolution between one-fourth year and 248 years.

The Planetary Configurations

The two *inferior planets*, Mercury and Venus, revolve inside the earth's orbit. Because their orbital periods are shorter than that of the earth, they overtake and forge ahead of the slower-moving earth. Relative to a stationary earth, they appear to move counterclockwise around the sun while swinging from one side of the sun to the other. The number of degrees that the planet is east or west of the sun is called the *elongation*. From its position closest to the earth at *inferior conjunction*, when it is in line with the sun, the planet swings rapidly outward to the west of the sun; during this time its phase changes from new to crescent. When the planet reaches its greatest angular distance west of the sun, it is conspicuous as a "morning star"; its phase is quarter. Thereafter, the planet appears to reverse its course as it moves toward *superior conjunction*. At this time it is farthest from the sun and in the same general direction, and its phase is full. Past superior conjunction the planet swings east of the sun on its way toward maximum eastern elongation when it becomes conspicuous as the "evening star" in the quarter

Figure 7.1   Relative sizes of the planets and satellites. From the Life Nature Library book, The Universe, *published by Time-Life Books. Drawing by Mel Hunter.*

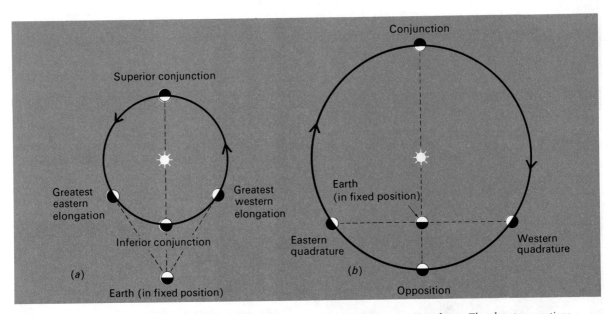

Figure 7.2 Configurations (aspects and phases) of (a) *an inferior planet and* (b) *a superior planet. The planetary motions shown are those viewed from the earth; however, viewed from the sun, they are all in the same direction—eastward.*

phase. Thence it turns back toward inferior conjunction to complete the circuit and the cycle of "lunar" phases.

Those planets whose orbits lie outside the earth's orbit are called *superior planets*. Since their orbital periods are longer than that of the earth, their motion, relative to a fixed earth, appears to be in a clockwise direction around the sun. When a superior planet is nearest to us and also brightest, it is in *opposition* and visible throughout the night. As the planet moves east of the sun, it passes through *eastern quadrature* when it is 90 degrees east of the sun. At this time it rises at noon and becomes an "evening star." Continuing on and now moving westward, it will reach *conjunction* when it is farthest from the sun at which time it rises and sets with the sun. It passes next through *western quadrature* when it is 90 degrees west of the sun. It rises at midnight and is now a "morning star." Finally, it reaches opposition when it is 180 degrees opposite the sun in the sky. The

only superior planet that exhibits a phase effect (gibbous) is Mars because of its relative closeness to the earth.

The true period of orbital revolution of a planet around the sun is known as the *sidereal period*. It represents the time taken by a planet to complete its circuit around the heavens relative to the stars. The time interval between similar configurations (opposition to opposition, for example) is known as the *synodic period*. It is different from the sidereal period because the earth advances in its orbit as the planet revolves around the sun.

The Satellites

The total number of known satellites in the solar system is thirty-two with all but three belonging to the Jovian planets. Jupiter has twelve moons, Saturn ten, Uranus five, Neptune two, Mars two, and the earth one. Six of them are comparable to our moon in size. The two moons of Mars rank among the

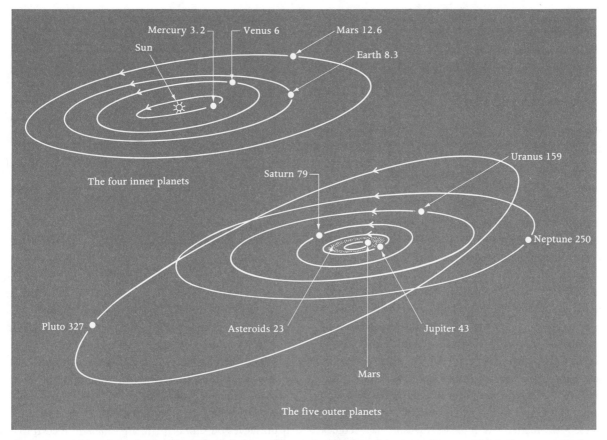

Mercury 3.2 — ┌ Venus 6   ┌ Mars 12.6
   Sun   ┌ Earth 8.3

The four inner planets

Saturn 79 ┐   Uranus 159

                              ● Neptune 250

Pluto 327 ●   Asteroids 23   Jupiter 43

                Mars

The five outer planets

Figure 7.3   Orbits of the planets. The scale of the lower diagram is 1/20 that of the upper diagram. The numbers correspond to the distances of the planets from the sun in light-minutes. (Adapted from a diagram by B. Lovell).

smallest known, with diameters of seven and fourteen miles. The nearer satellites tend to move in circular orbits in the planes of their primaries' equators and in the same direction as their primaries' rotation. The orbital motions of the outer satellites are more eccentric and more highly inclined to the equatorial planes of their primaries. The orbital motions of the four outer satellites of Jupiter and the most distant satellite of Saturn are *reversed* from the direction of their primaries rotation. (The only other moon with a retrograde orbit is the innermost satellite of Neptune.) It is thought that the outer satellites were captured by their primaries after the formation of the planets and their inner satellite systems.

The Asteroids or Minor Planets

These small solid objects orbit the sun in the same direction as the planets but in more eccentric paths with greater angles of inclination than the planets to the ecliptic plane. The vast majority of them are confined to the region between Mars and Jupiter. Most complete their orbital periods of revolution in three to six years at distances between two and three astronomical units from the sun. A few stragglers with shorter periods make close approaches to the earth, some within ten million miles of our planet. The size and number of the minor planets vary from the few between 100 and 620 miles down to tens of thousands below a mile in diameter.

The Comets

Unlike the planetary bodies, most comets move around the sun in far-ranging, highly eccentric orbits with periods of very long duration and at all angles of inclination. Their small masses make them easily susceptible to gravitational attractions by the planets. The giant planet Jupiter has been particularly influential in modifying the orbital paths of those comets that enter the Jovian gravitational neighborhood on their way around the sun. These have ended up as short-period comets in the range of 3.3 to 10 years compared to their original periods of revolution measured in the tens to hundreds of thousands of years. A comet is believed to consist of an icy conglomerate of frozen water and minor amounts of the primordial material, primarily methane, ammonia, and carbon dioxide, mixed with meteoritic matter. As it nears the sun, it becomes heated and forms an enveloping cloud of dust and vaporized gases. Closer in, the outward push of the solar wind, combined with the solar light pressure, drives away material which develops into a tail. In the rare bright comets, the long tail is an impressive sight in the heavens.

The Meteoroids and the Interplanetary Medium

Meteoroidal material ranges in size from irregular, solid lumps we call *meteorites* when they land on earth to tiny, invisible particles that flash through the atmosphere as *meteors*. The number of meteoroids increases immensely with diminishing size. All the particulate matter revolves around the sun in independent orbits. Small meteoroid particles having a cometary origin frequently orbit the sun in swarms.

The interplanetary medium consists of sparse gas, mostly protons and electrons, moving outward from the sun's atmosphere at a speed of several hundred miles per second. This ejected material constitutes the solar wind whose properties have been investigated with the aid of instrumented space probes and automatic recording devices left on the moon by the Apollo astronauts. Despite the enormity in numbers of the meteoroids and the cosmic dust and gas, interplanetary space constitutes a better vacuum than one produced in a terrestrial laboratory.

7.2 PLANETARY RESEARCH

Visual, Photographic, and Photometric Studies

Planetary studies are conducted with different observing techniques. Visual telescopic examination of surface or atmospheric markings is useful when certain minute details that cannot properly be resolved on photographs are to be scrutinized and drawn. For this kind of work high-altitude sites provide superior observing conditions. Direct photography is still the most widely used method since it preserves on film or plate a permanent record that can be studied at leisure. Photographs secured with passband filters, which confine the light to narrow spectral regions, yield useful information on the planets' surface or atmospheric chemistry. Polaroid filters and other polarizing devices, used in conjunction with photographic plates, enable astronomers to analyze the nature of the planetary surface or its atmosphere by the manner in which the reflected sunlight is polarized.

Spectral Studies

Spectrum analysis of a planet's light leads to important information about the chemical composition and physical conditions prevailing in planetary atmospheres. The atmospheric constituents are revealed by the presence of additional absorption lines originating in the planet's atmosphere. They are superimposed on the solar spectrum of the sunlight reflected from the planet's atmosphere and are sometimes difficult to separate from the very similar absorption lines originating in the sun's atmosphere. Improved heat-sensing detectors have greatly extended the study of planetary thermal emissions into the far infrared. They have provided new temperature data and information on the chemical compounds present in the planetary atmospheres.

Radio/Radar Studies

The normal thermal and abnormal (nonthermal) energy emitted by the planets in the millimeter, centimeter, and meter radio spectral regions has been investigated with radio telescopes. Radar mapping of Mercury and Venus in particular by means of pulsed radio signals has revealed new surface features not detectable by visual or photographic means. The signals are bounced back to earth as returning echoes, modified by the nature of the planetary terrain. A smooth reflecting surface, for example, returns an echo somewhat similar to the incident signal. If the surface is rough, the returning portion of the drawn-out echo arrives sooner from a higher region than from a lower region. Also, radar reflectivity is greater over rough terrain than over smooth ground depending upon the size of the irregularities. The returning wave train arriving from different

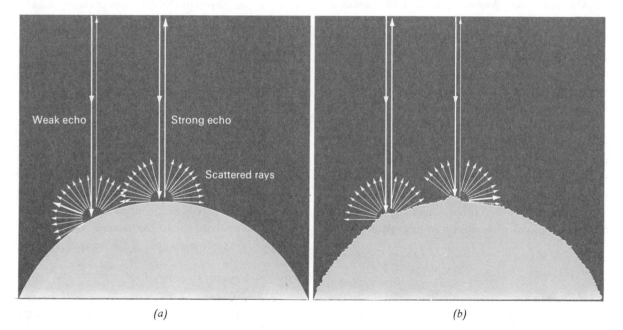

(a)   (b)

Figure 7.4   Mapping by radar. (a) *The signals are shown bouncing off a smooth surface. Only the center of the curved surface reflects a strong echo (thick arrow) back to earth. Where the surface curves away the rays bounce off at an angle, so that the planet's edges return only weak signals to earth. If, however, the radar rays bounce off irregularities such as mountains, the patterns are changed.* (b) *In what is otherwise an area of weak echoes, strong ones come bouncing back from the oblique surface. Radar rays striking at a different angle bounce their strongest signals off to one side, and only weak, scattered signals return to earth. (Redrawn from the Life Science Library book,* Planets, *published by Time Life books.)*

7 THE SOLAR SYSTEM: PLANETS AND SATELLITES

portions of the varied surface is analyzed in a computer, which leads to the construction of a radar map of the planet's surface.

Analysis of the Doppler change in radio frequency (caused by the planet's rotation) when a short-pulsed radio signal is bounced from the planet's surface leads to the precise period of a slowly rotating planet, not accurately available by optical methods. The returning radio wave coming from the part of the rotating planet's surface that is approaching the earth has its frequency slightly increased. The echo returning from the opposite side that is receding from the earth is slightly decreased in frequency.

Extraterrestrial Studies

One of the most promising methods of planetary research involves instrumented flybys, entry probes, orbiters, and landers. Infrared and ultraviolet spectrometers aboard these spacecraft provide clues to the composition, cloud structure, atmospheric and surface densities, pressures, and temperatures. Television cameras scan the surface details at close range. A magnetometer records the magnetic-field strength of the interplanetary medium as well as that of the planet. Future instrumented space probes should yield new insights into the physical, chemical, and possible biological properties of the planets.

Tables summarizing physical and orbital data for the planets and satellites appear in Appendices 8 and 9.

7.3 MERCURY ☿

Although one of the brighter objects in the heavens, Mercury remains an elusive naked-eye planet because of its closeness to the sun. Since the planet is well inside the earth's orbit, its maximum swing averages only 23 degrees outward from either side of the sun. Because of its swift orbital revolution around the sun, it remains clearly visible low above the horizon only for a few days after sundown or before sunup. It is best seen as an "evening star" during March and April and as a "morning star" during September and October.

Orbit of Mercury

The path of the planet is inclined at an angle of seven degrees to the plane of the earth's orbit. This angle is greater than that of any other planet except Pluto. Mercury is the nearest planet to the sun and is also the fastest-moving planet; it completes its orbital revolution in only 88 days. Its distance from the sun ranges from 29 million miles at perihelion to 43 million miles at aphelion. Its average distance is 36 million miles. The synodic period of the planet is 116 days. During this interval, as observed from the earth, it goes through the complete cycle of "lunar" phases.

Surface Features

The best optical telescopic observations of Mercury are made in broad daylight at high mountain observatories when the planet is well above the horizon. This avoids the poor viewing conditions encountered during the twilight period when the light of the planet must traverse the long path of turbulent air near the horizon. Observers of Mercury have reported seeing light and dark markings similar to those on the moon. Radar mapping shows the surface to be smoother than the moon's surface, with rougher areas concentrated in the equatorial zone.

Physical Properties

Mercury is the least massive ($\frac{1}{20}$ of earth's mass) and the smallest planet ($\frac{2}{5}$ of earth's diameter). Its mean density of 5.2 g/cm^3 nearly matches the earth's. The mass is derived from mathematical analysis of the gravitational disturbances that the planet exercises on comets, asteroids, and space vehicles during near approaches. The lack of any appreciable atmosphere results from the low surface gravity which

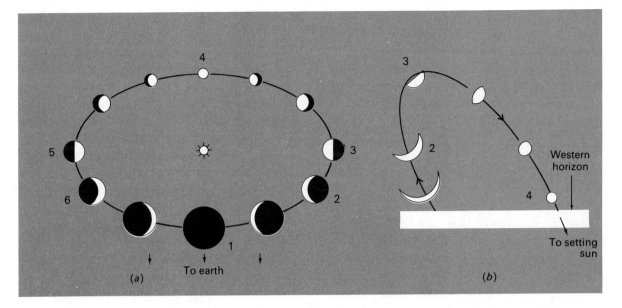

Figure 7.5   Changes in the apparent size and phases of an inferior planet (Mercury or Venus). (a) Appearance from earth:
1, inferior conjunction; 2, maximum brightness; 3, greatest elongation west; 4, superior conjunction; 5, greatest elongation east;
6, maximum brightness. (b) Changing positions and phases as an "evening star."

permits the escape of all but the heaviest gases. At noon the measured infrared temperature is 660°F; at midnight, on the dark side, it is −260°F. The somewhat higher night temperature than expected could be caused by the circulatory transfer of some heat from the sunlit side to the dark side through a small amount of atmosphere or heat conduction through the planet.

Rotation

In 1965 radio astronomers found from their Doppler radio observations that Mercury completes its rotation period in 58.6 days. This happens to be equal to two-thirds of its orbital period. Thus the planet completes three rotations on its axis during two orbital revolutions. This causes the sun to rise on the eastern horizon of Mercury and to set 88 days later on the western horizon. It is conjectured that

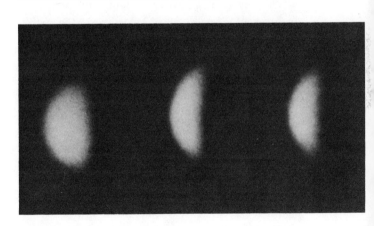

Figure 7.6   Mercury photographed at the Lowell Observatory on three different dates in June 1934. (Lowell Observatory Photograph.)

7 THE SOLAR SYSTEM: PLANETS AND SATELLITES

the rotation of Mercury must have been more rapid in the early history of the solar system. The sun apparently has exerted a sufficiently strong tidal pull on the planet's presumed bulge to slow its spin in the course of time so that Mercury's rotation is presently synchronized with its orbital period in the ratio of 3:2.

7.4 VENUS ♀

The second closest planet to the sun is a striking yellowish object in the sky, ranking third after the sun and moon in brightness. Like Mercury, Venus exhibits all the "lunar" phases, a phenomenon first discovered by Galileo in 1609 (mentioned earlier in Section 2.6). Its larger orbit, though still inside the earth's orbit, permits it to swing outward more slowly from the sun as viewed from the earth—about 47 degrees, twice as far as Mercury. Consequently, Venus remains visible as an "evening star" in our western sky or as a "morning star" in our eastern sky for weeks at a time.

Orbit of Venus

The path of Venus around the sun, which is inclined at the small angle of 3.4 degrees to the earth's orbit, is the most circular of any planet. Its orbital period is 225 days; the synodic period is 584 days. The distance of Venus from the sun is best determined by radar ranging and by radio transmission-receiving techniques from space probes. Its mean distance from the sun is 67.3 million miles. The minimum distance from the earth, which occurs at inferior conjunction, is 26 million miles. Although this is about nine million miles closer than Mars approaches the earth, we are unable to view its features at this time because the dark hemisphere is turned earthward. The maximum distance from the earth, which occurs at superior conjunction, is 160 million miles.

Telescopic Features

Venus is a heavily veiled planet whose surface is perpetually hidden by a thick atmosphere. Visual and photographic markings are indistinct and transient. Pulsed radio signals have been bounced from the planet to provide some clues concerning the nature of its surface. Radar maps obtained by this technique have disclosed mountainous areas. One such area is called Alpha, a bright roundish region in the southern hemisphere about 600 miles in diameter; another, called Beta, is an east-west chain of mountains even more extensive than Alpha. One equatorial mountainous locality exhibits a peak height of about two miles. A number of circular, smooth areas have been interpreted as resembling the lunar seas. In both hemispheres, regions of varying roughness and smoothness have been charted. On the whole, the planet's surface appears to have a rich and varied topography including cratered terrain.

Physical Properties

Venus has a diameter of 7,600 miles, smaller than the earth's by about 300 miles. Its mass, which is 82 per cent of the earth's mass, is most accurately derived from the perturbations it produces upon the trajectories of the close-approaching spacecraft. Its mean density is 5.2 g/cm^3, comparable to that of the earth or of Mercury. The surface temperature has been determined by means of microwave-instrumented flybys and entry probes, and from measurements made by ground-based radio telescopes. They independently confirm the extremely high surface temperature of nearly 900°F. About 85 miles above the surface, the temperature drops to -60°F. The night surface temperature does not differ appreciably from the day surface temperature. This probably results from strong atmospheric circulation that transports heat to the dark side of Venus. The planet's magnetic field, measured with spacecraft magnetometers, is extremely weak.

Most of our information concerning the physical and chemical characteristics of the planet has come

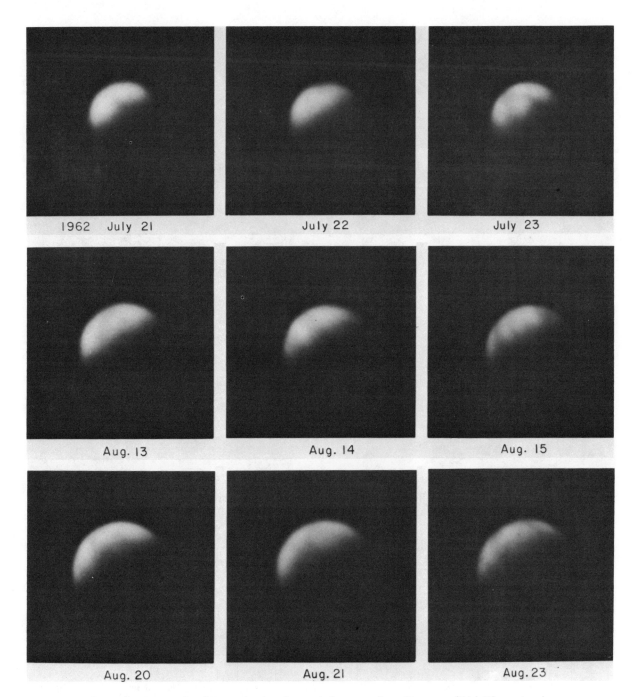

Figure 7.7 *Ultraviolet photographs of Venus showing changes in its atmosphere. (Courtesy of Lick Observatory.)*

7 THE SOLAR SYSTEM: PLANETS AND SATELLITES

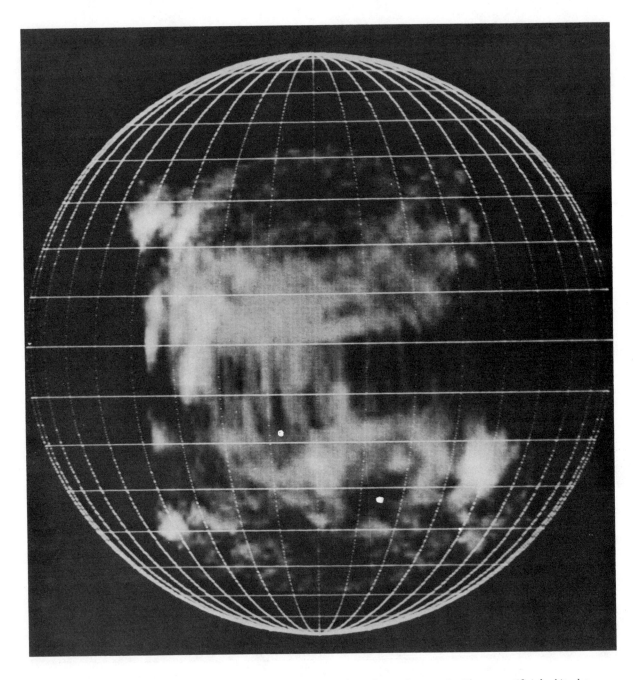

Figure 7.8   Radar map of Venus. The surface reflectivity is brighter from the rougher terrain. The two artificial white dots mark the centers of circular, dark features that resemble the seas on the moon. (Courtesy of Lincoln Laboratory, Mass.)

EXPLORING THE COSMOS

from the American flybys, Mariner 2 (1962) and Mariner 5 (1967), and from the Soviet entry probes, Venera 4 (1967), Veneras 5 and 6 (1969), Venera 7 (1970), and Venera 8 (1972). With the exception of the last two, the instrumented capsules released by the Russian spacecraft failed to function after spending up to 53 minutes in the dense atmosphere during their descent. Their sensing equipment apparently was damaged by the excessive heat and pressures encountered on the way down. The parachuted package of Venera 7, however, did land on the night side of Venus and telemetered data for 23 minutes before the signals faded away. Venera 8 landed on the sunlit side and telemetered information for 50 minutes before stopping. The data substantiated the previously determined high surface temperature. Instruments aboard the Venera 8 capsule detected radioactivity in the loose surface soil comparable to that of terrestrial granite. The surface density was found to be nearly 1.5 times that of water.

Atmosphere of Venus

During the nearly hour-long atmospheric descent of Venera 8's capsule, a jet-wind velocity of 110 miles per hour was recorded at an altitude of 27 miles. Below this level the wind velocity kept decreasing until it was only four miles per hour on the ground. The measured surface atmospheric pressure is about ninety times greater than the corresponding value on earth. The atmosphere contains about 97 percent carbon dioxide with traces of nitrogen, water vapor, ammonia, oxygen, carbon monoxide, hydrochloric acid, and hydrogen fluoride. It is natural to attribute the high surface temperature of Venus to the large amount of carbon dioxide. This gas is fairly transparent to incoming solar radiation but opaque to the outwardly reradiated infrared energy. This trapping of thermal radiation is similar to the greenhouse effect on earth but on a much larger scale. The carbon-dioxide content evidently was not reduced, as it was on earth, by reacting with primitive rocks to form into carbonates and absorption by the oceanic waters.

Rotation

Doppler radar observations have solved the mystery of Venus's rotation which could not correctly be obtained from optical or spectrographic observations because of its slow rate of spin. The planet rotates in a retrograde direction with its spin axis inclined only one degree from the normal to its orbit plane. (Retrograde in this sense refers to rotation that is reversed from that possessed by the other planets, excepting Uranus.) The rotation period is 243 days, 18 days longer than its orbital period. This makes the Venusian day 117 days long, consisting of 58.5 days of sunlight and 58.5 days of darkness. The spin-orbit relationship brings the *same* hemisphere of Venus toward the earth at every inferior conjunction. It is theorized that Venus originally possessed a direct rotation with a period comparable to the earth's and that the prolonged tidal influence of the earth and/or sun braked and ultimately reversed its rotation. This explanation has been criticized as being inadequate to account for the reversal of the Venusian spin. It is proposed instead that Venus collided with a moonlet moving originally in a retrograde orbit. The impact despun the planet and dissipated a large part of its rotational energy into internal heat while reversing the planet's spin.

7.5 MARS ♂

Earth-based telescopic views of the red planet seem to show earthlike characteristics—white polar caps expanding and contracting alternately and dark areas undergoing seasonal variations. The photographs transmitted to earth by the first Mars flyby, Mariner 4 in July 1965, revealed a waterless, cratered planet apparently resembling the moon. The extraordinary series of pictures of the Martian surface

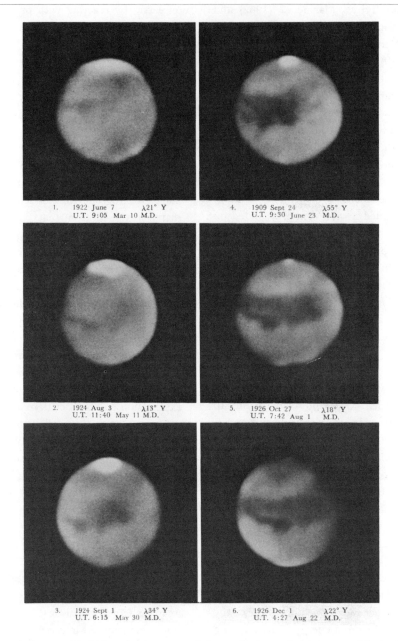

1.	1922 June 7	λ21° Y	
	U.T. 9:05	Mar 10 M.D.	
4.	1909 Sept 24	λ55° Y	
	U.T. 9:30	June 23 M.D.	
2.	1924 Aug 3	λ13° Y	
	U.T. 11:40	May 11 M.D.	
5.	1926 Oct 27	λ18° Y	
	U.T. 7:42	Aug 1 M.D.	
3.	1924 Sept 1	λ34° Y	
	U.T. 6:15	May 30 M.D.	
6.	1926 Dec 1	λ22° Y	
	U.T. 4:27	Aug 22 M.D.	

Figure 7.9   Earth-based photographs of Mars showing seasonal changes in the south polar cap and darkening of the blue-green areas. (Lowell Observatory Photographs.)

recorded by television cameras aboard Mariners 6 and 7 in 1969 and Mariner 9 in 1971–72 showed that Mars in many respects resembled neither the moon nor the earth. It is a different kind of planet.

Orbit of Mars

The orbital period of Mars around the sun is 687 days. Its path is inclined to the earth's orbit by the small angle of 1.85 degrees. Its distance from the sun varies from 128 million miles at perihelion to 155 million miles at aphelion; its mean distance is 141.6 million miles or 1.52 astronomical units. The interval between successive oppositions (the synodic period) is nearly $2\frac{1}{6}$ years. Because of the orbital eccentricity of Mars, the closest approach at opposition between earth and Mars occurs at intervals of fifteen or seventeen years when Mars is at or near its perihelion at the time both planets are in line on the same side of the sun. The most recent favorable opposition took place in August 1971 when Mars came within 35 million miles of the earth. During such a time even the most casual observer of the heavens is struck by the brilliant ruddy color of the planet, which far outshines the brightest stars.

Ground-Based Telescopic Features

Detailed maps of the numerous and varied features have been prepared in the past by many visual observers of the Martian scene. Scores upon scores of these markings carry Greek and Latin names indicative of the classical background of the early principal Martian observers, notably the Italian Giovanni Schiaparelli and the American Percival Lowell, who named many of these features.

Ordinary visual inspection reveals an orange disk on which are superimposed prominent white polar caps alternating in each hemisphere with the seasons. A color photograph of the planet is shown in Plate 5. Large, equatorial, grayish shadings streaked with darker mottlings are observed undergoing

seasonal changes in color and intensity. A so-called "wave of darkening" is observed to advance from the shrinking polar cap toward the equator as the markings intensify in shading and color. With the coming of summer the markings in the affected hemisphere begin to fade and the wave later begins to recede. The fine, delicate streaks known as the "canals" can only be observed occasionally when the air is momentarily quiet. Objects less than about sixty miles wide are not resolvable in earth-based telescopes. The Mariner pictures reveal the "canals" to be nothing more than the chance alignment of several dark-floored craters or irregular dark patches which the observer's eye unconsciously links together into a line resembling a canal. Ground-based observers have reported the presence of a light general haze and scattered white and yellow clouds in the rare Martian atmosphere. The "blue haze," so-

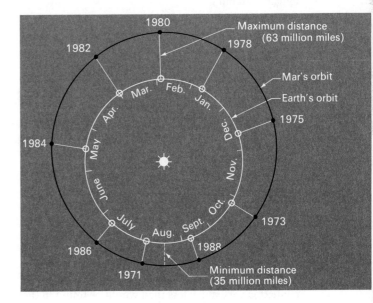

Figure 7.10 Orbits of earth and Mars showing the different distances of Mars at opposition.

called because its presence apparently obscures the surface details in photographs taken in blue and violet light, undergoes sudden clearings at times. Shortly after the close opposition of August 1971, a gigantic dust storm obscured the surface of Mars for several months. A similar dust storm occurred during the previous favorable opposition of the planet in 1956.

Physical Characteristics

Mars is a little more than one-half the earth's size with about one-ninth the earth's mass and a mean density about three-fourths the earth's density. The Martian day lasts 24 hours and 37.4 minutes. The rotation of the planet about its axis has produced a very slight degree of polar flattening. Since the tilt of Mars' axis from the perpendicular to its orbital plane is 25 degrees, the red planet experiences seasons in the same sense as earth does. Their duration is twice as long because the Martian year is 100 per cent longer than ours.

The south pole is always tilted toward the sun when Mars is closest to the sun. As a result its large ice cap recedes during the Martian summer as the frozen carbon dioxide evaporates and leaves behind a small permanent cap about 200 miles in diameter. On the other hand, the north pole is tilted toward the sun when the planet is farthest from the sun. Hence it retains a relatively large polar cap even during the Martian summer in the northern hemisphere.

The principal constituent in the thin Martian atmosphere is carbon dioxide; also present is some ozone, a minute quantity of carbon monoxide, and a trace of molecular nitrogen. A small, seasonally variable amount of water vapor has been detected together with its dissociation products, hydrogen and oxygen, at higher altitudes. The water-vapor content is very much less than would be found in the earth's desert air. The measured atmospheric pressure on the surface of Mars is 0.6 per cent of the earth's sea-level atmospheric pressure. The warmest daytime temperature is around 80°F at the Martian equator; at night it drops to −90°F. Over the polar caps, which are composed of frozen carbon dioxide ("dry ice"), it is −190°F.

The Mariner Findings

The first Martian flyby, Mariner 4 in 1965, recorded 22 pictures along a highly cratered strip somewhat resembling the surface of the moon. Mariners 6 and 7 flybys in 1969 transmitted back to earth 202 complete pictures covering about 10 per cent of the total surface down to a resolution of 300 yards. Certain features in the area of the south polar cap showed striking changes in brightness in the week between the Mariner 6 (July 31) and the Mariner 7 (August 5) passes. This phenomenon, which occurred in the early Martian autumn, undoubtedly represented a frost or atmospheric change. Two kinds of craters were observed: larger, eroded craters with flat bottoms and smaller, fresh-looking craters with rounded bottoms. Lacking were the serpentine rilles, the secondary craters, and the ray systems associated with main crater sites. The Martian craters contain fewer peaks and present a more subdued appearance than the lunar craters, presumably as the result of a weathering process.

When Mariner 9 arrived at Mars in November 1971, the great dust storm mentioned earlier was still in progress. The spacecraft was placed in a 12-hour orbit around Mars ranging between 1,025 and 10,600 miles from the Martian surface. By the end of the year the dust had settled sufficiently to permit the first televised views of the surface details. By the end of its photographic survey in October 1972 Mariner 9 had transmitted to earth some 7,300 remarkably clear pictures of the entire Martian surface. In the close-up views objects as small as one hundred yards in diameter were discernible.

A thin layer of haze was found to be continuously present at an altitude of thirty miles. Haze was also noted near the day-night boundary. Carbon dioxide clouds were observed over the north polar region and thin clouds over a large volcano near the equator. Certain light and dark elongated streaks and dark splotches, which appeared to change periodically within weeks, were interpreted to result from wind-blown dust alternately hiding and uncovering the surface details. That atmospheric winds were at work was clearly indicated by the presence of wave clouds, dust storms, and surface streaks. The peak wind velocities are estimated to be around 170 miles per hour.

Mars is not the geologically inactive planet that the pictures of the earlier Mariners had seemed to

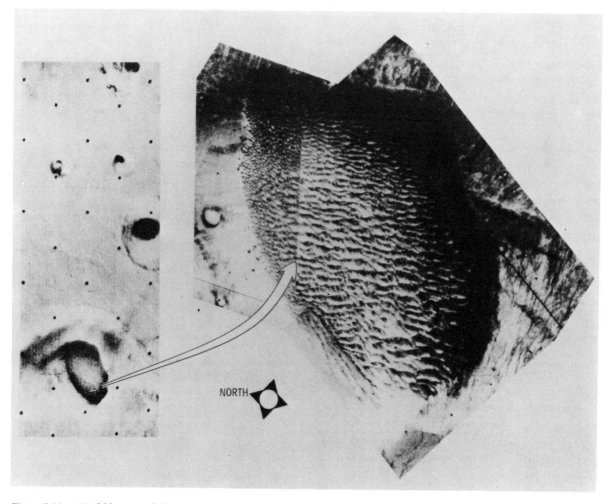

Figure 7.11 Wind-blown sand dunes inside a crater, 80 by 40 miles, in the Hellespontus region (330° E, 47° S). (Courtesy of NASA, Mariner 9.)

7 THE SOLAR SYSTEM: PLANETS AND SATELLITES

portray. Instead, Mars turns out to be a geologically complex and dynamically active planet still undergoing tectonic changes not unlike those on earth. Its terrain exhibits altitude differences of fifteen kilometers and a number of contrasting topographical features. The highly cratered areas, like those of the moon, are believed to be the oldest surface features. The most prominent cratered region surrounds the great basin long known as Hellas on Martian maps. Hellas is a circular, craterless area about 1,000 miles wide, one and one-half times the size of the largest lunar sea, Mare Imbrium. In Figure 7.14 it is the blank region centered at 290°E and 45°S.

A second type of topography is the large plateau region standing eight kilometers above the mean radius of the planet. It lies between about 60° and 100°W longitude and between about 30°S and 20°N latitude. Easily noticed is the spectacular rift valley cutting across the middle of the plateau. It is 2,500 miles long, 65 miles wide, and nearly four miles deep. At its western end, between 90° and 110°W, lies a complex pattern of intersecting fault valleys called the "chandelier region."

A third large area with different characteristics, known as Amazonis on Martian maps, appears in the upper left portion of the western half of the chart in Figure 7.14. This region, which is lightly cratered, resembles the Oceanus Procellarum basin on the moon. A distinguishing feature of this area is the presence of three large volcanoes running diagonally along the crest of a ridge called Tharsis and the spectacular isolated cone, Nix Olympica. This enormous volcano is three hundred miles across the base and about ten miles high.[1] It is surmounted by a bowl forty miles wide. Close-up pictures of its sides disclose a striated texture apparently formed by lava flowing down its slopes. To the northeast of Nix Olympica, centered at 110°W and 40°N, lies what may be the remains of

[1] It appears as a circular ring in the upper right of the Mariner 7 photo in Figure 1.1. See also Figure 7.12.

an eroded volcanic area. Also included in this third category of terrain are the extensive plains shown in the northeast part of the eastern half of the chart.

A fourth kind of topography, visible in the area bounded between 20°–50°W and 10°S to 20°N, is a plateau region marked by a complex of braided tributaries up to a kilometer in width and thousands of kilometers long. Erosion caused by water may have carved out the sinuous gorges and canyons.

The layered carbon dioxide south polar region constitutes a fifth type of Martian topography. A pitted region etched out near the south pole may have been formed by subsidence resulting from collapsed subsurface water ice which had melted. Although there is no evidence of surface water on the planet now, some scientists have conjectured that frozen water may exist underneath the polar cap. It is suggested that the laminated deposits may contain appreciable amounts of frozen water and/or carbon dioxide intermixed with dust. (See frontispiece to Chapter.)

Martian Satellites

The two little moons of Mars—Phobos, the inner one, and Deimos, the outer one—shed negligible moonlight on the Martian surface. Both satellites appear to be in synchronous rotation with the planet. Photographs of the satellites obtained by Mariner 9 show them to be potato-shaped with jagged, cratered surfaces. Phobos measures 13 by 16 miles. It orbits eastward, in the same direction that Mars rotates, in a period of 7 hours and 39 minutes at a distance of 3,675 miles from the surface of Mars. Since it revolves around Mars much faster than the planet rotates, it rises on the western horizon and sets on the eastern horizon $5\frac{1}{2}$ hours later. This is contrary to the motion of any other natural satellite in the solar system as observed from its primary. The other moon, Deimos, is about one-half the size of Phobos. It orbits Mars at a distance of 12,000 miles

Figure 7.12   Mosaic of Nix Olympica. The super volcano is about 300 miles wide at the base and is capped by a crater 40 miles in diameter. Nix Olympica is twice as broad as the most massive pile on earth. It is visible as a circular ring at longitude 134° W and latitude 18° N in Figure 7.14. (Courtesy of NASA, Mariner 9.)

Figure 7.13   Huge chasm with branching tributaries in Tithonius Lacus. This area is to the right of the "chandelier region" mentioned earlier. (Courtesy of NASA, Mariner 9.)

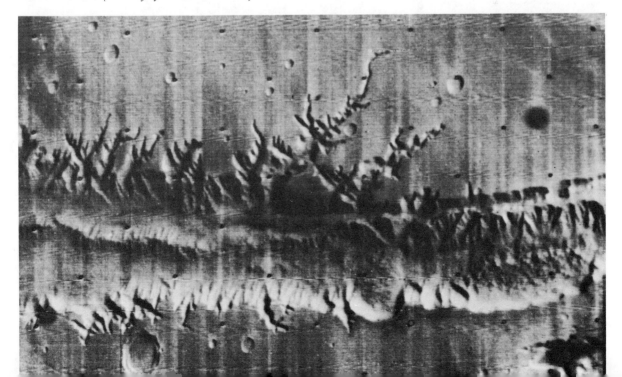

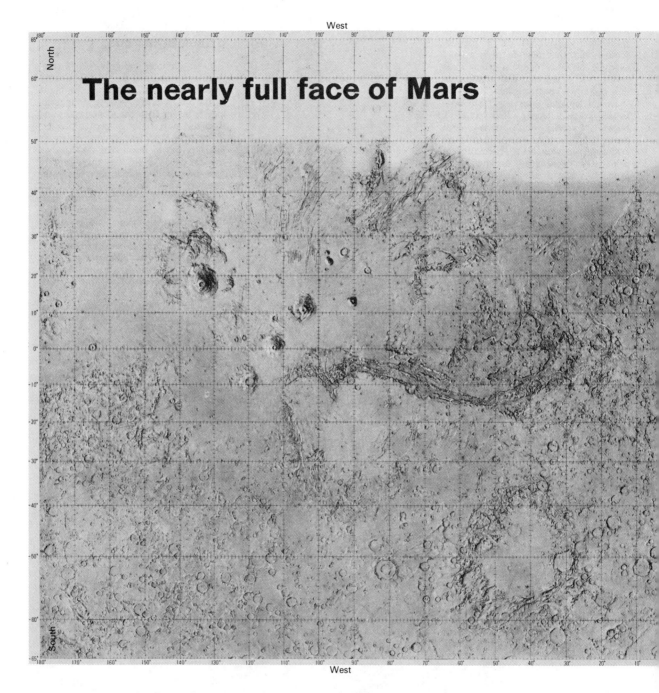

Figure 7.14   Topographical map of Mars between latitude 65° south and latitude 65° north. (Courtesy of NASA, Mariner 9.)

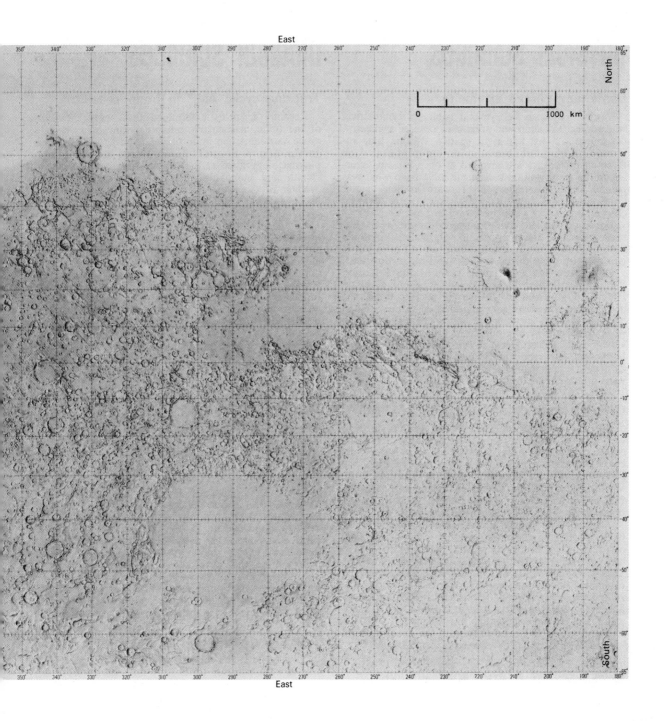

East

North

South

East

from the planet's surface in a period of 30.3 hours. Since its orbital period is somewhat longer than the rotational period of Mars, it rises on the eastern horizon and sets on the western horizon nearly three days later while going through its phases twice. The moons, which are very old as evidenced by their large amount of cratering, are probably asteroids captured after the planet was formed.

7.6 JUPITER ♃

The fifth planet from the sun, Jupiter is the largest and most massive planet in the solar system. In the nighttime sky it glows with a bright, steady, yellow light, outshining the stars. Although Jupiter is more than a thousand times larger than the earth, its mass is barely more than three hundred times that of the earth. It is attended by the largest collection of satellites of any planet, twelve in all.

Orbit of Jupiter

The great planet revolves around the sun at an average distance of 484 million miles (5.2 astronomical units) in 11.86 years. Its distance from the earth ranges from 601 million miles at conjunction to 367 million miles at opposition. The path of the planet is inclined to that of the earth by only 1.3 degrees. Its orbital eccentricity is about 5 per cent.

Telescopic Features

The telescopic view is that of a yellowish, somewhat flattened disk crossed by alternating light and dark atmospheric bands oriented parallel to the equator. The predominant colors of the dark belts are gray or brown, occasionally interspersed with blue, green, and red blotches. The lighter zones are yellowish in hue. The entire banded structure is constantly undergoing changes in color and intensity probably as the result of active local variations in the chemical compositions of the ingredients constituting the Jovian atmosphere. Conspicuous in the southern hemisphere is the oval Red Spot, 8,000 by 30,000

miles, floating in the deep atmosphere. One suggestion is that it may be the top of a partially liquefied stagnant column produced by a disturbed flow of material passing over a bump or depression, leading to an atmospheric irregularity. A color photograph of Jupiter appears in Plate 6.

Physical Properties

The diameter of Jupiter is 87,000 miles or about eleven times greater than the earth's diameter. Its mass has been determined by the application of

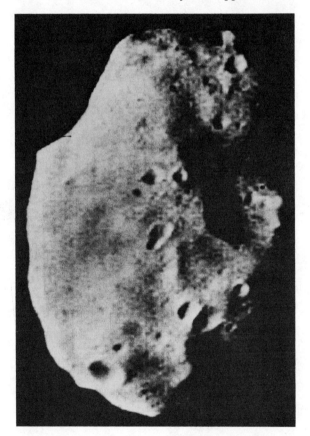

Figure 7.15   Martian satellite, Phobos, is pitted with more than a dozen small craters. The large crater at right center appears to have at least one small crater on its rim. (Courtesy of NASA, Mariner 9.)

Figure 7.16   The banded disk of Jupiter. (Courtesy of Lick Observatory.)

polar diameter, easily observable in a telescope. The measured radiometric temperature of $-190°F$ is undoubtedly that which exists near the top of its atmosphere. The hotter infrared radiation from the lower depths is mostly absorbed by the molecular gases before it reaches the topmost layers.

Jovian Radio Emission

Jupiter is the strongest radio emitter in the solar system after the sun. At times its radio activity rivals even the sun in intensity. Soon after the detection of radio emission in 1954, it was discovered that Jupiter possessed a well-defined magnetosphere with ionization belts similar to the Van Allen belts in the earth's magnetic field. Three different kinds of radio emissions have been observed: (1) the normal thermal centimeter radiation to be expected from a body absorbing and reradiating solar energy; (2) strong, fairly constant nonthermal centimeter radiation radiated by the electrons spiraling around the magnetic lines of force in the magnetosphere; (3) highly variable meter radiation, punctuated occasionally in bursts with energies up to ten million kilowatts. These bursts consist of beamed radiation intercepted by the earth when the planet's rotation brings the radio beam in line with the earth.

Chemical Composition and Internal Structure

The modified spectrum of the reflected sunlight emerging from the Jovian atmosphere reveals the presence of ammonia, methane, and molecular hydrogen. Spectrum analysis of the absorption bands of these molecular gases yields the following abundances: hydrogen is at least nine times more abundant then helium (the helium ratio is a theoretically calculated value since its spectral lines do not appear in the Jovian spectrum); hydrogen is 2,300 times more abundant than carbon and 15,000 times more abundant than nitrogen. Since these ratios are nearly the same in the sun, it appears that Jupiter has managed

Newton's modification of Kepler's third law from the periods and distances of its satellites. It has also been deduced from the gravitational disturbances that Jupiter exerts on the orbits of approaching asteroids. The value is 318 times that of the earth's mass, exceeding the combined masses of all the other bodies orbiting the sun. The mean density is one and one-third times that of water or about one-fourth the earth's density. Since its axis is tilted only three degrees from the normal to its orbital plane, the planet does not experience seasonal variations. The axial rotation period is 9 hours and 55 minutes, but all portions of the planet do not rotate in unison. The equatorial region completes its rotation about five minutes sooner than the adjoining higher latitudes. Also, mysterious slight speedups in certain other areas have been observed. The rapid rotation of the planet, coupled with its low density, has produced a flattening of about one-fifteenth in its to retain in cold storage the bulk of the primordial gases that were present in the solar nebula during the early formative stages of planetary development. The low density of the planet is attributable to the great preponderance of hydrogen. Some astronomers have suggested that the planet may have been a "stillborn" star that failed to materialize as another sun because its mass was not quite large enough to allow it to become a star.

One proposed model of Jupiter's structure begins with an outermost atmospheric layer consisting of the frozen-out crystals of ammonia. Below in successive strata lie a layer of ammonia clouds, followed by a substratum of ice crystals, then water droplets, and finally compressed water vapor down to a depth of 1,000 miles. At this level gravitational compression may have raised the temperature to several thousand degrees absolute. Underneath the atmospheric level, it is postulated that a shell containing a slurry mixture of water, hydrogen, and helium surrounds a large central core of highly pressurized solid hydrogen at a central temperature of 500,000°K. Unfortunately, we know less about the interior composition and construction of the major planets than we know about the sun's interior because the theoretical behavior of compressed gases at high temperatures is better understood than that of compressed matter at low temperatures.

Satellites of Jupiter

The four largest of the twelve known satellites of Jupiter, discovered by Galileo in 1609, are comparable to our moon in size.[1] They revolve in nearly circular orbits in the plane of Jupiter's equator with periods ranging from $1\frac{3}{4}$ days to nearly $16\frac{3}{4}$ days at between one-fourth million and about one million miles from the planet's center. Their motions can be followed nightly with a pair of binoculars. The fifth

---

[1] Two of the moons, Europa and Ganymede, were spectroscopically found in 1972 to be coated with water frost.

satellite, which was discovered visually in 1895 by E. E. Barnard at the Lick Observatory, is one of the smallest moons (~ 70 miles in diameter) and the closest. It orbits around the planet in the plane of the Jovian equator in the short time of twelve hours at 70,000 miles from its surface. The remaining seven small satellites, all subsequently discovered photographically, move in eccentric ellipses angled at 16–29 degrees to the plane of Jupiter's equator. Three of the moons are grouped in a narrow belt 7.13–7.35 million miles from the planet and revolve with periods of 250–264 days. The outer four satellites orbit in a retrograde direction around Jupiter in the range of 14 million miles with periods of 625–758 days.

Some unusual radio phenomena have been associated with two of the Galilean satellites: Io the first and Ganymede the third in order of distance from Jupiter. There is a rise of more than 100°F in the temperature of Jupiter's atmosphere where the shadow of Ganymede falls on the planet. This has been interpreted as resulting from a chemical breakdown that permits warmer material from below to well up into the shaded portion. Whenever Io is to one side of Jupiter as seen from the earth, there results an intense burst of meter wavelength radiation that persists for a couple of hours. Its source appears to be associated with disturbances in the Jovian magnetosphere induced by Io.

7.7 SATURN ♄

Saturn, the sixth planet in the order of distance from the sun, is one of the most remarkable objects in the heavens because of its rings. It outranks all the stars but Sirius and Canopus in brightness and shines with a steady, ashen color. Saturn is the second-ranking planet in the order of mass and size.

Orbit of Saturn

The planet swings around the sun in a slightly

eccentric ellipse in the period of 29.46 years at a mean distance of 887 million miles (9.4 A.U.). Its distance from the earth varies from 729 to 998 million miles, not enough to cause any appreciable change in its brightness. Its orbit is inclined only 2.5 degrees to the earth's orbital plane.

Telescopic Appearance

Viewed as it is at twice the distance of Jupiter, details on the noticeably flattened disk of Saturn still faintly resemble the banded, cloudy structure of Jupiter's atmosphere. The coloration is more restrained and the details are less distinct. On rare occasions there are sudden discernible changes, sometimes in the form of bright spots in the equatorial region. Saturn, photographed in color, appears in Plate 7.

Physical Properties

The mean diameter of Saturn, minus its ring system, is 72,000 miles. Its mass is 95 times the earth's mass. Its density is the lowest of any planet,

Figure 7.17   Saturn and its ring system. (Courtesy of Lick Observatory.)

0.7 times that of water, which leads to the well-known cliché that it could float in water. It rotates once in $10\frac{1}{2}$ hours on an axis that is inclined 26.7 degrees from the normal to its orbital plane, not very different from that of Mars or the earth. The combination of fast rotation and unusually low density has produced the largest degree of polar flattening of any planet, amounting to about one-ninth. Weak radio emission in the meter range has been detected emanating from the planet. The source is attributed to radiating electrons trapped within the magnetic field that is believed to surround the planet, similar to the action going on in the magnetosphere of Jupiter. Feeble thermal radiation is also present.

Composition of Saturn

The spectrum of Saturn exhibits stronger lines of methane than ammonia. The reduced visible proportion of ammonia results from the lower atmospheric temperature of Saturn. At the measured radiometric temperature of $-230°F$, the ammonia has crystallized into flakes. This leaves exposed the molecular hydrogen and the partly gaseous methane that are still well observable spectroscopically. The atmospheric chemistry and internal construction of Saturn are believed to be somewhat comparable to that prevalent in Jupiter. One proposed model for the Saturnian interior postulates a mixed shell of hydrogen-helium in the ratio of 11 : 1 and a solid hydrogen core starting about half-way to the center.

The Rings of Saturn

The circular rings of Saturn lie in a plane coincidental with Saturn's equator, whose angle of inclination to its orbital plane is nearly 27 degrees. During the 29.5-year period of the planet's revolution around the sun, the rings are observed obliquely at different angles from the earth. At intervals of a little over seven years they are alternately viewed in the maximum oblique position about half-way full

Figure 7.18   Various aspects of Saturn, 1933–1940. (Courtesy of Lick Observatory.)

on and edgewise when they practically disappear from sight. Their thickness may be only a fraction of a mile.

Four different rings have been identified: A, B, C, and D in the order of decreasing distance from Saturn. The dark, outermost ring A is 10,000 miles wide; its inside rim lies 44,000 miles from the surface

of Saturn. It is separated from the bright ring B by a blank space of about 2,500 miles called the *Cassini division*, named after its discoverer (1675). Ring B is 16,500 miles wide; its inside diameter lies 25,000 miles from the surface of Saturn. The third ring, C, known as the "crepe ring" because of its semi-transparency, is quite faint. It is about 13,000 miles

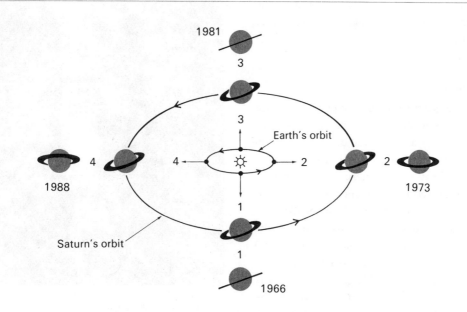

1981

3

3

Earth's orbit

4

4

2

2

1988

1973

Saturn's orbit

1

1

1966

Figure 7.19   Changing views of Saturn's rings. The dated sketches show the telescopic appearance of Saturn.

wide and is separated from ring B by a few hundred miles. The fourth and innermost ring, D, which is exceptionally faint and difficult to photograph, was discovered in 1969 by Pierre Guerin at Pic du Midi, a French observatory in the high Alps. It is separated from the crepe ring by approximately 2,000 miles.

The rings are composed of small particles believed to be coated with ammonia or water ice. Each particle pursues its independent orbit around Saturn in conformity with Kepler's harmonic law. This is evident in the spectral lines of the reflected sunlight through their Doppler shift, which decreases with the increasing radius of the ring system: the farther out, the slower the speed of the particles. A solid ring structure, on the other hand, would rotate fastest at its outer rim. The entire ring system lies within the critical distance known as the *Roche limit*, equal to 2.4 Saturnian radii. Inside this critical distance a

satellite would be subjected to the strong disruptive tidal pull of the planet. Whether the rings were formed inside the Roche limit by the breakup of a low-density satellite or whether unstable gravitational forces prevented the formation of a satellite is unknown.

The Cassini division corresponds to a particular place within the ring structure where a hypothetical particle would orbit in a period that is a simple fraction of the orbital periods of the inner satellites: namely, one-half, one-third, or one-fourth of the orbital periods of the second, third, and fourth satellites. A particle moving in this sensitive region is subjected by any one of these satellites to repeated gravitational disturbances that tend to drive it out of this region. For example, a particle in the Cassini division would have a period of 11.3 hours, half that of Mimas, the second innermost satellite. Whenever the two are closest, at every second round of the particle, Mimas exerts a gravitational perturbation that builds up repetitively to a point where the particle is forced out of its orbit.

Satellites of Saturn

Saturn possesses ten satellites ranging in distance from 60,000 miles to 8,040,000 miles with periods from three-fourths of a day to 550 days. All of them lie outside the Roche limit. Two of the moons are of particular interest. The innermost one, named Janus, was discovered by the French astronomer A. Dollfus in 1966. It orbits only 25,000 miles from the surface of Saturn and is barely outside the Roche limit. The seventh moon, Titan, is located 760,000 miles from the center of Saturn and is 1.5 times larger than our moon. It is the second largest satellite in the solar system, exceeded only by Ganymede in the Jupiter system. What makes Titan unusual is that it possesses an atmosphere that contains a considerable amount of methane as well as hydrogen. The other moons range in size from about 200 miles to 1,000 miles in diameter.

7.8 URANUS

Discovery of Uranus

"In examining the small stars in the neighborhood of H Geminorum I perceived one that appeared larger than the rest; being struck with its uncommon appearance . . . I suspected it to be a comet." So wrote William Herschel of England on the night of March 13, 1781, in his observing journal. After vainly trying to derive a cometary orbit for the object, astronomers realized that this was a new planet moving in a nearly circular orbit approximately twice as far away as Saturn. A check of older records revealed that the planet had mistakenly been charted as a star on many occasions during the preceding century. Just barely perceptible to the naked eye,

Figure 7.20 *Uranus and three of its five moons. (Courtesy of Lick Observatory.)*

it had escaped detection because of its very slow motion among the stars.

Orbit and Rotation

Uranus orbits the sun once in 84 years at a mean distance of 1.8 billion miles in a plane almost coincidental with the earth's orbital plane. Its diameter is 30,000 miles, its mass equals 14.5 earth masses, and its average density is 1.56 times that of water. One peculiarity about its $10\frac{3}{4}$-hour period of rotation is that its axis inclines at an angle of 82 degrees to a line drawn perpendicular to its orbital plane. We view its rotation in the reverse direction from that of any other planet except Venus. When its axis is in our line of sight at intervals of 42 years (one-half the sidereal period), we observe one or the other of its sunlit northern or southern hemispheres while the opposite hemisphere remains in continual darkness. One-quarter or three-quarters of its period later (21 and 63 years later), we observe both hemi-

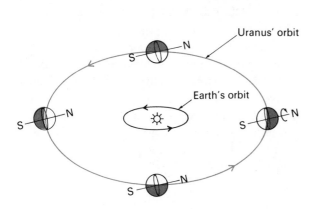

Figure 7.21   Hemispheric views of Uranus.

spheres equally when its axis points at right angles to our line of sight.

Telescopic Appearance and Physical Characteristics

Observed in a good-sized telescope, the slightly flattened disk is apple green in color. At its great distance of nearly two billion miles from the earth, it presents an almost featureless appearance. The little that can be observed seems to consist of indistinct bands with occasional vague markings. Both molecular hydrogen and methane have been identified spectroscpically in the atmosphere. Ammonia, which is unquestionably present, has been frozen out of the atmosphere, thus accounting for the absence of its spectrum. The somewhat higher density of Uranus (1.56 g/cm^3) may be caused by the presence of less hydrogen and helium and more ammonia and water in its composition. Its theoretically calculated equilibrium temperature is $-345°$F.

Satellites of Uranus

Uranus possesses five satellites with estimated diameters ranging from 100 to 800 miles. Their distances vary from 8,000 to 364,000 miles, corre-

sponding to orbital periods of 1.4 to 13.5 days. Since the moons revolve in the same direction as the planet, their motions are retrograde in the same direction as their primary. During the 84-year cycle of Uranus's revolution around the sun, their orbital movements are viewed at all possible angles to the line of sight between the edgewise and full projections.

7.9   NEPTUNE   Ψ

Mathematical Discovery of Neptune

For many years after the accidental discovery of Uranus in 1781, astronomers were perplexed that, even after allowing for the perturbations of Jupiter and Saturn, its orbital behavior was less predictable than that of the other planets. The discrepancy was finally resolved in 1845–46 by two young theoretical astronomers, John C. Adams in England and Urbain J. J. Leverrier in France. They arrived independently at the same conclusion: a disturbing body located beyond the orbit of Uranus was the culprit. Using only pencil and paper, both calculators succeeded in approximately pinpointing this unknown object, Adams a little earlier than Leverrier. Unfortunately, through misunderstanding and lack of proper sky charts, the search conducted at Adams' request in England was too prolonged by delays. Leverrier's results were communicated to J. G. Galle, the Berlin Observatory astronomer, who received the information on September 23, 1846. Within a half-hour, using the observatory's nine-inch refractor, Galle located the new planet as the interloper among a group of eight stars whose positions had been previously charted on a recently prepared map of the region. It was found within one degree of the predicted position and was about two times brighter than estimated and three astronomical units farther out than the predicted value. Though the honor of discovery was first accorded to Leverrier, followed by years of bitter controversy,

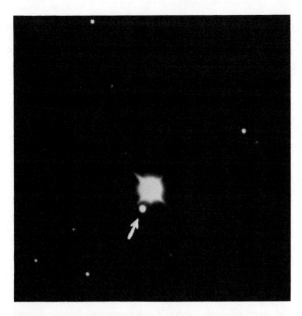

Figure 7.22   Neptune and its nearer satellite, Triton. (Courtesy of Lick Observatory.)

to its orbital plane in a period of approximately 16 hours. Its mass is 17.2 times greater than the earth's mass, and its average density is about 1.7 times that of water, in reasonable accord with the mean density of Uranus. Both hydrogen and methane have been spectroscopically detected in its atmosphere. Helium and ammonia are undoubtedly present but not spectroscopically observable. All of the ammonia and part of the methane have crystallized into solid matter at the prevailing atmospheric temperature of −360°F.

Satellites of Neptune

The larger of Neptune's two moons, Triton, orbits the planet at a distance of 220,000 miles in a direction opposite to the eastward rotation of the planet. Its period of orbital revolution around Neptune is 5.9 days. Triton's diameter is 2,600 miles with a mass nearly twice that of our moon and a slightly higher density of 3.5 g/cm^3. The smaller satellite, Nereid, is about 200 miles across. Every 360 days it swings around Neptune in a highly elongated ellipse ranging from 900,000 miles to six million miles from the planet. It has been suggested that the satellite was thrust into its present eccentric orbit from a more regular orbit during a close encounter with Triton.

7.10   PLUTO ♇

Discovery of Pluto

Percival Lowell, the founder of the observatory bearing his name, was convinced, on the basis of his calculations begun in 1905, that certain minute discrepancies still existed in the orbital motion of Uranus. (Neptune had not been observed long enough to provide useful data.) He concluded that the irregularities could be accounted for by the perturbative influence of an exterior planet. After

history now grants equal recognition to both these men.

Orbit and Telescopic Appearance

Neptune orbits the sun once in 164.8 years at a mean distance of 2.8 billion miles (30 A.U.). Its orbital path is nearly circular and is inclined at the small angle of 1.8 degrees to the plane of the earth's orbit. The telescopic image of Neptune is that of a very slightly flattened, bluish-green, almost featureless disk. Observers have at times noted irregular, indistinct markings and a bright equatorial zone vaguely similar to that of Uranus.

Physical Characteristics

The diameter of Neptune is 30,600 miles, virtually the same as that of Uranus. The planet rotates about an axis inclined 29 degrees from the normal several years of intermittent and unproductive search, the hunt was resumed in earnest in January 1929. The Lowell Observatory had recently acquired a thirteen-inch photographic refractor and had placed a young astronomer, Clyde W. Tombaugh, in charge of the new search program. After one year of photographing suspected star fields where the planet might be found, Tombaugh made the historic find in January 1930. He did this by comparing two plates of the same region exposed on different nights with a device called a blink comparator. This optical instrument makes it possible to detect small changes in the position or brightness of images by rapidly alternating the view from one photograph to the other.

The official announcement of Pluto's discovery was delayed for nearly two months during which time the Lowell astronomers carefully followed its slow movement among the stars. When they were positive that it was indeed a new planet beyond the orbit of Neptune, they announced its discovery on March 12, 1930. Careful reexamination of Lowell's calculations by later astronomers indicated that his conclusions were based upon questionable data and that the discovery was, in a way, an accident. Nevertheless, Lowell's important contribution was recognized and he was given credit posthumously for being instrumental in the search and discovery of Pluto. The first two letters of Pluto, the Greek god of the underworld, happen to be the initials of Percival Lowell, a double incentive for the naming of the ninth planet.

General Characteristics

Pluto moves around the sun once in 248.4 years at the mean distance of 3.675 billion miles (39.5 A.U.) in an eccentric ellipse inclined at the relatively high angle of 17.2 degrees to the earth's orbital plane. Its distance from the sun varies from 2.8 billion miles at

Figure 7.23   The blink comparator, used to detect changes in position and brightness of an object photographed at different times. Note the two plateholders in the center. (Lowell Observatory Photograph.)

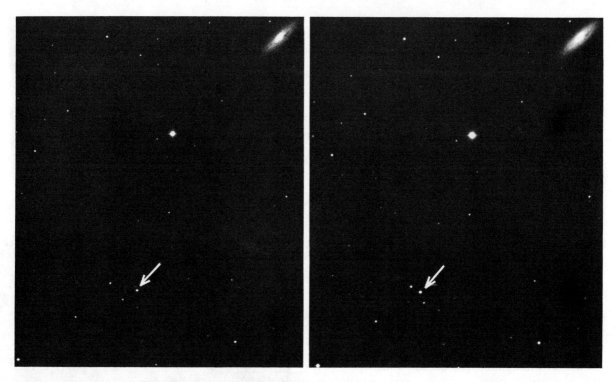

Figure 7.24   Positions of Pluto one day apart. (Courtesy of Lick Observatory.)

perihelion to 4.6 billion miles at aphelion. Photoelectric observations of its slightly varying brightness, presumably caused by uneven reflections of sunlight from its rough surface, reveal that the period of its rotation is 6.4 days. The planet's small disk, measured with the Hale 200-inch reflector, has a diameter of 3,700 miles. From the gravitationally derived mass of 0.11 earth mass units, the calculated mean density is about five times that of water, close to that of the earth. Its low surface gravity and extremely cold temperature of about −400°F would preclude the existence of a gaseous atmosphere. One explanation advanced to account for its relatively high-angled eccentric orbit and slow rotational spin supposes that it was a former satellite of Neptune that was gravitationally captured by the sun.

REVIEW QUESTIONS

1. Explain why the other planets in the solar system are not suitable as the abode of animal life.

2. Describe briefly the different techniques employed in studying the planets.

3. What are the surface and atmospheric conditions like on Venus?

4. How well can Mariner photos of Mars be reconciled with earth-based telescopic views? Where are the agreements and disagreements?

5. In what ways is the Martian terrain revealed to be similar and also different from terrestrial terrain?

6. Describe how the two little moons of Mars behave in the Martian sky.

EXPLORING THE COSMOS

7. Discuss the differences in the atmospheres of the following planets: (a) Venus; (b) Mars; (c) Jupiter.

8. What are the principal differences, physically and chemically, between the terrestrial planets and the Jovian planets?

9. What is one interpretation of the Great Red Spot on Jupiter?

10. Discuss the radio peculiarities existing in the magnetosphere of Jupiter.

11. What orbital differences are ·there among the satellites of Jupiter?

12. Explain why the rings of Saturn change their appearance during the course of the planet's revolution around the sun as seen from the earth.

13. How do we know that the rings of Saturn are composed of particles revolving in separate orbits around Saturn?

14. If there is anything unusual about Venus, Uranus, and Pluto, what might it be?

15. What are the prevailing ideas concerning the internal structure of the Jovian planets?

SELECTED READINGS

Bradbury, R., et al., *Mars and the Mind of Man,* Harper and Row, 1973.

Caidan, M., *Destination Mars,* Doubleday, 1972.

Clarke, A. C., and C. Bonestell, *Beyond Jupiter; The Worlds of Tomorrow,* Little, Brown, 1973.

Moore, P., *The New Guide to the Planets,* Norton, 1972.

Nourse, A. E., *Nine Planets,* Harper and Row, 1970.

Page, T., and L. W. Page, eds., *Wanderers in the Sky,* Macmillan, 1965.

Pickering, J. S., *Captives of the Sun,* Dodd, Mead, 1961.

Sagan, C., and J. N. Leonard, *Planets,* Life Nature Library (Time, Inc.), 1966.

Tucker, R. A. R., *The Paths of the Planets,* American Elsevier, 1967.

Whipple, F. L., *Earth, Moon, and Planets,* Harvard University Press, 1968.

Long-exposure photograph of Halley's comet as it appeared in 1910. The bright circular object to the right is the over-exposed image of Venus. Since the telescope followed the moving comet, the stellar images have short trails. (Lowell Observatory Photograph.)

THE SOLAR SYSTEM:
MINOR CONSTITUENTS
AND ORIGIN

Lo! from the dread immensity of space,
Returning, with accelerated course,
The rushing Comet to the Sun descends;
And, as he shrinks below the shading earth,
With awful train projected o'er the heavens,
The guilty nations tremble.

James Thomson (1700–1748),
Seasons, Summer

The discovery of the first asteroid in 1801 filled a void in the spacing of the planets required by an arithmetical rule called Bode's law. Today the total number of known asteroids is nearing 2,000, out of an estimated 50,000 smaller asteroids, most under a mile in diameter, orbiting between Mars and Jupiter.

Another class of minor bodies is the comets. Physically, they consist of small masses of frozen gases, not more than a few miles in diameter, contaminated with the more common heavier elements. Their tails develop as they are heated by the sun whose solar wind particles and light pressure expel the evaporated dust and gas from their heads. Two general species predominate: short-period comets traveling eastward around the sun in periods ranging from three to 200 years at low orbital inclinations to the ecliptic; and long-period comets swinging around the sun at all angles of inclination to the ecliptic in wide-ranging orbits with periods in hundreds to millions of years. The most famous but not the brightest is Halley's comet, which has been observed approximately every 75 years since 240 B.C. Its next scheduled appearance near the earth will be in 1985–86.

Small particulate matter orbiting the sun in the form of meteoroids, dust, and gas constitute a highly rarefied interplanetary medium lying in the plane of the planets' orbits. A grain-sized or smaller particle within this medium, when captured by the earth, produces a meteor trail as it passes through the earth's upper air. The larger bodies that survive atmospheric flight and land, namely the meteorites, are composed of nearly pure stone or iron, or a roughly equal admixture of both stone and iron. Their ages vary from many millions of years to about 4.6 billion years, the estimated age of the earth.

It is now generally accepted that the solar system was born when a gravitationally contracting solar nebula spawned a rotating disk of planetesimal fragments that accreted to form the planets. Although the details of planetary formation remain obscure, the prevailing view is that it occurs commonly elsewhere within our Galaxy.

8.1 ASTEROIDS

Bode's Law

In 1772 the German astronomer J. E. Bode called attention to a rule, originally discovered by J. D. Titius in 1766, to which the mean distances of the known planets seemed to conform. It has since become known as Bode's law, though it does not appear to possess the physical validity of a true law. In Table 8.1, illustrating Bode's law, the encircled numbers correspond to those objects that had not yet been discovered at the time. The fact that Uranus was found to fall very nearly in line with Bode's law when it was discovered in 1781 spurred the search for a planet existing between Mars and Jupiter at a distance of 2.8 astronomical units from the sun. (Note that the rule breaks down with Neptune and Pluto.)

Discovery of Asteroids

On January 1, 1801, the Sicilian astronomer G. Piazzi accidentally discovered an object whose orbital motion was verified to conform to that of a body located at 2.8 A.U. from the sun. The object was given the name of Ceres, Roman goddess of cereals. By 1807, after diligent search, three additional planetoids had been found having orbits near 2.8 A.U.: Pallas (1802), Juno (1804), and Vesta (1807). The six largest asteroids in the order of size are: Ceres (1), 620 miles; Pallas (2), 335 miles; Vesta (4), 320 miles; Davida (511), 218 miles; Eunomia (15), 155 miles; Juno (3), 133 miles. (The number in parentheses is the order of discovery.) Since 1845 at least one new minor planet has been discovered

Table 8.1 Bode's Law

Planet	Titius's Rule	Actual Distance from Sun (A.U.)	Distance Ratio
Mercury	$0 \times 0.3 + 0.4 = 0.4$	0.39	
Venus	$1 \times 0.3 + 0.4 = 0.7$	0.72	1:8
Earth	$2 \times 0.3 + 0.4 = 1.0$	1.00	1:4
Mars	$4 \times 0.3 + 0.4 = 1.6$	1.52	1:5
Minor planets	$8 \times 0.3 + 0.4 = \boxed{2.8}$	2.77 (Ceres)	1:8
Jupiter	$16 \times 0.3 + 0.4 = 5.2$	5.20	1:9
Saturn	$32 \times 0.3 + 0.4 = 10.0$	9.54	1:8
Uranus	$64 \times 0.3 + 0.4 = \boxed{19.6}$	19.18	2:0
Neptune	$128 \times 0.3 + 0.4 = \boxed{38.8}$	30.07	1:6
Pluto	$256 \times 0.3 + 0.4 = \boxed{77.2}$	39.46	1:3

annually. With the introduction of photographic techniques in the 1890's, they have been discovered by the dozens yearly, including old asteroids which have been temporarily lost because of orbital changes wrought by the planets.

Instead of a single planet occupying the slot at 2.8 astronomical units, thousands of small bodies are orbiting in the region between Mars and Jupiter. The name "asteroid" was originally applied to these objects by William Herschel because of their starlike appearance in the telescope. They are confined mostly in the zone between 2.1 and 3.5 A.U. with periods ranging from 3.3 to 6 years. Their orbits are less circular than those of the planets and their orbital planes are also more highly inclined to the ecliptic. Approximately 1,830 asteroids have been found up to the present time. They vary in size from Ceres (620 miles) to hundreds of lesser size on down to thousands that are only a mile or less in diameter. The total number of undiscovered smaller asteroids may run as high as 50,000.

General Characteristics

Photographic studies of the asteroids with different color filters reveal a considerable diversity in size, shape, and rotation among them. Most if not all

Figure 8.1   Tracks of two asteroids photographed at the Yerkes Observatory. (Courtesy of Yerkes Observatory.)

8 THE SOLAR SYSTEM: MINOR CONSTITUENTS

of the planetoids have irregular shapes as inferred from their variations in brightness. Their periods of rotation are measured in hours. Diameters are based on the estimates of brightness and an assumed percentage of reflectivity since all but the largest are too small to show a measurable disk.

Those minor planets which come close to the earth are particularly useful in providing more precise information concerning their dimensions, shapes, and rotational periods. One such planetoid, Eros, on its last approach to the earth in 1931 (14 million miles) was found to have an oblong shape about 15 by 5 by 5 miles, judged from its changing light and reflectivity as it tumbled in orbit. It was found to be spinning around its short axis in a period of 5 hours and 16 minutes. In June 1968, Icarus passed within 3.95 million miles of the earth. By bouncing radar signals from its surface, Icarus was found to possess an uneven, pitted surface about one-half mile wide and turning around in 2.5 hours. About a dozen asteroids are known to come close to the earth. One of them, Hermes, less than one mile in diameter, passed within twice the moon's distance from the earth (~500,000 miles) in 1937. Another one, Toro, with a period of only 1.6 years, appears to be gravitationally coupled during alternate intervals, measured in centuries, to the earth and then to Venus, forming a loose triple system, according to the Swedish astrophysicist H. Alfvén. The possibility of an errant minor planet colliding with the earth is extremely remote, but if such a collision were to occur, its destructive power could be equivalent to a 500,000-megaton bomb blast!

The Trojan Asteroids

In 1772 the French mathematical astronomer J. L. Lagrange solved a special case of the complex three-body problem in which the sun, a planet, and a smaller body each occupy one corner of an equilateral triangle. It was not until about a century later that actual objects fulfilling Lagrange's hypothetical solution were discovered. More than a dozen such asteroids are known and they carry the names of the famous Trojan war heroes and Greek warriors who participated in the siege of Troy as recorded in Homer's *Iliad*. These asteroids are trapped in a kind of gravitational vise; they are restricted to a slow oscillatory motion lasting many years about the vertex of the triangle while the sun and Jupiter hold their relative positions at the two other vertices. Thus Jupiter and the asteroids orbit the sun in Jupiter's period of twelve years with each group stationed approximately sixty degrees east or west of the planet.

Origin of the Asteroids

The mass of a minor planet is approximated from its estimated volume and an assumed moonlike density. The total mass content of all the asteroids is calculated to be not more than one-tenth of the moon's mass. The idea that the asteroids originated from the

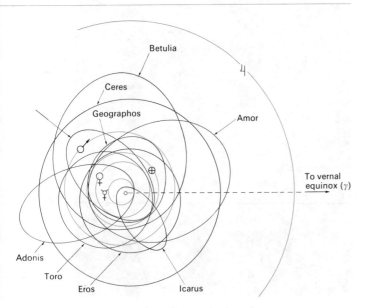

Figure 8.2 Orbits of unusual minor planets.

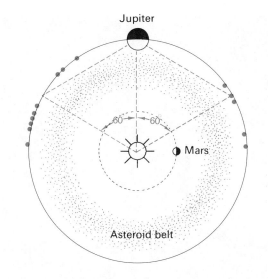

Figure 8.3 *The Trojan asteroids.*

breakup of a small body or from the failure of planetesimals to coalesce within the contracting solar nebula into a larger coherent body goes back for more than a century. Their proximity to Jupiter and its perturbative influence could have prevented any appreciable mass from forming. The probable consequence of Jovian action would be to modify the asteroidal orbits and increase the chances of collisions. During the course of time, fragmentation and splintering have multiplied the numbers of colliding asteroids. The asteroids are one of the key factors to our understanding of the past history of the solar system. Their number, size, density, composition, and distribution are important links in this chain of knowledge. The asteroids may be the best specimens of solidified primordial matter still present within the inner solar system.

8.2 COMETS

Comets appear unexpectedly in all parts of the sky. They are discovered accidentally on photo-

graphs taken for other purposes by professional astronomers or by amateur astronomers who methodically search for them. Comets are named after their discoverer or codiscoverers. The year 1970 produced a record number: seven new comets and the recovery of eleven old ones. Only rarely, perhaps once every other year or so, does a comet become bright enough to be seen with the naked eye. The spectacularly bright comets appear once or twice per decade.

General Appearance

The usual telescopic comet appears as a small, hazy object possessing a roundish nebulosity called a *coma* or *head* and occasionally a short tail. The brighter comet has more interesting features: an enlarged coma within which appears a small bright *nucleus* and a well-formed, usually curved, tail that points away from the sun. The size of the coma may vary from about 10,000 miles to well over one million miles. The nucleus, where the mass is concentrated, may range in diameter from a fraction of a mile to several dozen miles. The lengths of well-developed tails, which are usually formed at distances within the earth's orbit, are measured in millions of miles, sometimes exceeding 100 million miles.

That comets are flimsy structures of low density is demonstrated by the following observations: (1) they cannot be observed upon the solar disk when they pass in front of the sun; (2) stars are clearly seen through the tail and even through the outer portions of the head; (3) changes in brightness and size have been noted in the head but more pronounced alterations in the tail structure are observed from night to night; (4) they are easily susceptible to solar wind gusts and to tidal, gravitational, or other variable disruptive forces.

Orbits of Comets

The first positive evidence that comets were

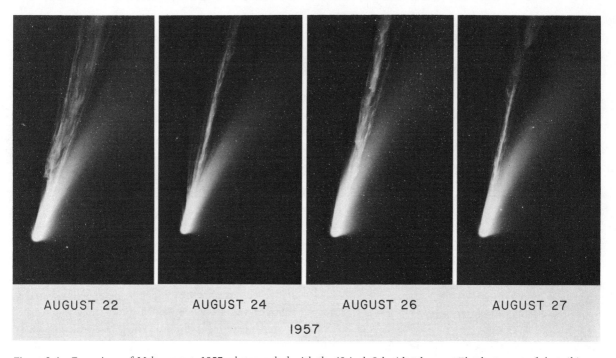

AUGUST 22   AUGUST 24   AUGUST 26   AUGUST 27

1957

Figure 8.4 Four views of Mrkos comet, 1957, photographed with the 48-inch Schmidt telescope. The dusty part of the tail is diffuse and slightly curved; the gassy part is filamentary and rectilinear. (Courtesy of Hale Observatories.)

extraterrestrial objects was provided by the six-teenth-century astronomer Tycho Brahe. From efforts to measure the parallactic displacement of the comet of 1577 among the stars between his observatory and other European centers, he concluded that the object was more distant than the moon. Johannes Kepler surmised from his observations of the bright comet of 1607 (later known as Halley's comet) that comets traveled along straight lines in space. It remained for Isaac Newton to demonstrate some eighty years later that comets are members of the solar system and move in elliptical orbits prescribed by the law of gravitation. If comets were found to be moving in parabolic or hyperbolic orbits (assuming that they were not forced into such orbits by planetary per-turbations), they would not be classified as belonging to the solar system (Section 2.7).

Periods of Comets

Comets fall into two groups, long-period and short-period comets, depending on the period of orbital revolution around the sun. The former group, which constitutes the majority of comets, travels in highly elongated ellipses inclined at all angles to the ecliptic plane. Their periods of orbital revolution range from hundreds to millions of years. The brighter members of this class rank among the most magnificent comets, with conspicuously long tails and well-defined nuclei. Several in this category graze the sun at closest passage, actually passing at high speed through the sun's outer atmosphere as they round the sun. They frequently undergo solar tidal disruption during this close encounter, and the fragmented parts travel as independent comets along nearly identical orbits at varying intervals up to

Figure 8.5   Comet Ikeya-Seki, 1965. This sun-grazing comet passed within 300,000 miles of the sun. (Courtesy of Smithsonian Astrophysical Observatory.)

inclination to the plane of the ecliptic, nearly all of them in the same direction as the planets. Their periods range from 3.3 to 200 years. Approximately half of them swing out from the sun only about as far as Jupiter. By tracing back mathematically the history of their orbital behavior, it was found that these objects were initially moving in long-period eccentric orbits which brought them on one critical occasion into a chance encounter with Jupiter. The great planet's attraction so modified their paths that they have become members of Jupiter's "family." They orbit the sun with their aphelia in the general vicinity of Jupiter.

Halley's Comet

When a bright comet appeared in the heavens during the late summer of 1682, Edmund Halley, the British astronomer, calculated its orbit according to the methods prescribed by his good friend Newton. Having also employed the same methods in deriving orbits for the bright comets of 1531 and 1607, he was struck by the similarity in their orbits. He concluded that the same comet had made three revolutions in an elliptical orbit in a period of $75\frac{1}{2}$ years. He predicted its return in 1758, but he died seventeen years before the comet returned as he had forecast. In March 1759 it passed perihelion, having been delayed by the perturbations of Jupiter and Saturn on its approach to the sun. For his recognition that this comet makes periodic returns to the sun's neighborhood, it has been named posthumously in his honor. A check of old records reveals that Halley's comet has been observed on every one of its returns since the year 240 B.C. The next appearance of Halley's comet in the vicinity of the earth will be in 1985–86. (A striking view of the comet appears in the frontispiece to this Chapter).

Physical and Chemical Properties of Comets

According to a structural model developed in

thousands of years apart. The brilliant Ikeya-Seki comet of 1965, which penetrated within 300,000 miles of the solar surface, was observed to split into two unequal parts as it rounded the sun. Other comets are known to have fissioned as a result of some other nontidal mechanism at much greater distances from the sun.

The second group of comets, numbering about a hundred, orbits the sun at small or moderate angles of

---

Figure 8.6   Portion of the Bayeux tapestry showing Halley's comet. "Behold the wonderful star" is inscribed along the top border of the tapestry, which depicts King Harold and his court attendants who regarded the appearance of the comet in 1066 as an evil portent. The association of this comet with Harold's defeat by William the Conqueror that same year is one of those superstitions that persisted for centuries. It was thought that the unexpected appearance of a bright comet heralded the death of royalty or other calamitous events. (Courtesy of The Bettmann Archive.)

detail by F. L. Whipple of Harvard, a comet is believed to consist of an icy core composed chiefly of water ice and lesser amounts of frozen methane, ammonia, and carbon dioxide, plus a small admixture of particulate matter and dust. This conglomerate, which constitutes the nucleus, is surrounded by outgassing material vaporized by solar heat to form the coma. As a comet approaches the sun, solar ultraviolet radiation becomes sufficiently intense to decompose the cold molecular substances into the simpler combinations of hydrogen, carbon, oxygen, and nitrogen. Their dissociated compounds are spectroscopically recorded as bright bands in the

cometary spectrum. Also present are the bright lines of a number of vaporized metals, principally iron, magnesium, silicon, and sodium. The emission lines and bands are superimposed on the weak background spectrum of the sunlight reflected from the cometary material. The expanded gases within the coma are driven away from the sun radially by solar wind and solar light pressure to form the tail which lengthens as the comet nears the sun. The curvature often noted in tails arises from differences in the outward flow of the gaseous material within the tail. A faster outflowing movement tends to produce a straighter tail. In 1970 ultraviolet sensors aboard

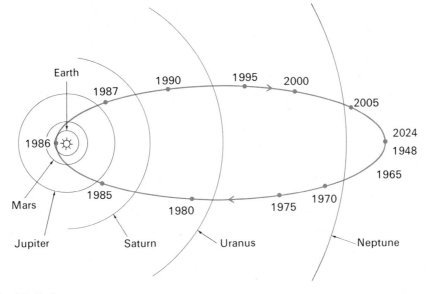

Figure 8.7   Orbit of Halley's comet.

instrumented earth-orbiting satellites detected huge halos around the heads of two comets emitting the ultraviolet light of hydrogen. One of the clouds had a diameter of eight million miles.

Origin of Comets

In 1950 the Dutch astronomer J. Oort advanced the notion, based on his study of the distribution of cometary orbits, that there exists a cometary cloud of not more than one hundred earth masses surrounding the sun at an average distance of 50,000 astronomical units. Detached from this great reservoir, as a consequence of perturbations by nearby stars, are small portions that begin to orbit the sun as long-period comets. Possibly around 100,000 comets would be expected to come close enough to the sun to be observable. The total number of comets is estimated to run into the billions.

8.3   METEOROIDS AND METEORS

At least 50,000 tons of cosmic debris pepper the earth daily in the form of billions of microscopic particles. We are aware only of those weighing a significant fraction of a gram as they produce the "shooting stars" that flash swiftly across the sky. The overwhelming majority of these particles striking the earth are too small to leave luminous trails in the atmosphere bright enough for us to observe.

Classification of Meteoroids

Small meteoritic particles are called *meteoroids* before they encounter the earth. Those bodies that are large enough to survive flight through the earth's atmosphere and land are called *meteorites*. The luminous trails of the smaller particles that are vaporized in the air are designated as *meteors*. In the order of increasing size and brightness, these are classified as:

(1) telescopic and radio meteors; (2) photographic or visual meteors; (3) fireballs or bolides.

Meteor Observations

Older visual observing methods have been replaced by more accurate photographic techniques. Valuable physical data can be obtained by placing two modified wide-angle Schmidt cameras with rapidly rotating shutters at widely separated stations. Each camera is directed toward a common part of the sky where the same meteor trails are photographed against the sky background. Analysis of the photographically chopped trails produced by the rotating-camera shutter system leads to estimates of particle size, mass, density, and orbital data. A network of sixteen unmanned stations in seven midwestern states continuously monitors the skies for bright flashes that may be associated with fireballs or bolides and meteorite falls whose locations can be pinpointed by triangulation.

Photographic observations are supplemented by radio/radar techniques which have the advantage of round-the-clock availability. A meteoroid passing through the atmosphere ionizes (electrically inflames) the air to a considerable distance from its path by virtue of its high speed. This is what we observe in the form of a luminous trail, rather than the tiny particle itself which is too small to be seen. Radio waves reflected from the ionized trail produce brief whistles in a receiver equipped with a beat-frequency oscillator. The whistles either increase or decrease in pitch depending on whether the particle is approaching or receding from the listener. This phenomenon is, of course, the well-known Doppler effect. Timing of the round-trip radar echoes and analysis of their profiles observed on an oscilloscope screen yield accurate information on meteor heights and velocities.

Velocities of Meteoroids

The velocities of meteoritic particles at the time of impact with the earth range from about 7 to 44 miles per second, depending upon their direction and the angle at which they strike the earth. The maximum speed at which a particle belonging to the solar system can strike the earth is around 45 mi/sec. Imagine a particle moving in a nearly parabolic orbit at the earth's distance at a speed of 25 mi/sec, just under the velocity of escape from the solar system. When it meets head on the earth, which is traveling at 18.5 mi/sec in its orbit, its relative speed seen from the earth becomes $(25 + 18.5) = 43.5$ mi/sec. There is a slight increase resulting from the gravitational attraction of the earth. For a particle moving in the same direction and overtaking the earth, the relative velocity is reduced to $(25 - 18.5) = 7.5$ mi/sec. From the observed speeds we conclude that the meteoroids are bona-fide members of the solar system. The slower-traveling particles are generally visible at a height of about 50 miles and disappear at 25 miles. The faster-moving ones appear and disappear at somewhat higher altitudes. Our atmosphere retards the entrance velocity of the particles and transforms their kinetic energy into radiated and frictional energy. What remains slowly filters down through the air as dust and solidified droplets of the melted meteoroids. Samples of this material have been recovered from high mountain sites and from the ocean bottoms.

Properties of Meteors

Spectral analysis of the meteors' incandescent tracks reveals the presence of vaporized gases in the form of the bright spectral lines of iron, sodium, magnesium, calcium, silicon, and several less abundant metals. Collected samples of upper atmospheric dust have been captured in sounding-rocket experiments. They exhibit a porous structure with densities lying between 0.01 and 1 g/cm^3, suggestive of a stony composition containing the metallic silicates. The average particle weighs a tiny fraction of an ounce and is microscopic in size. Nearly all of this particulate matter seems to be of cometary origin; the remainder possibly comes from asteroidal dust.

Meteor Showers

At certain times of the year meteor showers appear. They consist of swarms of "shooting stars" darting out of a small area in the sky and persisting for hours to days. On such occasions the earth is passing near or through a large group of particles moving in parallel paths around the sun. Owing to perspective, their tracks seem to diverge out of a small spot in the sky called the *radiant*, similar to the way railroad tracks appear to diverge from a point near the horizon. The shower is named after the constellation in which the radiant appears. If the meteoroids are more or less evenly scattered throughout the orbit, the meteor shower occurs annually

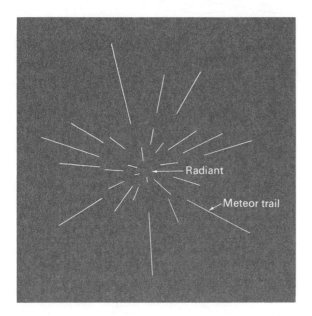

Figure 8.8   The effect of perspective causes the meteors to appear to diverge out of a small spot on the sky known as the the radiant.

when the earth cuts across the orbit; the Perseids are a prime example of such a shower. If the particles are concentrated in a small arc of the orbit, the shower occurs when the earth periodically intercepts the concentration; the Leonids constitute a swarm that appears most conspicuously at intervals of the orbital period of the swarm, 33 years. Some of the better-known showers are presented in Table 8.2.

Long ago astronomers found that some meteoroids travel in orbits very similar to those of certain comets, thus establishing a link between meteor showers and comets. The particle swarms are believed to be debris resulting from the evaporation and tidal disruption of old comets. On the night of November 13, 1833, the inhabitants of the southern part of the Atlantic seaboard witnessed an awe-inspiring sight. "Shooting stars" were observed plummeting down from the constellation of Leo at the rate of 100,000 or so per hour during a three-hour period. This spectacular display was produced when the earth encountered a swarm of meteors orbiting the sun in a period of 33 years and associated with the Temple comet (1866I) which has long since vanished. The succeeding meteoric displays of 1866, 1899, and 1932 grew progressively weaker until November 17, 1966, when a fairly good shower was observed in the southwestern part of the United States. Since the orbits of meteor swarms are easily perturbed by planetary attractions, it is not surprising that they disappear from the earth's neighborhood. Years later, through future planetary perturbations, they may be thrown into favorable positions relative to the earth, at which time they will reappear.

8.4   METEORITES

The falls of stones and irons from the heavens have been described many times in ancient chronicles. A Biblical reference appears in Joshua's account: ". . . the Lord cast down great stones from

Table 8.2 Certain Meteor Showers and Associated Comets

Name of Shower	Date of Maximum Display	Approximate Maximum Visual Hourly Count	Associated Comet	Period of Comet (years)
Lyrids	April 21	5	1861I	415
Eta Aquarids	May 4	5	Halley	76
Perseids	August 12	40	1862III	105
Draconids	October 10	Variable (low to high)	Giacobini-Zinner	6.6
Orionids	October 21	15	Halley	76
Taurids	November 1	5	Encke	3.3
Andromedids	November 14	low	Biela	6.5
Leonids	November 17	10	Temple	33
Ursids	December 22	15	Tuttle	13.6

heaven upon them unto Azekah, and they died." Primitive peoples are known to have worshiped these strange objects and to have fashioned tools of the iron specimens before iron ore was extracted from the ground. Nevertheless, the notion that stones falling from the sky came from outer space was considered preposterous even by astronomers as recently as two centuries ago. All doubt was finally dispelled in 1803 when, on April 26, a great shower of several thousand falling bodies was witnessed by many inhabitants in L'Aigle, France. The French Academy of Sciences immediately dispatched one of its members, who, after interrogating many witnesses, verified that the fall was indeed of extraterrestrial origin.

The majority of specimens have been discovered accidentally years after they have fallen. Out of some thirty-five different meteorite falls weighing over one ton, only four were actually seen descending. Very few of the hundreds of annual falls are ever recovered. Most of the meteorites land in the oceans or on unoccupied portions of the earth where it is unlikely their falls will be observed. There is no known record of any community having been destroyed or any individual positively having been killed by a falling meteorite, although there have been some close calls. Approximately 1,800 meteorite finds have been cataloged to date.

Meteorite Classification

The three general classes of meteorites, categorized according to their chemical and metallurgical properties, are:

1. Stones or *aerolites* composed chiefly of the silicates of iron, magnesium, aluminum, and other metals. These generally exhibit a relatively smooth brown or grayish fused crust indented with pits and cavities formed by passage through the air. Frequently embedded inside are small roundish globules called *chondrules*, which are composed of glassy minerals that could only have formed from hot molten droplets, presumably during an early stage in the development of the solar system.

2. Stony irons or *siderolites* consist of a matrix of stone and iron. Their brownish crust is sometimes broken by yellow olivine cavities. Inside, the iron may possess a veinlike or globular structure.

3. Irons or *siderites* are made up almost ex-

clusively of iron with varying proportions of nickel. These are easily identified by their characteristic pitted brownish exterior and large density. When cut, etched, and polished they usually exhibit a peculiar crystalline pattern known as Widmanstätten figures, whose likeness has no counterpart in terrestrially mined iron.

The largest known meteorite is an iron specimen still lying partly buried in the ground at Hoba in southwest Africa. Its date of fall is unknown. The meteorite is about $2\frac{1}{2}$ feet thick and measures 10 by 10 feet across the top; its estimated weight is 60 tons. A number of other irons weighing from 10 to 34 tons are on display in various museums throughout the world. The largest known stone, the Allende meteorite that fell in northern Mexico in February 1969, produced a brilliant luminous trail that separated into two pieces. Scattered fragments weighing a total of 3,000 pounds were picked up over an area of 100 square miles. The stones suffer the greatest amount of disruption because of their relative fragility compared to the irons.

Only an expert in the field of meteoritics can tell the difference between a stony meteorite and a terrestrial stone. Even though the great majority of the falls are stones, about 70 per cent of the recovered meteorites are irons because of their ease of identification. All the meteorites exhibit evidence of atmospheric ablation in their descent through the air, similar to the reentry of a manned space capsule. The rapid atmospheric passage aerodynamically shapes them, frequently into conical forms, as the fused material flows over the frontal surface. After the body has been slowed by its descent through the lower atmospheric layers, the material quickly hardens as the temperature falls before impact and it becomes cool enough to handle shortly after it hits the ground.

Radioactive dating of meteorites reveals ages in many instances that average in the tens of millions of years for the stones and 600 million years for the irons. These figures represent only the ages since the breakup of a larger mass. The oldest meteorite specimens are about 4.6 billion years old, which is also the accepted age of the earth. The chemical and mineralogical sequences existing among the different classes of meteorites strongly infer that they share a common heritage with the rest of the solar system.

Large Meteorite-Earth Encounters

Several dozen terrestrial craters formed in relatively recent times by meteorite strikes have been identified. At the conservative rate of one great collision in 10,000 years, at least 50,000 giant meteorites must have landed on earth during the past 500 million years. Many fossil craters may lie buried and unnoticed in the earth's crust. Most of them probably have been obliterated by the active weathering, erosion, and geological processes continually going on. One fossil crater in South Africa, known as the Vredevert Ring, is 130 miles in diameter and about 250 million years old. Near Winslow, Arizona, lies the Barringer Meteorite Crater, which was created by a 100,000-ton meteorite that must have devastated all plant and animal life within a large radius 20,000–50,000 years ago. The Barringer crater is 570 feet deep and is crowned with a raised rim four-fifths of a mile wide. More than thirty tons of shattered iron fragments have been picked up within a radius of four miles from the crater.

On February 12, 1947, a very large iron meteorite splintered over the region of Sikhote-Alin near Vladivostok, Russia. During its fall it produced a rain of fragments that littered an area of about two square miles. Some 200 pits and craters were formed and more than twenty-three tons of material were recovered.

At 7 A.M. on June 30, 1908, a tremendous fireball was observed flashing across the morning sky in

Figure 8.9   Meteorite specimens. (a) Polished section of the Allende meteorite shows fine-grained matrix with metal and most rounded chondrule inclusions. (b) Stone meteorite (carbonaceous chondrite), Allende, Mexico. It has a black fusion crust with lighter interior exposed where crust was probably removed on impact. (c) Polished and etched section of iron meteorite, Altonah, Utah. It displays the crystalline structure that is characteristic of iron meteorites. (d) Iron meteorite from Barringer Meteorite Crater has weathered and rusted appearance with cavities where material was removed probably while passing through the earth's atmosphere. (Courtesy of Smithsonian Institution, National Museum of Natural History.)

central Siberia. A great ball of flame brighter than the sun was seen to leap up from a forested region near the Tungusska River and was followed by an explosion powerful enough to level trees within a radius of thirty miles. The tremors were recorded on seismographs throughout Europe. The hurricane wind that was produced by the shockwave's after-effect tore off the roofs of houses hundreds of miles away and knocked down people and fences. Four hundred miles distant, horses could not stand on their feet. The London and Potsdam barographs recorded the atmospheric pressure waves from the blast twice around the world.

To this day no completely satisfactory explanation exists to account for an event of this magnitude—the greatest of its kind in modern times. The most common and possibly the most plausible suggestion is that a small comet of icy conglomerates struck the earth, dissipated its kinetic energy on the forest and the ground, and completely vaporized in the process.

Figure 8.10   Aerial view of Barringer Meteorite Crater. (Courtesy of F. Hatfield, Meteor Crater Museum.)

8 THE SOLAR SYSTEM: MINOR CONSTITUENTS

8.5 THE INTERPLANETARY MEDIUM

Interplanetary Dust

Although the space between the planets is a virtual vacuum by terrestrial standards, it is not completely devoid of gas and particles. The particulate matter is a mixture of particles blown out from the sun's atmosphere by the solar wind, micrometeoric debris scattered by comets, and granular powder strewn about from asteroid and meteorite collisions. Micrometeoroids greater than about one micron (one-millionth of a meter) in diameter tend to orbit the sun in inward-spiraling orbits; the smaller ones tend to be repelled by solar light pressure and solar wind.

Evidence of the existence of interplanetary dust comes from at least two sources. One is the well-known phenomenon known by the name of the *zodiacal light*. It is most easily observed in the northern hemisphere in the spring after sundown in the west and in fall before dawn in the east. It appears as a faint pyramidal band of light tapering upward from the eastward or western horizon along the line of the ecliptic. It has been photographed more clearly and in greater detail by astronauts in space as a tapering luminous streak extending for some distance on either side of the sun. The spectrum of zodiacal light is a faint replica of the solar spectrum, indicating that its source must be small particles lying in the plane of the earth's orbit and scattering the sunlight.

A very faint, slightly extended counterglow called the *gegenschein*, about ten degrees across, has been observed visually and has also been photographed opposite the sun's position in the night sky. It appears to come from a sparse concentration of particles optimally reflecting the sunlight toward the earth and positioned in this region possibly by the mutual gravitational attraction of the sun and the earth. More direct evidence of the existence of interplanetary dust is provided by space-vehicle experiments. Certain forms of penetration sensors are electronically arranged to count the number of micrometeorite impacts on exposed sensitized surfaces of the spacecraft. From the numbers of impacts registered it is estimated that the average distance between two interplanetary particles is about sixty-five feet in the space between the earth and the sun. In the vicinity of the planets, which act as a gravitational trap, the particle density is higher. In the asteroidal belt it must be still higher.

Interplanetary Gas

Most of the interplanetary matter exists in the gaseous state in the form of the solar wind. It consists of a continuous discharge of electrically charged gas particles, a plasma of protons and electrons, blasted outward from the sun's atmosphere at velocities of several hundred kilometers per second. During disturbed solar periods, the solar wind intensifies and becomes more gusty according to data telemetered from instrumented space probes. The effect of solar wind upon comets and its interaction with the earth's magnetic field was discussed previously in Sections 5.5 and 8.2.

8.6 ORIGIN OF THE SOLAR SYSTEM

Introduction

The circumstances surrounding the creation of the planetary system constitute one of the great unsolved enigmas in the annals of science. The theories that have been proposed to account for the origin of the solar system fall into two main categories: an accidental catastrophic event involving a fortuitous near-collisional encounter and a natural noncatastrophic alternative embodying a nebular condensation. Modifications and variations of the original ideas have been advanced to overcome the objections raised on various physical and dynamical grounds.

Before considering in historical perspective the suggested explanations of planetary genesis, let us examine the planetary arrangement within the solar system.

Architecture of the Solar System

It is unlikely that the design of the solar system could have materialized through some chance arrangement. Evidently, certain natural forces operated to create and shape the destiny of the solar system along the lines revealed in the following clues:

1. The planets are well isolated from each other; there is no bunching, as Bode's law shows (Section 8.1).

2. The orbits of the planets are nearly circular except for Mercury and Pluto, which may be a captured satellite of Neptune.

3. The orbits of the planets lie nearly in the same plane (Mercury and Pluto again excepted).

4. The planets revolve around the sun in the same direction that the sun rotates (from west to east).

5. With the exception of Venus and Uranus, the planets rotate around their axes in the same direction that the sun turns.

6. The terrestrial planets have high densities, moderate or no atmospheres, slower rotation, and few or no satellites; with the exception of Pluto they occupy the inner regions of the solar system.

7. The giant planets have low densities, thick atmospheres, many satellites, and rapid rotation; they occupy the outer regions of the solar system.

8. With some exceptions, the satellites revolve around their primaries in the same direction as their primaries.

Original Nebular Hypothesis

In 1755 the German philosopher Immanuel Kant proposed a logical interpretation of planetary creation by suggesting that the solar system was formed out of a huge, rotating, gaseous nebula undergoing slow contraction and condensation. In 1796 the celebrated French mathematical astronomer P. S. Laplace enlarged on this concept scientifically. It is known as the *nebular hypothesis*. Laplace theorized that as the slowly rotating large solar nebula contracted it was forced, by virtue of its increased rate of rotation, to flatten out and to spill material into an equatorial ring. Involved is the well-known principle of *conservation of angular momentum*, which requires a spinning body to rotate faster as its dimensions shrink. The angular momentum of a rotating body, which is a measure of its "quantity of rotation," remains unaltered internally. If the radius decreases, the velocity must increase to compensate for the reduction in radius in order to preserve the constancy of angular momentum. (This is what we observe when a spinning ice skater rotates faster as the outstretched arms are brought close to the body.) In the Laplacian version, when the centrifugal force acting on the outer rotating edge of the solar nebula exceeded the inward gravitational force of the nebular mass, a ring of gaseous matter was expelled, eventually coalescing into a planet. The process repeated itself, giving rise to a series of concentric rings which formed into the planets, while the main central portion condensed to become the sun. It is supposed that the satellite systems could have materialized within the ring structure prior to final development of the planets and that the asteroids were the shattered remains of a disrupted ring. The theory suffers from two principal defects. First, 98 per cent of the angular momentum resides in the orbital motions of the planets and there is no clear-cut mechanism by which the central mass could have transferred this amount of angular momentum to the planets. Second, a gaseous ring of this type would tend to disperse into space rather than pull itself together gravitationally to form a planet.

Encounter Theories

At the beginning of this century attempts to reconcile the nebular hypothesis with physical principles were temporarily abandoned. A different approach, the so-called *encounter theory*, was first speculated upon by the French naturalist Georges L. L. Buffon in 1745. It was revived and mathematically reinforced during the early part of this century by J. Jeans and H. Jeffreys in England and in a slightly different version by T. C. Chamberlin and F. R. Moulton in the United States. It was hypothesized that tidal gaseous filaments were pulled out of the sun by the sideswiping action of a passing star. The stellar visitor imparted a curved lateral motion to the strung-out hot material that later fragmented and solidified into planetesimals that coalesced into the planets by collisional accretion. This action accounts for the common direction of orbital motion of the planets and of the sun's rotation as well as for the planets' circular and nearly coplanar orbits. The planetesimal theory, however, also has serious failings. The ejected planetary material could not have acquired sufficient angular momentum nor would the hot gas have condensed into planets. Besides, the probability of a near encounter in our region of the Galaxy is vanishingly small, less than one in many millions.

Protoplanet Theory

By mid-century astronomers once more turned their attention to possible improvements in the nebular hypothesis. A new element was now introduced in the form of a small amount of dust in the cool gaseous nebula, thereby providing nuclei for the condensation of gas into larger aggregates which could accrete and solidify into the embryo planets.

(The presence of dust particles in the interstellar gas clouds out of which the stars are formed has been known for many years.) This modern version of the nebular hypothesis is called the *protoplanet hypothesis*. It was first formulated by C. F. von Weizsacker in 1945, then extended and modified by G. P. Kuiper and others in the years that followed.

It begins with a cool, rarefied, dusty cloud of gas possessing some degree of internal motion a fraction of a light-year in diameter. Random turbulent motions within the cloud induced instabilities leading to gravitational collapse. As the cool cloud contracted, its rotation increased and it began to flatten and shed material into its equatorial plane. With the rise in temperature due to compression of the solar nebula, the increased gas pressure halted further collapse. By this time the flattened outer disk extended some 30 A.U. from the main central bulge, the forming protosun, where most of the material was concentrated.

Gravitational effects caused the inner portions of the equatorial disk to rotate more rapidly than the outer parts. This created gravitational instabilities in the form of swirls and eddies which dissolved and reformed depending on their densities and on the strength of the solar tidal disruptive force. Eventually, some inchoate churning masses of gas and dust of sufficiently high density could withstand the disruptive forces and acquire additional material by accretion. Calculations indicate that the swirling eddies could coagulate into the protoplanets that would be spaced at discrete distances from each other. The reduced temperatures in the outer region of the disk would permit large quantities of hydrogen, helium, ammonia, methane, and water to condense and accumulate, thus accounting for the low densities of the Jovian planets. At distances beyond Neptune the quantity of nebular gas would be too sparse for planetary formation. Within the inner regions the higher temperatures of the contracting

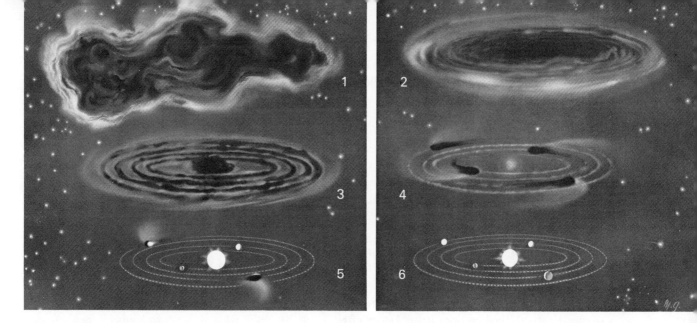

Figure 8.11 Birth of the solar system. Theoretical development of a family of planets and a central star from a cloud of interstellar gases is shown in this sequence. From the Life Nature Library book, The Universe, *published by Time-Life books. Drawing by Matt Greene.*

protosun would vaporize the lighter and more vola-tile material on the close-in terrestrial protoplanets. The protosatellites of the outer planets were pre-sumably formed on a miniature scale out of the left-over condensing planetary material. The asteroids and meteorites may have resulted from the failure of a small protoplanet to accrete because of the per-turbative tidal influence of Jupiter. The comets, still retaining their primordial ices, represent a fossil relic of the outlying primordial matter that constituted the original solar nebula.

Continued shrinkage of the primitive sun over a period of millions of years raised the sun's internal temperature from a few tens of thousands of degrees to several million degrees absolute when the first stages of nuclear burning were initiated. At this juncture the loss of the primordial gases by the terrestrial planets as a result of the rise in solar temperature coupled with the strong solar wind was severe compared to that suffered by the major

planets. The powerful tidal pull of the sun on the protoplanets during their early formative stage forced them to rotate originally in the same period that they revolved around the sun. As contraction of the protoplanets proceeded, their rotation increased sufficiently to become uncoupled from the sun. The original rotations of Mercury and Venus have subse-quently been modified.

The weakest link in the protoplanet hypothesis still remains the mode of transfer of angular momen-tum from the sun to the planets. If the angular momentum of the planets could somehow be re-turned to the sun, its present slow rotation of 2 km/sec would be increased to about 100 km/sec. As stars go, the sun is considered a "slow" rotator, presumably because of its loss of rotational energy to the planets during the period of planetary formation. A number of theorists have invoked the braking action of magnetohydrodynamic forces acting upon the sun through the interaction of the solar magnetic field with the ionized nebular gas in the disk. It is postulated that the magnetic lines of force spiraling outward from the rotating sun into the surrounding solar nebula would have exercised a magnetic drag on the spinning sun and served as conduits for transferring the angular momentum to the planetary discoid.

We have advanced a small part of the way toward an ultimate understanding of the origin of the solar system. Further progress will materialize from the unifying efforts of the geologists, mineralogists, and physicists engaged in the study of meteorites and lunar rock samples together with the astronomers who are developing improved theories on the formation of the stars. The genesis of a planetary system throughout space is believed to be the outgrowth of a frequent natural phenomenon that develops after an interstellar cloud has begun to contract into cool, globular condensations on their way to becoming stars. In recent years astronomers have discovered small, cool, dust envelopes around infrared stars within the interstellar clouds of the Milky Way. It is conceivable that some of these objects may be in the early stages of nebular condensation visualized in the protoplanet theory. The catastrophic theory as advocated in the planetesimal theory would account for no more than a few planetary systems in the Galaxy.

REVIEW QUESTIONS

1. What prompted the late eighteenth-century astronomers to search for a missing planet between Mars and Jupiter?

2. How are asteroids discovered? How many have we found so far? How big are they? How many more might there be? Why haven't the rest been discovered?

3. If Halley did not discover the comet bearing his name, why is it called Halley's comet?

4. What are the distinguishing orbital and brightness differences between the short-period and long-period comets?

5. Describe the change in the general appearance of a large comet as it approaches and recedes from the sun as viewed from the earth.

6. What is the present-day accepted version of the physical and chemical structure of the comets' three main components (nucleus, coma, and tail)?

7. Where do comets come from? How do we know that they belong to the solar system? Explain how it is possible for a comet to be forced into a hyperbolic orbit.

8. Describe what is likely to happen when a comet moving in a far-ranging orbit around the sun passes close to Jupiter.

9. If you were with a friend one night and both of you saw a "shooting star," how would you explain what actually happened to your friend, who has never taken a course in astronomy?

10. What is the distinction between (a) meteoroids; (b) meteors; (c) bolides; (d) micrometeorites; (e) meteorites?

11. How did astronomers prove that there was a physical connection between certain comets and meteor swarms?

12. Describe the physical structure and composition of the three classes of meteorites.

13. What evidence do we have that there have been actual collisions between the earth and large meteorites?

14. Why do we believe that the solar system is the product of a natural physical development and not the result of a chance encounter of the sun with another star?

15. Describe in general terms the various catastrophic and noncatastrophic theories of the origin of the solar system.

SELECTED READINGS

Hawkins, G. S., *Meteors and Comets*, McGraw-Hill, 1964.

Heide, F., *Meteorites*, University of Chicago Press, 1964.

Knight, D. C., *Meteors and Meteorites*, Watts, 1969.

Ley, W., *Visitors from Afar: The Comets*, McGraw-Hill, 1969.

McCall, G. J., *Meteorites and Their Origins*, Halstead, New York, 1973.

Page, T., and L. W. Page, eds., *Origin of the Solar System*, Macmillan, 1966.

Richardson, R. S., *Getting Acquainted with Comets*, McGraw-Hill, 1969.

Roth, G. D., *The System of Minor Planets*, Van Nostrand, 1962.

Watson, F. G., *Between the Planets*, Harvard University Press, 1956.

Solar eclipse of November 12, 1966, photographed at Pulcayo, Bolivia (altitude 13,000 feet). The overexposed image of Venus is at the bottom. (Courtesy of High Altitude Observatory, Colorado.)

OUR CLOSEST STAR:
THE SUN

Glorious the sun in mid-career;
Glorious th' assembled fires appear.

Christopher Smart (1722–1771),
Song to David

The sun's huge output of energy is supplied by the process of controlled thermonuclear fusion. Every second within the sun's superhot core 655 million tons of hydrogen are fused at a central temperature of about 13 million degrees absolute into 650 million tons of helium and 5 million tons of matter which is converted into energy and radiated into space. The piddling fraction of solar energy that the earth intercepts is enough to warm our planet and to sustain life. At present-day electric power rates, the earth's solar power bill amounts to $2.4 billion each second.

To investigate the sun's working conditions, we must employ telescopes appropriate to the spectral range under study (x-ray, ultraviolet, optical, and radio telescopes). The observational data provide a key to the proper understanding of the physical processes associated with various solar activities. Solar phenomena are constantly monitored from space observatories and probes as well as from ground stations through detailed inspection of normal and eruptive solar features and their radiated energy. This involves research on the solar atmosphere (the photosphere, chromosphere, and corona), sunspots, plages, flares, and the solar wind. The physical information derived from analysis of the solar spectrum yields important data about the sun's chemical composition, its magnetic activities, sunspot behavior, solar rotation, and atmospheric temperatures, densities, and pressures.

Definite correlations exist between the eleven-year sunspot cycle and the amount of solar ultraviolet radiation, the frequency of auroral displays, the changes in the earth's ionosphere, and the variations in the earth's surface magnetism. The aftereffects of disturbed solar conditions—flares, plages, and large sunspot groups—upon the terrestrial environment are being studied on a global scale at solar-monitoring observatories. Solar-terrestrial relationships, which involve many complex factors, are only partially understood at the present time.

9.1 RADIANT ENERGY OF THE SUN

Amount of Solar Energy

The sun is a gaseous, self-regulating, thermonuclear power plant equal in volume to $1\frac{1}{3}$ million earths. It pours forth energy into space in all directions at the stupendous rate of 380 trillion trillion watts or 3.8×10^{33} erg/sec.[1] (The erg is the scientific unit of energy. A two-gram caterpillar crawling at a rate of one centimeter per second exerts one erg of kinetic energy, a very small amount of energy by human standards.) The value of the solar energy was originally obtained by employing a highly efficient absorbing device called a *pyrheliometer*. It enables the astronomer to determine the amount of solar radiation that arrives over one square centimeter of the earth's surface within a certain interval of time in a direction perpendicular to the sun at the earth's mean distance. When appropriately corrected for atmospheric absorption, this quantity becomes the *solar constant* and is equal to two calories per square centimeter per minute or 1.39×10^6 erg/cm^2/sec. This value has been confirmed by sounding-rocket experiments which avoid the effects of atmospheric solar absorption.

The total energy emitted by the sun is equal to 1.39×10^6 erg/cm^2/sec multiplied by the number of square centimeters (2.73×10^{27} cm^2) on a spherical surface whose radius is the earth's mean distance from the sun. Since this represents the sun's radiation emitted in all directions at the earth's distance, it is equivalent to the energy radiated from the sun's surface. The total solar radiation therefore is $1.39 \times 10^6 \times 2.73 \times 10^{27} = 3.8 \times 10^{33}$ erg/sec, the figure

---

[1]One watt = 10^7 erg/sec = 0.24 calorie/sec.

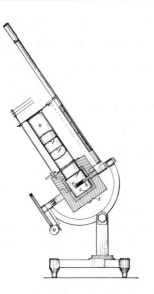

Figure 9.1   Pyrheliometer. A blackened, silvered disk inside the mercury-filled container at the bottom of the tube absorbs the solar rays. The rise in temperature of the liquid in a certain time interval is measured by a right-angled thermometer whose bulb is inserted in the mercury. (Courtesy of C. G. Abbot, The Sun, Appleton, New York, 1929.)

quoted in the second sentence of the preceding paragraph. Less than one-half of one-billionth of the sun's production is intercepted by the earth, but it is sufficient to warm our planet and to sustain life. The annual amount of power that man now generates on earth is equivalent to the amount that the earth receives from the sun in about twenty minutes.

Source of Solar Energy

The sun's generation of energy comes from the thermonuclear conversion of hydrogen to helium at a central temperature measured in millions of degrees. Every second within the sun's superhot inner core, a mass of 655 million tons of hydrogen is transformed into 650 million tons of helium and 5 million tons of mass-converted energy. The emergent radiation is equivalent to the production figure, 3.8×10^{33} erg/sec, mentioned earlier. In the core of the sun the energy derived from the fusion of hydrogen to helium consists of high-powered radiation mostly in the form of x-rays. By the time this flood of energy has worked its way through the maze of solar material to the surface after countless years of zigzag buffeting, it is largely degraded into the visible sunlight that we observe. Since the energy is radiated away from the surface at the same rate that it is being created, the sun is in effect a self-controlled fusion reactor. The hydrogen bomb is an example of an uncontrolled fusion process.

The Sun's Future

Present calculations indicate that the sun stands about midway in its lifespan and in its present mode of energy production. Since its inception as a thermonuclear generator, the sun has lost only about one-twentieth of its original mass of hydrogen during its five billion years of existence. In another five billion years or so, the hydrogen fuel within the central core will have been expended. Thereafter the sun will automatically adjust itself to the new working conditions by gravitational contraction of the burned-out hydrogen core now filled with deadweight helium. Compression will raise the internal temperature sufficiently to fuse the unused hydrogen into helium outside the core. As this process continues to envelop the layers closer to the sun's surface within a hundred million years, the sun will expand from a yellow star with its present dimensions to a giant red star with increased luminosity. The expanded sun may engulf the planets Mercury and Venus and seal the fate of life on the earth as its surface becomes too hot and its oceans evaporate. When the gravitationally contracting core reaches a central temperature of around 100 million degrees absolute, its accumulated helium will be synthesized into more complex atoms. The sun will subsequently undergo further changes in size and luminosity as more of its heavier-than-hydrogen nuclear fuel is consumed. The time will come when all the available nuclear fuel will be exhausted and thermonuclear reactions will cease, possibly within about seven billion years from now. The sun will gravitationally collapse into a small anemic star called a white dwarf, eking out a bare existence as a dying star. Long before this happens the earth, it is forecast, will experience a runaway greenhouse effect that will cause it to become enveloped in a highly pressurized steam bath, snuffing out all life that may have survived. Eventually, there will be no dark sky filled with bright stars because they too will have burned themselves out and vanished into faint obscurity as white dwarfs or rarer neutron stars. Only a scattering of long-lived faint red dwarfs will dominate the dark sky.

9.2 SOLAR STATISTICS

The following list summarizes pertinent information relating to the sun:

Mean distance from earth: 92,956,000 miles (149,598,000 km)

Maximum distance from earth: 94,506,000 miles (152,086,000 km)

Minimum distance from earth: 91,406,000 miles (147,097,000 km)

Diameter: 865,000 miles (1,391,000 km)

Mass: 1.99×10^{33} grams

Average density: 1.41 g/cm^3

Exposed portion of sun: photosphere—lowest visible layer; chromosphere—inner atmosphere; corona—outer atmosphere

Surface temperature: $5,760°K$ ($10,800°F$)

Total radiation: 3.8×10^{33} erg/sec

Color: yellow

Spectral class: G2 main sequence (G2V)

Angle between sun's equator and ecliptic: $7.2°$

Rotation: 25 days at equator; 35 days at poles

Chemical composition: about $\frac{9}{10}$ hydrogen; $\frac{1}{10}$ helium; small percentage of heavier elements

The Astronomical Unit

The mean distance of the earth from the sun is known as the *astronomical unit* (92,956,000 miles or 149,598,000 kilometers). It is one of the most important quantities in astronomy because it serves as the "yardstick" by which we measure the distances to the stars. Astronomers have employed several independent ways of determining the value of the astronomical unit. The more recent and most accurate methods use a radio beacon or other transmitting equipment aboard a sun-orbiting spacecraft to precisely track the vehicle. From its received signals and known space trajectory, the value of the astronomical unit can be derived by the methods of celestial mechanics. The other modern method uses radar to time the round trip of a pulsed signal reflected from Venus and thus to find its distance from the earth in miles. This information combined with the planet's known distance in astronomical units leads to the evaluation of the astronomical unit.

Solar Diameter, Mass, and Density

The linear diameter of the sun is obtained from its observed angular diameter of 0.533 degrees and the known distance by the same principle that was used in deriving the moon's diameter (Section 6.4). The computed value of the sun's diameter is 865,000 miles. The mass of the sun is 1.99×10^{33} grams, which is one-third million times greater than the mass of the earth.

The *solar mass* may be derived by applying Newton's modification of Kepler's third law of planetary motion to the earth and the sun (Section 2.7):

$$m_{\odot} + m_E = \frac{4\pi^2 d^3}{G \cdot P^2}$$

where $m_{\odot}$ = mass of sun; m_E = mass of earth; d = earth's mean distance from sun = 1.496×10^{13} centimeters; P = earth's period of revolution around the sun = 3.156×10^7 seconds; and G = gravitational constant = 6.667×10^{-8} cm^3/g · sec^2. On substituting the given figures, the result is $m_{\odot}$ = 1.99×10^{33} grams. (The earth's mass is insignificant and may be neglected.)

The average or *mean density* of the sun is found in the usual way: mass divided by volume. Hence

$$\text{mean density} = \frac{1.99 \times 10^{33} \text{ g}}{1.41 \times 10^{33} \text{ cm}^3} = 1.41 \text{ g/cm}^3$$

Solar Temperature

The sun's surface temperature, derived by several methods, averages out at 5,760°K. It is found with the aid of the radiation laws pertaining to an ideal radiator, which is very nearly the way the sun behaves. Such a body, called a *blackbody*, can absorb all the electromagnetic energy incident on it and reemit it at 100 per cent efficiency.

One of the three mathematical variants of expressing the blackbody radiation is called the *Stefan-Boltzmann law*. This law states that the radiation emitted from each square centimeter of the surface in one second of time is proportional to the fourth power of the temperature. The formula is:

$$E = 5.67 \times 10^{-5} \, T^4$$

where E = radiation in erg/cm^2/sec and T = temperature in degrees Kelvin. Dividing the total output of the solar energy (3.8×10^{33} erg/sec) by the sun's surface area (6.1×10^{22} cm^2) gives $E = 6.23 \times 10^{10}$ erg/cm^2/sec. Hence the effective surface temperature is:

$$T = \left(\frac{6.23 \times 10^{10}}{5.67 \times 10^{-5}}\right)^{\frac{1}{4}} = 5{,}750°K$$

Since the temperature varies somewhat over the solar disk and also at different visible depths, the effective temperature given by the Stefan-Boltzmann law may be regarded as a mean value over the entire solar disk. It will differ slightly from the values derived by the other methods.

One of the alternative methods utilizes *Wien's displacement law*, which is mathematically expressed as:

$$T = \frac{2.9 \times 10^7}{\lambda_{max}}$$

where λ_{max} is the wavelength in angstroms at which the radiation reaches its peak value. The observed peak value of the solar radiation occurs at 4,700 angstroms. Substituting λ_{max} in the foregoing formula gives $T = 6{,}200°K$.

The third method is based on *Planck's radiation law* for a blackbody. According to Planck's formula (which is too complex to present here), the theoretical energy distribution of a blackbody source differs for various temperatures as shown in Figure 9.2. The measured solar spectral intensities in the various wavelengths are matched against the Planck blackbody temperature curves for different temperatures. The best fit of the solar spectral-intensity values occurs at a temperature of 6,000°K.

Solar Rotation

The sun does not rotate as a solid body. The rotation period progressively increases from 25 days at the solar equator to nearly 35 days at the poles. This phenomenon, known as *differential rotation*, is believed to result from the influence of subsurface convection currents upon solar rotation. The observed movement, due to the sun's rotation, of the

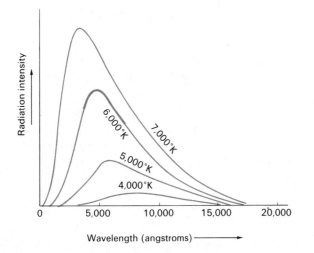

Figure 9.2 *Blackbody energy curves. The heavy line in the 6,000 K curve represents the observed distribution of energy in the visible portion of the solar spectrum. As the temperature increases, the peak radiation shifts toward the shorter wavelengths. This explains why the color of a glowing solid changes through the spectral colors from red to blue as its temperature rises. The maximum energy in the solar spectrum occurs in the yellow-green spectral region.*

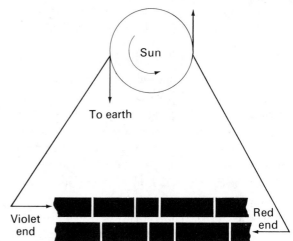

Figure 9.3 *Doppler shifts of opposite limbs at the solar equator. Displacement between limbs is 4 km/sec or 2 km/sec in relation to the sun's center.*

sunspots across the solar disk can be measured to find the length of time for the sun to complete one rotation on its axis. Another method that is applicable to all solar latitudes (sunspots rarely appear beyond forty degrees on either side of the solar equator) utilizes the Doppler frequency shift of the spectral lines from opposite limbs of the sun (Figure 9.3). Since the eastern edge of the sun rotates toward the earth and the western edge away from the earth, the measured difference in the Doppler wavelength displacement between the two limbs yields the relative velocity

between the opposite limbs. The measured limb velocity relative to the sun's center is 2 km/sec at the solar equator. Dividing the distance traveled in one rotation—that is, the solar circumference—by the velocity gives the time of one complete rotation at the equator. Hence

$$\text{Period of rotation} = \frac{2\pi \times \text{radius}}{\text{velocity}}$$

$$= \frac{2 \times 3.14 \times 6.96 \times 10^5 \text{ km}}{2 \text{ km/sec}}$$

$$= 25 \text{ days}$$

Solar Atmosphere

The ordinary direct telescopic view of the solar disk is that of the *photosphere*, marked here and there by the sunspots. This is the bottom level of the sun's

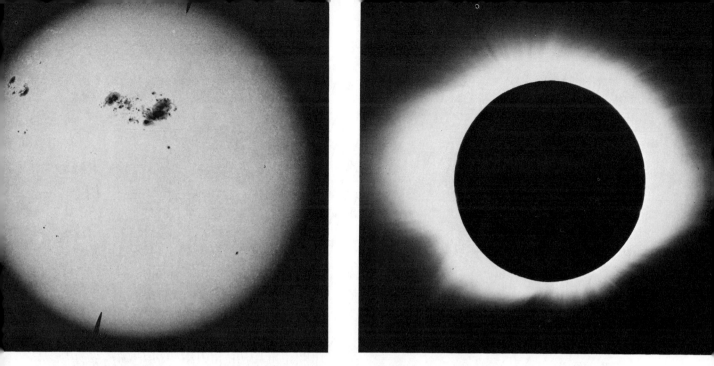

Figure 9.4   The sun: (a) *direct view;* (b) *eclipsed view. (Courtesy of Hale Observatory and Lick Observatory, respectively.)*

atmosphere. Lying above it is a well-defined, transparent, tenuous layer called the *chromosphere*, several thousand miles deep. This is topped by a rarefied superstratum, the *corona*, extending for millions of miles from the sun. Though these regions are differentiated by their differing physical properties, their boundaries are not sharply defined observationally; one region gradually merges into the other.

Our normal line of sight passes through the transparent gases of the corona, the chromosphere, and terminates some 200 miles into the photosphere before the photospheric gas becomes opaque. Below this level the energy of the outgoing solar radiation is sufficiently absorbed to prevent us from seeing farther into the sun's gaseous substrata. The light from the chromosphere and the corona beyond the solar limb is too weak to be seen against the bright glare of the sky adjacent to the sun. They become visible during a total eclipse of the sun when the moon

covers the solar disk. A detailed treatment of the solar atmosphere follows the discussion of the solar spectrum in the next section.

9.3   THE SOLAR SPECTRUM

Fraunhofer Spectrum

The spectrum of the visible solar disk displays a continuous band of colors from red to violet crossed by large numbers of dark lines. Nearly 600 of the most prominent lines were first mapped in 1814 by the German optical expert J. von Fraunhofer. He designated by letters the strongest absorption lines, beginning with A in the red and ending with K in the violet. As interpreted according to the third law of spectrum analysis (Section 4.3), the continuous radiation from the solar interior through the lower photospheric layers is absorbed in certain wavelengths by the different atoms in the upper portions

Figure 9.5   Layers of the sun's atmosphere. (From "Hot Spots in the Atmosphere of the Sun" by Harold Zirin. Copyright ©
1958 by Scientific American, Inc. All rights reserved.)

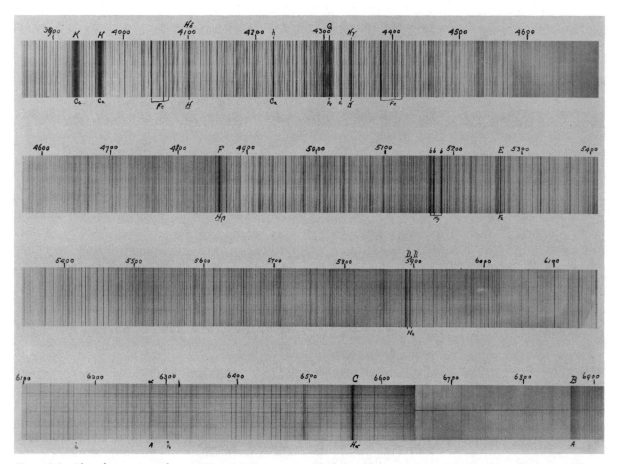

Figure 9.6 The solar spectrum from 3,900 to 6,900 angstroms. The lettered lines are those originally assigned by Fraunhofer. The chemical identification of several lines is shown. (Courtesy of Hale Observatories.)

of the photosphere and the adjoining chromosphere. In the uninterrupted bright regions, between the lines, the continuous radiation passes freely outward into space.

Ultraviolet and X-Ray Extensions

The major portion of the sun's radiation lies in the visible region where there is a good optical window in the earth's atmosphere. Scientists in recent years have employed instrument-borne sounding rockets and earth-orbiting satellites to explore the hitherto inaccessible ultraviolet and x-ray regions by means of sensitive detectors, narrow passband photography, and spectrum photography. The far ultraviolet spectrum shows a weak continuous background spectrum on which are superimposed many bright lines, mostly due to ionized atoms present in the hotter regions of the chromosphere. The solar x-ray emission in the still shorter wavelengths corresponds to a temperature of several hundred thousand degrees absolute, most of which originates in the coronal layers. The temperature of the solar gases

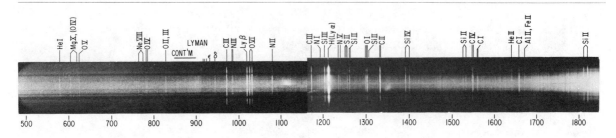

Figure 9.7   The ultraviolet spectrum of the sun showing bright lines, photographed from an Aerobee-Hi rocket on March 13, 1959. I indicates a neutral atom; II an atom that has lost one electron; III an atom that has lost two electrons and so forth. The horizontal scale is in angstroms. (Courtesy of Naval Research Laboratory.)

rises precipitously beyond the first several thousand miles above the sun's photosphere to over one million degrees absolute in the solar corona. The cause of this seemingly paradoxical behavior is dealt with in Section 9.7.

Infrared Extensions

In the long-wavelength region beyond the red end of the visible spectral region, there exist some partial atmospheric windows that permit investigation of the solar spectrum toward the microwave region. The deep infrared regions have been explored with sensitive heat-detection instrumentation in high-flying aircraft. Extraterrestrial measurement will be required to fully exploit the complete infrared spectral range down to the millimeter wavelengths.

The Radio Spectrum

From the millimeter wavelengths to the meter wavelengths a wide atmospheric window exists for radio observations. The quiet, undisturbed sun normally emits thermal (blackbody) radiation from the microwave region of about one centimeter to the long-wavelength region of about twenty meters. The solar atmospheric level at which energy is emitted

at the radio wavelengths is critically dependent on the density of the electrons and the wavelength of the radiation. The shortest waves (millimeters) originate in the cooler photospheric layer, the medium waves (centimeters) in the hotter chromosphere, and the longest waves (meters) in the still hotter coronal regions.

Three additional kinds of radio emission, identified as nonthermal in origin, have been observed whenever the sun is disturbed: (1) the very intense *radio bursts* lasting about a minute and radiating over many wavelengths, which are produced by the ejection of plasma (a high-energy mixture of charged particles) from the highly disturbed, active regions surrounding the sunspot groups; (2) long-lasting (hours to days) *noise storms* in the one- to ten-meter wavelengths, which are believed to originate from the interactions between magnetically trapped particles and moving plasma waves; (3) the centimeter-wavelength *slowly varying component*, partly thermal in origin and sometimes lasting for weeks, which is connected with the sunspot activity in the vicinity of the surrounding bright areas known as *plages*.

The Sun's Chemical Composition

Precise measurements of the wavelengths of the

absorption lines in the solar spectrum have enabled astronomers to identify nearly seventy elements out of the ninety-two natural elements, and almost twenty compounds. The identifications are based on laboratory analysis of the spectra of the elements. The missing elements, mostly the heavier ones, are probably present but their gases do not exist in sufficient abundance to be detected spectroscopically, or their spectral lines in the nonvisible regions have not yet been thoroughly explored. Measurements of the line blackness and width, coupled with theoretical knowledge of the probability that an atom will absorb radiation at the wavelength in question at a specified temperature, lead to an estimate of the relative abundances of the various elements present in the sun's atmosphere. It is found that, by number, hydrogen accounts for about 90 per cent, helium 9.9 per cent, and the remaining elements, 0.1 per cent. By weight, the respective figures are 70 per cent, 28 per cent, and 2 per cent.

9.4   THE PHOTOSPHERE

Observing the Photosphere

The photosphere is most conveniently studied by projecting the solar image on an observing screen by means of a fixed long-focus telescope. The largest solar telescope, located at the Kitt Peak National Observatory in Arizona, employs a 60-inch parabolic mirror with a focal length of 300 feet. It is housed in a partly submerged concrete tube structure that is inclined at 32 degrees to the horizontal in line with the earth's axis. A rotating flat mirror mounted at the top of the building tracks the sun across the sky. From this mirror the sunlight is directed by optical means to the long-focus parabolic mirror at the bottom of the 500-foot tube, then back to an underground observing room about half-way down the tube. The projected image of the sun's disk is nearly three feet in diameter. The Mt. Wilson

Observatory has two vertically mounted tower telescopes (seen in the left of the photograph in Figure 3.24). The taller 150-foot tower has an 80-foot well from which the sunlight is returned by means of a reflection grating to form a spectrum at the observing platform, as shown in Figure 9.8.

Photospheric Features

In ground-based photographs a number of details are clearly visible: the general granular appearance of the solar disk; the conspicuous sunspots; the darkening at the limb where the contrast is sufficiently heightened to permit viewing of the bright elevated patches called *faculae* (see Figure 9.4*a*). The limb of the sun appears darker than at the center because the tangentially viewed light from the edge of the sun comes from higher and cooler layers in the photosphere where the temperature is lower.

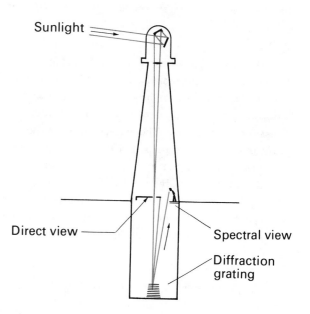

Figure 9.8   Optical path of sunlight in tower telescope.

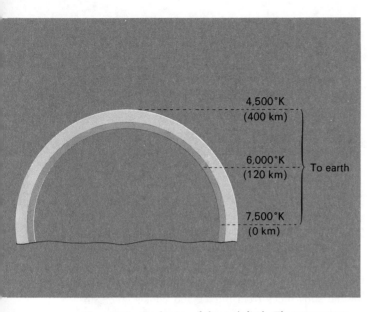

Figure 9.9   Darkening of the sun's limb. The temperature variation with depth of the photosphere is indicated. The number in parentheses is the height above the lowest level from which solar radiation reaches the earth.

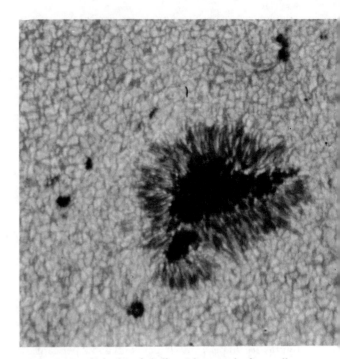

Figure 9.10   High-altitude balloon photograph of a small portion of the sun's photosphere. (Courtesy of Princeton University Observatory.)

The clearest pictures of the solar surface have been obtained with an air-borne reflecting telescope mounted in a balloon at heights of around sixteen miles where the finer details are not blurred by atmospheric turbulence. The high-resolution balloon photographs reveal a potpourri of bright granules averaging several hundred miles in diameter with dark interstices that give the surface its characteristic salt-and-pepper appearance. Photographic sequences show that the granules form, disappear, and reform in cycles lasting about eight minutes.

Physical Processes

The photosphere is in reality a bubbly, frothing sea of ascending bright and descending dark convection cells. The spectral lines of the bright granules shift to the violet while those of the inter-granular darker regions shift to the red at velocities under one mile per second. The observed Doppler shifts are in accordance with the interpretation that the bright granules are the tops of hot, rising gas currents that expand and cool to form the cooler, sinking gas currents of the darker interstices. More extensive Doppler studies over larger areas reveal the existence of supergranulation systems. These complex structures consist of rising and falling gas columns averaging 20,000 miles in diameter rhythmically pulsing within a period of several minutes. The pressure and density of the photosphere are obtained from the analysis of the widths and strengths of the absorption lines in combination with the photospheric temperature data. The average pressure of the hot photospheric gases is a few per cent of the earth's sea-level atmospheric pressure; the average photospheric density is about one ten-thousandth of the density of air at the earth's surface.

9.5 SUNSPOTS

Description

Sunspots are the most conspicuous features observed on the solar disk. Their existence was known centuries before the invention of the telescope. A typical sunspot possesses a cell-like structure consisting of a dark center called the *umbra* surrounded by a grayish filamentary region called the *penumbra*. The sunspot is intrinsically very bright; its umbral temperature is around 4,500°K. At this lower temperature the sunspot spectrum contains the molecular bands of additional compounds that are normally dissociated in the surrounding hotter photospheric regions. The umbra appears dark because it is viewed against an even brighter photospheric background whose temperature is 1,500°K higher.

Sunspot Formation

Sunspots initially develop within a matter of hours as small pores in the disturbed photosphere. They grow rapidly in size and generally aggregate into twin clusters of related groups containing an assortment of spots varying in diameter by thousands of miles. Frequently, one large dominating spot appears in each group. A typical spot builds up to a maximum diameter of 30,000 miles in a week or so, followed by a slower decline. The individual spots undergo slowly changing patterns from day to day, maintaining their cleavage into two separate groups almost to the end. The largest sunspot groups may cover an area extending over 200,000 miles (about one-fifth of a solar diameter). Sometimes they persist for several months.

The Sunspot Cycle

More than a century ago a German amateur astronomer named S. H. Schwabe discovered, over

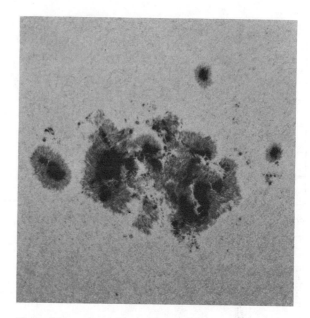

Figure 9.11 Large sunspot group of May 17, 1951. (Courtesy of Hale Observatories.)

an observing period covering twenty years, that the sunspots come and go in a cycle of about eleven years. The plotted sunspot number in Figure 9.12 is based on a formula that takes into consideration both the number of sunspot groups and the total number of individual spots. From the plot in the figure it is seen that the successive maxima are not of the same height and the interval between the peaks and troughs is not constant. In general, the rise toward the maximum has averaged 4.1 years while the decline toward the minimum has averaged 6.7 years. The intervals between maxima have varied from about 7.5 to seventeen years and between minima from 8.5 to fourteen years. The eleven-year period is an approximate mean value. As the eleven-year cycle progresses, the spots form closer to the equator with each succeeding year as shown in Figure 9.13. A rash of sunspots appearing in the

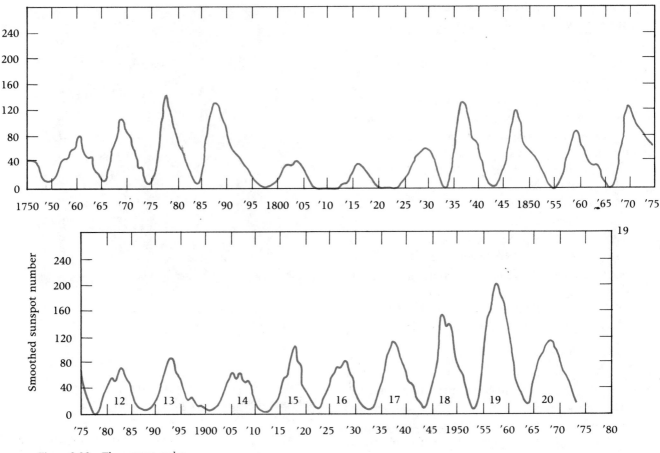

Figure 9.12   The sunspot cycles.

higher latitudes around 35°N or south heralds the beginning of a new cycle as the spots of the preceding cycle make their last stand near the solar equator.

Solar Magnetic Fields

The sunspots are the centers of intense magnetic fields. The swirls observed in the sunspot regions are caused by the gas currents moving along the curved magnetic lines of force surrounding the spot area. When light from a radiating source producing a line spectrum passes through a magnetic field, the lines split into two or more polarized components. The light within them vibrates in a straight line (linear polarization) or in a circular fashion (circular polarization), depending upon the directions of the magnetic lines of force. This phenomenon, known as the *Zeeman effect* in the laboratory, is minutely observed in the absorption lines of the sunspot spectrum by carefully examining their fine structure with high-dispersion spectrographs and with polarizing filters or other polarizing devices. The magnetic-field strength and polarity of a sunspot can be determined from the amount of line splitting and analysis of the

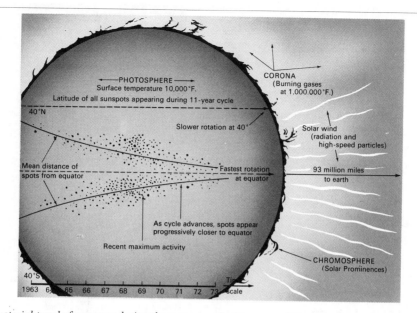

Figure 9.13 The equatorial trend of sunspots during the sunspot cycle. (Courtesy of Time Magazine. Redrawn by permission from a diagram by R. M. Chapin, Jr.)

kind of existing vibrations within the individual line components by means of polarizing measurements. It is found that the leading group of spots (in the forward direction of the sun's rotation) has the opposite polarity from the following group making up the trailing members. The opposite polarities are like those of the north and south ends of a horseshoe magnet. The measured field strength over the spot zone exceeds the earth's field several thousand times and is many times greater than the best commercially produced alnico magnets. (The unit of the magnetic-field strength is the *gauss*; the earth has an average field strength of $\frac{1}{2}$ gauss.) In the opposite hemisphere the polarities of the bipolar sunspot pair are reversed. The polarities in both hemispheres *reverse* in the following sunspot cycle. The sun as a whole possesses a general magnetic field several times stronger than the earth's field. However, the sun's general field reverses near the time of the sunspot maximum.

A completely satisfactory explanation of sunspot behavior and its associated magnetic-field phenomena is not yet available. At the present time the reasoning runs along the following lines first developed by Harold D. Babcock and Horace W. Babcock of the Hale Observatories. Distortions within the sun's magnetic field below the photosphere arise from the sun's unequal rotation. As the magnetic lines of force are pulled out and stretched unequally at the different latitudes, maximum stretching occurs at the solar equator where the rotation is swiftest. The magnetic lines eventually curl up into a twisted, undulating, ropelike structure below the photospheric surface. If a kink forms, the tortuous strands may arch up into the photosphere to create a bipolar sunspot group. The large temperature drop within the sunspot indicates that the normal convective flow of heat below the photosphere to the surface has been restricted by the presence of the localized intense magnetic field. The surface areas within this region receive less heat, as manifested in the appearance of the cooler sunspots. As the bipolar group of sunspots breaks up and decays, the field of the following spots of the bipolar group slants more toward the pole than that of the preceding spots of the bipolar group. There results a preferential migration of the following field remnants toward the polar regions that eventually reverse the sunspots' magnetic polarity opposite to what it was in the previous cycle. The period of complete reversal of the sunspot polarity is thus twenty-two years.

9.6 THE CHROMOSPHERE

The Flash Spectrum

For a few seconds after an eclipse of the sun becomes total, a thin pinkish fringe of light several

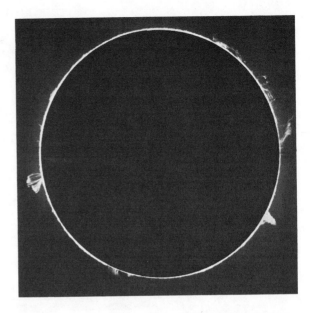

Figure 9.15 Solar chromosphere photographed in the light of the calcium K line with a spectroheliograph. Its color is pink when observed during the solar eclipse. The gaseous extensions are the prominences. (Courtesy of Hale Observatories.)

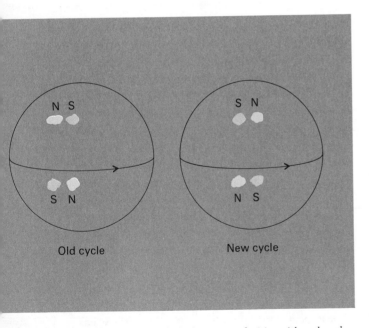

Figure 9.14 Reversal of sunspot polarities with each cycle.

thousand miles deep called the *chromosphere* suddenly appears beyond the obscured limb of the sun. Projecting from it here and there are rosy tongues of gas called *prominences* which may extend to heights of 100,000 miles or more. The chromospheric color results from the large amount of hydrogen gas emitting radiation in the principal hydrogen alpha line of the Balmer series.

A century ago it was found that, at the beginning of an eclipse, the normal dark-line spectrum is quickly replaced by a spectrum of bright lines named the *flash spectrum*. At this time the continuous spectrum disappears as the moon occults the solar disk, leaving exposed the sun's atmospheric fringe which produces the bright-line spectrum. The bright lines match the positions of the dark lines with a few exceptions. One notable exception was a bright orange line first observed during the eclipse of 1868. The unknown element responsible for its origin was named helium, after *helios*, the Greek word for the sun. It was not identified spectroscopically on earth until 1895. The appearance of certain helium lines not found in the Fraunhofer spectrum and the increased line strengths of a number of ionized metals in the flash spectrum are attributed to the higher temperature and lower density in the chromosphere.

Single-Color Views of the Chromosphere

Many interesting solar events can be monitored by photographing the sun's atmosphere in monochromatic light—that is, in radiation of a single wavelength. The Fraunhofer absorption lines are not completely black. There is still some light radiated within them though it is vastly weaker than in the unrestricted adjoining spectral regions. The depletion of light in the spectral lines is caused by atoms in the lowest chromospheric levels selectively absorbing the radiation moving upward from the photospheric regions and reradiating the energy in all directions (recall Figure 4.9). Although the net forward radiation in the spectral lines in any specific direction, say the earth's direction, is substantially reduced, it is still sufficient to photograph the sun in the wavelength of a prominent Fraunhofer line. The lines most commonly used are the red line of hydrogen alpha (C line) or either one of the two closely spaced violet lines of singly ionized calcium (H and K lines).

One type of single-color recording device, called a *spectroheliograph*, is a modified spectrograph mounted in the focal plane of a solar telescope. It slowly scans the solar disk and its near extension in the spectral light of one of the aforementioned lines. The finished picture is called a *spectroheliogram*. Another more common technique makes use of a specially designed telescope called a *coronagraph*, an instrument used primarily for study of the sun's

corona. It admits the sunlight through a narrow passband filter transparent only to the radiation in the region of the chosen spectral line. The coronagraph can only be used on high mountain sites where the air is sufficiently clean and transparent to reduce the glare of the sky to a level which permits photography of the faint outlying portions of the solar atmosphere. The combination of the filter and an appropriately placed occulting disk to create an artificial eclipse, together with certain precautions to prevent the passage of stray light, make possible the photography of the sun's atmosphere in the light of hydrogen or calcium. Without the occulting disk, the direct monochromatic view of the solar disk is obtained. The photograph of the sun secured with a narrow passband filter is called a *filtergram*.

Chromospheric Features

The bright, enhanced patches that hover around the sunspots in the spectroheliograms or filtergrams are called *plages*. They are composed of chromospheric gas that has been superheated to temperatures up to 100,000°K by the rapidly traveling waves of material flowing upward along the curled magnetic lines surrounding the sunspots. Time-lapse photography with the spectroheliograph or coronagraph reveals the spectacular movements of the glowing *prominences*. A series of short film exposures taken in succession over an interval of time, when run through a motion-picture projector at normal speed, provides a dramatic record of the continually changing solar atmospheric behavior that is lacking in the still pictures. The prominences assume various forms ranging from the almost stationary, quiescent bulges to the rapidly moving surges and the graceful loops flowing along the curving magnetic lines of force. The more active prominences ascend at speeds up to a thousand miles per second to heights of several hundred thousand miles. When projected against the solar disk, the prominences look like dark stringy

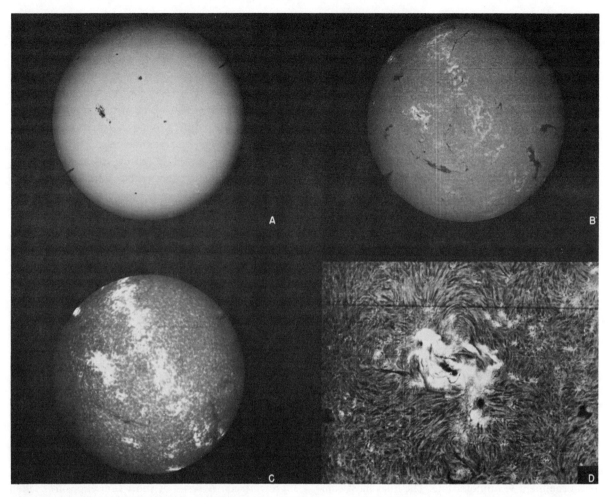

Figure 9.16   Four views of the sun: (a) *direct photograph;* (b) *hydrogen (alpha line) spectroheliogram;* (c) *calcium (K line) spectroheliogram;* (d) *plage region surrounding a sunspot group photographed in the light of the hydrogen alpha line. (Courtesy of Hale Observatories.)*

clouds absorbing radiation from below (see Figure 9.16b). Frequently, only downward motion is visible in an arched loop that may disappear inside a sunspot group, indicating that cooler and denser coronal material is draining toward the photosphere. The top portion of the arched magnetic lines of force that flow out of one bipolar group and into the other

bipolar group is capable of supporting the prominence against the normal pull of gravity for long periods of time.

When photographed in the shorter coronagraph exposures, the chromosphere is seen to be stippled with myriads of tiny jetlike spikes of gas, called *spicules*, that average about 500 miles across. Spicules

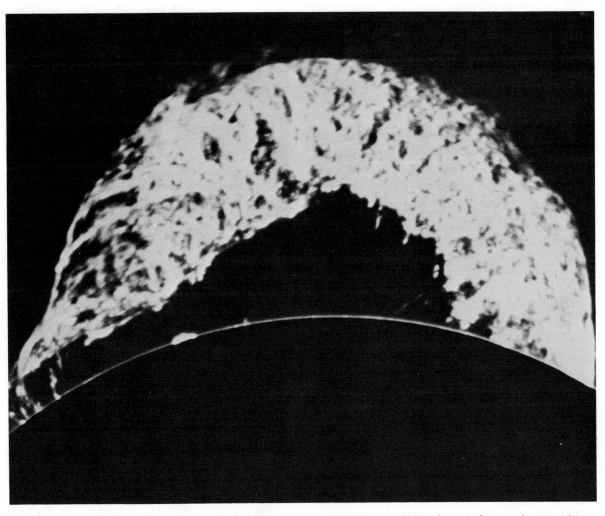

Figure 9.17   The great eruptive prominence of June 4, 1946. The prominence grew to a size almost as large as the sun within an hour; several hours later it disappeared completely. (Courtesy of High Altitude Observatory, Colorado.)

attain a maximum height of about 10,000 miles and then fade away or collapse within a matter of several minutes. Their total number at any one instant is estimated at about 400,000, covering a few per cent of the sun's surface at a given time. Their possible connection with granular movements in the photosphere remains obscure.

9.7   THE CORONA

Appearance

The corona is observed during the total phase of a solar eclipse as a large envelope of white, glowing gas extending outward sometimes several solar diameters. In the shorter exposures, coronal rays consisting of hot streams of the charged gas particles forming the solar wind are observed diverging outward from the polar regions along the curved magnetic lines of force. The outer configuration of the corona changes with the sunspot cycle. Near the time of the sunspot maximum, it assumes a circular form with streamers radiating in all directions. Near the time of the sunspot minimum, the corona extends for a greater distance along the equatorial region and terminates rather abruptly with shorter streamers curving out of the polar regions.

Coronal Spectrum

The coronal gases possess an extraordinary bright-line spectrum positioned on a weak, continuous spectrum which in turn overlies a faint Fraunhofer dark-line spectrum. This latter spectrum arises from the reflection of sunlight by interplanetary dust particles. The continuous spectrum is produced by the much smaller electrons scattering the sunlight in all the wavelengths. The approximately three dozen coronal emission lines originate in the peculiarly excited atoms of iron, calcium, nickel, and argon from which nine to fifteen electrons have been stripped in the superhot gaseous material under near-vacuum conditions. A temperature of at least one million degrees absolute is required to produce this high degree of ionization. The coronal lines are called *forbidden lines* because the atomic transitions that give rise to them normally occur very infrequently. Under the normal conditions of pressure and temperature that exist in the laboratory the forbidden lines are weak or absent, but the physical conditions for producing them are favorable in the corona. Because of the high temperature most of the coronal radiation should occur in the ultraviolet and x-ray spectral regions. This is substantiated in the x-ray photographs that reveal intense radiations whose source is well outside the photosphere of the sun.

Figure 9.18   *Solar corona photographed during the eclipse of March 7, 1970 near San Carlos Yautepec, Mexico (altitude 8,800 feet). (Courtesy of High Altitude Observatory, Colorado.)*

Origin of High Coronal Temperatures

What appears at first glance to be a paradoxical situation in which the temperatures of the chromospheric and coronal gases rise steeply rather than drop with increasing distance above the photosphere has been interpreted in the following manner. The major proportion of the heat contribution is believed to come from the energy of the shock disturbances created by the outward passage of sound waves

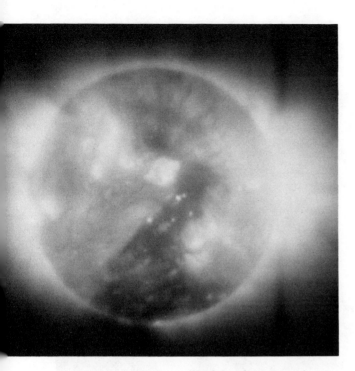

Figure 9.19   X-ray photograph of the solar corona taken during NASA aerobee rocket flight on Nov. 24, 1970. (Courtesy of American Science and Engineering, Cambridge, Mass.)

originating in the turbulent convection below the chromosphere. As the high-pressure shock fronts of these acoustic waves move into the chromosphere and into the corona, their energy is absorbed by the sun's outer atmosphere, causing the coronal material to become superheated. This creates a supersonic flow of gas composed mainly of ionized hydrogen that exits from the base of the corona in the form of the solar wind at a speed of several hundred kilometers per second. It is estimated that one million tons of discharged plasma leaves the sun every second. A contributing source of coronal heating is believed to come from the chromospheric spicules

(gas jets) generating shock waves that move into the base of the corona.

9.8   EFFECTS OF SOLAR DISTURBANCES

Solar Flares

A flare suddenly erupts as an intensely bright area in the plage region of the chromosphere, usually associated with a sunspot group. It emits radiation strongly throughout the entire electromagnetic spectrum. Most common during the periods of maximum spottedness of the sun, flares are graded according to their size, brightness, and behavior. They quickly pass through a period of great brilliance followed by a slower decline before fading away in a matter of minutes or hours. A major flare is the most violent kind of solar disturbance. The arriving ultraviolet and x-ray radiations play havoc with the earth's ionosphere by disrupting the normal flow of worldwide radio communications. The resulting ionospheric storms sometimes persist for days. Within twenty-four hours of the flare outburst, low-energy cosmic rays (charged particles) spiral into the polar regions of the earth causing polar radio blackouts. A long plasma tongue with a self-contained magnetic field temporarily stretches out from the sun and sweeps over the earth. All of these abnormal developments partially derange the earth's magnetosphere, create brilliant displays of the auroral lights, generate magnetic storms that upset compass needle readings, and induce excessive earth currents that interfere with land-wire communication. Radio emission from the sun is also noticeably stronger. In addition to solar flares, unusually active sunspot groups ruffle the terrestrial environment to a lesser degree.

Monitoring of unusual solar events has been expanded in recent years with the establishment of nearly fifty worldwide ground-based observatories and the launching of solar-orbiting spacecraft and

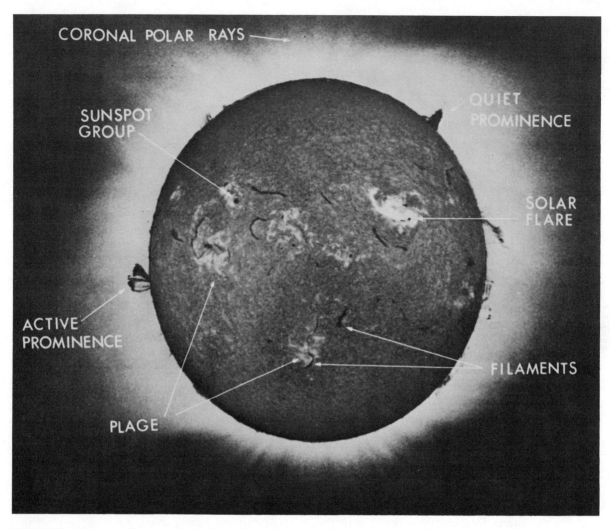

Figure 9.20   Composite filtergram of the solar disk and the chromosphere photographed in the light of the hydrogen alpha line superimposed on the inner corona. (Courtesy of Lockheed Solar Observatory.)

interplanetary probes. The latter are instrumented to detect the intensity and variations of the solar wind, the flux, power, and energy spectrum of the solar cosmic rays, flare phenomena, and general solar atmospheric activity in the terrestrially inaccessible short wavelengths.

Periodic Solar-Terrestrial Correlations

Certain solar-terrestrial interrelations known to be correlated with the eleven-year sunspot cycle are: (1) maximum and minimum receipt of solar ultraviolet radiation by the earth coincides respectively with the maximum and minimum of the sunspot

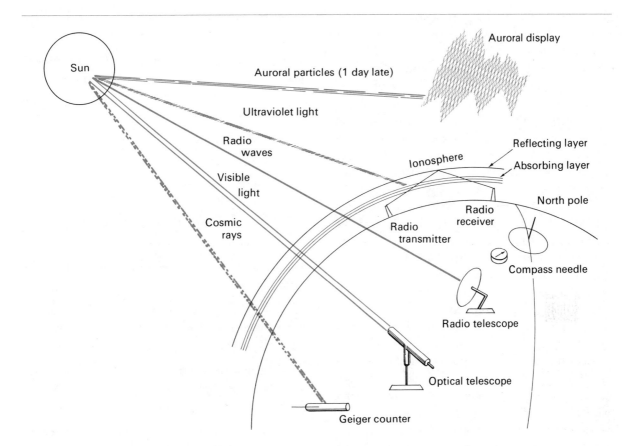

Auroral display

Auroral particles (1 day late)

Sun

Ultraviolet light

Radio
waves

Reflecting layer

Ionosphere

Absorbing layer

Visible
light

North pole

Radio
receiver

Cosmic
rays

Radio
transmitter

Compass needle

Radio telescope

Optical telescope

Geiger counter

Figure 9.21   Solar eruption with associated events. (Courtesy of the Royal Astronomical Society of Canada.)

cycle; (2) global radio communications at frequencies less than about thirty megahertz are at their best around the peak of the sunspot cycle because of the higher ionospheric electron densities which improve the long-range communications; (3) aurorae are most prominent at the time of the sunspot maximum; (4) terrestrial magnetic activity closely follows the ups and downs of the sunspot cycle; (5) the intensity of galactic cosmic rays diminishes near the time of the sunspot maximum as a result of the inter-

action between the charged particles and the strengthened interplanetary magnetic field which tends to deflect the particles (*Forbush effect*).

Attempts to link the sunspot cycle with fluctuations in the stock market, with wars, depressions, the growth of grain crops, and so on are scientifically unproved. Many years ago A. E. Douglas of the University of Arizona sought to establish a connection between the amount of rainfall and the sunspot cycle by examining the spacings between tree rings in old trees and ancient logs. He assumed that wider ring intervals would correlate with periods of heavier rainfall which might somehow be connected with the sunspot cycle. He managed to find several nonrandom cycles with periods ranging from five to twenty-three years. Although he was not successful in finding a close pattern between the growth of tree rings and the sunspot cycle, he did become expert in dating old wood from ancient Indian ruins in the southwestern states. J. R. Bray of New Zealand has called attention to the possible existence of a long periodic cycle of about 2,500 years. He believes it is correlated with the periods of past glacial advances and the temperature-related oxygen 18 isotopic data extracted from ice cores in Greenland. He concludes that the warmer climatic periods appear to be associated with higher sunspot activity and the cooler periods with lower sunspot activity.

Scientists are learning more about the complex and frequently obscure solar-terrestrial relationships through the present establishment of a worldwide coordinating network embracing the realms of atmospheric physics, space physics, solar physics, and extraterrestrial meteorology. Eventually, man should be able to forecast the immediate and long-range effects of solar events upon the earth for his own economic benefit.

REVIEW QUESTIONS

1. How do we know that sunspots are regions of intense magnetic activity?

2. What advantages does observing a total eclipse of the sun have over the normal means of observing the sun?

3. Suppose a major flare were to erupt on the sun while astronauts were exploring the lunar surface. Discuss the radiation dangers, if any, to which they might be exposed and whether there is any possibility of warning them in advance.

4. An x-ray photon created within the sun's superhot core has no chance of survival in getting through to the solar surface. How is it possible that x-ray photographs of the sun are commonplace?

5. What is the general picture of the photosphere?

6. Describe the behavior of the gases in the chromosphere. How deep is the chromosphere? How do we detect its existence?

7. How do we obtain a single-color hydrogen or calcium scan of the chromosphere?

8. Describe the prominence activity in the solar atmosphere.

9. How do we account for a coronal temperature of one million degrees Kelvin when the sun's surface temperature is only $6,000°K$?

10. When viewed at the time of a total eclipse of the sun, the chromosphere has a pinkish glow. Why? What does its spectrum show at this time?

11. How extensive is the corona? How does its appearance change with the sunspot cycle?

12. What gases have been identified in the coronal spectrum? What is so strange or different about their physical condition?

13. About how many elements have been identified in the solar spectrum? What technique is used to identify them?

14. How have astronomers determined the rotation period of the sun?

15. When do you predict the next maximum of the sunspot cycle will occur? The minimum that follows it?

SELECTED READINGS

Abetti, G., *The Sun*, Macmillan, 1957.

Ellison, M. A., *The Sun and Its Influence*, American Elsevier, 1968.

Gamow, G., *A Star Called the Sun*, Viking, 1964.

Kiepenheuer, K., *The Sun*, University of Michigan Press, 1959.

Menzel, D. H., *Our Sun*, Harvard University Press, 1959.

Moore, P., *Sun*, Norton, 1968.

Stetson, H. T., *Sunspots and Their Effects*, McGraw-Hill, 1937.

Lagoon nebula, Messier 8, in Sagittarius which lies in the richest part of the Milky Way. (Courtesy of Hale Observatories.)

THE GALAXY:
ITS STELLAR PROPERTIES

"Lo", quoth he, "cast up thine eye,
See yonder, lo! the galaxie,
The which men clepe the Milky Way
For it is white; and some parfay
Callen it Watling streete."

Geoffrey Chaucer (1340–1400),
The House of Fame

Photographic exploration at the beginning of the twentieth century disclosed that the structure of the Milky Way was far more complex than previously imagined. In the 1920's, as telescopes became larger and astronomers employed more efficient auxiliary equipment, a pattern revealing the large-scale structure of the system began to emerge. The Milky Way was a large, flat, rotating spiral galaxy containing dust, gas, and innumerable stars similar to thousands of other photographed galaxies. The sun is one star out of billions located well out from the center of the Galaxy. Centered around the Galaxy is a sparse extended distribution of stars called the galactic halo and a spheroidal scattering of some one hundred compact, large assemblages of stars called globular clusters. Today the galactic composition and the finer intricate details are being unraveled with radio, infrared, optical, x-ray, and gamma ray telescopes as additional surprises continue to unfold in a system once thought to be undecipherable.

Many important facts about the stellar constituency of our Galaxy have been revealed as a result of the labors of countless astronomers who over the years have ferreted out vital information about the stars: their distances, luminosities, space motions, space distributions, colors, temperatures, dimensions, masses, densities, spectral characteristics, ages, and chemical composition. From such data it is possible to find certain interrelations existing between the stellar properties. One of the most significant and rewarding discoveries has been the strong correlation between the temperatures or spectral classes of the stars and their intrinsic brightnesses, represented graphically by the Hertzsprung-Russell (H-R) or spectrum-luminosity diagram. Astronomers find this diagram useful in determining the distances of the stars (spectroscopic parallaxes) and in studying stellar evolution.

10.1 THE MILKY WAY: AN INTRODUCTION

On a clear, moonless night, well removed from the population centers, the casual observer would have no difficulty observing the Milky Way as a misty, irregular belt of varying brightness arching across the sky. In the temperate zones, different portions of this globe-circling band of stars are seen inclined at various angles to the horizon, depending on the time of year. In these regions about 30 per cent of the Milky Way remains below the horizon at all times. The only place on earth where it can be viewed in its entirety during the year is in the equatorial zone. Since some familiarity with the constellations is helpful in visualizing the location of the Milky Way features in different regions of the sky, we shall digress with a brief treatment of the constellations.

The Constellations

Eighty-eight constellations of all sizes are recognized today. (A luminescent sky map is placed in the back of this book.) As the mention of a certain country brings to mind its location on earth, so does the name of a constellation conjure up its approximate position in the sky. In the mid-latitudes of both hemispheres, one can view at sometime throughout the year at least four-fifths of all the constellations. Approximately one-half of them are within the Milky Way or adjoin its borders.

Our knowledge of the constellations is inherited from the Greeks who in turn were influenced by their civilized predecessors in Mesopotamia and the neighboring lands of the Near East. The Greek astronomers originally recognized forty-eight constellations. The remaining forty constellations, mostly those in the southern skies, were added in the seventeenth and eighteenth centuries by several map makers and astronomers. The brighter stars in a given constellation are designated by the small letters of the Greek alphabet, with the constellation name in the genitive of the Latin, in the approximate order of their decreasing brightness. This lettering scheme was introduced by J. Bayer who constructed a famous map of the heavens in 1603. The brightest stars also have special names of Greek, Latin, or Arabic origin. For example, α (alpha) Leonis, the brightest star in the constellation of Leo, is called Regulus; the second brightest star in Leo, β (beta) Leonis, is called Denebola. In 1928 the International Astronomical Union rectified the previously ragged constellation boundaries by having the boundary lines run north-south and east-west. The boundaries frequently zigzag to include as many stars as possible within the former constellations.

There are about 5,400 naked-eye stars in the skies of both hemispheres. When the twenty-four letters of the Greek alphabet were exhausted in specifying the individual stars within a particular constellation according to the Bayer rule, the letters of the Roman alphabet were sometimes employed, or, more frequently, the stars were simply numbered across the constellation from west to east in the star catalog of 1725 compiled by John Flamsteed, the first Astronomer Royal of England (example: 61 Cygni). For the fainter stars, their number in a star catalog suffices (example: Lalande 21185 is entry number 21185 in Lalande's catalog which includes entry numbers for the brighter stars as well). One class of stars whose brightness varies—namely, the variable stars—was given a special lettering classification by the German astronomers of the late nineteenth century. These stars carry either a single or double letter of the alphabet. For example, R Leonis is a well-known variable star in the constellation of Leo; SS Cygni is another well-known variable star in the constellation of Cygnus. Still other star nomenclatures are employed, sometimes confusing even to an astronomer. In all instances, however, the exact celestial coordinate positions (*right ascension* and *declination*, similar to longitude and latitude on earth) are tabulated along with the catalog number and the stellar data relating to the stellar brightness (magnitude), and other useful information. Appendices 10, 11, and 12 present further examples of star and constellation designations.

Visual and Pictorial Appearance of the Galaxy

During the late summer months in the mid-northern latitudes, one sees the Milky Way in its richest splendor in the southerly direction of the great star clouds of Sagittarius, for in that luminous blend of thickly strewn stars lies the way toward the center of our Galaxy. In the winter season one sees the dimmer and more sparsely occupied portion of the Milky Way in the southerly direction of Orion and upward toward Taurus, for that is the direction away from the galactic center.

It is not at all obvious from the appearance of the heavens that the sun is immersed within a star-studded, lens-shaped system that we call the Galaxy. Our edgewise view of it accounts for the banded appearance of the Milky Way. The concept of the Milky Way system in the rough form of a discoid had been advocated as early as 1750 by Thomas Wright of England. The first scientific evidence of its approximate form was obtained by William Herschel of England in 1784 on the basis of nearly seven hundred sample star counts distributed over the sky. He concluded that the sun occupied the approximate center of the stellar system, as did other astronomers for more than a century after him. It was not until 1917 that Harlow Shapley, then at the Mt. Wilson Observatory, discovered the eccentric position of the sun from his study of the distribution of the surrounding globular star clusters whose center he correctly assumed to be coincident with that of the stellar system.

In brief, our Galaxy is a gravitationally bound pinwheel structure of billions of stars. At the center lies the nuclear bulge from whose opposite

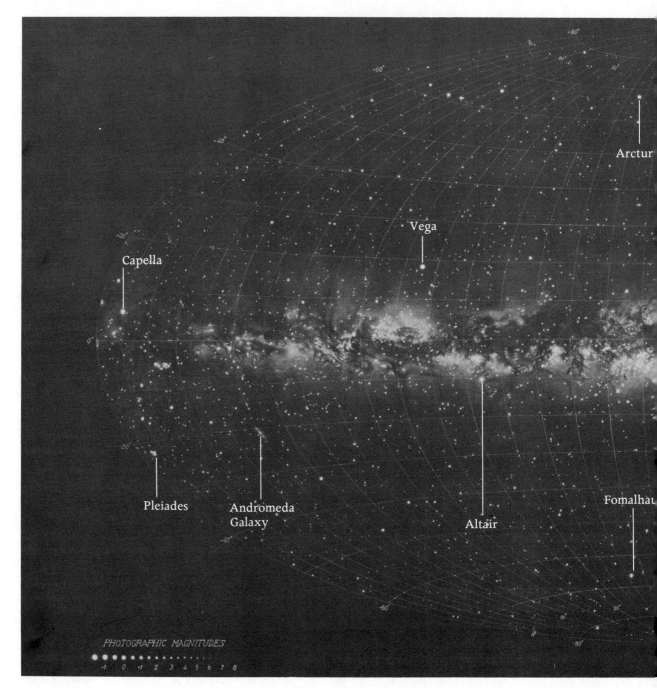

Figure 10.1   Panoramic view of the Milky Way. (Courtesy of Lund Observatory.)

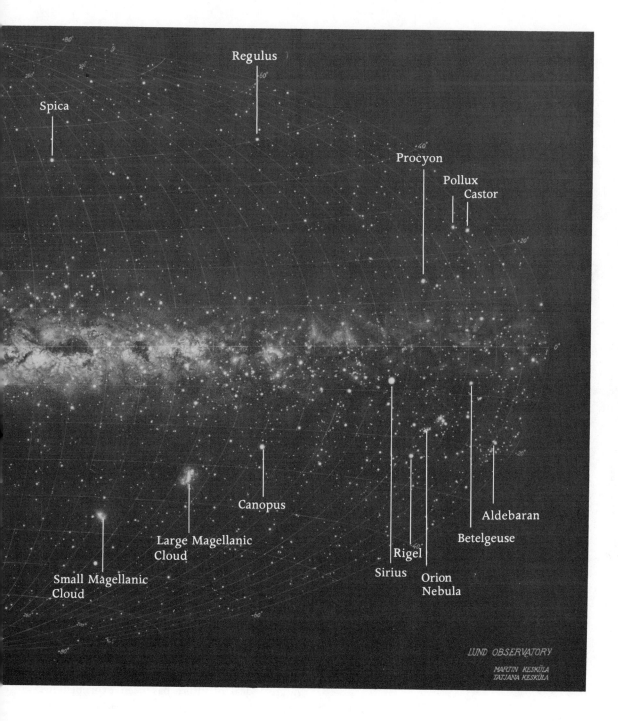

Spica

Regulus

Procyon

Pollux
Castor

Canopus

Large Magellanic
Cloud

Small Magellanic
Cloud

Rigel

Sirius

Orion
Nebula

Aldebaran

Betelgeuse

LUND OBSERVATORY

MARTIN KESKÜLA
TATJANA KESKÜLA

10 THE GALAXY: ITS STELLAR PROPERTIES

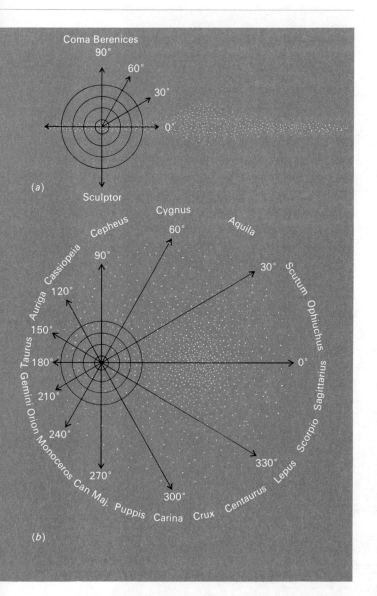

Figure 10.2 (a) *Schematic edgewise and* (b) *plan view of the Galaxy (center and discoid stellar portions.) Numerals represent galactic latitudes in diagram* (a); *galactic longitudes in diagram* (b). *The sun occupies the position at the center of the concentric circles.*

portions the spiral arms wind outward toward the periphery. They are delineated by an admixture of gas and dust, and rendered visible by the bright hot stars strung out along them. The individual stars revolve around the nucleus at various speeds dependent upon their distances from the center as dictated by the law of gravitation. A slightly flattened halo system of several billion stars and a spheroidal distribution of some one hundred globular clusters surround the main stellar discoid. A preview of the galactic arrangement may be obtained by referring to Figure 10.10.

10.2 STELLAR RESEARCH

Stellar Data

A number of twentieth-century optical and radio astronomers have been attempting to unravel the composite picture of the Galaxy by nibbling away piecemeal at its complex structure. For decades many more astronomers have been investigating the nature and properties of the stellar galactic membership. They have compiled a great body of valuable individual and statistical knowledge relating to star types and their kinematic, physical, and chemical attributes—a kind of stellar census of the population groups within the Galaxy. The information acquired deals with the following subjects: (1) distances, (2) space motions, (3) space distributions, (4) apparent and absolute luminosities, (5) colors and temperatures, (6) diameters, (7) masses, (8) densities, (9) spectral classes, (10) spectral-luminosity relations, (11) stellar atmospheres, and (12) chemical compositions. How these stellar data are obtained is described in the succeeding sections.

10.3 STELLAR DISTANCES

Trigonometric Parallax

A great deal of effort has been expended in deriving the distances of the stars by various means, for without this fundamental knowledge it is virtually impossible to evaluate many of the stellar characteristics. One basic technique, that of parallax, is easily understood by viewing against the background the apparent shift of the position of a pencil held at arms length with each eye alternately closed. The parallactic displacement becomes smaller as the distance of the pencil increases.

In principle, the minute apparent displacements in the photographed positions of the investigated star against the background of the distant stars are compared at intervals of six months when the earth is on the opposite sides of its orbit. The maximum parallactic shift occurs at the opposite ends of a base line whose length is equal to two astronomical units (diameter of the earth's orbit). With a telescope of focal length fifty feet, the total parallactic shift from the ends of the base line for the closest star, Alpha Centauri, is equal to 0.004 inch on the photographic plate. In practice, many photographs are secured at various times during a period of at least two years under exacting conditions. From careful measurements of the star's microscopic changes in position relative to the more distant stars by means of a finely machined measuring engine, the tiny parallax angle is extracted. Its measured value is slightly adjusted for the parallactic shift of the more distant background stars.

Insertion of the parallax angle, p, in formula 1 of Figure 10.3, which is easily derived by simple trigonometry, gives the distance of the star from the sun in astronomical units. Since the distance in astronomical units may rise to "astronomical" figures, astronomers prefer to employ two larger units of distance. One is the *light-year*, which corresponds to the distance that light travels in one year (velocity of light times number of seconds in one year = 5.88 $\times$ 10^{12} miles). The other is the *parsec*, which corresponds to the distance of a star whose parallax is one second of arc (1"). The parsec is the larger unit,

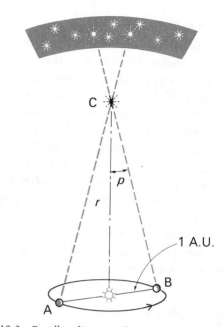

Figure 10.3 *Parallax diagram. If star C is viewed from points A and B on the earth's orbit six months apart, it will appear to have shifted its direction slightly with respect to the more distant stars. Measurement of the parallax angle, p, combined with knowledge of the earth's mean distance from the sun (= 1 A.U.), yields the distance of the star, r, by trigonometry:*

(1) Distance in astronomical units, r, (A.U.) = 206265/p"
(2) Distance in light-years, r, (L.Y.), = 3.26/p"
(3) Distance in parsecs, r (pc) = 1/p"
One light-year (L.Y.) = 5.88 $\times$ 10^{12} miles; one parsec (pc) = 3.26 light-years.

equal to 3.26 light-years. Appendix 10 lists the distances and other pertinent data relating to the twenty nearest stars.

Example: A certain star was found to have a measured parallax equal to 0.1 second of arc. What is its distance in (1) astronomical units, (2) in light-years, (3) in parsecs? From formula 1 (Figure 10.3), $r = 206265/0.1 = 2,062,650$ A.U.; from formula 2, $r = 3.26/0.1 = 32.6$ light-years; 0.1 from formula 3, $r = 1/0.1 = 10$ parsecs.

Limitation of Parallax Method

It is practically impossible to measure a parallactic shift smaller than 0.01 second of arc. This is equivalent to a displacement of about one-tenth the width of a human hair on photographic plates secured with the average long-focus telescope. This limit corresponds to a distance of about 300 light-years. The number of measurable parallaxes within this range is estimated to be not more than 50,000, of which some 6,000 have been measured. Fewer than 1,000 of these stars have parallaxes exceeding 0.05 second of arc (65 light-years). Fortunately, astronomers have devised a number of other methods for finding the distances of stars whose parallaxes are too small to be measured.

Distances of More Remote Stars

The most powerful technique makes use of the relationship that exists between the apparent brightness of an object whose true luminosity is known and its distance, by means of the inverse-square law of intensity of light. For example, if a light source is twice as distant as another of the same actual intensity, its apparent brightness is reduced by a factor of 4 (inversely as the square of 2, twice the distance); if three times as distant, the reduction is $3^2 = 9$ times; if four times as distant, the reduction is $4^2 = 16$ times, and so on. Hence, if the true brightness of a certain class of objects to which the subject star belongs is known, its distance can be calculated by means of the inverse-square law from its observed apparent luminosity. The method depends on the proper recognition of the subject star as an example of a specific kind of star whose true luminosity is known, thus permitting its use as a "standard candle." An example illustrating this technique is worked out in the section on magnitudes, Section 10.5.

Another less accurate method depends on the strengths of certain sharp interstellar absorption lines that are superimposed on the normal spectra of the distant hot stars. The interstellar lines arise from the absorption of the starlight as it passes through the intervening clouds of dust and gas on its way toward the earth. The strengths of the interstellar lines are roughly proportional to the distances of the stars. Still another technique used to determine the distances depends upon the orbital motions of binary stars or the group movements of relatively close star clusters. The process is too complex to describe here, but it involves the relationship that exists between their constituents' apparent angular motion, true linear motion, and distance.

10.4 STELLAR MOTIONS

One may ask: Do the stars move chaotically or is there a naturally organized stellar traffic pattern that tends to keep the stars in their places? There is, as we shall see, an individualized random motion, albeit slight, superimposed on a large common systematic movement shared by all the stars as they revolve around the center of the Galaxy.

Proper Motions

To evaluate the space motions of the stars projected on the sky, astronomers compare two photographs of the same star fields taken years apart with the same telescope in a machine called a *blink comparator* (shown in Figure 7.23). This device employs an optical arrangement that permits the viewer to look at each plate alternately in quick succession by flipping a lever. Stars which have changed their positions appear to jump with each flip of the lever. Their minute angular change in position between the two observing periods can then be measured. When reduced to the annual amount of angular change in seconds of arc, it is called the *proper motion*. In general, as would be expected, those stars that are closer to the sun tend to exhibit larger proper motions. Only a few hundred stars have proper motions greater than one second of arc per year. This is equivalent to about 1/2,000 of the sun's apparent diameter. Because of the great distances involved the observed movements are exceedingly tiny. The student may recall that Halley made use of a 1,700-year period in discovering the proper motions of several of the brightest stars (Section 2.8). The constellations that we see today looked the same to the ancients. Over a much longer period of time the star configurations familiar to us will change.

Radial Motions

The line-of-sight motion, or radial velocity, of a star is found from the Doppler shift of its spectral lines as described in Section 4.3. The measurement of radial velocities is independent of the distance. Most

Figure 10.4   Proper motion of Barnard's star between 1937 and 1962. (Lowell Observatory Photograph.)

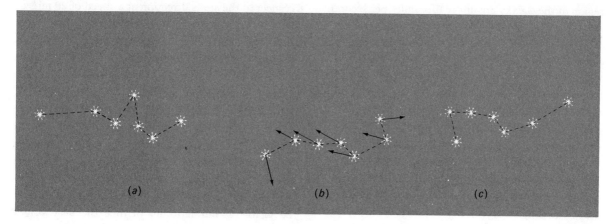

Figure 10.5   Changes in the appearance of the Big Dipper: (a) 100,000 years ago; (b) today; (c) 100,000 years from now. The five inner stars are parts of an open star cluster whose members are moving in parallel tracks in space.

10 THE GALAXY: ITS STELLAR PROPERTIES

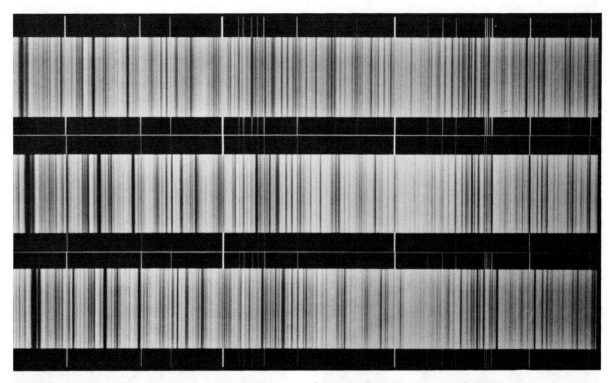

Figure 10.6 Spectra of low-, moderate-, and high-velocity stars (from top to bottom). (Courtesy of Lick Observatory.)

of the stellar radial velocities we observe within our region of the Galaxy are under fifty miles per second.

Space Motions

By mathematically combining knowledge of the star's distance in parsecs, its proper motion, and its radial velocity, the astronomer can find the true space motion of the star relative to the sun. It is instructive to examine how this procedure is applied to the sun's closest neighbor, Alpha Centauri. The observed data for Alpha Centauri are: distance, $r = 1.32$ parsecs; proper motion, $\mu = 3.68''$; radial velocity, $V_R = -14$ mi/sec. By calculation (see Figure 10.7), the tangential velocity, $V_T = 2.95 \times 3.68 \times 1.32 = 14$ mi/sec; the space motion, $V = \sqrt{V_R{}^2 + V_T{}^2} = \sqrt{(-14)^2 + (14)^2} = 20$ mi/sec. The

star is moving along a track angled 45 degrees with respect to the sun's direction at a speed of 20 mi/sec. By the year A.D. 30,000, Alpha Centauri's distance from the sun will have been diminished from its present value of 4.3 light-years to its minimum distance of 3 light-years (Figure 10.8). During the 28 millennia required to reach this minimum distance, its space motion will carry it along a path in the heavens that will place it in the constellation of the Southern Cross (Crux) around A.D. 14,000. Since Vega will be the north pole star then as a result of the precession of the equinoxes (Figure 6.10), the constellation of Crux with its altered configuration will be visible at our latitude. In time the very bright interloper, outshining the normal four stars of the Southern Cross, will move through the constellation on its way toward Hydra which it will reach around A.D. 30,000. Thereafter Alpha Centauri's distance from the sun will continue to increase as it next passes into the constellation of Cancer in A.D. 131,000. By that time it will have traveled slightly more than one-fourth the way around the sky.

Local and Galactic Solar Motions; Stellar Galactic Motions

It is possible to obtain meaningful information on stellar movements from the proper motions and the radial velocities even if the distances are unknown. From statistical analysis it is found that there is a general scattering of the nearby stars outward in the area around a certain point on the sky toward which the sun appears to be headed. There is a simultaneous general trend of the nearby stars in

the area toward the opposite point on the sky from which the sun appears to be receding. The celestial point toward which the sun is moving is called the *apex*; it lies in the constellation of Hercules within ten degrees of the bright star Vega. The opposite point on the sky is called the *antapex*; it lies in the constellation of Columba. The analysis from the radial velocities of the sun's neighbors further reveals that the sun is moving with respect to them at the relatively slow rate of twelve miles per second.

From data on stars at greater distances from the sun, it is found that the sun and its neighbors are moving in nearly parallel tracks at the high average speed of 170 miles per second around the nucleus of the Galaxy. This is taking place some 30,000 light-years from the galactic nucleus, about two-thirds of the radius of the Galaxy from its center. There are enough slight variations in the individual motions of the nearby stars, due to their gravitational interactions, to create the semblance of random move-

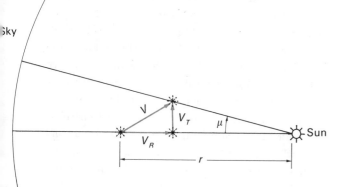

Figure 10.7 *Components of space motion:* r = *distance in parsecs;* μ = *proper motion;* V_R = *radial velocity;* V_T = *tangential velocity* = $2.95\mu \cdot r$ *(mi/sec);* V = *space velocity* = $\sqrt{V_R^2 + V_T^2}$

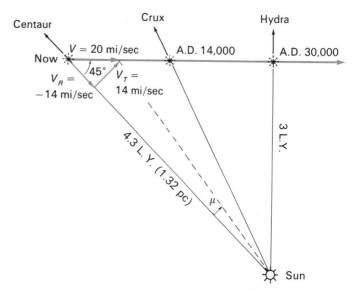

Figure 10.8 *Future space motion of Alpha Centauri.*

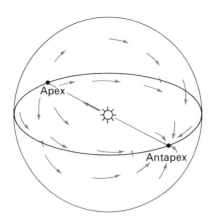

Figure 10.9   Effect of the sun's motion on the nearby stars. The stars appear to scatter outward from the point on the sky (apex) toward which the sun is headed—in the direction of the constellation Hercules, about 10 degrees from the bright star Vega. They appear to converge toward the opposite point in the sky (antapex) located in the constellation Columba.

ment within their local frame of reference. It is with respect to these nearby neighbors that we observe the sun's leisurely approach toward Vega.

The principal movement of the stars within the disk portion of the Galaxy is the Keplerian motion: the closer the star is to the main gravitational center of attraction (the nucleus of the Galaxy), the faster it moves. This behavior is similar to the planetary motions around the sun since the law of gravitation is the common "operator" in the solar system as well as in the galactic system. Within the nuclear bulge where the stellar density is greatest, the action approximates that of a solid structure: the farther the star is from the center, the faster it moves. The

individual stars well above or below the galactic plane, constituting the *halo population*, and the spherically distributed globular clusters move around the galactic center at all angles of inclination in highly eccentric ellipses. Their motions are analogous to the motions of the far-ranging comets orbiting the sun. A more detailed discussion of the galactic structure and its rotation is presented in Section 11.4.

10.5   STELLAR LUMINOSITIES

Apparent Stellar Magnitudes

Prior to the introduction of photography, the apparent brightness, or preferably the apparent *magnitude*, of a star could only be derived from visual estimates and measures. The original scale of brightness in terms of magnitude was first conceived by the ancient Greek astronomers. It is based on a logarithmic scale to which the eye naturally responds. Equal *ratios* of star brightnesses correspond to equal *differences* of magnitudes on the logarithmic scale. The old magnitude system was placed on a more accurate footing by astronomers of the last century; they established the modern scale of magnitudes on the following basis: Two stars whose ratio of brightness is 100:1 are said to differ by five magnitudes. From this rule it is possible, by means of a logarithmic formula, to construct a table of brightness versus magnitude as shown in Table 10.1. Some idea of the great range in magnitudes among the different celestial bodies may be obtained by examining Table 10.2. Note that the numerically larger negative values of magnitude denote brighter objects and the larger positive values, fainter objects. From Table 10.2 the difference in apparent magnitude between Sirius and Venus is $-1.4 - (-4.4) = 3$; according to Table 10.1, their ratio of brightness is 16:1—that is, Venus is sixteen times brighter than Sirius.

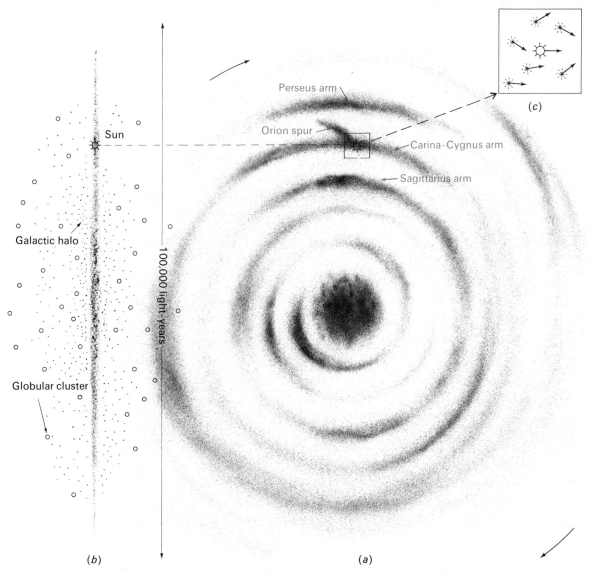

(b) |100,000 light-years| *(a)*

Perseus arm

Orion spur

Sun

Carina-Cygnus arm

Sagittarius arm

Galactic halo

Globular cluster

(c)

Figure 10.10   Idealized model of the Galaxy. (a) *Plan view: fragments of the spiral arms, shaded in blue, were first observed and mapped by optical astronomers. Figure 1 denotes the Sagittarius arm, 2, the Carina-Cygnus arm, 3, the Orion spur, and 4, the Perseus arm. The sun's position is marked by a small circle with a central dot. Later, radio astronomers tuned in on the 21 centimeter radiation from the neutral hydrogen clouds of the Milky Way and mapped many additional arms.* (b) *Edgewise view: the galactic halo appears as an ellipsoidal sprinkling of small white dots around the galactic disk. The surrounding globular clusters are represented by larger white dots. The dark central streak is caused by dust in the galactic plane obscuring the starlight. (Compare it with Figure 1.6 in Chapter 1.)* (c) *Localized view of the motions of the sun's neighbors: their slightly different motions around the galactic center are responsible for the observed local motion of the sun in the general direction of Vega with respect to its neighbors at 20 km/sec. The velocity of the sun and its neighbors around the galactic nucleus averages 270 km/sec toward Cygnus on a line approximately 90° from the direction to the galactic center in Sagittarius.*

10 THE GALAXY: ITS STELLAR PROPERTIES

Table 10.1	Brightness-Magnitude Values
Intensity Ratio	Magnitude Difference
1 : 1	0.0
1.6 : 1	0.5
2.5 : 1	1.0
4 : 1	1.5
6.3 : 1	2.0
10 : 1	2.5
16 : 1	3.0
40 : 1	4.0
100 : 1	5.0
400 : 1	6.5
1000 : 1	7.5
10,000 : 1	10.0
1,000,000 : 1	15.0
100,000,000 : 1	20.0

Table 10.2 Magnitudes of Selected Objects

Object	Visual	
	Apparent Magnitude	Absolute Magnitude
Sun	−26.8	+4.8
Full moon	−12.5	
Venus (at brightest)	−4.4	
Sirius (brightest star)	−1.4	+1.4
Alpha Centauri	−0.3	+4.7
Vega	0.0	+0.5
Antares	+1.0	−4.0
Andromeda galaxy	+3.5	−21.2
Faintest naked-eye star	+6.0	
Faintest star photographed by 200-inch reflector	+24.0	

The older visual methods of determining magnitudes have been superseded by the more accurate photographic and photoelectric methods. Astronomers have established a number of stellar magnitude sequences in various parts of the sky for this purpose. The magnitude sequences serve as calibrated standards of reference against which the magnitudes of other stars can be evaluated. A widely employed photographic procedure uses the relationship between image size on the plate and magnitude as shown in Figure 10.11. The magnitude measured on the ordinary blue-sensitive photographic plate is called the photographic magnitude or, more commonly, the blue magnitude. When measured on a yellow-sensitized plate in combination with a filter whose color sensitivity closely matches that of the eye, it is called the photovisual magnitude or, more commonly, the yellow magnitude; it corresponds to the older visual magnitude.

Absolute Stellar Magnitudes; Distance Modulus

In order to ascertain the real brightness differences existing between the stars, we must know their distances and apparent magnitudes. What is done in practice is to calculate mathematically by means of the inverse-square law of light (Section 10.3) the apparent magnitude that an object would have if it were placed at a chosen standard distance equal to ten parsecs (32.6 light-years). This computed value of magnitude is called the *absolute magnitude*. Intercomparison of the stars' luminosities at the same distance of ten parsecs naturally informs us what their actual brightnesses or absolute magnitudes are with respect to each other.

The formula for calculating the absolute magnitude of a celestial body is:

$$M = m + 5 - 5 \cdot \log r$$

where M = absolute magnitude, m = apparent magnitude, r = distance in parsecs, and $\log r$ = logarithm of r. The above equation may be solved for the distance r in the form:

$$\log r = \frac{(m - M) + 5}{5}$$

The difference between the apparent magnitude m and the absolute magnitude M $(m - M)$ is called the *distance modulus*. Its numerical value indicates how many times brighter or fainter the object is compared to its true brightness. Application of the inverse-square law of light leads to the object's distance. The principle involved is illustrated in the following example.

Example: A star belongs to a certain spectral class whose absolute magnitude $M = +5$; the star's observed apparent magnitude $m = +10$. What is the star's distance, r? The distance modulus $(m - M)$ $= 10 - 5 = 5$. This tells us that the star is five

Figure 10.11   Image size versus magnitude; the brighter the star, the larger and denser the image. In very bright stars, like the one near the top, a diffraction pattern with spokes is produced by the interposition of the supporting framework at the top of the telescope tube. (Courtesy of Lick Observatory.)

magnitudes fainter, or a hundred times less intense, than it is at the standard distance of ten parsecs. (From Table 10.1, a difference of five magnitudes, the distance modulus value, is equivalent to a brightness ratio of 100:1.) According to the inverse-square law of light, the star must be $\sqrt{100}$ or ten times farther than its standard distance of ten parsecs, or 10×10 $= 100$ parsecs distant.[1]

Color Magnitudes

The numerical value of the star's magnitude depends on the spectral region used in its determination. Special color filters used in conjunction with color-sensitive photographic emulsions, photomultiplier tubes, and infrared detectors provide the means for deriving the so-called color magnitudes: ultraviolet (U), blue (B), yellow or visual (V), red (R), near infrared (I), etc. One commonly used color-magnitude combination, known as the UBV system, covers the spectral range in three segments from 3,000 to 6,500 angstroms. The color magnitudes differ from one another in the same star because the stellar distribution of spectral energy varies with the wavelength according to the blackbody law of radiation. This makes it possible to derive the surface color temperatures of the stars from their color magnitudes, as will be described in Section 10.6.

The magnitudes so far discussed correspond to the amount of radiation within a given spectral range arriving at the surface of the earth. There is, however, a fundamental so-called *bolometric magnitude* that represents the *total* output of the star's radiation integrated over all the wavelengths received *outside* the earth's atmosphere. Unless it can be observed directly from properly instrumented artificial satellites, a theoretical correction, based upon the star's blackbody temperature, must be applied to the

---

[1] Those who have an acquaintance with logarithms can obtain the answer much more quickly: $\log r = (10 - 5 + 5)/5 = 2$; $r = 100$.

ground-observed magnitude. This correction compensates for the radiation lost in passing through the earth's atmosphere.

10.6 STELLAR TEMPERATURES AND COLORS

Color Temperatures

A convenient method of finding the surface temperature of a star is to compare two color magnitudes of the star. The difference in the two measured magnitudes is called the *color index*. A frequently determined color index is the B − V (blue minus yellow) difference in magnitudes. A blue star, for example, has a brighter blue magnitude on the normal blue-sensitive photographic emulsion than its yellow magnitude on the yellow-sensitive emulsion. The opposite is true for an orange or red star. Since the color index represents the difference in the amount of radiation between two separated narrow spectral regions of the blackbody energy curve of the star, the star's temperature can be determined. A number of blackbody energy curves are shown in Figure 10.12. Table 10.3 exhibits the relationship between color index and color temperature.

Spectral-Energy-Distribution Temperature

A more reliable but slower method of determining the star's surface temperature is to measure the change in intensity across its photographed spectrum (spectrogram). An output device records on a strip of paper the variations in the transmitted light of a slowly moving spot of light passing across the negative of the photographed spectrum. The recorded intensity distribution at the different wavelengths is matched to obtain the best fit against the calculated blackbody temperature curve based on Planck's law of radiation (Figure 10.12).

A newer technique involves continuous photoelectric spectral scanning by means of a slowly rotating grating that permits successive portions of the star's spectrum to pass over an array of photomultipliers sensitive to different spectral colors. The star's energy distribution in the various wavelengths can be recorded on paper, printed on cards, or binary coded for analysis by a computer.

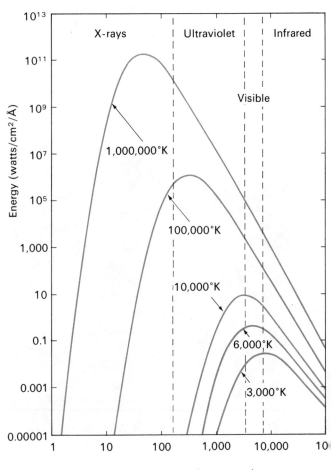

Figure 10.12 Blackbody energy curves according to Planck's radiation law.

Table 10.3 Relation between Color Index and Temperature

Color Index (B − V)	Color of Star	Color Surface Temperature
−0.6	Electric blue	30,000°K
−0.3	Blue	20,000°K
0.0	White	10,000°K
+0.3	Yellow-white	7,000°K
+0.6	Yellow	5,500°K
+1.0	Orange	4,500°K
+1.7	Red	2,600°K

10.7 STELLAR DIMENSIONS

Stellar Diameters

There are several ways of finding the sizes of the stars. One useful method is based on the star's surface temperature and its absolute bolometric luminosity. It can be shown by employing the Stefan-Boltzmann law of radiation (Section 9.2) that the radius of the star (R) varies with the square root of its luminosity (L) and inversely as the square of its temperature (T). The luminosity, L, is equal to the surface area of the star multiplied by the unit surface emission; that is, $L = 4\pi R^2 E$ where R is the star's radius and E is the surface emission in erg/cm^2/sec. From the Stefan-Boltzmann law, $E = 5.6 \times 10^{-5} T^4$. Hence $L \propto R^2 T^4$ from which $R \propto \sqrt{L/T^2}$. From the known values of L and T, the radius of the star can be calculated.

It is convenient to express the star's radius in terms of the sun's radius, thus eliminating the constant of proportionality. We may therefore write:

$$\frac{R_*}{R_\odot} = \sqrt{\frac{L_*}{L_\odot}} \left(\frac{T_\odot}{T_*}\right)^2 \qquad \begin{array}{l} * \to \text{star} \\ \odot \to \text{sun} \end{array}$$

Example: Barnard's star (the second closest star to the sun) has an absolute bolometric magnitude of +11.3 compared to the sun's which is +4.8. From the magnitude difference of 6.5 between the two bodies, we find according to Table 10.1 that the luminosity of Barnard's star is 1/400 that of the sun. The temperature of Barnard's star is $T_* = 2,900°K$; that of the sun is $T_\odot = 5,800°K$. Hence $L_*/L_\odot = 1/400$ and $T_\odot/T_* = 2$. Substitution of the numerical values in the above formula yields:

$$\frac{R_*}{R_\odot} = \left(\frac{5800}{2900}\right)^2 \sqrt{\frac{1}{400}} = 4 \times \frac{1}{20} = 0.2$$

Thus the diameter of Barnard's star is 1/5 of the solar diameter or 173,000 miles.

A direct measurement of the angular diameters of the largest stars was made many years ago by means of the stellar optical interferometer devised by the American physicist A. A. Michelson. The chief difference between the radio interferometer described in Section 3.3 and the optical interferometer is the replacement of the two radio antennas by two movable mirrors and the much shorter wavelengths of visible light. Starlight was reflected toward the main mirror of the 100-inch Mt. Wilson reflector from a movable mirror at each end of a long boom mounted on top of the reflector's tube. This produced a stellar image crossed by a set of dark interference fringes from each side of the star. The fringes could be made to disappear by adjusting the spacing between the movable mirrors. From the known critical separation of the mirrors, which caused the stellar image to become uniformly bright (disappearance of fringes), the angular diameter of the star could be calculated by means of a simple formula. The angular diameter of the star combined with the star's distance yielded the linear diameter of the star. A modernized version known as the intensity interferometer has been developed by the Australian astronomers R. H. Brown and R. Q. Twiss. It consists of two twenty-foot mirrors with variable spacing up to about 600 feet. The resulting fringe pattern produced by the interference of the starlight from the two telescopes is scanned by photoelectric multipliers. The output intensity fluctuations of the fringe pattern are analyzed electronically to yield the star's angular diameter. A third method of deriving stellar diameters is based on the orbital data obtained from certain kinds of double stars (Section 11.1).

10.8   STELLAR SPECTRA

Stellar Spectral Classes

One of the most fruitful avenues of exploration in all of astronomy has been in the spectral examination and classification of the stars into a well-ordered sequence. The first large-scale study of the spectra of the stars was a photographic survey of nearly one-quarter million stars inaugurated in 1884 at the Harvard College Observatory. It was finally completed forty years later. By placing a large thin prism in front of the telescope's objective lens, it is possible to photograph the spectra of many stars on a single plate as shown in Figure 10.13. The procedure was described in Section 4.6.

The Harvard astronomers were able to classify the stellar spectra into a progressive array which became known as the Harvard Draper spectral sequence. At the conclusion of the survey in 1924, when the relationship between the atomic structure and radiation was better understood, it was realized that the great diversity in the spectral patterns was due chiefly to temperature variations; it was not the result of abundance differences among the elements. The chemical elements are present in most stellar atmospheres in nearly the same proportions: an overwhelming amount of hydrogen, a small percentage of helium, and a much smaller percentage of the remaining elements.

Spectral Characteristics

Each spectral class in the Harvard classification is smoothly subdivided into ten parts from zero to nine. For example, the sun's spectral type is G2, 0.2 beyond G0 toward the next class, K. Table 10.4 lists the spectral classes and briefly describes their most distinguishing features.

Figure 10.13   Photographic negative of an objective-prism spectrogram of a star field. (Courtesy of Warner and Swasey Observatory.)

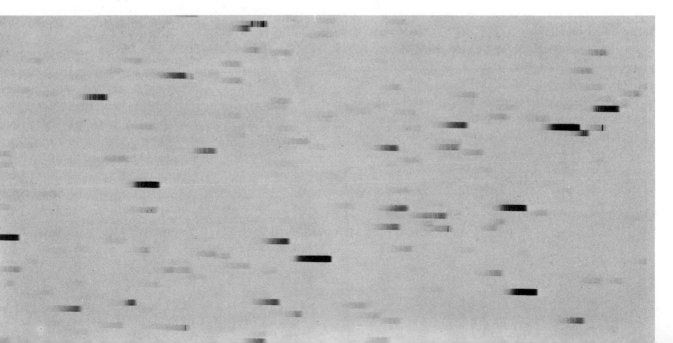

Table 10.4   The Spectral Classes

Spectral Type	Color	Average Temperature	Prominent Lines Present
O	~~Electric~~ blue	30,000°K	Ionized helium; multiple ionized oxygen, nitrogen, silicon; neutral helium; hydrogen weak
B	Blue	20,000°K	Neutral helium and hydrogen stronger; ionized oxygen, carbon, nitrogen, silicon
A	White	10,000°K	Hydrogen strongest; ionized calcium, iron, and titanium
F	Yellow-white	7,000°K	Hydrogen weakening; more ionized and neutral metals
G	Yellow	5,500°K	Hydrogen weaker; ionized calcium very strong; other ionized metals weaker; neutral metals stronger
K	Orange	4,500°K	Neutral atoms very strong; ionized calcium still strong; few ionized metals; hydrogen still weaker; some molecules appear
M	Red	2,600°K	Strong neutral atoms; hydrogen very weak; titanium oxide prominent

There are four minor classes constituting a very small percentage of the stars: (1) type W (Wolf-Rayet), the very hot-shell stars characterized by broad emission lines; this group is usually placed at the top end of the spectral divisions above type O; (2) and (3) types R and N, the cool red stars exhibiting prominently the absorption bands of carbon cyanogen (CN) and carbon hydride (CH) along with the low temperature lines of the neutral metals; (4) type S, the cool red stars possessing the conspicuous bands of zirconium oxide as well as the low temperature lines of the metals. These latter types are grouped at the low temperature end of the spectral sequence, usually after class M.

Line Intensities and Their Behavior

The observed dissimilarity in the stellar spectra comes from the uniquely selective manner in which the various atoms absorb and reradiate energy under different environmental temperatures. The stellar

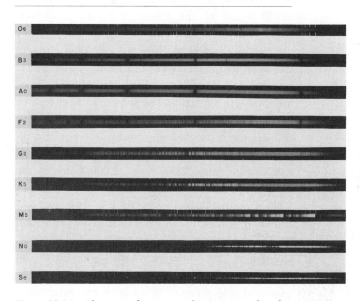

Figure 10.14   The spectral sequence, showing examples of each spectral class. (Courtesy of Hale Observatories.)

atmospheric pressure (in reality the electron pressure of the gas) exerts a minor influence on the spectral behavior. Decreased atmospheric pressure favors higher ionization; increased pressure diminishes the effect. In a hot environment a larger proportion of the atoms is ionized and excited to upper energy states owing to the presence of many high-energy photons and more energetic collisions between atoms. Most of the line radiations from the ionized atoms lie in the ultraviolet region leaving a sparse remainder in the visible portion of the spectrum. In a cooler environment those atoms requiring high-energy photons for excitation into upper levels are not present in significant numbers. Instead, the dominating low-energy photons control most of the excitation processes with the result that the majority of the atoms are excited into the lower energy states; only a minority with low ionization potentials may become ionized by losing an electron. The spectral lines from these neutral and singly ionized atoms, mostly those of the metals, are very numerous throughout the visible spectral region.

Let us examine the spectral role of hydrogen, the most abundant element present in the stellar atmospheres. We note that the hydrogen lines are of low strength at stellar temperatures in excess of 20,000°K, rise toward a maximum near 10,000°K, and decline more gradually toward the cooler temperatures. The photon energies corresponding to the temperature range 7,000°K to 15,000°K are of the right magnitude to excite many of the hydrogen atoms from the second to the third energy level and beyond (Figure 4.10). This gives rise to the absorption lines in the Balmer series and accounts for the great strength of the Balmer series in the visible region of the A and F spectral classes. In the hotter stars the overwhelming presence of the high-energy photons has left few hydrogen atoms with attached electrons. Those that still remain neutral account for the weak lines of the Balmer series. In contradistinction to hydrogen, the helium lines are present only in an environment containing an abundance of high-energy photons of the type available in the hottest stars. This results from the internal level structure of the helium atom which requires a greater amount of energy to excite the helium atoms.

10.9 THE SPECTRUM-LUMINOSITY (H-R) DIAGRAM

Correlation between Spectral Class and Absolute Magnitude

In 1911–1913 the Danish astronomer E. Hertzsprung and the American astronomer H. N. Russell independently demonstrated that a close connection exists between the spectral class of a star and its absolute magnitude. If we plot the stars' spectral classes (or temperatures or color indexes) horizontally against their absolute magnitudes (or luminosities) vertically, we find that the plotted points are not indiscriminately scattered over the diagram. Instead, they lie along well-defined tracks as illustrated in Figure 10.15.

It is obvious that stars of the same approximate spectral class or temperature come in different sizes. Consider, for example, the three M-type stars in Table 10.5, which are selected from the diagram (Figure 10.15). The diameters were calculated from the formula appearing in Section 10.7. The distinction between dwarfs, giants, and supergiants with respect to their sizes is made clear from the numbers of the last column. The figures show, as we would expect, that a more luminous star radiates energy over a larger surface area than a less luminous star of the same temperature.

Luminosity Classes

A refinement of the spectral classes into six different luminosity types was worked out by W. W. Morgan and P. C. Keenan of the Yerkes Observatory. It is based upon fine but observable distinctions in

1. *Types of Spectra (from* The Universe, *p. 47, Life Nature Library, published by Time Life Books).*
A continuous spectrum, *showing the familiar hues of the rainbow stretched out in a band of blending colors, is produced by a glowing solid or liquid, or by a hot gas under high pressure.*

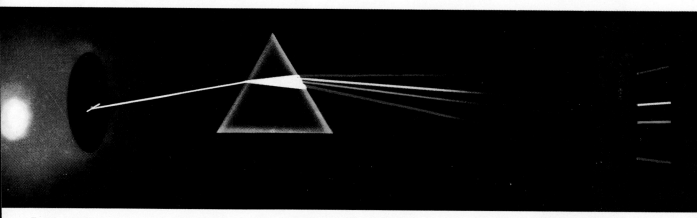

A bright line spectrum, *or emission spectrum, is produced by a hot gas of low density and pressure. Each chemical substance gives off a characteristic pattern of lines that differs from all the others and thus makes possible its identification like a set of fingerprints.*

A dark line spectrum, *or absorption spectrum, is caused by the presence of a cooler gas in front of a source producing a continuous spectrum. The cooler gas absorbs light precisely in the parts of the spectrum where it would emit bright lines if it were hot enough to radiate. The positions of the dark lines thus provide a clue to the composition of the gas.*

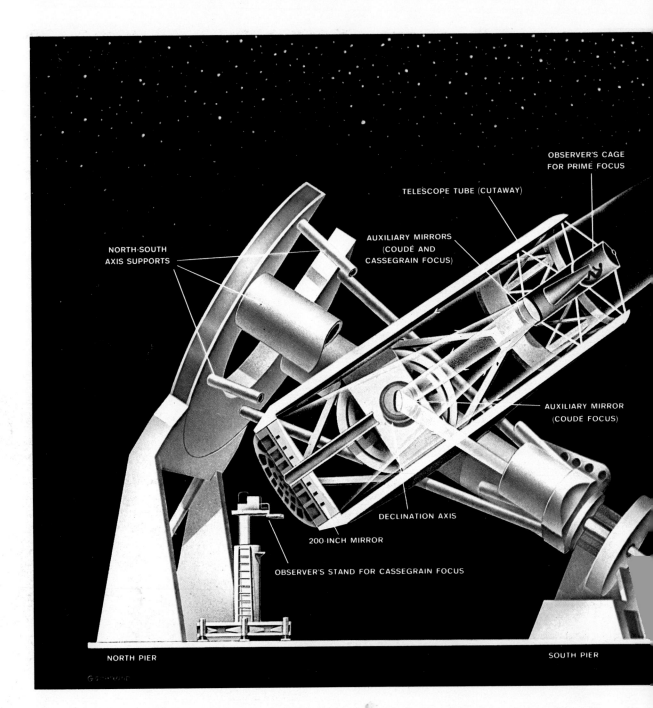

OBSERVER'S CAGE
FOR PRIME FOCUS

TELESCOPE TUBE (CUTAWAY)

AUXILIARY MIRRORS
(COUDÉ AND
CASSEGRAIN FOCUS)

NORTH-SOUTH
AXIS SUPPORTS

AUXILIARY MIRROR
(COUDÉ FOCUS)

DECLINATION AXIS

200-INCH MIRROR

OBSERVER'S STAND FOR CASSEGRAIN FOCUS

NORTH PIER

SOUTH PIER

2. *Spectroscopy with the Hale reflector. Light collected by the 200-inch mirror at the base of the telescope is focused into a bright beam and then guided into a special room filled with equipment for spectrum studies. The room is maintained at a constant temperature so that the by-now greatly concentrated beam of light will not be distorted by expansion or contraction of the instruments. In this drawing, the telescope is aimed at Sirius, the brightest star in the sky. At the lower right is projected*

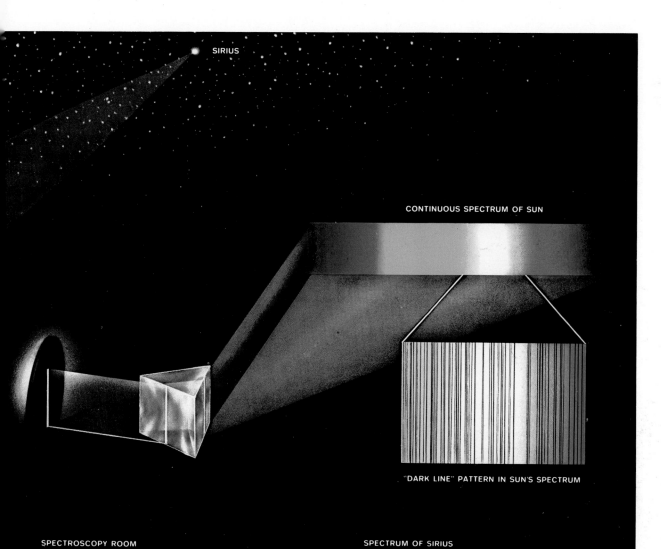

SIRIUS

CONTINUOUS SPECTRUM OF SUN

"DARK LINE" PATTERN IN SUN'S SPECTRUM

SPECTROSCOPY ROOM
FOR COUDÉ FOCUS

SPECTRUM OF SIRIUS

the spectrum of Sirius, revealing a pattern of dark lines identified as the spectrum of hydrogen. At the top right is a prismatic view of the spectrum of sunlight. Below that is a portion of the dark line spectrum of the sun obtained with a slit-and-prism combination. (From The Universe, *pp. 48–49,* Life Nature Library, *published by Time Life Books.)*

3. *The earth photographed from Apollo 16 (April 1972), showing an extensive cloud cover. However, much of Mexico and the southern half of the United States are clearly visible. (NASA)*

4. *View of the Lunar Module "Orion" and the Lunar Roving Vehicle at the Descartes landing site, photographed by astronaut Charles M. Duke Jr. of Apollo 16. Astronaut John W. Young can be seen directly behind the rover. The lunar surface feature in the left background is Stone Mountain. (NASA)*

5. *Mars photographed with the 120-inch reflector of the Lick Observatory. North is at the top. Both polar caps are visible. The dark markings spread across the ruddy Martian surface were once erroneously interpreted to be areas of vegetation. What the landscape of the planet is really like is shown in Figure 7.14.*

6. *Jupiter photographed with the 120-inch Lick reflector. The shadow of one of Jupiter's moons (the bright spot) is projected on the planet's disk. The red spot appears one-quarter inch below the satellite shadow.*

7. *Saturn photographed with the Mt. Wilson 60-inch reflector of the Hale Observatories.*

8. *Total eclipse of the sun photographed on July 10, 1972 by David Baysinger at Tuktoyaktuk, Northwest Territories, Canada.*

13. *Great nebula in Orion (Messier 42) photo-*
graphed with the Hale 200-inch reflector. The
Orion nebula is the birthplace of new stars some
1,500 light-years from the earth. Its overall
diameter is about 20 light-years. The nebula
consists mostly of glowing hydrogen gas with some
helium and lesser amounts of the heavier atoms
stimulated to fluorescence by the ultraviolet light
of its recently created stars. The phenomenon is
similar to the mechanism that causes certain
mineral substances to glow when irradiated with
ultraviolet ("black") light. In the nebula the
stellar ultraviolet light that strikes the atoms of
gas is absorbed and the energy is re-radiated in
the visible colors.

14. *Horsehead nebula in Orion (NGC 2024)*
photographed with the 48-inch Schmidt telescope
of the Hale Observatories. A large cloud of cool
dust is shown silhouetted against a backdrop of
glowing gas energized by nearby hot stars. The
stars and blue-white patch of nebulosity in the
obscuring portion of the photograph are obviously
foreground objects.

15. *North America nebula in Cygnus (NGC 7000) photographed with the 48-inch telescope of the Hale Observatories. The pinkish glow arises from hydrogen gas shining by the same mechanism that causes the gas in an emission nebula to radiate: the ultraviolet light of nearby hot stars, which is absorbed by the gaseous medium, is re-radiated in the visible region of the spectrum.*

16. *Pleiades and associated nebulosity in Taurus (Messier 45) photographed with the 48-inch telescope on Mount Palomar, Hale Observatories. The nebulosity around the brighter stars of the Pleiades star cluster contains dusty material which scatters (reflects) the starlight. The phenomenon is analogous to the color glow observed around a street lamp on a foggy night resulting from the scattering of the lamplight by the moisture particles. The color of the nebulosity is bluer than that of the stars because the shorter waves are scattered more strongly than the longer waves.*

17. *The Trifid nebula in Sagittarius (Messier 20) photographed with the 200-inch Hale reflector. The larger cloud on the right is an emission nebula, a conglomerate of dust and glowing gas stimulated to radiate in visible light by absorption of the powerful ultraviolet light of its immersed hot stars. Particularly noticeable are the branching dust lanes obscuring the view of the brighter background. The smaller blue cloud on the left is a reflection nebula, similar to that in the photograph of the Pleiades above.*

18. *Great galaxy in Andromeda (Messier 31) photographed with the 48-inch Schmidt telescope of the Hale Observatories. The Andromeda galaxy and its two elliptical satellites are about 2,200,000 light-years distant. The light by which we see these objects began its journey about the time man first appeared on our planet. The closely wound dust-streaked spiral arms glow blue with the light of the bright, young population I stars. The pinkish-white color of the central portion comes from the light of its old red population II stars. This major galaxy, about 130,000 light-years in diameter, is the nearest of the spirals. We view the galaxy at a rather sharp angle of about twelve degrees to the line of sight through a field of foreground stars inside our own Galaxy whose size and structure are comparable to that of our neighbor.*

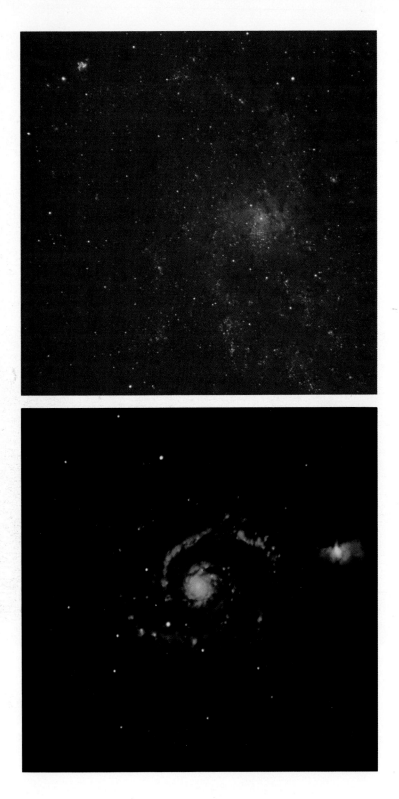

19. *The galaxy in Triangulum (Messier 33) photographed with the 200-inch Hale reflector. This spiral galaxy is another one of our neighbors within the Local Group. It is about 2,300,000 light-years distant and about three-fifths the size of our Galaxy. Its small nucleus is characteristic of those spirals with well-opened arms. Their bluish coloration comes from the presence of the giant and supergiant blue population I stars lighting up the spirally-strewn gas along the arms.*

20. *Whirlpool galaxy (Messier 51) photographed at the Flagstaff, Arizona station of the U.S. Naval Observatory. This Sc spiral, viewed face-on, is about ten million light-years distant. It exhibits a well-formed spiral structure rendered visible by the light of its blue supergiants. Although the upper coil crosses in front of the small irregular galaxy on the right, the two galaxies are evidently interconnected since they both possess the same velocity of recession.*

22. *Crab nebula in Taurus (Messier 1) photographed with the 200-inch Hale reflector. Its distance is about 5,000 light-years and its diameter, which is still growing, is six light-years. The lower of the two stars along the diagonal near the center is the gravitationally collapsed core of the supernova—a pulsar that flashes on and off thirty times per second.*

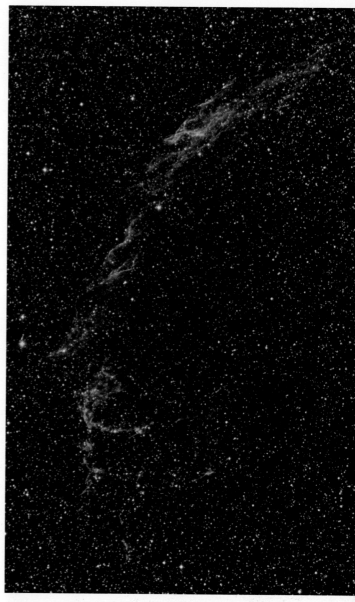

21. *Veil nebula in Cygnus (NGC 6992) photographed with the 48-inch Schmidt telescope of the Hale Observatories. This nebula is part of a larger loop which constitutes the remnant of a supernova (see Figure 14.1). It is about 2,500 light-years distant. The glowing luminescence is believed to result from the shockwave excitation created by the collision of the expanding material with pockets of interstellar gas and dust. This delicate lacework of gaseous filaments has been romantically described as a "soul floating heavenward."*

23. Abnormal galaxy in Ursa Major (Messier 82) photographed with the 36-inch Crossley reflector of the Lick Observatory. This galaxy, about ten million light-years away, is undergoing a violent explosion which is not too apparent in this colored reproduction. The black and white photograph in Figure 14.14 shows its explosive nature more clearly.

the strengths of certain critical absorption lines arising from physical variations of the stars within the same spectral subdivision. In Figure 10.16, note that though the spectra of the G8 supergiant, G8 giant, and G8 main-sequence stars are quite similar, there are some discernible differences in the indicated lines. These lines serve as sensitive indicators in sorting out the luminosity classes within a spectral subdivision. The luminosity classes are presented in the H-R diagram in Figure 10.17. According to this

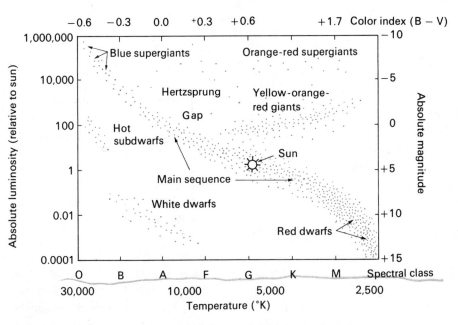

Figure 10.15   Schematic representation of the spectrum-luminosity diagram:

Blue supergiants—*bluest, most luminous, hottest; moderately large stars; low densities and large masses; very rare; example: Rigel.*

Red supergiants—*orange to red in color; the largest stars and among the brightest; large masses and extremely low densities; few in number; example: Betelgeuse.*

Giants—*yellow, orange, and red; considerably larger and brighter than the sun; average to larger than average masses and low densities; fairly scarce; example: Arcturus.*

Middle main-sequence stars—*white, yellow, and orange; stars higher than the sun on main sequence are somewhat larger, hotter, more massive, and less dense than the sun; plentiful in number; example: Sirius. Stars below the sun on the main sequence are somewhat smaller, cooler, fainter, less massive, and denser than the sun; plentiful in number; example: Epsilon Eridani.*

Red dwarfs—*coolest and reddest stars on the low rung of the main sequence; considerably fainter and smaller than the sun; small masses and high densities; the most abundant stars; example: Barnard's star.*

Hot subdwarfs—*quiescent novae, central stars of planetary nebulae, and other subluminous hot blue stars; solar-type masses and very high densities; fairly rare; example: central star of the Ring nebula in Lyra.*

White dwarfs—*mostly white and yellow; extremely faint and tiny by solar standards; enormously high densities; terminal evolutionary development; quite plentiful; example: the binary companion of Sirius.*

10 THE GALAXY: ITS STELLAR PROPERTIES

Table 10.5 Correlation between Intrinsic Brightness, Temperature, and Diameter of Three M-type Stars

Object	Absolute Luminosity relative to Sun	Temperature	Approximate Diameter relative to Sun
Red dwarf	0.01	3,000°K	0.4
Red giant	100	3,000°K	40
Red supergiant	10,000	3,000°K	400

scheme, now widely employed, the sun's spectral classification is G2V.

It therefore becomes possible to determine the *spectroscopic parallax* (or distance) of a star once its luminosity class is identified from its spectral appearance. The absolute magnitude M, corresponding to its spectral type and luminosity class, may be found from Figure 10.17. When subtracted from its apparent magnitude m, it is equal to $(m - M)$, the distance modulus from which the star's distance, or parallax, is derived according to the method outlined in Section 10.5.

Interpretation of the H-R Diagram

The significance of the Hertzsprung-Russell (H-R) diagram became clear when it was realized several decades ago that the diagram portrays the evolutionary development in the life histories of the stars. Aside from the inherent errors in the observational data, the broadened plots in the diagram represent a composite of slightly different evolutionary tracks resulting chiefly from marginal differences in the chemical compositions of the stellar populations. The physical explanation of the reason that the points in the diagram are not scattered at random is that the natural forces affecting the destinies of the stars confine them to the stable portions of the diagram while they are converting matter into radiant energy. The Hertzsprung gap represents a semistable region through which the evolving stars quickly pass. The subject of stellar evolution is treated at length in Chapter 12.

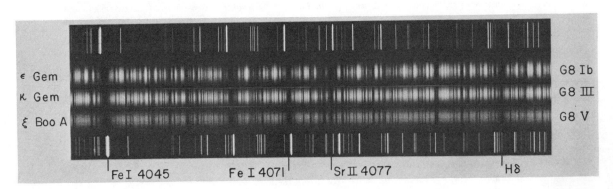

Figure 10.16 Differences in the appearances of certain sensitive lines between a supergiant, giant, and main-sequence star of the same spectral class (Courtesy of Lick Observatory.)

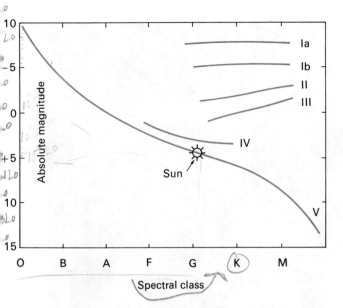

*Figure 10.17 Spectrum-luminosity classes (M-K system):
Ia, brightest supergiants; Ib, average supergiants; II, bright
giants; III, average giants; IV, subgiants; V, main-
sequence stars.*

REVIEW QUESTIONS

1. In their study of the stars, what vital physical data do astronomers seek out concerning stellar nature and properties?

2. Describe with the aid of a diagram the parallax method of determining the distance of a star.

3. What is one widely used method in finding the distances of stars too remote for the parallax determination?

4. What is the distinction between: (a) apparent magnitude and absolute magnitude; (b) photographic magnitude and photovisual magnitude; (c) bolometric apparent magnitude and apparent visual magnitude?

5. How is the color index or B − V magnitude of a star obtained? What is its significance?

6. Why does the color of a star change from red to blue as the temperature increases?

7. What data are needed to derive the true diameters of the stars? Is there an independent way of checking the results?

8. What is the relationship between: (a) spectral class and temperature; (b) spectral class and color index; (c) temperature and color index?

9. Account for the spectral dissimilarities existing in the stellar classes in terms of the concepts of atomic excitation and ionization and related temperature differences.

10. How did astronomers learn that stars with a great range in sizes exist?

SELECTED READINGS

Bok, B. J., and P. E. Bok, *The Milky Way*, Harvard University Press, 1957.

Bova, B., *Milky Way Galaxy: Man's Exploration of the Stars*, Holt, Rinehart, and Winston, 1961.

Branley, F. M., *The Milky Way: Galaxy Number One*, Crowell, 1969.

Merrill, P. W., *Space Chemistry*, University of Michigan Press, 1963.

Page, T., and L. W. Page, eds., *Stars and Clouds of the Milky Way*, Macmillan, 1968.

Page, T., and L. W. Page, *Starlight*, Macmillan, 1967.

Smart, W. M., *Some Famous Stars*, McKay, 1950.

Whitney, C. A., *Discovery of Our Galaxy*, Knopf, 1971.

Winter constellation of Orion and surrounding region. The three prominent stars in line form the belt of Orion. The nebula of Orion, appearing as the fuzzy object below the belt, lies in the scabbard of the mighty hunter. (Courtesy of Hale Observatories.)

THE GALAXY:
ITS CONSTITUENCY AND STRUCTURE

But when I lifted up my head
    From shadows shaken on the snow,
I saw Orion in the east
    Burn steadily as long ago.

From windows in my father's house
    Dreaming my dreams on winter nights,
I watched Orion as a girl
    Above another city's lights.

    Sara Teasdale (1884–1933),
    "Winter Stars,"
    Flame and Shadow (Macmillan, 1920)

Astronomers have classified the different stellar species that populate the Galaxy into two broad population groups: the younger population I stars and the older population II stars. They have ascertained the stars' numbers, distances, distributions, and studied their various properties and physical behavior. These stellar categories include the following principal classes: (1) variable stars such as the pulsating variables (called cepheids), long-period variables, irregular variables, and eruptive variables; (2) explosive stars such as the planetary nebulae, novae, and supernovae; (3) double stars comprising the visual, spectroscopic, and eclipsing binaries; (4) multiple stars merging into the larger stellar aggregations which include the open clusters, stellar associations, star clouds, and globular clusters.

The nonstellar constituency (the space between the stars) is known as the interstellar medium. It consists of a general mix of sparse gas and dust in lesser proportion. Most of the material is composed of hydrogen gas. Concentrations of this material appear as the bright and dark nebulae located largely in the outer spiral framework of the Galaxy. Existing within the interstellar medium are a number of localized sources of cool, complex compounds consisting mainly of various combinations of hydrogen, carbon, nitrogen, and oxygen aggregated in some instances into organic molecules of the type found in amino acids.

Some fragmentary spiral features of our Galaxy were originally derived from optical studies of the stellar distribution of the high-luminosity stars and their associated bright nebulosity. More detailed information has come from the radio analysis of the 21-centimeter radiation emitted by the neutral hydrogen. Optical and radio investigations reveal the Galaxy to be a large rotating spiral about 100,000 light-years in diameter. Surrounding it is a sparse ellipsoidal stellar halo intermingled with a spherical distribution of some one hundred globular clusters. The sun is situated approximately two-thirds of the galactic radius from the center in the disk portion of the Galaxy. Its period of revolution around the galactic center is about 220 million years. Within the Galaxy, stellar segregation is fairly evident. The oldest, metal-poor stellar populations II are concentrated in the globular clusters, in the galactic halo, and in the central regions; the youngest, metal-rich stellar populations I inhabit the outer spiral portions; an intermingling of mixed population groups exists throughout the disk portion of the Galaxy.

11.1 DIFFERENT STELLAR SPECIES

The Galaxy contains an assemblage of many kinds of stars of assorted sizes, masses, temperatures, colors, ages, and chemical compositions. At least four-fifths are main-sequence stars; the rest mostly constitute the white dwarfs, the rarer giants, and the still scarcer supergiants. Roughly half of the total stellar population consists of single stars; the remaining half comprises physically related stars ranging from double stars and multiple stars to clusters and group associations of stars. Certain stars whose light is not constant, such as the variable and eruptive stars, are singled out for special attention by astronomers because of their unusual characteristics. They make up less than one-tenth of 1 per cent of the stellar membership in the Galaxy.

Stellar Populations

A form of stellar segregation exists within the Galaxy. In many regions it is not sharply drawn but in its broadest category it embraces two distinct types of stellar groups called *population I* and *population II*. They are differentiated by dissimilarities in evolution, stellar properties, chemical composition, and location within the Galaxy. The first clue to their identification came from W. Baade's research on the Andromeda galaxy in the early 1940's when the Los Angeles area was blacked out during the early part of World War II. Employing red-filter photography with the 100-inch reflector, he managed to separate the hitherto unresolved central region of that galaxy into multitudes of red giant stars. These he named the population II stars to distinguish them from what he called the population I stars, the highly luminous blue supergiants located in the spiral arms (see Plate 18). The similarity of the population groups to those in our Galaxy was soon established. The population I stars within our Galaxy are associated with the bright, gaseous nebulae in the spiral arms. They represent a younger generation of stars than the older population II stars found in overwhelming numbers in the globular clusters, in the galactic halo, and in the nuclear regions of the Galaxy.

It is now realized, from accumulated observational data and from stellar evolutionary theory, that gradations between the two population groups do exist. The population types have been subdivided into the following categories based upon their evolutionary history and their galactic locations:

1. *Extreme population II* comprises the oldest stars, found chiefly in the galactic halo and in the globular clusters. Their average age is around 10 billion years; their proportion of the heavy elements is very low—about 1 per cent.

2. *Intermediate population II* tends to occupy the central bulge of the Galaxy and the lower stratum of the galactic halo. They vary in age, about 1.5– 10 billion years; their heavy-element concentration ranges from about 1 to 3 per cent.

3. *Intermediate population I* mostly inhabits the

Figure 11.1 Population I stars resolved in the outlying portions of the Andromeda galaxy, Messier 31. (Courtesy of Hale Observatories.)

Figure 11.2 Population II stars resolved near the nucleus of the Andromeda galaxy, Messier 31. (Courtesy of Hale Observatories.)

11 THE GALAXY: ITS CONSTITUENCY AND STRUCTURE

disk portion of the Galaxy. The majority are main-sequence stars about 0.2–10 billion years old; their heavy-element proportion is roughly 2–3 per cent. The sun is classed as a member of this group.

4. *Extreme population I*, confined strongly to the galactic plane, is frequently found in association with the gas and dust patches in the spiral arms. These are the youngest stars, with ages of 1–100 million years; their concentration of the heavy elements may be as high as 5 per cent.

Cepheid Variables

The present number of known variable stars of all classes is around 20,000. About half of them belong to a distinctive group comprising the pulsating variables. The so-called *classical cepheids*, numbering about 700, constitute one important subdivision of this group. The cepheids are named after the first star of their kind discovered, Delta Cephei. The classical cepheids are distinguished by the following characteristics: They are yellow supergiants of great brilliance; their light varies periodically over a range of about one magnitude during an interval of days to weeks; their spectra exhibit Doppler shifts in synchronization with the periodic changes in their light. The cyclic variations in light and velocity result from a small rhythmic expansion and contraction of their diameters: the more luminous the cepheid, the longer the period of variation. This extremely important correlation between period and brightness is known as the *period-luminosity relation*. It is represented graphically by a plot exhibiting the correlation in absolute magnitude with the period as shown in Figure 11.4 for the different types of cepheids. The precise calibration of the absolute-magnitude scale has been a difficult problem because no cepheid is close enough to have its parallax measured. Consequently, astronomers have resorted to less direct

methods in establishing the zero point of the absolute-magnitude scale.

The classical cepheids are the most luminous cepheids. Sparsely sprinkled about within the disk portion of the Galaxy, they constitute a small segment of the population I stars. Another less luminous group of cepheids with periods generally between ten and thirty days belongs to the population II membership. These are the *W Virginis cepheids* (named after their prototype), and they are found in the halo portion of the Galaxy and in several globular star

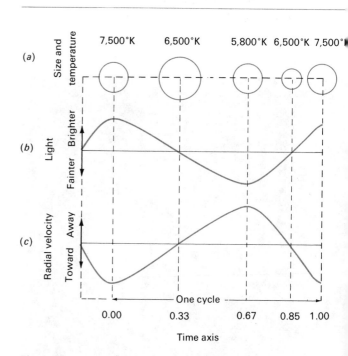

Figure 11.3 Typical cepheid variations during one light cycle. Stellar diameter changes are exaggerated in this drawing.

clusters. Still another population II group present in large numbers in the central and halo regions of the Galaxy constitutes a third class of cepheids known as the *RR Lyrae variables* (also named after their prototype). These are bluish-white giant stars considerably fainter than the other cepheids but nevertheless up to one hundred times brighter than the sun. Their pulsation periods average around one-half day.

The great value of the period-luminosity relationship lies in its application to the determination of distances. The cepheid variable stars serve as "standard candles" in evaluating the distances of newly discovered cepheids, whether in our Galaxy or in other galaxies. If the period and the apparent median magnitude of a newly discovered cepheid are derived from the photographic data, its distance can be calculated. (The median magnitude is the magnitude half-way between the maximum and minimum magnitudes.) Let us suppose an astronomer finds, after plotting the light curve (as in Figure 11.3*b*), that the period of a classical cepheid is five days and the apparent median magnitude, *m* is 7.3. There are distinguishing spectral and light characteristics that enable the astronomer to recognize the type of cepheid with which he is dealing. From the period-luminosity diagram in Figure 11.4 it is observed that a five-day classical cepheid possesses an absolute magnitude, *M* of -2.7. Hence the distance modulus: $(m - M) = 7.3 - (-2.7) = 10$. From the distance modulus formula in Section 10.5, the distance is found to be 1,000 parsecs. Since the absolute magnitudes of the RR Lyrae stars hover around $+0.5$, they also are useful as "standard candles" but at lesser distances.

Long-Period Variables; Irregular Variables

Another large fraction of the variable-star membership is composed of nearly 4,000 bright M-type

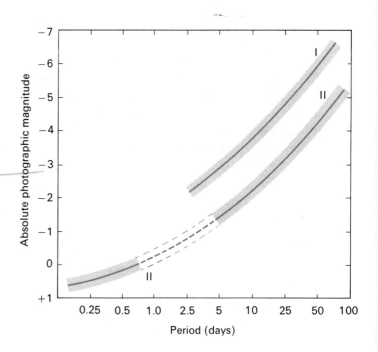

Figure 11.4   Period-luminosity relation: population I, classical cepheids; population II, W Virginis cepheids and RR Lyrae variables (short curve at lower left).

giants and supergiants. They exhibit cyclic light changes amounting to several magnitudes with a period of about a year. The most celebrated member of this group is the supergiant star Mira (Omicron Ceti). It varies between the second magnitude (about as bright as the pole star) and the ninth magnitude (sixteen times dimmer than the faintest naked-eye star) in a period of nearly a year. The accompanying spectral and velocity variations of the long-period variables are quite complex. The observed changes may be caused by some kind of imprecisely understood pulsating mechanism whose action is not identical to that of the cepheids. Infrared studies show the Mira-type stars to be surrounded by extensive envelopes from which gas and dust are being expelled.

Hundreds of other variable stars with a wide range of luminosities and colors exhibit such irregular and often baffling changes that the cause of their behavior remains obscure. In a number of instances the erratic behavior results from the interchange of atmospheric material between two nearly brushing components of a close double star, causing semi-periodic outbursts of luminosity. One small group of yellow supergiants, known as the R Coronae Borealis variables, contains a superabundance of carbon and a deficiency of hydrogen. They are completely unpredictable in their behavior. After long periods of quiescence that may last for years, they suddenly dim by several magnitudes and exhibit erratic fluctuations before returning to their normal brightness months or years later. Infrared studies indicate these stars possess envelopes of condensed carbon.

Eruptive Variables: Flare Stars; Novae

Some twenty main-sequence red dwarf stars, called *flare stars,* have been found to undergo sudden short-lived flare-ups in brightness up to several magnitudes. A rapid outburst builds up in a few seconds and gradually subsides within minutes. The flare phenomenon is probably caused by a localized high-temperature disturbance erupting on the star's surface in a manner similar to that of a solar flare.

The most spectacular eruptive stars are the novae and supernovae. Because of their special connection with pulsars, supernovae are discussed at length in Chapter 14. The sudden appearance of a nova in the heavens is signaled by a rapid rise in brightness amounting to tens of thousands of times within a few hours. Then follows a slow decline in light that may persist for a year before the star settles down to its former obscurity. The cause of this upheaval is fairly well understood. An aging, subluminous hot star of approximately solar mass has undergone a violent

Figure 11.5   Expanding nebulosity around Nova Persei 1901; photographed with the 200-inch Hale reflector in 1949. (Courtesy of Hale Observatories.)

superficial explosion as the result of internal instability. This unstable condition is brought about by the gradual exhaustion of its nuclear fuel and the consequent reduction in heat generation followed by a drop in the internal gas pressure. Equilibrium is restored after gravitational contraction causes a temperature rise that leads to a rapid expansion of the star's outer layers and their subsequent expulsion into space in the form of one or more rapidly expanding shells. Evidence of a blowout comes from the large observed Doppler shift of the absorption lines toward the blue in the spectrum of the nova. Shortly thereafter, widely broadened emission lines appear, indicating the ejection of a transparent gaseous shell at a high rate of speed, ocasionally up to 1,000 mi/sec. This is confirmed from the direct photographs secured much later, which show a growing envelope in the years following the outburst. It is estimated that not more than about 0.01 per cent of the star's material is blown off. Although the original prenova condition of the star is largely restored, in the due course of time, measured in tens or hundreds of thousands of years, it may repeat the performance a number of times. It is theorized that ultimately the star evolves into a white dwarf. Radio thermal energy from the expanding envelopes of ionized gas in two novae (Nova Delphini in 1967 and Nova Serpentis in 1970) was detected for the first time by radio astronomers at the National Radio Astronomy Observatory in Green Bank, West Virginia. It is estimated that our Galaxy experiences about thirty novae outbursts each year.

Planetary Nebulae

In one type of object, called a *planetary nebula*, a milder and slower type of ejection of surface material appears to have taken place. A planetary nebula consists of a small, hot, subluminous central star surrounded by a slowly expanding, frequently convoluted, nebulous shell of ionized gas moving outward at a speed of 10–20 mi/sec (see Plates 9 and 10). The nebulous envelope exhibits the bright-line spectrum of rarefied gases stimulated to fluorescence by the ultraviolet light of the central star. The star is presumed originally to have been a red giant of solar mass or less. Its hot, collapsed core has been transformed into the central star. It is believed to represent a brief interlude in the twilight of the star's existence before it ends its fusion-producing career and evolves into a white dwarf.

Binary and Multiple Stars

Possibly half of the stellar population consists of gravitationally linked stars orbiting each other. Among the sun's neighbors out to fifteen light-years, at least half are members of multiple systems. One commonly observed grouping in the Galaxy are the pairs called double or *binary stars* whose components range in separation from those in virtual contact with each other to a large fraction of a light-year apart. In any binary arrangement, each member swings around the common center of mass of the system (the barycenter) in an ellipse or circle. The more massive component moves in a tighter orbit than its less massive companion; the relative sizes of their orbits are in the inverse ratio of their respective masses. The relative motions of the system can be visualized by imagining how two unequal spherical ends of a dumbbell rod move when it is rotated around its center of balance. It is the same kind of action that was discussed earlier in connection with the earth and moon. (Section 6.4).

Binary systems are classified according to the instrumental methods of observing them. Three classes are differentiated: visual binaries, spectroscopic binaries, and eclipsing binaries. The information obtained from analyses of their orbital data varies somewhat with the type of binary. It includes the orbital dimensions, orbital shapes (eccentricities), periods of revolution, and orbital orientations with respect to the line of sight. In special instances, stellar data relating to diameters, masses, densities, and luminosites can be derived.

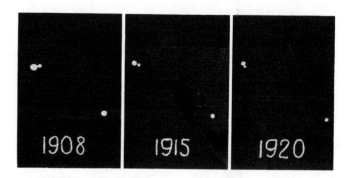

Figure 11.6   Orbital motion of the visual binary Kruger 60 during approximately one-quarter of its 44-year period. (Courtesy of Yerkes Observatory.)

---

11 THE GALAXY: ITS CONSTITUENCY AND STRUCTURE

In double stars with the greatest separations, both companions can be seen in the telescope and they are accordingly called *visual binaries*. The observed apparent path of one component around the other is the projection of the true orbit upon the plane of the sky. Yearly measurements of their apparent separations and angular movements around each other provide the necessary data to calculate their orbital parameters. It is found that the orbital dimensions vary from a few astronomical units to thousands of astronomical units corresponding to periods of revolution from several years to many thousands of years.

The binary nature of a system whose components cannot be resolved visually is revealed by the periodic oscillatory Doppler shifts in spectral lines of one or both components. These are the *spectroscopic binaries* whose orbits vary in size from a fraction of an astronomical unit to several hundred astronomical units. The corresponding periods of orbital revolution range from hours to several years. When the spectra of both components are visible, two alternating sets

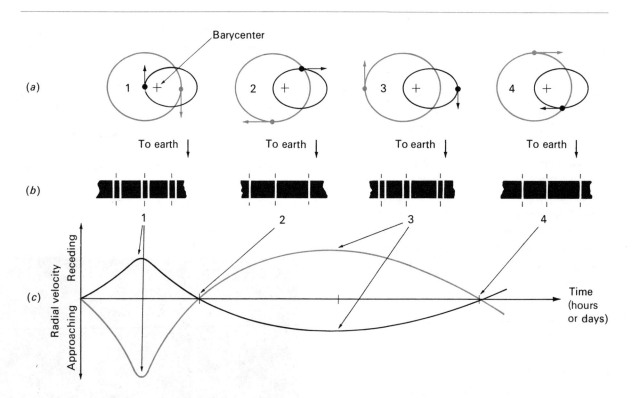

Figure 11.7 *Spectroscopic binary system.* (a) *Elliptic orbits of components; one component* (●) *is twice as massive as other component* (∘). (b) *Doppler line shifts of both components.* (c) *Velocity curves of both components; velocity of less massive companion shown in blue.*

of lines are periodically displaced in opposite directions (Figure 11.7b). Maximum shift occurs at intervals of one-half the period, when the orbital motion of the components is in the line of sight. Minimum shift occurs when they are moving across the line of sight one-quarter of a revolution later, at which time the two sets of lines merge. In most cases only the spectrum of the brighter component registers and one set of lines shifts periodically. The orbital information is derived by analyzing the velocity curve, a plot of the change in radial velocity during the period of revolution of the spectroscopic binary (Figure 11.7c).

In the closely paired stars whose orbital motions are viewed more or less edgewise, eclipses can be observed by photometric monitoring of the changes in light throughout the orbital revolution of the system. Such double-star systems are called *eclipsing binaries*. One companion periodically passes in front of the other, temporarily cutting off part or all of the light of the eclipsed star as shown in Figure 11.8. By analyzing the general shape of the light curve and the duration and amount of light diminution of the eclipses, it is possible to construct a scale model of the system. When the eclipsing binary is also observed as a spectroscopic binary, the combined data obtained from the light curve and the velocity curve lead to an evaluation of important stellar properties: the stars' actual diameters, their masses, densities, temperatures, and true orbital dimensions.

A small fraction of gravitationally linked systems involves more than two stars. The arrangement may consist of a distant third star revolving around a close pair or, more frequently, two close pairs, usually spectroscopic binaries, revolving around each other in a longer period. Other close combinations involving more than four stars are possible. One interesting multiple system is the second-magnitude star Castor in the constellation of Gemini. In a small telescope Castor is easily observed to be double; its period of revolution is about 400 years. The brighter visual component is a spectroscopic binary with a period of 9.2 days. The fainter visible companion is also a spectroscopic binary whose period is 2.9 days. A nearby ninth-magnitude star called Castor C, 1.2 minutes of arc away, orbits the visual pair in many thousands of years; it is an eclipsing binary with a period of 0.8 day. Thus all three classes of binaries are represented in the sextuple system of Castor.

Mass-Luminosity Relation

One very important quantity, the stellar mass, cannot be obtained from isolated single stars because their insignificant gravitational effects upon other stars are not observable. In visual binary systems, application of Kepler's modified third law of motion, combined with knowledge of the stars' mean angular separation, distance, and orbital period, leads to an evaluation of the stellar masses.

In this instance, Newton's version of Kepler's third law may be written: $m_1 + m_2 = d^3/P^2$, where m_1 and m_2 are the respective masses of the components in units of the sun's mass, d is their average separation in astronomical units (obtained by multiplying the mean angular separation in seconds of arc by the distance in parsecs), and P is the orbital period of revolution in years. The observed motion of each companion around the barycenter yields the mass ratio, m_1/m_2, similar in principle to that used in calculating the ratio of the moon's mass to that of the earth (see Figure 6.9a). Knowledge of the combined mass of the system and the mass ratio yields the individual masses.

Example: The observational data for the binary system of Sirius are as follows: $d = 20$ astronomical units, $P = 50$ years, m_1 (Sirius)/m_2 (companion) = 2.3. Hence, $m_1 + m_2 = (20)^3/(50)^2 = 3.2$; this value, combined with $m_1/m_2 = 2.3$, or $m_1 = 2.3m_2$, gives:

$$m_1 \text{ (Sirius)} = 2.2 \text{ solar masses}$$
$$m_2 \text{ (companion)} = 1.0 \text{ solar mass}$$

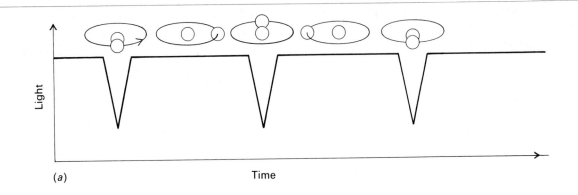

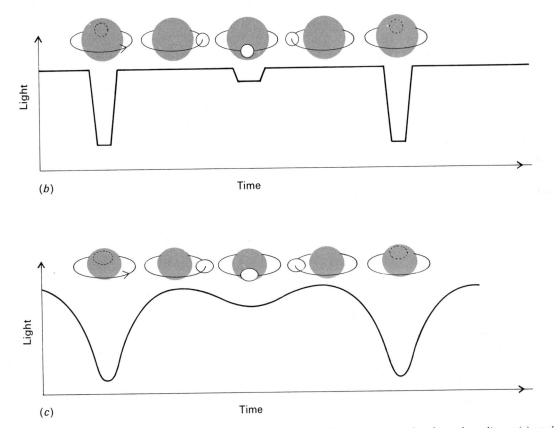

Figure 11.8 Representative eclipsing binary systems: (a) partial eclipses; (b) alternating total and annular eclipses; (c) total and annular eclipses of tidally distorted companions.

A similar analysis can be applied with some modification to certain cases of spectroscopic and eclipsing binaries. Here there is the added advantage that the distance does not enter into the calculations since the true dimensions of the orbits are known from the velocity data. From the preceding information a significant correlation between the mass and the absolute luminosity of a star has been established for stars on the main sequence. It is known as the *mass-luminosity relation*. This relationship has also been derived theoretically from the fundamental laws governing the behavior of matter and radiation within the stellar interiors. Note in the diagram that the more massive stars shine more brightly, which follows from the simple fact that a greater stellar mass has more matter to convert into energy per unit time and therefore possesses a higher luminosity. It also uses up its nuclear fuel faster and burns itself out sooner.

The correspondence between mass and luminosity exhibited in Figure 11.9 breaks down for the non-main-sequence stars, whose internal structures differ from those of the main-sequence stars. Although the range in luminosities is very large, roughly from one-millionth to 30,000 times the sun's brightness, the masses exhibit a very modest range from several hundredths to about seventy-five solar masses. There is a critical minimum mass below which a contracting gaseous body cannot become hot enough to initiate thermonuclear fusion and radiate as a star. There is also a maximum limit set by the outward force of radiation pressure that restricts the mass content of a star.

11.2 STELLAR GROUPINGS

Open Clusters

In the disk portion of the Galaxy are found hundreds of gravitationally related multistar assemblages called *open clusters* (formerly known as *galactic*

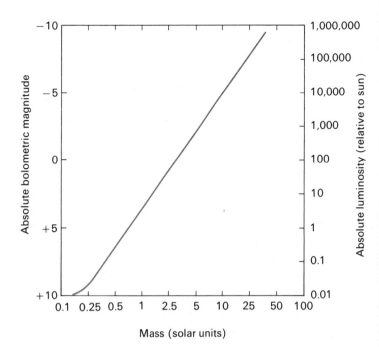

Figure 11.9   Mass-luminosity relation for main-sequence stars.

clusters). Their total number is estimated to be around 15,000. Open clusters are arranged in somewhat loose swarms embedded within the mainstream of the stellar population. Their membership runs from a score to many hundreds of stars spread out over several tens of light-years. Their stellar constituency consists of population I stars covering a considerable spread of colors and luminosities. The ages of the clusters vary from a few million to ten billion years. The oldest open-star clusters are the more compact groups which have managed to withstand the various disruptive forces operative within the Galaxy over the past billions of years. In photographs of the youthful clusters the brilliant blue giants predominate. In those of the middle-aged clusters, the main contribution comes mostly from the yellow-white main-sequence stars; their bright blue stars have long since evolved into white dwarf or neutron stars.

Stellar Associations

In the outer regions of the Galaxy, a number of sparse aggregations of highly luminous O and B stars called *stellar associations* are found scattered within the concentrations of gas and dust in the spiral arms of the galactic disk. Their dimensions vary up to several hundred light-years in diameter. One estimate places their number at seven hundred. There is strong evidence that the youthful stars which populate these assemblages have had a recent common origin. The individual members are rapidly separating from each other as a consequence of the outward radial expansion from the association center, the presumed point of origin. It appears that these associations are highly unstable aggregations with a maximum life expectancy of a few million years before they completely disperse into the mainstream of the Milky Way.

Globular Clusters

The largest and most highly concentrated assemblages of stars are the *globular clusters*. About 120 of them surround our Galaxy in a vast spheroidal arrangement centered on the galactic nucleus. The largest globular clusters may contain up to one million stars packed within a diameter of several hundred light-years. The nearest globular cluster is Messier 4, about 8,000 light-years from the sun. In photographs the red giants dominate because of their greater luminosity even though they may exist in fewer numbers than the main-sequence stars. The Orbiting Astronomical Observatory (OAO-2) has detected the presence of a number of hot, luminous

Figure 11.10   Open star cluster in Cancer. (Courtesy of Hale Observatories.)

Figure 11.11   Globular star cluster in Hercules, Messier 13. The total number of stars in this aggregation may be as high as one million. (Courtesy of Hale Observatories.)

blue members. Their ultra-violet light does not register on earth-based photographs, because of the heavy atmospheric selective absorption of the light. Despite the appearance of crowding in the pictures, the individual stars, though more closely spaced than in the solar neighborhood (up to 300 times), are far enough apart to avoid collisions. They tend to swing in almost rectilinear orbits in a pendulumlike motion from one side through the center to the other side of the cluster.

Let us summarize the distinguishing features that make the globular clusters a unique stellar breed. They are composed of the oldest population II stars; their spectra in general reveal an exceptionally low metal content compared with the stars of the disk population; they are spheroidally scattered around the center of the Galaxy; and they move in far-ranging elliptical orbits about the galactic center at all angles to the plane of the galactic disk.

11.3 INTERSTELLAR DUST, GAS, AND MOLECULES

In the early part of this century astronomers believed that interstellar space was fairly transparent and consequently any dimming or reddening of the starlight could be ignored. Later, in the 1930's, it was discovered that the distant stars were dimmed and reddened more than the nearer stars by the passage of their light through an interstellar absorbing medium. The interstellar matter consists of a mixture of atomic and molecular gases and fine dust particles which are largely concentrated in irregularly shaped clouds of low temperature, ranging in diameter from 0.1 to 50 light-years. The dust in interstellar space consists of widely separated microscopic particles whose composition and properties are unlike the dust with which we are familiar on earth. The absorption of starlight is due almost entirely to the dusty material that permeates the interstellar medium. The gaseous component is fairly

transparent to the passage of starlight. Altogether, interstellar matter occupies no more than ten percent of the volume of our Galaxy.

Interstellar Dust

In long-exposure photographs of the Milky Way, irregular patches of dark nebulae partially or completely obscure the view of the starry background. One lengthy region consists of an in-depth complex of dozens of isolated and interconnected dark clouds stretching about half-way around the middle of the galactic band from Cygnus to Crux. This obscuring strip forms the Great Rift that divides the Milky Way into two branches (see Figure 10.1). In many regions the dark nebulosity often separates into tangled absorbing lanes cutting across sections of the bright gaseous nebulae. Much of this material has probably been expelled from the stars by stellar winds or by more violent means. A cube 3,000 miles on an edge contains about one gram of this stuff. There is only one dust grain for every million million hydrogen molecules. Despite their extremely low density, the dark clouds are remarkably opaque because of the accumulated effect of the light extinction produced by the passage of starlight through an enormous path length of the absorbing material. The intensity of the starlight is cut down about 50 per cent in passing through 2,000 light-years of the more heavily obscuring regions of the Galaxy. The blue colors are affected more than the red colors, hence the color of a distant star whose light has been selectively scattered appears not only dimmer but redder than it actually is. If a suitable correction is not applied to the observed magnitude of a distant star, the distance calculated from the distance modulus $(m - M)$ comes out too great. Unfortunately, astronomers are hampered by the uneven and spotty distribution of the absorbing material which is concentrated mostly in or close to the galactic plane. The interstellar haze clinging close to the galactic

Figure 11.12   The Milky Way in Ophiuchus, a complex of stars, dark clouds, and bright nebulosities. (Courtesy of Yerkes Observatory.)

plane prevents us from viewing our full share of extragalactic objects in this direction. In edge-on spiral galaxies this haze appears as the dark lane passing centrally across the galaxy (Figure 1.6 and Figure 10.10b).

From the amount of reddening, scattering, polarization, and spectral absorption of the starlight, astronomers have concluded that the dust grains have diameters of the order of one hundred-thousandth of an inch. They appear to consist of an assortment of graphite, iron particles, silicon carbide, silicates, and frozen gases (ices). Polarization studies indicate that at least some of these grains are elongated and aligned with the weak interstellar magnetic field. The dust contributes about 1 per cent of the total mass of the interstellar medium. It is believed that most if not all of the interstellar dust comes from the condensation of material blown out from the stellar envelopes and atmospheres. The chemistry and exact origin of interstellar dust are not clearly understood at the present time.

Interstellar Gas

The gaseous component of the interstellar material, which consists mostly of hydrogen, exists both in the ionized and neutral condition. Its density may vary from less than one atom per cubic centimeter in the regions between the dust lanes to several thousand atoms per cubic centimeter in the bright gaseous nebulae. In the dark neutral hydrogen clouds, the density may reach 100,000 atoms/cm^3. If the air expelled in one exhalation of a person's breath were allowed to expand into an evacuated cubical enclosure one mile on an edge, the resulting density would exceed that in most parts of the interstellar medium.

Ionized Hydrogen Gas (HII Regions)

To considerable distances from the hot O and B stars, hydrogen gas is ionized by the stars' strong ultraviolet radiation. Such regions of ionized hydrogen are designated as *HII regions*. The absorption by the hydrogen of the ultraviolet photons emitted by these hot stars removes the electrons from the atoms and ionizes the hydrogen. In the course of their wanderings, the free electrons are momentarily recaptured by the hydrogen nuclei. As the captured electrons cascade down into the various atomic levels, they release the photons that give rise throughout the electromagnetic spectrum to many lines in the various hydrogen series, among which is the well-known Balmer series. The radiation that is observed in the bright gaseous nebulae consists, to a considerable extent, of the integrated light of the various spectral line emissions created by the process of ultraviolet absorption of the starlight and the subsequent recombination of the electrons with the ions.

In addition, certain atoms, chiefly ionized oxygen, nitrogen, and neon, can be stimulated to emission through infrequent encounters with free electrons which may excite the atoms into rare low-lying metastable levels. These are long-lived atomic levels having lifetimes up to several hours instead of the ordinary one hundred-millionth of a second. In the rarefied medium such atoms that have been "kicked upstairs" in this manner by electron collisions will endure for long periods in the excited metastable states without interruption. They will then spontaneously drop down to the bottom levels. This process gives rise to the so-called *forbidden lines* prominent in the red, green, and ultraviolet portions of the bright-line nebular spectrum. They are "forbidden" in the sense that their production is inhibited except under conditions approaching a vacuum.[1] The interstellar cloud of gas exhibiting a bright-line spectrum (Figure 11.13) is properly called an *emission nebula*. See Plates 13 and 15 for excellent examples of emission nebulae.

Neutral Hydrogen Gas (HI Regions)

Where there is an insufficient supply of ultraviolet light to ionize the gaseous material, the hydrogen within it remains cold and neutral. Such regions of unionized hydrogen are called *HI regions*. The dust particles within a cool nebula simply scatter and reflect the light of the embedded star or stars (see Plate 16). Since blue light is scattered more strongly than red light, the color glow around the star or stars is slightly bluer than the incident starlight. The effect is somewhat similar to the glow of light around a street lamp on a foggy night when the lamplight is scattered by the watervapor particles. Since the spectrum of the nebula is a weak, diluted replica of the absorption spectrum of the associated star or stars, this type of gas cloud is called a *reflection nebula*. In those regions far removed from any activating stars, the interstellar patches of gas and dust

[1] The action is similar to that observed in the bright-line spectrum of the solar corona (Section 9.7).

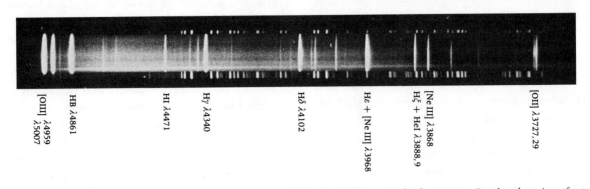

[OIII] λ4959 λ5007

HB λ4861

HI λ4471

Hγ λ4340

Hδ λ4102

Hε + [Ne III] λ3968

[Ne III] λ3868
Hζ + HeI λ3888.9

[OII] λ3727.29

Figure 11.13   Bright line spectrum of Orion nebula photographed by A. B. Wyse at Lick Observatory. Bracketed entries refer to forbidden lines. Roman numeral indicates atomic state: I, neutral; II, singly ionized; III, doubly ionized. The continuous background spectrum arises from the scattering of the starlight by the dust particles. (Courtesy of G. H. Herbig.)

reveal themselves as the dark, diffuse nebulae randomly scattered throughout the Milky Way.

The discovery in 1951 of a radio spectral line at 21 centimeters (1,420 megahertz) emitted by the cool neutral hydrogen opened up a new era of exploration of the Galaxy and its structure. Its presence had been predicted seven years before by the Dutch astronomer H. van de Hulst.

Electrons and protons behave like tiny rotating gyroscopes. About once in eleven million years, on the average, the spinning electron will spontaneously reverse its spin from the one in which it was aligned with the spinning proton. This drops the atom into the lower of the two closely split levels of the ground state of the atom with the release of a 21-centimeter photon. Eventually, after a chance encounter with a stray atom, the spinning electron may flip over and once more align itself with the spinning proton awaiting another spin reversal millions of years later. Even though the time lag is inordinately long for the production of a 21-centimeter photon, there is always a ready supply of the 21-centimeter

radiation available along the enormously long path length in the direction of the earth to make the line easily observable.

Analysis of the profiles and the Doppler shifts of the 21-centimeter line in many directions of the Milky Way have enabled radio astronomers to map the distribution of the neutral hydrogen within the Galaxy in considerable detail. Sections of the spiral-arm structure, previously identified in optical observations of the bright nebulosities associated with the hot luminous stars, have been greatly extended. A number of additional arms have been discovered in the 21-centimeter surveys. Radio observations have also revealed the existence of hydrogen streamers or jets projecting out from the galactic disk.

Other Neutral Gases

Starlight passing through the distant, cool, interstellar gaseous material is selectively absorbed in a few low-temperature spectral lines observed superimposed on the normal spectra of the hotter stars. These so-called *interstellar lines* are easily differ-

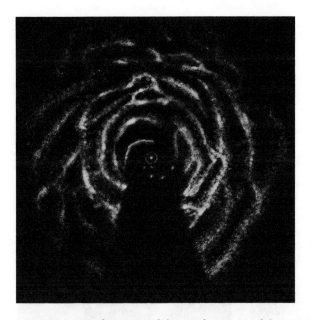

Figure 11.14   Radio picture of the spiral structure of the Galaxy derived from the 21-centimeter observations made by Dutch and Australian radio astronomers. The sun is represented by the small white dot and enclosed circle above the center of the Galaxy. (Courtesy of G. Westerhout.)

entiated from the few spectral lines of the O and B stars and many novae by their usually narrow widths and differently displaced Doppler line shifts. They become more difficult to identify in the line-rich later spectral classes. Frequently, several sets of Doppler-shifted interstellar lines appear, indicating that the starlight has passed through a succession of separate intervening clouds moving at different speeds to the line of sight (Figure 11.15). In the visual spectral region astronomers have identified traces of the following substances: atomic sodium, calcium, iron, potassium, titanium, molecular cyanogen, and neutral and ionized carbon hydride. In the ultraviolet spectral region, molecular hydrogen and carbon monoxide have been identified. Since 1964 radio astron-

omers have observed the high-level recombination lines of hydrogen, helium, and carbon arising from small upper-level atomic transitions between the closely crowded energy levels near the series limit. A captured electron may, for example, become momentarily trapped in the 110th level of the hydrogen atom before cascading down to the 109th level to emit a radio photon at six centimeters.

Interstellar Molecules

Since 1963 radio astronomers have been discovering a surprising number of compounds, including many organic ones, in the centimeter and millimeter microwave region in the cold interstellar clouds. By the end of 1972 twenty-seven molecules containing various combinations of hydrogen, carbon, nitrogen, and oxygen had been identified from approximately fifty radio spectral lines. Some of the familiar compounds are ammonia (NH_3), hydroxyl (OH), water (H_2O), carbon monoxide (CO), cyanogen (CN), formaldehyde (H_2CO), and methyl alcohol (CH_3OH). Two compounds, CH_3C_2H and CH_3CHO, contain a record number of seven atoms. Several sulfides including the familiar hydrogen sulfide (H_2S), and one metallic oxide, silicon monoxide (SiO), have also been discovered. Compared to the ubiquitous hydrogen, the molecules are present in small proportions—less than one part in one thousand of hydrogen. In a few instances the spectral lines are observed in absorption instead of in emission, whenever their compounds happen to lie in front of a galactic or extragalactic source emitting continuous radiation. (In 1971 OH was discovered in the exploding galaxy, M82, and in the galaxy, NGC253; in 1972 CO was found in the nearby galaxy, M33).

A number of specific molecules are being produced in a dense cloud, known as B2, near the galactic center in Sagittarius and in the Orion nebula. Other sources of production appear to be more randomly distributed in localized regions of the interstellar clouds. Some are concentrated in tiny regions comparable to the dimensions of the solar system. Their processes of formation and chemical stability remain a mystery. Possibly the enveloping dust clouds prevent the ultraviolet starlight from reaching these molecules and dissociating them. They could still be dismembered by the more penetrating x-rays and cosmic rays; or they could be removed by adhering to the surface of dust grains after striking them. It appears that some imperfectly understood mechanism is creating them in far greater abundances than by the ordinary process of collisional accretion. These interesting discoveries have opened up a new interdisciplinary field known presently as *astrochemistry* or *molecular astronomy*. Some of the molecular ingredients are found in the chemical structure of the organic compounds associated with living matter.

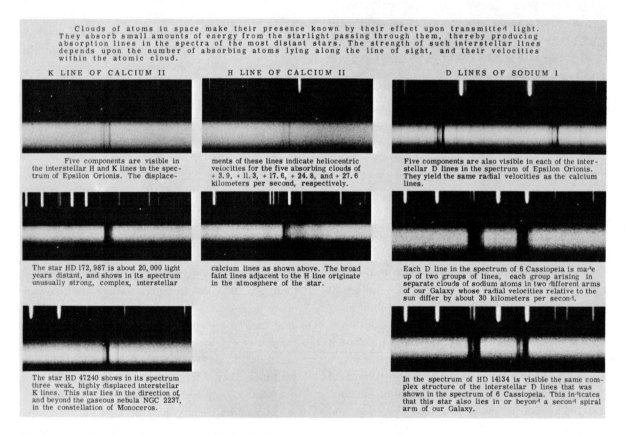

Clouds of atoms in space make their presence known by their effect upon transmitted light. They absorb small amounts of energy from the starlight passing through them, thereby producing absorption lines in the spectra of the most distant stars. The strength of such interstellar lines depends upon the number of absorbing atoms lying along the line of sight, and their velocities within the atomic cloud.

K LINE OF CALCIUM II   H LINE OF CALCIUM II   D LINES OF SODIUM I

Five components are visible in the interstellar H and K lines in the spectrum of Epsilon Orionis. The displacements of these lines indicate heliocentric velocities for the five absorbing clouds of + 3.9, + 11.3, + 17.6, + 24.8, and + 27.6 kilometers per second, respectively.   Five components are also visible in each of the interstellar D lines in the spectrum of Epsilon Orionis. They yield the same radial velocities as the calcium lines.

The star HD 172,987 is about 20,000 light years distant, and shows in its spectrum unusually strong, complex, interstellar calcium lines as shown above. The broad faint lines adjacent to the H line originate in the atmosphere of the star.   Each D line in the spectrum of 6 Cassiopeia is made up of two groups of lines, each group arising in separate clouds of sodium atoms in two different arms of our Galaxy whose radial velocities relative to the sun differ by about 30 kilometers per second.

The star HD 47240 shows in its spectrum three weak, highly displaced interstellar K lines. This star lies in the direction of, and beyond the gaseous nebula NGC 2237, in the constellation of Monoceros.   In the spectrum of HD 14134 is visible the same complex structure of the interstellar D lines that was shown in the spectrum of 6 Cassiopeia. This indicates that this star also lies in or beyond a second spiral arm of our Galaxy.

Figure 11.15   *Multiple interstellar lines of ionized calcium and neutral sodium in the spectra of several stars. (Courtesy of Hale Observatories.)*

11.4 ROTATION OF THE GALAXY

Evidence of Rotation

The flattening of our Galaxy is a consequence of its rapid rotation about an axis passing through the center of the nuclear bulge. The first observational clues of the galactic rotation were obtained by B. Lindblad and J. H. Oort in 1926–27 from their studies of the motions of the stars. Oort succeeded in uncovering a pattern of movement among the stars that indicated a Keplerian motion within the Galaxy. Stars closer to the center than the sun orbit around the galactic center faster than the stars farther out from the sun—as do the planets around the sun. What is observed is the radial component of the difference in orbital velocity between the sun and a star in any given direction within the galactic plane.

The observed radial motions of the nearby stars agree with the theoretical stellar pattern deduced from the differential galactic rotation as shown in Figure 11.16. Stars in the 45 and 225-degree sectors appear to be receding from the sun; stars in the 135 and 315-degree sectors appear to be approaching the sun; those in the 0, 90, 180, and 270-degree sectors show no differential radial motion. Stars whose average distance from the sun is 1,000 parsecs exhibit a maximum differential radial motion of about 15–20 km/sec; those whose average distance from the sun is greater show the expected larger effect. These stars are in general closer to the galactic center where the rotation is faster, and also farther from the galactic center where the rotation is slower, than is the first group.

Galactic Dimensions and Rotation Data

Analysis of the differential rotational movements observed among the stars by optical astronomers and among the neutral hydrogen clouds by radio astronomers at various distances from the sun yields the following data:

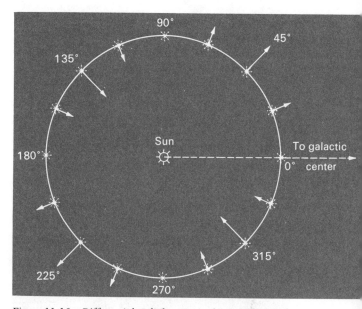

Figure 11.16   Differential radial motions of nearer stars which result from galactic rotation.

Diameter of Galaxy: 100,000 light-years

Diameter of galactic halo: >100,000 light-years

Distance of sun from galactic center: 30,000 light-years

Thickness of nuclear bulge: 16,000 light-years

Thickness of disk: 3,000 light-years

Mass of Galaxy: 170,000 million solar mass units

Mean density of matter in Galaxy: 10^{-23} g/cm^3 or 0.1 solar mass units per cubic parsec

Velocity of sun around center: 170 miles per second

Period of sun's revolution: 220 million years

Direction toward center of Galaxy: constellation of Sagittarius

It will be helpful at this point to re-examine the pictorial schematic of the Galaxy shown in Figure 10.10.

The figures presented are not definitive; they are constantly being revised as astronomers accumulate more extensive and accurate data. They do indicate that our stellar system is a galaxy of major size, constructed along the same lines as our large neighbor in the constellation of Andromeda some two million light-years distant (Plate 18).

11.5 OVERVIEW OF THE GALAXY

Gross Structure

Let us review the large-scale features that characterize our Galaxy. Its general appearance is that of a flattened, spiral-shaped assemblage of some 200 billion single, multiple, and clustered stars of assorted types stretching across a diameter of 100,000 light-years. The stellar system is largely segregated into two main population groups of older and younger stars. The central bulge of densely populated, metal-deficient old stars tends to rotate like a solid structure out to a distance of about 20,000 light-years. The younger, metal-enriched stars inhabiting the outer spiral arms revolve independently around the galactic center in approximately circular orbits. The sun, a yellow, middle-aged star, is located in the galactic suburbs, about two-thirds of the galactic radius from the center. It orbits around the center at a speed of 170 miles per second in a period of 220 million years.

It is estimated that at least 95 per cent of the galaxian mass is locked up in the stars. The remainder consists of gas and cold dust grains strewn about more sparsely in the regions between the spiral arms than along the arms where it appears in clumps and patches. In many places it remains dark; in other places it is rendered visible by the radiation from the recently created, hot young stars embedded within these clouds. The main bulk of the galactic material is concentrated in the nuclear bulge. Surrounding the spiral discoid is an ellipsoidal configuration of several billion old stars forming the halo population, and an outer, nearly spherical aggregation of about 120 globular clusters filled with the oldest stars.

Some Finer Details

A small, brilliant galactic core called Sagittarius A, not visible optically, has been observed radiating strongly in the x-ray, ultraviolet, infrared, and microwave spectral regions. The following description is derived from the radio observations of neutral hydrogen. Receding outward from the core at decreasing speeds is a broken, ring-shaped shell of hydrogen gas with velocities between 30 and 130 mi/sec. The mechanism by which this gas is replenished remains unclear. Gaseous material also appears to be moving inward from the direction of the galactic halo into the discoid. In addition, eruptive movements of gas have been observed streaming outward at an angle about 7,000 parsecs from the galactic center. They form a turned-up and turned-down extension on opposite sides of the Galaxy.

Optical astronomers first identified sections of the spiral arms by tracing the regions where the O and B stars and their associated emission nebulosities are most prominent (see Figure 10.10). These bright gaseous condensations delineate the spiral features of the Galaxy. The closest arm whose inner edge skirts the sun is the *Carina-Cygnus arm*. It arcs over a considerable angle some 3,000 light-years farther out than the sun. Near the sun it bulges outward in a short extension called the *Orion spur*. A second arm, known as the *Perseus arm*, extends in the same general direction nearly 4,000 light-years beyond the first arm, closer to the edge of the Galaxy. A segment of a third inner arm called the *Sagittarius arm* has been observed closer to the galactic center than the sun at a distance of several thousand light-years from the sun. As Figure 11.14 reveals, the radio view of our Galaxy's spiral structure not only encompasses these three arms but adds many more hydrogen lanes, resulting in a tangled spiral pattern.

REVIEW QUESTIONS

1. What are the physical and luminosity differences between the cepheids of population I, population II (W Virginis type), and RR Lyrae variables?

2. Why do astronomers attach so much importance to the period-luminosity relation that exists between the period of pulsation of a cepheid and its absolute magnitude?

3. Name two kinds of mildy erupting variables and describe their behavior.

4. Differentiate observationally between the three classes of binary stars.

5. Explain how it might be possible for a binary system to be all three: a visual binary, a spectroscopic binary, and an eclipsing binary.

6. What kind of orbital and physical data relating to the components of a binary can be derived?

7. How is the velocity curve of a spectroscopic binary obtained? The light curve of an eclipsing binary? What use is made of these curves?

8. The mass-luminosity relation reveals that the more massive the star, the more brightly it radiates. Can you explain why?

9. Discuss the differences in the space distributions between the open clusters, the globular clusters, and the stellar associations.

10. Why is the light of distant stars reddened in passing through the interstellar medium? What evidence is there that interstellar dust is the culprit?

11. Describe the physical state and appearance of the interstellar clouds in the vicinity of the hot, luminous O and B stars, and in the regions far removed from such stars.

12. Since the gas component of the interstellar medium is transparent to starlight, how is its existence revealed?

13. How have radio astronomers succeeded in tracing the spiral structure of the galaxy from their observations of neutral hydrogen?

14. Draw a schematic plan view and edgewise view of the galaxy, showing its general structural features; also locate the sun's position.

15. Indicate in your sketches for question 14 the approximate locations of the different population groups: population I; population II; halo population; globular clusters.

SELECTED READINGS

Bok, B. J., and P. F. Bok, *The Milky Way*, Harvard University Press, 1957.

Dufay, J., *Galactic Nebulae and Interstellar Matter*, Dover, 1968.

Glasby, J. S., *The Dwarf Novae*, American Elsevier, 1970.

Glasby, J. S., *Variable Stars*, Harvard University Press, 1968.

Hey, J. S., *The Evolution of Radio Astronomy*, Science History Publications, 1973.

Jaki, S. L., *The Milky Way: An Illusive Road for Science*, Science History Publications, 1973.

Page, T., and L. W. Page, eds., *Stars and Clouds of the Milky Way*, Macmillan, 1968.

Payne-Gaposchkin, C., *Variable Stars and Galactic Structure*, Athlone, 1954.

Smith, F. G., *Radio Astronomy*, Penguin, 1960.

Unusual gaseous nebula in Serpens photographed in red light with the 200-inch Hale reflector. The tiny dark spots (globules) projected against the bright background are believed to be gravitationally collapsed condensations of gas and dust that will some day begin to radiate as stars. (Courtesy of Hale Observatories.)

STELLAR INTERIORS
AND EVOLUTION

So may we read, and little find them cold:
Not frosty lamps illuminating dead space,
Not distant aliens, not senseless Powers.
The fire is in them whereof we are born;
The music of their motion may be ours.

George Meredith (1828–1909),
Meditation under Stars

The stabilizing forces that keep a star in equilibrium involve the equality between the downward weight of the overlying layers and the upward thrust of the gas and radiation pressure together with the proper distribution of the flow of energy through the star. The secret of stellar longevity lies in the thermonuclear fusion of matter into energy deep inside the stars, in accordance with Einstein's equation, $E = mc^2$ (energy equals mass multiplied by the velocity of light squared). Because c^2 is such a large number, 9×10^{20} $(cm/sec)^2$, a prodigious amount of energy can be extracted from a tiny bit of matter.

Application of the natural laws governing the interactions between matter and energy enable astronomers, guided by the observed physical properties that the stars display, to trace the life histories of the stars. The stars develop along certain well-defined evolutionary tracks exhibited in the H-R color-luminosity diagram. The more massive stars live from a few million to several hundred million years because they exhaust their nuclear fuels at a prodigious rate. The less massive stars can exist for billions of years because they consume their nuclear fuels more sparingly.

Although there is strong observational evidence that stars are created within the dust-laden gas clouds of interstellar space, the mechanics of star formation are not well understood. It is believed that denser pockets of interstellar material condense into dark blobs called globules. They contract gravitationally, heat, and within a relatively short time, depending on their masses, form into protostars that evolve toward the main sequence from the right. They settle down on the main sequence and spend most of their lives there, fusing hydrogen into helium for millions to billions of years. After exhaustion of the hydrogen in its central core, the star leaves the main sequence and tracks upward to the right as it expands to become a red giant on its way toward the red-giant tip. During this period both hydrogen in the surrounding shell and helium within the core burn at a much higher temperature because of core contraction. As further nuclear burning of hydrogen into helium and helium into carbon and the heavier elements proceeds, the star tracks back and forth along the horizontal branch of the H-R diagram over long periods of time, hunting for a stable configuration. While it pursues this course it may temporarily emerge as a short-period, pulsating, cepheid variable (RR Lyrae star). The star continues to undergo successive internal adjustments as it synthesizes the heavier elements from its dwindling stock of nuclear fuels. Eventually a stage is reached where stars, like the sun and stars of lesser mass, can no longer generate energy through their internal thermonuclear processes. Shorn of their ability to support through gas pressure the pressing weight of the overlying layers, they die quietly as they gravitationally collapse into small, dense, white dwarfs. Their internal heat slowly bleeds away and they end their lives as black dwarfs—stellar corpses. The more massive stars may terminate their existence by exploding as supernovae and gravitationally collapsing into tiny neutron stars with densities a million billion times that of water. It is even possible, according to relativity theory, for the most massive stars to undergo such a complete catastrophic collapse near the end of their life cycles that they may disappear into black holes. The vast majority of the stars, however, live relatively quiet lives from birth to death.

12.1 INSIDE THE STARS

The fundamental problem of probing the structure and behavior of matter and energy inside the stars may be stated as follows: Given the known facts about the stars—namely, their diameters, masses, luminosities, and temperatures—and assuming a reasonable chemical composition for them, what can be learned about their internal physical conditions and structures and their evolutionary history? Application of the appropriate physical laws enables us to predict the observed evolutionary pathways of the stars in the spectrum-luminosity (H-R) diagram (Figure 12.1). Theoretical exploration of stellar interiors rests on certain assumptions made with regard to the basic physical processes operative within the stars. We shall now describe the processes that govern the lives of the stars and maintain their existence over long periods of time measured in millions to billions of years. In exploring the interior of a star, we begin first with a description of the internal forces that maintain the star's stability throughout most of its history.

Hydrostatic Equilibrium

At all points within a stable star the net downward gravitational pressure is balanced by the net outward gas pressure. If this were not so, the star would expand if the gas pressure exceeded the gravitational pressure, or it would contract if the reverse were true, until equilibrium between these two forces was restored. The gravitational pressure arises from the weight of the overlying gas layers. The gas pressure is the sum total of the forces imparted by the incessantly colliding gas particles moving at enormous velocities as a result of the high internal temperatures. The gas pressure thus may be regarded as the buoyant force that supports the weight of the overlying layers and prevents the star from gravitationally collapsing. In the hottest stars the momentum of the hard-driving photons produces an intense radiation pressure that supplements the gas pressure in supporting the overlying mass burden.

The behavior of the normal stellar gas conforms to the simple ideal expressed in the *perfect-gas law*,

well-known to the student of physics or chemistry. This law states that the pressure of the gas is proportional to its density and temperature inside a closed vessel. (The star's material is enclosed in the form of a sphere by its self-gravitation.) Under ordinary conditions the perfect-gas law fails when the density of the gas is greater than about one-tenth that of water. In the normal stellar interior, despite the high density which may exceed the density of water by a factor of at least one hundred times, the intense heat has stripped the electrons from the atoms; the bare nuclei and the free electrons dash wildly about at great speeds still consistent with ideal gas conditions. Use of the perfect-gas law simplifies mathematical treatment of the stellar interior. Another simplification that eases the burden of calculation relates to the chemical composition of the star. The bulk of the gaseous material for most stellar models consists of a high proportion of hydrogen, a lesser amount of helium, and a very small percentage of the heavier elements. A typical stellar composition

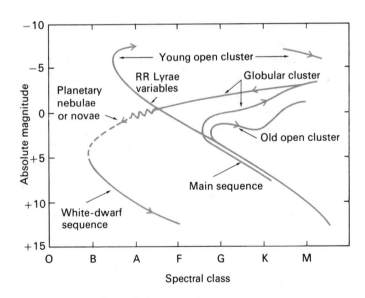

Figure 12.1   Stellar evolutionary trackways.

---

12 STELLAR INTERIORS AND EVOLUTION

by weight might be: hydrogen, 70 per cent; helium, 28 per cent; heavy elements, 2 per cent.

Thermal Equilibrium

So long as the star continues to produce energy by burning its nuclear fuel at the same rate that energy is radiated from its surface, the star remains thermally stable. As the heat flows steadily outward from the center, local thermal equilibrium prevails to keep the temperature constant at any point within the star by means of a naturally regulated, thermostatic-control system. If the leakage of energy through a certain region were suddenly to increase or decrease, the temperature would change and a chain reaction would follow in which the hydrostatic equilibrium would be upset. This would lead to an instability which, if not checked, would result eventually in an explosion or implosion. This does not happen, however, except in extreme circumstances, and internal stability is thus automatically restored by the regulatory adjustment in hydrostatic equilibrium to compensate for the change in the thermal equilibrium.

In a thermally stable star, a distinction must be made regarding the most efficient mode of energy transport under the different physical conditions. One possibility is by conduction, as in the transfer of heat along a metal rod. For normal gaseous interiors this mode is totally ineffective and inefficient. A second and likely method is by convection through the circulation of heated gas between the hotter and cooler regions. (The movement of hot air ducted into the rooms of a house from a central furnace is an example of convection.) In regions where the temperature change with depth is fairly rapid, convection cells form within the unstable, turbulent gas; thus convection will be facilitated and will become the principal means of energy transport. Within a convective zone the different atomic constituents are well mixed as a result of the continual stirring process.

A third mode of energy transmission is by means of radiation. (The radiant heat from an electric heater without a fan is an example of energy transport across a room by radiation. The addition of a blower would also provide convection.) Deep inside the star the high-energy electromagnetic radiation produced by thermonuclear fusion in the core of the star is passed outward within the radiative zone by the photons. Along the way they are continually being scattered by the free electrons or absorbed by the atoms and reradiated. In the radiative region there is very little mixing and the original chemical separation of the elements is maintained.

Hindrance to the Flow of Radiation (Opacity)

The continual interchange between the electromagnetic radiation and matter deep inside the star, through the process of absorption and reemission of the photons and their constant buffeting by the electrons and atoms, impedes the progress of the outward flow of radiant energy. The action is crudely analogous to that of falling raindrops encountering air resistance as gravity pulls them downward. The resistance to the flow of radiation is called the *opacity*; it tends to regulate the outward flow of radiation. If the opacity were not present, that is, if the interior gases were not opaque due to lack of absorption of energy, the star would be transparent and we could see through it. Most of the high-powered original radiation formed within the star's core is so degraded in encountering resistance on its way out that it is rendered relatively harmless by the time it leaves the surface of the star. The sunlight that we receive on earth may have begun its outward journey through the sun ten million years ago in the form of lethal x-ray radiation deep inside the sun's interior.

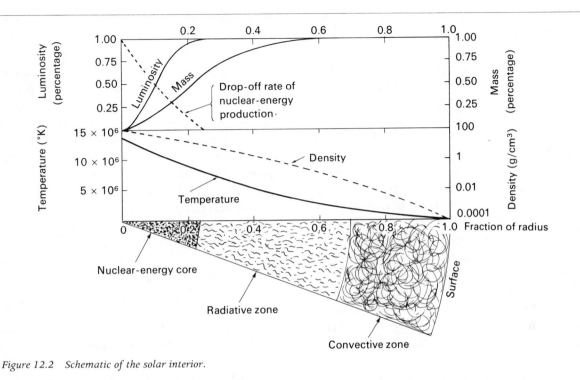

Figure 12.2   Schematic of the solar interior.

12.2   THERMONUCLEAR ENERGY PRODUCTION

Early Attempts to Account for the Source of Stellar Energy

It was known over a century ago that the amount of energy radiated by the sun during its lifetime could never have been supplied by the ordinary process of combustion similar to the burning of wood or coal. Even under the most efficient production of energy by any known chemical process, the sun would have burned itself out in less than 40,000 years. Heat energy is available by the conversion of potential energy through gravitational compression. This becomes a vital source of energy upon which the star draws during certain periods in its evolution. Calculations inform us that the sun, on the basis of gravitational contraction alone, would not have survived for more than about thirty million years.

The Atomic Nucleus as the Source of Energy

It was therefore necessary to discover a way by which a star could keep shining for billions of years. The secret lay in the fusion of a lightweight element into a heavier element at a rate slow enough to last for that length of time. Since hydrogen was known to be present in overwhelming abundance, it naturally became suspect as the necessary fuel. In 1937–38 the nuclear physicists H. Bethe and C. F. von Weizsäcker independently suggested a process whereby hydrogen nuclei could be converted into helium to release sufficient quantities of energy to keep the stars shining so long.

The rate of nuclear fusion is critically dependent on the temperature and the density of the gas. Higher temperature facilitates the rate of energy production; higher density increases the frequency of collisions between nuclei which stand a better chance of fusing. From this it follows that the rate of the nuclear reactions will be greatest in the star's central region. It will gradually fall to zero at a critical distance from the center where the temperature and density are too low to initiate further nuclear reactions. In the sun, for example, 80 per cent of its nuclear energy is generated within a region of the core extending out to 15 per cent of the sun's radius and containing 20 per cent of its mass (see Figure 12.2). The proper nuclear reaction rate within a star is maintained under stable conditions by means of an automatic feedback system. If more energy were to be produced than the star could radiate from its surface, the core would overheat and expansion would occur. This would be followed by a cooling that would reduce the nuclear rate.

There are two principal methods by which hydrogen is fused into helium to provide energy: the proton-proton (p-p) chain and the carbon-nitrogen-oxygen (CNO) cycle. In main-sequence stars less massive than about 1.2 solar masses, the proton-proton chain is the dominant mode of energy production. In the more massive main-sequence stars where the central temperatures are higher, the carbon-nitrogen-oxygen cycle operates in the deep interiors. We will now describe the proton-proton chain that supplies most of the nuclear energy in solar-type stars. The rest of the energy comes from the carbon-nitrogen-oxygen cycle which becomes increasingly less influential with decreasing mass.

The Proton-Proton Chain Reaction

Within the hydrogen burning core, whose temperature averages about eleven million degrees absolute, two protons (H1) will collide very fre-

quently and violently. Only after overcoming their electrostatic repulsion do they manage to coalesce into a deuteron (H2) with the emission of a positron (e^+) and a neutrino (v, "nu"). This happens on an average of once in several billion years per pair of protons. The deuteron is the nucleus of the double-weight isotope of hydrogen; the positron is a positively charged electron; the neutrino is a massless, chargeless particle that carries away energy with the speed of light. In each nuclear reaction presented below, the subscript represents the atomic number and the superscript represents the atomic weight; the subscripts and the superscripts must balance on each side to maintain the proper energy balance before and after the reaction. The first step in the nuclear reaction is written:

$$_1H^1 + _1H^1 \rightarrow _1H^2 + _1e^0 + v$$

The neutrino passes through the star unchallenged but the positron ($_1e^0$ or e^+) immediately encounters an electron (e^-) and the two particles annihilate each other to form two gamma-ray photons. Next another proton collides with a deuteron to fuse into a helium nucleus (He3) with the emission of a gamma ray (γ) on an average of once every four seconds:

$$_1H^1 + _1H^2 \rightarrow _2He^3 + \gamma$$

Finally two helium nuclei of atomic weight 3 collide and fuse into an ordinary helium nucleus (He4), ejecting two protons. This takes place about once every million years. Hence:

$$_2He^3 + _2He^3 \rightarrow _2He^4 + _1H^1 + _1H^1$$

A total of six protons entered into the production of two helium 3 nuclei out of which a single helium 4 nucleus was formed while two protons were returned to the pool (see Figure 12.3a). Despite the long interval of time required to complete the process, there is such a colossal amount of hydrogen available within the stellar interiors that the individual contributions

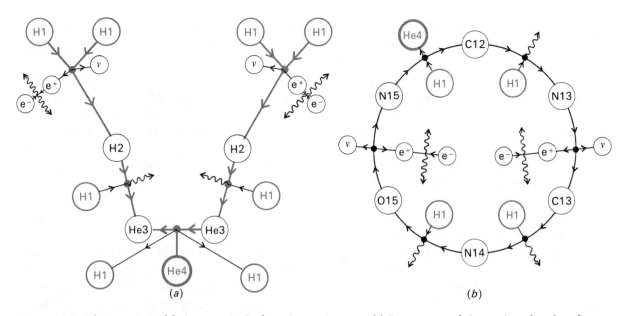

Figure 12.3   The two principal fusion processes in the main-sequence stars. (a) *Proton-proton chain reaction takes about five billion years to complete and predominates in solar-type and cooler stars.* (b) *Carbon-nitrogen-oxygen cycle takes about seven million years to complete and predominates in stars hotter than the sun. Key to symbols:*

H1 = *proton (hydrogen 1 nucleus)* e^+ = *positron*
H2 = *deuteron (hydrogen 2 nucleus)* e^- = *electron*
He3 = *helium 3 nucleus* v = *neutrino*
He4 = *helium 4 nucleus* γ = *gamma-ray photon (*~~➔*)*

add up to an enormous sum of energy created each second.

Conversion of Matter into Energy

The mass of the end product, He 4, weighs 0.71 per cent less than the combined mass of the four protons (4 × H 1) that were engaged in the reaction. The small amount of mass lost is converted into energy in accordance with Einstein's famous equation, E(energy) = m(mass) × c^2(velocity of light squared). For example, one gram of hydrogen is converted into 0.9929 gram of helium plus 6.4×10^{18} ergs of energy from 0.0071 gram of hydrogen. In practical units, the sun is consuming each second 655 million tons of hydrogen to produce 650 million tons

of helium and 5 million tons of mass-converted radiation which is equivalent to 3.8×10^{33} erg/sec. Even at the low conversion efficiency of 0.71 per cent there is enough hydrogen in the stellar core to keep a star like the sun shining on the main sequence for at least ten billion years. In the last five billion years of its existence it has used up about one-half of the hydrogen in the core, an amount equal to 5 per cent of its total quantity of hydrogen. Hence 0.035 per cent of the solar mass has been converted into energy (.71 × .05). In the meantime the sun has been accumulating helium within its core. What happens next is discussed briefly later in this section and more fully in Section 12.5.

In stars exceeding 1.2 solar masses, the carbon-nitrogen-oxygen (CNO) cycle predominates at a central temperature of about twenty million degrees absolute. There are six steps in the process before four protons are fused to produce helium as the end product plus energy. In the CNO cycle the successive steps are: carbon 12 → nitrogen 13 → carbon 13 → nitrogen 14 → oxygen 15 → nitrogen 15 → carbon 12 + helium 4. (See Figure 12.3b). The cycle is closed with the return of the original carbon that served as a catalyst. Beginning with carbon 12, fusion with a proton following a collision occurs about once every one million years to create unstable nitrogen 13 which ejects a gamma photon. The nitrogen 13 decays within minutes into carbon 13 with the release of one neutrino and one positron which encounters an electron, resulting in their mutual annihilation into two gamma rays. After an average interval of a couple of hundred thousand years, carbon 13 fuses with a proton and changes into nitrogen 14 with the expulsion of a gamma photon. Several million years later the nitrogen 14 manages to unite with a proton to create unstable oxygen 15 with the release of a gamma photon. Within a couple of minutes oxygen 15 decays into nitrogen 15 with the ejection of one neutrino and one positron which meets the same fate as its predecessor. Finally, after an average wait of about 10,000 years, nitrogen 15 fuses with a proton and splits into helium 4 and carbon 12 which is available for the next round of fusion.

The difference in the rate of energy production between the p-p chain and the CNO cycle at various temperatures is shown in Figure 12.4. The p-p chain is less temperature-sensitive than the CNO cycle. The p-p chain proceeds at a reaction rate that is proportional to the fourth power of the temperature; the CNO cycle proceeds at a rate that is proportional to the seventeenth power of the temperature. Up to about sixteen million degrees absolute, the proton-proton reaction dominates. Beyond that temperature

the carbon-nitrogen-oxygen cycle takes over with an energy-production rate of 10 ergs per gram per second. The average rate for the sun is understandably less, about 2 ergs per gram per second. (Our bodies radiate heat more efficiently than that!) The two curves in Figure 12.4 explain why the more massive stars with their higher internal temperatures consume their hydrogen at a faster rate, resulting in greater luminosities and shorter lifespans.

Neutrino Production

The neutrinos that are created within the stellar interiors pass freely outward into space because of their low probability of interaction with matter. They carry away a small fraction of the energy of visible light. Interplanetary space is filled with solar neutrinos which invisibly flood the earth in enormous quantities. Perhaps one out of 100,000 billion billion neutrinos that go through a man's body during his lifetime might be absorbed by him! The detection of solar neutrinos would provide astronomers with firsthand information on the sun's energy-generating

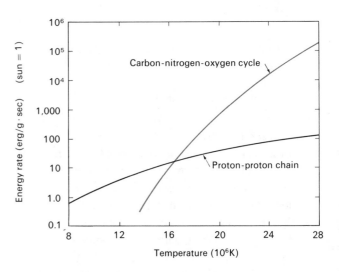

Figure 12.4   Stellar energy-production rates (after H. Bethe and H. Reeves.)

mechanism which until now has been obtained by indirect methods.

One scheme that has been devised to detect solar neutrinos employs a huge tank containing 100,000 gallons of a common dry-cleaning solvent. It is located in a South Dakota gold mine one mile underground to shield it from non-neutrino particles. When one of the populous chlorine atoms in the solvent absorbs a neutrino, it is transformed into radioactive argon whose decay can be monitored with a proportional counter. The observed capture rate of neutrinos is about one-tenth of the predicted number of two neutrinos per day. The disagreement between the observed and theoretical rates has not yet been satisfactorily explained.

Production of the Heavy Elements

After the consumption of the hydrogen in the stellar core, the star undergoes a series of successive internal adjustments later in its evolutionary history, leading to the production of the heavier elements. Following hydrogen exhaustion in the stellar core and a consequent rise in temperature due to gravitational compression, helium-burning occurs at a central temperature between 80 and 100 million degrees absolute to produce carbon. Termination of each stage of nuclear fuel-burning is followed by gravitational contraction which raises the core temperature to initiate the next round of nuclear burning. At temperatures of 600 to 700 million degrees, carbon burning gives rise to a number of nuclear reactions that result in the creation of oxygen, neon, sodium, and magnesium. The time scale of the "cooking" process is accelerated in the successive syntheses of the heavier elements. For example, while the hydrogen-burning stage may endure for about ten billion years in a solar-mass star, the carbon and oxygen stages of burning may last for only a hundred to a thousand years.

At central temperatures approaching one billion degrees, oxygen burning yields silicon, phosphorus, and sulfur. Successive synthesis of the still heavier elements continues beyond one billion degrees up to iron, during which time the remaining hydrogen in the outer shell of the star has been nearly entirely consumed. Beyond iron it is possible for the heaviest elements to be synthesized through successive neutron capture at still higher temperatures when a sufficient supply of neutrons becomes available. Depending upon a number of factors following fuel exhaustion, a star may die quietly as a white dwarf; or explode violently as a supernova leaving behind a surviving neutron star; or gravitationally collapse into a configuration called a *black hole*. In the latter situation the star has crushed itself out of visible existence by becoming extremely dense within a tightly enclosed region of space from which its radiation cannot escape into external space.

12.3 COMPUTATION OF STELLAR MODELS

Computer Solution

The basic processes which describe the behavior of matter and the energy flow within the stars are expressed in the formal language of a number of complex mathematical equations. These equations deal with: (1) the changes in pressure from the surface of the star inward toward the center; (2) the corresponding changes in temperature; (3) the corresponding changes in mass content; and (4) the corresponding changes in luminosity. The solutions of these equations require the services of electronic computers which can quickly process them within a matter of minutes.

Briefly, the operations entail a series of steps starting with the initial values pertaining to the star's known observational data: its mass, luminosity, surface pressure, and surface temperature. Beginning with the first shell below the surface of the star, the changing values of the aforementioned four quantities are calculated within the first layer. The values obtained for the bottom of the first layer are inserted anew in the equations and a solution of these four parameters is derived for the next shell. The process is repeated, step by step, for each successive shell down through to the final zone at the center of the star. Here the calculated values of the pressure and temperature should be appropriate to the nuclear generation of energy, and the mass and luminosity should fall to zero. If not, a certain amount of "juggling" of the proper proportion of the chemical elements is permitted until a satisfactory solution for a particular structural model can be found.

Because of the present uncertainties in the chemical composition and in at least two of the other variables—namely, the opacity and nuclear-energy processes—the final solution for a particular stellar model may not be a perfect one. The test lies in how well these models can predict the evolutionary courses of the stars in the spectrum-luminosity diagram. A representation of one solar model appeared in Figure 12.2. Astronomers have succeeded in calculating a number of satisfactory models for stars of differing masses throughout most of their lifetimes in attempts to fit them at the appropriate places in the H-R diagram. One of the most interesting findings arising out of the study of the stellar interiors is the variety of stable configurations that a star can assume during its lifespan in response to changes in its physical and chemical status. This amazing ability of a star to adjust itself automatically to altering circumstances through a natural feedback system is in reality governed by the basic laws of physics.

12.4 BIRTH AND EARLY EVOLUTION OF THE STARS

A convincing theory of stellar evolution should account in a general way for the genesis of star formation, the life cycles of the stars, and the forces that guide their destinies and determine their stellar properties. More specifically, it should be able to explain the strong observed spectral-luminosity correlation exhibited by the stars on the H-R diagram and the wide diversity that exists between the stars of different masses, sizes, luminosities, and densities. In a way the study of stellar evolution can be compared to the situation that would confront a mythical Martian who has been transplanted to earth. Having never seen a tree before, he could exercise his acute powers of observation and sound reasoning in reconstructing the life history of a tree by a walk through a forest. From his careful examination of the acorns lying on the ground, the tender sproutlings, the saplings, the fully mature trees, the decaying, denuded trees, and the fallen patriarchs, he could, by analytical biological deduction, theoretically develop a satisfactory model of the evolution of a tree even though he could not witness its actual growth.

Stellar Birth

There is strong observational evidence supported by theoretical computations that the stars are created out of the pools of cool gas and dust present in the interstellar clouds. The rate of star formation within the interstellar cloud is highly dependent on several factors: the gas density, dust distribution, temperature, and the degree of internal turbulence. The precise physical mechanism by which the stars originate within the interstellar medium is not yet fully understood. It is believed that within one of the denser regions of an interstellar cloud, an excess of dust and gas collects into a pocket which gravitationally attracts additional material from the surrounding environment. The formed blob may be a large or small mass depending on the degree of internal turbulence and how effectively it has retained the captured infalling material.

Many small, dark spots or blobs to which B. J. Bok of the University of Arizona first called attention in 1948 have been photographed against the bright star-studded background and luminous clouds of the Milky Way. They are called *globules* (see frontispiece to this chapter). It is conjectured that they represent an early stage in the condensation of matter into protostars formed within the interstellar cloud. Their diameters range from about twenty-five to one thousand times the dimensions of the solar system. Let us follow the history of one of these globules, destined to become the sun.

Protostar Development of the Sun

Having accreted matter from its surrounding cloud, the globule is now a small fraction of a light-year in diameter with a core density of at least 10^{-19} g/cm^3. It consists mostly of cool molecular hydrogen, some helium, a small percentage of the heavier elements, and dust grains. As the globular material shrinks due to its self-gravitation, the core of the newly formed protostar eventually becomes sufficiently opaque to restrict the normal outward flow of heat. According to a mathematical analysis carried out by R. B. Larson of Yale, the resulting rise in temperature generates a shockwave disturbance that causes the protostar to brighten rapidly and temporarily halt the infall of accreting material. The embryo star continues to heat internally by gravitational contraction as the molecular hydrogen dissociates into atomic hydrogen. Continued heating evaporates the dust grains and liberates the electrons from the atoms. These processes subtract from the kinetic energy needed to provide sufficient gas pressure to support the weight of the overlying layers. The resulting drop in gas pressure brings about a gravitational collapse of the core, which slows down as the temperature and pressure begin to climb. By the time the core has accreted all its surrounding matter, its central density is almost that of the present sun but it is still opaque to visible light. The protosun now evolves downward on the Hayashi track, all the while growing fainter at nearly

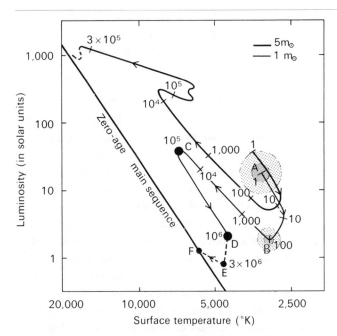

Figure 12.5   *Pre-main-sequence evolution of the sun (lighter line) and of a star five times more massive than the sun (heavier line), according to theoretical calculations by R. B. Larson. The numbers on the tracks represent years since the collapsing globule began to emit escaping infrared radiation. The approximate relative sizes of the protosun enroute to the main sequence are also shown. The dashed portion constitutes the radiative era when most of the energy is transported outward by radiation instead of by convection. A: central core forms from rapidly condensing cloud; B: shockwave disturbance initiates steep rise in brightness of embryonic sun; C: one-half the mass has accreted in the stellar core after which the protosun tracks downward as its luminosity decreases with but a small drop in temperature; D: core has accreted nearly all its mass from infalling matter. Main source of energy still comes from gravitational contraction. Radiative phase begins as sun becomes optically visible at start of downward Hayashi track; E: termination of Hayashi phase of evolution. Hydrogen burning commences during pre-main-sequence stage on approach to the main sequence; F: sun arrives on zero-age main sequence several million years later, completely stabilized with hydrogen burning well under way.*

constant surface temperature. Heated material from the center of the young sun surges outward, stirred by convection as the hot gas currents move toward the surface.

Final Pre-Main-Sequence Development

Toward the end of the Hayashi track, convective circulation within the young star gradually dies out. It is supplanted by a growing radiative core out of which energy is transported by radiation instead of the mixing of the gas currents as in convection. This change is brought about by a rapid rise in the central temperature as the result of continued gravitational compression until a core temperature of hundreds of thousands of degrees is attained. At this stage, the light nuclei (first deuterium, followed by lithium, beryllium, and boron), which are present in small quantities, are quickly consumed by reacting with the protons to produce small amounts of helium and initiate the production of thermonuclear energy.

During this period the protosun has become less opaque and would be optically visible as a newly emerging star with its surrounding dust cloud radiating strongly in the infrared. In several instances, G. H. Herbig of the Lick Observatory, and later other astronomers, have witnessed within a matter of years a partial clearing away of the dust to reveal developing stars presumably formed out of the rapid collapse of globules. More recently, radio astronomers have detected microwave emission from minute clouds of hydrogen and water molecules apparently collapsing and giving birth to new stars possibly with attendant planetary systems.

Supporting evidence that the source of stellar birth lies within the gas-dust clouds comes from the close coexistence of the T Tauri variable stars and the heavily veiled clouds from which they have unquestionably descended. T Tauri variables possess different characteristics from the older, more stable stars. They exhibit erratic changes in brightness and apparently possess dusty envelopes. Sometimes found intermingled with the T Tauri stars are the very young, brilliant O and B stars. The Orion nebula is a typical breeding ground for the production of both the more slowly evolving T Tauri stars and the rapidly evolving blue supergiants.

Finally, when the central temperature of the young sun has risen through gravitational compression to several million degrees, it is high enough to ignite the proton-proton chain and hydrogen burning has begun. It has taken the sun a few million years from scratch to reach the hydrogen burning stage. Before long, the sun will have arrived at the main sequence with the thermonuclear conversion of hydrogen to helium well under way and contraction completely halted. It has presently settled down on the main sequence for a long, uninterrupted period of stability that is scheduled to last for at least ten billion years.

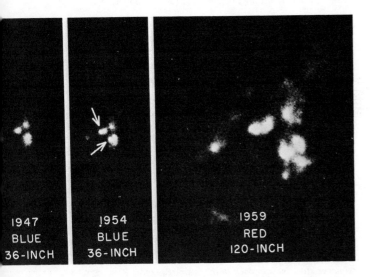

1947
BLUE
36-INCH

1954
BLUE
36-INCH

1959
RED
120-INCH

Figure 12.6   Herbig-Haro objects—possible examples of newly evolving stars. (Courtesy of Lick Observatory.)

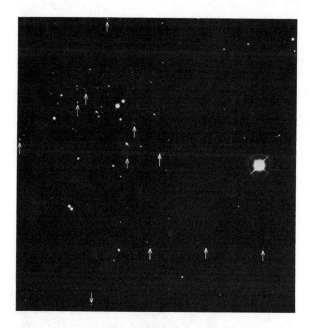

Figure 12.7   *T Tauri stars (arrows) in a very young cluster photographed in infrared light. (Courtesy of Lick Observatory.)*

Pre-Main-Sequence Evolution of Stars with Different Masses

The time required to attain the stable, hydrogen-burning condition from its globule stage is dictated by the amount of mass the star accumulates as revealed in Table 12.1. Stars exceeding the sun's mass evolve more rapidly above, while those under the sun's mass evolve more slowly below, the sun's track on their way to the main sequence. Over two solar masses the Hayashi stage is bypassed altogether. Stars with masses less than about one-fifth of the solar mass are underacheivers. Satisfactory thermonuclear fusion is never consummated because their internal temperatures are too low. They arrive far down on the main sequence in a wholly convective state, continually contracting toward a degenerate

condition of extremely high density. Thereafter they proceed slowly and inevitably to their terminal fate —that of a white dwarf. The minimum mass needed to reach the lowest rung on the main sequence is not less than about one-tenth of the sun's mass. Below that value the object would bypass normal stellar development and possibly end up as a cold black dwarf or a Jovian-sized planet.

When a large interstellar blob fragments into a number of globules with differing masses, the various stars will arrive on the main sequence at different times. The more massive luminaries will settle down first in beadlike formation according to their masses in the upper-left portion of the main sequence. Their less massive companions will eventually be strung out progressively to the right of the lower half of the main sequence. This theoretical prediction of stellar behavior is borne out, for example, in the youthful open cluster, NGC 2264, according to data derived by M. F. Walker of the Lick Observatory. In his plot the hotter, more massive stars have already assembled on the main sequence while the cooler, less massive stars are still to the right of the main sequence. As expected, a number of T Tauri variable stars are members of the cluster (Figure 12.8).

Table 12.1   Approximate Time to Reach Hydrogen-Burning Stage from the Globule Stage

Solar Mass Units	Approximate Time Interval
0.2	1 billion years
0.5	150 million years
1.0	3 million years
2.0	2 million years
4.0	500,000 years
10.0	100,000 years
30.0	30,000 years

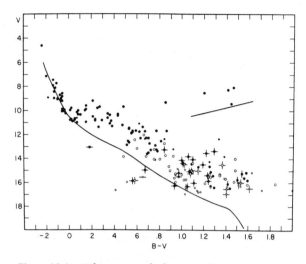

Figure 12.8 Color-magnitude diagram of the young cluster NGC 2264. The long line is the zero-age main sequence and the short line is the giant branch. The crosses represent the T Tauri stars. (Courtesy of M. F. Walker, Lick Observatory.)

12.5 LIFE ON THE MAIN SEQUENCE

Zero-Age Main Sequence

The string of successive positions that the newly evolved stars of differing masses reach on the main sequence from the right as shown in Figure 12.8 is called the *zero-age main sequence*. It is convenient to date the star's age from this position since the time consumed by each star in evolving to the main sequence is a very small fraction of its entire life cycle. The physical and chemical alterations taking place within the star at this time are slower than at any other period of its history. This is why the star spends most of its life on or near the main sequence and it explains why this portion of the H-R diagram is the most crowded region.

The approximate period that a star spends on the main sequence is proportional to its mass and inversely proportional to its luminosity. With this as a guide the last column of Table 12.2 has been calcu-

lated, based on the time the sun is expected to remain on the main sequence (ten billion years).

Development beyond the Zero-Age Main Sequence

As hydrogen burning continues for millions to billions of years depending on the stars' masses, the central core is slowly changing its chemical composition. There is a gradual depletion of hydrogen accompanied by a growing accumulation of inert helium. This leads to a slight increase in the mean molecular weight within the core. There is a consequent rise in the central temperature and a corresponding advance in the rate of nuclear fusion. As the star automatically adjusts itself to these changing conditions, the luminosity increases and the star begins to evolve upward and slightly to the right of the zero-age main-sequence line, as shown in Figure 12.9. By this time the star has consumed about 12 per cent of its total quantity of hydrogen. The more massive the star, the greater is the displacement and the sooner it is accomplished. What happens following the exhaustion of hydrogen in the core is described next.

12.6 EVOLUTION BEYOND THE MAIN SEQUENCE

The Turnoff Point

The inert helium that has accumulated in the core reduces the gas pressure because there are fewer particles occupying the core—one helium nucleus in place of four hydrogen nuclei. The star's interior is forced to contract gravitationally to re-establish equilibrium. This in turn raises the temperature which starts the hydrogen burning in a shell surrounding the core as the carbon-nitrogen-oxygen cycle begins to take over. The star has reached a critical point on the H-R diagram known as the *turnoff point* in attempting to maintain its stability. It does this by expanding its outer envelope as it reacts to the new flood of energy coming up from the compressed core. The time since its departure from

Table 12.2 Approximate Time Spent by Stars on Main Sequence

Spectral Class	Surface Temperature (°K)	Mass (solar units)	Luminosity (relative to sun)	Time Duration (years)
O7	35,000	25	80,000	3×10^6
B0	25,000	15	10,000	1.5×10^7
A0	10,000	3	60	5×10^8
F0	7,000	1.5	6	2.5×10^9
G0	5,800	1.0	1	10^{10}
K0	4,800	0.8	0.6	1.3×10^{10}
M0	3,500	0.4	0.02	2×10^{11}

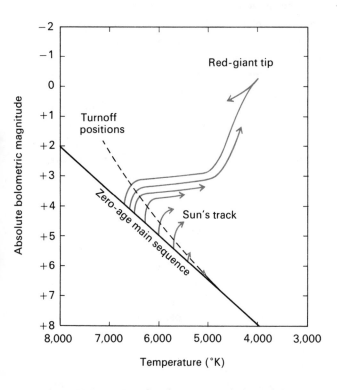

Figure 12.9 Projected evolutionary tracks beyond the main sequence for stars between 0.6 and 1.3 solar masses (adapted from data by A. R. Sandage).

the zero-age main sequence to the turnoff position decreases with increasing mass.

Evolution toward the Giant Stage

As the star expands it brightens but it becomes redder because its expansion increases faster than its luminosity. Having moved off the main sequence upward and to the right, it is on its way to becoming a red giant. The electrons within the core reach a degenerate state characterized by an enormously high density as they are squeezed into the smallest space possible by the rising gas pressure. Unlike the behavior in a perfect gas (Section 12.1), the pressure of the electron gas is now independent of the temperature. The motions of the electrons are confined to smaller limits even though their velocities can approach the velocity of light. Energy within the degenerate core is now transported by *conduction*, similar to the flow of heat along a metal rod.

As the core temperature rises, imparting its heat to the surrounding burning hydrogen, the star continues to track toward its full development as a red giant. For a star of the sun's mass, the time interval between the turnoff point and the beginning of the red-giant stage is about one billion years. For a star of 0.7 solar mass units, it is about 2.5 billion years. At the red-giant terminus, the so-called *red giant tip*, solar-type stars may reach a luminosity a thousand times brighter and a diameter fifty times larger than the sun's present values.

The Helium Flash

After a solar-type star has spent about 300 million years in the red-giant stage, drastic changes take place in the star's internal structure when it reaches the red-giant tip. The helium core, which now contains about one-half the star's mass, begins to fuse into carbon at a temperature of 80 to 100 million degrees absolute by means of the triple-alpha process. This process involves the simultaneous collision of three helium nuclei to form carbon 12. The continued heating of the helium-degenerate core does not increase the pressure as it would in a normal gas. Consequently, the star's natural feedback mechanism in regulating itself is inoperative. The core temperature rises so precipitously that a thermal runaway quickly develops. The star undergoes a violent structural adjustment known as the *helium flash* during which the core temperature peaks to more than 300 million degrees. After a few thousand years the central temperature declines to about 100 million degrees. The star has finally settled down to a stable configuration on the zero-age portion of the horizontal branch of the H-R diagram (Figure 12.10). It is now quietly burning helium within its core while hydrogen burning continues in a wider surrounding shell than before.

Rapid Evolution of the More Massive Stars

Stars with masses exceeding several times the sun's mass evolve rapidly from the blue-supergiant stage on the main sequence horizontally across the H-R diagram toward the red-supergiant stage (refer to Figure 12.1). Following hydrogen exhaustion in the core, gravitational contraction forces the inert helium core to shrink until the temperature is high enough to initiate the fusion of helium into carbon. Helium exhaustion is followed by another round of

core contraction which forces the star's envelope to expand enormously, decreasing its surface temperature. The star very rapidly evolves at nearly constant luminosity to the right in the upper part of the H-R diagram toward the red end where carbon burning is taking place. It is now a red supergiant. The swift evolution following departure from the main sequence accounts for the relative absence of stars in the Hertzsprung gap (refer to Figure 10.15).

12.7   LIFE ON THE HORIZONTAL BRANCH

Fate of Least Massive Stars

Stellar activity for the lowest mass stars (less than 0.3 solar mass) on the horizontal branch is nonexistent. Their central temperatures never become high enough to start helium burning. Theoretically, they can exist as cool, red dwarfs for many tens of billions of years well down at the tail end of the main sequence before evolving into red degenerate dwarfs and ultimately into white dwarfs. None of these stars presumably has arrived at this condition within the estimated age of the Galaxy (about fifteen billion years).

Fate of Solar-Mass Stars

The subsequent evolution of a star of mass comparable to the sun during its tenure on the horizontal branch of the H-R diagram has been worked out by Icko Iben, Jr., of the Massachusetts Institute of Technology for the population II type of star. The typical star, having expanded to a diameter about fifty times that of the sun with a luminosity one thousand times brighter during the peak of its red-giant stage, is quietly burning helium in a tiny core at the center and hydrogen in a thin shell beyond. Energy is transported by conduction through the degenerate helium core and thence by radiation the remainder of the way. The star spends about 100 million years on the horizontal branch. During this

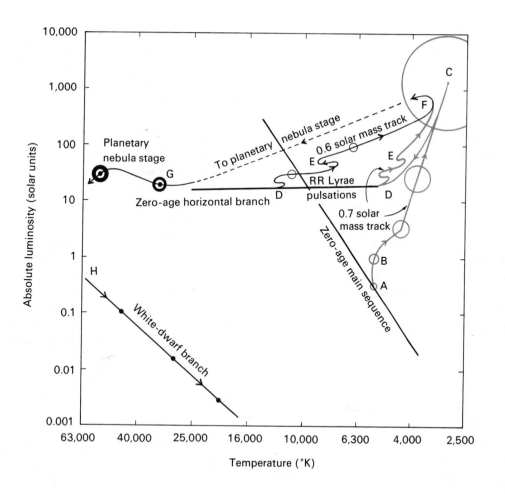

Figure 12.10 *Evolutionary tracks beyond the main sequence. Steps in the evolutionary sequence are:*

A: *main-sequence hydrogen burning.*

B: *hydrogen exhaustion; stellar core filled with inert helium.*

B → C: *hydrogen burning in shell outside inert helium core.*

C: *helium ignition at red-giant tip.*

C → D: *helium-core flash rapidly moves star to D.*

D → E: *helium burns in core while hydrogen burns farther out as star tracks back and forth seeking a stable configuration.*

E: *helium exhaustion in core; helium starts to burn in surrounding shell.*

E → F: *core consists of inert carbon and oxygen; helium continues burning in surrounding shell; an intermediate zone is composed principally of helium beyond which lies a hydrogen-burning shell and an outer envelope containing the original composition of the star.*

F → G: *uncertain path that may transform star into a planetary nebula.*

G → H: *star eventually evolves into white-dwarf stage as all its available nuclear energy is exhausted.*

12 STELLAR INTERIORS AND EVOLUTION

time it may swing alternately back and forth between the red end and the blue end several times while hunting for a stable configuration. Within the so-called narrow instability strip it rhythmically pulsates as an RR Lyrae variable as its diameter expands and contracts in a cycle of hours.

The next step in the star's evolutionary development is somewhat unclear. The stellar core has been transformed into an inert carbon-oxygen mixture while helium and hydrogen farther out are burning in separate shells. It is conjectured that a condition of oscillatory instability may eventually be reached that is severe enough to cause material outside the helium shell to be vigorously ejected in the form of an expanding envelope surrounding the hot-core remnant of the star. The object now resembles a planetary nebula (see Plates 9 and 10). The hot central star, already very dense, is on its way toward evolving into a white dwarf.

Fate of More Massive Stars

The evolutionary path pursued by stars with masses somewhat greater than the sun's mass beyond the red-giant stage has not yet been worked out theoretically in detail because of physical uncertainities and mathematical complexities. It is doubtful, however, that such stars can evolve uninterruptedly into white dwarfs if they fail to shed a sufficient amount of matter through some kind of ejection mechanism. Instead they may undergo ungovernable nuclear reactions terminating in one or more nova outbursts, or if sufficiently massive, they may explode as supernovae.

12.8 COLLAPSED DYING STARS

White Dwarfs

As the star approaches the white-dwarf stage, no longer able to sustain itself by nuclear reactions due to the exhaustion of its available fuels, gravitational collapse follows. This is finally halted when the enormous pressure exerted by the dense electron gas in a state of degeneracy stabilizes the stellar structure. The physical properties of white dwarfs were first investigated mathematically by S. Chandrasekhar of the University of Chicago. One of the interesting consequences that follows from Chandrasekhar's theory is that the white dwarf contracts into a *smaller* size, the *larger* its mass. For example, a white dwarf containing 0.4 solar mass has a radius equal to 1.5 per cent of the sun's radius; one with 0.8 solar mass has a radius equal to 1 per cent of the sun's radius. The theoretical Chandrasekhar limit is reached for a white dwarf with 1.4 solar mass and zero radius. From this it follows that a star whose mass exceeds 1.4 solar mass connot evolve into a white dwarf unless it disposes of its excess mass by continuous ejection of matter during its red-giant term or by more violent means through the explosive ejection of material during a later evolutionary stage.

There is no correlation between the radius of a white dwarf and its surface temperature. Neither is there any correlation between the temperature and the spectral class as in normal stars. The color "white" is a misnomer; it was first applied to the white companion of the double star Sirius. A star of solar mass contracting into a white dwarf begins as a small, hot, blue object. As it gradually cools, slowly releasing its internal heat by conduction through the degenerate gas, it changes color from blue to red. The evolutionary tracks of the white dwarfs are parallel to the main sequence but well over to the left and below the upper portion of the H-R diagram (Figure 12.10).

The discoverable white dwarfs are relatively close to the sun; their faint luminosity renders them invisible at greater distances even in the largest telescopes. Out of the twenty nearest stars, two are white dwarfs, the binary companions of Procyon and Sirius. The total number of known white dwarfs is approximately two hundred. A conservative estimate places their total number in the Galaxy at not less than one billion. Most of them must be descendants of the old population II stars which have by now evolved into white dwarfs during the fifteen billion years or so of the Galaxy's existence.

The white-dwarf companion of Sirius is 10,000 times fainter than Sirius. Its mass is equivalent to the sun's mass, but its luminosity is only 0.2 per cent that of the sun and its diameter only 85 per cent of the earth's diameter. Its mean density is three million times the density of water and its central density is about one billion times that of water, near the upper limit for white dwarfs. (The central density of a neutron star, in turn, may exceed that of the white dwarf by a factor of one billion.) Eventually, in the course of billions of years, the internal supply of heat conducted outward to the surface of the white dwarf will finally be exhausted as the star cools down. It will gradually fade into obscurity until it becomes an extinct black dwarf along a one-way, irreversible track. It is not known whether such highly dense stellar corpses exist in our Galaxy.

Neutron Stars

The evolutionary destiny of the more massive stars is believed to lead to a more violent end after a series of internal adjustments during the synthesis of the heavier elements. These adjustments, which are regulated by the gravitational forces, occur during periods of successive core exhaustion of the heavier elements from carbon up through iron 56. It is a stop-and-go process; the ash of each previous stage ignites at a higher temperature and a new interlude of stability reigns. When the fuel is exhausted, contraction follows until the temperature is high enough to fire the next heavier ash, and so on as the periods of stability grow shorter. The energy released per gram during the various fusion stages from helium to iron amounts to only about one fifth that released in the fusion of hydrogen to helium.

Further gravitational contraction within the degenerate iron core builds up the temperature to several billion degrees. At approximately seven billion degrees, iron breaks down into helium, subtracting energy from the central core and refrigerating it in the process. This leads to further internal compression followed quickly by complications (described in Section 14.2) that cause the star to lose control and to blow up in a cataclysmic explosion that releases the equivalent of a solar mass in the form of a brilliant supernova. The rapidly expanding luminous shell of gas leaves behind a kernel of degenerate neutrons compacted into a density up to 100 billion tons per cubic inch. The core has become a neutron star. Stars with the largest masses may collapse so energetically that they fall into black holes. The post-supernova phase of the star's existence or its black hole finale is treated in greater detail in Section 14.2.

12.9 OBSERVATIONAL EVIDENCE OF STELLAR AGING

Comparison of Theory with Observation

The clusters serve as the key in unraveling the evolution of the stars. The color-luminosity (H-R) diagrams of the clusters furnish the best sources on stellar aging since we are dealing with a group of stars that began their existence at about the same time in the same place. This makes it possible to observe the differences in the aging process of the individual stars according to their distributions in the H-R diagrams. The distance factor is eliminated because the cluster stars are observed at the same distance from the sun. Hence individual spectral-luminosity differences on an H-R diagram are real even if the distance of the cluster is unknown. In order to compare the actual differences between the clusters as a whole, we must, of course, know their distances. The result of such a comparison appears in Figure 12.11. The globular cluster data provide us with observational checks of the theoretically predicted evolutionary tracks of the stars between the main sequence and the blue end of the horizontal branch. The open-cluster data perform the same function between the pre-main-sequence stage of development to the red-giant tip. The observed color-luminosity plots conform quite closely with the predicted relation between temperature and luminosity.

Evaluating the Age of a Cluster

As the individual stars within the cluster evolve, they distribute themselves in accordance with their

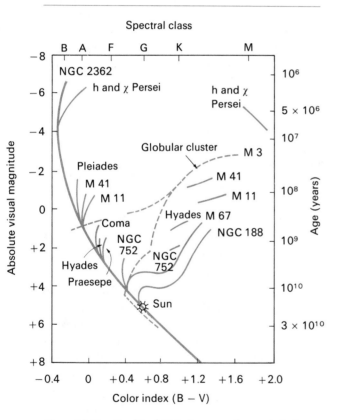

Figure 12.11   Combined H-R diagrams of several clusters.

masses along the main sequence, beyond the turnoff point, onto the giant branch, and along the horizontal branch. The age of the cluster is found by locating the position of the turnoff point. This critical place corresponds to the maximum luminosity attained by those cluster members still burning hydrogen within their cores. The composite H-R diagram (Figure 12.11) reveals the connection between the position of the turnoff point and the age of each cluster.

The youngest cluster is NGC 2362, whose estimated age is less than two million years. None of its supergiants has yet crossed the Hertzsprung gap. In the next youngest cluster, h and χ Persei (a twin cluster), some of the former blue supergiants have evolved into red supergiants as described in Section 12.6. These massive luminaries may end their first-stage careers in a blaze of glory as supernovae. They presumably pass on to a second career as pulsing neutron stars or pulsars. The oldest open cluster, NGC 188, is well advanced in years as is the globular cluster, M3, whose stars in addition occupy the horizontal branch. They are both over ten billion years old, not quite as old as the Galaxy. We note that the sun has not noticeably budged from the main sequence during its lifetime of five billion years. It still has another five billion years to go before it reaches the turnoff point. The slight displacement in the main sequences of the open and globular-type clusters is attributed to differences in the chemical composition of each kind of cluster. Those clusters with a higher metallic content evolve on a track slightly above the main-sequence track of the metal-deficient clusters.

Conclusion

The current theory of stellar evolution accounts fairly well for the various paths of development exhibited by the stars. We have a good understanding of the gravitational and nuclear forces operative within the stars. The theory enables us to follow the resultant changes in structure and development from stellar birth to near exhaustion of the available nuclear fuel. It is not by any means a perfect theory nor does it apply equally well to all the major portions of the star's lifespan. During the initial stages and beyond the horizontal branch of the H-R diagram, the evolutionary picture is somewhat obscured. It becomes clearer again after the development of the white-dwarf stage toward extinction. The most detailed and accurate theoretical analysis has been directed toward the most advanced stellar age groups with the longest evolutionary history since these naturally provide us with the best checks of the theory of stellar evolution. It is found that the ages of the oldest members of the Galaxy, namely the globular clusters, are compatible with the estimated age of the Galaxy, which is believed to be in the neighborhood of fifteen billion years.

REVIEW QUESTIONS

1. Explain how a sunbeam striking the ground may have begun its long journey as an x-ray photon inside the sun.

2. How do the two balancing forces that keep a star in hydrostatic equilibrium react on each other?

3. Describe the three modes of energy transport inside a star. Under what conditions does each of them operate best?

4. Explain why the perfect-gas law still prevails in normal stellar interiors since it is known to fail when the density of an ordinary gas reaches a density of one-tenth that of water.

5. How is it possible to obtain an enormous amount of energy from the conversion of the lighter elements into the heavier elements?

6. How many protons are fused in a stellar interior to produce helium plus energy? At what tempera-

tures does the proton-proton chain reaction operate best? The carbon-nitrogen-oxygen cycle?

7. Why do the more massive stars shine more brightly than the less massive stars? Why are their life cycles shorter than their less massive counterparts?

8. What evidence is there that the stars are created out of a concentrated interstellar mix of gas and dust?

9. Describe in a general way the evolutionary history of the sun from its birth inside an interstellar cloud as a globule to its full-fledged status as a main-sequence star.

10. What sort of unstable conditions are the recently created stars likely to experience on their way toward the main sequence? Have we discovered any such stars?

11. Why do stars spend most of their lives on the main sequence?

12. What is meant by the turnoff point above the zero-age, main-sequence line? What is so significant about this position?

13. Describe the probable post-main-sequence evolution of the sun after it leaves the main sequence until it arrives on the horizontal branch of the H-R diagram.

14. What is the probable terminal fate of the most massive stars?

15. Describe the sun's predicted evolution after it has exhausted its available stock of nuclear fuel.

SELECTED READINGS

Jastrow, R., *Red Giants and White Dwarfs*, Harper and Row, 1971.

Lynds, B. T., ed., *Dark Nebulae, Globules, and Protostars*, University of Arizona Press, 1971.

Meadows, A. J., *Stellar Evolution*, Pergamon, 1967.

Page, T., and L. W. Page, eds., *Evolution of Stars*, Macmillan, 1967.

Struve, O., *Stellar Evolution*, Princeton University Press, 1950.

The Whirlpool galaxy, Messier 51, and its satellite in Canes Venatici. (Courtesy of Hale Observatories.)

THE GALAXIES IN SPACE

The world, the race, the soul—
  Space and time, the universes
All bound as is befitting each—all
  Surely going somewhere.

Walt Whitman (1819–1892),
Leaves of Grass

The true nature of the spiral and oval nebulae was not observationally established until the early part of this century when larger reflecting telescopes were employed. Definite proof that these nebulae were extragalactic objects came in 1923–24 when Hubble found a small, irregularly-shaped cloud in Capricornus and two large spiral nebulae, one in Andromeda and the other in Triangulum, to be well outside the Milky Way system. From extensive photographic data, Hubble showed that the vast majority of the galaxies could be classified into three major groups: spiral, elliptical, and irregular.

In the last half-century a large amount of information on the galaxies has been gathered with telescopes of ever-increasing apertures, including the numbers and types of galaxies, space distributions, sizes, luminosities, motions, masses, rotations, structures, stellar and gas-dust compositions. Survey plates reveal many regions where the galaxies bunch into clusters containing from scores to thousands of individual galaxies. Our Galaxy is a member of a small cluster of at least twenty known galaxies called the Local Group. Its overall dimensions are some three million light-years. There is some evidence that certain clusters of galaxies may themselves be members of supercluster systems spread out over enormous regions of space up to 150 million light-years in diameter.

One of the great scientific discoveries of the twentieth century was Hubble's discovery that the galaxies are receding at speeds proportional to their distances from us. This is interpreted as a general expansion of the universe. It causes the galaxies to separate from each other like ink spots on a balloon being inflated. From the expansion rate (55 km/sec/megaparsec) it is calculated that the age of the universe is nearly eighteen billion years. A tentative picture of the evolutionary development of the galaxies out of the primordial material that

constituted the early universe has just begun to emerge.

13.1 INITIAL IDENTIFICATION OF THE GALAXIES

Early Investigations

The examination and classification of the galaxies scattered throughout space began in earnest in the early days of the present century when photography was employed with the reflecting telescope, an instrument ideally suited for this kind of work. Prior to the advent of photography, astronomers had visually observed and cataloged a wide assortment of small, nebulous patches and stellar knots, whose forms, dimensions, and luminosities they had described. But they had failed to perceive the true nature of these objects whose detailed structure and extent are most advantageously revealed on photographic exposures.

Charles Messier, the French comet hunter, assembled the first catalog of 103 of these objects in 1781. He carefully described their telescopic appearance to avoid mistaking them for comets which he wished to discover. A more extensive catalog of star clusters and nebulae, listing some 5,000 entries, was published in 1864 by John Herschel, whose father, William, had previously recorded about half of them in an earlier catalog (1802). The most comprehensive of the older catalogs presently in use are the New General Catalog (NGC) and the two supplemental Index Catalogs (IC), compiled by the Danish astronomer J. L. E. Dreyer between the years 1888 to 1908.[1] The entire number of clusters and nebulae entered in these catalogs, which are composed of the brightest objects down to the twelfth magnitude, is around 13,000. One modern catalog, based on the 48-inch Schmidt photographic survey, lists 34,000 galaxies

[1] In regard to catalog numbering, M 13 is Messier's thirteenth catalog entry for the great globular cluster in Hercules, which is NGC 6205, entry number 6,205 in Dreyer's New General Catalog.

brighter than magnitude 15.1. This number is dwarfed by the total number, running into the uncounted millions, that can be photographed with modern reflecting and Schmidt telescopes at the limit of their capabilities.

Galactic or Extragalactic Nebulae?

More than two centuries ago Thomas Wright and Emanuel Swedenborg had imaginatively suggested that the small gaseous condensations observed in telescopes might be other stellar systems like our own. In 1755 Immanuel Kant pursued this idea further when he theorized that the nebulous, lens-shaped objects were distant Milky Way systems (island universes) which were distributed at random angles of inclination to the line of sight. Furthermore he reasoned, these systems of stars appear misty by virtue of their great distances from us.

Lord Rosse's mid-nineteenth-century drawings revealed a spiral pattern in several nebulae observed with a 72-inch reflector (then the world's largest) located on his Irish estate. The first substantial evidence that the spiral nebulae were stellar systems came in 1915 when V. M. Slipher of the Lowell Observatory spectrographically recorded the presence of absorption lines displaced by large amounts in fifteen spiral nebulae. Eleven of them had recessional velocites up to 700 miles per second. The spectra of dark lines on a continuous background were the kind that would be expected from the composite spectral light of thousands or millions of individual stars. In at least two instances the spectral lines were slightly tilted, a true indication of internal rotation. It was becoming clear from their distinct spiral forms and from the large Doppler shifts of their spectral lines that these objects constituted a different stellar category.

If the spirals were indeed stellar aggregations, why was it not possible to resolve them into separate stars with the largest telescopes of the early twentieth century? The fact that a dozen bright novae and supernovae had been found in the spiral nebulae when no other stars could be seen should have served as an indication of the great distances of these objects. Were the spiral and lens-shaped, elliptical nebulae extraneous to our Galaxy as H. D. Curtis of the Lick Observatory advocated or were they in reality related to our Galaxy as H. Shapley of the Mt. Wilson Observatory argued? (Reference relative to their debate on this question was made in Section 2.9.) The issue was settled definitively by 1924 when E. Hubble of the Mt. Wilson Observatory succeeded (1) in resolving the irregular, nebulous structure, NGC 6822, in Capricornus and the peripheral por-

Figure 13.1   Four galaxies in Leo—three spirals and one elliptical. (Courtesy of Hale Observatories.)

13 THE GALAXIES IN SPACE

Figure 13.2   The Andromeda galaxy, Messier 31, and its two elliptical companions. (Courtesy of Lick Observatory.)

tions of the two large spirals, M 31 in Andromeda and M 33 in Triangulum, into discrete stars, and (2) in deriving distances based on their cepheid variables that placed these objects well beyond the confines of our Galaxy.

13.2   CLASSIFICATION OF THE GALAXIES

The Hubble Sequence

From his extensive collection of plates, Hubble chose approximately 600 well-defined bright galaxies upon which to base a classification system. He arranged them in an orderly sequence resembling a tuning-fork configuration. The order of his original presentation is sometimes reversed so that the elliptical galaxies terminate the progression instead of initiating it as shown in Figure 13.4. The irregular galaxies have since been included to close the prongs of the fork. The present arrangement is based on several progressive criteria: (1) type of stellar populations present; (2) configuration of the spiral-arm structure; (3) proportion of gas and dust present;

(4) size of the nucleus; (5) degree of flattening. We shall now describe the individual characteristics and dissimilarities among the various classes.

Irregular Galaxies

The irregular galaxies, which constitute about 3 per cent of the known galaxies, exhibit little symmetrical form. One group labeled Irr I contains a good proportion of highly luminous blue stars, star clusters, and interminglings of gas with very little dust. A second group, Irr II, is characterized by a greater deformity, fairly conspicuous dust lanes, and a composite spectrum of white, unresolved stars.

Figure 13.3 Galaxy in Triangulum, Messier 33. (Courtesy of Lick Observatory.)

Spiral Galaxies

Two distinct kinds of spirals are recognized: the *normal spirals* (S) and the less numerous *barred spirals* (SB). Although most of the conspicuous galaxies are the spirals, they are not in the majority. There are many more elliptical and irregular galaxies of low luminosity that are difficult to observe and identify at the greater distances. In the normal spirals two or more arms wind outward from regions on opposite sides of the nucleus. In the barred spirals the arms emerge from the ends of a straight arm or bar passing through the center. Both kinds are graded by the tightness of the arms and the size of their nuclei; the more loosely wound spiral has a smaller nucleus. In the *c* and *b* subdivisions, clumps of bright gaseous knots, interspersed with highly luminous population I stars, are strung out along the arms like beads. In the central regions the older population II stars predominate. The obscuring dust lanes exhibit a somewhat ragged appearance. In those spirals that are viewed edgewise, the opaque material is strikingly revealed as the long dark streak threading across the middle of the galaxy. The *a* category possesses a somewhat smooth and unresolved texture of older population classes with little evidence of bright nebulae or gaseous knots and associated bright stars. In the S0 type of galaxy, there appears a smooth, abbreviated extension without spiral structure beyond the nucleus. The edgewise view displays a very flat appearance without the characteristic dark streak. In place of the elongated bar, the galaxy has a stump often surrounded by a faint halo or ring structure without spiral arms.

Elliptical Galaxies

The elliptical galaxies (E) are recognized by their oval form, the absence of a spiral structure, and a smooth, symmetrical appearance. They are the most abundant of all the galaxies and vary in size from dwarfs to giants. The number beside the E designa-

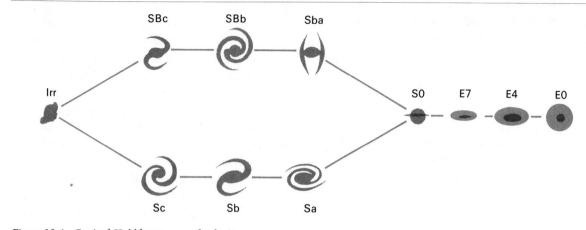

Figure 13.4   Revised Hubble sequence of galaxies.

tion indicates the degree of flattening from 7, the maximum, to 0, the minimum (spherical). The absence of population I stars and the missing dust streak across the middle of the spindle point to the lack of youthful stellar membership. The closest ellipticals have been successfully resolved into stars of the older generation population II types. Globular clusters have also been photographed around the nearby giant elliptical galaxies. The dwarf ellipticals exhibit a sparser and much less compact stellar distribution than their larger counterparts.

Significance of the Galaxian Classification

Within each individual galaxy stellar evolution proceeds at various rates, but the galaxies as a whole do not necessarily evolve from one form into another as the Hubble classification might suggest. It is conjectured that the elliptical galaxies evolved out of spherical blobs of condensed primordial material (mostly hydrogen and helium) as protogalaxies with little angular spin. Such protogalaxies, endowed with some degree of turbulence, could retain their ellipsoidal symmetrical configuration and quickly evolve into stars without undergoing gravitational

collapse into a flattened disk. On the other hand, the spirals, which may have begun their existence also as spherical protogalaxies, initially possessed a large amount of internal rotational energy that helped bring about their eventual collapse into their present spiral forms. The spherically distributed globular clusters and the semiflattened halo system evidently were formed before the collapse was completed. Following the collapse into a disk, star formation spreads outward from the center which is ultimately depleted of most of its original star-forming material. The last stars to materialize are created in the interstellar gas-dust patches residing mainly in the galactic outskirts where the spiral arms are so prominent. The Hubble sequence may be regarded (1) as a dynamical arrangement dependent upon the degree of internal rotational motion and turbulence, and (2) as a population sequence governed by the progress of evolutionary development within each galaxy.

Abnormal Galaxies

In recent years astronomers have discovered a number of peculiar galaxies that do not fit the Hubble classification scheme because of their optical or radio

ELLIPTICALS, made up primarily of older stars, range from E0-type spheres of stars (left), clustered tightly toward their centers, to flying-saucer-shaped E7's (right).

SPIRALS, seen fullface (left) or in profile (right), range from tight, big-hubbed Sa's (top) to loose, small-hubbed Sc's (bottom). The Milky Way is an intermediate Sb type.

BARRED SPIRALS' arms trail from spindle-shaped spherical hubs. Sometimes (right) the arms are thick, sometimes (left) they are fine-drawn and encircle the hub.

IRREGULARS are shapeless unclassifiable galaxies. Most of them contain turbulent gas clouds and brilliant blue stars, but some are poor in gas and contain old red stars.

Figure 13.5   Types of galaxies. (From The Universe, Life Science Library, *Courtesy of Time-Life, Inc.)*

13 THE GALAXIES IN SPACE

abnormalities. Some of these consist of tattered strings of interacting galaxies easily recognized by their torn and fragmented appearance. Their malformed features indicate a high degree of instability that may have resulted from the disintegration of a larger unstable mass into separate sections which resemble the broken links of a chain. Other peculiar galaxies take the form of tidally distorted parcels connected frequently by luminous bridges of stars and dust. The heavy concentration of bright blue stars in the midst of surrounding gas and dust suggests that these objects are in an early stage of evolution. Still other galaxies with optical or radio differences include the bright, extralarge elliptical galaxies, the N-type galaxies with starlike nuclei, the Seyfert galaxies which possess tiny bright cores exhibiting broad emission spectra, and the exploding galaxies. Nearly all of them are strong radio emitters and some are strong x-ray and infrared emitters of the

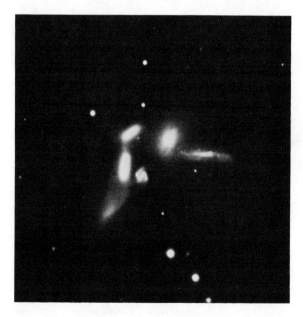

Figure 13.6 Interacting galaxies with connecting bridges in Serpens. (Courtesy of Hale Observatories.)

type connected with violent events. The abnormalities associated with these unusual galaxies are treated in the following chapter.

13.3 DISTANCES TO THE GALAXIES

Relative Numbers of Different Galaxies

Several billion galaxies lie within the range of the largest modern telescopes. In the polar regions of our Galaxy where the light obscuration is a minimum, there are places where the galaxies actually outnumber the foreground stars within our own Galaxy. Many thousands of galaxies are sufficiently close to permit a detailed examination of their structural patterns. Such studies reveal that the total number of elliptical galaxies in a given volume of space must greatly exceed the number of spiral galaxies. Out of twenty presently known galaxies, including our own Galaxy, which constitute a small local cluster known as the Local Group, the great majority are elliptical galaxies and the remainder are about equally divided between the spiral and irregular galaxies. Certain clusters of galaxies have been found to consist almost entirely of elliptical and S0 galaxies.

Methods of Deriving Galaxian Distances

It is hardly surprising, in view of the enormous expanses involved (up to 100,000 times the diameter of our Galaxy), that the distances to the remote galaxies are at best crude estimates. The distances to the neighboring galaxies beyond the Local Group, however, are fairly well established. The accuracy naturally diminishes with increasing distance. Just as the precise determination of the astronomical unit (the earth's mean distance from the sun) sets the scale of our stellar system, so must there be an accurate ''yardstick'' for measuring the galaxian distances in the universe. Invaluable cosmic data depend on the reliability of the yardstick. For example, the linear dimensions, spatial distributions, intrinsic luminosities, and masses of the galaxies; the physical and evolutionary differences among them; the mean density of matter in the universe, its rate of expansion, and the type of cosmological world model—all these depend on the correct scale of distance.

Distance Indicators

The determination of distances presently rests on the assumption that similar objects in our Galaxy and in other galaxies have the same physical characteristics. Suitably chosen objects can serve as "standard candles" of known luminosity derived from our investigations of them in our own Galaxy. The observed apparent luminosity of a recognized standard candle in a distant galaxy, combined with its absolute (true) luminosity, leads to the distance of the galaxy in which the object appears. The principle involved utilizes the inverse-square law of light in which the distance of a body is obtained from its apparent and absolute magnitudes by way of the distance modulus $(m - M)$ as described in Section 10.5. Table 13.1 lists a number of different kinds of standard candles and the maximum distances to which they may be employed in estimating distances to the exterior galaxies with the 200-inch Hale reflector. The cepheid variables remain our most dependable criterion in deriving distances. We are presently restricted in their use to only about thirty of the closer galaxies where we can single them out.

Example: The apparent magnitude (corrected for interstellar absorption) of an object identified in a distant galaxy as an extremely bright blue supergiant star is $m = 21$. From Table 13.1 its absolute magnitude $M = -9$. Hence the distance modulus is $(m - M) = 21 - (-9) = 30$, which from the formula in Section 10.5 corresponds to a distance of ten million parsecs (32,600,000 light-years).

When it is impossible to distinguish any kind of isolated object in a galaxy, a judgment of distance is made on the basis of the galaxy's total luminosity, on the basis of its surface brightness, its apparent size, or its mass-to-light ratio. The precaution is taken to recognize the particular class of galaxy involved since there is a great diversity in the brightness and dimensions of the galaxies. The indiscriminate lumping of all of them into one group would lead to serious errors in distance. Photographically, the image of a galaxy at the threshold of visibility is distinguishable from the pointlike appearance of a star image by its fuzziness or nonspherical shape. The distance to a large cluster of galaxies is considerably more reliable.

Table 13.1 Distance Indicators

Brightest of Its Type (standard candles)	Absolute Magnitude (M)	Approximate Maximum Distance (light-years)
RR Lyrae variables	0	1,400,000
Population II red giants	−3	5,000,000
Cepheids	−6	20,000,000
Blue supergiants	−9	80,000,000
Novae	−9	80,000,000
Globular clusters	−10	130,000,000
H II emission nebulae	−12	320,000,000
Supernovae	−19	8,000,000,000

In this instance we can select, say, the observed average apparent magnitude of the ten brightest galaxies as a luminosity criterion instead of depending upon a single galaxy. If we adopt their absolute mean magnitude to be $M = -21$, based upon knowledge gained from similarly constituted nearer clusters, we can derive the distance of the cluster. At the very least we can obtain fairly good estimates of the relative distances of such clusters by comparing the apparent luminosities of their respective brightest members or some other common luminosity characteristic. In small clusters a comparison between the absolute magnitude of the M 33 spiral in the Local Group and the apparent magnitude of the third brightest cluster member provides a rough estimate of distance.

13.4 GALAXIAN DATA

Galaxian Separations

The average separation between observed isolated galaxies is several million light-years. It is undoubtedly less when proper allowance is made for the suspected preponderance of undiscovered dwarf-sized galaxies. Within the local cluster to which mention was made in the preceding paragraph, the average separation is under one million light-years. Inside the central volume of a heavily populated large cluster it may be only of the order of tens of thousands of light-years. It has been suggested that at such close distances, collisions between galaxies have stripped away their original gaseous trappings while leaving the stars intact. This would account for the scarcity of spiral structures in these assemblages.

Galaxian Diameters, Luminosities, and Masses

The range in size, total brightness, and mass of the galaxies is very large as revealed in Table 13.2. The largest and smallest galaxies are the elliptical galaxies. The true dimensions of the galaxies are derived from their apparent diameters and known distances. The measured apparent magnitudes of the galaxies combined with their known distances yield their absolute luminosities by means of the standard formula, $M = m + 5 - 5 \cdot \log r$, in Section 10.5.

An estimate of the galaxian masses can be found most easily from the Doppler-line shifts in those spirals that are viewed more or less edgewise. One measures the difference in radial velocity at the opposite rotating edges (approaching and receding edges in the line of sight as viewed from the earth). The differential velocity together with the known radius of the galaxy enables us to calculate the mass from Kepler's modified third law of motion. Twin galaxies whose members orbit each other offer another opportunity to evaluate the galaxian masses. The observed radial-velocity differences of the pair, combined with their known separation, lead to estimates of their masses also with the aid of Kepler's third law. The method is similar in principle to that employed in deriving the masses of the binary stars (Section 11.1). A third method utilizes the amount by which the composite spectral lines in a galaxy are broadened as a consequence of its internal rotation. The assorted Dopper line shifts of the individual stars moving around the center of the galaxy at different speeds tend to widen the spectral lines. This effect provides a measure of the galaxian mass which dictates the degree of its internal motion and hence the amount of line broadening.

Table 13.2 reveals that a significant correlation exists between the masses and the luminosities of the various types of galaxies, namely, the mass-to-luminosity ratio. Its value serves as an important indicator of the kinds of stellar populations present within the different galaxies. Differences in the mass-luminosity ratio reflect the changing compositions of the colors and spectral types that make up the different population groups among the various classes of galaxies. It averages up to fifty for the ellipticals, about ten to thirty for the spirals, and one to ten for

Table 13.2 Galaxian Diameters, Luminosities, and Masses (relative to Our Galaxy[a])

Data	Irregular Galaxy	Spiral Galaxy	Elliptical Galaxy
Diameter range	1/20–1/4	1/5–$1\frac{1}{2}$	1/50–4
Luminosity range	1/1500–1/15	1/200–1	1/20,000–5
Mass range	1/2000–1/2	1/100–$1\frac{1}{2}$	1/1,000,000–50
Mass-luminosity ratio in solar units	1–10	10–30 (highest in the centers)	10–50 (highest in the giant ellipticals)

[a] Our Galaxy: diameter = 100,000 light years; luminosity = 20 billion suns; mass = 170 billion solar masses.

the irregular galaxies. A high value signifies the presence of a larger proportion of faint dwarf stars whose mass contribution is much greater than that of the scarcer, more luminous stars.

13.5 SPATIAL DISTRIBUTION OF THE GALAXIES

In the first quarter of the twentieth century there was a growing awareness that the apparent scarcity of spiral and elliptical nebulae in the vicinity of the galactic plane might be caused by obscuring haze in the Milky Way. It had not yet been decided whether these objects were constituents of our Galaxy or external bodies and whether their absence in the galactic plane was an optical illusion or a physical attribute of our Galaxy. After Hubble proved that these nebulous bodies were extragalactic objects (1924), there was no a-priori reason to doubt the uniform distribution of the galaxies in space. The natural inference could be drawn that the apparent observed unequal distribution of the galaxies was illusory as Hubble proceeded to demonstrate.

The Zone of Avoidance

From sample counts of some 44,000 galaxies photographed with the 100-inch Mt. Wilson reflec-

tor, Hubble established that there was indeed an apparent gradual thinning out of the number of galaxies toward the galactic plane as shown in Figure 13.7. The *zone of avoidance* is attributed to the presence of interstellar dust concentrated in the plane of the Galaxy. The large flare within the zone on the extreme right coincides with the direction toward the center of the Galaxy in Sagittarius. The optical view of the nucleus is hidden from sight by the accumulation of intervening obscuring matter. Further confirmation of the general obscuration comes from the pronounced reddening and dimming of the distant stars, clusters, and galaxies located in the vicinity of the plane of the Milky Way. In traversing the line of sight from the outside toward our position in the Galaxy, an external object is dimmed by about 30 per cent in the vertical direction to the galactic plane. It is dimmed by increasing amounts in the direction away from the normal until near or total extinction is encountered in the plane of the Galaxy.

True Space Distribution of the Galaxies

When the counts were rectified by corrections for the interstellar absorption, Hubble demonstrated that the galaxies, at least to a first approximation, were scattered equally in all parts of the sky. Later and more detailed investigations of galaxian counts at greater distances, however, have revealed places

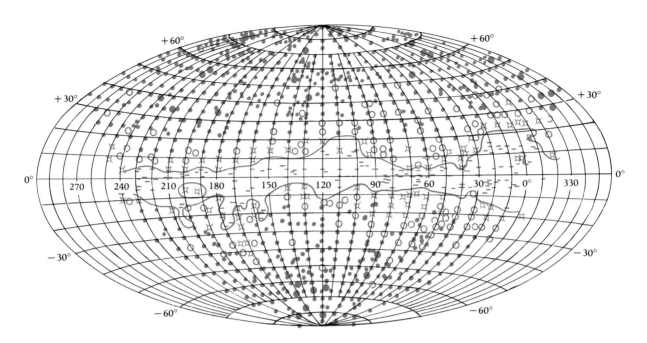

Figure 13.7 Apparent distribution of the galaxies. (Hubble diagram). The zone of avoidance, which outlines the obscuration, is centered on the galactic plane. Vacant areas in the diagram were too far south to be accessible from California. Key to symbols:

- ● *above average number*   ○ *very few galaxies*
- · *average number*   — *no galaxies*
- ¤ *below average number*

were scattered equally in all parts of the sky. Later and more detailed investigations of galaxian counts at greater distances, however, have revealed places where the galaxies appear to be strewn up to one hundred times more densely in certain regions than in others. There is a definite tendency to cluster in groups and in large clouds containing anywhere from a handful to hundreds or even thousands of these enormous assemblages. It is very noticeable when one examines the apparent distribution of the galaxies brighter than the thirteenth magnitude. There are strong concentrations in the form of large clumps of galaxies in the polar directions of our Galaxy where

the obscuration is a minimum. It appears that the largest observable structural features in the universe, namely, the huge congregations of clusters, may have overall diameters of 150 million light-years. Over still larger regions, around one billion light-years in diameter, the average deviations from a uniform distribution are considerably reduced and the universe assumes more of a homogeneous character. Thus localized inhomogeneities on a vast scale exist within the framework of the largescale isotropic distribution of the galaxies in the universe. One of these minor inhomogeneities within a large aggregation known as the local superstructure is the so-called Local

Group. Our Galaxy is a member of this group whose diameter is about three million light-years.

13.6 THE LOCAL GROUP OF GALAXIES

Composition and Distribution

There are twenty known members identified as belonging to the Local Group (see Table 13.3). In 1968 the Italian astronomer P. Maffei discovered on infrared photographs close to the galactic plane two heavily veiled, nebulous objects. They were subsequently identified in 1970 as a large elliptical galaxy and a large spiral galaxy by a team of astronomers from the University of California and the California Institute of Technology. These two galaxies appear to lie several million light-years outside the presently accepted boundary limits of the Local Group.

The present membership may not be a complete count because of the possible existence of other nearby galaxies hidden by the obscuring material or undetected by reason of being very faint dwarf or subdwarf systems with low stellar concentrations.

Table 13.3 The Local Group of Galaxies

Galaxy	Type	Distance (light-years)	Diameter (light-years)	Absolute Visual Magnitude	Mass (solar units)
Our Galaxy[a]	Sb-Sc		100,000	−20.5	1.7×10^{11}
Large Magellanic Cloud[a]	Irr I	160,000	30,000	−17.7	2.5×10^{10}
Small Magellanic Cloud[a]	Irr I	180,000	25,000	−16.5	
Ursa Minor system[a]	E4 dwarf	220,000	3,000	−9?	10^5
Sculptor system[a]	E3 dwarf	270,000	7,000	−11.8	3×10^6
Draco system[a]	E2 dwarf	330,000	4,500	−9	10^5
Leo II system	E0 dwarf	750,000	5,200	−10	10^6
Fornax system	E3 dwarf	800,000	15,000	−13.6	2×10^7
Leo I system	E4 dwarf	900,000	5,000	−10.4	3×10^6
NGC 6822	Irr I dwarf	1,500,000	9,000	−14.8	
NGC 147[b]	E6	1,900,000	10,000	−14.5	
NGC 185[b]	E2	1,900,000	8,000	−14.8	
NGC 205[b]	E5	2,200,000	16,000	−16.5	
NGC 221 (M 32)[b]	E3	2,200,000	8,000	−16.5	2×10^9
Andromeda I[b]	E0 dwarf	2,200,000	1,630	−11	
Andromeda II[b]	E0 dwarf	2,200,000		−11	
Andromeda III[b]	E0 dwarf	2,200,000	2,500	−11	
NGC 224 (M 31, Andromeda galaxy)[b]	Sb	2,200,000	130,000	−21.2	2.6×10^{11}
NGC 598 (M 33)[b]	Sc	2,300,000	60,000	−18.9	10^{10}
IC 1613	Irr I dwarf	2,200,000	16,000	−14.7	

[a]Clustered together near our Galaxy.
[b]Clustered together near the Andromeda galaxy. Andromeda I, II, and III were discovered in 1971; their quoted values are preliminary. Another object called Andromeda IV may be an appendage of M 31.

The largest members of the Local Group are the three spiral galaxies, M 31, our Galaxy, and M 33 in that order. The smallest members are the dwarf elliptical galaxies. The three-dimensional space distribution of the Local Group is such that our Galaxy is near one edge of a slightly flattened system with the majority of its members lying in the south galactic hemisphere. One subgroup is centered around our Galaxy and another around the Andromeda galaxy. From analysis of the radial velocities of the member galaxies it appears that our Galaxy possesses a random motion of about 60 mi/sec compared to the mean velocity of the Local Group.

The Magellanic Clouds

Our closest extragalactic neighbors are the two naked-eye objects in the southern skies known as the Clouds of Magellan. They were named in honor of Ferdinand Magellan whose ship made the first circumnavigation of the earth in 1522. Both the Large Magellanic Cloud (LMC) and the Small Magellanic Cloud (SMC) provide astronomers with a fertile field of investigation because of their proximity and the diversity of the objects they contain. Although the angular separation between the clouds is about 25 degrees in the sky, they are in reality a physically related double system. They are immersed in a common envelope of neutral hydrogen emitting the characteristic 21-centimeter radio line. The central plane of the large cloud is tilted nearly 90 degrees to the line of sight; we view the small cloud at an oblique angle. Both galaxies possess a ragged disk-like structure somewhat flattened by rotation. They contain stars of all descriptions and ages, including thousands of cepheid variables as well as gaseous nebulae and star clusters. Very prominent in the large cloud is the preponderance of blue and red supergiants and the obscuring dust. In two instances differences have been noted between similar objects in the Magellanic Clouds and those in our Galaxy:

(1) in the distribution of the periods, colors, and magnitude variation of the cepheid variables, and (2) in the appearance of a concentration of blue giants in certain globular clusters of the clouds instead of the usual red giants of population II.

The Andromeda Galaxy, M 31

The Andromeda galaxy, visible as a faint, hazy spot with the unaided eye, is the largest member of the Local Group (Figure 13.2). Its longest angular dimension covers nearly five degrees in the sky, the distance between the two end stars in the bowl of the Big Dipper. The central plane of the galaxy is inclined at a rather sharp angle of 12 degrees to the line of sight. On short exposure photographs, a small, brilliant nucleus appears quite similar to the one detected in the infrared and microwave observa-

Figure 13.8   The Magellanic Clouds are visible to the naked eye in the southern latitudes. In the photograph the Large Cloud, in Doradus, has an apparent diameter of twelve degrees; the Small Cloud, in Tucana, has an apparent diameter of eight degrees. (Courtesy of Harvard College Observatory.)

tions of our galactic nucleus. Two spiral arms wind out of the nuclear bulge over several turns and are well delineated in the photographs. Many gaseous knots and open-star clusters are observed in the outlying disk portion. The dust lanes exhibit chaotic patterns and obscure large regions of the stellar background. The central region is dominated by the population II red giants and the outlying portions by the bright blue population I supergiants. In the intermediate areas between the arms, which are relatively free from obscuration, there is a general mix of both population groups. These regions are sufficiently transparent to permit the viewing of remote galaxies in the distant background. Completely surrounding the galaxy are more than two hundred globular clusters. An average of about two dozen novae appear annually. Only one supernova has been detected; it was observed in 1885 in the nuclear region and rose to a peak brightness some 10,000 times brighter than the most luminous supergiants in the galaxy.

Analysis of the Doppler shifts in the spectrum of the central portion reveals gas moving outward from the center at speeds of 60–120 mi/sec in an expanding ring similar to the gaseous movements in the nuclear regions of our Galaxy. As in our Galaxy, the nuclear bulge of the Andromeda galaxy rotates like a solid wheel while the disk portion moves in accordance with Keplerian motion. An estimate of the total mass of the system can be derived by applying Kepler's modified third law of motion on the assumption that most of its mass is concentrated at the center. The value found is 2.6×10^{11} solar masses, one and one-half times the mass of our Galaxy. In practically every respect, our stellar system and the Andromeda system are remarkably alike in their major features, physical characteristics, and composition.

The two small satellite companions, NGC 205 and NGC 221, are typical elliptical galaxies resolved into myriads of population II stars. The three new satellites, discovered in 1971 by S. Van den Bergh, are extremely faint dwarf spheroidal systems each believed to consist of several hundred thousand old population II stars.

The Dwarf Galaxies

The Ursa Minor, Sculptor, Draco, Leo, and Fornax systems each exhibit a featureless aggregation of several million loosely concentrated stars symmetrically arranged about a sparsely populated center. Their principal constituents are the population II red giants and a lesser number of RR Lyrae cepheids. The two irregular dwarf galaxies, NGC 6822 and IC 1613, present a different appearance: a ragged formation of very young stars embedded in small gas pockets and a mixture of diverse population groups.

13.7 CLUSTERS OF GALAXIES

Some Representative Clusters

Beyond the immediate confines of the Local Group are the relatively close pair of Maffei galaxies mentioned previously and two small groups out to several million light-years. Within a radius of about fifty million light-years are distributed about fifty cluster groups. Among them is the giant Virgo cluster about fifty million light-years distant. It is composed of some 2,500 galaxies stretching across an expanse of space about seven million light-years in diameter and containing a number of local condensations of galaxies with many double and triple systems. According to G. de Vaucouleurs, the distribution of the entire collection of all these preceding groups forms an enormous flattened super-system which he calls the *local supercluster*. The center lies in the region of the Virgo cloud. Its overall diameter is about 130 million light-years; its collective mass is estimated to be 10^{15} solar masses. The Local Group, which is located near the edge of the supersystem,

Figure 13.9 An intrinsically faint, small, dwarf, elliptical galaxy in Sextans, photographed with the 200-inch Hale reflector. (Courtesy of Hale Observatories.)

Large-Scale Distribution

Investigations of the distribution of faint galaxies by G. Abell from the Mt. Palomar 48-inch Schmidt photographic data and by C. D. Shane and his co-workers from the photographic survey conducted at the Lick Observatory with the 20-inch twin refractor disclose the widespread clumping of matter in the universe. The clustering of galaxies has been found to be so prevalent that, aside from the possible presence of invisible intergalactic material, it constitutes the dominant arrangement of matter throughout much of space. Astronomers have discovered countless numbers of clusters ranging in size from the dwarf assemblages to the enormous multi-aggregations having diameters up to 150 million light-years, comparable in size to the local supercluster mentioned previously. On a still vaster scale, averaged over an interval of one billion light-years, the universe appears to be more homogeneous.

The Contradiction in Galaxian Masses

Attempts to estimate the individual masses of the galaxies within a cluster have led to conflicting results. Two common methods are based upon the observed Doppler line shifts arising from the internal motions of the individual galaxies and from the differential velocities of the physically linked pairs of galaxies as described in Section 13.4. A completely independent way of calculating the average galaxian masses within a cluster depends upon the random motions of the member galaxies constituting the cluster. The greater the total mass of the cluster, the stronger is the gravitational force of the assembled membership. This results in a higher spread of velocities. The average galaxian masses derived from an analysis of the observed velocity differences arising out of the large random motions comes out many times greater than the masses obtained from the internal rotations of the individual galaxies or

revolves around the center at a speed of 250 mi/sec.

One of the most impressive rich clouds is the cluster in Coma Berenices whose distance is estimated to be 310 million light-years. Its members are scattered over a region of space in excess of ten million light-years in diameter with a slight concentration toward the center. It is characterized by a symmetrical distribution of many hundreds of galaxies, mostly of the S0 and elliptical types. The more compact the cluster, the higher is the percentage of elliptical galaxies. Another large aggregation of galaxies, about 470 million light-years distant, is the Hercules cluster. Both the Virgo and Hercules systems exhibit little central concentration or symmetry. They contain a high percentage of spiral and irregular galaxies and large numbers of peculiar galaxies of the type associated with unstable configurations.

from the differential velocities of the double galaxies. In the latter two instances, the derived masses include only the matter content within the individual galaxies; the velocity-dispersion method includes matter that may be extraneous to the galaxies. Thus it is possible to resolve the disagreement between the conflicting methods of calculating the masses by postulating the existence of a large amount of invisible intergalactic material distributed within the cluster. We shall return to the puzzle of the missing matter in Sections 13.9 and 16.8.

13.8 THE LAW OF RECESSION OF THE GALAXIES

Discovery of the Red Shifts

The first clue to a remarkable discovery relating to the galaxies was uncovered by V. M. Slipher in the early part of this century. Upon extending his earlier work (Section 13.1) he found unusually large red shifts up to 1,100 mi/sec in the absorption spectral lines of all but two of the forty-three nebulae he investigated. Even larger recessional velocities were found for the fainter galaxies observed by the Mt. Wilson astronomer M. L. Humason. Not long afterward, Hubble succeeded in estimating the distances

Figure 13.10   Central region of the cluster of galaxies in Coma Berenices, whose distance is estimated to be 310 million light-years; photographed with the 200-inch Hale reflector. (Courtesy of Hale Observatories.)

Table 13.4   Representative Clusters of Galaxies

Cluster	Estimated Number of Observable Galaxies	Approximate Distance (light-years)[a]	Radial Velocity (mi/sec)
Virgo	2500	50,000,000	+710
Perseus	500	220,000,000	+3,300
Coma	1500	310,000,000	+4,300
Hercules	100	470,000,000	+6,700
Corona Borealis	500	950,000,000	+13,500
Bootes	150	1,700,000,000	+24,400
Hydra	?	2,700,000,000	+38,000

[a]The distances of the last six clusters are provisional.

for a number of galaxies whose radial velocities had been measured. When the velocities were plotted against the distances, a straight-line relationship emerged: the *farther* the galaxy is, the *faster* it is moving away from us. The only exceptions were several nearby galaxies, including members of the Local Group, which exhibited velocities of approach. It was obvious that a fundamental phenomenon was operative in the universe, one that overcame the random motions of the galaxies with increasing distance and which became evident beyond the immediate galaxian neighborhood.

Hubble Law of Recession

If interpreted literally, the proportional velocity-distance relationship, known as the *Hubble law of recession*, signifies that the universe is expanding. We shall reserve discussion of its cosmological implications to the chapter on cosmology (Chapter 16). Hubble's original results have been extended by a number of investigators at the Hale and Lick Observatories to include hundreds of additional more distant galaxies and several dozen more distant clusters.

Hubble's law may be expressed mathematically by this simple expression:

$$V = H \cdot r$$

in which the radial velocity V is proportional to the distance r; H is called the Hubble constant and its value depends on the slope of the line. From the straight-line relationship between V and r it follows that a galaxy that is two billion light-years away is receding twice as fast as a galaxy that is one billion light-years distant. The velocity-distance relation can be used to estimate the distance of a remote galaxy for a given value of H from its red-shifted spectral lines when the distance indicators of Table 13.1 are unresolvable.

As we shall see in Chapter 16, the numerical

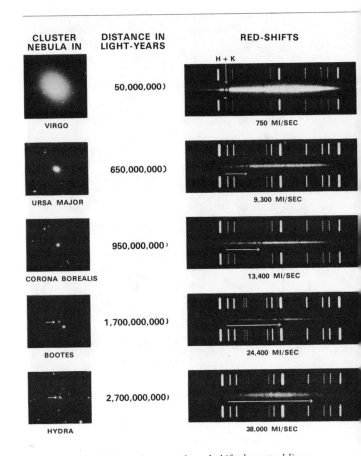

CLUSTER NEBULA IN	DISTANCE IN LIGHT-YEARS	RED-SHIFTS
VIRGO	50,000,000	750 MI/SEC
URSA MAJOR	650,000,000	9,300 MI/SEC
CORONA BOREALIS	950,000,000	13,400 MI/SEC
BOOTES	1,700,000,000	24,400 MI/SEC
HYDRA	2,700,000,000	38,000 MI/SEC

Figure 13.11   Relation between the red-shifted spectral lines of the galaxies and their distances. Arrows indicate shift for calcium lines H and K. One light-year equals nearly 6 trillion miles or 5.9×10^{12} miles. (Courtesy of Mount Wilson and Palomar Observatories.)

value of H and any departure from the straight-line plot have an important bearing on the type of cosmological model that prevails in the universe. A recent estimate of the Hubble constant places its value at 55 km/sec/megapc, or 10 mi/sec for each one million light-years of distance. The reciprocal of the Hubble constant, $1/H = r/V$, can be used to approxi-

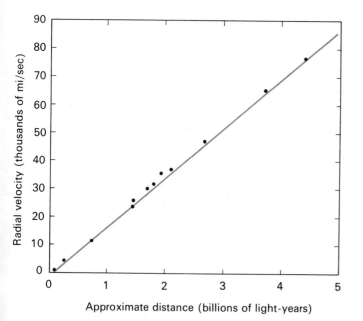

Figure 13.12 Velocity-distance relation (derived from cluster data).

condensed out of the turbulent primordial gas clouds that formed within the early expanding universe. It is theorized that these huge unstable condensations collapsed gravitationally into one of two forms: (1) a symmetrical, dense cluster of galaxies resembling the Coma cluster which is stabilized by the presence of its slower rotating elliptical membership and reduced internal random motions, or (2) an elongated, semistable formation resembling the Virgo cluster with its large complement of faster rotating spirals and higher internal motions. It is possible that cluster groups may still be forming from intergalactic material, most of which remains undetected. The Dutch astronomer J. H. Oort, a leading expert in the studies of the galaxies, estimates that only 3 per cent of the intergalactic gas is presently contained in the galaxies.

Evolution of the Galaxies

The course of galaxian development is influenced by various factors: the density and temperature of the primordial gas, its degree of turbulence, and the rate of accretion of intergalactic matter. Protogalaxies with little net spin evolved into the elliptical galaxies while those with greater amounts of rotational energy eventually collapsed into the spiral galaxies. In the procession from the elliptical to the spiral galaxies, there is a smooth gradation from high to low average densities (except for the dwarf ellipticals which are thinly populated) with a corresponding change in color from all red to mixed red and white to blue-white at the fringes of the spirals, depending on the population groups. In the gas-impoverished elliptical galaxies, star birth has virtually ceased. Star formation within the spiral galaxies appears to begin in the halo and central regions before it can spread into the outlying spiral arms. It is not certain to what extent the gravitational and magnetohydrodynamic forces play a role in shaping and preserving the structure of the spiral arms long

mate the age of the universe (assuming a constant uniform expansion). This is permissible since r/V represents distance divided by velocity which is equal to the time since the expansion began. Let us determine the approximate time since the expansion began by employing the value of $H = 55$ km/sec per 10^6 parsecs. This reduces to $H = 5.62 \times 10^{-11}/$ year. Hence the approximate age of the universe is $1/H = 0.178 \times 10^{11}$ years $= 17.8$ billion years. This value is compatible with the ages of the oldest globular clusters in our Galaxy ($\sim$13–15 billion years). The age of the universe is less if the expansion has slowed down with time.

13.9 EVOLUTION OF CLUSTERS AND INDIVIDUAL GALAXIES

Formation of Clusters

One current view is that the clusters of galaxies evolved from larger unstable structures that were after their formation. As in vortex motion, the arms trail behind in the rotation. Rotation would normally be expected to wind up the arms after several revolutions. Theoretical calculations with electronic computers indicate that the arms could evolve from disturbed gravitational fields within the protogalaxy. Their longevity remains an unanswered question.

Stellar Evolution within the Galaxy

The globular clusters of our Galaxy are believed to have been created first out of the large gravitationally contracted pockets of gas formed within the slowly rotating protogalaxy. Further condensation of the protogalaxy pulled matter toward the central regions. This increased the rotation and caused the protogalaxy to assume an ellipsoidal shape. The older halo population II stars were formed during this period of contraction. Final gravitational collapse produced the rapidly spinning spiral-structured discoid of the young population I stars. All classes of objects moving around the galactic center tend to occupy the volumes of space which they originally inhabited at the time of their condensation. This explains why the globular clusters, which were formed some distance from the galactic plane, move in highly elongated elliptic orbits around the galactic center, whereas the disk population moves in more nearly circular orbits around the galactic center.

In order to account for the enriched material (heavier elements) of the older population types, it is postulated that in the early formative period of the Galaxy a considerable number of short-lived, supermassive stars were initially created out of the fragmentation of the hydrogen-helium gas mixture within the protogalaxy. Rapid synthesis of the heavier elements within the stars' interiors was followed by explosive nucleosynthesis of the still heavier elements during supernovae outbursts, which violently ejected this material into the gaseous interstellar medium.

Out of this "contaminated" gaseous mixture originated the population II stars. They in turn synthesized within their interiors more of the heavy elements, some of which were subsequently expelled into interstellar space by the actions of their stellar winds or eruptive processes. Out of this further enriched gaseous environment evolved the old population I stars and finally the young population I stars inside the gas-dust residue still present in the exterior portions of the spiral galaxy. The newly created population I blue supergiants born in the spiral arms will never live through one rotation of the Galaxy.

Conclusion

Let us summarize the evolutionary changes taking place within a galaxy: (1) the stars eventually exhaust their nuclear fuels at different rates and terminate their lives peaceably or violently depending upon their masses; (2) less interstellar material becomes available for stellar creation despite its recycling; (3) the stellar matter changes gradually in chemical composition toward an increase in the heavier elements; (4) with advancing age the galaxy as a whole becomes redder as its luminous blue giants rapidly evolve and fade away; (5) dynamical changes induced by the gradual disappearance of interstellar matter and the slowing down of extreme stellar motions by the general gravitational field occur within the galaxian structure. One of the incompletely answered questions relating to the evolution of the galaxies involves the precise roles of the physical agents responsible for the great diversity in the mass content and the variations in structure of the galaxies.

REVIEW QUESTIONS

1. How was it established that the spiral galaxies were extragalactic objects?

2. What, if anything, does the Hubble sequence of galaxies represent?

3. Describe briefly the general appearance of the three principal classes of galaxies (spiral, elliptical, and irregular).

4. Discuss the distribution of the population types within the three types of galaxies in the Hubble sequence.

5. What is the range in the diameters, luminosities, and masses of the galaxies? Where does our Galaxy fit in the picture?

6. What is meant by the "zone of avoidance"? Why does it exist?

7. Explain how certain distance indicators can be used as "standard candles" in estimating the distances to the galaxies.

8. Discuss the findings that have been made regarding the clustering of the galaxies.

9. How do we know that there is a relatively small clustering of galaxies known as the Local Group?

10. Where does the Local Group of galaxies fit within the present picture of the "local supercluster"?

11. What is the Hubble law of recession of the galaxies? What is its significance?

12. How does stellar evolution proceed within a spiral galaxy? Use our Galaxy as a basis for discussion.

SELECTED READINGS

Asimov, I., *Galaxies*, Follett, 1968.

Hodge, P. W., *Galaxies and Cosmology*, McGraw-Hill, 1966.

Page, T., and L. W. Page, eds., *Beyond the Milky Way*, Macmillan, 1969.

Roman, C., *Discovery of the Galaxies*, Grossman, 1969.

Shapley, H., *Galaxies*, Harvard University Press, 1967.

Woltjer, L., ed., *Galaxies and the Universe*, Columbia University Press, 1968.

A black hole is a curled region of space enclosing a collapsed object, from which neither matter nor light can escape into external space. In this black-and-white reproduction of an original color painting by Helmut Wimmer, a light ray is being sucked into the hole by the tremendous gravitational field of a superdense, gravitationally collapsed star.

COSMIC VIOLENCE

Twinkle, twinkle, quasi-star
Biggest puzzle from afar
How unlike the other ones
Brighter than a billion suns
Twinkle, twinkle, quasi-star
How I wonder what you are.

George Gamow (1904–1968)

The early optical explorations of the universe seemed to indicate that it was a quiet, orderly cosmos filled with well-behaved galaxies. Then astronomers discovered rare, isolated, violent events taking place within our Galaxy and in other galaxies in the form of novae and supernovae. When radio astronomers started probing the heavens in the late 1940's the picture of the universe began to change rather abruptly. Powerful new sources of radio energy were now being discovered farther in space than ever before. While radio astronomers pointed the way and optical astronomers followed in their tracks, the observational evidence kept mounting that the abnormal emission from radio galaxies, certain overactive galaxies, and exploding galaxies indicated a universe that appeared more violent the more deeply it was penetrated.

This impression became more firmly rooted following the radio discovery of the powerfully energetic quasi-stellar objects and the optical disclosure that these mystery sources appear to be at great cosmological distances, based on the interpretation of the large red shifts of their spectral lines. If this cosmological explanation is correct, a view not shared by all astronomers, we are looking back in time toward the early period in the history of the universe when it was filled with great unrest and turbulence.

Within our own Galaxy came the next surprising and unexpected discovery of the pulsars. These are believed to be the collapsed hulks of supernovae that apparently have turned into ultradense, rapidly rotating, neutron stars only a few miles wide. And now, guided by relativity theory, we have taken the final leap. Might there not be totally collapsed objects that have shrunk past a certain critical size known as the gravitational radius *and disappeared into* black holes? *Under these conditions they would wrap themselves in a completely closed region of curved four-dimensional space and vanish from sight. As John B. S. Haldane once perceptively stated: "My suspicion is that the universe is not only queerer than we suppose, but queerer than we* can *suppose."*[1]

14.1 THE VIOLENT UNIVERSE

In the galactic niche that we occupy the behavior of matter is quite placid in comparison with its action elsewhere. In other parts of the Galaxy isolated events do occur, principally those accompanying the novae and supernovae. The aftereffects of a more turbulent era through which the Galaxy passed during its early formative stage are still present in the form of expelled gas, enhanced gamma-ray and infrared radiation, and nonthermal radio emission emanating from the galactic center. Farther out in deep extragalactic space we encounter cataclysmic outbursts associated with the strong radio sources and the quasars which serve as portents of the turbulent beginnings experienced during the early history of the universe.

The Scale of Cosmic Violence

The word "violence," used in the present context to describe the extraordinary events taking place in various parts of the universe, is not the product of unnatural forces. Rather it is the workings of the natural physical laws operating in an exotic realm so far removed from our limited terrestrial experiences that it strains our imagination in attempting to derive a rational explanation for its behavior.

In setting the stage of cosmic violence that exists in the universe, we cite these relatively modest figures first: the energy released by a one-megaton hydrogen bomb is about 4×10^{22} ergs in a flash; in an average solar flare, about 10^{28} erg/sec; by the sun, 2×10^{33} erg/sec; by the most luminous superstar, about 10^{38} erg/sec.

[1] *Possible Worlds and Other Papers*, Harper, 1928.

Table 14.1   Scale of Cosmic Violence

Object	Estimated Energy Output	
	Rate (erg/sec)[a]	Total Amount Expended (ergs)
Our Galaxy (nonviolent)	4×10^{43} (optical) ; 10^{38} (radio) ; 10^{37} (x-ray)	10^{61} [b]
Galactic center	3×10^{41} (infrared) ; 10^{40} (gamma ray)	10^{58}
Nova	10^{39} (optical) at maximum light	10^{45}
Supernova (Crab nebula)	10^{36} (optical) ; 10^{37} (x-ray) ; 6×10^{33} (gamma ray) ; 10^{34} (radio)	10^{50}
Seyfert galaxy (NGC 1275)	10^{45} (optical) ; 4×10^{45} (x-ray) ; 10^{47} (infrared)	10^{59} [c]
Exploding galaxy (M 82)	10^{55} (optical)	10^{58} [c]
Quasar (3C 273)	10^{46} (optical) ; 6×10^{48} (infrared) ; 10^{46} (x-ray)	10^{60} [c]

[a]To convert to kilowatts, divide by 10^{10}.
[b]Nuclear-energy production in stars during last fifteen billion years.
[c]These violent events occur over a much shorter interval (10^5–10^8 years).

14.2   SUPERNOVAE

Discovery of Supernovae

Supernovae have been discovered in scores of galaxies. A total of three hundred were cataloged by the end of 1971. The approximate frequency of their occurrence varies from six per century in the brightest and largest spirals to one every two centuries in the faintest spirals. Estimates of the number of supernovae that have appeared in our Galaxy have been at variance. Over two dozen have been identified so far. According to historical records, at least fourteen supernovae have been observed during the last two millennia in our Galaxy. This corresponds to a rate of one event nearly every one and one-half centuries. The actual rate of occurrence may be higher by a factor of at least two. Many galactic radio sources may possibly be the sites of old supernovae explosions. Their optical identification is difficult, if not impossible, because the ejected material has expanded to such a great distance that it has become invisible optically. However, the rapidly expanding remnants of the expelled cloud of gas, colliding with distant pockets of interstellar material, could be shock-excited into luminescence. This may be what happened in the Loop nebula in Cygnus. The enormous Gum nebula extends over fifty degrees across the southern sky. It is about 2,300 light-years in diameter with its closest edge only some 325 light-years from the earth. According to the investigations of S. P. Maran of NASA and his co-workers, the nebula represents the expanded ionized region of hydrogen gas that was excited by a moving pulse of ultraviolet and x-ray emission which left the site of the explosion of the supernova Vela X between 11,000 and 20,000 years ago. The discovery of a pulsar (a rapidly pulsing radio star) within the Vela X supernova remnant provides further evidence that pulsars appear to be the collapsed high-density cores of violently exploding massive stars.

Three other supernovae remnants in the form of very large broken rings or arcs have been identified: a radio loop centered on the north celestial pole, the North Polar Spur extending from the constellation of Aquila northward, and the Cetus Arc covering the constellations of Cetus and Aquarius. Several well-authenticated supernovae that have appeared in our Galaxy are the Crab nebula of A.D. 1054 in Taurus,

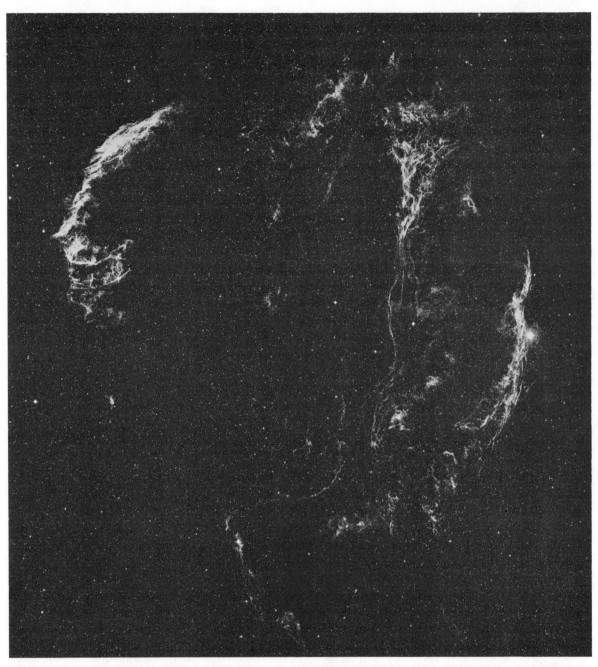

Figure 14.1   *The Loop nebula in Cygnus, photographed in red light with the 48-inch Schmidt telescope. The photograph reveals the remnants of a supernova explosion about 2,500 light-years distant. (See Plate 21 for a color view of the left portion of this nebulosity.) (Courtesy of Hale Observatories.)*

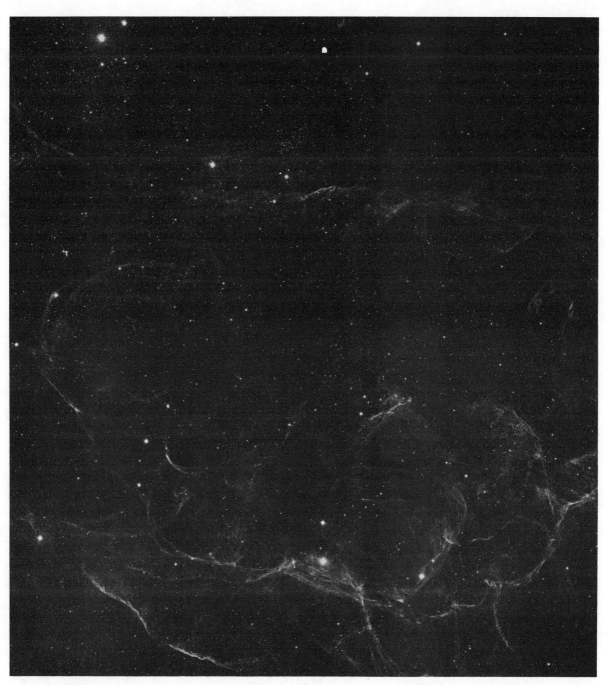

Figure 14.2   The ultraviolet network of nebulosity associated with the Vela pulsar and supernova remnant in the Gum nebula. (Courtesy of Bart J. Bok of the University of Arizona.)

14 COSMIC VIOLENCE

distant 5,000 light-years; Tycho Brahe's supernova of A.D. 1572 in Cassiopeia, distant 10,000 light-years; Kepler's supernova of A.D. 1604 in Serpens, distant 20,000 light-years; Cassiopeia A supernova, distant 11,000 light-years; the Loop nebula in Cygnus (mentioned above), distant 2,500 light-years; the supernova of A.D. 1006 in Lepus, distant 10,000 light-years.

Two kinds of supernovae are recognized: (1) type I which attains a maximum luminosity of about a hundred million suns and is believed to herald the demise of a hydrogen-deficient population II star; (2) type II which reaches a maximum brilliance up to twenty million suns and which may signal the end of the fuel-burning era of an enriched, heavy-element, population I star. A supernova is a catastrophic event of such magnitude that it stands out in isolated splendor at maximum light in a distant galaxy whose other stars cannot be resolved. The photographs and the light curve of one very bright supernova that appeared in a remote galaxy are shown in Figures 14.3 and 14.4. Typically, there is a tremendous rise in brightness within a few days toward a peak, followed by a gradual decline that lasts for months and sometimes for years.

Theory of Supernova Formation

According to theoretical calculations a supernova originates in a star of advanced age whose mass exceeds the Chandrasekhar limit of 1.4 solar mass (see Section 12.8). Toward the end of the star's metamorphosis into a supernova, the accelerated thermonuclear reactions within the star's rapidly dwindling supply of nuclear fuel last only weeks to days to minutes as the star attempts to maintain its equilibrium. Unable to cope with the fast-changing internal conditions, the star becomes unstable and gravitational collapse ensues, resulting in still higher temperatures. This generates a great outflow of neutrinos from the highly compressed core. With further compression a stage is reached when the neutrinos can no

longer freely escape into space and carry away energy with them. Instead they are absorbed in the star's outer layers. This causes the surrounding regions containing the lighter nuclei (carbon, oxygen, neon, etc.) to heat up to a temperature of several billion degrees while the central core temperature rises precipitously to tens of billions of degrees. Within seconds the outer layers of the star are blown off in a catastrophic explosion that releases an enormous flux of high-powered radiation and high-

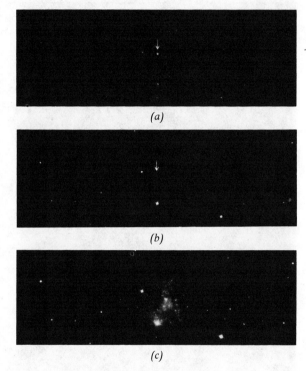

(a)

(b)

(c)

Figure 14.3   Supernova in Galaxy, IC 4182, type I, in Virgo. (a) September 10, 1937—peak brightness; exposure 20 minutes; outshines entire Galaxy which is not recorded during exposure time. (b) Nov. 24, 1938—about 400 days after maximum brightness; exposure 45 minutes; Galaxy faintly recorded. (c) Jan. 19, 1942—about 1,600 days after maximum brightness; exposure 85 minutes; supernova too faint to be detected in Galaxy which is clearly recorded in the longer exposure. (Courtesy of Hale Observatories.)

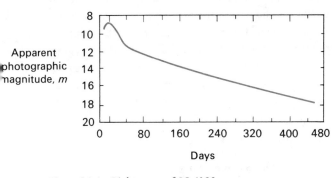

Apparent photographic magnitude, m

Days

Figure 14.4 Light curve of IC 4182.

energy particles, mostly cosmic rays and neutrons, accompanied by an intense shock-wave disturbance. The outburst is so violent that the energy liberated is equivalent to the total amount that the sun expends in a hundred million years. The material expelled represents a considerable fraction of the star's mass. The rapidly expanding luminous cloud radiates strongly throughout the entire electromagnetic spectrum. The broad emission lines observed in the spectra of the supernovae are interpreted as the Doppler shifts resulting from the explosive outward movement of the gases propelled from the star at velocities up to several thousand miles per second. The implosive reactive force generated by the shock wave imparts such high velocities to the degenerate electrons within the stellar core that they react with the protons to form neutrons. With the removal of the electrons which had provided the supporting pressure against further gravitational collapse, the core contracts still further as it becomes saturated with neutrons in a degenerate condition approaching a density of 10^{14} g/cm^3. A rapidly spinning, superdense, central remnant survives as a neutron star a few miles in diameter in the form of a pulsar. In only a few instances, however, has a pulsar been observationally identified within a supernova remnant. Why

more pulsars cannot be spotted in the vicinity of supernovae remains open to question.

Nucleogenesis of the Heavier Elements

At the prevailing higher central temperatures in stars of greater mass than the sun, the elements up to the stable iron group (atomic number ~ 26) are synthesized by the fusion of the lighter elements. Some of the fusion products react with helium to produce unstable nuclei which release neutrons. Beyond iron the still heavier elements can be built up by the slow fusion of these neutrons with successive nuclei as far as lead and bismuth (atomic number 83). For the still heavier nuclei, it has been difficult to account for their production in normally evolving stars. Such elements, even if produced by slow neutron capture, undergo too rapid radioactive decay to persist in sufficient numbers. What is needed is a large supply of neutrons reacting rapidly with the heavier nuclei to produce the heaviest atoms. Calculations indicate that the most likely source of free neutrons would be found in a superhot supernova core from which the emerging neutrons rapidly react with the remaining nuclei to create the heavy elements when the star blows up. The expanding cloud, enriched with the heavy elements, permeates the interstellar environment and "contaminates" it. In this way, successive generations of stars formed from the enriched interstellar clouds will contain a higher proportion of the heavier atoms from this process than the older stars. This mechanism has been alluded to earlier in Section 13.9.

Black Holes

The current theories of supernova formation predict the possibility of the most massive stars collapsing so energetically that they shoot through the "event horizon" and disappear into a *black hole*. The powerful gravitational force of the collapsed core overwhelms the gas pressure. The relativistic explanation of this weird stellar fate is that the intense gravitational field surrounding the collapsed superdense object curves space so completely around it that its light cannot escape into the external world and so it vanishes from sight. Relativity theory predicts that this kind of complete collapse would be viewed by a distant observer to be contracting indefinitely toward the critical boundary between visibility and invisibility known as the *Schwarzschild* or *gravitational radius*. The calculated radius of the Schwarzschild sphere for the collapsed sun is slightly under two miles. (The sun is not the kind of star that will experience such a collapse.) Outside the Schwarzschild limit the collapse can be halted short of the gravitational radius in the white dwarfs and the neutron stars whose masses are well under those of the most massive stars.

An unwary spaceship caught in the gravitational clutches of the curled-up field of a black hole would be sucked into it never to escape. According to the theoreticians who have investigated the properties of black holes with the aid of the theory of relativity, several kinds of black holes are possible, some with exotic space geometries. Black holes constitute the end product in the hierarchy of gravitationally collapsed objects, after the neutron stars. Even though an object disappears into a black hole, it is not isolated gravitationally. One place to look for black holes is in binary systems where the existence of an invisible black hole companion of the proper mass could be detected gravitationally from the orbital motion of the visible component. Another possibility is that gas streaming from one component into its close blackhole companion might radiate detectable x-ray emission. J. Wheeler of Princeton University has theorized that a massive star collapsing into a black hole might emit a pulse spectrum of oscillations in the form of gravitational radiation. Gravity waves are discussed in the next chapter (Section 15.5).

Although some thirty-five years elapsed before neutron stars were discovered after their predicted existence, the first of the black holes is now believed to have been discovered (October 1972), within $3\frac{1}{2}$ decades of their prediction. The x-ray source, Cygnus X-1, may be the black hole companion of a nearby blue supergiant star, physically associated with it as part of a binary system.

14.3   THE CRAB NEBULA

Identification as a Supernova

The most celebrated supernova and the one that has been most studied by optical, radio, infrared, and x-ray astronomers is the Crab nebula. It has been a fruitful source of surprising discoveries. In 1921 J. C. Duncan at the Mt. Wilson Observatory found that the nebular filaments in this object were expanding at a rate that suggested a possible explosive origin about 900 years earlier. This estimate of its birthdate coincided very nearly with the date of A.D. 1054 when, according to old Chinese chronicles, a "guest star" suddenly appeared in the constellation of Taurus and remained visible to the naked eye for many months. The combination of the outward displacements (proper motions) of the filaments observed over the years and their Doppler-shifted spectral lines yields a distance of about 5,000 light-years for the object. Its present visible diameter is about six light-years.

Two different kinds of emissions have been observed: (1) the optical bright lines characteristic of the planetary nebulae appear in the spectrum of the expanding filamentary network; (2) the continuous emission spectrum that originates in the so-called "amorphous" region. The bright-line spectrum is produced by the capture of electrons by the ionized atoms; as the electrons cascade down into the lower atomic levels, they emit the photons that give rise to the emission lines. The continuous emission, which is spread throughout the electromagnetic

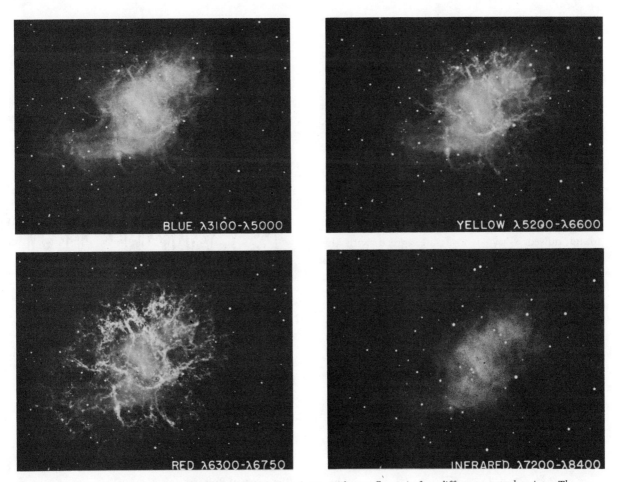

Figure 14.5   The Crab nebula photographed with the 100-inch Mt. Wilson reflector in four different spectral regions. The filamentary network and associated "amorphous" region are most clearly seen in the red photo. A color photograph of the Crab nebula appears in Plate 22. (Courtesy of Hale Observatories.)

spectrum, comes from the highly polarized synchrotron radiation. This kind of nonblackbody radiation is emitted by fast-moving electrons spiraling along the magnetic lines of force that permeate the nebula (Figure 14.6). It is theorized that the electrons are ejected from the rapidly rotating core remnant of the supernova and are accelerated to high velocities by the expanding electric and magnetic fields present in the nebula.

Discoveries in the Crab Nebula

The Crab nebula was one of the first discrete radio sources to be discovered (1948). In 1968 radio astronomers at the National Radio Astronomy Observatory in West Virginia found that a source within the nebula was emitting sharp, discontinuous radio pulses whose rate was later established to be thirty times per second. Within a year the source was pinpointed as coming from one of the two central stars in the nebula (see Plate 22). This type of pulsing radio star belongs to a class of objects called *pulsars* (to be discussed in the next section). It was also observed to be flashing optically at the same frequency as the radio pulses—thirty times per second. The Lick astronomers shortly afterward devised an ingenious method to reveal photographically the blinking phenomenon of the pulsar (Figure 14.8).

The Crab nebula was also the first discrete x-ray source to be discovered in the heavens during a Naval Research Laboratory sounding-rocket flight in 1963. In 1969 the Naval Research Laboratory scientists found pulsed x-rays whose rate agreed with the optical and radio observations. The Crab nebula emits about one hundred times more energy in the x-ray region than in the optical region. The optical radiation in turn is about a hundred times more intense than the radio emission. In 1972, astronomers found that the Crab nebula was also emitting gamma radiation at a rate slightly less than its radio flux.

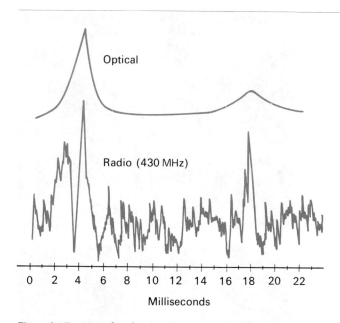

Figure 14.7 *Optical and radio "light curves" of Crab nebula. The radio curve shows a split down the middle of the main pulse. The ragged appearance of the radio curve results principally from the scintillation effects in the interstellar medium.*

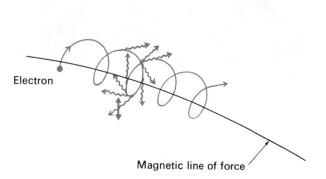

Figure 14.6 *Mechanism of synchrotron radiation, which occurs along the spiral path of the electron (shown only for one loop in the diagram). The double arrow ($\updownarrow$) shows the vibrating plane of polarized light which is perpendicular to the magnetic line of force and to the direction of radiation.*

14.4 PULSARS

Discovery of Pulsars

During the course of a search in 1967 at the University of Cambridge in England with a newly designed sensitive radio telescope, a strange object was discovered in the constellation of Vulpecula to be pulsing with a precise period of 1.337 seconds. It was subsequently designated CP 1919, in which CP stands for Cambridge Pulsar, the latter word being the name chosen for the pulsing object; 1919 corresponds to the right ascension of its position in the sky. Within a few weeks after the initial discovery, A. Hewish, the director of the radio observatory, and his colleagues found three additional pulsars. Some ninety pulsars have now been discovered with periods ranging from 0.033 to 3.75 seconds. Of this number only two optical pulsars have been identified: the Crab nebula and the x-ray pulsar, Hercules X-1, whose period is 1.238 sec. It undergoes a 6-hour eclipse every 40 hours by a blue subgiant observable companion known as HZ Herculis.

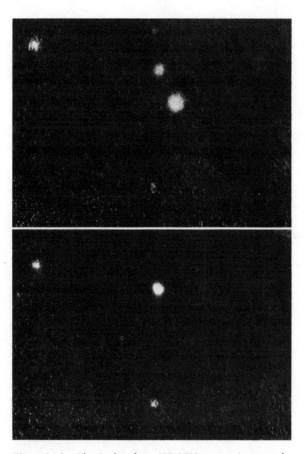

Figure 14.8   The Crab pulsar, NP 0532, at maximum and minimum light. This body flashes on and off about thirty times per second. (Photographed by J. Wampler and J. L. Miller with the 120-inch Lick reflector, courtesy of Lick Observatory.)

Pulsar Observations

The pulsar record for one Cambridge pulsar, CP 0950, with a period of 0.2530646 second appears in Figure 14.9. Although the pulse frequency of the pulsars is very precise (better than one part in one hundred million), the pulse amplitude, shape, and width vary considerably from one pulse to another. In general, pulsars with periods greater than one second have double peaks. The individual pulses exhibit a complex structure, containing a number of subpulses of short duration as small as one hundred-millionth of a second (Figure 14.9b). The duration of the pulses ranges from several thousandths of a second to about one-tenth of a second. For about 99.9 per cent of the time, the pulsar energy output remains "quiet" as we observe it. The energy of the pulses varies appreciably over the radio spectrum; it tends to decrease toward the shorter wavelengths. The amount of radio energy emitted during one burst is from one million to ten billion times greater per square centimeter each second than the sun emits from a similar area per second.

Scintillation Effects

The trace in Figure 14.9b clearly reveals the phenomenon of scintillation (twinkling) as the radiation passes through the drifting interstellar clouds and the interplanetary plasma of the solar wind. This phenomenon becomes noticeable when the source has very small dimensions. The action is similar to the terrestrial atmospheric twinkling of starlight that issues from a point source like a star as opposed to the steady average light from the disk source of a planet. If the sun suddenly ceased shining, the pulse duration of its turned-off light would be smeared out over an interval of two seconds. The radiation from the center of the solar disk, which bulges out closest to us, would disappear first. It would be followed in succession by the light from the ever-widening zones out to the sun's limb. The

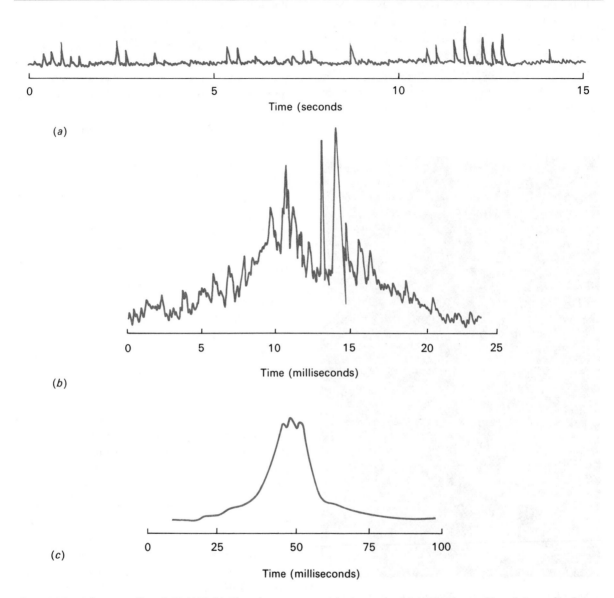

Figure 14.9   Pulsar recording of CP 0950. (a) The pulses occur at precise intervals of 0.2530646 second but their amplitudes
vary. (b) Fine structural details recorded with 1,000-foot dish telescope at Arecibo, Puerto Rico, at a frequency of 195 megahertz.
(c) Average pulse envelope, averaged over many pulses. (From "Pulsars" by A. Hewish. Copyright © October 1968 by
Scientific American, Inc. All rights reserved.)

last disappearing flash would arrive from the limb since the edge is farthest from us. It is clear from the sharp pulsar peaks that the energy is coming from a very small region. For a pulse duration of one hundred microseconds (0.0001 sec) the diameter corresponds to about eighteen miles, the distance that light travels in 0.0001 second.

The presence of electrons in interstellar space affects the velocities of the different radio waves: the longer the wavelength, the slower the velocity. The radio waves emerging from a sharp pulse are therefore dispersed along the way into a train of waves. The shorter waves arrive on earth before the longer waves. The amount of delay depends on the frequency of the radiation, the interstellar electron density, and the path length. The difference in arrival time between the extreme ends of the radio spectrum may be as much as sixty seconds. From the observed delay time and a reasonable value of the electron density (~ 0.1 electron per cubic centimeter), the distance to the pulsar (the path length) can be obtained. Calculations of this kind reveal that the pulsars are relatively close to us with an average distance of about 3,000 light-years. They are distributed in or near the plane of the Galaxy.

Theoretical Model of a Pulsar

There is common agreement that the pulsars are the rapidly rotating magnetized neutron cores of the supernovae, as first proposed by T. Gold. It is hypothesized that the swiftly contracting stellar core, following the supernova outburst, conserves its magnetic and rotational energy and thereby becomes a rapidly spinning, highly magnetized, superdense body. Its concentrated magnetic field is at least one million million times stronger than the earth's magnetic field and its rate of spin may be over one million times faster that the earth's rotation. Only a tiny body of the order of five to twenty miles in diameter

packed at an enormous density approaching the nuclear density could survive disruption.

According to the theory, the star's high rotational speed provides the reservoir of energy needed to maintain the continuous flow of charged particles (plasma) streaming from the magnetic poles of the neutron star. The intense magnetic field forces the star's plasma envelope to rotate with the star. In the so-called "lighthouse model," the charged particles in the plasma are accelerated along the magnetic lines of force of the star's spinning dipole (similar to the dipole of a bar magnet). As they pass through the region where the spin of the rotating plasma approaches the speed of light, the particles emit radiation in the form of a highly directed cone of light

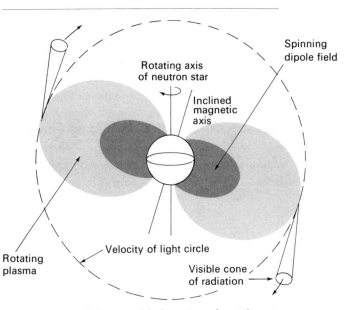

Figure 14.10 *Lighthouse model of rotating pulsar. The axis of the rapidly rotating neutron star must be properly oriented for us to catch the flash of radiation whenever one of the rotating beams sweeps past our line of sight. Otherwise we will not detect any pulses. From (Lighthouse Model of a Rotating Pulsar by A. Hewish). Copyright © 1968 by Scientific American, Inc. All Rights Reserved.*

spinning with the star. When the searchlight beam sweeps across the line of sight to the earth, it is viewed as a pulse every fraction of a second or so.

The theory predicts that the braking effect of the magnetic field will slow down the pulse rate by dissipating the rotational energy of the star. The prediction has been confirmed by observations conducted over a period of time in at least a dozen pulsars. They have shown a decrease in the pulse rate between 0.3 and five parts in 10^{15} per period of pulsation. Since the pulsars with the shortest periods are the youngest, it follows that the Crab nebula, which has the shortest period discovered so far (0.033 sec), must be the youngest pulsar. It is slowing down at about 12.5-millionths of a second per year. This corresponds to an energy loss of 10^{38} ergs per second, about 100,000 times more than the sun loses by radiation each second. Approximately the same loss occurs from its synchrotron radiation and nebular expansion. The average age of the remaining pulsars, omitting the Crab and Vela pulsars, is about two million years. It is not surprising therefore that their expanding envelopes of gases have enlarged beyond the point of optical visibility. The failure to detect optical pulsations in all but two pulsars may be an indication that the light flashes are a transient phenomenon that occurs only during the pulsar's early history.

A theoretical model of the interior of a neutron star has been derived by M. A. Ruderman of Columbia University. Ruderman pictures the small degenerate central core as consisting of an unknown mixture of neutrons, protons, mesons, and strange heavy particles of the kind observed in the breakup of atomic nuclei with the large particle accelerators. Its superdense material ($\sim 10^{15}$ g/cm^3) is packed inside a volume whose diameter is about four kilometers and whose temperature is ten billion degrees Kelvin. This density is equivalent to the nucleus of the atom. Surrounding the central core is a superfluid about ten kilometers thick composed mainly of neutrons with the frictionless properties that liquid helium 3 displays near absolute zero. Overlying the superfluid is a rigid crust of heavy nuclei several kilometers thick with a preponderance of neutrons in the bottom portion. The outer skin is a lattice of atoms only a few centimeters thick.

It was noted that the Vela pulsar, which had been pulsing regularly at eleven times per second, suddenly speeded up during one week at the end of February 1969 by 208-billionths of a second. A speedup was also observed in the Crab pulsar. The Ruderman theory postulates that as the star slows down in its rotation, the reduced centrifugal force tends to increase the sphericity of the star. The rigid crystallized crust undergoes accumulated stresses that finally cause it to rupture to a depth of less than one centimeter, producing what is called a "starquake." Within a fraction of a second, the resettlement of the star's structure results in a temporary speedup of the crust.

14.5 OVERACTIVE GALAXIES

Seyfert Galaxies

The typical Seyfert galaxy (named after Carl Seyfert who discovered them in 1943) is a fairly large spiral with an unusually small, active nucleus. Evidence that a strongly energetic region within the nuclear core, only a light-year or less in diameter, is undergoing violent reactions comes from its variable optical emissions which at times are extraordinarily intense. Several of these galaxies are also powerful variable radio, infrared, and x-ray emitters. It is estimated that 1 or 2 per cent of the spirals are Seyfert galaxies. Further confirmation of the abnormal activity is obtained from the broadened spectral lines that indicate the nuclear expulsion of ionized matter in the form of clouds at high velocities from the center. What process or processes are responsible for the synchrotron radiation that accompanies the emission is not yet clear. Except for their lesser total luminosities, the Seyfert galaxies possess a number of characteristics similar to the quasars. Perhaps Seyfert galaxies represent an early disruptive stage through which all spirals, including our own, must pass.

N Galaxies and Compact Galaxies

N galaxies have some properties in common with Seyfert galaxies and with quasars. They consist of a bright, sharp nucleus surrounded by a small nebulous envelope. About a dozen of them have been identified, all apparently at great cosmological distances as interpreted from the large red shifts of their spectral lines. They exhibit rapid fluctuations in brightness and color, at times within a period of a few days, indicating that the variable sources must be less than a light-week in diameter. Other signs that relate them to the quasars and the Seyfert galaxies are the presence of strong, bright spectral lines and the large output of radio energy. A very distant Seyfert galaxy might resemble an N galaxy.

Another more abundant kindred type of galaxy is the compact galaxy first observed by F. Zwicky of the Hale Observatories. It usually resembles a very small elliptical galaxy with a high surface brightness and a stellarlike nucleus.

14.6 EXPLODING GALAXIES
Observed Radio Emission

In their probes of the sky, radio astronomers have detected two distinct kinds of radio emissions: *thermal* and *nonthermal*. Thermal radiation grows progressively weaker with increasing wavelengths in accordance with the blackbody distribution of energy extended into the radio spectral region (Figure 10.12). This type of continuous radio energy is quite prevalent in our Galaxy as well as in other galaxies. It arises from interactions between the free electrons and ions (mostly protons) during close encounters within the interstellar medium. In the process the electrons, while escaping capture by the ions, are stimulated to radiate energy over a wide range of wavelengths, much of which appears in the radio region. Many of the electrons are the products of the disintegration of atomic nuclei colliding with cosmic-ray particles. Thermal radiation also occurs in the bright gaseous nebulae similar to the Orion nebula. Here the electron supply comes mainly from the ionization of atoms induced by the ultraviolet light of their evolved hot stars. The greater the motions of the electrons, the higher is the output of thermal energy.

There are isolated galactic sources like the Crab nebula and other supernova remnants, or the galactic nucleus, whose radio energy is not thermal. Unlike thermal radiation, its intensity *increases* toward the longer wavelengths. The observed nonthermal energy is frequently ascribed to synchrotron radiation which is emitted by rapidly moving electrons spiraling around the magnetic lines of force (Figure 14.6). The same kind of radio emission is present in many galaxies whose optical appearance and spectral behavior are often unusual. The Seyfert galaxies mentioned earlier are one example.

Peculiar Radio Galaxies

The output of nonthermal radio emission from these abnormal galaxies is anywhere from one to ten million times greater than the ordinary radiation from a normal galaxy. More than half of the optically identified discrete radio sources are strong radio galaxies of this type. At least three kinds of peculiar radio galaxies are recognized: (1) giant elliptical galaxies with string-like protrusions in the form of jets or other abnormal extensions; (2) galaxies of curious optical appearance whose radio-emitting regions are displaced from their optical source; and (3) highly distorted galaxies suggestive of explosive events. The positions of the radio-emitting regions vary with different galaxies. There may be a small, intense, radio-emitting center coinciding with the optical center; a strongly radiating tiny core and a weaker large envelope as in M 87 (Figure 14.11); or a double emitting source on either side of the optical region as in Cygnus A (Figure 14.12). A more complex structure is found in the elliptical galaxy, Centaurus A. Here a widespread obscuring lane passes through the middle of the galaxy but the radio picture is that of two small, intense radio sources on either side of the dust lane and two weaker and much larger elliptical radio sources well separated on opposite sides of the optical image (Figure 14.13).

The giant elliptical galaxy, M 87, a member of the Virgo cluster and about fifty million light-years distant, is an unusual object. On long exposure photographs its appearance is normal, with many globular clusters distributed around it. Its radio out-put is ten thousand times greater than that of our Galaxy. Its small, intense radio core, noted in the preceding paragraph, is only one-fourth light-year in width. It is believed to be undergoing repeated explosions. The surrounding weaker radio halo, which is more than 100,000 light-years in diameter, is presumably produced by the high-velocity particles ejected continuously from the nucleus during the last million years or so. In the short photographic exposures, a luminous blue jet containing a string of compact knots appears to streak out some distance from its center. The light within the jet is strongly polarized, consisting of synchrotron radiation. A faint counterjet on the other side of the galaxy has also been photographed. The inference is drawn that short-lived explosive forces are responsible for the ejection of matter at high speeds from the parent

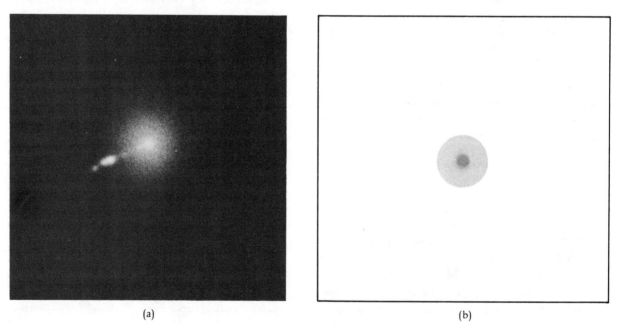

(a)   (b)

Figure 14.11   Giant elliptical galaxy in Virgo, M 87, also known as Virgo A by radio astronomers. (a) Optical picture in short exposure shows a small, intense central core and a luminous jet. A long exposure photograph shows that it is surrounded by many globular clusters. Distance about 50 million light years. (b) Radio picture reveals a tiny bright core surrounded by a weaker halo not quite as large as the visible portion. (Photograph, courtesy of Lick Observatory.)

nuclei of such peculiar galaxies. It is estimated that the material expelled amounts to as much as ten to one hundred solar masses per year.

One of the most remarkable objects is the peculiar radio galaxy, M 82, about ten million light-years distant (Figure 14.14). The velocities of the Doppler-shifted emission lines originating in the drawn-out filaments perpendicular to the principal axis of the galaxy point to a cataclysmic explosion that took place 1.5 million years earlier. It is estimated that about five million solar masses (about 1/25,000 of the mass of our Galaxy) were violently ejected from the center. The luminous material is emitting strongly polarized synchrotron radiation which energizes the hydrogen and other atoms in the filaments to produce their observed bright-line spectra.

It is difficult to account for the prime source of the intense radio emission observed in the strongest radio sources. Something like one trillion solar masses of hydrogen equivalent to one hundred average-sized galaxies would have to be converted into energy by the ordinary inefficient process of thermonuclear fusion to equal the observed amount of radio energy. Two other far more efficient conversion methods are possible: release of potential energy by gravitational collapse or matter-antimatter annihilation which is virtually 100 per cent efficient. Exactly how either of these two mechanisms can be invoked is not clear.

14.7 QUASI-STELLAR OBJECTS

In the years since their discovery in 1960, the quasi-stellar objects (QSO's), or *quasars* as they are popularly called, still largely remain an enigma. One

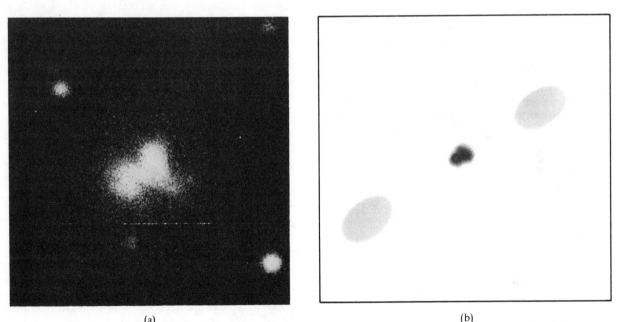

(a)

(b)

Figure 14.12   Radio galaxy Cygnus A. (a) Optical picture shows a fuzzy double object. Distance about 500 million light years. (b) Radio picture reveals two external sources shown in light blue color. This object was the first discrete radio source discovered outside our Galaxy (1945). (Photograph, courtesy of Hale Observatories.)

14 COSMIC VIOLENCE

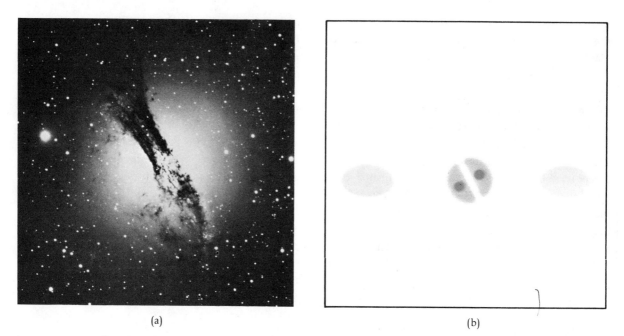

(a)   (b)

Figure 14.13   Radio galaxy Centaurus A. (a) Optical picture shows a strong obscuring lane cutting across the middle of the galaxy. Distance about 15 million light years. (b) Radio picture reveals two small, intense radio cores (dark blue) on a line perpendicular to the dust band and a fainter, large elliptical region (light blue) on either side of the optical image. (Photograph, courtesy of Hale Observatories.)

group, the quasi-stellar radio sources (QSS's), is characterized by strong radio emission. It is distinguished from a second type known as the radio-quiet objects (also called blue stellar objects or blue compact galaxies), which are not radio emitters. These two classes of inconspicuous, apparently starlike bodies possess not only considerably red-shifted spectral lines but extraordinarily powerful radiation concentrated in a region that may be as small as a fraction of a light-year in diameter.

Discovery of QSO's

By 1960 the high degree of pinpointing accuracy developed through the technique of radio interferometry (Section 3.3) enabled optical astronomers to direct their telescopes precisely onto the suspected radio objects and to positively identify them. The

QSO's, which resemble ordinary stars, had actually been photographed on star-field plates many times prior to their identification without raising any suspicion about their characteristics. The first optical recognition of a quasar was made in 1960 with the 200-inch Hale reflector on an object labeled 3C 48, the forty-eighth entry in the third Cambridge Radio Catalog (see Figure 14.15). Although it looked like an ordinary star of the sixteenth magnitude, its bright-line spectrum and those of three other similar objects proved undecipherable at the time.

In 1962 Maarten Schmidt of the Hale Observatories obtained a spectrogram of the small, thirteenth-magnitude radio source, 3C 273, accurately pinpointed by Australian radio astronomers with the 210-foot radio dish antenna at Parkes, Australia (see Figure 14.15). Within weeks he succeeded in un-

Figure 14.14   Exploding galaxy, M 82, shows filaments extending 25,000 light-years outward from the center. (Courtesy of Hale Observatories.)

sured by means of radio telescope interferometry are often less than 0.002 second of arc. Some nebulous extensions have been photographed in a few of the nearer QSO's. Despite their apparent tiny sizes, the radio images are frequently structured and noncircular. Many possess a hierarchy of minute, discrete components; others have extended radio sources on either side of the optical center, somewhat reminiscent of the radio galaxies. Very long baseline radio interferometer measures have disclosed the rapid separations of closely spaced, minute sources apparently resulting from explosions within the quasar.

In some instances two sources appear to be separating from each other at a speed greater than the velocity of light. This illusory effect has one possible geometrical explanation. For example, the beam of a rotating searchlight playing across the patchy clouds in the night sky gives the impression of a luminous disturbance in very rapid motion. In a somewhat analogous manner, rapidly separating gas clouds within the quasar, interacting with the ambient plasma and its associated magnetic field, develop outwardly moving shockwave disturbances that appear to travel faster than the velocity of light.

The prime source for estimating the distances of the remote quasars from their measured redshifted line spectra is the Hubble law of recession (Figure 13.12). The nearest quasi-stellar object is a radio-quiet object about twenty million light-years distant. From his sampling, Schmidt found that the counts of QSO's increased much faster with distance than if their distribution in space were uniform. This finding agreed with an earlier distribution count made of radio sources by the British radio astronomers Ryle and Clark. According to Schmidt's analysis, the quasi-stellar objects were formed in largest numbers within a couple of billion years after the universe began its expansion. At that time the universe contained about one thousand times

raveling the puzzle when he recognized in the bright-line spectrum the characteristic spacing of the first three lines of the Balmer series of hydrogen. They were displaced to the red by a large Doppler shift corresponding to a velocity of 15 per cent of the velocity of light. With the logjam broken, astronomers soon decoded their earlier spectrograms which also revealed very large red shifts for a number of recognized emission lines.

Appearance and Distribution of QSO's

About two hundred quasi-stellar objects had been spectroscopically examined by the end of 1971. Slightly more than half of them are QSS's and the remainder are the radio-quiet objects. Nearly all of the observed quasi-stellar objects have a starlike optical appearance. Their angular diameters mea-

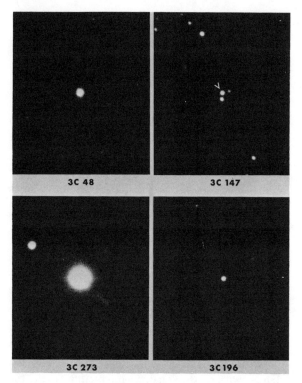

3C 48   3C 147

3C 273   3C 196

Figure 14.15   Four quasi-stellar radio sources photographed with the 200-inch Hale reflector. (Courtesy of Hale Observatories.)

more quasars than now. Out of some fifteen million of these objects, which some believe are the short-lived, brilliant cores of galaxies, most would have burned themselves out by the time their light could reach us.

Energy Flux within QSO's

The most striking physical condition about the quasi-stellar objects is the incredible flood of energy that is gushing out of a source confined to a volume of space that appears to be less than a light-year in diameter. In some instances the energy is a hundred times greater than from our whole Galaxy. That the radiating region must be small is also confirmed by the twinkling in the radio light similar to the scintillation effects observed in the pulsars (Section 14.4).

The scintillation effect is superimposed on a slower time fluctuation caused by changes in brightness observed in many QSO's within a region that may be only light-days in diameter. The variability of the QSO's in the optical and radio emission is unpredictable. From an examination of old plates, some show changes amounting to a few tenths of a magnitude in days to weeks and even in years; others show larger changes within days or months. There appears to be no correlation between the optical and radio fluctuations. The maximum energy appears to peak in the infrared. The radiation is believed to be mainly synchrotron radiation emission of the type that is associated with disruptive forces.

Spectral Characteristics and Velocity Shifts

The spectra of the QSO's include the bright lines of a number of familiar ionized elements (carbon, magnesium, oxygen, neon, silicon, helium) and hydrogen, overlying a continuous spectrum whose source is ascribed to synchrotron radiation. All the lines are displaced by very large amounts toward the red. Their identification is based upon certain recognized patterns of the emission-line spacings observed in the rarefied envelopes of the planetary nebulae, novae, and other hot sources as well as from laboratory sources. At least two lines are needed for identification and measurement of the red shift. The measured line shifts range from a few per cent up to 91 per cent of the velocity of light. This is nearly eight times the red shift of the most distant ordinary galaxy observed.

The maximum shift so far recorded is $\Delta\lambda/\lambda = 3.56$. In this instance the ultraviolet Lyman alpha line, whose normal wavelength is 1,216 angstroms, has been shifted to 5,540 angstroms in the blue-green spectral region. Hence $\Delta\lambda/\lambda = (5540 - 1216)/1216 = 3.56$. For large velocities a relativistic Doppler formula is used (see Section 15.3, formula 5b). When solved for v/c the answer is $v/c = 0.91$, that is, the object is receding at a speed equal to 91 per cent of the velocity of light.

In several dozen quasi-stellar objects, a number of narrow absorption lines appear, usually with redward displacements different from those of the bright lines. Even more puzzling is the discovery that certain sets of absorption lines possess slightly different velocities. As before, the identifications of these lines is found from their accurately known laboratory wavelength measurements and from their recognized patterns and spacings in the spectra of the rarefied gas clouds surrounding a hot radiating source. One quasar contains seven different sets of absorption lines grouped around the red shifts, $\Delta\lambda/\lambda = 1.365, 1.596, 1.656, 1.671, 1.674, 1.956,$ and 2.202. An obvious interpretation of these differences is that the absorption arises from a series of thin shells moving outward at different speeds amounting to appreciable fractions of the speed of light. On the other hand, if the absorption is not physically related to the QSO's, it presumably originates in the intergalactic medium. Since the absorption lines are close to the redward displacement of the emission lines, the first of the hypotheses is the more acceptable view. The proper explanation of the divergent line shifts is not yet resolved.

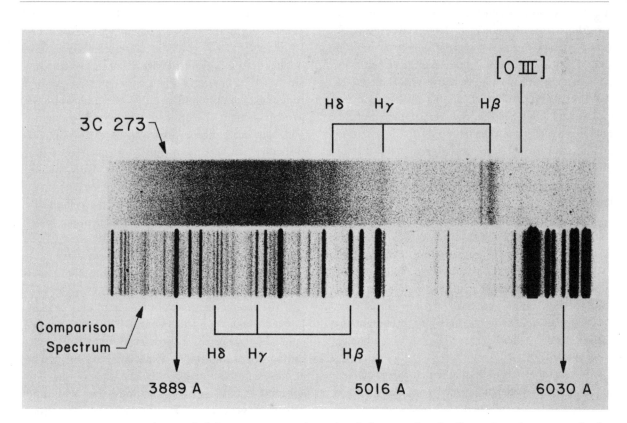

Figure 14.16   Spectrogram (negative) of the quasar 3C 273 obtained with the 120-inch Lick reflector. Note the pronounced red shift of the Balmer hydrogen lines (Hβ, Hγ, and Hδ) in relation to the comparison spectrum. (Courtesy of Lick Observatory.)

Are the Red Shifts Truly Cosmological?

Many astronomers believe that the Doppler shifts of the spectral lines in the quasi-stellar objects correspond to true velocities arising out of the expansion of the universe. Other astronomers hold different opinions. They reason that these objects may not be so distant after all. This would reduce their enormous power output and bring them more reasonably in line with other sources. One non-cosmological interpretation, known as the local Doppler hypothesis, is that these bodies were violently expelled at high velocities from nearby galaxies or from the center of our Galaxy. Observations of strings of galaxies, including some quasars, give the impression of having been ejected in opposite directions from the nuclei of large active galaxies. If the quasars were ejected from nearby centers, it should follow that some would exhibit velocities of approach which have not been observed. H. C. Arp of the Hale Observatories, from his analysis of the quasar data, contends that the apportionment of the quasar red shifts and their non-uniform distribution on the sky are not representative of very distant objects; furthermore, he finds, quasars associated with nearby galaxies do not have the expected high luminosities.

Another suggestion attributes the observed red shifts of the QSO's to the well-known red shift associated with strong gravitational fields (Section 15.5). This hypothesis requires the existence of supermassive stars, which could not maintain a stable configuration long enough to account for all the QSO's in existence, or clusters of gravitationally collapsed stars such as neutron stars. No such bodies have been observed.

In several instances dissimilar velocities between a quasar and an apparently allied galaxy or group of galaxies have been observed. Differences up to about 12,500 mi/sec have been measured. In each case the quasar is red-shifted more than the galaxy. If enough similar discrepancies can be substantiated, other than to attribute them to chance alignments of bodies at different distances, this could cast doubt on the cosmological interpretation that the red shifts are due *entirely* to the expansion of the universe. Some unknown secondary effect, possibly dependent upon the type of galaxy, may also be involved. However, one quasar within a cluster of galaxies about three billion light-years away was found to exhibit the same amount of red shift as the brightest galaxy in the cluster.

If the cosmological interpretation is accepted, how are the vast stores of energy pouring out of such distant but incredibly small regions accounted for? Gravitational collapse of a cluster of massive, contracting objects with a combined mass of one trillion solar masses could be converted into radiation in quantitative agreement with the observed amounts $(10^{36}$–10^{38} kilowatts). The enormous mass content required to supply millions of QSO's could raise the average density of matter in the universe enough to endanger our concepts regarding its expansion. The difficulty can be circumvented by imagining a continual series of successive collapses of many rotating bodies over a long period of time. Their extremely rapid axial rotations, acquired after the collapse by virtue of conservation of angular momentum, might provide a reservoir of sufficient kinetic energy convertible into radiation. The idea possesses some merit in accounting for the violent erratic luminosity changes observed in many quasars.

Thermonuclear reactions are out of the question. It would take the conversion of the entire mass of our Galaxy to produce the energy content of a QSO during its presumed life expectancy of 100,000 to at most ten million years. The QSO's would have to consume masses greater than their own estimated masses to generate their observed energies! Other possibilities that have been considered involve the production of radiation by matter-antimatter annihilation or through unstable plasma clouds radiating in a magnetic field.

Conclusion

Let us summarize what is tentatively known about the quasi-stellar objects: (1) their spectra consist of a number of bright lines (many of them forbidden lines) superimposed on a continuous emission background presumably consisting of synchrotron radiation; a smaller proportion also contain sharp absorption lines displaced a little differently from the bright lines; (2) their spectral lines are Doppler-shifted toward the red by large amounts; (3) they radiate strongly throughout the entire electromagnetic spectrum; their energy, which is confined to very small dimensions, appears to peak in the infrared spectral region; (4) the quasars emit radio energy not quite as strongly as the optical energy; the class of QSO's called the radio-quiet quasars (otherwise known as the blue stellar objects) emit no detectable radio energy; (5) the lifetimes of the QSO's are brief; (6) they are not composed of stars but rather of tiny, massive, rapidly separating cores, as interpreted from the radio observations; and (7) less well established, they may be the primeval condensations that formed the active center of newly created galaxies during an earlier, more violent stage of the universe.

REVIEW QUESTIONS

1. How do we differentiate between nonviolent and violent sources?

2. Describe the series of cataclysmic events that may befall a massive population I star when it has exhausted its available nuclear fuels.

3. Why is the Crab nebula so important to astronomers and physicists?

4. How can a radio astronomer identify a certain object as a quasar rather than as a pulsar or a radio galaxy?

5. How have astronomers determined that pulsars and quasars are very small bodies? Which are smaller: pulsars or quasars? How do we know?

6. What evidence is there that the nuclei of Seyfert galaxies are unstable structures of high-energy content?

7. What are the arguments in favor of the thesis that the quasi-stellar objects are cosmologically very distant?

8. What are the counterarguments that the quasi-stellar objects are not as far away as their red-shifted lines indicate?

9. Why do we have difficulty accounting for the high energy content of the QSO's?

10. Explain why it is unlikely that our sun will ever become a supernova.

11. What causes gravitational collapse in a star? What physical circumstances may bring it to a halt before complete collapse into a black hole?

12. Which, in your opinion, has the greater prospect of being discovered first: a black hole or a black dwarf? By what technique could either one be discovered? Is there any way to distinguish between them?

SELECTED READINGS

Bova, B., *In Quest of Quasars*, Macmillan, 1970.

Burbidge, G. R., and M. Burbidge, *Quasi-stellar Objects*, Freeman, 1967.

Calder, N., *Violent Universe*, Viking, 1970.

Hoyle, F., *Galaxies, Nuclei, and Quasars*, Harper and Row, 1965.

Kahn, F. D., and H. P. Palmer, *Quasars, Their Importance in Astronomy and Physics*, Harvard University Press, 1967.

Albert Einstein (1879–1955), interpreter of the cosmos. Copyright © by Philippe Halsman.

INTRODUCTION TO RELATIVITY THEORY

Nothing puzzles me more than time and space; and yet nothing troubles me less.

Charles Lamb (1775–1834),
in a letter to Thomas Manning (1810)

In 1887 an historic experiment was performed by the American scientists Michelson and Morley to detect the absolute motion of the earth by timing the relative speed of light in different directions within the ether space. It was found that the velocity of light was the same in all directions, regardless of the velocity of the source, thereby making it impossible to determine the absolute motion of the earth. Physicists were left in a quandary until Einstein developed his special theory of relativity in 1905 relating to uniform velocities between moving observers (inertial frames of reference). The theory dispensed with the notion of the ether and absolute motion in space. The constancy of the velocity of light for all observers was accepted as a fact of nature in the theory. Einstein's mathematical derivation of the relativistic expressions of length, mass, and time involves a term called the Lorentz contraction factor, $\sqrt{1 - (v^2/c^2)}$, where v/c is the velocity of an observer relative to the velocity of light. This factor modifies the measurements of length, mass, and time made by observers moving at different speeds with respect to each other in space.

In 1916 Einstein extended his special theory to include the accelerated motions between observers. Into this general theory he introduced the principle of equivalence. It asserts that a gravitational force is indistinguishable from an inertial force arising from accelerated motion. Einstein's general theory of relativity deals with the spatial geometry of four dimensions in which the three dimensions of space are physically linked with the fourth dimension of time. This is in contrast to the Newtonian space of three dimensions divorced from time. According to the Newtonian concept, moving bodies react on each other at a distance governed by the law of gravitation. According to relativity theory, bodies move in space subject to the local structure or curvature of four-dimensional space.

The larger the mass of the body, the greater is the associated local curvature.

The space-time continuum exists in three forms: zero curvature of flat Euclidean space; positive curvature of closed spherical space; negative curvature of open-ended hyperboloidal space. Astronomers have not yet succeeded in determining the kind of universe in which we live. So far, out of the various observational tests of the theory of relativity, none has ever disproved Einstein's predictions.

15.1 CONCEPTS OF SPACE AND TIME

Introduction

Astronomy and the theory of relativity have had a long and profitable relationship. Certain astronomical phenomena, which we will discuss later in the chapter, provided some of the earliest tests of Einstein's theory of relativity. One of the most profound applications of the theory lies in the field of cosmology where it has served to elucidate the nature of the physical world on the cosmic scale. Relativity theory has explained to astronomers how stars manage to keep shining so long through their thermonuclear conversion of matter into energy. One need hardly mention the significant role it has played in advancing the frontiers of nuclear and atomic physics as well as those of gravitational astronomy. Here the theory of relativity can satisfactorily account for physical effects associated with high velocities that the older classical theory of Newton cannot properly predict.

Newtonian vs. Einsteinian Views

Man's commonsense perceptions of the natural phenomena do not always serve him adequately in describing the laws of nature. The Newtonian description of the laws of physics implies that the spatial dimensions are independent of time; in other words, the measurements of length and time are the same for all observers in space. Einstein's theory of relativity relates the three dimensions of space with the fourth dimension, time. Length and time measurements are not absolute but relative to each other. Thus two observers in motion relative to each other will see the same series of events occurring at different places and at different times within their respective coordinate systems of measurements, or frames of reference. The concept of "relativity" is involved because one cannot drop anchor in the universe; all motion is relative.

In the Newtonian view space is characterized by three numbers, the spatial coordinates, x, y, and z— that is, place without regard to time t. A body in motion receives its orders on how to move remotely from the law of gravitation. However, the law is silent when the body moves uniformly. Four-dimensional Einsteinian space is conceived as a world of *events*, time and place together, described by four numbers, the spatial coordinates, x, y, z and the time coordinate t. In the relativistic view a body moves *uniformly* or *nonuniformly* according to whatever the structure of the space-time geometry happens to be in its vicinity. The path of a body moving in the space-time world of four dimensions is called a geodesic world line or *geodesic*. A geodesic is the shortest distance between two points in four-dimensional geometry, analogous to the great circle's route being the shortest distance between two points on a sphere. We view space as the three-dimensional surface of a four-dimensional hyperstructure in the same way that imaginary flat creatures would view their "flatland" as the two-dimensional surface of a three-dimensional sphere.

15.2 THE SPECIAL THEORY OF RELATIVITY

Basic Postulates of the Special Theory

Albert Einstein published his mathematical theory of special relativity in 1905 when he was 26 years old and working as a patent examiner in the Swiss patent office in Bern. The special theory deals with *uniform* motions between observers or with what is referred to as inertial frames of reference. In 1916 he completed the more general theory of relativity which takes into account nonuniform (accelerated) motions between observers. In order to develop the mathematical formulation of his special theory of relativity, Einstein laid down the following postulates:

1. The laws of physics are the same for all observers in inertial frames of reference.

2. The velocity of light (186,282 mi/sec or 299,792 km/sec) is the same for all observers in space.

Further comments are in order. Two observers moving uniformly relative to one another are said to occupy inertial frames of reference enjoying equal physical status. Neither observer will be able to detect motion of his own system by means of any experiments conducted in his system. Einstein's contribution was to generalize this effect by making it applicable to all physical phenomena, whether they be mechanical, optical, or electromagnetic in nature.

The Michelson-Morley Experiment

At this point we must digress briefly to discuss the results of a famous experiment (1887) which had a bearing upon the theory of relativity. Space was imagined to be filled with a stationary, invisible medium called the *ether* which served as the carrier of electromagnetic waves (as air does for the transport of sound waves). According to this notion the earth's true (absolute) velocity could be measured with respect to this stationary medium by timing the speed of light in various directions. The American physicists Michelson and Morley sought to detect a difference in the speed of a light beam propagated parallel to the earth's motion around the sun and one simultaneously transmitted in the perpendicular direction over the same distance. They employed an interferometer, a device that was capable of measuring a round-trip time difference as short as 10^{-16} second over a reflected light path of eleven meters. The problem is similar to timing the roundtrip of two swimmers exerting the same effort in a river race; one swims up- and downstream while the other swims directly across stream and back the same distance. According to the simple mathematics of the problem, the swimmer moving at right angles to the river bank would return sooner to the same starting point than the swimmer moving up- and downstream. In the case of light, the time spent moving across the earth's path, back and forth, was calculated to be $\sqrt{1 - (v^2/c^2)}$ shorter than the time spent moving parallel to the earth's path in the same direction and in the opposite direction; here v is the absolute velocity of the earth's orbital motion and c is the velocity of light. It was reasoned that the minute difference in the relative speeds of the light beams in the perpendicular directions would lead to an evaluation of the earth's absolute motion in space.

No matter in what directions the light was propagated or at what time of year the experiment was performed, the result was the same. There was no measurable time difference over the same interval of distance between the light beams in any direction. This experiment proved that the absolute velocity of the earth in space cannot be found because the velocity of light is independent of the relative velocity of the light source and the observer. This is Einstein's postulate 2. The ether was no longer necessary.

Einsteinian vs. Newtonian Velocities

It is of interest to compare one aspect of relativistic and Newtonian motions. According to Einstein, if v_A and v_B represent the space velocities of two observers A and B respectively, their relative velocity, v_{AB}, is:

$$v_{AB} = \frac{v_A + v_B}{1 + \frac{v_A \cdot v_B}{c^2}} \qquad \text{(Einstein)}$$

where c is the universal symbol for the velocity of electromagnetic waves (186,300 mi/sec in rounded figures). This formula follows from the linking together of the fourth dimension of time with the three dimensions of space. If A's and B's velocities are insignificant in comparison with the velocity of light (v_A/c and $v_B/c \sim 0$), the above formula reduces to

$$v_{AB} = v_A + v_B \qquad \text{(Newton)}$$

which is the Newtonian expression under any conditions. If two spaceships are approaching each other at speeds of 100,000 mi/sec and 150,000 mi/sec respectively, their relative velocity of approach, v_{AB}, is *not* the sum, 250,000 mi/sec (Newton), but 174,560 mi/sec (Einstein). Radio signals exchanged between the two ships will be received at the same speed (186,300 mi/sec). This follows from Einstein's postulate 2. Let us consider the extreme situation. If two light beams are transmitted simultaneously in opposite directions from the same point, they will recede from each other at the relative velocity of light ($c = 186,300$ mi/sec) and *not* at 372,600 mi/sec ($= 2c$). This may be verified by substituting $v_A = v_B = c$ in Einstein's formula and obtaining $v_{AB} = c$. There is no way yet discovered by which an object can travel faster than light in the special theory of relativity.[1]

Time Dilation

Another well-known consequence of relativity is that time is slowed down by the factor $\sqrt{1 - (v^2/c^2)}$ where v/c is the observer's velocity relative to that

[1] Hypothetical particles called tachyons that move faster than light have been postulated but never found.

of light. It is called the *Lorentz contraction factor*.[1] This slowing down of time has been named *time dilation*. The faster an observer travels relative to the speed of light, the slower his clock appears to run as seen by another observer whose own clock is seen by the first observer to be running slow. Neither observer is aware of this effect on his own clock. Time contraction is unimportant for all ordinary speeds ($v/c \sim 0$) but it must be reckoned with at speeds which are significant fractions of the velocity of light. Time dilation affects all physical phenomena, whether dynamical, atomic, or electromagnetic in nature, in which the time element enters as a factor.

It is not difficult to develop the formula for time dilation as can be seen from the following illustration (see Figure 15.1). Imagine a rocket ship about to whiz through a long motionless space tunnel that also serves as a laboratory. At the instant the rocket ship is completely inside the laboratory, a flash bulb is fired at point O in the rocket ship and is simultaneously observed in the same spot at P on the floor of the laboratory. Let the clocks in both places read zero at that instant. The rocket man (B observer) watches the beam move vertically up and down in his ship a distance $2L$ where L is the distance between his floor and the ceiling mirror. The round-trip time for the light pulse in the rocket-ship frame is:

$$(1) \qquad t_B = \frac{2L}{c} \quad (c = \text{velocity of light})$$

The laboratory man (A observer) sees the light beam move by way of his ceiling mirror M_A along a diagonal path PM_AR. It is received at point R on the floor of the laboratory frame at the same spot Q where the rocket man observed the returning flash. During this time the rocket ship moved forward the distance $x_A = v \cdot t_A$ where v is the ship's velocity and t_A is the time interval of the light flash in traveling the

[1]Named after the Dutch physicist who first developed it in 1904 from his mathematical analysis of electromagnetism.

distance PM_AR inside the laboratory. By the Pythagorean theorem, the length of the diagonal $PM_A = RM_A = \sqrt{L^2 + (\frac{1}{2}tv_A)^2}$. Hence, the total time interval is:

$$(2) \qquad t_A = \frac{2\sqrt{L^2 + (\frac{1}{2}vt_A)^2}}{c}$$

Squaring equation 2 and substituting it in equation 1 in order to eliminate L, we obtain:

$$t_A^2 = \frac{4L^2}{c^2} + \frac{v^2 t_A^2}{c^2} = t_B^2 + \frac{v^2 t_A^2}{c^2}$$

or
$$t_A^2 \left(1 - \frac{v^2}{c^2}\right) = t_B^2$$

from which it follows that:

$$(3) \qquad t_A = \frac{t_B}{\sqrt{1 - \dfrac{v^2}{c^2}}}$$

If the space ship's velocity is $3/5$ c and the rocket man measures the round-trip time interval of the light flash to be one ten-millionth of a second, then according to formula 3 the laboratory man records it to be 25 per cent longer or time-dilated.

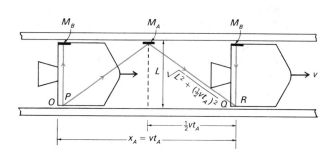

Figure 15.1   Behavior of light ray in rocket ship and space lab.

Relativistic Units of Length, Mass, and Time

In addition to the time-dilation effect, Einstein derived two other important formulas involving length l and mass m. These, together with the previous expression 3, are:

$$(4a) \qquad l_A = l_B \sqrt{1 - \frac{v^2}{c^2}}$$

$$(4b) \qquad m_A = \frac{m_B}{\sqrt{1 - \frac{v^2}{c^2}}}$$

$$(4c) \qquad t_A = \frac{t_B}{\sqrt{1 - \frac{v^2}{c^2}}}$$

where $\sqrt{1 - v^2/c^2}$ = the Lorentz contraction factor; l_A, m_A, t_A are the relativistic length, mass, and time interval measured by an observer for an object in motion, as compared to its measured length, mass, and time interval, l_B, m_B, and t_B respectively, by an observer to whom the object appears at rest.

Observer A will measure a shorter length in the direction of motion for the moving object than will observer B to whom the object appears stationary. For example, observer A would note that B's rocket ship has contracted in length while passing through the laboratory compared to the length of a similar rocket ship at rest in the laboratory. Actually, there is no *physical* contraction of B's rocket ship. A's measurements are influenced by the Lorentz contraction which arises from distortions within the space geometry frame of the moving body. In addition, observer A will measure a greater mass for the moving body than will observer B; and observer A will measure a longer time interval between two events than will observer B for the same two events. This last effect is what we found to exist between the rocket man B and the laboratory man A in the preceding section. If two observers are in motion relative to each other, both will note corresponding changes in length, mass, and time with respect to each other. This follows from the mathematical development relating to Einstein's postulate wherein the identity of the laws of nature remain unaltered in both frames of reference.

15.3 SOME RELATIVISTIC CONSEQUENCES

Increase of Mass

The Stanford linear accelerator is capable of accelerating electrons along a straight tube nearly two miles long close to the speed of light (0.9999999992 c). The tube is very long because of the huge amounts of additional power required to accelerate the electrons as they gain mass through their increased velocities. The final electron mass at the end of the run is 83,000 times greater than normal. If Newtonian physics prevailed, the same electron speed could be attained in a tube length of slightly under one inch!

Slowdown of Time

An observation that confirms the time-dilation effect occurs in connection with the disintegration of muons into lighter particles. Muons are elementary particles about two hundred times heavier than electrons with a laboratory-measured half-life of 1.5-millionths of a second. They are produced as one of the by-products of a collision between a cosmic-ray particle and the nucleus of an atmospheric atom at heights of around forty miles. At their speed, close to the speed of light, they would take 200-millionths of a second to reach sea level traveling downward in a vertical direction. If there were no time dilation, they would decay before they reach the ground; however, a sizable fraction of them survive flight to the ground. Their longevity is increased because their clock time as observed by us is running forty-four times slower than their laboratory earth time as a result of their high velocity.

Relativistic Doppler Formula

An important modification of the Doppler effect mentioned in Section 4.3 is necessary when the relative speed of recession or approach is an appreciable fraction of the velocity of light. The correspondence between the nonrelativistic and relativistic forms is:

(5a) $\quad z = \dfrac{\Delta\lambda}{\lambda} = \dfrac{v}{c} \quad$ (nonrelativistic)

(5b) $\quad z = \dfrac{\Delta\lambda}{\lambda} = \sqrt{\dfrac{1 + (v/c)}{1 - (v/c)}} - 1 \quad$ (relativistic)

where $\Delta\lambda$ = measured wavelength shift at λ, v = radial velocity of object, and c = velocity of light. If a redward shift from 3,000 to 9,000 angstroms is observed in a quasar, $\Delta\lambda/\lambda = (9000 - 3000)/3000 = 2$ and its recessional velocity is $\frac{4}{5}c$, the correct value calculated from equation 5b. If these values are inserted in the incorrect equation 5a, the velocity is twice the speed of light ($v/c = 2$), a physical impossibility. It is often convenient to express the red shift as the proportional shift in wavelength, z or $\Delta\lambda/\lambda$.

Astronomers Find Fountain of Youth

Astronomer Tom is planning to leave the earth on a round-trip space flight to star S, twelve light-years distant, at a rocket speed of three-fifths the velocity of light ($v = \frac{3}{5}c$). (See Figure 15.2.) At the same time, astronomer Dick is to leave in the opposite direction on a round-trip space voyage to star T, also twelve light-years away, at a rocket speed of four-fifths the velocity of light ($v = \frac{4}{5}c$). The third man, Harry, will remain on earth to monitor their flights. Before takeoff the three men synchronize their clocks. To avoid undue complications in the recording of the travelers' clock times, we will assume that the periods of acceleration at the beginning of the outward and return paths and the periods of

deceleration in approaching each star or the earth are extremely brief in comparison with the length of time spent in moving at constant velocity and may therefore be neglected.

According to Harry's prediction, Tom will be gone for forty years and Dick for thirty years. On his return to earth, however, Tom will claim that he has been away thirty-two years by his clock time, and Dick will assert that he has been gone only eighteen years by his clock time. To clarify these conclusions, consider Tom's situation. It takes a light ray twenty-four years to make the round trip between earth and star S. Tom, traveling at $\frac{3}{5}c$, will accomplish the feat in $24/\frac{3}{5} = 40$ years, judged by Harry's earth clock. But since Tom's clock runs slow by the contraction factor, $\sqrt{1 - (\frac{3}{5})^2} = \frac{4}{5}$, Tom's round-trip time will be $\frac{4}{5} \times 40 = 32$ years according to Tom's clock.

Suppose all astronomers are twenty years old at the start. When Dick returns to earth, he finds that Harry is fifty years old while he is thirty-eight years old. When Tom returns, Harry is now age sixty and Tom is fifty-two. When Tom and Dick meet again on earth, Tom will be only four years older than Dick because Dick returned sooner than Tom by ten earth years. Since biological aging involves the time element in molecular cell growth, it is presumed that the ages quoted here are biologically correct.

Figure 15.2 Astronomers' space trip.

The Clock Paradox

This illustration of the difference in age between an earthbound observer and a space traveler is called the "clock paradox." It has been argued that by the principle of reciprocity the earth may be considered to be moving relative to the fixed inertial frame of the spaceship so that the earth rider could end up younger than the space traveler. When the situation is analyzed properly by means of the Doppler principle and signal flashes recording the passage of time from one frame of reference to another, it can be shown that the space traveler does indeed age more slowly than the stay-at-home. Near-immortality, however, will never be achieved simply by moving at a speed close to the velocity of light in one direction. An observer who exits from an inertial frame of reference with a uniform or accelerated velocity relative to it must subsequently return to it so that his time lags behind the time of the observer who remains in the inertial frame. The clock paradox conclusion has been verified in the laboratory. In one experiment a group of muons accelerated in a magnetic merry-go-round at $0.9965\,c$ experienced lifetimes twelve times longer when they returned to their starting positions than the "stay-at-home" muons who remained behind at the same starting point.

A further confirmation was obtained in October 1971 when two physicists flew four cesium atomic clocks, once eastward and once westward, around the world on commercial airlines. Relative to the reference clocks at the U. S. Naval Observatory, the transported clocks lost 59-billionths of a second during the eastward trip (in the same direction as the earth's rotation) and gained 273-billionths of a second during the westward trip. These values were in reasonable accord with those predicted from the theory of relativity after applying the necessary corrections for the variations in latitude, speed, and altitude along the different aircraft routes.

15.4 THE GENERAL THEORY OF RELATIVITY

The Principle of Equivalence

The next great advance that Einstein made in his theory of relativity was to generalize it in 1916 by making it applicable to observers moving non-uniformly with respect to each other. The fundamental laws of nature, Einstein reasoned, remain invariant throughout the universe in all frames of reference, whether they are accelerated or not.

Newton had shown from his second law of motion that the force necessary to accelerate a body is proportional to its "inertial" mass. (Inertial relates to the resistance offered by a body to an applied force.) He was also aware that the gravitational force on a body is proportional to its "gravitational" mass. Otherwise, bodies of different masses would not fall to the ground at the same rate—that is, with constant acceleration. Galileo, according to the story, earlier had demonstrated that balls of different composition (weight) dropped from the Leaning Tower of Pisa hit the ground at the same time. In 1890 Baron von Eötvös experimentally proved to a high degree of precision that inertial mass and gravitational mass are equivalent, a coincidence that had long been taken for granted. It was Einstein who aided in its interpretation. He concluded that it is impossible to distinguish between the effect of an inertial force or a gravitational force upon accelerated motion. Einstein incorporated this concept in his *principle of equivalence,* which states that a gravitational force can be replaced by an inertial force arising out of accelerated motion without any change in the physical activity involved. We shall illustrate this important point by the following imaginary demonstration.

Imagine a Newtonian observer inside a rocket ship constantly accelerating at one *g*. Under one *g* of acceleration the observer "feels" at home as on earth. He holds a ball in one hand. (It does not matter whether it is a tennis ball or a billiard ball.) When the ship is in position 1 (Figure 15.3) the occupant releases the ball. It continues to move upward with the velocity the ship had at the moment of release as shown by the successive positions along the broken line in Figure 15.3. If the rocket ship were moving upward at *constant* velocity, the ball would remain suspended in the same place since both the ship and the ball move the same amount. This is described as a "free fall" environment. Since the rocket ship is accelerating, the floor moves upward faster than the ball, colliding with the ball in position 4. The occupant who is a prisoner inside his spaceship attributes this effect to the force of gravity.

An Einsteinian observer, however, has been watching what is going on inside the spaceship from a vantage point outside the ship. His explanation of the sequence of events is simple. All those actions going on inside the rocket ship are accountable on the basis of the accelerated motion of the ship. Who needs the force of gravity, he asks? Einstein pointed out that each observer has a right to his own description of events. It is permissible to replace the force of gravity by a "fictitious force," that is, by an inertial force due to an accelerated motion. An inertial force is not a real force but an effect resulting from the non-uniform motion of the observer's frame of reference. An example of a "fictitious force" arising from an accelerated motion is one experienced by a person standing on the floor of a merry-go-round in motion. He "feels" a force that tends to move him toward the rim; it is called the centrifugal force.

Geometry of Four-Dimensional Space

The relativist pictures gravitation as an outgrowth of the space-time properties involving the curvature of four-dimensional space. Spatial curvature is influenced by the presence of material bodies. In the absence of mass, the curvature of nearby space is zero and a body in this kind of space moves

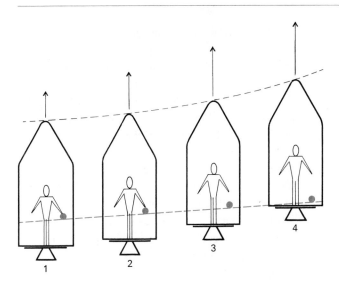

Figure 15.3 *Experiment in accelerated rocket ship.*

uniformly in a straight line. In the curved space geometry surrounding a large mass, less massive bodies move in this "warped" space naturally along a geodesic, the shortest distance in the four-dimensional continuum. The elliptic paths of the planets are geodesics in the space curvature surrounding the sun. What we call gravitation is nothing more that the natural behavior of bodies moving within the geometrical framework of the space-time world. In the Newtonian view the body moves according to action from a distance dictated by a force called the law of gravitation. In the Einsteinian view a body moves freely in response to the local field structure of curved space-time. In the vast majority of situations, Newtonian theory suffices to describe physical events except where the velocities involved approach the velocity of light. There are, however, several important astronomical differences between classical and relativity theory that will be explored in Section 15.5.

The Curvature of Space

If two-dimensional beings (flat, paper-doll creatures living in "flatland") knew how to evaluate the properties of their space geometry, they would know on what kind of surface they actually live. They might accomplish this by traveling great distances along the surface of their space world and noting how the curvature changes in value from point to point. (It is assumed that their measuring apparatus will not be affected by changes in position.) They could then decide whether they lived in the world of Euclidean geometry of zero curvature or whether their world is non-Euclidean and exhibits positive or negative curvature. These are the only options open to them. The three choices are shown in Figure 15.4.

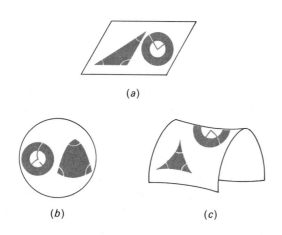

(a)

(b)   *(c)*

Figure 15.4 Two-dimensional world models: (a) *flat space (Euclidean), zero curvature* (k = 0), *three angles of triangle = 180°, area of circle = πr^2, circumference of circle = $2\pi r$;* (b) *spherical surface, positive curvature* (k > 0), *three angles of triangle > 180°, area of circle < πr^2, circumference of circle < $2\pi r$;* (c) *hyperboloidal surface, negative curvature* (k < 0), *three angles of triangle < 180°, area of circle > πr^2, circumference of circle > $2\pi r^2$.*

Do we three-dimensional beings, living on the surface of a four-dimensional hyperstructure, have a way of determining the curvature of its hyperstructure? We also have three choices available to us: (1) the universe has zero curvature ($k = 0$), and it is flat, infinite in extent, and Euclidean; (2) the universe has positive curvature ($k > 0$), and is finite in extent but unbounded, like a sphere without a boundary; (3) the universe has negative curvature ($k < 0$), and is hyperbolic and open-ended. Some relativists have raised the specter of a more complicated universe, in which the four-dimensional manifold of space-time is immersed in a kind of superspace that could involve as many as ten or more dimensions. As we shall see in the following chapter on cosmology, the observational evidence in favor of any specified world model is inconclusive.

15.5 OBSERVATIONAL TESTS OF THE THEORY OF RELATIVITY

Gravitational Red Shift

In his general theory of relativity, Einstein showed how an object in a gravitational field would contract, gain mass, and slow down in its clock time. Implied in the last item, that of time dilation, is the effect of a gravitational field on vibrating atoms. Relativity predicts how much the wavelength of the radiation emitted by an atom is lengthened, or shifted to the red, in the presence of a gravitational field. The relative change in wavelength ($\Delta\lambda/\lambda$) is proportional to the mass of the attracting body divided by its radius ($\propto m/R$). (See Figure 15.5.)

The phenomenon is of practical astronomical interest because it involves a photon of light whose change in wavelength can be measured as it escapes from the surface of a star. The effect is not easily observable in the sun, but if the gravitational field is sufficiently intense, as it would be for a white dwarf of solar mass and small size (m/R large), it can be measured. The gravitational red shift has been observed in several white dwarfs which are components of binary systems. In these instances it is possible to differentiate between the redward gravitational displacement of the spectral lines and the Doppler shift arising from the combined orbital and barycentric radial motions of the system. The measured red-shifted value is in satisfactory accord with the values predicted from the theory.

The gravitational red shift has been verified with greater accuracy in the physics laboratory by comparing the frequency of gamma rays emitted by radioactive cobalt at two different distances from the earth's surface, seventy-two feet apart. (The phenomenon associated with the release of gamma rays in the crystal of a heavy radioactive atom such as cobalt is called the *Mössbauer effect*.) Closer to the earth's surface the gravitational field is stronger than at a higher altitude. The frequency of the gamma photons is therefore reduced, or their wavelength increased, as they ascend to a high altitude where the clock time

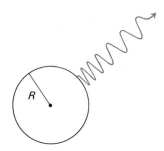

Figure 15.5 Photon escaping from surface of white dwarf —wavelength of escaping photon lengthens as it leaves surface. Since a small fraction of the energy of the photon is used to escape from the strong gravitational field of the star, its outgoing energy is slightly diminished; the frequency, which is proportional to the energy of the photon (E = hf), is thereby decreased and its wavelength increased. Hence the absorption lines in the white dwarf's spectrum should exhibit a small redward shift.

is less dilated. The minute change in frequency was found to agree with the amount predicted to within 3 per cent.

Precession of Mercury's Orbit

The perihelion of Mercury's orbit shifts forward in the direction of the planet's revolution around the sun as the result of perturbations by the other planets (Figure 15.6). After mathematical allowances based on the Newtonian theory had been made by astronomers of the last century for the advance of the perihelion in the orbit of Mercury, the observed value per century still exceeded the calculated value by forty-three seconds of arc. One way to remove the discrepancy was to increase the mass of Venus by an inadmissible one-seventh or to postulate the existence of a never-discovered planet called Vulcan circling inside Mercury's orbit. The difficulty was resolved in 1915 by Einstein, whose theory accounts for the additional forty-three seconds of arc per century.

The general theory of relativity predicts that the orbit of a planet rotates in its own plane as does the classical theory of Newton. In either theory the perihelion change is most pronounced in the case of Mercury's orbit. Einstein's equations for the elliptic motion of a planet orbiting around the sun include an extra term not present in the Newtonian equations. The contribution of this additional term is a tiny fraction of the amount resulting from the perturbative effects. It adds up to one extra revolution in three million years in the precession of Mercury's orbit. In the relativistic view, the planet, by virtue of its eccentric orbital motion, periodically moves into a stronger and weaker gravitational field where it encounters varying properties of the space-time structure surrounding the sun.

Gravitational Deflection of Starlight

Another comparison between classical and relativistic physics is afforded during a total eclipse of

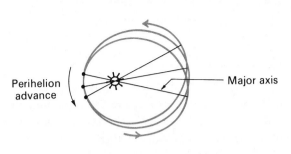

Figure 15.6   Apsidal rotation of Mercury's orbit.

the sun. According to Newtonian calculations a ray of light from a star, considered as a moving stream of photons[1] grazing the limb of the sun, would be deflected outward 0.875 seconds of arc as viewed from the earth by the sun's gravitational field. From the relativistic point of view, space is "warped" around the sun because of the curvature of space and a ray of light will consequently travel along a geodesic path in the four-dimensional medium. When this factor is taken into account, the deflection of starlight is exactly twice that given by Newtonian theory because of the added effect introduced by the geometry of four dimensions.

The first observational test to check the validity of the relativistic prediction was made by British astronomers in 1919 during a total solar eclipse in Brazil. For many years thereafter it became a standard procedure to conduct this test at every total eclipse of the sun. A photograph taken of the darkened sky around the eclipsed sun reveals the presence of the nearby bright stars. Another photograph of the same area is obtained at night a few months earlier or later with the same telescope (the sun is in a different place in the sky then). The normal and displaced star

[1] The photon is treated as a particle whose mass is equal to its energy divided by the velocity of light squared ($m = E/c^2$).

positions are then compared. The amount of deflection naturally decreases with increasing distance from the sun's limb. In every instance the verdict has favored relativity theory though the difficulties of the measurement and the resulting uncertainties have not made it a crucial test.

Radio/radar checks on the bending of radio waves in the vicinity of the sun also tend to confirm Einstein's prediction. In one test a very slight delay in the receipt of radar signals reflected from the surfaces of Mercury and Venus was observed when the planets were on the far side of the sun. This results from the solar-influenced curvature of space which causes a slight bending of the path of the signal as it passes the sun on its way toward the earth. The delaying effect was more recently observed at the time the Mars Mariners 6 and 7 were on the far side of the sun in the spring of 1970, 250 million miles from the earth. They were interrogated by radio signals transmitted from the 210-foot Goldstone radio dish in southern California under the supervision of the Jet Propulsion Laboratory radio astronomers. The maximum round-trip time for the signals was 43 minutes. The observed delay due to the bending of the signal path in the vicinity of the sun was 204 microseconds compared with 200 micro-

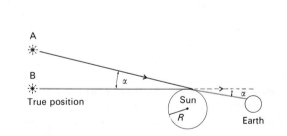

Figure 15.7   Gravitational bending of starlight grazing the sun's limb. Point A shows apparent position; B, true position; deflection angle α = 0.875 second of arc (Newton) or 1.75 seconds of arc (Einstein).

Figure 15.8 Comparison of star positions during an eclipse and when there is no eclipse. The four crosses correspond to the deflected star positions on the eclipse plate. The four asterisks represent the true star positions when the sun is not present. Star displacements are greatly exaggerated.

utmost precaution must be exercised to isolate the apparatus from nongravitational disturbances. According to Weber, he has succeeded in detecting gravity waves simultaneously in his Maryland laboratory and at the Argonne National Laboratory near Chicago on a frequency of 1,660 hertz (cycles per second). In 1972 he recorded simultaneous responses on two different frequencies: in Maryland on 1,030 hertz and at Argonne National Laboratory on 1,650 hertz. The majority of the gravity waves appears to be coming from the direction of the galactic nucleus in Sagittarius. The observed vibrations correspond to a cyclic change in the length of the cylinders amounting to one hundred-trillionth of an inch. Further confirmation of Weber's results is needed before there is general acceptance of these findings. In the meantime many other gravity-wave detectors responding to different frequencies are being constructed by other investigators as the search for gravity waves widens.

15.6 THE SCIENTIFIC AND HUMANITARIAN EXCELLENCE OF EINSTEIN

Einstein, the Physicist

Einstein's contributions to science embrace more than his theory of relativity. In 1905, at the age of 26, he published three trail-blazing papers. The first one dealt with Brownian movement. In 1827 Robert Brown, an English botanist, had observed through a microscope the zigzag paths of tiny pollen-grain particles in a drop of water being buffeted by the much smaller invisible atoms and molecules in the fluid. Einstein worked out the correct mathematical expression for this action on the basis of the natural thermal motions possessed by the atomic and molecular particles about the time the structure of the atom was first being probed. Another paper reinforced the quantum concept of light, developed by Max Planck in 1900, by his theoretical treatment of the

seconds predicted by relativity theory, a most satisfactory agreement. (One microsecond equals one-millionth of a second.)

Gravitational Radiation

One prediction that Einstein made and which had lain dormant for nearly half a century because it was considered too difficult to verify was that extremely weak gravitational waves are radiated in space with the velocity of light by rapidly accelerated or spinning bodies. They are possibly detectable with sensitive apparatus. Large astronomical objects undergoing violent activity perhaps offer the best opportunity for uncovering them. More than a decade ago J. Weber devised delicate recording equipment to pick up infinitesimal oscillations on the surfaces of large aluminum cylinders produced by the gravitational waves when they strike the cylinders. The photoelectric phenomenon that had recently been discovered. For this contribution Einstein was awarded the Nobel Prize in physics in 1921. Finally, there was his third and most famous contribution, the special theory of relativity. In 1917 Einstein also provided a deeper insight into Planck's law of radiation (Figure 10.12) by deriving it on the basis of the probabilities of atomic transitions between energy states.

The theory of relativity has exerted a more profound effect on the course of modern physics and on our understanding of the physical world than any theory ever developed. It has correctly accounted for certain astronomical phenomena that defied explanation on Newtonian principles. It has opened up a new theoretical door in the field of high-energy astrophysical phenomena associated with the quasars, pulsars, and black holes. It has rewarded us with a firmer grasp of the cosmological forces shaping our universe. It has led the way to one of the most important technological developments in history, the utilization of nuclear energy. And it has revealed a structural beauty in nature that belied our intuitive senses. Although the theory of relativity has been successful in accurately representing and correctly predicting observational and experimental data, it need not be regarded as the "final word." It is, however, the most plausible theory that best describes those events that lie within the realm of our present experience. (There are a number of competing theories but none has yet been found to be experimentally superior to Einstein's theory.)

Einstein, the Humanitarian

Besides being one of the most profound thinkers of all time, there was another side to the genius of Einstein. As a person he was by nature a man of unpretentious disposition. He was also a pacifist with a deep concern for the welfare of his fellow beings. Let us read what Einstein himself has said:

> Concern for man himself and his fate must always form the chief interest of all technical endeavors, concern for the great unsolved problems of the organization of labor and the distribution of goods—in order that the creation of our mind shall be a blessing and not a curse to mankind. Never forget this in the midst of your diagrams and equations.[1]

As an émigré from Nazi Germany in 1933, he temporarily abandoned his pacifistic views during the war with Germany. He believed the use of force to be justified against an enemy that was determined to destroy his people (the Jews). Einstein later felt that he had made a great mistake in his life when he recommended in his famous letter to President Roosevelt in 1939 that the atom bomb be produced because of the possibility that the Germans might do so first. As it turned out, the German effort did not materialize.

Einstein was filled with a deep reverence for the works of nature and once stated, "The most incomprehensible thing about the world is that it is comprehensible." According to one of his collaborators,[2] he was somewhat appalled by the great strides in the expansion of scientific knowledge that took place in the first half of the twentieth century and concluded that though we know so much more we correspondingly understand so much less. He thought of himself more as a philosopher than as a scientist. In a way Einstein followed the philosophical precepts of the Greek philosophers who attempted to account for natural phenomena on the basis of logical deductions instead of experimentation. He was successful where the ancients failed because he ingeniously employed the powerful analytical tools of mathematics developed in the course of two thou-

[1] From an address delivered at the California Institute of Technology in 1931.
[2] C. Lanczos in *Einstein: Physics and Reality*, Interscience Publishers, 1965.

sand years since Plato and Aristotle, combined with an unerring sense of cosmic perception.

Lord C. P. Snow, who was acquainted with Einstein, gives us this assessment of him:

> Einstein was the most powerful mind of the twentieth century, and one of the most powerful that ever lived. He was more than that. He was a man of enormous weight of personality, and perhaps most of all, of moral stature. . . . I have met a number of people whom the world calls great; of these, he was by far, by an order of magnitude, the most impressive. He was—despite the warmth, the humanity, the touch of the comedian—the most different from other men.[1]

REVIEW QUESTIONS

1. How does one explain the negative result of the Michelson-Morley experiment?

2. What were the two postulates of the special theory of relativity?

3. What is meant by time dilation or time contraction?

4. Discuss the significance of the Lorentz contraction factor $\sqrt{1 - (v^2/c^2)}$. in relativity as applied to measurements of length, mass, and time.

5. What is the difference between an inertial frame of reference and a noninertial frame of reference?

6. How would you describe the difference between Newtonian space and Einsteinian space-time?

7. State the principle of equivalence in your own words. Illustrate it by means of an example.

8. How does Einstein look at gravity in comparison to Newton?

9. Describe the properties of the three forms of space curvature.

10. Give a brief account of the observational verification of Einstein's theory of relativity by astronomers.

11. Explain how it is possible for a father to return from a space voyage younger than the grandchildren he left behind.

12. We have measured time-dilation effects and mass-increase effects at relativistic speeds but not length contraction. Why is that?

SELECTED READINGS

Barnett, L., *The Universe and Dr. Einstein*, Morrow, 1957.

Chester, M., *Relativity: An Introduction for Young Readers*, Norton, 1967.

Coleman, J. A., *Relativity for the layman*, Macmillan, 1959.

Gamow, G., *Mr. Tompkins in Paperback*, Cambridge University Press, 1965.

Gamow, G., *Mr. Tompkins in Wonderland*, Macmillan, 1940.

Gardner, M., *Relativity for the Millions*, Macmillan, 1966.

Struble, M., *The Web of Space-Time. A Step-by-Step Exploration of Relativity*, Westminster Press, 1973.

Whitrow, G. J., ed., *Einstein, The Man and His Achievement*, Dover, 1973.

[1] From a review by C. P. Snow, which appeared in the *Financial Times* of London, of the book *The Born-Einstein Letters, 1916–1955*, translated by Irene Born, Walker and Co., 1971.

Astronomer Hubble (1889–1953), explorer of the cosmos. (Cover portrait courtesy Time Magazine; copyright Time Inc. 1948.)

COSMOLOGY

Man is not born to solve the problems of the universe, but to find out where the problems begin, and then to take his stand within the limits of the intelligible.

J. W. von Goethe (1749–1832)

The weakest of the four basic forces that govern the behavior of matter, is by normal standards, the gravitational force. However, in the universe-at-large it becomes the most powerful force because its strength increases with increasing mass. What role has the gravitational force played in structuring the universe? Indeed, how was the universe created and how has it evolved? The general theory of relativity, depending on certain starting assumptions, leads to several classes of solutions of the world model: the static model, first developed by Einstein but since discarded after Hubble's later discovery of the expansion of the universe based on the recession of the galaxies; the nonstatic or time-dependent models which may take the form of the open-ended hyperbolic universe, the spherically closed universe, the pulsating universe, the flat Euclidean universe, or the steady-state universe. The overriding question is: Can we determine from the various cosmological models proposed which particular model best fits the observed galaxian data in which Hubble's law of recession of the galaxies plays a central role?

The recently discovered low-temperature (3°K) microwave radiation that fills the cosmos seems to be confirming evidence that the presently recognized universe began with the explosion of the primeval fireball about eighteen billion years ago. Unfortunately, the critical differences existing between the various time-dependent world models can only be distinguished at extreme cosmological distances. At these distances the observed galaxian or quasar data (essentially the relationship between the recessional velocities and the corrected apparent magnitudes of the galaxies) are too uncertain to render a positive decision. The determination of our world model must await more precise observational data.

16.1 THE STUDY OF THE UNIVERSE

The Controlling Forces in Nature

Four kinds of basic forces have been found in nature to interact with particles in various ways. There is the strong nuclear force, a kind of "nuclear glue," that holds the protons and neutrons inside the nucleus together against the electrostatic repulsive force of the positively charged protons. Within the nuclear domain ($\sim 10^{-13}$ cm) the density is one billion tons to the cubic inch. Next is the electromagnetic force, about a hundred times weaker but with a larger range within the atom as a whole ($\sim 10^{-8}$ cm) and indeed functioning well beyond the atomic limits. It holds the positive nucleus and the surrounding electrons together and it helps to bind the atoms within the molecules. The electron configuration of the atom determines the gross structure and properties of matter. Modern technology would not have been possible without the utilization of the electromagnetic force that actuates most of the machines upon which our civilization depends. The third force is the weak nuclear force, a million million times weaker than the electromagnetic force. It is the least understood of the four forces. It operates within the nuclear and atomic realms and gives rise to the phenomenon of radioactive decay. Finally, there is the gravitational force, the weakest force of all, 10^{40} times weaker than the electromagnetic force! Yet the universe of matter on the macroscopic scale is ruled and shaped by it because it grows in strength with increasing mass. In astronomical bodies it is the dominant force.

The Cosmological Problem

Cosmology is concerned with the study of the origin, structure, and evolution of the universe. The fundamental problem in cosmology is to develop from the general theory of relativity a theoretical time model of the universe that can be subjected to observational testing. This involves knowledge of crucial physical factors: the mean density of matter in space, the exact Hubble law of recession, and the time rate of expansion of the universe. The present dilemma lies in our inability to secure sufficiently reliable physical data on the outermost galaxies and quasars to provide a satisfactory observational test of the proposed cosmological models.

16.2 THE FIRST COSMOLOGICAL MODELS

The Cosmological Principle

One of the basic assumptions made in developing the first cosmological models of the universe is the following postulate, known as the *cosmological principle*: All observers in space see the universe in its essential features the same way. The relativist would say: The universe is invariant under translations and rotations and is therefore homogeneous and isotropic. From this statement it follows that our sample of the universe, except for local variations, is assumed to be no different from another sample selected at random in a different place in the universe.

Einstein's Static Cosmological Model

In the cosmological model that he developed in 1917, Einstein found a solution for a static universe—that is, one that did not change with time. This was a reasonable approach before the expansion effect had been discovered. He naturally assumed that the random motions of the galaxies canceled out and that the average density of matter smeared out over the universe remained constant. The model he preferred was a spherically closed universe with matter thinly spread out rather than a flat, infinite universe. The universe was pictured as finite in extent but boundless in the same sense that a sphere is limited in size but without an edge or boundary. Einstein found it necessary to introduce a slight repulsive force acting between the galaxies, so he incorporated a cosmological constant (Λ) in his field equations. This was done to prevent the universe from collapsing through its self-gravitation and thus remain static. In his formula the radius is inversely proportional to the square root of the mean (smeared out) density of matter (ρ). To this day it is not a precisely known quantity. For the estimated values of ρ between 10^{-29} g/cm^3 to 10^{-31} g/cm^3, the calculated radius of Einstein's model lies between 10 billion and 100 billion light-years respectively.

The De Sitter Cosmological Model

An alternative solution of Einstein's field equations was found shortly afterward by the Dutch astronomer Willem de Sitter. He went to the other extreme: an infinite universe in which the density of matter was so low it could mathematically be regarded as empty. At large distances De Sitter found the cosmological constant to correspond to a repulsive force tending to expand the universe. De Sitter's model consisted of a Euclidean universe with no beginning and no ending, practically empty forever, and expanding with time to infinity. Although the model did not fit reality, it was the forerunner of the later nonstatic models that are prevalent today. A static universe cannot remain in equilibrium because of the motion of matter (galaxies) within it and its radiation. The slightest movement involving the interaction between matter and energy would unbalance it and cause it to expand or contract.

Discovery of an Expanding Universe

Hubble's discovery of the law of recession of the

galaxies in 1929 (Section 13.8) motivated cosmologists to seek a solution predicated upon an unstable, expanding universe. This is the so-called evolutionary or exploding model that unfolds with time. The nonstatic solutions need not require the employment of the cosmological constant. For the sake of simplicity, its value is usually set equal to zero in the mathematical development of time-based models. The abandonment of the cosmological constant was a great relief to Einstein, who was esthetically displeased with his initial employment of it. He is said to have confessed that his introduction of the cosmological constant was the greatest blunder of his life.

An Analogy to the Expanding Universe

In Figure 13.12, Section 13.8, it was noted that the velocity of recession of a galaxy was proportional to its distance; the farther away a galaxy is, the faster it is receding from us. This same phenomenon is observable from any other galaxy (the cosmological principle) and is interpreted as a true Doppler effect arising out of the expansion of the universe.

A two-dimensional analogy of this concept can be visualized in the example of tiny, flat microbes located on an ink spot (their galaxy). They are distributed more or less uniformly with other ink spots (other galaxies) on the surface of a balloon that is being inflated (their expanding universe). They picture themselves as living in "flatland." Let us suppose that at a certain time there are four observed scattered galaxies, G_1, G_2, G_3, and G_4 distant from the home galaxy, G, of the microbe astronomers. They occupy the positions shown in Figure 16.1a and their initial distances are given in the second column of Table 16.1. It is assumed that the four galaxies under observation are originally examined over a region of space small enough to be considered essentially flat. One second later, the balloon has doubled in size and the distances have doubled as shown in the third column of the table. In the last column we note that the speed of recession of the four galaxies observed from the home galaxy grows as fast as their distance increases. This is the Hubble law of recession shown in Figure 13.12. It is observed the same way from each galaxy with respect to the others as implied in the cosmological principle.

If, as the balloon continues to expand, our discriminating microbe astronomers were to measure the velocities of the very remote galaxies, they might discover that the straight-line relation between the velocity and the distance no longer holds true. Suppose that for the most distant galaxies our microbe astronomers find that the velocity increases faster than the distance, causing the distance-velocity line to curve upward slightly. This could be one indication that their supposedly flattened two-dimensional universe is positively curved (that is, it turns back on itself), leading to a closed universe. The student may recall a method of determining the positive curvature of a static, two-dimensional, spherical surface by finding the three angles of a large triangle to be greater than 180 degrees (Figure 15.4).

16.3 TIME-DEPENDENT COSMOLOGICAL MODELS

The Friedmann Models

Beginning with A. Friedmann in 1922, Abbé G. LeMaître in 1927, and others, a number of theoretical cosmologists have derived mathematical solutions based on the nonstatic solutions of Einstein's field equations. One solution found by Friedmann without the use of the cosmological constant led to a contracting universe and another to an expanding universe. Actually, a greater diversity of Friedmann models results when the cosmological constant is different from zero. These are too complex for consideration here; the main cosmological features are present in the simpler models in which the cosmological con-

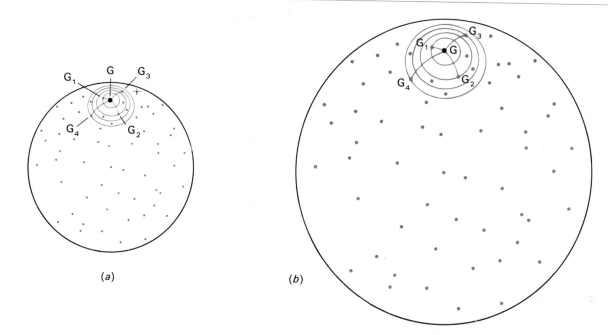

Figure 16.1   Recession of the galaxies on a two-dimensional surface. (a) Partially inflated balloon showing apparent distribution of galaxies at a certain time; (b) the same balloon after further inflation showing the apparent distribution of galaxies one second later. (The balloon analogy is inexact in one respect: although the space between the galaxies stretches, the galaxies themselves do not expand.)

stant is zero. The solution of the Friedmann equations in the framework of the general theory of relativity leads to three different models as shown in Figure 16.2.

The Hyperbolic Universe

In the hyperbolic, open-ended model, the expansion settles down to one that increases roughly with the time ($R \propto t$). There is but one expansion

Table 16.1   Recessional Motion of the Galaxies

Galaxy	Original Distance from Home Galaxy, G (inches)	Distance from Home Galaxy One Second Later (inches)	Speed of Recession (in/sec)
G_1	1	2	1
G_2	2	4	2
G_3	3	6	3
G_4	4	8	4

16 COSMOLOGY

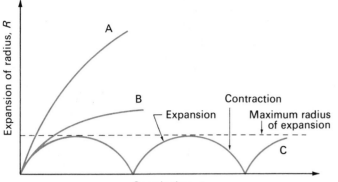

Figure 16.2   Friedmann models (cosmological constant = zero): A, k = −1 (hyperbolic universe); B, k = 0 (Euclidean universe); C, k = +1 (closed spherical universe).

starting from a restricted space-time region called a "singularity," perhaps with a "big bang" out of a superdense core of superhot matter. The total amount of matter present in the universe is insufficient to halt the expansion through self-gravitation; it proceeds inexorably toward infinity. There is no return because the velocity of expansion is too great. As space stretches out with the expansion, the smeared-out density of matter decreases as the distances between the galaxies increase. There will be photons of light arriving from distant objects whose photons just manage to reach us. They will be red-shifted almost beyond the point of perception. This outermost limit of observability is called the *event horizon* in the language of relativity. It does *not* represent an edge to space; there is no edge any more than there is a center to the universe. Stated another way, the center is everywhere, the circumference nowhere. Beyond the event horizon lie the unobservable bodies whose photons never get here because the expansion is proceeding faster than their light can reveal. An analogous situation is one in which a runner on an expanding race track finds the finish line receding too rapidly for him ever to catch up with it.

The Flat Euclidean Universe

The scenario for a Euclidean zero-curvature model begins at a singularity with the supposed "hatching of the cosmic egg." The expansion is proportional to the two-thirds power of the time ($R \propto t^{\frac{2}{3}}$). It is therefore expanding more slowly than the hyperbolic model. The expansion eventually comes to rest at infinity as the density falls to zero. From an infinite density at the origin of time, the Euclidean universe has presently reached a mean density of 6×10^{-30} g/cm^3 after nearly eighteen billion years of expansion (corresponding to a Hubble constant of 55 km/sec/megapc).

The Oscillating Universe

Instead of a single, unique beginning, the pulsating evolutionary model expands and contracts alternately over an indefinite period of time. In this kind of universe there exists a finite amount of matter, a finite limit to space, and a finite time of oscillation. As its expansion slows down because of self-gravitation, the universe eventually reaches a maximum critical size dependent upon its mean density. Contraction then takes over, slowly at first, then accelerating toward a spectacular climax as all matter in the universe collapses toward a superheated, superdense state. This is followed by a bounce or rebound into a second round of expansion. After the end of each cyclic period, estimated to endure for many billions of years, the universe is reconstructed all over again. Some theorists have speculated that the new evolving universe need not be the same in its physical details as the previous experience. It could reemerge with different particle and chemical properties in which only the fundamental constants of nature—namely, the velocity of light, the gravitational constant, and the Planck constant of radiation —would remain unchanged; or it might collapse into a black hole and be transformed into a strange, new universe.

16.4 THE STEADY-STATE MODEL

The Perfect Cosmological Principle

A novel deployment of the field equations of the general theory of relativity was effected by Fred Hoyle. It was based upon the original research by H. Bondi and T. Gold in 1948 to devise a nonstatic model of the universe whose general appearance remains unaltered *forever*. This is the steady-state model of continuous creation. An extension of the cosmological principle in time is invoked to arrive at the perfect cosmological principle: not only does the universe appear the same to all observers *but it looks the same in perpetuity*.

Continuous Creation

In the steady-state-model there is no singularity nor is there a beginning or an end. Space expands exponentially with time toward infinity. The Hubble constant (H) does not vary with time as in the exploding models. The galaxies are created, evolve, and die while the average matter density in space remains constant. In order that the galaxian population, or smeared-out density of matter, remain constant, it is necessary to assume that new matter in the form of hydrogen is continuously being created. This compensates for the expansion which tends to thin out matter. The average rate of creation in a large-sized classroom would be about one hydrogen atom in fifty million years, a rate hopelessly beyond detection. Since galaxies are being formed at a steady rate to keep pace with the expansion, the average separation between the galaxies remains unchanged with the passage of time.

16.5 THE AMBIPLASMA WORLD MODEL

The Symmetrical Universe

An interesting cosmological theory in which it has been proposed that the universe began with an *equal* proportion of matter and antimatter has been advanced by O. Klein and H. Alfvén, Swedish astrophysicists. They base their work on the well-known symmetry existing between particles and antiparticles as verified in particle-accelerator experiments. For every particle—a proton, neutron, electron, etc. —there exists a corresponding antiparticle—namely, an antiproton, antineutron, antielectron (positron), etc. An antihydrogen atom therefore would contain a negatively charged antiproton and a positively charged orbiting electron or positron. Its spectral identification would be the same as that of the normal hydrogen atom, consisting of a positively charged proton and a negative orbiting electron.

The major hurdle in the Klein-Alfvén model is to provide an inhibiting agent that would prevent the mutual destruction of matter and antimatter in close proximity. The theory assumes that initially there existed a highly attenuated plasma consisting mostly of protons and antiprotons with a scattering of electrons and positrons occupying a spherical region about two trillion light-years in diameter. The ambiplasma density was originally too low for particle encounters to occur. Self-gravitation of the cloud eventually reduced its size to several billion light-years, at which time particles and antiparticles began to collide and annihilate each other to produce radiation. When the cloud had gravitationally collapsed to a diameter of a couple of billion light-years, the radiation pressure of the photons overcame the gravitational attraction and caused the cloud to expand. During the expansion phase of the universe, the cloud fragmented into a mixture of matter and antimatter which formed into protogalaxies. The theory projects the possible separation of the ambi-plasma into regions of matter and antimatter from which the galaxies containing only one kind of matter are formed. This raises the question of whether antigalaxies exist in space. If the Andromeda galaxy is an antigalaxy, we have no way of discriminating spectroscopically this possibility because the spectral lines of both kinds of matter would appear at identical wavelengths with the same intensities. Unlike matter and antimatter, the photon of radiation is its own antiphoton.

16.6 WHICH COSMOLOGICAL MODEL?

The Preferred Model

Most astronomers favor the exploding type of universe in one form or another. If the amount of so-far-undiscovered, nonluminous material consisting of unformed intergalactic matter, dead galaxies, and black holes turns out to be appreciable, it would raise the mean density of matter and increase the self-gravitation of the universe. The pulsating model might then possibly become the preferred cosmology. The steady-state model in its original presentation has fallen into disfavor for several reasons. The counts of several thousand radio sources, which are detectable at great distances, reveal that these remote sources appear to be more numerous in a given volume of space than are the closer sources. This is contrary to the prediction of the steady-state cosmology which requires that the counts remain steady in all regions of space. The steady-state theory also implies that, on the average, the types of galaxies should be the same for the remote galaxies as well as for the nearer ones. Among the several hundred quasi-stellar objects spectroscopically examined so far, none fits the original Hoyle description of a wide assortment of galaxian types of different ages. Like the radio sources, the number distribution of the quasi-stellar objects adds up to strong evidence in support of the exploding models. Finally, the presence of the low-temperature, background microwave radiation (to be discussed in the next section) follows logically as a consequence of the fireball explosion. The isotropic low-energy, microwave radiation, which is a relic of the primeval fireball explosion that was created at the time of the big bang, cannot be reconciled with the steady-state theory. The theory assumes that the universe was never in a superdense condition from which the fireball originated.

Modified Steady-State Model

Hoyle has since introduced what he calls a "radical departure" from his original steady-state theory in an attempt to bring it in line with recent observational data, particularly with respect to counts of distant radio sources. By introducing a "C field" into Einstein's field equations, he obtains a solution which indicates that a vast region of matter called a bubble oscillates in density within the large-scale, steady-state condition. The bubble fluctuates between a high density of 10^{-8} g/cm^3 and a low density of 10^{-30} g/cm^3 or less as the bubble expands and contracts inside the expanding universe. A localized bubble pulsates between bounces that never reach a singular point beyond the point of no return (the so-called "gravitational radius") during its extreme contracted value. We are presently living inside one bubble at the time of low density. Hoyle speculates on the possible existence of other bubbles besides our own that possess physical properties whose values are outside the range of our perception.

The Robertson-Walker Solutions of Cosmological Models

H. P. Robertson and A. G. Walker have derived a useful equation from Einstein's field equations that permits an observational test of the cosmological world models. Their equation relates the apparent bolometric magnitudes of the galaxies to the red-shifted factor, z or $\Delta\lambda/\lambda$, the Hubble constant, H, and a deceleration parameter called q. This latter factor is connected with the rate at which the expansion is slowing because of the self-gravitation of the universe, which tends to brake the expansion. The Robertson-Walker equation graphically takes the form of a red shift ($\Delta\lambda/\lambda$) versus magnitude plot instead of the red shift (velocity) versus distance plot as in the original graph of the law of recession (Figure 13.12). The distance estimates of the remote galaxies obtained by extrapolation of certain distance indicators employed in the closer galaxies are replaced by the corrected apparent magnitudes of the galaxies, a more easily derived datum. Recall that distance and magnitude are related to each other through the inverse-square law of light (Section 10.3).

The observed apparent magnitudes obtained from the photometric measures on the photographic plates must be corrected for the following effects: (1) loss of light in passing through the earth's atmosphere (the bolometric correction); (2) variation in galaxy size because of poorly defined galaxian boundaries in photometric measurements; (3) the red-shifted light which affects the colors and luminosities of the galaxies; (4) dimming by interstellar absorption within our Galaxy; (5) possible evolutionary changes since the galaxies are viewed at different cosmological distances and may exhibit differing stellar compositions, colors, and luminosities as a result of aging.

The plot of the Robertson-Walker equation for several values of q is shown in Figure 16.3. The type of world model follows from the numerical evaluation of the two parameters: the Hubble constant H and the q factor or the mean density of matter ρ which is related to the q factor. The dependence of the form of the world model on the q factor is shown in Table 16.2. The constant k defines the type of world curva-

ture: $k > 0$ represents positive curvature; $k = 0$ represents the absence of curvature in flat space; $k < 0$ represents negative curvature (refer to Section 15.4 for review). For models where q is greater than $\frac{1}{2}$ ($k = +1$) the expansion will eventually cease and contraction will take over. For $q = \frac{1}{2}$ ($k = 0$) the expansion decelerates to infinity where it comes to rest as the mean density reaches zero. For q between zero and less than $\frac{1}{2}$ ($k = -1$) the universe keeps expanding forever with finite velocity as the density approaches zero. In the steady-state model, $q = -1$ and the mean density remains constant as the universe expands to infinity.

Once sufficiently reliable observational data can be reasonably fitted to one of the theoretical curves in the plot of Figure 16.3, the type of world model follows. One major difficulty lies in the proper determination of the corrected apparent magnitudes of the remote galaxies, there being five different corrections each with present uncertainties up to 0.2 magnitude. The observational data collected by A. Sandage of the Hale Observatories for forty-two clusters of galaxies, employing the brightest cluster member as the "standard candle," show the expected straight-line takeoff with the correct slope for the closer galaxies. There may be a slight departure from linearity for the farthest galaxies corresponding to an uncertain value of q of about $+1$. This would indicate a positively curved, closed universe. The most distant object plotted in Figure 16.3 is receding at a velocity of two-fifths the speed of light.

More recently, W. A. Baum of the Lowell Observatory employed a Hubble diagram based on his measurements of the apparent diameters of thirty-three elliptical galaxies in four distant clusters. The result of his plot of the red shift against the apparent diameters, which require fewer corrections than the apparent magnitudes, indicates a preliminary value of $q = +0.3$, corresponding to an open-ended, hyperbolic universe. The work in evaluating the

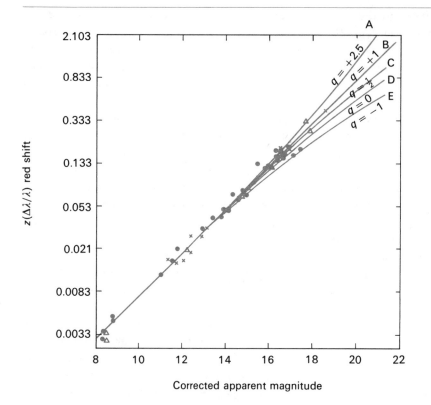

$z (\Delta\lambda/\lambda)$ red shift

Corrected apparent magnitude

Figure 16.3   Hubble diagram for first-ranked galaxies in clusters (adapted from diagram by A. Sandage). Key to symbols:
• = nonradio objects, x = radio objects (both with 200-inch telescope); Δ = nonradio objects (data by W. A. Baum); A =
closed spherical universe; B = closed spherical universe; C = Euclidean universe; D = open-ended hyperbolic universe;
E = steady-state universe.

fundamental parameters, the Hubble constant H, and the deceleration factor q must of necessity proceed slowly because the optical research in this field is limited to a handful of the world's largest reflectors. Within a score of years it is possible that sufficiently reliable values of H and q might be forthcoming to inform us on the true nature of our physical world. This assumes that there will be no upsetting discoveries or unexpected developments in the meantime.

16.7   LOW-ENERGY COSMIC BACKGROUND RADIATION

Discovery of Microwave Radiation

This low-temperature radiation was discovered accidentally in 1965 by two Bell Telephone radio engineers, A. A. Penzies and R. W. Wilson. They were investigating the source of radio noise in the incoming radio signals from the earth-orbiting communication satellites picked up by the telephone

Table 16.2   Cosmological Models

Model	k	q	Mean Density $\rho(g/cm^3)^b$	Type of Universe
Exploding[a]	+1	$>\frac{1}{2}$	$>5 \times 10^{-30}$	Closed spherical (oscillating)
Exploding[a]	0	$\frac{1}{2}$	5×10^{-30}	Euclidean (flat, infinite)
Exploding[a]	−1	0 to $<\frac{1}{2}$	$<5 \times 10^{-30}$	Hyperbolic (open, infinite)
Steady state	0	−1	5×10^{-30}	Infinite and timeless

[a]Cosmological constant (Λ) is zero.
[b]For $H = 50$ km/sec/megapc.

company's twenty-foot horn antenna at Holmdel, New Jersey. This discovery is reminiscent of a similar occurrence over thirty years earlier in which another Bell Telephone engineer accidentally detected radio noise coming from our Galaxy while seeking the cause of radio interference on the company's transmission lines (Section 3.3). It so happened that microwave cosmic radiation was being theoretically reinvestigated in 1965 by R. H. Dicke and his Princeton co-workers. They learned that Penzies and Wilson had observationally detected it about the same time, a strange coincidence not too uncommon in science. Its possible presence had been first theoretically predicted by G. Gamow in 1934 and later elaborated upon by R. A. Alper and R. C. Herman in 1948.

The 3°K Blackbody Microwave Radiation

In retracing the history of the expanding universe, one cannot avoid the general conclusion that matter was more densely packed in the past. In the beginning it must have congregated into a hot, superdense state that exploded in a violent reaction (the big bang) accompanied by a high-powered blast of high-frequency radiation (the primeval fireball). The constant chase of the fireball's original high-frequency photons toward the receding event horizon of the expanding universe during the last many billions of years has lengthened their wavelengths into the microwave millimeter region. The entire universe is bathed in this cosmic radiation arriving from all directions in space. By the cosmological principle, observers elsewhere in distant places should also detect it coming from everywhere.

The theory predicts that (1) the observed radiation of the fireball should correspond to blackbody radiation at a temperature of several degrees above absolute zero; (2) the radiation should be isotropically distributed—that is, the same in all directions. These predictions appear have been confirmed observationally. A plot of the microwave spectral distribution showing the observational points on the blackbody curve appears in Figure 16.4. The optical measurements made of wavelengths less than one millimeter are uncertain. They do not indicate a downward turn in the radiation plot near one millimeter. If confirmed by future observations, which must be conducted outside the earth's atmosphere, they could cast some doubt on the straightforward interpretation that the microwave radiation is a relic of the primeval fireball.

An interesting calculation that can be derived from the present temperature of the fireball (3°K) and the mean density of matter in the universe ($\rho \sim 10^{-29}$–10^{-31} g/cm^3) leads to the prediction that about 23–28 per cent of helium by weight was formed out of the primeval hydrogen within a few minutes after the explosion. This happens to be in close agreement with the percentage of helium in the sun, in the population I stars generally, and in the ionized regions of our Galaxy and of other galaxies. The question of the production of helium in the stars is pursued further in the next section.

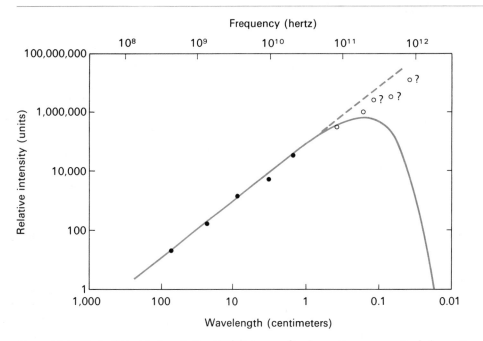

Figure 16.4   Fireball blackbody radiation (2.7°K): ● = *radio observations;* ○ = *optical observations (CN, CH, CH+).*

16.8   THE BIG BANG AND THE EVOLVING UNIVERSE

Theoretical research on the history of the early universe following the event of the fireball explosion began with the initial probes by G. Gamow and his colleagues several decades ago. Their work was later extended by a number of other investigators. The early stages of the big-bang model provide high-energy physicists with an opportunity for theoretically exploring the behavior of matter and radiation under extreme physical conditions unattainable on earth. We shall follow the evolution of the universe along the lines laid down by E. R. Harrison of the University of Massachusetts.

Evolution of the Universe

Like the ancient cosmologists, Harrison begins with a state of chaos. All matter in the universe was concentrated in a superdense core with a density of 10^{94} g/cm^3 and a temperature in excess of 10^{30} degrees absolute. His proposed timetable extended to the present era appears in Table 16.3. The initial superdense, hot cosmic fluid is a mix of the so-called strongly interacting elementary particles composed of hadrons (mesons, protons, neutrons, etc.) and a smaller proportion of photons and lighter-weight leptons (muons, electrons, neutrinos, etc.). There is present an almost equal division of matter and anti-matter with a slight preponderance of matter over antimatter by one part in one billion. If matter and antimatter were equally proportioned at the start, the annihilation of matter, it is argued, would be virtually complete and the universe would have consisted of radiation and very little matter. Since it

Table 16.3 Evolution of the Universe since Birth

Epoch	Time	Density (g/cm³)	Temperature (°K)	Action
Chaos	10^{-44} sec	10^{94}	10^{32}	Unimaginable
Hadron era	10^{-44}–10^{-4} sec	10^{94}–10^{14}	10^{32}–10^{12}	Annihilation of heavier elementary particles produces fireball
Lepton era	10^{-4}–10 sec	10^{14}–10^{4}	10^{12}–10^{10}	Annihilation of lighter elementary particles continues fireball
Radiation era	10 sec–10^{6} yr	10^{4}–10^{-21}	10^{10}–3×10^{3}	Fireball stage ends as radiation decouples from matter
Galaxian era	$>10^{6}$ yr	$<10^{-21}$	$<3,000$	Quasars and clusters of galaxies condense
Present era	$>10^{10}$ yr	10^{-29}–10^{-31}	3	Galaxies and stars have formed and are still forming

is not the case, there may have been a tiny but significant initial asymmetrical distribution of particles and antiparticles. In the present description of events there is nothing to prevent the universe from being fragmented into islands of matter and antimatter.

At the near instantaneous origin of time, the fireball erupts from the annihilation conversion of the hadrons into the powerful gamma radiation. The lepton era begins after the lowest mass hadrons, the pions, have annihilated each other. It continues with the destruction of the lighter-weight particles. It ends with the annihilation of the electrons as the produced neutrinos break away to form a ghost world of their own, moving about eternally and independently of the other universal constituents. About ten seconds after the start of the fireball explosion, the radiation era begins and expanding space is becoming filled mostly with photon radiation and neutrinos. The powerful gamma radiation is decoupled from matter. The photons are now set free to move about in the expanding universe forever after. In the words of Harrison: "Matter is like a faint precipitate suspended in a world of dense light."

During the radiation era matter consists principally of protons and neutrons; the neutrons combine with the protons to produce deuterium followed by the synthesis of helium. By this time, with the lowered temperature, the electrons have been captured by the protons to form atoms; the protons and the electrons can no longer scatter the light of the photons. The universe now becomes transparent. The fireball radiation that flooded the expanding universe during the first million years presently appears as the fossilized relic of the past in the form of the microwave radiation.

Production of Helium

The percentage of helium created depends critically upon the present values of the mean matter density in space and the temperature of the fireball. The calculated abundance ratio of helium to hydrogen leads to an estimated value of 25 per cent by weight. This corresponds to a ratio of ten hydrogen atoms to one helium atom, which is approximately the abundance ratio in the later-generation stars, including the sun. The predicted abundance values for the heavier elements, however, are too low in comparison with the observed values derived from the stellar spectral-line measurements. It would appear that they were principally created by thermonuclear reactions within the central cores of the stars. The first-generation stars of population II that have evolved into the blue-white region of the horizontal branch of the H-R diagram (Figure 12.1) have temperatures high enough to bring out the helium lines. They have an observed hydrogen-to-helium ratio considerably less than the value predicted by the big-bang model. The young population I stars reveal a higher abundance ratio as would be expected with later-generation stars. The predicted helium-to-hydrogen ratio can be lowered by accelerating the expansion of the universe. This would provide less time for nuclear reactions but it results in an overproduction of deuterium. The relative contributions of the helium formed in the early stages of the universe and the helium synthesized subsequently in the stellar interiors still remain to be settled.

Formation of the Galaxies

The galaxian era began with the dominance of matter over radiation when the universe was about one million years old and about one-thousandth of its present size. (There are still hundreds of millions of times more photons and neutrinos roaming around in the universe than there are protons and neutrons.) How was this primordial matter having a density of less than 10^{-21} g/cm^3 and a relatively low temperature distributed in space and how was it formed into galaxies? Did the finger of God as the Director of the Universe stir this matrix to form eddies or pockets of condensed gas as James Jeans once expressed it? Or did local inhomogeneities in the chaotic gas develop as the result of random turbulence or shock waves within the medium? The galaxies supposedly condensed out of the churning primordial eddies. On the other hand, P. J. E. Peebles of Princeton has hypothesized that the perturbative gravitational effects existing during the early stages of the expansion gave rise to oscillating density wavelets he calls "wrinkles" and to larger density aggregates he calls "knobs." In this view the largest wrinkles coagulated into clusters of galaxies after the radiation was uncoupled from the primeval matter. The smaller wrinkles continued to oscillate and eventually smoothed out in time. The more massive knobs may have pinched off and gravitationally collapsed into black holes, becoming useless for galaxy cluster formation.

Figure 16.5 Cosmological models of the universe. (From top to bottom.) (a) In the big bang, open-ended version, the universe was hatched from an exploding superdense, superhot "primeval atom" some 15 to 20 billion years ago. As the universe expands toward infinity, the galaxies spread out and the average density of matter diminishes. (b) In the pulsating version, the universe expands and contracts rhythmically in a period amounting to many billions of years. There is enough matter present so that the self-gravitation of the universe brings the expansion to a halt after which contraction sets in. At some unspecified distance from the point of origin a new cycle of expansion and contraction begins and repeats itself indefinitely. (c) In the steady state version, as the universe expands the galaxian population remains constant. Old galaxies disappear and new galaxies are formed so that the universe presents an unchanging appearance. This requires that new hydrogen be created spontaneously in order that the average density of matter remain the same as the universe expands. (Reprinted from "How It All Began," Newsweek, May 25, 1964. Drawing by Mel Hunter.)

(a)

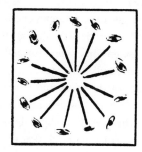

(b)

(c)
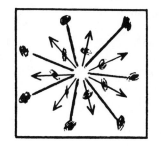

J. H. Oort has called attention to the uneven distribution of the galaxies brighter than the thirteenth magnitude in groups of clusters about 100 million light-years in diameter. He regards this as evidence that large-scale, inhomogeneous structures of 10^{14} to 10^{15} solar masses similar to the Virgo cloud and its extensions were formed during the highly turbulent conditions prevailing in the early universe. Masses of this size could survive the disruptive forces of shock disturbances and the radiation pressure of the fireball. A slight density enhancement in the primordial material, possibly aided by a localized slight retardation in the expansion of the universe, might "snowball" into a density large enough to condense into a large-scale structure that would eventually collapse into groups or chains of clusters.

It is conjectured that the majority of the galaxies were formed, following the high production rate of their energetic precursors (the quasars and the radio galaxies), at about one-fourth to one-fifth of the present age of the universe. According to Oort, the inward radial currents of a whirl of galactic size arising from the general turbulence generated by the fireball would locally retard the expansion of the universe sufficiently to permit the accumulation of matter. It would then collapse gravitationally to become a galaxy in which stars would form. There would still be an inflow of gas from the surrounding environment on a reduced scale that would continue for a long time. This is presumably what is now taking place in our own Galaxy. Astronomers have speculated that most of the matter in the universe may be locked up in the black holes and/or in the nonvisible ionized intergalactic gas whose temperature is estimated to lie between 100,000°K and 1,000,000°K. At the present time it is not known what proportion of this gas, if any, contributes to the observed diffuse x-ray radiation that has been detected coming from everywhere in space.

Cosmic Abundance of the Elements

The spectroscopic analysis of astronomical bodies from galaxies to stars and nebulae, combined with the chemical analysis of meteorites, provides the basis for an evaluation of the relative abundance of the elements. Table 16.4 lists the thirteen most plentiful elements in the universe.

Our chemical sampling of the universe reveals that hydrogen comprises about 91 per cent and helium about 9 per cent of all matter in space.[1] What little remains, including an undetermined amount of helium, has been created largely by thermonuclear reactions during a later epoch within the interiors of the stars. These synthesized elements have been partially expelled from the stars by stellar winds or by more violent means to produce the chemical mix of interstellar matter out of which succeeding generations of stars have been created (see Section 13.9).

[1] By weight the approximate percentages of hydrogen, helium, and the rest are 66, 27, and 7 respectively.

Table 16.4 The Most Abundant Elements

Element	Relative No. of Atoms
Hydrogen	500,000
Helium	50,000
Oxygen	3,140
Nitrogen	230
Carbon	115
Neon	35
Iron	25
Silicon	15
Magnesium	13
Sulfur	5
Nickel	2
Aluminum	1.3
Calcium	1

REVIEW QUESTIONS

1. What four basic natural forces rule the cosmos? Describe their roles.

2. If gravity is the weakest of the four forces, why is it so dominant within the universe at large?

3. What is modern cosmology all about? What was ancient cosmology concerned with?

4. What is the difference between a static and a non-static universe? Why is a static universe physically impossible?

5. Why is the red shift of the galaxies interpreted to be a consequence of the expansion of the universe?

6. Describe the possible variations of the time-dependent world models: hyperbolic, spherical, Euclidean, oscillating.

7. Why has it been so difficult to decide from observational data what the world model of the universe is?

8. What is the cosmological principle? The perfect cosmological principle?

9. Describe the steady-state model. What are its drawbacks?

10. What two important parameters must be evaluated in order to determine the correct world model?

11. What is the evidence in favor of the big-bang version?

12. Explain the origin of the low-temperature ($3°K$), isotropic, microwave radiation.

13. Describe the probable course of events *within* the first million years after the big bang according to the present interpretation.

14. Describe the probable course of events *after* the first million years following the big bang according to the present interpretation.

15. What impressions have you gained from this chapter concerning the modern viewpoint of cosmological genesis compared with the ancient views?

SELECTED READINGS

Bonnor, H., *The Mystery of the Expanding Universe*, Macmillan, 1964.

Dickson, F. P., *The Bowl of Night*, MIT Press, 1968.

Gamow, G., *The Creation of the Universe*, Viking, 1952.

Hodge, P. W., *Concepts of the Universe*, McGraw-Hill, 1969.

Kilmister, C., *The Nature of the Universe*, Dutton, 1971.

Schatzman, E., *The Origin and Evolution of the Universe*, Basic Books, 1966.

Singh, J., *Great Ideas and Theories of Modern Cosmology*, Dover, 1961.

Smart, W. M., *Riddle of the Universe*, Wiley, 1968.

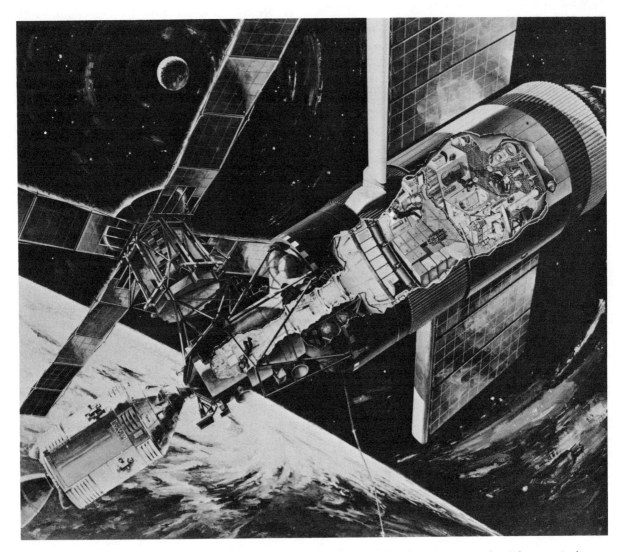

Skylab—manned earth orbital space station. The large cylindrical module extending from the upper right to the center is the orbital workshop. It has two solar-array wings for power generation and contains complete quarters for the three-man crew during all mission operations. The Apollo Telescope Mount, which houses a solar observatory, is shown at left center with its four deployed solar panels. The command-service module, which serves as the astronauts' ferry vehicle between earth and Skylab, is at the lower left. (Courtesy of NASA.)

SPACE ASTRONOMY

The exploration of the cosmos—the moon and the planets—is a noble aim. Our generation has the right to be proud of the fact that it has opened the space era of mankind.

Anatoly A. Blagonravov (1894–), member of the Soviet Academy of Sciences engaged in space research, *Bulletin of the Atomic Scientists,* September 1969

Man's first view of the heavens in the previously inaccessible short wavelengths took place in 1946. A V-2 rocket-borne spectrograph ascended to a height of sixty miles above the desert sands of New Mexico and returned with film of the ultraviolet spectrum of the sun. Behind this achievement lay centuries of random experiments with rockets except for the concerted Nazi experimentation during World War II with V-1 and V-2 rockets.

The space age began with the launching of the world's first artificial satellite, Sputnik 1, by the USSR in October 1957. Our national commitment to space research began officially with the establishment of the National Aeronautics and Space Administration (NASA) in 1958. Since that time our government has orbited hundreds of scientifically instrumented space vehicles and approximately two dozen manned spacecraft in the exploration of outer space. NASA operates three worldwide networks, one for orbiting satellites, a second for interplanetary vehicles, and a third for manned flights. Each network is separately involved in the tracking, telemetry, communications, and command functions of its respective vehicles.

Since the 1950's atmospheric sounding balloons and sounding rockets have returned with much useful solar data in the ultraviolet and x-ray regions. Instrumented sounding rockets have led to the discoveries of a large number of x-ray sources, many identified with known supernovae remnants and with several abnormal galaxies. The greatest wealth of detailed astronomical information in the short wavelengths has come from the orbiting solar observatories, orbiting geophysical observatories, and orbiting astronomical observatories.

The Skylab station is equipped with a large solar telescope. Its three-man crew will conduct a number of ultraviolet and x-ray solar studies, a survey of the earth's resources; and many bio-logical, technological, and scientific experiments. It has cost the government $25 billion to put men on the moon and a comparable amount to launch its unmanned instrumented spacecraft during a decade and a half of operation. The ordinary citizen may well inquire whether the expenditures of men, time, resources, and money have been worth the effort.

17.1 HISTORICAL BACKGROUND

Introduction

In 1946, after World War II, man's first glimpse of the universe in the short wavelengths beyond the reach of ground-based optical equipment began modestly with the sun. Employed for that research were the upper atmospheric sounding rockets, including modified captured German V-2 war rockets. Since that time astronomical observations above the earth's obscuring blanket of air have been extended throughout the ultraviolet, x-ray, and gamma-ray spectral regions by means of instrumented space vehicles. They have revealed the presence of hitherto unknown galactic x-ray stars, plus x-ray and gamma-ray extended sources. The other end of the electromagnetic spectrum in the partially obstructed micron region is presently being explored with infrared telescopes mounted aboard high-flying aircraft. This research has expanded our knowledge concerning stellar birth, radiation from the galactic center, and the excessive energy prevalent in the cores of the highly energetic extragalactic sources. In the recent past, an imposing array of interplanetary probes, orbiting solar, geophysical, and astronomical observatories, lunar orbiters and landers, Venus flybys and entry probes, and Mars flybys and orbiters have returned a wealth of information undreamed of a few years ago. Yet all of our celestial triumphs would not have been possible without the labors of the early rocket pioneers.

Brief History of Rocketry

The birth of the space age rests upon the accomplishments of many individuals and groups who have experimented with rockets since the Chinese created them in the thirteenth century. Throughout history and indeed to this very day, rockets and firearms have frequently been in competition with each other in warfare. By the end of the nineteenth century opposing armies had found rifle fire and artillery fire so superior to the often erratic rocket fire that rockets were virtually abandoned as military weapons.

It was not until World War II that rockets were again revived as a dangerous war weapon by the Germans in the form of the 46-foot long V-2 rocket. They had obtained much of their theoretical and practical knowledge about rockets from the American rocket experimenter Robert H. Goddard (1882–1945), who was a physics professor at Clark University in Massachusetts. His peaceful efforts in utilizing rockets as a scientific aid in exploring space were largely ignored in his native country. Goddard's principal contributions were incorporated in a Smithsonian Institution publication entitled *A Method of Reaching Extreme Altitudes* (1919). In concluding his report Goddard expressed the belief that a ten-ton rocket carrying magnesium powder could be fired to land on the moon and explode in a brilliant flash that might be visible in a large telescope, a suggestion that was ridiculed as a crackpot idea at the time.

Two other pioneer contemporaries of Goddard were Russian school teacher Konstantin Ziolkowski (1887–1935) and Rumanian-German physicist Hermann Oberth (1894–   ). As early as 1903, Ziolkowski had published a theoretical paper later entitled *The Rocket into Cosmic Space*, dealing with rocket principles. In Oberth's published article, *The Rocket into Interplanetary Space* (1923), he predicted that rockets could be constructed to overcome the earth's gravity and transport machines and men into space.

At the end of World War II, the United States shipped many of the captured German V-2 rockets and parts to the White Sands Proving Grounds missile base in New Mexico. Our military authorities felt that the immediate need of gaining operational experience in the handling and firing of large rockets was of paramount importance. In turn, this would lead to improvements in guidance control and tracking techniques for future ballistic missiles and rockets of our own manufacture. As a by-product, the experiments would add immeasurably to our knowledge of the largely unexplored upper atmosphere. To achieve the aforementioned goals, we fired from the White Sands range between 1946 and 1951 about sixty instrumented rockets obtained from the assembled stockpiles of captured V-2's.

In the late 1940's a beginning had been made in the field of atmospheric studies by such civilian governmental research agencies as the Naval Research Laboratory in Maryland and the Langley Research Center in Virginia. Their scientists, together with those from the private sector interested in exploring the upper atmosphere and extraterrestrial phenomena, were invited by the military authorities in charge of the V-2 program to conduct a number of experiments in upper atmospheric research. On October 24, 1946, an instrumented V-2 rocket carried a small ultraviolet grating spectrograph designed by the Naval Research Laboratory scientists to a height of sixty miles. During its ascent, a camera, whose film was later recovered, made a running record of the ultraviolet extension of the solar spectrum down to 2,200 angstroms for the first time in astronomical history.

Dawn of the Space Age

Until 1958, the year after the world's first artificial satellite, the Soviet Sputnik 1, had blazed its path across the sky, our country had no official space organization. Neither had it formulated any national policy to conduct explorations in space. Prior to this time our space activities had been directed for the most part by the armed services which had a vital stake in developing rockets and guided missiles as a national security measure. In 1958, at the urging of President Eisenhower and the Science Advisory Committee which he had appointed in 1957 to survey the possibilities of developing a national program in space exploration and space technology, the 85th Congress enacted into law the National Aeronautics and Space Administration (NASA) agency. One of the primary objectives set forth in the Act was "to acquire scientific knowledge on the environment of our solar system and Galaxy which will lead to a better understanding of the physical universe and man's role in it."

In a report issued in March 1970 by the President's Science Advisory Committee, the original goals and programs laid down by its predecessors over a decade earlier were reiterated and extended to include the following objectives:

1. Contribute to the economic strength and security of the nation and provide beneficial services through an expanded program of earth-oriented research and applications of space science and technology.

2. Explore the solar system with emphasis on a phased program of lunar exploration, the search for extraterrestrial life, and a diversified program of planetary exploration.

3. Use the unique features of space platforms outside the earth to expand our knowledge of the universe and basic physical laws through space astronomy and space physics research.

Other recommendations dealt with expanding the opportunities for civilian application of space, developing a suitable biomedical reserach program, and improving international cooperation in space activities. In December 1963 the General Assembly of the United Nations unanimously approved a resolution declaring that space is open and free to all states for exploration, that nothing in space can be owned by any one country, and that the exploration of space should be directed toward the betterment of the human race.

17.2 ROCKET ACTION

Rocket Principles

A rocket engine operates on the principle of action and reaction as expressed in Newton's third law of motion (Section 3.5). Some well-known examples of this principle are the backward recoil of a rifle when the bullet leaves the muzzle or the rotary lawn sprinkler actuated by the backward reaction of the squirting water jets. If the neck of an inflated balloon is held to prevent the compressed air from escaping, nothing happens because the internal gas pressure is equally balanced in all directions. But when the neck is released, the air rushes out (action) and the balloon moves in the opposite direction (reaction) because the gas pressures are now unequal in these directions.

In a rocket engine a liquid propellant mixture of fuel and oxidizer (hydrogen and oxygen, for example) is pumped into the rocket's combustion chamber where it explodes to produce a hot blast of gases directed outward at high speed through the bell-shaped exhaust nozzle. The force of the reaction produces a thrust that accelerates the rocket forward as burning continues until it reaches maximum velocity at burnout. It is not technologically practical nor economically possible to construct a single-stage chemical rocket with a very high proportion of its weight in the propellants. The difficulty is overcome by employing a multistage rocket in which each successive stage adds its velocity increment toward

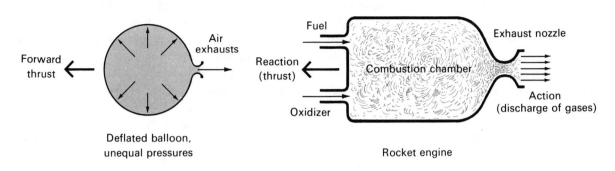

Figure 17.1 *Principle of action and reaction.*

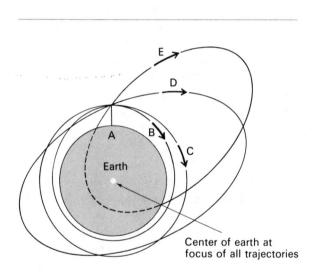

Figure 17.2 *Rocket trajectories: A, launch point; B, elliptic orbit (injection approximately horizontal with a velocity of slightly under 5 mi/sec); C, circular orbit (injection horizontal to earth's surface at 5 mi/sec); D, elliptic orbit (injection angle >0° with a velocity somewhat over 5 mi/sec but less than escape velocity of 7 mi/sec); E, intercept orbit (injection angle too high).*

the final desired velocity needed to inject the payload into orbit. The type of orbit desired is determined by the final injection velocity and the angle of injection relative to the horizontal at the earth's surface.

Launch Sequence and Orbital Injection

A frequently employed rocket system for boosting astronomical payloads into orbit is the Atlas-Centaur combination. It stands about 120 feet high and is about 10 feet in diameter. The duostage rocket weighs about 150 tons and delivers over 500,000 pounds of thrust. Each stage carries an automatic control-and-guidance section, separate fuel and oxidizer tanks, a propellant-pumping system, and a combustion chamber with small vernier rockets attached on the outside for control purposes. The upper Centaur stage in addition carries the payload which is installed in the protective nose section that drops off before final injection of the payload into orbit. The Atlas first-stage rocket consists of two booster engines which fire first. Following their burnout, the large single sustainer engine takes over. Liquid oxygen and RP-1 kerosene (a jet-aircraft type of fuel) are the employed propellants that provide a thrust of 500,000 pounds. After burnout of the Centaur second stage, which utilizes liquid oxygen and liquid hydrogen as the oxidizer and fuel respectively, the payload is detached to continue on its assigned trajectory. Prior to injection of the payload into orbit, an automatic guidance system has altered the direction of flight from the vertical at launch to pitch-over and finally to the near horizontal.

17.3 SPACECRAFT OPERATIONS

Control and Guidance

During the sequence of events that occurs in flight before the payload is placed in orbit, the rocket stages must be controlled and guided. No

Figure 17.3   Atlas-Centaur rocket on the launch pad at Cape Kennedy. This is the rocket that has boosted various astronomical spacecraft into orbit. (Courtesy of NASA.)

rocket can be expected to follow a prescribed course because many disturbing factors tend to cause the rocket to yaw, pitch, and roll. An autopilot system monitors the rocket's flight pattern and with the aid of an electronic computer applies the necessary corrections during powered flight by means of small vernier thrustor rockets to keep the vehicle in its predetermined path.

Once the payload is in orbit, radio command signals from ground stations or automatic timing devices can maneuver the spacecraft by means of small, electronically actuated, jets. The correct orientation of the payload, the pointing and proper maintenance of any of its parts such as antennas, solar panels, sensors, star trackers, telescopes, etc., can be sustained by the following devices, singly or in combination: (1) spin rockets or gas jets; (2) earth, sun, and star sensors; (3) star sights; (4) gyro systems; (5) momentum wheels; (6) magnetic devices; (7) horizon scanners. The methods of control and guidance depend upon the designs and missions of the spacecraft, ranging from the earth satellites and space probes to the manned vehicles.

NASA Global Networks

NASA maintains a worldwide system of tracking and data-gathering that is divided into three categories: (1) Manned Space Flight Network located at the Johnson Space Center in Houston, Texas; (2) Satellite Network located at the Goddard Space Flight Center in Greenbelt, Maryland; and (3) Deep Space Network located at the Operations Control Center at the Jet Propulsion Laboratory in Pasadena, California.[1] Each network operates out of a "central control," a complex of men and machines that monitors, directs, and coordinates the operations of the space-

---

[1] An optical tracking network employing about a dozen modified Schmidt (Baker-Nunn) cameras stationed around the world is operated for NASA by the Smithsonian Astrophysical Observatory in Cambridge, Massachusetts.

Figure 17.4   Central control room of the 210-foot diameter paraboloid antenna at Goldstone, Calif. The antenna is designed for spacecraft tracking and communication at outer-planetary distances. The precision and power of this antenna, however, has led to its additional use in radar mapping of Venus and Mars and in pulsar and quasar observations. (Courtesy of Jet Propulsion Laboratory.)

instructing the equipment within it to perform certain operations.

17.4   SPACE RESEARCH IN ASTRONOMY

Balloon Astronomy

The first balloon observations of the sun were made during two flights in the fall of 1957 under Project Stratoscope I, directed by M. Schwarzschild of Princeton University. A 12-inch reflector was carried aloft by a 130-foot Skyhook balloon to an altitude of nearly twenty miles above 95 per cent of the earth's atmosphere. An electronically actuated system kept the telescope pointed to the sun while several thousand pictures of the sun's surface were recorded. The telescopic equipment and the camera films were recovered by a parachute drop. Since the focal settings of the telescope were uncertain because of heating and other factors, it was necessary to automatically shift the focal settings in the hope of securing a number of in-focus pictures. In 1959 four Stratoscope flights, this time instrumented with a ground-controlled, radio-command system, employing televised manipulation of the telescope's pointing and focal settings, returned with a couple of hundred of the most detailed photographs of the solar surface ever obtained (see Figure 9.10).

In the early 1960's several Stratoscope II ascents with larger Skyhook balloons were made for the purpose of spectroscopically analyzing the Martian and Venusian atmospheres in the ultraviolet and infrared spectral regions. Some flights carried observers, the others automated equipment, including a 36-inch reflecting telescope. The most conclusive findings from all these attempts were the detection of water vapor in the infrared spectrum of the Martian atmosphere (confirmed shortly after by ground-based spectrograms) and its probable infrared detection in the form of ice crystals in the Venusian atmosphere. Later Stratoscope II flights directed by

craft under its command and the associated ground stations in its network. The networks perform the missions of tracking, telemetering, communicating, and commanding via a global linkage system using all forms of communications. Tracking refers to the monitoring of the spacecraft's trajectory (position, velocity, direction) by means of the incoming radio signals from the spacecraft. Telemetry deals with the radio reception of the measured information from the scientific instruments and sensors aboard the space vehicle. Communicating relates to the message contacts between the ground stations, astronauts, central control, etc. Commanding involves the technique of relaying radio instructions to the spacecraft, instructing it to execute certain maneuvers or the Princeton group were employed to secure high-resolution photographs of Jupiter, Uranus, the resolved nucleus of the Andromeda galaxy, the unresolved nucleus of its companion, M 32, and a Seyfert galaxy. In recent years balloons have been used sporadically in the study of x-ray, gamma-ray, and cosmic ray sources. They have detected gamma rays coming from the center of the Galaxy and x-rays from several variable sources.

Sounding-Rocket Astronomy

Rocket flights, though of short duration (minutes) compared to balloon flights (hours), possess the important advantage of ascending five times higher (100 miles). Sounding rockets depend exclusively on telemetry rather than on partial telemetry and parachute recovery of the data. They are relatively easy to instrument and are economically operable. Since 1949, under the direction of H. Friedman and his associates at the Naval Research Laboratory, great advances have been made in obtaining direct x-ray and hydrogen Lyman alpha views of the solar surface and its near atmospheric extensions. They have photographed the entire solar ultraviolet and adjoining x-ray spectral regions. With other experimenters they have succeeded in detecting the shortest solar x-rays, down to 0.1 angstrom, with sensitive Geiger counters, scintillation counters, and other types of counters.

The first ultraviolet views of the night sky, including the diffuse radiation from Lyman alpha, were recorded by the Naval Research Laboratory scientists in 1956. Later, with improved equipment and techniques, the same group succeeded in mapping the ultraviolet radiation from two discrete sources. One was an extended area in Orion and the other a bright area surrounding the first-magnitude star Spica. Since 1962 rocket-borne instruments have photographed the ultraviolet spectra of a number of young stars in the Orion nebula. They have detected

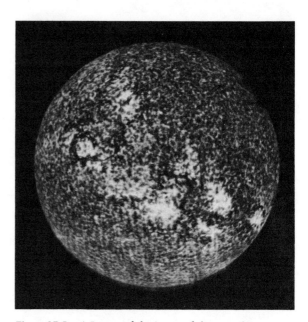

Figure 17.5   A Lyman alpha image of the sun taken on July 10, 1972 from an Aerobee rocket. (Courtesy of U.S. Naval Research Laboratory.)

x-ray radiation in the form of a uniform diffuse background that covers the sky. About fifty galactic x-ray sources were discovered with sounding-rocket apparatus by 1972. Most of them were concentrated in the Milky Way constellations of Sagittarius, Scorpius, and Cygnus. At least fourteen of these sources have been identified; these include the peculiar blue variable stars, Scorpius X-1 and Cygnus X-2 (the X designation stands for x-ray); several supernovae: the Crab nebula, Tycho's supernova, Cassiopeia A, the Cygnus loop, and Vela X-2. A number of extragalactic x-ray sources have also been identified: the radio galaxies M 87 and M 84 in the Virgo cluster, Centaurus A, two Seyfert galaxies, NGC 1275 (Perseus A) and NGC 4151, and the quasar 3C 273.

Satellite Astronomy

Despite the large disparity in cost between a

sounding rocket and an artificial satellite, the great advantage of the latter lies in the continuous monitoring of events over different regions of extraterrestrial space for long periods of time. Between October 1958 and March 1960, the United States launched a series of five Pioneer sun-orbiting space probes of which only the last two, Pioneers 4 and 5, were successful. Their mission was to investigate solar activity, the interplanetary medium, and the sun's influence on the earth's environment. A second series of improved Pioneers began with Pioneer 6 in December 1965 and continued through Pioneer 9 in November 1968. Some of these Pioneers were still functioning in solar orbit in 1972. The latter Pioneer experiments have dealt with the detection of solar flares, solar wind, solar plasma intensities, and the interplanetary magnetic field.

A long and extensive series of wide-ranging, earth-orbiting Explorer satellites began in January 1958 and is still going on. In the past the spacecraft equipment has recorded: (1) cosmic-ray intensities and directions; (2) micrometeoroid counts, sizes, and velocities; (3) the structure, extent, and magnetic-field strength of the earth's magnetosphere; (4) velocity distribution and intensities of incoming solar particles; (5) earth's upper atmospheric composition, temperatures, and densities; (6) solar ultraviolet and x-ray radiation; (7) extrasolar x-rays and gamma rays. For the first time Explorer 11 recorded gamma-ray photons coming from various directions with no marked preference for the plane of the Milky Way. The x-ray satellite, Explorer 42 (named Uhuru), launched off the coast of Kenya in December 1970, has detected well over one hundred x-ray sources, many of them variable in intensity. Most of them have not yet been identified optically. Several x-ray objects are components of short-period eclipsing binary systems. One of them, Cygnus X-3, undergoes brief, unpredictable radio flare-ups. The noneclipsing binary component, Cygnus X-1, may be a black

hole into which matter, sucked from its nearby blue-supergiant companion, radiates x-rays. About thirty x-ray sources are apparently of extragalactic origin. Included among those definitely identified are a number of overactive galaxies, several discrete objects in the Magellanic Clouds, the Andromeda galaxy, the quasar 3C 273, and the Virgo, Coma, and Perseus cluster of galaxies. The x-ray radiation found in the clusters may be coming from hot intergalactic gas within the clusters or from synchrotron emission.

Orbiting Solar Observatory (OSO)

An important family of space vehicles is known by the name of observatory satellites. They are the most sophisticated and complex of their type ever launched.[1] The program was initiated in March 1962 with the launching of the first Orbiting Solar Observatory (OSO-1) into a nearly circular orbit at an altitude of 350 miles. The mission of this spacecraft was to record: (1) the intensities and spectral range of the sun's wavelengths in the x-ray and gamma-ray regions; (2) the enhanced x-ray emission during solar flare outbursts; and (3) the solar-wind flux. During its 1,000 hours of operation it recorded 75 solar flares and subflares.

The standard satellite configuration consists of a central shaft with a drum at the bottom containing a number of experiments, power supplies, radio equipment, and the position stabilization control apparatus. The latter consists of end-mounted compressed nitrogen gas containers and jets on the shaft extensions to correct for deficiencies in stabilization of the spacecraft. Mounted on the center shaft is the semicircular array housing the hundreds of solar cells on panels that constantly face the sun as directed by the solar sensors. The drum rotates at thirty revolutions per minute to provide maximum gyroscopic stability. The top section carries additional experiments and is pointed at the sun.

[1] Excluded from the discussion are the Orbiting Geophysical Observatories.

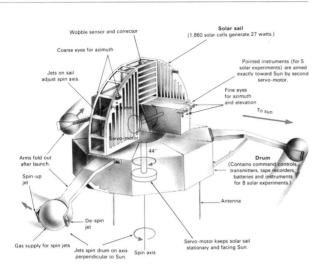

Wobble sensor and corrector

Coarse eyes for azimuth

Jets on sail
adjust spin axis.

Solar sail
(1,860 solar cells generate 27 watts.)

Pointed instruments (for 5
solar experiments) are aimed
exactly toward Sun by second
servo-motor.

Fine eyes
for azimuth
and elevation

To sun

Servo-motor

44″

Arms fold out
after launch.

Spin-up
jet

De-spin
jet

Gas supply for spin jets

Jets spin drum on axis
perpendicular to Sun.

Spin axis

Drum
(Contains command controls,
transmitters, tape recorders,
batteries and instruments
for 8 solar experiments.)

Antenna

Servo-motor keeps solar sail
stationary and facing Sun.

Figure 17.6   Orbiting Solar Observatory (OSO). (Courtesy of Time *Magazine. Redrawn by permission from a diagram by R. M. Chapin, Jr.)*

OSO-2, launched in February 1965, contained equipment for eight experiments involving ultraviolet spectroscopy, solar x-ray and gamma-ray measurements, solar corona intensities, and zodiacal light polarization. OSO-3, launched in March 1967, carried equipment for nine experiments to investigate the solar activity in the same spectral regions as its predecessors. A new addition was an ultraviolet solar-disk scanner. The next four solar observatories were launched in the following four years. They added a new dimension with the inclusion of ultraviolet and x-ray spectroheliographs designed to secure monochromatic views of the solar disk and its atmospheric extensions in the light of certain spectral lines.

Orbiting Astronomical Observatory (OAO)

The most sophisticated and costly of the astronomical satellites has been the Orbiting Astronomical Observatory. Out of four launches only two were successful: OAO-2 in December 1968 and OAO-Copernicus (OAO-C) in August 1972. The latter, the fourth and final observatory satellite of the series, was named to commemorate the approaching 500th anniversary of the great Polish astronomer who was born in 1473. The first failed in April 1966 because of a power-supply malfunction. The third, a complex satellite costing $83 million, aborted in November 1970 because the protective nose cone cover failed to jettison on schedule.

OAO-2, which was boosted into a circular orbit 480 miles high by an Atlas-Centaur two-stage rocket, carried a 1,000-pound scientific payload. The satellite housed four 12-inch reflectors and associated color filters designed to measure photometrically the ultraviolet radiations of thousands of stars in four separate spectral bands. It also carried three 16-inch and four 8-inch reflectors to record on command the ultraviolet spectral-energy distribution and photometric intensities of selected objects (galaxies, gaseous nebulae, novae, planets, comets, etc.). The radio commands for pointing to any specified celestial body are issued from the Goddard Space Flight Center in Maryland. The satellite's useful life ended in 1973.

Among the findings so far revealed are higher ultraviolet temperatures for the hot young stars than expected from their visible spectral intensities; extensive mass loss from the atmospheres of the O and B supergiant stars; an ultraviolet excess from the center of the Andromeda galaxy and from several other galaxies; considerable variation in interstellar light absorption from star to star; the presence of bright blue stars on the horizontal branch of the H-R diagram in the globular clusters; and the existence of an immense Lyman alpha hydrogen cloud surrounding the head of the comet Togo-Sato-Kosaka of 1969.

OAO-Copernicus is equipped with a 32-inch ultraviolet reflector and a cluster of three small x-ray telescopes designed to investigate the short-wavelength radiation down to one angstrom. It circles the earth once every 100 minutes at an altitude of 460 miles. One of the spacecraft's principal functions is to learn more about the physical and chemical nature of the interstellar medium from the way in which gas and dust absorb and scatter the stellar ultraviolet light. Another important objective is to examine more closely the radiation from the hot young stars and from the newly discovered x-ray sources. When the occasion arises, the observatory's ultraviolet telescope will be aimed at specific targets of opportunity with an accuracy equivalent to pinpointing a baseball from a distance of 130 miles.

17.5 PLANETARY EXPLORATION

Planetary Missions to the Nearby Planets

During the 1960's Venus had been investigated by two U. S. Mariner flybys and four USSR Venera flybys and entry probes; Mars, by three U. S. Mariner flybys. In the latter part of 1971 the United States placed Mariner 9 and the Soviet Union placed Mars 2 and Mars 3 in orbit around Mars. Their purpose was to obtain information on the nature of the Martian terrain, the atmospheric composition and structure, the ground and atmospheric variations in temperature, and the general seasonal phenomena. The results of the experiments were discussed in Section 7.5. The American Viking soft landers scheduled for the mid-1970's will conduct automatic experiments dealing with the physical, chemical, and biological conditions on Mars. Probes will search for organic compounds and living organisms in the Martian soil. In late 1973 a Mariner flyby is scheduled to be orbited to curve around Venus which will decelerate it toward a future rendezvous with Mercury. The relative positions of the two planets must be in a favorable position for this double flyby.

Trajectories for Encounter with Venus or Mars

Shorter flight times on more direct paths are possible with the nuclear and ion rocket-powered vehicles of the future. The only practical method available at the present time for launching a spacecraft toward any planet is by means of chemical

Figure 17.7   Orbiting Astronomical Observatory (OAO-Copernicus), the fourth and final spacecraft in the series, was successfully orbited on August 21, 1972. The large flat surfaces on either side of the vehicle are the solar panels. (Courtesy of NASA.)

propulsion. Nearly all of the propellant is consumed to power the space vehicle long enough to permit it to escape from the earth. The vehicle thereafter becomes a satellite of the sun as it is directed into a long, unpowered, coasting orbit, known as a transfer orbit, toward a rendezvous with Venus or Mars. The resulting "minimum energy" orbit is the one that uses the least amount of rocket propellant, a precious commodity, to inject the spacecraft into its transfer orbit. Some deviations from the minimum-energy orbit, leading to an earlier rendezvous of perhaps a month, are possible, depending on the available propellant supply and the payload weight. A small amount of rocket energy is kept in reserve to provide mid-course corrections for a more precise trajectory while the vehicle is enroute to the planet or for terminal guidance in the event a soft landing or an orbit around the planet is intended.

Aiming a spacecraft toward a planetary target on a long, curved, coasting path (the transfer orbit) is a delicate and difficult task. Both earth and planet are in motion around the sun at different speeds and in different directions. The problem is similar to that of a gunner on a rotating merry-go-round firing at a fast-flying duck. Planet and earth must be in the correct relative positions when the rocket firing takes place, which must be in the proper direction and at the correct velocity. The optimum target launch dates or "windows" for Venus and Mars occur at intervals corresponding to the synodic periods of the planets: 584 days for Venus and 780 days for Mars.

For the flight to Venus the departure must be *opposite* to the earth's orbital motion to curve the path inward toward Venus. This permits the vehicle's orbital velocity acquired from the earth's orbital velocity of 18.5 mi/sec at escape time to be reduced by the velocity required to escape from the earth (7 mi/sec). The resultant velocity of about 11 mi/sec relative to the sun causes the craft to fall toward the sun to a rendezvous with Venus about four

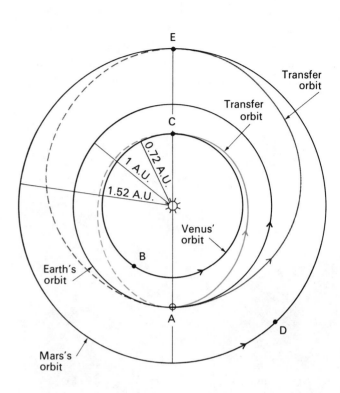

Figure 17.8   Idealized minimum-energy orbits to Venus and Mars. Circular and coplanar orbits are assumed.
Rendezvous position is 180 degrees around the sun from the launch point. The transfer orbit for Venus is a half-ellipse whose mean distance is the average distance between Venus and earth: (1 + 0.72)/2 A.U. = 0.86 A.U. The transfer orbit for Mars is a half-ellipse whose mean distance is the average distance between Mars and earth: (1 + 1.5)/2 A.U. = 1.25 A.U. In both instances the travel time is equal to one-half the period of the complete ellipse, easily derived from Kepler's third law of planetary motion. A, launch position from earth; B, Venus at time of launch; C, rendezvous of space craft with Venus four months later; D, Mars at time of launch; E, rendezvous of spacecraft with Mars 7.5 months later.

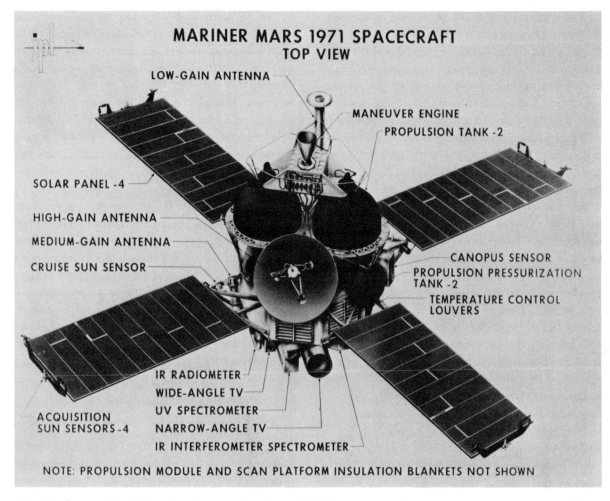

MARINER MARS 1971 SPACECRAFT
TOP VIEW

LOW-GAIN ANTENNA

MANEUVER ENGINE
PROPULSION TANK -2

SOLAR PANEL -4

HIGH-GAIN ANTENNA

MEDIUM-GAIN ANTENNA

CRUISE SUN SENSOR

CANOPUS SENSOR
PROPULSION PRESSURIZATION
TANK -2
TEMPERATURE CONTROL
LOUVERS

IR RADIOMETER
WIDE-ANGLE TV
UV SPECTROMETER
ACQUISITION
SUN SENSORS -4
NARROW-ANGLE TV
IR INTERFEROMETER SPECTROMETER

NOTE: PROPULSION MODULE AND SCAN PLATFORM INSULATION BLANKETS NOT SHOWN

Figure 17.9   Mars Mariner 9 orbiter spacecraft. (Courtesy of NASA.)

months after launch. For the flight to Mars the departure must be in the *same* direction as the earth's orbital motion. The resultant velocity relative to the sun after escape from the earth is approximately 25 mi/sec. This forces the vehicle to swing outward from the sun along its transfer orbit toward a rendezvous with Mars seven to eight months after launch.

Exploration of the Outer Planets

A Pioneer 10 spacecraft was launched early in March 1972 on a Jupiter-oriented mission that will take it within 90,000 miles of the planet after nearly two years. Between July and February 1973 it had penetrated entirely through the asteroid belt and had recorded about seventy non-damaging collisions with tiny particles. A second spacecraft, Pioneer 11, is expected to be orbited in 1973; it will arrive in Jupiter's vicinity in 1975. The Pioneer spacecraft is instrumented for thirteen different experiments to permit exploitation of phenomena both enroute and close at hand. During the approximate 100-hour period in swinging around Jupiter, it will photograph the giant planet in red and blue light and measure the ultraviolet and infrared radiation. The cloud structure and the Great Red Spot will be analyzed physically and chemically, the magnetosphere and its activity monitored, the intense radiation belts explored, the thermal balance and the hydrogen-helium content of its atmosphere investigated, and the gravitational field of the planet evaluated.

The spacecraft is expected to exit the solar system with a velocity of seven miles per second relative to the sun. The probability of Pioneer 10 encountering another civilized planetary system in space is exceedingly remote. It would take a little more than 100,000 years to reach the vicinity of the nearest star. A message from earth was engraved, however, on a plate mounted on the skin of the vehicle. (See the frontispiece to Chapter 19.)

The relative positions of the earth and the planets beyond Jupiter are favorable for a so-called "grand tour" of the outer planets during the latter part of this decade. Once every 175 years, the outer planets line up along an arc like a curved string of pearls. This particular arrangement serves as a gravitational leverage in accelerating an approaching space vehicle from one target planet to the next one. The first opportunity comes in September 1977 when a launched spacecraft could reach Jupiter in February 1979. The great planet would then accelerate the space vehicle toward the next planet, Saturn, which it would reach in September 1980. Saturn would in turn accelerate the probe toward Pluto, which it would reach in March 1986. Thence it would pass

out of the stellar system to become an interstellar tramp subject to the gravitational whims of the nearby stars. A second grand tour could begin in November 1979, and the spacecraft would reach Jupiter in April 1981, Uranus in July 1985, and Neptune in November 1986. Without the planets' gravitational push, the flight times would be decades long. Budgetary restrictions, however, are limiting the investigations of the outer planets to Jupiter and Saturn missions with Pioneer or Mariner-type spacecraft.

The remainder of the present century will bear witness to the continued exploration of the solar system through the medium of various instrumented spacecraft missions. We should like to know more fully its chemical distribution, its physical properties, and its origin. It would also be of great scientific importance to seek the answers by means of experiments as to whether the dynamical laws and the general theory of relativity are precisely followed extraterrestrially.

17.6 MANNED SPACE STATIONS

Skylab Space Station

The Skylab space platform is scheduled to be launched in May 1973. The station will be manned by rotating three-man crews of which one member will be a scientist. They will perform a number of carefully selected scientific, technological, and biomedical experiments. The station consists of a workshop assembly joined to a command-service module. The workshop section will be launched into a nearly circular, 270-mile orbit by a two-stage, 30-story tall Saturn V rocket. The module will be launched one day later by a 20-story tall Saturn IB rocket. The overall length of the 90-ton clustered system is 118.5 feet with a diameter varying between 10 and 21.6 feet. Compared to a Soviet space laboratory that was trial-orbited in June 1971, the American station is about twice as long, weighs nearly three times as much, and contains about four times the working space.

Apollo Telescope Mount (ATM)

Of astronomical interest is the Apollo Telescope Mount solar observatory. It houses eight instruments designed to investigate solar phenomena not generally visible from ground stations. The 22,000-pound ATM structure is nearly fifteen feet long and seven feet at its maximum width. It is provided with an environmental-control system, gyroscopic stabilization, a deployment-pointing arrangement, solar-array and battery electric-power units, data and communications systems, and a variety of ultraviolet

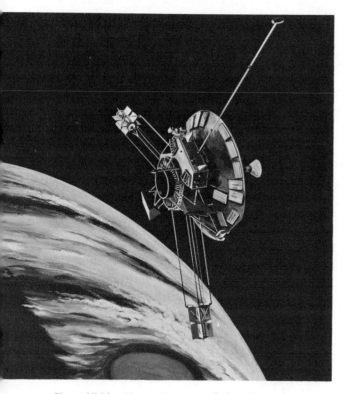

Figure 17.10   Pioneer 10 spacecraft flying by Jupiter in vicinity of the Great Red Spot. (Courtesy of NASA.)

and x-ray astronomical instrumentation. Photographs will be made on the brightness, form, and polarization of the solar corona, the ultraviolet and x-ray emissions from solar flares will be recorded, and narrow-band spectral scans will be made of the solar atmosphere and the disk.

Other Astronomical Science Experiments

Included in the science experimental package aboard the Skylab station are other studies of astronomical importance. These involve an ultraviolet sky survey of Milky Way star fields and clouds; galactic x-ray mapping to locate x-ray sources and to investigate the general x-ray background radiation in space; studies of the intensity and polarization of the zodiacal light and the gegenschein region; and photography of the ultraviolet airglow of the earth's upper atmospheric layers.

17.7   FUTURE SPACE RESEARCH IN ASTRONOMY

Proposed Projects

A Space Science Board consisting of sixteen scientists encompassing a wide range of diversified interests in the new subdisciplines of astronomy was set up in 1970 by NASA to investigate the future prospects of an expanding research program in space astronomy. They recommended: (1) that the research in x-ray and gamma-ray astronomy be enlarged with the aid of more sophisticated earth-orbiting spacecraft employing specialized equipment since explorations in these areas cannot be conducted from the ground; (2) the mounting of a 120-inch reflector in a manned earth-orbiting observatory to be kept updated by means of periodic earth-shuttle visits; (3) intensified efforts in research and development and in the operation of more efficient infrared detectors; (4) further radio observations from earth-orbiting radio observatories employing

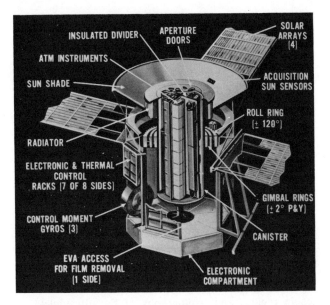

INSULATED DIVIDER
APERTURE DOORS
SOLAR ARRAYS (4)
ATM INSTRUMENTS
ACQUISITION SUN SENSORS
SUN SHADE
ROLL RING (± 120°)
RADIATOR
ELECTRONIC & THERMAL CONTROL RACKS (7 OF 8 SIDES)
GIMBAL RINGS (± 2° P&Y)
CONTROL MOMENT GYROS (3)
CANISTER
EVA ACCESS FOR FILM REMOVAL (1 SIDE)
ELECTRONIC COMPARTMENT

Figure 17.11   The Apollo Telescope Mount (ATM) is a solar observatory equipped to observe, monitor, and record the structure and behavior of the sun, particularly during periods of solar-flare activity. (Courtesy of NASA.)

very-long-base line interferometry; also a radio telescope operating in the longest wavelengths beyond the atmospheric cutoff; (5) continued observations with higher-resolution apparatus of the solar and planetary surfaces from space satellites; and (6) the inclusion of cosmic-ray particles and fields research in the space experiments. One of the major projects mentioned, the large space telescope, is expected to be launched by 1980. Except for the earth-orbiting station and its associated shuttle system, no further American manned space missions after Apollo 17 are planned for the remainder of the 1970's.

Pros and Cons of Space Exploration

Many scientists have questioned whether the manned projects have been worth the costs in returned scientific or technological rewards. They argue that we should proceed in space exploration with reduced emphasis on manned expeditions but with increased reliance on automated and remotely controlled spacecraft in future projects.

There have been various arguments concerning the ultimate value of space research by scientists and nonscientists alike. Each of the following statements was made by a well-respected and distinguished scientist:

If we did not go to the moon, we would be lesser people.

Space exploration is one of man's greatest adventures and the USA must participate with brilliance and boldness.

What has been accomplished with manned exploration is not worth a thousandth part of what has been spent.

The expenditures in putting a man on the moon are scientifically unjustified.

We cannot predict precisely what values this knowledge of space will bring, but men are not going to be satisfied *not* to acquire as much knowledge as they can.

The hope for national prestige does not really adequately support a decision to undertake the exploration of space.

It is a program of the military-industrial complex, which they have frantically attempted to wrap up in the mantle of science to gain prestige and support.

If the preceding quotations sound contradictory, there is, nevertheless, an element of substance in varying degrees in all of the statements. The economic benefits of aerospace spinoffs since the space age began have been largely taken for granted. Space-related achievements include the development of high-speed computers and thermoelectric devices in heating and cooling systems; and substantial improvements in optics, plastics, glassware, epoxy resins, medical technology, miniaturized electronic components, communication equipment, fabrication of hard materials, and many other processes, materials, and devices. It is impossible to predict what the long-range beneficial factors in space-related activities will be upon our national economic and socio-political fabric any more than we can do so for scientific research in general. Imaginative scientific investigations in space can lead to the expansion of man's intellectual growth and to the enrichment of the world's storehouse of scientific knowledge. Such goals are under attack by certain elements in our society. They believe that the space funds, which amount to 0.3–0.5 per cent of the gross national product, should be spent relieving the miseries on earth. Nevertheless, it is not unreasonable to expect that our descendants will honor those spirits who had the vision and courage to venture into the open-ended frontiers of space toward a more enlightened understanding of man and his universe.

REVIEW QUESTIONS

1. What event or events revived modern interest in rockets after their use had been practically abandoned at the end of the nineteenth century?

2. Do you believe that the stated objectives expressed by the President's Advisory Committee are still valid? Explain your answer.

3. How does a rocket work? How is it possible for the rocket to acquire a velocity in excess of the exhaust velocity of the gases?

4. Describe how the Mariner spacecraft is placed in a transfer orbit so that it can rendezvous with Venus or Mars.

5. Why must we employ a multistage rocket instead of a large single-stage rocket in order to launch a spacecraft into orbit?

6. Describe several experiments undertaken in the the Orbiting Solar Observatories.

7. What are the relative advantages of balloons, sounding rockets, and artificial satellites in space exploration?

8. What new celestial information have astronomers accumulated from the Orbiting Astronomical Observatory (OAO-2)?

9. Discuss some of the planetary space projects planned for the coming decade.

10. Debate the pros and cons of the following questions: (a) Is manned space exploration financially justified? (b) Is it scientifically justified? (c) Should we continue to spend less money in the future on space exploration even if the USSR forges ahead of us?

SELECTED READINGS

Clarke, A. C., *Promise of Space,* Harper and Row, 1968.

Ely, L. D., *Space Science for the Layman,* Thomas, 1967.

Hodge, P. W., *The Revolution in Astronomy,* Holiday House, 1970.

Ley, W., *Events in Space,* McKay, 1969.

von Braun, W., *Space Frontier,* Holt, Rinehart, and Winston, 1971.

von Braun, W., and F. I. Ordway III, *History of Rocketry and Space Travel,* Crowell, 1966.

Imaginary creatures on another world propel themselves by ingesting the nutrients from the ambient medium and expelling the waste products in spurts. (From The Planets, *Life Science Library, courtesy of Time-Life, Inc.).*

EXOBIOLOGY:
LIFE ON OTHER WORLDS

Through the vast reaches of space and time, part of the matter of the universe has evolved into living matter, of which a tiny part is in the form of brains capable of intelligent reasoning. As a result, the universe is now able to reflect upon itself. In this respect, at least, the whole evolutionary chain of events is endowed with meaning.

—*Astronomy and Astrophysics for the 1970's,* volume 1, Report of the Astronomy Survey Committee, National Academy of Sciences, 1972

The plurality of habitable worlds is a notion that extends back for centuries. One older idea, known by the name of panspermia, *supposes that the seeds of life are present in the form of micro-organisms in interstellar space, ready to invade any hospitable planet they encounter. The presence of amino acids in the meteorites and the discovery of certain organic molecules in the interstellar clouds cannot by themselves prove that life exists. The possibility of its creation outside the solar system would be enhanced by the discovery of the amino acids among the interstellar compounds. Despite the fact that we have no solid evidence of life in extraterrestrial space, it would be scientifically absurd to deny its existence somewhere in space. Within the decade we should know if any kind of life exists on Mars when an automated biochemical laboratory is deposited on its surface.*

In searching for the most promising stellar life-supporting candidates among the sun's neighbors, we have developed certain criteria of acceptance. Rejected for various reasons are all but the main-sequence, solar-type stars with spectral classes ranging between F2 and K5. On this basis possibly one to ten stars within a distance of one thousand light-years harbor planets that are congenial to higher orders of life. We can only vaguely guess at the evolved forms into which other extrasolar beings have developed. Some scientists have envisioned advanced galactic societies capable of creating artificial automata with integrated brains and computer-directed control over events beyond our imagination to conceive.

18.1 THE CHEMISTRY OF LIFE

Introduction

How did life originate on earth? Are there other habitable worlds? Can we find any clues to the existence of life elsewhere in space? Have we any physical evidence regarding the formation of solar systems? Are they a common occurrence in the universe? These are some of the perplexing questions concerning life that countless generations have wondered about and asked themselves in the past— questions that are closer to being answered than ever before.

Before discussing the prospects of life elsewhere, let us briefly review the process of spontaneous generation that is commonly believed to have led to the establishment of life on our planet through chemical and biological evolution. Though not all biologists unite on all the factors involved in the definition of life, most of them agree that life is different from nonlife in some or all of these vital respects: (1) replication or the ability to reproduce itself; (2) evolution by chance mutation or otherwise; (3) ability to absorb nutrients from the surrounding environment and to extract energy for growth, internal storage, and later utilization; (4) awareness of external environmental conditions and reactions to these conditions; (5) possession of a cellular structure capable of sheltering its internal activities.

The Terrestrial Chemistry of Life

A widely accepted version of the early development of terrestrial life assumes that the earth, at an early stage of its existence, was endowed with a primitive atmosphere consisting of ammonia, methane, water vapor, and perhaps some hydrogen. At a later stage a secondary atmosphere was formed by the outgassing of nitrogen, carbon dioxide, and water vapor from the earth's interior. Synthesized from the primeval and secondary constituents, with the aid of solar ultraviolet radiation, electrical discharges (lightning, etc.), and other energy sources, were the amino acids, the carbohydrates, and the other organic molecules. These atmospheric compounds were washed down by the rains into the warm seas. Here in the beneficial, nourishing "soup," over a long period of time, the more complex organic molecules, the proteins, nucleic acids, polysaccharides, and lipids—the basic ingredients of life—were fashioned into the first living cells. (Refer to Section 5.7 for a review.)

On earth the chemistry of life is based on the element carbon and the solvent water, supplemented with the biologically important atoms of nitrogen, phosphorus, and sulfur. Carbon possesses the property of self-linkage (chain-building) and ease of combination with other biologically significant atoms, namely, hydrogen, oxygen, and nitrogen, to a marked degree. Water with its low viscosity and high liquidity is the ideal solvent in the chemistry of the organic compounds. From water come the hydrogen bonds needed to provide the structural stability within the long strings of proteins, nucleic acids, and other polymers. The watery environment and the moderate temperatures that permitted the carbonaceous molecules to remain stable were the keystone factors in the development and continuance of life on earth. The carbohydrate composition of terrestrial life is revealed in the following statistic: oxygen, 70 per cent; carbon, 18 per cent; hydrogen, 10.5 per cent; others, 1.5 per cent.

It has been theorized that an alternate life chemistry might be based on the element silicon with ammonia as a substitute for water and fluorine gas as a possible replacement for carbon dioxide. However, the versatility of molecular combinations and the physical conditions under which they can exist would be considerably restricted in comparison with carbon and water. In a competing environment, carbon life would eradicate silicon life because of its greater adaptability and flexibility.

In other planetary environments possessing a terrestrial chemistry, life processes would be subject to a number of physical factors. These include the thermal range of the liquidity of water which is dependent on the atmospheric pressure, the stability of organic structures at high temperatures and low atmospheric pressures, the oxygen content, and the salinity of the water. One might set the temperature limits roughly between the freezing and boiling points of water and the pressure limits approximately between almost zero and high oceanic pressures up to about 1,000 earth atmospheres. But it is not likely that any complex organisms could survive at the extreme values quoted. Still, simple organisms and plants do exist on earth in unexpected places and under inhospitable conditions. B. Parker of the Virginia Polytechnic Institute has found evidence of microorganisms thriving within their own ecosystems in terrestrial clouds. It is possible that bacteria and other simple organisms can exist in the harsh Martian environment, in the warmer regions of Jupiter's atmosphere, or in the high-level Venusian clouds but hardly on the torrid surface of Venus where the temperature is 900°F.

18.2 LIFE ELSEWHERE IN THE SOLAR SYSTEM

Discovery of Amino Acids

Of great biological significance was the 1970 discovery of amino acids in a recently fallen (1969) Australian meteorite by C. Ponnamperuma and his colleagues at the Ames Research Center of NASA in California. Extraterrestrial amino acids have since been found in two other meteorites (1971). Only six of the eighteen identified amino acids in the meteorites are found in living cells on earth. The discovered amino acids are almost an equal mixture of "right-" and "left-handed" molecules. "Left-" or "right-handed" refers to the direction of rotation of the plane of polarization when a beam of polarized light passes through the material. The amino acids on earth are left-handed; hence, the finding lends support to the contention that the meteoritic amino acids are of extraterrestrial origin. Since planetary life forms would contain either left- or right-handed amino acids exclusively, it follows that the mixture of both types in the meteorite specimens must be of chemical origin and not of biological origin. It is further concluded, on the basis of the meteorites' ages (4.5 billion years), that the amino acids were present when the earth was formed.

In addition to the amino acids, a number of hydrocarbons were discovered, some similar to those on earth and others of nonbiological origin. The presence of hydrocarbons in meteorites had been reported several years earlier. It was found that a higher proportion of the carbon 13 isotope was present in the Australian meteorite than is known to exist in terrestrial organisms. Table 4.1 reveals that terrestrial carbon 13 is about 1 per cent as plentiful as terrestrial carbon 12.

Martian Life

The thermally habitable zone in the solar system, where life might flourish on a terrestrial type of planet, has been placed between Venus and Mars. The rejection of Venus as a suitable abode because of its high surface temperature leaves Mars as the only candidate for biological exploration. According to a theoretical chemical analysis undertaken by S. I. Rasool and C. de Bergh, if the earth had formed only six million miles closer to the sun, it could have ended up as a hot and sterile planet. This would not be true if the earth had formed farther out from the sun by the same amount.

In August and September 1975, NASA plans to launch two instrumented spacecraft called Vikings to search for life on Mars. Part of each space vehicle will remain in orbit around the planet to explore its atmospheric and surface conditions. The capsule portion, which will contain a biological laboratory, will be detached and make a soft landing on the Martian surface. The biological hunt will be confined mainly to testing for the possible presence of soil microorganisms. Two television cameras will scan the surface periodically to investigate possible activity of the microflora and microfauna that may be present.

One interesting automated experiment involves the inoculation of the Martian soil samples with a rich variety of nutrients to investigate the metabolic processes of the microorganisms. Their respiration products will be monitored and identified by means of various life-detector systems. Employed for this purpose will be analysis of the gas exchange in the atmosphere of the growth medium, gas chromatograph observations of the volatile products of an incubated heated soil sample, and mass spectrometer measurements of the incubated soil species. Radioactive carbon dioxide introduced into the culture medium will be absorbed by the soil organisms and generate radioactive carbon at a rate that is proportional to their reproduction rate, an activity that is easily monitored with a suitable detector. Unfortunately, we do not know the proper growth culture for Martian organisms; they might be killed by the introduction of inappropriate terrestrial nutrients. Whatever the methods of analysis, the results will be telemetered from the capsule back to earth via the orbiting portion of the spacecraft.

The ideal arrangement would be to collect samples and return them to earth for analysis with all the available sophisticated techniques that are carried out with the lunar samples. It is of paramount importance that contamination of the Martian surface by organisms transported from earth be avoided at all costs through adequate sterilization of the spacecraft and its instruments. By the same token, suitable safeguards should be established to prevent back-contamination, that is the introduction outside the testing laboratory of Martian microbes from the samples returned to earth. These precautions were advocated as early as 1959 by a United Nations committee appointed to formulate legal principles to be observed in the exploration of outer space.

In 1970 N. H. Horowitz and his co-workers at the California Institute of Technology found that a laboratory mixture of Martian gases (carbon dioxide, 97 per cent, carbon monoxide and water vapor, 3 per cent), and sterilized soil exposed to ultraviolet radiation yielded three organic compounds extracted from the soil. These were formaldehyde (H_2CO), acetaldehyde (CH_4CO), and glycolic acid ($HOCH_2$-$COOH$). The first two compounds have been discovered in the interstellar clouds of our Galaxy. The results of the experiment may be in conflict with the previously held thesis that the synthesis of organic compounds under primitive planetary conditions requires a reducing atmosphere—that is, one in which the hydrogen reactions predominate.

The excellent pictures returned by the Mars Mariners spacecraft in 1969 and 1971–72 neither proved nor disproved the existence of biological activity on the red planet. By way of comparison, a search was undertaken by Carl Sagan and his co-workers for evidence of life on earth, based on the study of thousands of weather-satellite photographs. Only two positive identifications of human artifacts could be found from heights of several hundred miles: some swaths cut through a forest in Ontario by loggers and a recently completed interstate highway, number 40, in the state of Tennessee.

Life beyond Mars

The search for life in the solar system more distant than Mars appears unrewarding at the present time in the light of our biological ignorance concerning the major planets. In the investigations of the outer planets described in Section 17.5, provisions could be made for the detection of biologically significant substances, presumably in the form of the amino acids and other similarly related organic structures. For example, scientists have speculated on the possible existence of organic molecules within the warmer atmospheric levels of Jupiter which possesses the gaseous compounds necessary for their production.

18.3 LIFE BEYOND THE SOLAR SYSTEM

Introduction

The notion that life may exist on other worlds is not new. Its roots can be traced as far back as the Greek philosophers, many of whom believed in the habitability of other worlds. The concept of extraterrestrial life was greatly expanded, following the remarkable revolution in scientific thought and experimentation that ushered in the seventeenth century, by many eminent scientists and philosophers who advocated the plurality of habitable worlds. In the succeeding centuries, descriptions of extraterrestrial living beings and accounts of their activities began to appear in the works of literature in ever-increasing numbers. Perhaps no book on the subject of extraterrestrial life ever made a greater impression on the general public than Camille Flammarion's popular publication, *On the Plurality of Habitable Worlds*, in the latter half of the nineteenth century. The French astronomer claimed that the planets were created specifically to engender life. Another astronomer whose works gripped the public imagination along the same lines was Percival Lowell, the founder of the Lowell Observatory in Arizona. He observed and wrote extensively about Mars in the belief that the Martian canals had been constructed by a race of intelligent beings in order to transport the water from the melting polar caps toward the equatorial regions for the growth of crops. Two of Lowell's most popular works were entitled *Mars and Its Canals* (1906) and *Mars as an Abode of Life* (1910).

Panspermia

The theory that the seeds of life are eternally present in the universe appears to have gained popular acceptance during the late nineteenth and early twentieth centuries. According to this concept, known as *panspermia* (omnipresent life), living organisms are not spontaneously generated from non-living matter but are transmitted from planet to planet. In 1907 the Swedish chemist S. A. Arrhenius elaborated on the idea further by postulating that microorganisms (spores or bacteria) attached to dust particles were widely dispersed in interstellar space. They were readily available to fertilize any hospitable world they encountered through their wanderings as they were propelled about by the light pressure of the stars. It is difficult to imagine how such isolated organisms floating around in space could survive the radiation hazards of cosmic rays, gamma rays, and other incident shortwave radiation. Perhaps they could find sanctuary deep inside the denser interstellar clouds which could protect them from most external damaging radiation. Still, how the recently discovered organic compounds in the interstellar clouds manage to persist against the odds of dissociation and the radiation hazards remains a mystery (Section 11.3). Caution must be exercised against interpreting the presence of these organic compounds as proof of biological activity rather than as the product of chemical action. In one experiment a gaseous mixture of several interstellar compounds (ammonia, methanol, and formaldehyde or formic acid) was irradiated with ultraviolet light and crystallized into a large number of amino acids. It is noteworthy that amino acids were synthesized without the presence of water. It remains to be seen whether the biology of the earth could have evolved directly from interstellar organic molecules which may have been present on earth initially, or whether it developed from the primitive ingredients mentioned in Section 18.1. An exciting discovery would be the detection of amino acids in interstellar clouds.

Implantation of Living Organisms

A very old idea is that life on earth may have originated from the organisms embedded in fallen meteorites. Having survived the rigors of space, they would now be in a position to thrive and evolve in the receptive environment of the earth. Curiously, one of the organic ingredients existing in the interstellar clouds, formaldehyde, was found in 1972 to be present in the large stone meteorite that fell in northern Mexico in 1969 (Section 8.4).

T. Gold of Cornell University suggested over a decade ago that life on earth could have been transplanted accidentally when space voyagers from a distant planet visited a sterile earth in a remote period. The bacterial organisms within the garbage they left behind found suitable conditions for their growth and expansion into higher organisms. This highly speculative idea became known as the "garbage theory." One is reminded of the great monumental artifact, left behind on the moon by visitors from another world long before the dawn of civilization on earth, awaiting its recovery by a future team of earth scientists as fictionalized in the film *2001, A Space Odyssey*.

Another idea, called *planetary engineering,* under discussion by microbiologists deals with the possibility of implanting terrestrial organisms on potentially suitable sterile worlds. A hypothetical situation might be one in which Mars is seeded with organisms to create plants that could produce enough oxygen to develop a more suitable environment capable of being colonized by man. Implantation may already be a fait accompli among well-advanced interstellar societies who may have succeeded in biologically seeding infertile planets.

Search for Life among the Nearby Stars

If we wished to select those stars in the solar neighborhood where life might exist, how would we proceed? S. S. Huang of Northwestern University has proposed certain criteria that might be employed to look for stars with possible planetary systems.

Binary and multiple stars, which constitute about half of the stellar population, would be ruled out because the orbits of planets around these stars would not be sufficiently stable for them to remain continuously within a thermally habitable zone. Another large stellar group, the hotter stars, would be rejected on the grounds that their lifetimes are too short (less than one billion years) to permit the slow evolutionary biological development of their planets.

The final selection therefore would embrace those main-sequence stars between spectral classes

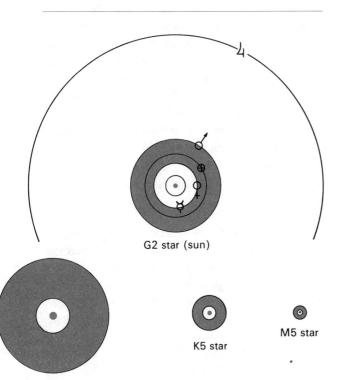

Figure 18.1   Thermally habitable zones around certain stars shown in blue. From (Life Outside the Solar System by Su-Shu Huang). Copyright © 1960 by Scientific American, Inc. All Rights Reserved.

F2 and K5 where the best opportunity of supporting advanced forms of life exists. These stars rotate more slowly than do the hotter main-sequence stars, presumably as a consequence of the transfer of their angular momentum (rotational energy) to the planets during the formation of a planetary system. The habitable zone around the cool, red dwarf stars of spectral class M would be too small and close to the star. A planetary body that near to its parent star might be forced into synchronous rotation with the star so that the same hemisphere would be continuously exposed to it. Consequently, it would be too hot on one side and too cold on the other side to support life. Furthermore, a fraction of the late dwarfs are flare stars whose radiations might endanger life in their vicinity.

Out of 54 stars within five parsecs (16.3 light-years) only three stars meet the prescribed qualifications. These are the main-sequence stars Epsilon Eridani (K2), Epsilon Indi (K5), and Tau Ceti (G8). Three dwarf M-type stars and one component of a visual binary (61 Cygni) have unseen companions; they are excluded on the preceding grounds. One of the single red dwarfs, Barnard's star, has two invisible planetary bodies of approximately Jovian mass revolving in circular orbits with periods of 12 and 26 years well outside the thermally habitable zone of the parent star. The only optical technique presently available in the search for planetary bodies involves photographic measurements over long periods of time. One searches for minute, periodic deviations or irregularities in the stellar proper motions caused by the orbital movements of planets around their stellar primaries. The periodic motion is in reality the movement of the star about the barycenter of the star-planet system. It is discoverable in situations where the mass ratio of planet to star is not insignificant. That was how the planets were detected around Barnard's star by P. van de Kamp (1969) after four decades of photographically checking the proper

South

North

Figure 18.2   The sky motion (proper motion) of Barnard's star. The left image of each pair of field stars, including Barnard's star, was secured one year earlier than the right image. Note that Barnard's star in the center exhibits a change in position (mostly south), whereas the other stars show no evidence of proper motion. The proper motion of Barnard's star has a minute periodic wiggle caused by the presence of its planetary companions as shown in Figure 18.3. (Courtesy of Sproul Observatory, Swarthmore College.)

motion of that star. Its barycentric movement amounts to one ten-thousandth of an inch on the photographic plates (Figure 18.3).

If we adopt the solar neighborhood as a representative sample in which three stars out of 54 within five parsecs have potentially habitable planets, the average distance between the biologically suitable stars turns out to be eighteen light-years. Within a radius of 1,000 light-years, one would expect to find 55 stars possessing suitable planets harboring some

kind of life. Out of that number it is optimistically estimated that at least ten intelligent societies may have evolved.

The optimum biological conditions that would provide the widest latitude for the development of life would be found on those planets endowed with a hydrosphere containing water as a universal solvent and an oxidizing atmosphere with the proper optical windows. On the physical side, too large a planet would retain an oversupply of the reducing gaseous compounds and hydrogen. Too high a surface gravity would require a strong skeletal-supporting structure and might result in sluggish creatures. This kind of reasoning leads to an upper limit of about twice the earth's size as a planet with the best physical requirements. Even if the key molecule, DNA, is present, it is quite possible that the evolved biological species on other planets would be different in many respects from the terrestrial life forms because of the enormous number of chance combinations of nucleotides available in the structure of DNA.

18.4   POSSIBLE FORMS OF EXTRASOLAR LIFE

What Kind of Intelligent Species?

Life in the universe became possible during the course of the expanding universe only after the galaxies had formed and their created stars had existed long enough to synthesize the heavy atoms needed for the production of life. A novel idea advanced by Brandon Carter of Princeton University is that the emergence of life is governed by the choice of the fundamental constants of nature (the velocity of light, c, the gravitational constant, G, and the Planck constant, h). The auspicious period in the evolution of the universe when the biological development is most favorable depends on the values of these universal constants; they determine the properties of matter and radiation which in turn dictate the mechanics of stellar structure and evolu-

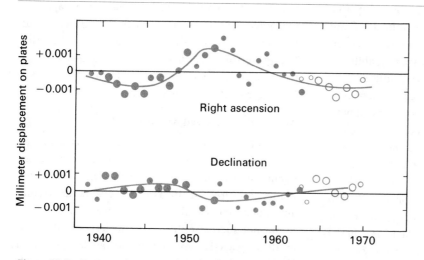

Figure 18.3   Barycentric motion of Barnard's star caused by the presence of one or more invisible, gravitationally disturbing bodies. The size of each dot is proportional to the annual number of plates. The circles represent projected positions since 1963. (Courtesy of P. van de Kamp).

tion that makes life possible. This structuring of life in the universe in accordance with the universal constants of nature has been called the "biological principle."

There are logical reasons for believing that any planetary form of life would stem from autocatalytic chemical reactions that would evolve within the favorable ambient medium into proteinlike structures. In autocatalysis, one of the products in the reaction serves to accelerate the reaction, thus speeding up the whole process of assembly. (In ordinary catalysis, a chemical is involved that speeds up the chemical reaction without being consumed in the reaction.) The amassed configurations in turn would escalate into self-assembled microsystems that would in time develop into primitive multicellular biological organisms. Sophistication in living forms will increase in proportion to their adaptability to react to changes in their environment based upon their ability to store and recall experiences without the time-consuming trial-and-error methods.

It is tempting to think, in view of the universal similarity in the chemical composition of the elements, that DNA may be the ubiquitous molecule that masterminds life elsewhere. Given sufficient time, the flowering of an intelligent species on a suitable planet is fairly certain to develop. But into what forms would such creatures evolve? If we employ the earth as a representative sample, wherein living forms have developed a universality of similar structures, we might suspect that a highly evolved, land-based extrasolar species, also subject to gravity and electromagnetic radiation like ourselves, would inherit some common biological characteristics. It need not resemble man too closely. There are reasons for believing that a marine environment would be less propitious for the development of a superior species. On the other hand, airborne animals of any large size would require too much energy to remain aloft to the detriment of their food-finding abilities.

The evolved intelligent creatures would have to possess a body structure within which a central nervous system operated. They would be equipped with sensory organs not all necessarily like ours. Though they would enjoy the advantages of mobility and manipulative ability, they need not have the same symmetrical appendages as earthlings. There would be an upper biological limit to physical size, for too bulky a creature demands a large energy source for locomotion; in addition, the time taken for a nerve pulse to travel from a remote area of its body to the brain would take too long for the creature to react quickly enough to bodily danger. Very small beings might evolve to a high degree of intelligence if their ancestors were not forced to compete against larger and more powerful adversaries for survival.

Evolutionary Track in Man

Some biologists insist on the "nonrepeatability of evolution." This concept implies that if man were wiped off the face of the earth, nature would not repeat itself in the identical pattern by fashioning another man because, under similar circumstances, the causal chain of evolutionary sequences would be different the second time around. Had the evolutionary chain of events on earth been different, so the argument goes, there would be no *Homo sapiens* as we know him today. Acceptance of this premise leads to the view that extrasolar beings need not possess hominid characteristics.

The great leap forward on earth was accomplished in the last few million years when a humanoid creature learned to walk upright and to free his hands for the delicate manipulation of tools. This made it unnecessary to fight like an animal with his mouth which was set free to develop a vocal appara-

tus. As man's brain evolved and his mental capacities expanded, there developed in time a collective culture and civilization that set him apart from all other living creatures. He has presently reached a social, technical, and scientific plateau from which to embark on extraterrestrial ventures.

Artificially Conceived Automata

Looking into the future, one may visualize an advanced civilization capable of constructing intelligent, self-reproducing automata with integrated brains and directional mastery of events far beyond any computer capabilities that we can imagine. Might not such a sophisticated society already exist in those galactic environs where stellar evolution first began in the halo and central regions of the Galaxy, long before our sun was created? Could an artificially conceived brain concocted by these superintelligent denizens, for example, direct the synthesis of the organic molecules in the interstellar clouds into living cellular structures? To illustrate how far the speculation has gone in this direction, the following paragraph is quoted from *Intelligence in the Universe* by R. A. MacGowan and F. I. Ordway III (Prentice-Hall, 1966) in their chapter on "Extrasolar Intelligence":

> It can be hypothesized that there may be a single superintelligent automaton centrally located in the Galaxy. New automata growing in other parts of the Galaxy may be striving to emigrate to the central brain with maximum speed. This can be expected if integration of automata is technically feasible and always mutually advantageous. If this situation prevails, it would be impossible for us to predict the precise physical characteristics of the centralized galactic super brain.

REVIEW QUESTIONS

1. What elements and environment would constitute the basic ingredients of life on another biologically suitable planet?

2. Discuss the significance of the presence of the amino acids in meteorites; the presence of organic molecules in interstellar space.

3. Describe the plans of NASA to explore the biology of Mars.

4. What is the theory of panspermia? What are the arguments for and against it?

5. Suppose Mars were inadvertently seeded with earth organisms that began to thrive and multiply in the Martian environment. Would that be good or bad? Explain your answer.

6. What are reasonable criteria for selecting a stellar candidate among the sun's neighbors with a suitable habitable zone?

7. How was it shown that Barnard's star has planetary bodies circling it?

8. What can we surmise concerning the possible forms that extrasolar beings might evolve into?

9. What is meant by the "nonrepeatability of evolution"?

10. Discuss the possibility of a life form developing in a silicon-ammonia medium as opposed to a carbon-water medium.

SELECTED READINGS

Allen, T., *The Quest—A Report on Extraterrestrial Life*, Chilton, 1965.

Berendzen, R., ed., *Life Beyond Earth and the Mind of Man*, NASA, Scientific and Technical Information Office, 1973.

Bova, B., *Planets, Life, and LGM (Little Green Men)*, Addisonian, 1970.

Cade, C. M., *Other Worlds Than Ours*, Taplinger, 1967.

Dole, S. H., *Habitable Planets for Man*, American-Elsevier, 1970.

Firsoff, V. A., *Life Beyond the Earth*, Basic Books, 1963.

MacGowan, R. A., and F. I. Ordway III, *Intelligence in the Universe*, Prentice-Hall, 1966.

Moffat, S., and E. A. Shneour, *Life Beyond the Earth*, Four Winds Press, 1966.

Shklovskii, L. S., and C. Sagan, *Intelligent Life in the Universe*, Holden-Day, 1966.

Sullivan, W., *We Are Not Alone*, McGraw-Hill, 1964.

Young, R. S., *Extraterrestrial Biology*, Holt, Rinehart, and Winston, 1966.

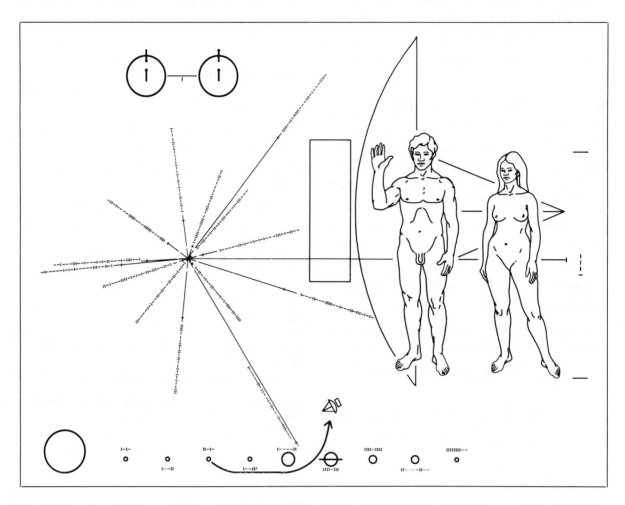

Identification plaque on Pioneer 10. The earth's identification card (designed by Carl Sagan, Linda Sagan, and Frank Drake) is engraved on a 6 × 9-inch, gold-anodized aluminum plate mounted on the skin of Pioneer 10. The message reveals that the hydrogen atom in interstellar space (upper left) emits 21-centimeter radiation, which serves as the connecting link of measurement between ourselves and another society and sets the scale for the human dimensions and those of the spacecraft behind the two figures. The man has his right arm raised in the universal gesture of friendliness. The fourteen diverging radial lines are binary-coded clues to the possibly identifiable pulsars that reveal the time of launch and earth's position in the Galaxy. The long horizontal line extending to the right indicates our distance from the galactic center. The bottom set of circular figures shows that the inhabitants of the third planet from their star launched the spacecraft to sweep by the fifth planet (Jupiter) on its way into interstellar space. (Courtesy of Carl Sagan.)

INTERSTELLAR SPACEFLIGHT
AND COMMUNICATION

There is no easy way to the stars from the earth.

Seneca (c. 3 B.C.–A.D. 65),
Hercules Furens, Act II

The technological and biological difficulties involving interstellar spaceflight appear impossible to overcome. Consider a proposed round-trip space voyage to Tau Ceti, one of the biologically suitable stars about twelve light-years distant, at four-fifths the speed of light. Even though the time-dilation factor is favorable (eighteen years round-trip contracted time), a 100 per cent efficient photon engine would require an initial spaceship weight of 41,000 tons of propellant for a 100-ton payload. The high relativistic speed of the spacecraft through the interstellar medium would also require many tons of outside shielding to minimize the radiation hazards for the ship's occupants. Consequently, the only other means of establishing contacts with other extrasolar societies open to us is through interstellar communication by electromagnetic exchanges of signals.

Attempts to detect extraterrestrial signals go back to the beginning of the century. The last modern effort, known as Project Ozma, took place in 1960 when the 85-foot radio dish at the National Radio Astronomy Observatory in West Virginia failed to detect the presence of artificial signals coming from two prime stellar candidates, Tau Ceti and Epsilon Eridani, about twelve light-years away. Calculations based upon reasonable physical premises hint that there may be at least 100,000 civilizations in our Galaxy capable of interstellar communication.

It has been suggested that since our communicative phase of civilization is only a few decades old we should not attempt to transmit but to listen. Instead we should look for signals leaking out from normal global transmissions of alien worlds. We could also listen for extrasolar signals possibly being transmitted in our direction on frequencies close to that of the natural 21-centimeter radiation of neutral hydrogen (around 1400 megahertz). Advanced societies who are also instrumented in this spectral region for the similar purpose of studying the hydrogen distribution in the Galaxy might be inquiring: "Is there anyone out there?" *Even if interstellar intercourse is established with another galactic civilization, the time interval between the transmission of a message and its received response might be measured in centuries.*

19.1 INSURMOUNTABLE HURDLES OF INTERSTELLAR FLIGHT

Difficulty of Realization

Because of the vast stellar distances, the enormous technological barriers, and the unknown biological factors involved in interstellar flight even to the nearest stars, human space travel seems hopeless of achievement for a long time to come, if at all. Let us begin modestly with a spaceship making a round-trip flight to the nearest star, Alpha Centauri, 4.3 light-years distant, at a constant speed of thirty miles per second. This is slightly more than the velocity needed to escape from the solar system at the earth's distance from the sun. The round-trip journey would last 53,400 years. The only possible recourse is to employ rocketships traveling at speeds that are appreciable fractions of the velocity of light to shorten the trip and to take biological advantage of the time-dilation effect (Section 15.2). Let us re-examine the prospects of a high-velocity trip to Alpha Centauri.

If it were possible to accelerate the spaceship continuously at a constant rate of one g (equivalent to the acceleration we experience on earth), the passengers would experience no great discomfort. The best technique would be to reverse the acceleration half-way out and come to rest in the vicinity of Alpha Centauri; on the return trip accelerate at one g half-way and decelerate at one g toward the earth the rest of the way. The round-trip earth time would be twelve years; the contracted time aboard the spacecraft, which would attain a maximum speed of 95 per cent the velocity of light, would be 7.2 years.

Round-Trip Flight to the Center of the Galaxy

Let us employ the same technique in constantly accelerating to or decelerating from the half-way point at one g for the round-trip spaceflight to the center of the Galaxy (30,000 light-years distant). One finds, according to the mathematics of relativity theory, that it is biologically possible from the aging standpoint. The space travelers would return to earth about forty years older only to discover that it is 50,000 earth years since they departed from the earth. Their maximum speed at the half-way point (15,000 light-years) would be within 0.0000005 per cent of the velocity of light. The power requirements for even less ambitious rocketship interstellar flights are overwhelmingly prohibitive as the following illustration will show.

An Interstellar Flight to Tau Ceti

To demonstrate the insuperable difficulties of interstellar flight at high relativistic speeds, let us investigate the spaceship's power requirements for Dick's round-trip flight to a star twelve light-years away at a rocket speed of four-fifths the velocity of light as described in Section 15.2. The distance chosen is approximately the distance to Tau Ceti, one of the biologically suitable stars referred to in Section 18.3. In optimizing Dick's interstellar flight program we will choose the best energy source possible even though it may never be achieved in practice. The most efficient rocket engine conceivable is a photon rocket powered by the controlled annihilation of equal amounts of matter and antimatter. We now address ourselves to this problem: How much propellant would a rocketship need for a payload weight of 100 tons (about twice the weight of the Apollo moonship) to make a round-trip flight to Tau

Ceti, twelve light-years away, at a speed of 80 per cent the speed of light?

The spaceship will leave the earth at rest velocity and (1) accelerate rapidly to $\frac{4}{5} c$, coasting nearly all the way; then (2) decelerate quickly near the target star and turn around; (3) accelerate rapidly to $\frac{4}{5} c$, coast again during most of the return trip; and finally (4) decelerate quickly near the earth back to zero velocity on earth. Each of these four actions involves a mass ratio of 3.0 : 1.[1] When solved according to relativity mechanics, these four stages call for a total initial spaceship weight of 8,100 tons, all of which except the 100-ton payload is expended by the time Dick returns home thirty earth years later.

There are other physical difficulties besides the large initial tonnage required and the hopeful survival of Dick through the periods of rapid acceleration and deceleration, let alone the biological factors involved. At its maximum speed of 80 per cent the velocity of light, the exposed frontal section of the spaceship will be blasted by about forty million million atoms per second on each square foot even though the interstellar space density, mostly hydrogen, is about one atom per cubic centimeter. This high count arises mainly from the relative velocities of encounter between the moving ship with the atoms and partly from the Lorentz contraction factor, $\sqrt{1 - (v^2/c^2)}$, which decreases the spacing between the atoms. The resultant erosional bombardment is less than the flux of a high-intensity proton accelerator. But it would require concrete shielding material several feet thick to protect the astronaut inside. The total weight of the spaceship therefore becomes only of academic interest. Furthermore, to add to the complications, it would be necessary to employ a duostage, chemical-nuclear combination to launch the spaceship from a point far enough from

---

[1] Mass ratio here is equal to the weight at the start of each action divided by the mass left after each acceleration or deceleration.

the earth. This would avoid radiation damage of the earth from the high-frequency radiation produced by the annihilation of matter which would be comparable to that of nuclear detonations.

If we were to employ the most efficient chemical propulsion system available today for the interstellar flight, the requirements would be beyond belief. Present-day maximum rocket-exhaust velocities are between two and three miles per second. To achieve the final velocity of four-fifths the velocity of light, a one-ton payload would require a propellant weight of $10^{32,000}$ tons! Since the estimated total mass of the universe is $\sim 10^{50}$ tons, the entire proceeding is a mathematical exercise in futility. The conclusion to be drawn from these findings is that close contact with extrasolar beings may not be realized for centuries, if ever. Therefore, the only other stratagem open to us in the foreseeable future is to attempt to establish electromagnetic exchanges with other communicative societies. Assuming that the economical use of power is universally practiced, one may conclude that the least expensive way to engage in interstellar intercourse is by the exchange of long-distance radio signals.

19.2 EXTRATERRESTRIAL COMMUNICATION

In the last decade or so the query: "Are we alone?" has been recast into an affirmative reply: "We are not alone" in space. Yet we have no direct proof of that belief any more than our predecessors had although we have since acquired a few promising leads. Even the uninitiated person, however, and certainly the student who has traveled the road of astronomy so far, doubts that we are the sole intelligent inhabitants of the vast universe. In this day of scientific enlightenment, man has cast aside forever the ancient anthropocentric convictions of his self-inflated, self-centered importance in nature's arena.

Early Attempts at Interplanetary Communication

Before the days of radio communication in the last century, various methods of signaling our presence to other worlds in the solar system had been proposed: huge bonfires in the form of simple geometrical patterns such as squares or triangles; a ten-mile-wide strip of pine forest in Siberia in the form of a right triangle; huge mirrors from which to reflect the sunlight; a twenty-mile, circular ditch filled with water over which kerosense would be poured and set burning; a powerful concave mirror that would focus sunlight on Mars and burn simple numbers in the desert sands of the planet; a network of large mirrors strategically positioned in several European cities to conform to the configuration of the Big Dipper in Ursa Major as a possible sign of intelligence on earth.

In 1899 an eccentric electrical pioneer, Nikola Tesla, constructed a laboratory in Colorado in an abortive attempt to transmit powerful electrical signals into space and to detect any possible replies. His apparatus consisted of a large primary coil 75 feet in diameter and a 200-foot mast topped by a three-foot copper ball. He alternately introduced powerful surges of electricity into the copper ball and into the ground, believing that the earth's magnetic field would increase the power of his signal. Incandescent lights were set glowing 26 miles away but there were no detectable extraterrestrial responses to his efforts at the time, although a year later he claimed to have picked up interplanetary signals.

In 1921 G. Marconi believed that he had detected regular pulsed signals from outer space in the high-meter band while aboard his experimental communication yacht, the Electra. In 1924, when Mars was in close opposition to the earth (35 million miles), David Todd, professor of astronomy at Amherst College, got the U. S. government to turn off its high-powered transmitters for five minutes before every hour between August 21 and August 23. During these five-minute silent periods he used a special receiver tuned between 5 and 6 kilometers[1] to record on tape any signals coming through. He was aided in his efforts by other listeners throughout the country. Out of a melange of dots, dashes, and jumbled code groups, nothing definite could be ascribed to an extraterrestrial source. Todd had earlier proposed that an abandoned mine shaft in Chile be converted into a telescope by filling a 50-foot bowl at the bottom with mercury. The heavy liquid would be set in rotation to form a natural parabolic reflector at whose focus would be positioned a powerful light source to transmit an intense beam of light to Mars when the planet passed overhead. Astronomers duly criticized this arrangement as unworkable. Today's optical systems would utilize lasers for signaling purposes but at the present state of the art they are not powerful enough for extrasolar communication. Recall that laser beams are presently being reflected from special corner reflectors placed on the moon in connection with certain experiments (Section 6.2).

Modern Attempts to Locate Artificial Signals

Following the spectacular improvements in radio-telescope design and observing techniques after World War II, a few astronomers and physicists had begun to entertain privately the feasibility of detecting extrasolar signals from intelligent sources on other worlds. The subject finally surfaced into the open in a British scientific journal, *Nature,* in September 1959 when physicists G. Cocconi and P. Morrison of Cornell University presented logical reasons why some effort should be given to the search for artificial interstellar signals in outer space.

The following year the first and only attempt

[1] It is now known that such long waves are reflected back into space by the ionosphere (Section 4.1, p. 70).

so far in this country to detect artificial signals in space was conducted under the guidance of F. D. Drake at the National Radio Astronomy Observatory at Green Bank, West Virginia. This undertaking was called *Project Ozma* after the legendary princess in the imaginary land of Oz. The 85-foot radio dish was aimed at Tau Ceti and Epsilon Eridani (two prime candidates whose qualifications were discussed in Section 18.3) during 150 hours of unrewarding observing from May through July 1960 (Figure 19.1).

At some future time when radio astronomers, employing more sensitive equipment and improved techniques of reception, have extra hours to spare on a problem whose odds against success are overwhelming, careful listening may once more be resumed out to distances of hundreds or thousands of light-years. In the meantime there remains always the slim chance that we might accidentally: (1) stumble onto artificial signals being randomly directed toward us and other likely targets; (2) intercept signals being exchanged between two other worlds or between a cruising spaceship and its parent planet; (3) pick up signals from an automated probe monitoring our solar system and reporting to its home station, or querying us, or mimicking our communications to gain recognition; and (4) eavesdrop on a galactic network exchanging information among its member societies.

19.3 NUMBERS OF COMMUNICATIVE CIVILIZATIONS

Calculating the Number of Communicative Societies

Let us examine further the possibilities of interstellar communication. It is of interest, in order to appraise our chances of success, to make an intelligent inquiry into the possible number of communicative civilizations within our Galaxy. A communicative society is defined as one that is technologically competent and sufficiently motivated to engage in an interstellar dialogue. A general formula expressing

Figure 19.1   The 85-foot radio telescope and receiving equipment used in Project Ozma (1960). (Courtesy of National Radio Astronomy Observatory.)

the number of such galactic communities in terms of several uncertain factors and probabilities has been developed as follows:

Evolutionary factors → astronomical biological sociological

$$N = \overbrace{n_s \cdot f_s \cdot n_p} \cdot \overbrace{f_b \cdot f_i} \cdot \overbrace{f_c \cdot f_l}$$

where

N = the number of communicative civilizations in the Galaxy.

$n_s = 2 \times 10^{11}$, the estimated number of stars in the Galaxy.

$f_s = 0.1$, the fraction of stars that have developed biologically suitable planetary systems. Ruled out are: (1) the binary and multiple stars which constitute approximately 50 per cent of the stellar population for the reason that the orbital motions of planets would be too complex or unstable to permit the uninterrupted biological development of life; (2) the hotter, more rapidly

rotating stars with lifespans too short to develop biologically active planetary systems, which constitute some 10–15 per cent of the stellar population; (3) the red dwarfs in whose close biospheres the planets would be locked in synchronous rotation with the parent stars and the white dwarfs with their lifeless planets, if any; their combined percentage number is estimated at 25–30 per cent of the total population. That leaves about 10 per cent for the solar-type stars (F–K).

n_p = 1, the number of planets in each planetary system suitable as an abode of life. Such planets must be in the thermally habitable zone surrounding the parent sun where the appropriate physical conditions, temperature, atmosphere, water, etc., are conducive to the support and maintenance of life. In the solar system two such planets, earth and Mars, are inside the life zone. As a conservative figure we estimate one planet per system as the average number with a suitable environment for the germination of life.

f_b = 1, the fraction of congenial planets on which life actually emerges. Let us assume that biological evolution follows the pattern on earth, beginning with an atmospheric mix of methane, ammonia, and water vapor enveloping a warm, watery planet and leading to the production of the amino acids and the subsequent highly complex organic molecular structures that constitute all life processes. The factor f_b may then be set equal to unity on the assumption that life will, under the proper conditions, eventually gain a foothold, flourish, and evolve into a myriad of thriving forms sooner or later.

f_i = 1, the fraction of biological species that evolves into a technically competent culture ultimately capable of engaging in interstellar communication. Given two or three billion years of effort, the probability that nature will create at least one type of intelligent species similar or even superior to *Homo sapiens* is 100 per cent. Hence the factor f_i is set equal to 1.

f_c = 0.5, the fraction of extrasolar societies that are stimulated to attempt interstellar communication. There could exist civilizations not interested in exchanging messages with their fellow space neighbors. Our own interstellar communicative curiosity extends back only several decades during our 6,000 years of civilization. In the absence of any information to the contrary, we will assume that one out of every two competent galactic societies is presently a communicative society. Hence f_c = 0.5.

f_l = 10^{-5}, the ratio of the life expectancy of the communicative species to the biological age of the planet. This is the most uncertain factor of

all to evaluate. Reviewing the possibilities of self-destruction by nuclear holocaust between competing technologies fighting each other for world supremacy, biological disasters occasioned by ill-advised genetic engineering, aberrations in the planet's ecology and climatology resulting from stupidities and blunders, terrestrial and extraterrestrial catastrophes, and other unforeseen calamities befalling a civilized society, one is tempted to predict that the moments of civilized glory may be brief indeed in the lifespan of an intelligent species. There is no assurance that the prevailing good sense of even a superior intelligence will be able to control its own destiny indefinitely. It is not unlikely that there could be a succession of recurring cycles of civilization, each arising Phoenix-like out of the ashes of the preceding civilization during the planet's history. One could optimistically assume a longevity of the communicative phase equal to 300,000 years. Let us be more restrictive by assuming a longevity of 30,000 years which will reduce the number of communicative societies by a factor of ten. Using the earth as a sample on the basis of collected scientific evidence, we take the duration of a habitable planet during its biological stage of development to be three billion years. The factor f_l is therefore equal to the ratio of 30,000 to 3,000,000,000 or 10^{-5}.

Finally, we find the number of communicative, technologically advanced galactic societies to be

$$N = 2 \cdot 10^{11} \cdot 10^{-1} \cdot 1 \cdot 1 \cdot 1 \cdot 0.5 \cdot 10^{-5} = 1 \cdot 10^5$$

We conclude that there ought to be approximately 100,000 civilizations in our Galaxy able and willing to communicate with each other. Not all of them will be within our range, because the time required for a transmitted electromagnetic signal to reach us and for us to reply may exceed the communicative span of an intelligent species. Nevertheless, there should be a sufficient number of communicative societies within reach to make interstellar communication worth a try. Since most of the primordial hydrogen in the Galaxy has already condensed into stars, star formation and its attendant planetary developments are, some fifteen billion years later, proceeding at a decelerated pace.

19.4 COMMUNICATIVE OPTIONS

Shall We Listen or Transmit?

It is more advantageous for us at present to listen for extrasolar signals than for us to transmit them. In our incipient stage of electronic technology it is too impractical for us to inquire, "If there is somebody out there, where are you?" Presumably there are advanced galactic societies with the capabilities and the will to transmit as well as to receive; otherwise, interstellar communication would never materialize. Perhaps the messages that older, more accomplished cultures have been transmitting for centuries have by now reached the solar system. The most advanced celestial communities would avail themselves of energy sources far more sophisticated and powerful than any we can dream of today, perhaps even using the energy output of their parent sun by modulating its light as a method of signaling.

R. N. Bracewell of the Stanford Radio Astronomy Institute has theorized that advanced civilizations might prefer to send automated probes or synthetic intelligent automata to biologically suited solar systems. In this way they might uncover existing technical societies that could engage in conversation with the elaborately computerized automata aboard the visiting probes. The discovery of a technological community could be relayed to the probe's home planet directly or by way of an already existing galactic communicative network. Even if the com-

municative society can overcome the financial drawbacks in undertaking an interstellar search that may not be rewarded for centuries, it will be faced with the problem of selecting the proper targets. The buckshot technique of transmitting or listening in all directions with an isotropic antenna system is useless. The radio-telescope design will be in the form of a large array and will have to possess an extremely sharp beam pattern into which power can be concentrated, permitting it to be aimed precisely at specific stars. Our own chances of reception will be improved at least one hundred thousand times if we can detect signals out to 1,000 light-years compared to ten light-years. To accomplish this purpose, B. M. Oliver, a radio engineer, has proposed the *Project Cyclops,* consisting of a gigantic array of at least 1,000 100-meter dishes spread out over a circular area ten miles wide, costing several billion dollars. Such an installation would be capable of intercepting beamed messages out to 1,000 light-years or detecting the normal "radio leakage" from transmissions broadcast by advanced societies up to distances of 100 light-years.

Proper Choice of Communication Frequencies

The decision as to which microwave spectral region to employ for interstellar discourse is not a difficult one to make. Radio astronomy dictates that a suitable choice of wavelengths lies between three and thirty centimeters where the effects of atmospheric absorption and cosmic background noise are at a minimum. A large radio telescope on the moon, could, of course, cover a much wider spectral range. A logical frequency of universal significance would be in the vicinity of 1,420 MHz (21 cm) which is the emitting frequency of the dark, neutral hydrogen clouds outlining the spiral arms of our Galaxy. Other galactic inhabitants are supposedly conducting similar surveys of the hydrogen distribution. With both our and their receivers tuned to the same spectral region, the receipt of coded transmissions by either side would ensure the best chance of successful detection.

It has been hypothesized that the total output from all the television stations beaming programs from the United States during the last two and one-half decades might be detectable as a point source of radio emission reaching a daily crescendo for a few hours (corresponding to prime terrestrial observing time) at distances up to 25 light-years. In order to locate the signal, a stellar eavesdropper would have to filter out the much stronger radio noise from the sun and Jupiter. Given our receiving equipment, a civilization many thousand light years away could detect signals beamed from the 1,000-foot dish at Arecibo, Puerto Rico. Even if communication were established with another world, it might take centuries to exchange messages. Perhaps the first step we should take in acknowledging the contact with an alien society is to transmit a duplicate of the received message back to the source to inform it that its inquiry has been received and deciphered.

FLASH!

A coded radio message (Figure 19.2) coming from the direction of Epsilon Eridani has been picked up by radio astronomers on a frequency of 1,426 MHz. (Courtesy of B. M. Oliver who composed and interpreted the imaginary message.)

The message consists of a long string of pulses and spaces continually repeated every 22 hours and 53 minutes, evidently the rotation period of the transmitting planet orbiting around Epsilon Eridani. The message was deciphered by substituting the figure "1" for the pulses and "0" for the blanks, similar to the binary code system used in computer processing. The message contains 1,271 entries, the product of two prime numbers, 31 and 41. There are two choices of arranging the groupings: 41 groups horizontally and 31 vertically, or 31 groups horizontally and 41 vertically. The first choice leads to the satisfactory solution presented in Figure 19.3.

We note the configuration of bipeds, a father and mother holding a child between them. The circle of dots at the upper left is their sun; the planets are numbered in code language from one to eight vertically down the left edge. The male primate points to the fourth planet, his home planet. The configuration of dots at the top represents hydrogen 1, carbon 6, and oxygen 8, indicating that life on that planet, like ours, is based on carbohydrate chemistry. The wavy line beginning with planet 3 and the middle, fishlike shape below in the center reveal that it possesses a watery environment with marine life. The creature on the right has her arm upraised toward the binary 6 which denotes the number of fingers and presumably a counting system based on the number 12 in contradistinction to our ten fingers and a duodecimal system. The symmetrical series of dots and spaces in the lower-right portion of the diagram between the head and the foot evidently refers to the size of the bipeds. The horizontal line in the center indicates *eleven* units of some kind. Since the only unit in common between us is the wavelength of 21 centimeters on which the message is transmitted, we conclude that these beings are 21×11 cm $(= 231$ cm$)$ tall or about $7\frac{1}{2}$ feet tall.

Exchange of Knowledge

Once electromagnetic exchanges are instituted between ourselves and a galactic community, it would be possible to transmit all the world's knowledge in a matter of days. Let us estimate that about ten million books have been written by mankind. If the average book contains 250 pages and each page has 2,000 characters, the total volume of man's cultural output equals 5×10^{12} signs. If our language is made up of 100 different symbols which may be represented by slightly less than seven binary digits

```
1000000000000000000000000000000000000000001000011100000000000000100
0000000010001000000001000100000000000000000000000000000000000000010
0010000100000010000000000001000000000000100010000001000100100100010000
0100010001000000001110000000000000100000000000010000000000000000000
000000000000000000000000000000000000000000000000000010000000000010
0010000011000100000000000000000000000000000000000000000000000011000
0110000110000110000110001000000000100100100100100100100100100100010
0101010010010000110000110000110001100001100000000001000000000001
1111010000000000000001000000000000100000100000000000001011011
10010000000000000001111101000000000000000000000000000100000000000
0000001000100111000000000000010100000000000000010100100001100101010
1110010100000000000000010100100001000000000001001000000000000000000
01001000001000000000011111000000000000111110000011101010100000
10101000000000000101010000000100000000000010001010000000010100010
0000000000000000001000100100010001001101100111011011011010010000010010
001010101000100010000000000000001000100010010010010010001000100000
10000000000001110000011111000001110000000011111010000001010101000001
010000010001000000010000000000010000010000111000010000001000001100
000000100000100010001000100000100000100001100001000001000100010010010010
0100000100001100000000011000001101100011011000001100111
```

Figure 19.2   Coded message received from Epsilon Eridani. (Courtesy of B. Oliver.)

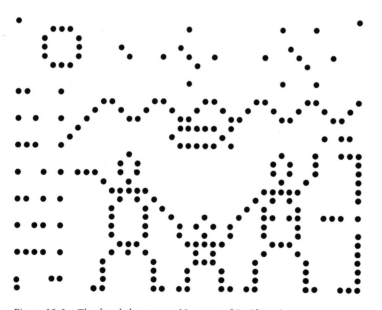

Figure 19.3   The decoded message. (Courtesy of B. Oliver.)

$(2^7 = 128)$ and if each sign were coded in the binary system, the total number of bits to be transmitted amounts to about 4×10^{14} with room to spare for an explanatory preface. A bandpass of 100 MHz centered on 1400 MHz would suffice for the transmission of all of man's works to a distant stellar outpost in about 46 days. Given enough time, social biological, and technological information could be exchanged between ourselves and an older, wiser civilization for the betterment of earthlings who have not yet been able to alleviate their own miseries on the most beautiful planet in the solar system.

REVIEW QUESTIONS

1. Why is interstellar flight such an impossible dream?

2. What advantage does a space voyager gain if he can make a round-trip flight from the earth to another extrasolar world at relativistic speeds?

3. Discuss the early attempts to communicate with extraterrestrial beings.

4. What was Project Ozma? Is it worth trying again today?

5. What is a reasonable guess as to the possible number of communicative societies inhabiting the Galaxy? How is this figure arrived at?

6. Should we try to transmit coded signals to other worlds or should we instead listen for them? Give the reasons for your answer.

7. Explain why the spectral region around 1400 megahertz might be a suitable choice for extrasolar communication.

8. When the pulsars were first discovered, the thought naturally occurred that "little green men" were trying to talk to us. Why was this notion soon abandoned?

9. What are the possibilities that artificial signals may be picked up accidentally?

10. Do you believe that interstellar communication may be going on somewhere in our Galaxy, or do you dismiss this idea as too preposterous for serious discussion?

SELECTED READINGS

Cameron, A. G. W., ed., *Interstellar Communication*, Benjamin, 1963.

Cole, D. W., and R. G. Scarfo, *Beyond Tomorrow*, Amherst Press, 1965.

Kaplan, S. A., ed., *Extraterrestrial Civilizations* (translated from Russian), National Technical Information Service.

MacVey, J., *How We Will Reach the Stars*, Macmillan, 1969.

Sagan, C., ed., *Communication with Extraterrestrial Intelligence*, MIT Press, 1973.

Shklovskii, L. S., and C. Sagan, *Intelligent Life in the Universe*, Holden-Day, 1966.

Cone nebula in Monoceros, photographed in red light with the 200-inch Hale reflector. It is located on the southern fringes of the young star cluster, NGC 2264. (Courtesy of Hale Observatories.)

EPILOGUE

The highest wisdom has but one science—the science of the whole—the science of explaining the whole creation and man's place in it.

Leo Tolstoy (1828–1910)
War and Peace

As a science astronomy has always prided itself on its deep philosophical and cultural values inspired by the search into the cosmic nature of man's origin. Today's astronomy goes much further in illuminating the relationship between our terrestrial existence and our cosmic environment. Astronomy is no longer an "ivory tower" profession engaged in solely by astronomers seeking to unravel the mysteries of the universe. Its ranks have been augmented by scientists from other disciplines presently exploring related new frontiers in exobiology, cosmic chemistry, high-energy astrophysics, and astrogeology, all of which are leading to exciting developments.

Exploration of the universe with new and more powerful kinds of telescopes on earth and in space, together with technological improvements in the recording of observational data, has revealed a universe far more complex and grandiose than we had imagined. The dramatic discoveries that have given us fresh insights into the nature of the universe have also conspired to present us with new cosmic riddles. We have entered what has been called the "golden age of astronomy," which gives promise of more cosmic surprises awaiting discovery in the future.

20.1   IN RETROSPECT

The Emergence of Man

The human species is the product of a long evolutionary experiment that supposedly began with the big bang about eighteen billion years ago. "We are the descendants of the exploding fireball that initiated the present stage of the universe."[1] From the expanding primeval matter that pervaded the early universe were formed the galaxies. Then came

---

[1] Quotation by Princeton physicist J. A. Wheeler. The remainder of the paragraph is the substance of Professor Wheeler's related remarks during a talk given at the Ames Research Center of NASA in July 1971.

the stars. For the development of life and the evolution of man the heavy atoms were necessary. Their synthesis required several billion years of "cooking" time in the stars during the continued expansion of the universe. Had the velocity of expansion been too rapid, the primordial matter within it would have thinned out too quickly for it to condense into galaxies, stars, and finally planets on which life could sustain itself. Had the expansion been too slow, the universe would have collapsed before life had a chance to develop anywhere. The universe evolved the way it did because we are here!

Man has begun to lift the veil of mystery surrounding his particular occupancy on the third planet in the order of distance from his parent star, which glows in near isolated splendor in the outskirts of the vast stellar organization that he calls the Galaxy. The everlasting questions concerning the basic universal laws of nature, the evolution of the solar system and of the universe, and the riddle of life are closer to being answered than ever before.

Man's Place in the Universe

Where does *Homo sapiens* stand in the universal hierarchy? Let us compare man with the enormous range of values exhibited by different objects throughout the universe (Table 20.1).

Role of Man

The history of man's pursuit toward a better understanding of himself and his environment, de-emphasizing his centralized role in the universe along the way, has been marked by a number of epoch-making changes. These have come about as a result of man's discovery of certain scientific truths— but not without struggle, hostile opposition, and even martyrdom against the popularly held views of his time. The changes wrought in man's social order and in his mode of life as a consequence of these developments have been infinitely more lasting and

Table 20.1 Universal Range of Matter, Time, and Energy

(a) Object	Diameter
Proton or electron	10^{-13} cm
Atom	10^{-8} cm
MAN (height)	180 cm
Neutron star	2.5×10^6 cm
Earth	1.3×10^9 cm
Sun	$\begin{cases}1.4 \times 10^{11}\text{ cm} \\ 4.7\text{ light-sec}\end{cases}$
Galaxy	1×10^5 light-yr
Universe	$\sim 4 \times 10^{10}$ light-yr

(b) Object	Distance from Earth
MAN	0 cm
Moon	$\begin{cases}3.8 \times 10^{10}\text{ cm} \\ 1.37\text{ light-sec}\end{cases}$
Sun	$\begin{cases}1.5 \times 10^{13}\text{ cm} \\ 8.3\text{ light-min}\end{cases}$
Nearest star	4.3 light-yr
Nearest galaxy	1.6×10^5 light-yr
Farthest observable object (quasar)	$\sim 15 \times 10^9$ light-yr

(c) Object	Mass (grams)
Electron	9×10^{-28}
Hydrogen atom	1.7×10^{-24}
DNA molecule	$\sim 10^{-17}$
MAN	7×10^4
Mountain	$\sim 10^{11}$
Earth	6×10^{27}
Sun	2×10^{33}
Galaxy	4×10^{44}
Observable universe	$\sim 10^{53}$
Entire universe	$\sim 10^{56}$

(d) Object	Average Density (g/cm³)
Universe (smeared-out density)	$\sim 10^{-30}$
Galaxy (smeared-out density)	$\sim 10^{-23}$
Supergiant star	10^{-7}
MAN	~ 1
Sun	1.4
White dwarf	10^5
Neutron star	10^{14}
Black hole	$> 10^{15}$

(e) Object	Time (sec)
Mean lifetime of neutral pion	10^{-16}
Period of vibration of radio wave from broadcast station	10^{-6}
MAN's heart beat	1
One day	8.6×10^4
One year	3.2×10^7
MAN'S lifespan	10^9
MAN on earth	10^{14}
Age of earth	1.5×10^{17}
Age of universe since big bang	$\sim 6 \times 10^{17}$

(f) Object	Energy (ergs)
Molecule at room temperature	6×10^{-14}
Particle at sun's center	10^{-9}
Fly in motion	10^4
MAN walking	10^8
Ton of coal burned	10^{17}
One-megaton H-bomb	4×10^{22}
Strong earthquake	$\sim 10^{27}$
Sun's output in one day	3×10^{39}
Supernova (total)	10^{49}
Quasar (during estimated life of one million years)	10^{60}

beneficial to the human experience than any achieved by violence and physical conquests.

Perhaps the most significant and ennobling scientific influences that have elevated the human spirit and upgraded man's material welfare have been:

—the Copernican revolution which displaced the earth as the center of the universe

—the discovery of the law of gravitation followed by the great experimentalists and mathematicians who developed the powerful analytical tools that have created our present technological civilization

—the Darwinian biological revolution which altered man's concept of himself as the center of the living terrestrial world

—the theory of relativity and the laws governing the behavior and structure of matter which have provided a deeper insight into the enigma of the cosmos on both the microscopic and the macroscopic scale

—the biochemical revolution involving the recognition of the basic molecular processes that bind all terrestrial life in the unifying signature of the genetic code

—the exploration of outer space—man's grandest adventure—whose ultimate consequences to the human race cannot yet be foretold

20.2   IN PROSPECT

Unsolved Riddles in Our Galaxy

In spite of impressive advancements in our understanding of cosmic phenomena, many major parts of the cosmic puzzle are still unclear. Included among these perplexities within our own Galaxy are:

—the origin and durability of interstellar organic molecules

—the exact chemical composition of interstellar dust grains

—the clarification of the initial stages of stellar evolution up to the main sequence and the terminating evolutionary developments beyond the horizontal branch of the H-R diagram

—the precise mechanisms involved in the explosions of the supernovae and their relationship to the neutron stars and the pulsars

—the internal physical conditions and composition of the pulsars together with the precise mode of pulsed-energy production

—the possible existence of black holes

—the nature of the recently discovered x-ray stars and other x-ray sources, and the diffuse x-ray background radiation

—the inflow and outflow of circulatory material within the Galaxy

—the formation and preservation of the spiral arms of the Galaxy

—the correct structural model of the Galaxy

Unsolved Riddles in Extragalactic Space

In the deeper reaches of space problems still awaiting satisfactory solutions include:

—the nature and role of the quasars, the radio galaxies, and the overactive galaxies in the evolutionary development of the universe, and their high-energy sources

—the formation and evolution of the clusters of galaxies as well as the individual galaxies

—the proper distributions of the galaxies and their types throughout space

—the mystery of the hidden intergalactic matter

—the origin of the big bang (if it did indeed occur)

—the possible nonuniformity in the expansion of the universe

—the kind of universe we live in, and whether it is closed or open

Conclusion

Though man may resolve older questions he must expect also to encounter new enigmas and strange discoveries in the distant future as he sharpens his reasoning powers, improves his measuring probes and techniques, and widens his horizon of percep-tion. He has already set foot on one of the prize bodies in the solar system, the moon. Because of its relatively unchanging nature during the past several billion years, it has begun to yield a few tantalizing clues on the origin of the earth-moon system and, in fact, on the early history of the solar system. In the future, man will look longingly beyond the solar system toward the stars. Will they be out of reach forever?

It is most fitting that we end our exploration of the cosmos by quoting A. S. Eddington's final remarks from his classic book, *Space, Time, and Gravitation* (Cambridge University Press, 1920):

We have found a strange foot-print on the shores of the unknown. We have devised profound theories, one after another, to account for its origin. At last, we have succeeded in reconstructing the creature that made the foot-print. Lo! it is our own. (NASA)

APPENDICES

APPENDIX 1   SCIENTIFIC NUMBER NOTATION

Powers of Ten

Word	Number	Power	Prefix
trillion	1,000,000,000,000	10^{12}	tera
billion	1,000,000,000	10^9	giga
million	1,000,000	10^6	mega
thousand	1,000	10^3	kilo
hundred	100	10^2	hecto
ten	10	10^1	deca
unit	1	10^0	
tenth	0.1	10^{-1}	deci
hundredth	0.01	10^{-2}	centi
thousandth	0.001	10^{-3}	milli
millionth	0.000,001	10^{-6}	micro
billionth	0.000,000,001	10^{-9}	nano
trillionth	0.000,000,000,001	10^{-12}	pico

Illustrative Examples

The arithmetical operations involving very large and very small numbers are simplified by means of a few easy rules as revealed in the following examples:

1. $584,000 = 584 \times 10^3 = 58.4 \times 10^4 = 5.84 \times 10^5 = 0.584 \times 10^6$ etc.

2. $0.00000485 = 485 \times 10^{-8} = 48.5 \times 10^{-7} = 4.85 \times 10^{-6} = 0.485 \times 10^{-5}$ etc.

Operations with Powers of Ten

1. Multiplication (add exponents):
$$10^{-3} \times 10^2 \times 10^4 = 10^{-3+2+4} = 10^3$$

2. Division (subtract exponents):
$$\frac{10^4}{10^2} = 10^{4-2} = 10^2$$

3. Raising power or extracting root (multiply exponents): $(10^2)^5 = 10^{10}$; $(10^{-2})^4 = 10^{-8}$; $(10^{-10})^{\frac{1}{2}} = 10^{-5}$

Complete Examples

1. $$\frac{(4 \times 10^2)^2}{2 \times 10^4} = \frac{4^2 \times 10^4}{2 \times 10^4} = \frac{16}{2} \times 10^0 = 8$$

2. $$\frac{(64 \times 10^{-2})^{\frac{1}{2}}}{\sqrt{16 \times 0.02}} = \frac{64^{\frac{1}{2}} \times 10^{-1}}{4 \times 2 \times 10^{-2}} =$$
$$\frac{\sqrt{64} \times 10^1}{8} = \frac{8}{8} \times 10^1 = 10$$

3. $$\frac{0.662 \times 2,400,000}{0.0007 \times 120}$$
$$= \frac{6.62 \times 10^{-1} \times 2.4 \times 10^6}{7 \times 10^{-4} \times 1.2 \times 10^2}$$
$$= \frac{6.62 \times 2.4 \times 10^5}{7 \times 1.2 \times 10^{-2}} = 18,914$$

APPENDIX 2   SIMPLE ALGEBRAIC OPERATIONS

Mathematical Symbols

$\propto$	proportional to	$>$	greater than
$\approx$	very nearly equal to	$<$	less than
$\sim$	roughly or approximately equal to	$=$	equals

Ratio and Proportion

1. $y \propto x$ means: y is proportional to x, or y varies directly as x

2. $L \propto 1/d^2$ means: L is inversely proportional to the square of d, or L varies inversely as the square of d

3. $F \propto M \cdot m/r^2$ means: F varies directly as the product of M and m and inversely as the square of r

4. The proportionality sign $\propto$ is removed by introducing a constant of proportionality. Thus in the above examples:

$$y = cx \qquad L = \frac{k}{d^2} \qquad F = \frac{GMm}{r^2}$$

5. The following are different forms of the same quantities:

$$pv = RT, \; p = \frac{RT}{v}, \; v = \frac{RT}{p}, \; T = \frac{pv}{R}, \; \frac{p}{R} = \frac{T}{v}, \; \frac{v}{R} = \frac{T}{p}$$

Transposition of Terms

Reverse the sign of the term when transposing it to the other side of an equation. Examples:

1. $20x - 5 = 10x + 15$ transposed reads $20x - 10x = 15 + 5$ or $10x = 20$; hence $x = 20/10 = 2$

2. $6t - 55 + 9 = 41 - 2t + 9$ or $6t + 2t = 41 + 9 + 55 - 9$ or $8t = 96$; hence $t = 96/8 = 12$

Units of Length
Table 1

Unit	km	m	cm	μ	Å	in	ft	mi
1 kilometer (km) =	1	1000	10^5	10^9	10^{13}	39,370	3280.83	0.6214
1 meter (m) =	0.001	1	100	10^6	10^{10}	39.37	3.28083	6.214×10^{-4}
1 centimeter (cm) =	10^{-5}	0.01	1	10^4	10^8	0.3937	0.03281	6.214×10^{-6}
1 micron (μ) =	10^{-9}	10^{-6}	0.0001	1	10^4	2.54×10^4	—	—
1 angstrom (Å) =	10^{-13}	10^{-10}	10^{-8}	10^{-4}	1	3.937×10^{-9}	—	—
1 inch (in) =	2.54×10^{-5}	0.0254	2.54	2.54×10^4	3.937×10^7	1	0.08333	1.58×10^{-5}
1 foot (ft) =	3.05×10^{-4}	0.3048	30.48	—	—	12	1	1.89×10^{-9}
1 mile (mi) =	1.60934	1609.34	160,934	—	—	63,360	5280	1

Table 2

Unit	pc	L.Y.	A.U.	km	cm	mi
1 parsec (pc) =	1	3.2617	206,265	3.0857×10^{13}	3.0857×10^{18}	1.917×10^{13}
1 light-year (LY) =	0.3066	1	63,240	9.4605×10^{12}	9.4605×10^{17}	5.878×10^{12}
1 astronomical unit (AU) =	4.848×10^{-6}	1.582×10^{-5}	1	1.446×10^8	1.496×10^{13}	9.2956×10^7

Units of Mass
Table 3

Unit	g	kg	mt	oz	lb	st
1 gram (g) =	1	10^{-3}	10^{-6}	.0353	2.2046×10^{-3}	—
1 kilogram (kg) =	10^3	1	10^{-3}	—	2.2046	1.1023×10^{-3}
1 metric ton (mt) =	10^6	10^3	1	—	2204.62	1.10231
1 ounce (oz) =	28.35	—	—	1	0.0625	—
1 pound (lb) =	453.6	0.4536	—	16	1	0.0005
1 short ton (st) =	9.072×10^5	907.185	0.9072	—	2000	1

Examples of Unit Rates

1. 0.1 gram per cubic centimeter = 0.1 g/cm^3

2. 200 miles per second = 200 mi/sec = 200 mps

3. 1/1,000 pound per square inch = 0.001 lb/in^2

4. 32 feet per second per second = 32 ft/sec/sec = 32 ft/sec^2

5. 100 ergs per square centimeter per second = 100 erg/cm^2 · sec or 100 erg/cm^2/sec

APPENDIX 4   SCIENTIFIC CONSTANTS; CONVERSION FACTORS; ARC MEASUREMENT; GEOMETRICAL RELATIONS

Physical Constants

Quantity	Symbol	Value
Velocity of light in vacuum	c	2.998×10^{10} cm/sec[a]
Gravitational constant	G	6.667×10^{-8} cm³/g·sec²
Planck's constant	h	6.625×10^{-27} erg·sec
Mass of hydrogen atom	m_H	1.673×10^{-24} g
Mass of proton	m_p	1.6725×10^{-24} g
Mass of electron	m_e	9.109×10^{-28} g

[a] The latest measured value (1972) is 299,792,456.2 ± 1.1 meters/sec.

Astronomical Constants

Object or Quantity	Value
Mass of earth	5.977×10^{27} g
Mean radius of earth	6.371×10^8 cm
Mass of sun	1.989×10^{33} g
Radius of sun	6.960×10^{10} cm
Solar luminosity	3.85×10^{33} erg/sec
Astronomical unit	1.49598×10^{13} cm
One sidereal year	365.256 days = 3.156×10^7 sec

Conversion Factors

These units are defined in the Glossary, Appendix 16.

1 angstrom (1 Å)	$= 10^{-8}$ cm
1 calorie	$= 4.185 \times 10^7$ ergs
1 electron volt (ev)	$= 1.602 \times 10^{-12}$ erg
1 erg	$= 1$ g·cm²/sec²
1 kilowatt-hour (kw-hr)	$= 3.6 \times 10^{13}$ ergs
1 photon (energy)	$= 1.986 \times 10^{-8}$ erg/Å
1 watt	$= 10^7$ erg/sec

Arc Measurement

One circle contains 360 degrees (360°)

one degree
$(1°)$ = sixty minutes of arc $(60')$

one minute of arc
$(1')$ = sixty seconds of arc $(60'')$.

Geometrical Relations

1. Area A of a circle of radius r or diameter d:

$$A = \pi r^2 = 3.14r^2 = \pi d^2/4 = 0.785d^2$$

2. Circumference C of a circle of radius r or diameter d:

$$C = 2\pi r = 0.628r = \pi d = 3.14d$$

3. Surface area S of a sphere of radius r:

$$S = 4\pi r^2 = 12.57r^2$$

4. Volume V of a sphere of radius r:

$$V = 4/3\ \pi r^3 = 4.19r^3$$

Temperature Scales

All molecular motions stop at lowest possible temperature.

Conversions between Temperature Scales

1. $F = 9/5\ C + 32 = 9/5\ K - 460$

2. $C = 5/9\ (F - 32) = K - 273$

3. $K = 5/9\ (F + 460) = C + 273$

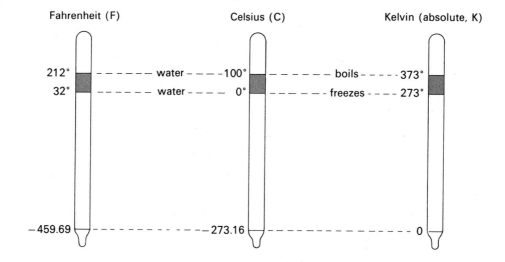

APPENDIX 5   GREEK ALPHABET

alpha:	A	α	iota:	I	ι	rho:	P	ρ
beta:	B	β	kappa:	K	κ	sigma:	Σ	σ
gamma:	Γ	γ	lambda:	Λ	λ	tau:	T	τ
delta:	Δ	δ	mu:	M	μ	upsilon:	Υ	υ
epsilon:	E	ε	nu:	N	ν	phi:	Φ	ϕ
zeta:	Z	ζ	xi:	Ξ	ξ	chi:	X	χ
eta:	H	η	omicron:	O	o	psi:	Ψ	ψ
theta:	Θ	θ	pi:	Π	π	omega:	Ω	ω

Atomic Number	Element	Symbol	Atomic Weight	Atomic Number	Element	Symbol	Atomic Weight
1	Hydrogen	H	1.008	44	Ruthenium	Ru	101.07
2	Helium	He	4.003	45	Rhodium	Rh	102.905
3	Lithium	Li	6.939	46	Palladium	Pd	106.4
4	Beryllium	Be	9.012	47	Silver	Ag	107.868
5	Boron	B	10.811	48	Cadmium	Cd	112.40
6	Carbon	C	12.011	49	Indium	In	114.82
7	Nitrogen	N	14.007	50	Tin	Sn	118.69
8	Oxygen	O	16.000	51	Antimony	Sb	121.75
9	Fluorine	F	18.998	52	Tellurium	Tc	127.60
10	Neon	Ne	20.179	53	Iodine	I	126.904
11	Sodium	Na	22.990	54	Xenon	Xe	131.30
12	Magnesium	Mg	24.305	55	Cesium	Cs	132.90
13	Aluminum	Al	26.981	56	Barium	Ba	137.34
14	Silicon	Si	28.086	57	Lanthanum	La	138.91
15	Phosphorus	P	30.974	58	Cerium	Ce	140.12
16	Sulfur	S	32.064	59	Praseodymium	Pr	140.91
17	Chlorine	Cl	35.453	60	Neodymium	Nd	144.24
18	Argon	A	39.948	61	Promethium	Pm	(145)
19	Potassium	K	39.102	62	Samarium	Sm	150.35
20	Calcium	Ca	40.08	63	Europium	Eu	151.96
21	Scandium	Sc	44.956	64	Gadolinium	Gd	157.25
22	Titanium	Ti	47.90	65	Terbium	Tb	158.92
23	Vanadium	V	50.941	66	Dysprosium	Dy	162.50
24	Chromium	Cr	51.996	67	Holmium	Ho	164.93
25	Manganese	Mn	54.938	68	Erbium	Er	167.25
26	Iron	Fe	55.847	69	Thulium	Tm	168.93
27	Cobalt	Co	58.933	70	Ytterbium	Yb	173.04
28	Nickel	Ni	58.71	71	Lutetium	Lu	174.97
29	Copper	Cu	63.546	72	Hafnium	Hf	178.49
30	Zinc	Zn	65.38	73	Tantalum	Ta	180.95
31	Gallium	Ga	69.72	74	Tungsten	W	183.85
32	Germanium	Ge	72.59	75	Rhenium	Re	186.2
33	Arsenic	As	74.922	76	Osmium	Os	190.2
34	Selenium	Se	78.96	77	Iridium	Ir	192.22
35	Bromine	Br	79.904	78	Platinum	Pt	195.09
36	Krypton	Kr	83.80	79	Gold	Au	196.97
37	Rubidium	Rb	85.47	80	Mercury	Hg	200.59
38	Strontium	Sr	87.62	81	Thallium	T1	204.37
39	Yttrium	Y	88.905	82	Lead	Pb	207.19
40	Zirconium	Zr	91.22	83	Bismuth	Bi	208.98
41	Niobium	Nb	92.906	84	Polonium	Po	(209)
42	Molybdenum	Mo	95.94	85	Astatine	At	(210)
43	Technetium	Tc	98.906	86	Radon	Rn	(222)

When atomic weight is not accurately known, the weight of the most stable isotope is given in parentheses.

Atomic Number	Element	Symbol	Atomic Weight	Atomic Number	Element	Symbol	Atomic Weight
87	Francium	Fr	(223)	97	Berkelium	Bk	(247)
88	Radium	Ra	226.02	98	Californium	Cf	(251)
89	Actinium	Ac	(227)	99	Einsteinium	Es	(254)
90	Thorium	Th	232.04	100	Fermium	Fm	(257)
91	Proactinium	Pa	231.04	101	Mendelevium	Md	(256)
92	Uranium	U	238.03	102	Nobelium	No	(254)
93	Neptunium	Np	237.05	103	Lawrencium	Lr	(257)
94	Plutonium	Pu	239.05	104	Rutherfordium	Rf	(259)
95	Americium	Am	(243)	105	Hahnium	Ha	(260)
96	Curium	Cm	(247)				

APPENDIX 7   WORLD'S LARGEST OBSERVATORIES

Reflecting Telescopes

Observatory	Aperture (inches)	Completed or Under Construction (UC)
Zelenchakskaya, Caucasus, USSR	236	UC (1974)
Hale, Mt. Palomar, Calif.	200	1948
Kitt Peak National, Ariz.	158	1973
Inter-American, Cerro Tololo, La Serena, Chile	158	UC (1974)
Siding Spring, New South Wales, Australia	150	UC (1974)
French Pyrenees	144	UC
European Southern, La Silla, Chile	144	UC
Lick, Mt. Hamilton, Calif.	120	1959

Refracting Telescopes

Observatory	Aperture (inches)	Year Completed
Yerkes, Williams Bay, Wisc.	40	1897
Lick, Mt. Hamilton, Calif.	36	1888
Paris, France	33	1896
Astrophysical, Potsdam, Germany	31.5[a]	1899
Allegheny, Pittsburgh, Pa.	30	1914
Mt. Gros, Nice, France	30	1887
Pulkovo, Leningrad, USSR	30	1886

[a] Half of twin-mounted telescope; other half is 20-inch refractor.

Schmidt Telescopes

Observatory	Aperture (inches)	Completed or Under Construction (UC)
Tautenberg, Thuringen, Germany	53 (80″ mirror)	1960
Siding Spring, New South Wales, Australia	49.5 (72″ mirror)	UC (1973)
Mt. Palomar, Calif.	49 (72″ mirror)	1948
European Southern, La Silla, Chile	39.4 (64″ mirror)	1973
Uccle, Belgium	33 (46″ mirror)	1958
Hamburg, Germany	32 (47″ mirror)	1955

Steerable Radio Telescopes

Observatory	Aperture of Dish (feet)	Year Completed
Max Planck Institute, Germany	326	1970
National Radio Astronomy, W. Va.[b]	300	1962
Jodrell Bank, England	250	1957
CSIRO, Parkes, Australia	210	1961
Jet Propulsion Laboratory, Goldstone, Calif.	210	1966

[b] Movable in north-south elevation only.

Fixed Radio Telescope

Observatory: NAIC, Arecibo, Puerto Rico
Aperture of spherical dish: 1,000 feet
Year completed: 1963

Radio Interferometers

Observatory	Configuration	Completed or Under Construction (UC)
National Radio Astronomy, Datil, New Mexico	Nine 82-ft. diam. dishes along each branch of a Y configuration; overall dimensions, 26 miles	UC
University of Sydney, Fleurs, New South Wales, Australia	Crossed array in N-S and E-W directions; each array has 32 25-ft. diam. dishes and is one-fourth mile long	UC
Mullard Radio, Cambridge, England	Eight 42-ft. diam. dishes in line, 3.1 miles long	1972
Westerbork, Holland	Twelve 66-ft. diam. dishes in line, one mile long	1971
Stanford Radio Astronomy Institute, Stanford, Calif.	Five 60-ft. diam. dishes in line, 675 feet long	1971
National Radio Astronomy, Green Bank, West Virginia	Three 85-ft, diam. dishes in line, 1.4 miles long	1965
Mullard Radio, Cambridge, England	Three 60-ft. diam. dishes in line, one mile long	1964

Multi-element Radio Antenna Structures

Observatory	Overall Dimensions	Completed
University of Sydney, Canberra, Australia (Mills Cross telescope)	Two crossed-wire mesh arms each one mile long	1965
Simferopol, Crimea, U.S.S.R.	1600 × 1600 feet	1964
Mullard Radio, Cambridge, England	1500 × 66 feet	1958
Meudon, Nancy, France	1000 × 115 feet	1963
Vermillion River, University of Illinois, Danville, Illinois	600 × 400 feet	1962
Lebedev Physics Institute, Serpuhkov, U.S.S.R.	328 × 131 feet (2)	1963
Ohio State University, Delaware, Ohio	340 × 70 feet	1961

Data	Mercury	♀ Venus	⊕ Earth	♂ Mars	♃ Jupiter	♄ Saturn	♅ Uranus	♆ Neptune	♇ Pluto
Orbital Data									
Distance from sun (AU)	0.387	0.723	1.00	1.52	5.20	9.54	19.18	30.06	39.44
Sidereal period (yrs)	0.241	0.615	1.00	1.88	11.86	29.46	84.01	164.79	247.69
Synodic period (days)	115.9	224.7	—	779.9	398.9	378.1	369.7	367.5	366.7
Inclination of orbit to ecliptic	7.0°	3.4°	0.0°	1.85°	1.3°	2.5°	0.8°	1.8°	17.2°
Orbital eccentricity	0.206	0.007	0.017	0.093	0.048	0.056	0.047	0.009	0.250
Average orbital velocity (mi/sec)	29.7	21.7	18.5	15 0	8.1	6.0	4.2	3.4	2.9
Physical Data									
Diameter (earth units)	0.38	0.95	1.00	0.53	11.04	9.17	3.79	3.85	0.50
Mass (earth units)	0.05	0.82	1.00	0.11	318.0	95.1	14.5	17.3	0.11
Mean density (g/cm^3)	5.2	5.2	5.5	4.0	1.3	0.7	1.6	1.7	4.9
Rotation period	59^d	243^d	23.94^h	24.62^h	9.84^h	10.23^h	10.8^h	16^h	6.4^d
Surface gravity (earth units)	0.39	0.91	1.00	0.38	2.64	1.13	1.01	1.17	0.44
Inclination of equator to orbit	?	1°	23.45°	25.2°	3.1°	26.7°	82°	29°	?
Oblateness	0	0	0.003	0.005	0.067	0.105	0.007	0.025	0
Velocity of escape (mi/sec)	2.67	6.40	6.95	3.27	35.7	22.0	13.5	14.3	3.3
Albedo	0.06	0.75	0.39	0.15	0.50	0.50	0.66	0.62	low
Solar energy received (earth units)	6.7	1.91	1.00	0.043	0.037	0.011	0.003	0.001	0.0006
Approximate mean temperature (°F)	600	850	+55	−60	−190	−230	−345	−360	−400
Atmospheric gases observed (principal constituents in blue)	—	CO_2, O_2, HCL, CO, HF O, NH_3, N_2	N_2, O_2, CO_2, H_2O, A, O_3, etc.	CO_2, H_2O, H, O, O_2, CO, C, N_2, O_3	CH_4, NH_3, H_2	CH_4, NH_3, H_2	CH_4, H_2	CH_4, H_2	—

Planet and Satellite	Average Distance from Planet (mi)	Period of Revolution (days)	Orbital Eccentricity	Diameter (mi)	Discoverer	Year
Earth						
Moon	238,860	27.32	0.055	2,160		
Mars						
Phobos	5,825	0.32	0.021	14	A. Hall	1877
Deimos	14,580	1.26	0.003	7	A. Hall	1877
Jupiter						
V. Amalthea	112,000	0.50	0.003	70	E. Barnard	1892
I Io	261,900	1.77	0.000	2,290	Galileo	1610
II Europa	416,600	3.55	0.000	1,790	Galileo	1610
III Ganymede	664,600	7.16	0.002	3,120	Galileo	1610
IV Callisto	1,169,000	16.69	0.008	2,770	Galileo	1610
VI Hestia	7,130,000	250.6	0.158	60?	C. Perrine	1904
VII Hera	7,290,000	259.6	0.207	20?	C. Perrine	1905
X Demeter	7,350,000	263.5	0.130	10?	S. Nicholson	1938
XII Adrastria[a]	13,000,000	625	0.169	10?	S. Nicholson	1951
XI Pan[a]	14,300,000	714	0.207	15?	S. Nicholson	1938
VIII Poseidon[a]	14,600,000	735	0.378	30?	P. Melotte	1908
IX Hades[a]	14,700,000	758	0.275	15?	S. Nicholson	1914
Saturn						
X Janus	99,100	0.75		200	A. Dollfus	1966
I Mimas	115,200	0.94	0.020	300?	W. Herschel	1789
II Enceladus	147,700	1.37	0.004	350?	W. Herschel	1789
III Tethys	182,900	1.89	0.000	630	G. Cassini	1684
IV Dione	234,300	2.74	0.002	550	G. Cassini	1684
V Rhea	327,100	4.52	0.001	810	G. Cassini	1672
VI Titan	758,400	15.94	0.029	2,980	C. Huyghens	1655
VII Hyperion	918,700	21.26	0.104	200?	W. Bond	1848
VIII Iapetus	2,210,000	79.32	0.028	700?	G. Cassini	1671
IX. Phoebe[a]	8,040,000	550.37	0.163	150?	W. Pickering	1898
Uranus						
V Miranda	80,700	1.41	0.000	200	G. Kuiper	1948
I Ariel	119,100	2.52	0.003	500	W. Lassell	1851
II Umbriel	165,900	4.14	0.004	400	W. Lassell	1851
III Titania	272,100	8.71	0.002	700	W. Herschel	1787
IV Oberon	363,900	13.46	0.001	600	W. Herschel	1787
Neptune						
Triton[a]	219,500	5.88	0.000	2,300	W. Lassell	1846
Nereid	3,461,000	359.42	0.750	200?	G. Kuiper	1949

[a]Retrograde motion.

Designation	Distance (LY)	Proper Motion (sec of arc)	Radial Velocity (km/sec)	Apparent Visual Magnitude[a] A	B	Visual Luminosity[a] (sun = 1) A	B	Spectral Type[a] A	B	Remarks
Sun				−26.81		1.0		G2V		
Alpha Centauri	4.3	3.68	−23	0.00	+1.4	1.3	0.36	G2V	K5V	b
Barnard's star	6.0	10.30	−108	+9.54		0.0004		M5V		c
Wolf 359	7.7	4.84	+13	+13.66		0.00001		M6eV		d
Lalande 21185	8.3	4.78	−86	+7.47		0.005		M2V		e
Sirius	8.7	1.32	−8	−1.42	+8.7	20	0.0017	A1V	wd	f
Luyten 726-8	9.0	3.32	+29	+12.5	+12.9	0.00006	0.00004	M5.5eV	M6eV	g
Ross 154	9.6	0.67	−4	+10.6		0.00037		M4.5eV		d
Ross 248	10.3	1.58	−81	+12.24		0.00010		M5.5eV		d
Epsilon Eridani	10.8	0.97	+15	+3.73		0.27		K2V		h
Luyten 789-6	10.9	3.27	−60	+12.58		0.00008		M5.5eV		d
Ross 128	10.9	1.36	−13	+11.13		0.00005		M5V		
61 Cygni	11.1	5.22	−64	+5.19	+6.02	0.073	0.034	K5V	K7V	i
Procyon	11.3	1.25	−3	+0.38	+10.7	6.7	0.0005	FIV-V	wd	j
Epsilon Indi	11.4	4.67	−40	+4.73		0.12		K5V		
BD +43˚44	11.7	2.91	+18	+8.07	+11.04	0.0058	0.00037	M2.5eV	M4eV	k
Σ 2398	11.7	2.29	+8	+8.90	+9.69	0.0064	0.0013	M4V	M5V	l
Tau Ceti	11.9	1.92	−16	+3.50		0.39		G8Vp		m
CD −36˚15693	11.9	6.87	+10	+7.39		0.011		M2V		
BD +5˚1668	12.3	3.73	+26	+9.82		0.0013		M4V		
CD −39˚14192	12.8	3.46	+21	+6.72		0.024		M0V		

[a]A = brighter component; B = fainter component.

[b]AB system is visual binary, period 80 years; a third member is Proxima, 2.2° away: apparent magnitude, +10.68; luminosity, 0.00007; spectral type, M5eV (flare star).

[c]Has two invisible planetary bodies circling it in periods of 12 and 26 years; masses 0.8 and 1.1 Jupiter's mass, respectively.

[d]Flare star; e signifies bright lines present in spectrum.

[e]Unseen companion, period about 8 years.

[f]The wd signifies white dwarf; visual binary, period 50 years.

[g]Visual binary, period may be about 50 years.

[h]An invisible body, several times the mass of Jupiter, circles it in a period of 25 years.

[i]Visual binary, period about 720 years; has unseen component.

[j]Visual binary, period 41 years.

[k]Visual binary, component A is a spectroscopic binary.

[l]Visual binary.

[m]The p signifies spectrum peculiarity.

Star	Bayer Designation	Right Ascension (1965)	Declination (1965)	Trig. Parallax	Distance (LY)	Proper Motion (″)	Radial Velocity (km/sec)	Visual Magnitude A	Visual Magnitude B	Visual Luminosity (sun = 1) A	Visual Luminosity (sun = 1) B	Spectral Type A	Spectral Type B	Remarks
Sirius	α CMa	6h43m.6	−16°40′	+0″374	8.7	1.32	− 7.6 var	−1.42 var	+ 8.7	20	0.002	A1 V	wd	a
Canopus	α Car	6 23 .2	−52 41	0.017	100	0.02	+20.5	−0.72		1300:		F0 Ib-II		
Rigil Kent	α Cen	14 37 .2	−60 42	0.754	4.3	3.68	−22.7 var	+0.01	1.4	1.3	0.36	G2 V	K5V	b
Arcturus	α Boo	14 14 .1	+19 22	0.090	36	2.28	− 5.2	−0.06		100		K2 IIIp		
Vega	α Lyr	18 35 .8	+38 45	0.123	26	0.34	−13.9	+0.04		50		A0 V		
Capella	α Aur	5 14 .1	+45 58	0.073	45	0.41	+30.2 S	+0.05	10.2	75:	60:	G5 III:	M IV	c
Rigel	β Ori	5 12 .9	− 8 14	0.004	900:	0.00	+20.7 var	+0.14 var	6.6	50000:	100:	B8 Ia	B9	d
Procyon	α CMi	7 37 .5	+ 5 19	0.283	11.5	1.25	− 3.2	+0.37	10.7	6.7	0.001	F5 IV-V	wd	e
Betelgeuse	α Ori	5 53 .3	+ 7 24	0.005	500:	0.03	+21.0 var	+0.41 var		13000:		M2 Iab		
Achernar	α Eri	1 36 .4	−57 25	0.023	120:	0.10	+19	+0.51		600:		B5 V		
Hadar	β Cen	14 01 .3	−60 12	0.002	500:	0.04	−12 S	+0.63	4	9000:	400:	B1 III		f
Altair	α Aql	19 49 .1	+ 8 46	0.194	16.8	0.66	−26.3	+0.77		9.8		A7 IV-V		
Acrux	α Cru	12 24 .6	−62 54	—	400:	0.04	− 6	+1.39	1.9	3000:	1700:	B1 IV	B3	g
Aldebaran	α Tau	4 33 .9	+16 26	0.048	68	0.20	+54.1	+0.86 var	13	150	0.002	K5 III	M2 V	h
Spica	α Vir	13 23 .3	−10 59	0.019	230:	0.05	+ 1.0S	+0.91 var		250:	?	B1 V		i
Antares	α Sco	16 27 .3	−26 21	0.019	500:	0.03	− 3.2 var	+0.92 var	5.1	8000:	170:	M2 Ib	B4e V	j
Pollux	β Gem	7 43 .2	+28 07	0.093	35	0.62	+ 3.3	+1.16		30		K0 III		
Fomalhaut	α PsA	22 55 .7	−29 48	+0.144	23	0.37	+ 6.5	+1.19	6.5	12	0.09	A3 V	K4 V	k
Deneb	α Cyg	20 40 .2	+45 09	−0.013	1600:	0.00	− 4.6 var	+1.26		50000:		A2 Ia		
—	β Cru	12 45 .7	−59 30	—	500:	0.05	+20 var	+1.28 var ?		5000:		B0 IV		l

Note: Values in **bold-face type** are obtained directly from the trigonometric parallaxes; all others are derived from the spectroscopic luminosities. Spectral types are on the Morgan-Keenan (Yerkes) system. Roman numerals following the type indicate the luminosity class, as: Ia, bright supergiant; Ib, less luminous supergiant; II, bright giant; III, giant; IV, subgiant; V, dwarf. In column 8 a value followed by S is the center-of-mass velocity of a spectroscopic binary system; one followed by "var" is the mean velocity for a star whose radial velocity varies but probably not as a result of orbital motion in a binary system.

*a*α CMa: The orbital period of the visual binary is 50 years.

*b*α Cen: The orbital period of the AB system is 80 years. Component C, Proxima Centauri, is 2.°2 distant. It is a flare star (V645 Cen) of type dMe, visual magnitude 10.68, and visual luminosity 0.00007.

*c*α Aur: The spectrum of Capella is composite. The two stars form a spectroscopic binary with a period of 104 days. The distant companion II (12′ from the bright star) is a physical companion. It is itself a close binary of visual magnitudes 10.2 and 13.7, and corresponding luminosities 0.012 and 0.0005

*d*β Ori: Component B is a spectroscopic binary with a period of 10 days and both stars are B9; it has been suspected of being a close visual binary.

*e*α CMi: On the basis of its mass and magnitude, the companion is a white dwarf. The spectrum has been observed. The orbital period is 41 years.

*f*β Cen: The separation of the two stars is 1″.

*g*α Cru: The separation of AB is now about 4.5″; both components are spectroscopic binaries. The mean radial velocities of the two systems are −11.2 and −0.6 km/sec respectively. Another star, C, mag 5.3 and type B4, is 202″ distant but is not a physical member of the system.

*h*α Tau: Component B is 30″ from A.

*i*α Vir: The star is a spectroscopic binary with a period of 4.0 days. Shallow eclipses of about 0.1 mag have been observed.

*j*α Sco: The companion is about 3″ from A.

*k*α PsA: The companion, HR8721, is 2° from the bright star.

*l*β Cru: The star is a variable of the β CMa type with a period of approximately 4 hours.

Source: Compiled from data furnished by C. E. Worley in Leaflet No. 431, Astronomical Society of the Pacific, May 1965.

Latin Name	Latin Genitive	Abbreviation	English Equivalent	When Visible in Evening[a]	First-Magnitude Stars
Andromeda	Andromedae	And	Andromeda	Aut, win, *N*, S	
Antlia	Antliae	Ant	Air pump	Spr, N, *S*	
Apus	Apodis	Aps	Bird of paradise	Year, S	
Aquarius	Aquarii	Aqr	Water bearer	Aut, N, S	
Aquila	Aquilae	Aql	Eagle	Sum, N, S	Altair
Ara	Arae	Ara	Altar	Year, S	
Aries	Arietis	Ari	Ram	Aut, win, N, S	
Auriga	Aurigae	Aur	Charioteer	Win, *N*, S	Capella
Boötes	Boötis	Boo	Herdsman	Sum, N, S	Arcturus
Caelum	Caeli	Cae	Chisel	Win, N, *S*	
Camelopardus	Camelopardis	Cam	Giraffe	Year, S	
Cancer	Cancri	Cnc	Crab	Win, spr, N, S	
Canes Venatici	Canum Venaticorum	CVn	Hunting dogs	Spr, *N*, S	
Canis Major	Canis Majoris	CMa	Large dog	Win, N, S	Sirius
Canis Minor	Canis Minoris	CMi	Small dog	Win, N, S	Procyon
Capricornus	Capricorni	Cap	Sea goat	Aut, N, S	
Carina	Carinae	Car	Keel of Argonauts' ship	Year, S	Canopus
Cassiopeia	Cassiopeiae	Cas	Cassiopeia	Year, N	
Centaurus	Centauri	Cen	Centaur	Spr, N, *S*	Alpha & Beta Centauri
Cepheus	Cephei	Cep	Cepheus	Year, N	
Cetus	Ceti	Cet	Sea monster	Aut, win, N, S	
Chamaeleon	Chamaeleontis	Cha	Chameleon	Year, S	
Circinus	Circini	Cir	Compasses	Year, S	
Columba	Columbae	Col	Dove	Win, N, *S*	
Coma Berenices	Comae Berenices	Com	Berenice's hair	Spr, N, S	
Corona Australis	Coronae Australis	CrA	Southern crown	Sum, N, *S*	
Corona Borealis	Coronae Borealis	CrB	Northern crown	Sum, N, S	
Corvus	Corvi	Crv	Crow	Spr, N, S	
Crater	Crateris	Crt	Cup	Spr, N, S	
Crux	Crucis	Cru	Cross (southern)	Year, S	Acrux & Beta Crucis
Cygnus	Cygni	Cyg	Swan	Sum, aut, *N*, S	Deneb
Delphinus	Delphini	Del	Dolphin	Aut, N, S	
Dorado	Doradus	Dor	Swordfish	Year, S	
Draco	Draconis	Dra	Dragon	Year, N	
Equuleus	Equulei	Equ	Little horse	Aut, N, S	
Eridanus	Eridani	Eri	River	Win, N, S	Achernar
Fornax	Fornacis	For	Furnace	Win, N, S	
Gemini	Geminorum	Gem	Twins	Win, N, S	Pollux
Grus	Gruis	Gru	Crane	Aut, N, *S*	
Hercules	Herculis	Her	Hercules	Sum, N, S	
Horologium	Horologii	Hor	Clock	Year, S	
Hydra	Hydrae	Hya	Sea serpent	Spr, N, S	

[a] In temperate zones around mid-latitude 35° north or south: N, visible in north temperate zone; S, visible in south temperate zone; *N*, most favorable for northern viewers (higher in sky); *S*, most favorable for southern viewers (higher in sky). The designation "year" means visible above horizon all year round at latitude 35° N or 35° S. All or nearly all the constellations are visible in the equatorial (torrid) zone during part of the year. Only the constellations approximately north of declination 24° S or south of declination 24° N are visible in the northern or southern latitudes respectively in the frigid zones.

Latin Name	Latin Genitive	Abbreviation	English Equivalent	When Visible in Evening[a]	First-Magnitude Stars
Hydrus	Hydri	Hyi	Water snake	Year, S	
Indus	Indi	Ind	Indian	Year, S	
Lacerta	Lacertae	Lac	Lizard	Aut, *N*, S	
Leo	Leonis	Leo	Lion	Spr, N, S	Regulus
Leo Minor	Leonis Minoris	LMi	Little lion	Spr, *N*, S	
Lepus	Leporis	Lep	Hare	Win, N, S	
Libra	Librae	Lib	Scales	Sum, N, S	
Lupus	Lupi	Lup	Wolf	Sum, N, *S*	
Lynx	Lyncis	Lyn	Lynx	Win, spr, *N*, S	
Lyra	Lyrae	Lyr	Lyre	Sum, aut, *N*, S	Vega
Mensa	Mensae	Men	Table mountain	Year, S	
Microscopium	Microscopii	Mic	Microscope	Sum, aut, N, *S*	
Monoceros	Monocerotis	Mon	Unicorn	Win, N, S	
Musca	Muscae	Mus	Fly	Year, S	
Norma	Normae	Nor	Level	Sum, N, *S*	
Octans	Octantis	Oct	Octant	Year, S	
Ophiuchus	Ophiuchi	Oph	Serpent bearer	Sum, N, S	
Orion	Orionis	Ori	Orion	Win, N, S	Rigel & Betelgeuse
Pavo	Pavonis	Pav	Peacock	Year, S	
Pegasus	Pegasi	Peg	Winged horse	Aut, N, S	
Perseus	Persei	Per	Perseus	Aut, win, *N*, S	
Phoenix	Phoenicis	Phe	Phoenix	Aut, N, *S*	
Pictor	Pictoris	Pic	Easel	Year, S	
Pisces	Piscium	Psc	Fishes	Aut, N, S	
Piscis Austrinus	Piscis Austrini	PsA	Southern fish	Aut, N, S	Fomalhaut
Puppis	Puppis	Pup	Stern of Argonauts' ship	Win, N, *S*	
Pyxis	Pyxidis	Pyx	Compass of Argonauts' ship	Spr, N, S	
Reticulum	Reticuli	Ret	Net	Year, S	
Sagitta	Sagittae	Sge	Arrow	Sum, aut, N, S	
Sagittarius	Sagittarii	Sgr	Archer	Sum, N, S	
Scorpius	Scorpii	Sco	Scorpion	Sum, N, *S*	Antares
Sculptor	Sculptoris	Scl	Sculptor's shop	Aut, N, S	
Scutum	Scuti	Sct	Shield	Sum, N, S	
Serpens	Serpentis	Ser	Serpent	Sum, N, S	
Sextans	Sextantis	Sex	Sextant	Spr, N, S	
Taurus	Tauri	Tau	Bull	Win, N, S	Aldebaran
Telescopium	Telescopii	Tel	Telescope	Sum, N, *S*	
Triangulum	Trianguli	Tri	Triangle	Aut, win, N, S	
Triangulum Australe	Trianguli Australis	TrA	Southern triangle	Year, S	
Tucana	Tucanae	Tuc	Toucan	Year, S	
Ursa Major	Ursae Majoris	UMa	Great bear	Year, N	
Ursa Minor	Ursae Minoris	UMi	Small bear	Year, N	
Vela	Velorum	Vel	Sail of Argonauts' ship	Spr, N, *S*	
Virgo	Virginis	Vir	Virgin	Spr, N, S	Spica
Volans	Voltantis	Vol	Flying fish	Year, S	
Vulpecula	Vulpeculae	Vul	Fox	Sum, aut, N, S	

APPENDIX 13   OWNING YOUR OWN TELESCOPE

Observing through a telescope the craters and mountains of the moon, the changing phases of Venus, the belts of Jupiter and the motions of its satellites, the rings of Saturn, the sunspots, the Orion nebula, the Pleiades open star cluster, the Hercules globular cluster, the double star Castor, the Andromeda galaxy, and a host of other wondrous heavenly sights is a source of never-ending pleasure. Many thousands of lay persons who have made their own telescopes or bought them find skygazing a fascinating hobby.

Your investment in a telescope should be carefully considered in view of your particular requirements. This involves the amount of money you wish to spend, the size, type, and quality of the instrument, and how often and where it will be used. It is recommended before making any purchase that you seek advice from any of the following sources that may be in your locality: amateur astronomy club, astronomy hobby store, staff members of a planetarium, or an astronomy teacher. Useful information on telescopes, kits, and their parts can be gleaned from the telescope advertisements in *Sky and Telescope* magazine and in the Edmund science catalog which is freely available by writing to Edmund Scientific Co., Barrington, N. J. 08007.

For amateur use a reflecting telescope is generally preferable to a refracting telescope. A 4-inch refractor, for example, costs several times more than a 4-inch reflector. A 6-inch reflector would be a satisfactory choice for good overall optical viewing. For those who are mechanically inclined and wish to build their own telescope, the saving in cost is about one-half the cost of the least expensive 6-inch reflector on the market (about $200, 1973 prices).

The standard 6-inch Newtonian reflector has a tube length of several feet and possesses a fairly heavy equatorial mounting tripod for good stability. There are several very lightweight Schmidt-Casse-grain telescopes of excellent quality available at a considerably higher cost. Their lightness and short tube length renders them easily transportable to good viewing sites outside the population centers with their annoying sky pollution problems.

The following references should be helpful in obtaining and using a telescope.

Telescope Information

1. *Sky and Telescope* magazine (available in libraries).

2. Edmund catalog (free); Edmund Scientific Co., Barrington, N. J. 08007.

3. *Making Your Own Telescope*, by A. J. Thompson; Sky Publishing Corp., Cambridge, Mass. 02138 (1947).

4. *Telescopes for Skygazing*, by H. E. Paul; American Photographic Book Publishing Co., New York (1965).

5. *Telescopes; How to Make and Use Them*, by T. Page and L. W. Page; Macmillan, New York (1966).

6. *Standard Handbook for Telescope Making*, by N. E. Howard; Thos. Y. Crowell Co., New York (1959).

7. *All About Telescopes*, by Sam Brown; Edmund Scientific Co., Barrington, N. J. 08007. Additional information in inexpensive brochures may be obtained from the same company. Consult the Edmund catalog.

Locating Celestial Bodies

1. *Celestial Objects for the Common Telescope*, two volumes in paperback edition, by T. W. Webb; Dover Publications, New York (1962).

2. *A Field Guide to the Stars and Planets*, by D. H. Menzel; Houghton Mifflin Co., Boston (1964).

3. *A Beginner's Guide to the Skies*, by R. N. Mayall and H. W. Mayall; G. P. Putnam's Sons, New York (1960).

4. *Stargazing with Telescope and Camera*, by G. T. Keene; H. W. Wilson Co., New York (1962).

References

The following reference sources probably will be consulted most frequently:

1. Books: *Subject Guide to Books in Print; Paper Bound Books in Print*, plus monthly supplement, *The Month Ahead; Book Review Digest; Technical Book Review Index; Essay and General Literature Index* (extracts from books); *Science Books* (quarterly, published by the American Association for the Advancement of Science); *A Guide to Science Reading* (paperback), H. J. Deason, editor (contains bibliography of over 1,300 paperbound books in science; every student should have this inexpensive copy).

2. Periodicals (magazines, journals, and newspaper articles): *Readers' Guide to Periodical Literature; Social Sciences and Humanities Index; Book Review Index* (periodicals); *New York Times Index* (newspaper articles); *Applied Science and Technology Index; Science for Society* (an excellent bibliographical source containing pertinent books and periodical references, published by the American Association for the Advancement of Science, 1970).

3. Almanacs and yearbooks: *Information Please Almanac; New York Times and Encyclopedic Almanac; World Almanac and Book of Facts.*

4. Encyclopedias: *Chamber's Encyclopedia; Collier's Encyclopedia; Columbia Encyclopedia; Encyclopedia Americana; Encyclopedia Britannica; The New Popular Science Encyclopedia of the Sciences,* published by Popular Science editors.

5. Science dictionaries: *McGraw-Hill Encyclopedia of Science and Technology; Van Nostrand's Scientific Encyclopedia; Dictionary of Astronomical Terms* (paperback), A. Wallenquist, American Museum Science Books, 1966.

6. Biographical dictionaries: *Biography Index; Current Biography; American Men of Science; World's Who in Science.*

Essay Material and Projects

The listed bibliographic material is helpful but not necessarily complete. The student is encouraged to use the reference sources described in the preceding section.

1. Keep a scrapbook or file of items of astronomical interest that appear in the newspapers and periodicals. Comment on the new developments and discoveries that may be in conflict with the statements in the textbook or not included in the book. It is suggested that you turn in the collected material for examination by your instructor at the end of the term. (He may find some new information that he can use in his class.)

2. Inquire among your classmates and professors as to the reality of the schism existing between the nonscientific and scientific elements in our society. Compare the viewpoints of the liberal-arts students with the science and engineering students. Report on the attitudes among students concerning the relative merits of the science-technology establishment and the nonscience humanistic community.

3. Take a poll among the students to determine what proportion of them are true believers in astrology, what proportion treat it as a harmless pastime, and what proportion ridicule it as nonsensical. Also consult the card-catalog file in your public library to determine the relative number of books carried on astrology and astronomy. (Of course, your college library would not be expected to house any books dealing with the practice of astrology.) Discuss your findings and if you find an upsurge in astrology, how do you account for it?

4. Can you identify the astronomical bodies referred to in these quotations? (Extra credit if you locate the sources.)

"sovereign mistress of the true melancholy"—Shakespeare

"of this great world both eye and soul"—Milton

"this majestical roof fretted with golden fire"—Shakespeare

"golden fruit upon a tree all out of reach"—G. Eliot

"a seat where the gods might dwell"—Milton

"the governess of the floods"—Shakespeare

"maker of sweet poets"—Keats

"that orbèd continent, the fire that severs day from night"—Shakespeare

"that orbèd maiden with the white fire laden"—Shelley

"the God of life and poesy and light"—Byron

"the forget-me-nots of the angels"—Longfellow

"a corpse upon the road of night"—Sir Richard Burton

5. Take a closer look at the purported polarization that exists between the humanistic and scientific worlds as propounded by the authors whose works appear below. Prepare a summary of their views.

The Two Cultures and the Scientific Revolution, C. P. Snow, Cambridge University Press, 1959; *The Two Cultures and a Second Look,* C. P. Snow, Cambridge University Press, 1969; *Two Cultures? The Significance of C. P. Snow,* F. R. Leavis, Random House, 1963; *Science and the Shabby Curate of Poetry* (Essays about the Two Cultures), Martin Green, Norton, 1965; *The Making of a Counter Culture.* Theodore Roszak, Doubleday, 1969.

6. Science has been criticized as arrogant, cocksure, unresponsive to the social order, an elitist profession, self-worshiping, indifferent to the humanistic tradition, pontifical, and doctrinaire. Would you agree with any of these pronouncements? Amplify your remarks.

Source material: *Science Is a Sacred Cow,* Anthony Standen, Dutton, 1950; *Science Is Not Enough,* Vannevar Bush, Morrow, 1967; *The Role of Science in Civilization,* R. B. Lindsay, Harper and Row, 1963 (Chapter 3: Science and the Humanities); *Personal Knowledge,* Michael Polanyi, University of Chicago Press, 1958; *Science and Culture,* Gerald Holton, editor, Houghton Mifflin, 1965; *Where the Wasteland Ends,* Theodore Roszak, Doubleday, 1972; *Social Control and the Uses of Science,* Nigel Calder, Simon, 1970.

7. Suppose all astronomical research were to cease by having astronomers suspend their operations for the remainder of the century. Can you predict what the short- or long-range consequences would be upon society? Would it matter much to the majority of the world's population? To the humanistic world? To you personally?

8. Many more students have read Shakespeare's *Macbeth* than have studied Kepler's laws of planetary motion. Both great men published their work at about the same time. Elaborate on the influences each one has had upon our culture and civilization. Whose work, in your opinion, has had the more profound effect on the quality of modern life?

9. Present the scientific arguments in favor of the plurality of habitable worlds. Is it in conflict with the religious beliefs of any faith? Despite the fact that we have no direct evidence of intelligent life elsewhere, is there any reason to doubt its existence?

10. There are three excellent science-fiction novels whose titles bear the name *Andromeda,* one of the well-known constellations. All of them involve the ultimate security of life on this planet. The books are:

A for Andromeda, Fred Hoyle, Harper, 1962. (Strange signals from the direction of Andromeda contain scientific information unknown to man and imperil life on earth.)

Andromeda Breakthrough, Fred Hoyle and John Elliot, Harper and Row, 1965. (Concerns an alien, computer-created girl named Andromeda and her involvement with British scientists trying to prevent the earth from being destroyed by an unknown force that is jeopardizing life on earth.)

The Andromeda Strain, Michael Crichton, Knopf, 1969. (A world biological crisis ensues when a mysterious capsule containing lethal microorganisms lands in Arizona and causes widespread deaths while frantic scientists search for an antidote.)

You are asked to read one of Hoyle's two works and the novel by Crichton and to comment on the books' scientific plausibility, the authors' writing style, and to level any criticism, good or bad, that you as a reviewer wish to present.

11. Two of the world's greatest scientists possessed contrasting personalities: Newton and Einstein. Compare Newton's personal behavior with that of Einstein, their views on science, ethics, religion, philosophy, and their lives in general.

Source material (Newton): *Isaac Newton*, I. Bernard Cohen, *Scientific American*, December 1957, page 73; *Newton: His Life and Work*, E. N. Andrade, Doubleday, 1958; *Isaac Newton: A Biography*, Louis T. More, Dover, 1934; *Isaac Newton*, John D. North, Oxford University Press, 1967; *A Portrait of Isaac Newton*, Frank E. Manuel, Harvard University Press, 1968.

Source material (Einstein): *Out of My Later Years*, Albert Einstein, Littlefield, 1950; *Einstein: His Life and Times*, Phillip Frank, Knopf, 1953; *Albert Einstein*, Leopold Infeld, Scribner, 1950; *Albert Einstein: Creator and Rebel*, B. Hoffman, Viking, 1972; *Einstein; The Life and Times*, Ronald W. Clark, World, 1971.

12. There are several popular astronomy periodicals and pamphlets published in the United States and one in Canada on a monthly or bimonthly basis:

Sky and Telescope, Sky Publishing Corp., Cambridge, Mass.; *The Griffith Observer*, Griffith Observatory, Los Angeles, Calif.; *Mercury*, Astronomical Society of the Pacific, c/o California Academy of Sciences, San Francisco, Calif.; *Modern Astronomy*, Buffalo, N.Y.; *Astronomy*, Milwaukee, Wisc.; *The Journal of the Royal Astronomical Society of Canada*, Toronto, Canada.

Your task is to examine carefully the past several issues of each of the above publications your library possesses and to submit a report on the informational character and general excellence of the articles, irrespective of the format and general attractiveness of the publication.

13. Do you believe that a conflict may exist between modern cosmological theories of the universe and a person's deep religious beliefs? Is it possible to reconcile the apparently contradictory viewpoints between the Biblical and scientific explanations of genesis? Are you affected personally by any doubts on the matter?

14. Stonehenge consists of a large system of half a dozen concentric circles of stones or holes whose ruins rest on England's Salisbury Plain. Mainly through the research of astronomer Gerald S. Hawkins it is now known that Stonehenge served as an astronomical observatory at least 3,000 years ago. Write an account of its use in ancient times and how Professor Hawkins helped to unlock the secrets of Stonehenge.

Source material: *Stonehenge Decoded*, G. S. Hawkins and J. B. White, Doubleday, 1965; *Stonehenge*, R. J. C. Atkinson, Pelican Books, London, 1960; *Mystery of Stonehenge*, F. M. Branley, Crowell, 1969.

15. What discovery or concept in the history of astronomy, in your judgment, has had the most profound influence upon our present civilization? If you think there has been no single unique effect

but that several significant astronomical developments have been involved, give the reasons for your answer.

16. There are many allusions to the stars, comets, planets (benign or evil), and other astronomical reminders in Shakespeare's plays and Milton's poetry. Some of them are famous quotations. Quote the references that you can find in their works.

17. Kepler was one of the most imaginative and interesting scientists who ever lived. He managed to perform his astronomical research despite great personal hardships. Write an account of his experiences based on a reading of his biography.

Source material: *Watershed: A Biography of Johannes Kepler*, Arthur Koestler, Doubleday, 1960; *John Kepler,* Angus Armitage, Roy Publications, 1967.

18. Your school or public library may possess an astronomy textbook that was printed more than a quarter of a century ago. Read the section in the book that deals with stellar evolution and compare it with the present views. Then do the same for the sun. Comment on the relative differences of the changing views of each subject during the interval in question.

19. Radio astronomy is one of the most active and prolific fields of research in physical science. Prepare a brief report on the history of its development since the end of World War II.

Source material: *Radio Astronomy*, F. G. Smith, Penguin (paperback), 1960; *Radio Astronomy*, J. L. Sternberg and J. Lequex, McGraw-Hill, 1963; *Radio Astronomy*, Frank Hyde, Dufour, 1962; *Exploration of Space by Radio*, R. H. Brown and B. Lovell, Chapman and Hall, 1957; *Exploration of Outer Space*, A. C. B. Lovell, Harper, 1962.

20. Compare your present views of the universe as you approach the end of this course with any preconceived notions you entertained before enrolling in the course. In what area have your ideas about the universe changed the most?

21. The ancient Mayan civilization is said to have been as highly advanced in astronomical knowledge as any of the older cultures of the past prior to the Greek era. Can you locate and comment on any information concerning this subject?

22. Galileo did not invent the telescope. Most sources credit a Dutch spectacle-maker, Jan Lippershey, with having first constructed a telescope in 1608. There is evidence that the development of "perspective glasses" took place in England prior to their use on the continent. Prepare a brief account of the circumstances surrounding the invention of the telescope and its first use in astronomy.

One reference: *The New Astronomy and English Imagination*, Marjorie Nicholson, Cornell University Press, 1956.

23. A great deal of nonsense has been written on the subject of flying saucers. Some say that they are as real as rainbows; others are firm believers that they represent extraterrestrial visitations. The public libraries have dozens of publications dealing with UFO's (unidentified flying objects). If you should ever sight a flying saucer, contact Dr. J. A. Hynek, an authority on ufology, Astronomy Department, Northwestern University, Evanston, Illinois. Prepare a brief dissertation on the subject, presenting both sides of the controversy.

Source material: *A Scientific Study of Unidentified Flying Objects,* E. U. Condon, Dutton, 1969; *UFO's: A Scientific Debate*, C. Sagan and T. Page, eds., Cornell University Press, 1973; *Anatomy of a Phenomenon: A Scientific Appraisal*, J. Vallee, Regnery, 1965; *The World of Flying Saucers: A Scientific Examination of a Major Myth of the Space Age*, D. H. Menzel, Doubleday, 1963; *The UFO Experience: A Scientific Inquiry*, J. A. Hynek, Regnery, 1972.

24. In *Love's Labour's Lost,* Shakespeare comments on the work of astronomers, opening with these two lines:

"Study is like the heaven's glorious sun
That will not be deep-searched with saucy looks"

Locate the rest of the quotation and paraphrase Shakespeare's remarks.

25. In the village of Nova Brunsviga there is a flourishing astronomical society consisting of eight members—Mr. Mercury, Mr. Mars, Mr. Jupiter, Mr. Saturn, Mr. Uranus, Mr. Neptune, Mr. Pluto, and Miss Venus. Each planet of the solar system is observed by one and one member only; no member observes the planet bearing his name. We have discovered the following facts:

1. Mercury's observer sends his observations to the *Nova Brunsviga Echo,* and Mars's observer sends his to the editor of *The Observatory.*

2. Mr. Neptune observes four satellites belonging to his planet.

3. The heavenly namesakes of the observers of Venus and Neptune are neighbors in the solar system.

4. Jupiter is outside his observer's heavenly namesake's orbit.

5. Mr. Saturn has no interest in Neptune; five years ago he mistook Venus for his planet; since then he has given up observing in disgust.

6. Miss Venus and Mr. Jupiter observe neighboring planets.

7. Mr. Pluto is building a telescope and hopes it will be ready for the next opposition of his planet.

8. Miss Venus consults Sir William Herschel's observations of her planet.

How are the planets distributed among the eight observers? (From *The Observatory* of July 1934.)

26. Prepare an oral report for presentation to the class on exploring the possibilities of acquiring a telescope for one's own pleasure. Consult the reference sources given in Appendix 13. List the prices of the various models available and where they may be purchased. Also provide information on the kit assemblies and parts available for those wishing to build their own telescopes.

27. What are your feelings concerning the "tyranny of scientific progress" as expressed by these famous persons and the Biblical source?

Lord Byron:
> "Knowledge is not happiness, and science
> But an exchange of ignorance for that
> Which is another kind of ignorance."

George Bernard Shaw: "Science is always wrong. It never solves a problem without creating ten more."

Einstein: "Why does this magnificent applied science which saves work and makes life easier bring so little happiness? The simple answer runs: Because we have not yet learned to make sensible use of it."

Hendrik W. van Loon: "I have come to have very profound and deep-rooted doubts whether Science, as practiced at present by the human race, will ever do anything to make the world a better and happier place to live in, or will ever stop contributing to our general misery."

Ecclesiastes: "He that increaseth knowledge increaseth sorrow."

Source material: *Scientists in Search of Their Conscience,* A. R. Michaelis and H. Harvey, eds., Springer-Verlag, 1973.

28. How might you convince a skeptic that an astronomer can predict the fortunes of the stars far more successfully than an astrologer can predict the fortunes of human beings?

APPENDIX 15   BIBLIOGRAPHY

Textbooks

Abell, G., *Exploration of the Universe,* Holt, Rinehart, and Winston, 1969.

Abell, G., *Exploration of the Universe: Brief Edition,* Holt, Rinehart, and Winston, 1973.

*Alter, D., C. H. Cleminshaw, and J. G. Phillips, *Pictorial Astronomy*, Crowell, 1969.

Baker, R. H., and L. W. Frederick, *Astronomy*, Van Nostrand Reinhold, 1971.

*Baker, R. H., and L. W. Frederick, *An Introduction to Astronomy*, Van Nostrand, 1968.

Birney, D. S., *Modern Astronomy*, Allyn and Bacon, 1969.

*Brandt, J. C., and S. P. Maran, *New Horizons in Astronomy*, Freeman, 1972.

*Dixon, R. L., *Dynamic Astronomy*, Prentice-Hall, 1971.

Huffer, C. M., F. E. Trinklein, and M. Bunge, *An Introduction to Astronomy*, Holt, Rinehart, and Winston, 1973.

*Hynek, J. A., and N. C. Apfel, *Astronomy One*, Benjamin, 1972.

*Inglis, S. J., *Planets, Stars, and Galaxies,* Wiley, 1972.

*Jastrow, R., and M. H. Thompson, *Astronomy, Fundamentals and Frontiers,* Wiley, 1972.

Menzel, D. H., F. L. Whipple, and G. De Vaucouleurs, *Survey of the Universe,* Prentice-Hall, 1970.

Pananides, N.A., *Introductory Astronomy,* Addison-Wesley, 1973.

Payne-Gaposchkin, C., and K. Haramundanis, *Introduction to Astronomy*, Prentice-Hall, 1970.

*More elementary texts.

Wyatt, S. P., *Principles of Astronomy*, Allyn and Bacon, 1971.

General Astronomical Information

Flammarion Book of Astronomy, Simon and Schuster, 1964.

Gingerich, O., ed., *Frontiers in Astronomy*, Freeman, 1970.

Glasby, J. S., *Boundaries of the Universe,* Harvard University Press, 1971.

Hoyle, F., *Astronomy*, Doubleday, 1962.

Kopal, Z., *Man and His Universe*, Morrow, 1972.

Menzel, D. H., *Astronomy*, Random House, 1970.

Meyert, A., and H. Zimmermann, *A Concise Encyclopedia of Astronomy*, American Elsevier, 1968.

Rohr, H., *The Beauty of the Universe*, Viking, 1972.

Ronan, C. A., *Discovering the Universe,* Basic Books, 1971.

Rudaux, L., and G. De Vaucouleurs, *Larousse Encyclopedia of Astronomy*, Prometheus, 1959.

Young, L. B., *Exploring the Universe*, Oxford University Press, 1971.

Star Charts and Maps

Dexter, W. A., *A Field Guide to Astronomy without a Telescope*, Houghton Mifflin, 1971.

Mayall, R. N., and M. W. Mayall, *Beginners' Guide to the Sky*, Putnam, 1960.

Menzel, D. H., *Field Guide to the Stars and Planets,* Houghton Mifflin, 1964.

Norton, W. W., *Star Atlas*, Sky Publishing Corp., Cambridge, Mass., 1971.

Neely, H. M., *Primer for Star Gazers,* Harper, 1946.

Olcott, W. T., *A Field Guide to the Stars and Planets*, Putnam, 1954.

Periodicals for Students

Mercury, bimonthly journal of the Astronomical Society of the Pacific, San Francisco, Calif.

Science News, weekly, 1719 N Street N. W., Washington, D. C.

Scientific American, monthly, New York, N. Y.

Astronomy, monthly, P.O. Box 1305, Milwaukee, Wisc., 53201.

Modern Astronomy, monthly, 18 Fairhaven Dr., Buffalo, N.Y., 14225.

Sky and Telescope, monthly, Sky Publication Corp., Cambridge, Mass.

Griffith Observer, monthly, Griffith Observatory, Los Angeles, Calif.

Journal of the Royal Astronomical Society, bimonthly, Royal Astronomical Society of Canada, Toronto.

The Strolling Astronomer, bimonthly, Box 3AZ, University Park, New Mexico 88001.

Celestial Observer, quarterly, 10444 El Comel Dr., San Diego, Calif., 92124.

Absolute magnitude: equivalent to the apparent magnitude a celestial body would have if placed exactly 10 parsecs (32.6 light-years) from the sun.

Absolute zero: the theoretical temperature at which the molecules of a substance have their lowest possible kinetic energy. It corresponds to $0°K$ on the Kelvin (absolute) scale, $-273°C$ on the Celsius (centigrade) scale, and $-460°F$ on the Fahrenheit scale. See Appendix 4.

Absorption spectrum: a continuous spectrum that is crossed by dark lines.

Achromatic: relatively free from any color defect in an optical system.

Aerolite: a stony meteorite composed mostly of metal silicates.

Algae: one-cell or multicell aquatic plants found in damp places. Examples: seaweeds, green scum on ponds, shaded walls, tree trunks, etc.

Alpha particle $(_2He^4)$:   the nucleus of the helium atom possessing two protons and two neutrons.

Alt-azimuth: applies to the mounting arrangement of a telescope that permits it to be rotated horizontally and vertically.

Altitude: the vertical angle of a body above the horizon.

Ambiplasma: a high-temperature, ionized gas containing an equal mixture of positively and negatively charged particles.

Amino acids: the constituents of proteins containing the amino (NH_2) and carboxyl (COOH) groups of compounds.

Angstrom: a unit of length in spectroscopic wavelength measurements equal to 10^{-8} centimeter. Its symbol is Å.

Angular momentum: a measure of the quantity of rotation possessed by a spinning body about an axis or point.

Anorthosite: a granular, igneous rock composed chiefly of feldspar minerals consisting of silicates of aluminum with potassium, sodium, or calcium constituents.

Antapex: the point on the sky from which the sun appears to be receding relative to its stellar neighbors. It is exactly opposite to the apex in the heavens.

Antimatter: matter which is identical in its behavior to ordinary matter except that it contains the oppositely charged or neutral counterparts of ordinary matter. Example: the normal proton carries a positive charge; the antiproton carries an equal but negative charge.

Aperture: equivalent to the diameter of a telescope objective or radio dish or antenna structure.

Apex: the point on the sky (not far from the bright star Vega) toward which the sun appears headed relative to its stellar neighbors at the speed of 12 miles per second.

Aphelion: the point in the elliptic orbit where a planet or comet is farthest from the sun.

Apparent magnitude: the apparent brightness of a celestial body based on a logarithmic scale of luminosity.

Apsides (line of):   the major axis of an elliptic orbit.

Association: a sparsely populated cluster of physically related stars having a common origin.

Asteroid: see **minor planet**. Also called a **planetoid**.

Astrobiology: the study of living forms in space.

Astrochemistry: also known as *molecular astronomy*; the chemistry of the compounds discovered in the interstellar clouds.

Astrodynamics: the branch of astronautics that applies the principles of gravitational mechanics to the motions of space vehicles.

Astrogeology: the study of the composition, interior, and surface structure of other solid worlds (Mars and the moon are prime examples).

Astrometry: the division of astronomy that deals with the precise determinations of the positions, motions, and parallaxes of the heavenly bodies.

Astronautics: the science that is concerned with rocket and spaceflights.

Astronomical unit: the mean distance between the earth and the sun; its value is 1.496×10^{13} centimeters or 92,956,000 miles.

Astrophysics: the field of astronomy that is concerned with the physical, chemical, and thermal properties of the celestial bodies accessible to direct observation by means of various detection equipment throughout the electromagnetic spectrum.

Atomic clock: an electronically actuated mechanism whose clock rate is precisely governed by the naturally occurring vibration frequencies of certain atoms (cesium, rubidium, hydrogen) or molecules (ammonia).

Autocatalysis: the process that automatically produces more catalysis to aid in the further production of the substance.

Azimuth: horizontal arc from the north point of the horizon measured clockwise to the object's position projected on the horizon.

Ballistic: refers to a projectile or missile fired in the earth's atmosphere as it describes an elliptical trajectory.

Balmer series: the series of lines in the visible and ultraviolet spectral regions arising from transitions between the second energy level of the hydrogen atoms and its higher levels.

Barycenter: the center of mass around which two bodies orbit.

Basalt: a dense, igneous rocklike material composed chiefly of iron and magnesium silicates.

Beta particle: same as the electron.

Biosphere: that portion of the earth's atmosphere, ground, and water where life can flourish.

Bipolar group: refers to a large sunspot group which is divided into two portions with opposite magnetic polarities.

Bit: shorthand for "binary digit." Based on the powers of the binary number 2 as employed in computer science.

Blackbody: an ideal body capable of absorbing all the radiation falling on it and reemitting it without loss.

Black hole: a superdense configuration which a body assumes when it collapses gravitationally in such a way that its powerful gravitational field prevents its radiation from emerging into the external space.

Blazed: refers to a particular shape and size of the finely spaced grooves of a grating that permits a beam of light to be thrown into a single spectrum without wasting its light into other spectral orders.

Blink comparator: an optical device that permits any two similar regions of a pair of photographic plates to be rapidly viewed alternately in order to detect changes in brightness or positions of objects on the plates.

Bolide: an unusually bright meteor that sometimes explodes with a loud sound into fiery fragments.

Bolometer: a thermal detector employed to measure infrared radiation.

Booster: the main or higher stages of a rocket that propel the payload vehicle into orbit.

Breccia: an impacted mixture of lunar soil and rock fragments.

Bright-line spectrum: an emission spectrum of bright lines observed in the spectrum of an incandescent gaseous body at low pressure.

Burnout: moment when the propellant (fuel and oxidizer) of a rocket stage is completely consumed.

Calorie: the amount of heat required to raise the temperature of 1 gram of water 1°C.

Carbohydrate: a compound that contains carbon and water in various proportions, forming sugars, starches, and cellulose in living plants.

Cassegrain: the optical arrangement that permits light rays from the primary mirror of the reflecting telescope to be reflected back through the central hole of the mirror by means of a small convex mirror placed in front of the prime focus.

Catalysis: the process that produces a reaction between other substances by means of a chemical which remains unchanged during the reaction.

Catalyst: a substance that promotes or accelerates a chemical change in a reaction without itself being consumed in the process.

Celestial equator: the great circle that represents the extension of the earth's equator projected onto the sky.

Celestial mechanics: the field of astronomy that deals with the gravitational motions of the celestial bodies.

Cellulose: the basic constituent of the cell wall in green plants.

Cepheid: a pulsating variable star of the giant or supergiant class with a period of pulsation between a fraction of a day and 50 days.

Chandler wobble: the minute bodily shifting of the earth with respect to its axis of rotation in a roughly circular, nearly annual motion up to 50 feet in diameter.

Chandrasekhar limit: the theoretical limit (1.4 solar masses) below which a star can evolve presumably without mishap into a white dwarf.

Chondrule: a small, glasslike, round body found in stony meteorites. It is believed to have crystallized from molten droplets present during the initial stages of condensation of the solar nebula.

Chromatic aberration: the color defect due to the failure within an optical system to bring the different wavelengths to a common focus.

Chromosome: the threadlike string of genes which is part of every nucleus in a living cell.

Chromosphere: the pinkish portion of the sun's atmosphere lying immediately above the photosphere.

Codon: a triplet of three adjoining nucleotides that specifies one of the amino acids in the DNA chain.

Color index: the difference in magnitudes between two spectral colors of the celestial object (most often between the blue and yellow colors).

Color-luminosity diagram: the Hertzsprung-Russell plot of the stars in which the abscissa is the color index and the ordinate is the apparent or absolute magnitude.

Coma: (1) the gaseous envelope immediately surrounding the nucleus of a comet; (2) an optical aberration most prevalent in mirrors in which stellar images near the edge of the field of view have a cometlike appearance.

Continental drift: the gradual separation of the continents due to sea-floor spreading during the last 200 million years at the rate of about an inch per year.

Continuous spectrum: the uninterrupted band of emission produced by a body radiating energy over a continuous range of wavelengths.

Continuum (atomic): the continuous spectral region adjacent to the head of the series limit of the atom's spectral lines. It arises from an ionized condition of the atom involving transitions of electrons between the various energy levels and points beyond the last energy level of the atom.

Continuum (space): the space-time environment in four-dimensional space.

Corona: the outermost portion of the sun's atmosphere best observed during a total eclipse of the sun.

Coronagraph: a special telescope carefully designed to photograph the chromosphere and inner corona of the sun without the intervention of an eclipse of the sun.

Correlator: a device that electronically mixes the inputs of two radio signals to produce a multiplied output.

Cosmic rays: highly energetic particles impacting upon the earth's atmosphere. They consist mostly of protons with a sprinking of heavier atomic nuclei originating in outer space.

Cosmological constant: a mathematical term involving a repulsive force which Einstein introduced into his field equations in the general theory of relativity to counteract the self-gravitation of the universe.

Cosmology: the branch of astronomy concerned with the origin and evolutionary development of the universe.

Coudé (focus): an optical system that permits the beam of light from the primary mirror of the reflecting telescope to be directed down the hollow polar axis of the instrument to a remote focal position that remains fixed regardless of the position of the telescope (see Figure 3.7d).

Cytoplasm: the slightly viscous fluid that surrounds the nucleus of the cell.

Dark-line spectrum: same as absorption spectrum.

Deceleration parameter (q): a negatively varying quantity that is a function of the rate of slowdown of the expanding universe and the Hubble constant, H.

Declination: the celestial coordinate that corresponds to the angular distance of a body north or south of the celestial equator.

Deferent: in the Ptolemaic system, the large circle centered on the earth upon whose circumference the center of a smaller circle (epicycle) revolves, carrying the planet on its rim.

Degenerate gas: a very high-density, high-temperature condition of matter different from the perfect-gas condition in which the electrons or nucleons are restricted in the number of energy states they may occupy.

Differentiation (geological): the physical and chemical separation of an inhomogeneous medium into various layers.

Dipole (antenna): a metal rod or wire antenna that is one-half wavelength in length at the specified operating frequency.

Dipole (magnetic): a magnetized object that possesses north and south magnetic poles. A bar magnet and the earth are two examples.

Dipole field: the magnetic field surrounding the magnetic dipole of a body (similar to the magnetic lines of force of a bar magnet).

Dispersion: the spreading of the light into its various wavelengths as, for example, by a prism or grating.

Distance modulus: the difference between the apparent magnitude (m) and the absolute magnitude (M) of a celestial body; that is, $m - M$, from which its distance may be derived by application of the inverse-square law of light intensity.

DNA: deoxyribonucleic acid, the inheritance material consisting of long chains of nucleotides present in the chromosomes of all living matter.

Doppler effect: the apparent shift in wavelength or frequency as a result of the relative line-of-sight motion between the observer and the source of radiation.

Dwarf (star): a star of moderate mass and luminosity on the main sequence. (The sun is a yellow dwarf star.)

Dynamic: relating to forces in motion.

Dyne: the scientific unit of force; it represents the force needed to accelerate a mass of one gram one centimeter per second each second.

Eccentricity: in an ellipse, the numerical ratio of the distance of the focus from the center of the ellipse to the length of the semimajor axis. Its value is always less than 1 for an ellipse; equal to 0 for a circle; equal to 1 for a parabola; greater than 1 for a hyperbola.

Eclipsing binary: two generally close stars orbiting each other in a plane viewed edgewise, or nearly so, from earth, resulting in the mutual eclipse of one star by the other.

Ecliptic: the great circle extension of the earth's orbit upon the celestial sphere; the same as the apparent yearly path of the sun in the sky.

Ecology: the study of the interactions of living things with their environment.

Electromagnetic: pertaining to the field of radiation produced by oscillating electric or magnetic currents.

Electron: the negatively charged particle that is the basic outer component of the atom.

Electron volt: the kinetic energy gained by an electron moving across an electric potential of one volt.

Ellipse: the closed path traced by a moving point whose distance from two fixed points (loci) remains constant.

Emission nebula: a bright, gaseous nebula exhibiting a bright-line spectrum.

Emission spectrum: a spectrum containing bright lines.

Enzyme: a protein molecule that acts as a catalyst.

Epicycle: the smaller circle in the Ptolemaic system along which the planet moves while the center of the circle (the epicycle) revolves about its deferent.

Equatorial mounting: the telescope arrangement that permits the instrument to be rotated about an axis parallel to the earth's axis of rotation in order to follow the rotation of the sky by means of a clock-drive system.

Equinoxes: the two points of intersection between the celestial equator and the ecliptic. These are the vernal equinox through which the sun passes on or about March 21, and the autumnal equinox through which the sun passes on about September 23 (see Figure 2.1).

Erg: the scientific unit of energy; it is defined as the work expended by a force of one dyne moving through a distance of one centimeter.

Eruptive variable: a variable star characterized by sudden explosive or erratic light outbursts.

Euclidean: refers to the space geometry as perceived by our senses.

Event: an occurrence specified by *both* time and place in the space-time world of four dimensions in the theory of relativity.

Event horizon: that division in relativistic space beyond whose realm no photons of light will ever reach us.

Evolutionary cosmological model: the time-dependent expanding model of the universe that evolves from its superhot state of highly condensed matter originally contained in a small volume of space.

Excite: to energize an atom or molecule from a lower to a higher energy state by absorption of a quantum of energy.

Exobiology: the study of extraterrestrial life in space.

Exosphere: the outermost fringe of the earth's atmosphere.

Exploding galaxy: a galaxy undergoing a violent outward eruption of matter.

Extra-: beyond the body in question. For example, extraterrestrial: outside of the earth; extrasolar: outside of the sun or solar system; extragalactic: outside of our Galaxy.

f (number): the focal length of a lens or mirror divided by its aperture. The smaller the f number, the greater the speed of the optical system.

Faculae: enhanced bright regions best observed near the sun's edge.

Filtergram: a photograph of the solar disk and/or its atmosphere obtained with a narrow passband filter.

Fireball: an exceptionally brilliant meteor.

Flare: a sudden energetic eruption of radiation on the sun.

Flare star: an orange or red dwarf star that exhibits sudden, brief, unpredictable outbursts of radiation.

Flash spectrum: the bright-line spectrum of the sun's chromospheric layer momentarily observed after the start and before the finish of the total phase of the eclipse.

Focal ratio: the focal length of a lens or mirror divided by its aperture.

Forbidden lines: spectral lines originating in a gaseous medium of exceedingly low density where the probability of occurrence is high compared to that under ordinary laboratory conditions.

Fraunhofer lines: the most prominent dark lines in the solar spectrum first mapped by J. Fraunhofer in 1814.

Frequency: the number of electromagnetic waves that pass by a given point each second.

Fringes: the alternating bright and dark spacings resulting from the interference (reinforcement and cancellation) of the electromagnetic waves of radiation with each other.

Fusion: the thermonuclear synthesis of the heavier elements from the lighter ones.

Galactic cluster: an open star cluster in the Galaxy.

Galactic equator: the great circle in the sky passing through the central plane of the Milky Way.

Galactic halo: the outer, nonflattened stellar portions of a galaxy.

Galactic latitude: the number of degrees of an object above or below the galactic equator.

Galactic longitude: the number of degrees of an object measured along the galactic equator northward from the direction of the galactic center.

Gamma rays: the highest-energy photons of radiation possessing the shortest wavelengths, less than about 0.1 angstrom unit.

Gauss: the scientific unit of magnetic-field strength.

Gegenschein: the faint counterglow patch of light observed in the night sky opposite to the sun's direction.

Geiger counter: a gas-filled tube electronically set so that the gas becomes ionized and hence electrically conductive when a charged particle or photon enters the tube. The resulting short pulse of electric current generated activates a counter.

Gene: a unit in the chromosome that uniquely determines a set of inheritance characteristics.

Geocentric: centered on earth.

Geodesic: pertaining to measurements on the earth's surface. In the theory of relativity, a *geodesic* represents the shortest distance between two points in four-dimensional space.

Geosphere: the solid portion of the earth.

Giant (star): a large-sized star of higher than average luminosity.

Globular cluster: a compact spheroidal assemblage of tens of thousands of stars found in the halo portion of a galaxy.

Globule: the small, roundish patch of dark nebulosity that may be the precursor of a protostar.

Grating: an optical surface (transmissive or reflective) upon which is ruled a large number of finely spaced grooves. A beam of light impinging upon it is broken into several spectral orders on each side of the central image.

Gravitational collapse: the rapid compression of a body whose gravitational force greatly exceeds its normal outward-balancing gas-pressure force.

Gravitational deflection of light: the slight bending in the light path experienced by a light ray skimming past the limb of a massive body.

Gravitational radius (or **Schwarzschild radius**): the critical radius reached by a collapsing body immediately before disappearing into a black hole.

Gravitational red shift: the red shift in wavelength experienced by a photon leaving the surface of a massive object, as predicted by the theory of relativity.

Gravitational radiation (or **gravity waves**): weak oscillations, traveling with the speed of light, emitted by a highly accelerated body, as predicted by the theory of relativity.

Great circle: the trace produced on the surface of a sphere by a plane passing through its center.

Greenhouse effect: the warming effect that a planet experiences between its surface and atmospheric layers as a result of the trapping of the solar infrared radiation.

H I region: the volume of interstellar space where the hydrogen remains neutral and optically dark.

H II region: the volume of interstellar space occupied by ionized hydrogen.

Hadrons: the heavyweight class of elementary particles ranging from the mesons to the protons, neutrons, and still heavier particles up to nearly 3,000 electron masses.

Halo (galactic): the ellipsoidal distribution of population II stars centered on the Galaxy.

Hayashi track: the fairly rapid downward evolutionary route in the H-R diagram followed by the young star prior to reaching the main sequence. It is characterized by a decrease in luminosity at approximately constant temperature.

Heliocentric: centered at the sun.

Helium flash: the violent, rapid fusion of three helium nuclei into carbon that occurs in the dense helium core of a red-giant star prior to its emergence on the horizontal branch of the H-R diagram.

Hertzsprung gap: the nearly vacant region existing between the upper portion of the main sequence and the left end of the giant branch in the H-R diagram.

Horizontal branch: the upper, approximately horizontal, portion of the H-R diagram followed by stars evolving from the red-giant stage toward the blue to white semistable pulsating, or planetary nebula, or nova stage.

Hour angle: the arc along the celestial equator measured westward from the observer's meridian to the hour circle passing through the object.

Hour circle: any great circle on the celestial sphere passing through both celestial poles.

H-R (Hertzsprung-Russell) diagram: the graph that exhibits the relationship between absolute magnitudes (plotted vertically) and the temperatures, or spectral classes, or the color indexes of the stars (plotted horizontally).

Hubble constant: the constant of proportionality (H) in the Hubble law of recession of the galaxies. Its presently determined value is close to 50 km/sec/megaparsec.

Hubble law of recession: the proportional relationship between the velocities (red shift) of the galaxies and their distances.

Hydrocarbon: any chemical containing a mixture of carbon and hydrogen.

Hydrosphere: the water portions of the earth.

Hydrostatic equilibrium: the balance that exists between the pressure forces and the gravitational forces within the different layers of a star.

Hyperbolic: pertains to the open-ended curve of a conic section formed by the intersection of a plane with a right-circular cone at any angle between the axis of the cone and its slant edge.

Hyperstructure: the superspace structure that envelops a space structure of lower order.

Igneous: adjectival description of molten lava or basalt rock that has solidified.

Image tube: an electronic device in which the optical image falls on a photocathode surface to emit electrons whose flow can be intensified and magnetically guided to fall on a fluorescent screen where it is recorded by a camera. The use of an image tube results in shorter exposure times than with photographic plates.

Inclination: angle between the orbital planes of two bodies; or the angle of the equator of a body with respect to its orbital plane.

Inertia: the reluctance of a body (proportional to its mass) to change its state of motion when a force acts upon it.

Inertial force: the force needed to overcome the inertia of a body in order to change its motion.

Inferior conjunction: the position of an inferior planet, as viewed from the earth, when it is between the sun and the earth.

Inferior planet: a planet (Mercury or Venus) whose orbit lies inside the earth's orbit.

Infrared: that portion of the electromagnetic spectrum extending from the visible red end toward the longer wavelengths up to about one millimeter.

Interferometer: an optical instrument that is used to examine the fringe patterns of light produced by the constructive and destructive interference of light waves from a source of small angular dimensions.

Interstellar lines: dark lines superimposed on the spectra of the stars resulting from the absorption of the starlight in passing through the interstellar clouds.

Invariant: unchanging under any conditions.

Ionization: the stripping from an atom of one or more of its electrons.

Ionosphere: the upper atmospheric region from about 35 to 250 miles where the air is ionized into discrete layers (D, E, F_1, and F_2 layers).

Irregular galaxy: a galaxy without a symmetrical form of the type exhibited by a spiral or elliptical galaxy.

Isotope: an atom similar to another atom with the same number of protons but with a different number of neutrons in the nucleus.

Isotropic: the same in every direction.

Jovian planet: refers to one of the major planets (Jupiter, Saturn, Uranus, or Neptune).

Keplerian (motion): the undisturbed orbital motion of a body around another in conformity with Kepler's planetary laws of motion.

Kilowatt-hour: expenditure of 1,000 watts of power in one hour of time.

Kinematics: the field of physics concerned with the descriptive study of motion without regard to its cause.

Kinetic energy: the energy of motion possessed by a moving body. It is equal to one-half the product of its mass and the square of its velocity.

Kinetic gas temperature: the temperature that a gas assumes as the result of the distribution of velocities of the gas particles.

Lander: an instrumented vehicle or capsule ejected from a space vehicle that lands on an extraterrestrial body.

Leptons: the lightweight class of elementary particles that constitute the electrons, muons, and their associated neutrinos.

Light curve: a graphical plot that shows the change in the magnitude of a variable star (plotted vertically) vs. the time (plotted horizontally).

Light-year: the distance that light travels in one year ($= 9.46 \times 10^{12}$ kilometers or 5.88×10^{12} miles).

Line of apsides: the line joining the perihelion and aphelion points of the elliptic orbit. It represents the major axis of the ellipse.

Line of nodes: the line joining the opposite nodes of an orbit.

Lipid: a fatty acid or substance that can be extracted from tissue by a fat solvent such as ether or hot alcohol.

Lithosphere: the stony crust and upper mantle of the earth down to an approximate depth of 30 miles.

Lobe: the radio-antenna pattern inside of which signals can best be received.

Local Group: the small group of bunched galaxies, including our Galaxy, consisting of 20 known members spread over a diameter of about three million light-years.

Local supercluster: the apparent clumping of a supersystem of galaxies scattered over a volume of space about 130 million light-years in diameter. The Local Group is one subunit of the supercluster.

Long-period variable: a red variable star with an amplitude variation of several magnitudes over a period between approximately 200 to 400 days.

Lorentz contraction factor: the term $\sqrt{1 - (v^2/c^2)}$, first introduced by the Dutch physicist H. A. Lorentz. It appears in the formulas for relativistic length, mass, and time intervals (v = velocity of the observer relative to the velocity of light, c).

Lyman alpha line: the first spectral line of the ultraviolet Lyman series at 1,216 angstroms, produced by electron transitions between the ground level and the next (second) level of the hydrogen atom.

Lyman series: the ultraviolet hydrogen series of spectral lines arising from transitions to or from the ground level of the atom (see Figure 4.11).

Magellanic Clouds: the pair of irregular galaxies visible to the naked eye in the southern skies. They are our closest extragalactic objects.

Magnetic field: the region surrounding a magnetized body which acts upon electrical particles or currents within its range.

Magnetic pole: one of the two diametrically opposite points of a spherical body, or the end points of a bar magnet, where the flux of the magnetic lines of force is a maximum.

Magnetohydrodynamics (MHD): the branch of physics that deals with the behavior of a plasma (electrified gas) moving through a magnetic field.

Magnetometer: an electronically actuated instrument that detects and measures the magnetic-field strength of any object.

Magnetosphere: the complete magnetic field that surrounds the earth or any other magnetized planet.

Magnitude: the brightness of a celestial body based on a logarithmic scale of intensity to which the eye naturally responds.

Main sequence: the major distributional segment of the stars running diagonally across the H-R diagram from the upper left to the lower right.

Major axis: the longest diameter of the ellipse; also called the **line of apsides.**

Manifold: a mathematician's reference to an n-dimensional space-time continuum.

Mantle: the intermediate layer between the core of a solid astronomical body and its outer crust.

Mare: the Latin name for *sea* (plural: *maria*); one of the dark markings on the moon.

Mascon: a concentrated mass lying below the crust of the moon or a solid planet; it gravitationally disturbs a spacecraft flying over it.

Mass: the amount of matter contained in a body. It is a measure of the inertia displayed by a body when acted upon by a force.

Mass unit: the standard reference against which the atomic masses are compared. It is equal to $\frac{1}{12}$ the mass of the carbon 12 isotope ($= 1.6604 \times 10^{-24}$ gram).

Meridian (celestial): the great circle on the sky that passes through the observer's zenith and the north-south points of the horizon.

Mesosphere: the intermediate atmospheric layer above the stratosphere extending approximately between 20 and 60 miles above the earth's surface.

Meteor: the luminous trail left behind by the passage of a tiny cosmic particle (meteoroid) through the earth's atmosphere.

Meteorite: an extraterrestrial metallic or stony object that survives flight through the earth's atmosphere and lands on the ground.

Meteoroid: a solid particle or body of small dimensions in extraterrestrial space.

Meteor shower: the bright streaks appearing to radiate from a common point in the sky caused by a swarm of meteoroids entering the earth's atmosphere.

Micro-: one-millionth.

Micron: a unit of measurement equal to one-millionth of a meter.

Microwave: the radio spectral region in the millimeter to centimeter wavelengths.

Milli-: one-thousandth.

Minor planet: one of the thousands of small solid bodies revolving in orbits chiefly between Mars and Jupiter.

Momentum: the product of a body's mass and its velocity ($= mv$).

Monochromatic: corresponding to light of a single wavelength or color.

Muon (or mu-meson): an elementary charged particle of about 207 electron masses with a half-life of about 1.5-millionths of a second. It decays into an electron and a neutrino.

Mutation: a change in the hereditary material (genes) produced at random by environmental influences or other factors.

Negative curvature: a space continuum whose curvature is hyperbolic and open-ended of infinite dimensions. In the three-dimensional version, the surface is saddle-shaped.

Neutrino: an elementary particle without mass or charge emitted during the process of a nuclear reaction.

Neutron: a neutral elementary particle of about the same mass as the proton which together with the neutron forms the basic constituents of atomic nuclei.

Neutron star: a gravitationally collapsed star of very small dimensions and enormously high density, composed mainly of neutrons.

Node: one of the two points of intersection, 180° apart, between the orbit of a celestial body and a plane of reference such as the ecliptic, for example.

Nova: a star that suddenly erupts into an object of great brilliance that surpasses the sun's luminosity by a factor of hundreds of thousands to millions of times.

Nucleic acid: the substance of the DNA molecule.

Nucleon: refers to either the proton or neutron inside the atomic nucleus.

Nucleotide: one of the four bases within the double-twisted DNA chain. These are adenine (A), thymine (T), cytosine (C), and guanine (G). In RNA, thymine is replaced by uracil (U).

Nucleus: the central portion of the atom, a comet, a galaxy, or a cell.

Nutation: the small 18.6-year period of oscillation superimposed on the earth's 25,800-year period of precession.

Objective: the main lens or mirror of the telescope.

Objective prism: the thin, large prism placed in front of the telescope objective. It produces a spectrum of each star in the field of view of the telescope.

Observatory satellite: an earth-orbiting satellite of the class: orbiting astronomical observatory (OAO); orbiting geophysical observatory (OGO); orbiting solar observatory (OSO).

Olivine: a common earth mineral composed chiefly of the silicates of magnesium and iron.

Opacity: the reduction in the intensity of the light as it passes through the various layers of a medium (in stars through the different gaseous layers).

Open star cluster: a somewhat loose assemblage of stars, numbering dozens to hundreds, with various degrees of central condensation. In our galaxy it is also known as a **galactic cluster.**

Opposition: the position of a superior planet when it is closest to the earth. At this time it is 180° from the sun's direction.

Orbit: the path of a body subjected to the gravitational force of another body.

Orbiter: a space vehicle placed in orbit around an extraterrestrial body such as the moon or a planet.

Organic compounds: pertaining to the carbon compounds; they are biologically important in living organisms.

Oxidizer: the rocket propellant that combines with the fuel to produce a strong combustible discharge which flows out of the rocket nozzle to give it forward thrust.

P (seismic) waves: the longitudinal waves of an earthquake that causes the earth's inner material to expand and contract alternately. Also called *primary*, or *pressure*, or *compression waves.*

Panspermia: the theory that microorganisms floating in space or attached to interstellar dust particles can germinate and start the evolutionary chain of life when they encounter a hospitable sterile planet.

Parallax: the apparent shift in the position of an object when observed from two different places.

Parsec: the distance of a body whose parallax equals one second of arc.

Passband filter: a filter that is transparent to electromagnetic radiation in a very narrow spectral range.

Peculiar galaxy: an abnormally shaped galaxy and/or one that emits nonthermal radiation.

Perfect cosmological principle: the proposition in the steady state theory that the universe looks the same everywhere at all times.

Perfect gas: an ideal gas whose pressure increases directly with the temperature and the density.

Perihelion: the point in the path of a body orbiting the sun where it is closest to the sun.

Perturbation: a disturbance in the normal movement of an orbiting body arising from an external force, usually gravitational in nature.

Photoconductor: any light sensor that converts light into a flow of electrons.

Photometer: an instrument used to measure the intensity of a light source.

Photomultiplier: a small, evacuated tube within which a photoelectric cell and its multiplying stages are mounted to provide an amplified flow of electric current when the cell is exposed to light.

Photon: the unit carrier of electromagnetic radiation.

Photosphere: the light-emitting, visible surface of the sun.

Photosynthesis: the buildup of organic compounds within plants by their absorption of water, carbon dioxide, and solar energy.

Pion (or **pi-meson**): a charged elementary particle with a mass equal to 270 electron masses. Inside the atomic nucleus it serves as the "glue" that holds the protons and neutrons together.

Plage: a bright, disturbed area of the solar surface observed usually in the light of the hydrogen alpha line of the Balmer series or the Fraunhofer K line of calcium.

Planck's constant (h): the universal constant that connects the energy of the photon (E) to its frequency (f) through the equation, $E = hf$.

Planetary nebula: a slowly expanding envelope of gas surrounding a small, hot, central star.

Planetesimals: small, solid bodies which are believed to have formed during the condensing stage of

the solar nebula that evolved into the planetary system we know today.

Planetoid: one of the alternate names for **asteroid** or **minor planet.**

Plasma: a hot, electrically charged (ionized) gas.

Polar axis: the axis of an equatorially mounted telescope about which the telescope can be swung to follow the diurnal motions of the stars. The polar axis is always parallel to the earth's axis of rotation.

Polarized radiation: electromagnetic radiation whose vibration is confined to a fixed plane (plane-polarized light) or to one which rotates (circularly polarized light).

Polar wobble: see **Chandler wobble.**

Polymer: a giant molecule formed from thousands of smaller molecules linked together.

Population types: the classification of the stars into two main groups, population I and population II, and intermediate types based upon differences in age, chemical composition, spectral properties, velocities, and location in the Galaxy.

Population I: the younger stars found in greatest numbers in the outer portions of the galactic disk.

Population II: the older stars mainly inhabiting the central and halo portions of the galactic system.

Positive curvature: a space continuum whose curvature is spherical or ellipsoidal, resulting in a closed universe.

Positron: a positively charged electron or anti-electron.

Precession of equinoxes: the conical movement of the earth's axis of rotation in a period of 25,800 years. The phenomenon causes the equinoxes to slide westward along the ecliptic about 50 seconds of arc per year. It is produced by the gravitational pull of the sun and moon, tending to bring the earth's equatorial bulge into their plane (the ecliptic plane); the spinning earth acts like a gyroscope and resists this force, thus resulting in the conical motion of its axis.

Precession of Mercury's orbit: the slow eastward rotation of the line of apsides of the planet in its own plane as a consequence of the planetary perturbations upon the orbit of Mercury.

Primeval fireball: the high-powered explosion from a superhot, superdense state of condensed matter that supposedly initiated the expansion of the universe.

Principle of equivalence: Einstein's declaration that a gravitational force cannot be distinguished from an inertial force; hence a gravitational field can be replaced by an accelerated system. This principle is one of the cornerstones of the general theory of relativity.

Proper motion: the angular change of the star's direction from the sun in one year of time.

Protein: a large molecule composed of hundreds to thousands of amino acids joined together by peptide links making up the DNA molecule.

Proto-: refers to the embryo condensation of an evolving body such as a planet, star, or galaxy.

Proton: the positively charged particle that is part of the nucleus of every atom. It is 1,836 times heavier than the electron.

Proton-proton (p-p chain reaction): the sequence of thermonuclear reactions that builds up helium from hydrogen with the release of energy inside the cores of the main-sequence stars.

Pulsar: a very small, rapidly pulsating, radio star that is believed to be the neutron core remnant of a supernova explosion.

Pyrheliometer: a thermometer type of instrument used to measure the intensity of the solar radiation.

q **(deceleration parameter):** the term in the mathematical treatment of the expansion of the universe related to its slowdown imposed by the self-gravitation of the universe (see **deceleration parameter**).

Quadrature: the configuration of the moon or a planet corresponding to its position when it is 90° from the earth-sun line.

Quantum: a finite or discrete amount of a quantity. The term is frequently applied to the discrete bundle of energy possessed by the photon.

Quasar: the popular designation for a quasi-stellar object.

Quasi-stellar object (QSO): the general class of stellar-appearing objects believed by most astronomers to be very distant, because of their large red shifts, and also highly luminous. One group, quasi-stellar sources, emits strong radio energy; the other group, often called blue stellar objects, emits no detectable radio energy.

Radial velocity: that component of an object's motion that lies in the line of sight, producing the Doppler shift in the spectral lines of the body.

Radiant: the place in the sky from which the meteors diverge during a meteor shower. The shower is named after the constellation in which the radiant appears.

Radioactive: the adjective used to describe the

spontaneous breakdown of certain atomic nuclei (normally the heaviest atoms) into lighter nuclei with the ejection of alpha particles, electrons, and gamma photons.

Radio galaxy: a galaxy that emits strong radio radiation.

Reflection nebula: a dusty gas cloud that reflects the light of the nearby stars.

Refraction: the change in the direction of light rays when passing from one medium into another of different density.

Regolith: the pulverized debris on the lunar surface produced by the meteoritic bombardment of the surface material during the eons of time.

Regression (of the nodes): the westward (backward) slippage of the nodes of the orbit of an easterly revolving body with respect to a fundamental plane of reference. Most often the regression of the nodes refers to the 18.6-year cycle of the moon's nodes sliding westward along the ecliptic.

Resolving power: the ability of a telescope to separate the fine details in an image.

Retrograde motion: the apparent westerly motion of a planetary body as viewed from the earth, contrary to its usual easterly movement among the stars.

Right ascension: a coordinate in the equatorial system of measurement. It measures the arc along the celestial equator from the vernal equinox eastward to the hour circle of the celestial body. It is similar to the measurement of longitude on earth.

Rille: a canyon or gorge found in the surface of the moon or Mars.

S (seismic waves): the transverse waves of an earthquake that causes the earth's material to vibrate perpendicular to the direction of travel of the waves. Also called *secondary* or *shear* waves.

Schwarzschild radius: the critical radius reached by a gravitationally collapsing body between the point of visibility as a highly compressed body and nonvisibility as a black hole.

Scintillation: the twinkling effect observed when light from a very small radiating source passes through a turbulent medium.

Scintillation counter: a device consisting of a fluorescent substance that emits a tiny flash of light when struck by a fast-moving particle. The light is amplified by a photocell that records its intensity.

Seismic: pertaining to earthquakes.

Seismograph (seismometer): an earthquake-recording instrument that measures the intensity of the seismic waves and their variation with time.

Seyfert galaxy: a special class of spiral galaxy that exhibits intense, irregular, electromagnetic radiations within a small, active nucleus.

Sidereal period: represents one complete revolution of a celestial body with respect to a fixed point in the heavens, such as a star.

Siderite: a type of meteorite consisting mostly of nickel and iron with traces of other metals.

Siderolite: a type of meteorite containing a mixture of stone and iron.

Sign of the zodiac: one of the twelve equally spaced constellation divisions (30° in length), centered on the ecliptic, through which the sun passes monthly in succession (see Figure 2.2).

Silicates: mineral compositions largely containing silicon and oxygen.

Skylab station: the 28-ton, earth-orbiting space station housing a scientific laboratory and a crew of three astronauts for the purpose of conducting elaborate extraterrestrial scientific investigations.

Solar wind: the continuous stream of charged particles (mostly protons and electrons) ejected from the sun at high velocities.

Sounding rocket: an instrumented rocket that ascends up to a maximum altitude of about 100 miles before falling back to the earth's surface.

Space-time: the four-dimensional world of space and time as visualized in the theory of relativity. An **event** is located in the space-time continuum analogous to a *point* in three-dimensional space.

Space velocity (space motion): the true motion of the star in space relative to the sun.

Spectrogram: the photographic plate on which the spectrum of an object is recorded by the telescope.

Spectrograph: basically the same as the spectroscope except that the eyepiece is replaced by a photographic plate for recording the spectrum.

Spectroheliogram: a photograph of the sun taken with a spectroheliograph.

Spectroheliograph: a spectrograph modified to photograph the solar disk or the chromosphere in the light of a single spectral line, either in the red hydrogen alpha line or the violet H or K line of calcium.

Spectroscope: an optical instrument containing a prism or grating with appropriate lenses to permit direct viewing of the spectrum of a radiating source (see Figure 4.15).

Spectroscopic binary: a double star whose components are not separately observed in a telescope but whose binary character is revealed by the periodic Doppler shift of the spectral lines.

Spectroscopic parallax: the derivation of the star's distance (or parallax) from knowledge of its apparent magnitude and its absolute magnitude on the basis of its spectral characteristics.

Spectrum: the separation of the energy of a radiating source into its component wavelengths by means of a prism, grating, or other dispersing device.

Spectrum-luminosity diagram: the Hertzsprung-Russell diagram that exhibits the relationship between the absolute magnitudes of the stars and their spectral classes.

Spherical aberration: the failure of light rays striking all parts of a lens or mirror with spherical surfaces to converge at the same focal setting.

Spicule: a small, spikelike protrusion arising within the chromosphere as shown in the monochromatic views at the edge of the sun.

Static universe: a nonexpanding or noncontracting universe in equilibrium.

Steady-state cosmology: the model of the universe in which it is assumed that the density of matter within it remains constant as the universe expands.

Stefan-Boltzmann law: a formula that relates the amount of emission (E) by a blackbody to the fourth power of its temperature (T): $E \propto T^4$.

Stellar association: a sparse aggregation of young population I stars found in the outer gas-dust regions of the Galaxy.

Stratosphere: the narrow atmospheric zone that lies above the lowest level of the earth's atmosphere, the troposphere. It extends from about 7 to 15 miles above sea level and has a constant temperature of $-67°F$.

Strömgren sphere: the ionized hydrogen region, or H II region, surrounding one or more stars that is activated by their ultraviolet light.

Strong nuclear force: the nuclear "glue" or binding force that holds the nucleons together against the disruptive repulsive force of the positively charged protons. It operates within the nuclear domain ($\sim 10^{-13}$ centimeter).

Sugar: a class of the carbohydrate compounds that is soluble in water and has a sweet taste.

Sunspot: a dark marking visible on the sun's surface. Although the sunspot temperature is about 4,500°K, it appears dark by comparison with the brighter and hotter photospheric background of 6,000°K.

Supergiant (star): an unusually large and highly luminous star.

Superior conjunction: the position of a superior planet, as viewed from the earth, when it is in the same direction as the sun and farther away from the sun.

Superior planet: a planet whose orbit lies outside the earth's orbit.

Supernova: an exploding star that suddenly attains a luminosity up to 100 million times the sun's brightness.

Synchrotron radiation: the continuous polarized radiation emitted by fast-moving electrons spiraling around the magnetic lines of force in the presence of a magnetic field.

Synodic month: the period of the moon's phases (29.53 days).

Synodic period: the time interval between consecutive similar configurations of a planet as, for example, between successive inferior conjunctions or oppositions.

Tangential velocity: the component of the star's motion that is at right angles to the line of sight. It is also known as *transverse velocity* or *cross motion*.

Technology: the field that transforms scientific principles into practical applications for everyday life in the modern world.

Tectonics (plate): the study concerned with the movements of the segments of the earth's lithosphere (continents and minor land masses) along the top of the earth's fluid mantle.

Telemetry: the technique of remote measurement.

Thermal equilibrium: the balancing condition between incoming and outgoing radiation that keeps the internal temperature of the star constant at any point.

Thermal sensor: any heat-measuring device.

Thermocouple: a heat-measuring apparatus consisting of two strips of different metals joined together at one end. A meter connected to the free ends registers the current generated when the juncture is exposed to infrared radiation.

Thermosphere: the atmospheric layer extending from about 60 miles to 250 miles. It is characterized by a constantly rising gas-kinetic temperature with height.

Tidal force: the unequal gravitational pull exerted upon the various parts of a body tending to deform its shape.

Time contraction: the slowing down of the clock rate of an object moving at high relativistic velocity.

Time-dependent cosmological model: any nonstatic model of the universe that evolves (contracts or expands) with time.

Tower telescope: a solar-telescope arrangement in which a tower-mounted rotating mirror following the sun reflects the sunlight into a long focus lens or mirror system which forms an enlarged image of the solar disk for study.

Trench: a deep rift or fracture produced at the edge of a continental plate when it collides with an oceanic plate.

Triangulation: a surveying operation in which the base angles from a carefully measured base line to a distant point can be determined. A trigonometric solution gives the distance of the remote object from either end of the base line.

Trojan asteroid: one of a group of stable, orbiting, minor planets located at or near the vertex of an equilateral triangle with Jupiter and the sun occupying the other vertices. One group lies approximately 60° east of Jupiter; the other, approximately 60° west of Jupiter.

Troposphere: the bottom layer of the earth's atmosphere where our weather takes place. Its height averages about 7 miles.

T Tauri variable: a low-temperature dwarf star with bright emission lines subject to erratic changes in light. It is found in the vicinity of dark nebulosity and is believed to be the forerunner of a main-sequence star.

Turnoff point: the critical departure position where an evolving star turns off the main sequence after exhausting its core supply of hydrogen and is on the way to becoming a red giant.

UBV system: the standardized magnitude and color system employed by astronomers for comparing intensities in the ultraviolet (U), blue (B), and yellow or visual (V) spectral regions.

Ultraviolet: the portion of the electromagnetic spectrum that extends from the shortest visible waves at about 3,900 angstroms to about 100 angstroms.

Umbra: the dark central region of a sunspot. In an eclipse it is the dark central part of the shadow cast by an illuminated body.

Variable star: any star that intrinsically exhibits periodic or nonperiodic changes in light.

Velocity of escape: the minimum initial speed required for an object to leave permanently the region of an attracting body.

Vernal equinox: the point of intersection on the sky between the sun's path (ecliptic) and the celestial equator reached by the sun on about March 21 of each year (see Figure 2.2).

Visual binary: a physically related double star whose components can be resolved in a telescope.

Visual magnitude: the magnitude corresponding to the measurement of the visual light in the approximate spectral range of 4,000–7,000 angstroms.

Watt: a unit of power equivalent to the expenditure of ten million ergs per second.

Wavelength: the distance between successive crests or troughs of a wave.

Wave mechanics: the mathematical theory of quantum mechanics that forms the basis of the modern concept of atomic phenomena in terms of the interactions of radiation with matter.

Weak nuclear force: the basic nuclear force involved in the phenomenon of radioactive decay. It is characterized by a slow nuclear reaction rate (for example, 17 minutes on the average for neutron decay into a proton, electron, and antineutrino) in comparison to the strong nuclear force which reacts in a very short time (as when a neutron is ejected from a nucleus in 10^{-21} second).

White dwarf (star): a star that has collapsed gravitationally into a small, very dense and faint object after expending its nuclear fuel.

Wien's (displacement) law: the simple formula stating that the wavelength at which the peak energy of a radiating blackbody occurs varies inversely with the temperature of the body. As the temperature rises, the maximum of the blackbody's energy curve is displaced toward the shorter wavelengths.

Wobble: the small observed bodily shifting of the earth with respect to its axis of rotation; known also as the **Chandler wobble.**

W Virginis star: the prototype of a special class of cepheid variables belonging to population II.

X-rays: electromagnetic radiation whose wavelengths are approximately between 1 and 100 angstroms. Their spectral region lies between the gamma and ultraviolet wavelengths.

Zeeman effect: a splitting or widening of the spectral lines of a radiating source in the presence of a magnetic field. The phenomenon was discovered in the laboratory by the Dutch physicist P. Zeeman in 1896.

Zenith: the point in the sky that is immediately overhead. More precisely it is determined by the extension of the surveyor's plumb line to the sky as directed by gravity.

Zenith tube (telescope): a vertically mounted telescope accurately instrumented to photograph stars in or near the zenith for the purpose of time and latitude determinations.

Zero-age main sequence (ZAMS): the principal branch in the H-R diagram reached by stars which have evolved to the point of stability as the result of hydrogen burning.

Zero curvature: the flat space continuum that is characterized by Euclidean geometry where there is no ''warping'' of the space structure as in positive or negative curvature.

Zodiac: the circling band of twelve equal constellation divisions or signs centered on the ecliptic (the apparent path of the sun); see Figures 2.2 and 2.3.

Zodiacal light: the faint band of light that tapers upward from the horizon, following the course of the ecliptic. It apparently results from the reflection of the sunlight by the interplanetary dust in the plane of the earth's orbit.

Zone of avoidance: the irregular band along the Milky Way where few or no galaxies appear as a consequence of the severe obscuration of light by the interstellar dust in or near the galactic plane.

INDEX

INDEX